Western Australia

Sally Webb
Ilsa Colson

LONELY PLANET PUBLICATIONS
Melbourne • Oakland • London • Paris

WESTERN AUSTRALIA

To Christmas Island (1500km)
& Cocos (Keeling) Islands (2037km)

INDIAN OCEAN

Ashmore Reef

Cartier Island

Joseph Bonaparte Gulf

NORTHERN TERRITORY

KUNUNURRA
Spot wildlife on a cruise down the Ord River

Kununurra

Wyndham

Aboriginal Land

DRYSDALE RIVER NATIONAL PARK

Kimberley Plateau

PURNULULU (BUNGLE BUNGLE) NATIONAL PARK

Halls Creek

WOLF CREEK CRATER NATIONAL PARK

Aboriginal Land

Lake Willis

Lake Mackay

Lake MacDonald

Cape Londonderry

Bonaparte Archipelago

Nature Reserve

Aboriginal Land

Gibb River Rd

Derby

Great

Northern

Fitzroy Crossing

Hwy

Ord River

Fitzroy River

GREAT SANDY DESERT

Canning Stock Route

Percival Lakes

Gary Hwy

GIBSON DESERT

Gibson Desert Nature Reserve

GIBB RIVER ROAD
Experience rivers, rough riding and homestead hospitality

Collier Bay

Cape Leveque

Broome

Northern Hwy

Great

Kidson Track

Lake Dora

RUDALL RIVER NATIONAL PARK

Lake Auld

Lake Disappointment

Canning Stock Route

Lake Waukarlycarly

BROOME
Get a feel for the perils and pleasures of pearl diving

Marble Bar

Newman

Pilbara

Aboriginal Land

Great Northern Hwy

River

KARIJINI (HAMERSLEY RANGE) NATIONAL PARK

COLLIER RANGE NATIONAL PARK

THE PILBARA
Travel near-empty roads through a haunting landscape

Port Hedland

Wickham

Roebourne

Karratha

Dampier

MILLSTREAM CHICHESTER NATIONAL PARK

Hwy

North West Coastal

Hamersley

Range

Witteroom

Tom Price

Paraburdoo

EXMOUTH
Swim with whale sharks the experience of a lifetime

Barrow Is

Onslow

Exmouth

Exmouth Gulf

North West Cape

NINGALOO MARINE PARK

Tropic of Capricorn

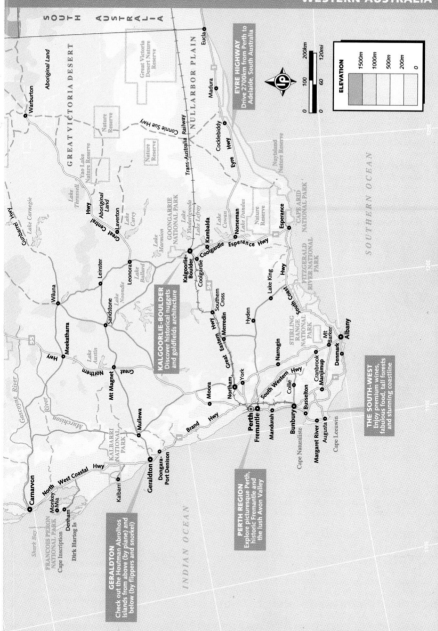

Western Australia
3rd edition – February 2001
First published – April 1995

Published by
Lonely Planet Publications Pty Ltd ABN 36 005 607 983
90 Maribyrnong St, Footscray, Victoria 3011, Australia

Lonely Planet Offices
Australia Locked Bag 1, Footscray, Victoria 3011
USA 150 Linden St, Oakland, CA 94607
UK 10a Spring Place, London NW5 3BH
France 1 rue du Dahomey, 75011 Paris

Photographs
Many of the images in this guide are available for licensing from
Lonely Planet Images.
email: lpi@lonelyplanet.com.au

Front cover photograph
Dolphins at Monkey Mia (Martin Cohen)

ISBN 0 86442 740 9

text & maps © Lonely Planet 2001
photos © photographers as indicated 2001

Printed by SNP Offset (M) Sdn Bhd

Contents – Text

2 Contents – Text

CORAL COAST & THE PILBARA 282

THE KIMBERLEY 307

GLOSSARY 337

ACKNOWLEDGMENTS 339

INDEX 346

MAP LEGEND back page

METRIC CONVERSION inside back cover

Contents – Maps

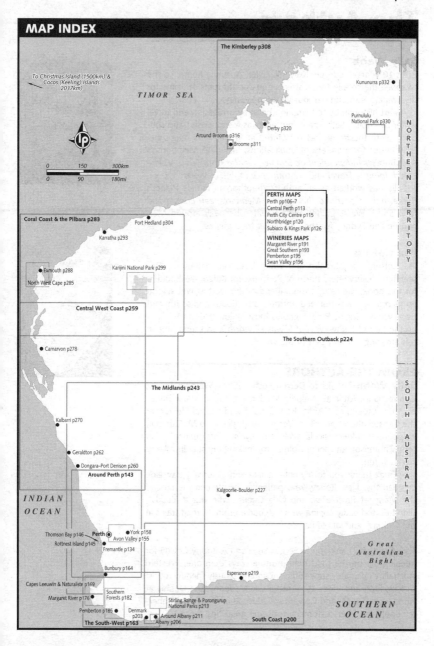

MAP INDEX

To Christmas Island (1500km) &
Cocos (Keeling) Islands
2037km)

TIMOR SEA

The Kimberley p308

Kununurra p332 ●

Purnululu
National Park p330

Derby p320 ●

Around Broome p316
● Broome p311

PERTH MAPS
Perth pp106–7
Central Perth p113
Perth City Centre p115
Northbridge p120
Subiaco & Kings Park p126

WINERIES MAPS
Margaret River p191
Great Southern p193
Pemberton p195
Swan Valley p196

Coral Coast & the Pilbara p283

Port Hedland p304 ●

Karratha p293 ●

● Exmouth p288
North West Cape p285

Karijini National Park p299

Central West Coast p259

N O R T H E R N   T E R R I T O R Y

The Southern Outback p224

● Carnarvon p278

S O U T H   A U S T R A L I A

The Midlands p243

● Kalbarri p270

● Geraldton p262
● Dongara–Port Denison p260

Around Perth p143

Kalgoorlie–Boulder p227 ●

INDIAN OCEAN

Thomson Bay p146 — Perth ⊙ ● York p158
Rottnest Island p145 ● Avon Valley p155
Fremantle p134

Great Australian Bight

Bunbury p164 ●

Capes Leeuwin & Naturaliste p169

Southern
Forests p182

Esperance p219 ●

Margaret River p176 ●

Pemberton p185 ●   Denmark
p203 ●

Stirling Range & Porongurup
National Parks p213
● Around Albany p211

The South-West p163   Albany p206 ●   **South Coast p200**

SOUTHERN OCEAN

0   150   300km
0   90   180mi

The Authors

Sally Webb

After 10 years in Europe, Sally still called Australia home, so she swapped the cobblestoned streets and ancient ruins of Rome for skyscrapers, surf and harbour views in Sydney.

An art historian by training, journalist by profession and travel writer by choice, Sally spent four years as a staff writer and sub-editor with the Rome-based *Wanted in Rome* news magazine. Sally writes for a variety of publications, including Melbourne's *Age*, Britain's *Independent on Sunday*, *Qantas Club*, *Vive*, *Vogue Entertaining & Travel* and *Australian Gourmet Traveller*.

Sally has worked as an author/co-author on Lonely Planet's *Rome*, *Italy*, *Corfu and the Ionians*, *Mediterranean Europe* and *New South Wales* guides and has eaten her way around Melbourne and Sydney for the *Out to Eat* food guides.

Ilsa Colson

Ilsa Colson is a journalist and writer based in Melbourne. Researching 'everywhere north of Perth except Kalgoorlie-Boulder' for this book, she caught the tail end of the wettest wet season on record. She was pursued northward by floods and southward by a cyclone. She no longer ignores those yellow 'Floodway' signs on the side of highways. But it was all worth it to spend time in this amazing, ancient part of the world.

FROM THE AUTHORS

Sally Webb Thanks to Derren Foster at the Walpole Tourist Centre; Gary Muir at Walpole Wilderness Tours; Klaus Tiedemann at Esperance CALM; Beth Schultz and Rachel Siewert at the Conservation Council of Western Australia; Brad McCahon in Kalgoorlie-Boulder; Nicola Wells (for cycling information); and John Thompson and Jenni Holmes for making my stay in Albany so much fun.

A huge thank you to my entertaining and observant travelling companions: Jack Stoney, who patiently chauffeured me around the Margaret River area; and Orla Guerin, who, for a 'paddy', didn't do too badly coping with Kalgoorlie brothels, road trains in the Outback and lots of bad coffee.

Ilsa Colson Thank you to Fergus Shiel and Anthony Colson for keeping me on the right road in more ways than one; Western Australia's invariably super-efficient and fabulously friendly tourist offices; Fran and Peter at Karratha CALM, Jenny and Debbie at Kununurra CALM, and Cervantes CALM; and Wendy at Kimberley Books (and her customers) for some great tips.

This Book

Between them, authors Sally Webb and Ilsa Colson covered the entire 2.5 million sq km of Australia's largest state in their research for this 3rd edition of *Western Australia*. They updated and added to the work of Jeff Williams, who wrote the previous two editions. Craig McKeough tasted his way around Western Australia's wine regions to produce the new wineries special section.

FROM THE PUBLISHER

Rebecca Turner planned and commissioned this book, which was produced in Lonely Planet's Melbourne office. Editing was coordinated by Kim Hutchins, with unflappable guidance from Hilary Ericksen, and the able help of Bruce Evans and Cherry Prior. Kusnandar coordinated design, layout and mapping, with the assistance of Jane Hart. Kusnandar also compiled the climate chart. Jenny Jones provided final-hour help with the maps, and Joanne Newell assisted with indexing.

Matt King coordinated the illustrations, which were drawn by Pablo Gastar, Kellie Hamblet, Martin Harris, Ann Jeffree, Kate Nolan and Mick Weldon. Glenn Beanland, Jane Hart and Valerie Tellini selected and organised the photographs, and Vicki Beale and Jenny Jones designed the cover. Lisa Borg provided support during layout. Thanks to Iain Young, who cast his expert eye over the wildflowers special section at short notice.

THANKS
Many thanks to the travellers who used the last edition and wrote to us with helpful hints, advice and interesting anecdotes. Your names appear in the back of this book.

Foreword

ABOUT LONELY PLANET GUIDEBOOKS

The story begins with a classic travel adventure: Tony and Maureen Wheeler's 1972 journey across Europe and Asia to Australia. Useful information about the overland trail did not exist at that time, so Tony and Maureen published the first Lonely Planet guidebook to meet a growing need.

From a kitchen table, then from a tiny office in Melbourne (Australia), Lonely Planet has become the largest independent travel publisher in the world, an international company with offices in Melbourne, Oakland (USA), London (UK) and Paris (France).

Today Lonely Planet guidebooks cover the globe. There is an ever-growing list of books and there's information in a variety of forms and media. Some things haven't changed. The main aim is still to help make it possible for adventurous travellers to get out there – to explore and better understand the world.

At Lonely Planet we believe travellers can make a positive contribution to the countries they visit – if they respect their host communities and spend their money wisely. Since 1986 a percentage of the income from each book has been donated to aid projects and human-rights campaigns.

Updates Lonely Planet thoroughly updates each guidebook as often as possible. This usually means there are around two years between editions, although for more unusual or more stable destinations the gap can be longer. Check the imprint page (following the colour map at the beginning of the book) for publication dates.

Between editions up-to-date information is available in two free newsletters – the paper *Planet Talk* and email *Comet* (to subscribe, contact any Lonely Planet office) – and on our Web site at www.lonelyplanet.com. The *Upgrades* section of the Web site covers a number of important and volatile destinations and is regularly updated by Lonely Planet authors. *Scoop* covers news and current affairs relevant to travellers. And, lastly, the *Thorn Tree* bulletin board and *Postcards* section of the site carry unverified, but fascinating, reports from travellers.

Correspondence The process of creating new editions begins with the letters, postcards and emails received from travellers. This correspondence often includes suggestions, criticisms and comments about the current editions. Interesting excerpts are immediately passed on via newsletters and the Web site, and everything goes to our authors to be verified when they're researching on the road. We're keen to get more feedback from organisations or individuals who represent communities visited by travellers.

Lonely Planet gathers information for everyone who's curious about the planet – and especially for those who explore it first-hand. Through our guidebooks, phrasebooks, activity guides, maps, literature, newsletters, image library, TV series and Web site we act as an information exchange for a worldwide community of travellers.

Research Authors aim to gather sufficient practical information to enable travellers to make informed choices and to make the mechanics of a journey run smoothly. They also research historical and cultural background to help enrich the travel experience and allow travellers to understand and respond appropriately to cultural and environmental issues.

Authors don't stay in every hotel because that would mean spending a couple of months in each medium-sized city and, no, they don't eat at every restaurant because that would mean stretching belts beyond capacity. They do visit hotels and restaurants to check standards and prices, but feedback based on readers' direct experiences can be very helpful.

Many of our authors work undercover, others aren't so secretive. None of them accept freebies in exchange for positive write-ups. And none of our guidebooks contain any advertising.

Production Authors submit their raw manuscripts and maps to offices in Australia, USA, UK or France. Editors and cartographers – all experienced travellers themselves – then begin the process of assembling the pieces. When the book finally hits the shops, some things are already out of date, we start getting feedback from readers and the process begins again...

WARNING & REQUEST

Things change – prices go up, schedules change, good places go bad and bad places go bankrupt – nothing stays the same. So, if you find things better or worse, recently opened or long since closed, please tell us and help make the next edition even more accurate and useful. We genuinely value all the feedback we receive. Julie Young coordinates a well-travelled team that reads and acknowledges every letter, postcard and email and ensures that every morsel of information finds its way to the appropriate authors, editors and cartographers for verification.

Everyone who writes to us will find their name in the next edition of the appropriate guidebook. They will also receive the latest issue of *Planet Talk*, our quarterly printed newsletter, or *Comet*, our monthly email newsletter. Subscriptions to both newsletters are free. The very best contributions will be rewarded with a free guidebook.

Excerpts from your correspondence may appear in new editions of Lonely Planet guidebooks, the Lonely Planet Web site, *Planet Talk* or *Comet*, so please let us know if you *don't* want your letter published or your name acknowledged.

Send all correspondence to the Lonely Planet office closest to you:

Australia: Locked Bag 1, Footscray, Victoria 3011
USA: 150 Linden St, Oakland, CA 94607
UK: 10A Spring Place, London NW5 3BH
France: 1 rue du Dahomey, 75011 Paris

Or email us at: talk2us@lonelyplanet.com.au

For news, views and updates see our Web site: www.lonelyplanet.com

HOW TO USE A LONELY PLANET GUIDEBOOK

The best way to use a Lonely Planet guidebook is any way you choose. At Lonely Planet we believe the most memorable travel experiences are often those that are unexpected, and the finest discoveries are those you make yourself. Guidebooks are not intended to be used as if they provide a detailed set of infallible instructions!

Contents All Lonely Planet guidebooks follow roughly the same format. The Facts about the Destination chapters or sections give background information ranging from history to weather. Facts for the Visitor gives practical information on issues like visas and health. Getting There & Away gives a brief starting point for re-searching travel to and from the destination. Getting Around gives an overview of the transport options when you arrive.

The peculiar demands of each destination determine how sub-sequent chapters are broken up, but some things remain constant. We always start with background, then proceed to sights, places to stay, places to eat, entertainment, getting there and away, and getting around information – in that order.

Heading Hierarchy Lonely Planet headings are used in a strict hierarchical structure that can be visualised as a set of Russian dolls. Each heading (and its following text) is encompassed by any preceding heading that is higher on the hierarchical ladder.

Entry Points We do not assume guidebooks will be read from beginning to end, but that people will dip into them. The tradi-tional entry points are the list of contents and the index. In addition, however, some books have a complete list of maps and an index map illustrating map coverage.

There may also be a colour map that shows highlights. These highlights are dealt with in greater detail in the Facts for the Visitor chapter, along with planning questions and suggested itin-eraries. Each chapter covering a geographical region usually begins with a locator map and another list of highlights. Once you find something of interest in a list of highlights, turn to the index.

Maps Maps play a crucial role in Lonely Planet guidebooks and include a huge amount of information. A legend is printed on the back page. We seek to have complete consistency between maps and text, and to have every important place in the text captured on a map. Map key numbers usually start in the top left corner.

Although inclusion in a guidebook usually implies a recommen-dation we cannot list every good place. Exclusion does not necessarily imply criticism. In fact there are a number of reasons why we might exclude a place – sometimes it is simply inappropriate to encourage an influx of travellers.

Introduction

There is nowhere else I'd rather be…I am at the beach looking west with the continent behind me as the sun tracks down to the sea. I have my bearings.

Tim Winton, *Land's Edge* (1993)

Western Australia, more commonly known by its acronym WA ('double-u ay'), is a state of incredible contrasts: sophisticated cities and ghost towns; the rugged Kimberley and the billiard-table-flat Nullarbor; the lush green forests of the south-west and the sunbaked red and brown hues of the arid centre; and the brilliant blue waters of the oceans and the dazzling white saltpans on the fringe of civilisation.

Australia's largest state, WA is isolated by desert from the population and power centres in Australia's east. There's a feeling that the west is somehow different, almost a separate country.

It is packed with wonders, many of which are just being 'discovered'. Chances are you will be the only person swimming in the idyllic lagoons of Ningaloo Reef on a particular day; you might be one of a handful of people who camp inside a gorge in the spectacular Purnululu (Bungle Bungle) National Park in a month; when fishing, you'll have a couple of hundred kilometres of beach to yourself; and you and your travelling companion could be the only people who see a particular huge expanse of wildflowers in bloom this year.

The only remaining frontier in nondesert Australia is in the north of WA. The Kimberley, remote, rugged and three times the size of England, is still the least-populated

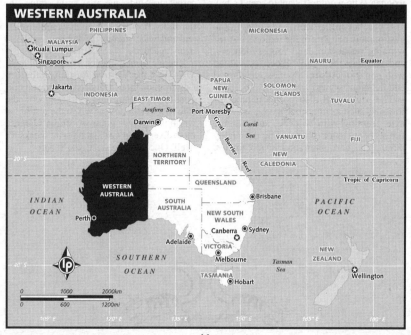

WESTERN AUSTRALIA

11

area of northern Australia. To the south is the equally wild Pilbara. The spectacular Hamersley Range includes memorable views over gorges of the Karijini National Park. Sandwiched between the Kimberley and the Pilbara is the exotic town of Broome, now a major tourist mecca.

The hub of WA is its cosmopolitan capital city, Perth, which is packed with classy hotels, excellent restaurants and great shops. Perth's wide range of activities and entertainment options includes symphony orchestras, hip nightclubs and beautiful ocean beaches. Not far away is the vibrant, historic port of Fremantle, and a short ferry ride will take you to get-away-from-it-all Rottnest Island. Within two hours' drive of Perth there are the pretty towns of the Avon Valley and the world-class windsurfing beaches of Lancelin.

The south-west of the state attracts the most visitors. It is a favourite short-break destination for Perth residents – and no wonder. Who wouldn't want to spend a few days lazing on (or surfing the waves of) the best beaches in the west, indulging in the gastronomic delights of the region's award-winning restaurants and food producers, and washing the whole experience down with some of Australia's most celebrated and delicious wines?

The south-west also boasts natural attractions such as limestone caves, archipelagos teeming with wildlife, and sublime forests of ancient trees including the mighty jarrah, giant karri, marri and the rare tingles.

The well-preserved former whaling town of Albany, WA's first settlement, offers a glimpse of the state's historic past. King George Sound, off Albany, is one of several places in the state for spotting whales.

Along the magnificent south coast, some of WA's best coastal parks, such as the World Biosphere Reserve at Fitzgerald River and the rugged Stirling and Porongurup Ranges, offer unsurpassed walking and adventure sports. Heading north to the goldfields region, there's once-thriving ghost towns and the feisty frontier city of Kalgoorlie-Boulder.

The state is the perfect ecotourism destination. Shark Bay, renowned for its friendly dolphins at Monkey Mia, has an additional wealth of flora and fauna which has led to its designation as a World Heritage Area. Marine life at unforgettable Ningaloo Reef includes the world's largest fish, the whale shark; manta rays; humpback whales; turtles; and dugongs.

Throughout WA, stunning wildflowers carpet the landscape after spring rains; approximately 12,000 species are found within the state. Birdlife and animals are prolific and the wide variety of habitats supports many species.

There's something for every traveller in WA. Why the Western Australian Tourism Commission thought it needed to spend millions on an ad campaign starring supermodel Elle McPherson to sell WA to the rest of the world is anyone's guess. Australia's largest, most diverse and fascinating state speaks for itself. Once you go west, you'll agree.

Facts about Western Australia

HISTORY

Australia was the last great landmass to be discovered by Europeans. Long before the British claimed it as their own, European explorers and traders had been dreaming of the riches to be found in the unknown – some said mythical – southern land *(terra australis)* that was supposed to form a counterbalance to the landmass north of the equator. The continent they eventually found had already been inhabited for tens of thousands of years.

The Archaeological Record

It is generally accepted that the first humans came to Australia across the sea from South-East Asia. Exactly when colonisation took place is the subject of hot debate, with the favoured options being 35,000–45,000 and 55,000–60,000 years ago.

If the Aborigines island-hopped from South-East Asia it is likely that the north-west of the continent (the present Kimberley) was their first landfall. They would have spread from here to all parts of the continent and, ultimately, across to Tasmania.

There is much evidence to indicate that Aboriginal people lived as far south in WA as present-day Perth at least 40,000 years ago. The state has a rich archaeological record, including a camp site (39,500 years old) unearthed at Swan Bridge, stone tools (30,000 years old) gathered from the Devil's Lair near Cape Leeuwin, and ochre mined from Wilgie-Mia (30,000 years ago) in the Murchison district.

There is a great deal of evidence of a sophisticated culture farther south, with examples of Aborigines' daily food-gathering; many shell middens (remains of shellfish meals), quarries and fish traps remain.

About a dozen local groups of the Nyungar people occupied the area of the Swan River Valley and it is estimated that there was more than another dozen tribal groups between Geraldton and Esperance. The Aborigines travelled along *bidi* (tracks) to trade or meet for feasts and ceremonies.

The Europeans

The Portuguese, traversing the Indian Ocean in the 15th century, may have been the first

---

The Dreaming

Creation stories explain the origins of Australian Aboriginal peoples, reinforcing the belief that they have inhabited the continent since the beginning of time.

The creation period is often referred to as the Dreaming. It was the time when spiritual beings (also known as ancestral spirits) travelled across the land forming natural features and instituting laws and rituals. In the Kimberley region of Western Australia (WA), the Wandjina, Marlu the Great Kangaroo and the Maletji Dogs are all ancestral spirits. Warlu the Rainbow Snake and Mangela are ancestral spirits from the Pilbara. Other local areas have their own creation stories and ancestral spirits which are depicted in rock art: The Jaburara of the Burrup Peninsula etched the Climbing Men into the rock of Murajuga and the Ngaluma people etched images of ancestral spirits in the dolerite rocks of Depuch Island (the Aboriginal name is Womalantha), a site where ceremonies are performed.

But the Dreaming is not simply the past – it is also the present and the future. After creating life and everything associated with it, the ancestral spirits entered the land to dwell there or formed themselves into natural features. Aborigines thus have strong spiritual links with particular tracts of land; it is possible that every major geographical feature you see in your travels in WA will have some special significance for Aborigines in that area. Since it is believed that ancestral spirits still live in the land, taking care of sacred sites is an essential part of maintaining life, health and social order.

Europeans to discover the west coast of Australia. A 16th-century book talks about a voyage to the Kimberley coast, and a Portuguese map, dated 1602, indicates a landing in the region of Collier and Brunswick Bays.

The region's position near the Indian Ocean trade routes led to very early European contact. The first Europeans known to have landed on or near the coast of Western Australia (WA) were Dutch. Dirk Hartog sighted land near Shark Bay on 25 October 1616. He and a party of fellow Dutch rowed ashore from the *Eendracht* and landed on the island that now bears his name. At what is now called Cape Inscription he left a pewter plate recording the landing.

The first navigator to really chart the west coast was Abel Tasman. In 1644, with the ships *Limmen*, *Zeemeeuw* and *Bracq*, Tasman sailed up the north-west coast from near Exmouth Gulf, continuing farther north towards the Gulf of Carpentaria.

William Dampier was the first Englishman to chart the coast of WA. A buccaneer and passenger of the *Cygnet*, he landed at the subsequently named Cygnet Bay (near the modern-day Dampier Peninsula) in 1688. Dampier's 1697 publication *New Voyage Around the World* prompted funds for a subsequent trip in 1699 to what was then known as New Holland. On board the ship HMS *Roebuck*, he charted from the Houtman Albrohos Islands as far north as Roebuck Bay, Broome.

In 1696 another group of Dutch navigators – Willem de Vlamingh in the *Geelvinck*, Gerrit Collaert in the *Nijptangh* and Cornelius de Vlamingh in the *Het Weseltje* – searched New Holland for a group of survivors from a Dutch East India Company ship lost in 1694. They sighted the coast on Christmas Day and landed on the mainland at Cottesloe Beach. Exploring parties ventured inland, saw the black swans and gave the river on which Perth is now sited its name. Willem de Vlamingh also mistook the quokkas (small wallabies) on the island west of Perth for rats and named the place *Rotte-nest* ('rat's nest').

De Vlamingh sailed north and landed on Hartog Island, where he substituted the Hartog Plate with one of his own, then continued as far north as Exmouth Gulf before heading for Batavia (Jakarta).

European exploration at Rottnest Island, 1697

Later Exploration

In 1791 George Vancouver, in command of the *Discovery* and *Chatham*, sailed within sight of land at Cape Nuyts. He discovered and named Cape Chatham, and two days later found the harbour of King George Sound, where he formally took possession of the country for Britain.

The following year a French expedition transported by two ships – the *Recherche* and *L'Espérance* – visited the west coast looking for traces of the French explorer La Perouse, who had disappeared in 1788. The place names Esperance and Archipelago of the Recherche relate to this visit by the French, as does Point d'Entrecasteaux, named after the captain of the *Recherche*.

In 1800 the French navigator Nicolas Baudin set out to survey the southern coast of Australia. His two ships *Le Géographe* and *Le Naturaliste* anchored in Geographe Bay, near present-day Busselton, on 27 May 1801. Baudin explored the coast as far as Shark Bay, where, today, the naturalist of the expedition, François Péron, is remembered in the name of the cape at the tip of the peninsula.

Colonisation

It was probably the exploration by French mariners such as Baudin that prompted colonists on the eastern coast of Australia to take interest in the vast west. Reports of a dry, barren land had previously discouraged attempts at settlement and it was not until 1826 that Major Edmund Lockyer, some troops and a small party of convicts were sent from Sydney in the brig *Amity* to establish a small military outpost at King George Sound. This outpost (present-day Albany) was not intended to be permanent and in 1831 the garrison and convicts were withdrawn.

Also in 1826, Captain James Stirling had sailed to the area of the Swan River to see if it was suitable for settlement. Stirling was enthusiastic about its potential; he pushed for the establishment of a colony when he returned to Britain in 1828. In November 1828, Captain CH Fremantle, in command of HMS *Challenger*, sailed to take possession of the territory. On 2 May 1829, at the mouth of the Swan River, he formally annexed all territory outside the colony of New South Wales (NSW) for the Crown.

Stirling's proposals had received much publicity in Britain and many people flocked to take advantage of the favourable terms of settlement: one acre of land for every one shilling and sixpence (equal to $0.15 today but worth considerably more then) of equipment, money or stock that potential settlers took with them. Stirling was appointed lieutenant governor of the settlement, and was provided with administrators and the 63rd Regiment.

The *Parmelia* and *Sulphur* transports arrived in Cockburn Sound on 1 June 1829 and the new colony was officially proclaimed on 18 June. By the end of 1830 there were about 1500 settlers.

The first 10 years of colonisation proved arduous. The land given to the settlers was often of poor quality, food was scarce and money was in short supply. In 1848 there were more than 40,000 people in the colony but just over a thousand labourers. Shortages eventually led the colony to ask the British government for help in the form of convict labour.

Aboriginal Resistance

During the long history of Aboriginal occupation of WA, hunting and gathering was done successfully in small nomadic groups, despite the often harsh environment. However, colonisation proved to have dire consequences for the local Aborigines, especially the Nyungar people of the south-west.

In 1829 the Swan River settlement was established on land known already to the Nyungar as Mooro; the site of Perth at the foot of Mt Eliza was known as Boorloo. After seeing the settlers shoot their food sources such as kangaroo, the Aborigines took cattle and sheep in response. But under European law they were seen as thieves.

Aboriginal–European relations reached their nadir during Governor Stirling's control. In 1832–33, the Aborigines began forming groups in order to resist the settlers.

In October 1834 an official expedition led by Stirling, designed to eliminate resistance by the Nyungar – led by the warrior Calyute, set out for the Murray River. The Nyungar were ambushed and many were killed. Two of Stirling's men were wounded and one, Captain Ellis, died later of his wounds. The Battle of Pinjarra (as it came to be known) lasted for about an hour and a half; the wounded Aborigines were hunted down and killed. About 50 were slain but Calyute survived. Nyungar resistance effectively ended at that point and the following year the Murray River leaders pledged their support to Governor Stirling and the Crown.

The Convicts

The first group of convicts transported to WA at the request of the colony arrived off Fremantle in the *Scindian* on 1 June 1850. It was at this time that transportation was ending in the eastern colonies – 1840 in NSW and 1852 in Tasmania.

Many convicts were set to work constructing public buildings and roads in Perth and Fremantle. Works from this period include the gaol at Fremantle, a road linking Perth to Albany, Government House, the Perth Town Hall, the Pensioners Barracks and a summer residence for the governor on Rottnest Island.

Convicts worked for the government until eligible for a conditional pardon or 'ticket-of-leave' (four years for a seven-year sentence, and five years, three months for a 10-year sentence) when they could do wage labour, virtually as free men, for other settlers. They were also subject to certain reporting conditions and could not return to Britain.

The first comptroller-general, Captain Edmund Henderson, oversaw the operation until 1863. When an ex-comptroller-general of convicts in Tasmania and a veteran of Norfolk Island, Dr JS Hampton, arrived to take over as governor, the convicts were treated more strictly. The settlers spread out from Swan River to Champion Bay, Bunbury, Busselton and Albany, with convicts providing labour.

Transportation of convicts to WA ceased by January 1868 with the 37th transport, the *Hougoumont*. On board the ship were 63 Irish Fenians, including the writer and editor John Boyle O'Reilly. In 1869 O'Reilly escaped from Bunbury on a US whaler. From New York he helped organise the rescue of six other Fenians – the *Catalpa* picked them up near Rockingham in 1876. More than 9600 convicts were sent to WA, their labour important to the development of the colony.

'Cinderella' Colony

Compared with the colonies in the east, WA was very poor, prompting the reference 'Cinderella' colony. But its apparent poverty did not deter further exploration.

Explorers had been hard at work since 1839 when George Grey walked from Shark Bay to Perth. Edward John Eyre's party set out from South Australia (SA) in 1840, with Eyre and an unwilling Aborigine, Wylie, finally reaching Albany in 1841 after food shortages had forced them to depend on Wylie's hunting and food-gathering ability. In 1861 Frank T Gregory set out from Nickol Bay (near modern-day Karratha) along the Fortescue River to the Hamersley Range.

The Forrests – John and Alexander – were active explorers for 10 years from 1869 to 1879. In 1869 John led an expedition in search of Ludwig Leichhardt and got as far inland as Lake Ballard; in 1870 he and four others travelled from Perth to Adelaide. In 1873 a party led by Peter Warburton left Alice Springs in an attempt to cross to Perth, nearly starving to death before they reached the north-west coast near the Oakover River. In 1875–76 Alexander and Ernest Giles crossed the continent from SA to Perth, and in 1879, Alexander, in a much-feted expedition, went from De Grey River to Daly Waters in the Northern Territory (NT).

As new regions were discovered, systems of roads, railways and telegraph lines were established to link communities. Perth was connected to the Overland Telegraph Line in 1877, providing communication with London and Adelaide.

The Baron of Bunbury

John Forrest, later Lord Forrest, Baron of Bunbury, was born near Bunbury in 1847. He is the giant of Western Australia's modern history, having achieved fame in the fields of exploration and politics. In physical appearance he was also a giant, with a huge frame, bushy whiskers and an equally dominating presence.

In 1869 he led an expedition to search for Ludwig Leichhardt's party and reached the Lake Ballard area north of modern-day Kalgoorlie-Boulder. Next, in 1870, he became the first to follow the Great Australian Bight west to east when he travelled from Perth to Adelaide.

On his third expedition in 1874, Forrest explored the hinterland from which flow the Gascoyne, Murchison, Ashburton, De Grey and Fitzroy Rivers. From there he pushed on across the Gibson Desert to the Peake telegraph station on the Adelaide-to-Darwin telegraph line, thus completing a more northerly west-to-east crossing. He published an account of his journeys, *Explorations in Australia*, in 1875.

As commissioner of Crown lands and surveyor-general from 1883 to 1890, Forrest made a fourth expedition, in 1884, to a large part of the Kimberley plateau. In 1890 he entered politics as the state's premier, heading a coalition of independent members of parliament (there were no political parties in the state at that time).

Forrest resigned from state politics in 1901 and entered the first federal parliament as Australia's postmaster-general in the first federal ministry. Later he held portfolios for defence, home affairs and treasury and was, for a brief period, acting prime minister. His two chief political successes were the goldfields water supply scheme and the transcontinental railway. In 1918, the year of his death, he became the first Australian-born citizen to be raised to the British peerage.

Gold Rushes

Gold was discovered at Halls Creek in the remote Kimberley in 1885. In 1886 diggers on the Queensland fields made the anticlockwise trek towards new riches. The terrain in the Kimberley was inhospitable and the track from the wharves at Wyndham and Derby the most ferocious that miners in Australia had yet negotiated.

The Pilbara was next to reveal its riches. In 1888 diggers swarmed over Pilbara Creek, fanning out through the dry gorges to Marble Bar, Nullagine and the Ashburton River.

Gold was found near Nannine, inland from Geraldton, in 1890. The Murchison field now bloomed and Cue, Day Dawn, Paynes Find, Lake Austin and Mt Magnet joined the list of gold towns in the Outback.

More discoveries followed, especially around Southern Cross in the Yilgarn. Major strikes were made in 1892 at Coolgardie and a year later at nearby Kalgoorlie.

Coolgardie's period of prosperity lasted only until 1905 and many other gold towns went from nothing to populations of 10,000, then back to nothing in just 10 years. Of all the goldfield areas, Kalgoorlie-Boulder remains the only large town. However, WA profited from the gold boom for the rest of the century. Gold put WA on the map and finally gave it the population to make it viable in its own right, rather than just an offshoot of the eastern colonies.

Economic depression and unemployment often attracted fossickers back to the gullies and rivers, especially during the Great Depression. In other places mining never actually stopped – witness the Golden Mile in Kalgoorlie-Boulder.

Federation, WWI & Later

The colony of WA adopted a new constitution in 1890 and the gold discoveries brought wealth and independence to the state. Initially there was scepticism about whether or not the eastern colonies would care about the remote west in a federation. But when it came to vote to federate, the eastern diggers on the west's goldfields ensured a 'yes' vote. The new Australian constitution was accepted and WA retained its boundary at the 129th meridian. The first premier was the explorer Sir John Forrest (see the boxed text 'The Baron of Bunbury' earlier in this chapter).

During WWI, WA came to national focus when many of the state's young people joined volunteers from the eastern states in the rush to enlist. Albany and Fremantle were the major embarkation points for several flotillas of troops, horses and equipment, before the ships sailed direct to Sri Lanka and on to the Middle East. (The story is poignantly and poetically told in Peter Weir's film *Gallipoli*, which is largely set in WA.)

Soon after WWI ended, a wheatbelt between Perth and the eastern goldfields was established, and there was rapid expansion in primary production. The Depression of the 1930s hit WA hard; wheat and wool prices fell dramatically, affecting local manufacturing of farmers' supplies, and many workers lost their jobs and were forced to go on the 'dole' (unemployment benefit).

The Depression heightened feelings of neglect in the west and added to the perception that the isolated state had lost much because of Federation. During the 1930s, discussion about secession from the Federation occurred, with proponents blaming the eastern states for the prevailing economic woes. Electors in the compulsory 1933 referendum voted by almost two to one to leave the Australian Commonwealth; only six electoral districts – five in the goldfields and the Kimberley – of 50 recorded a 'no' majority. Secession never occurred, as WA was deemed to have no legal right to request legislation on the constitution. The referendum, however, was an important signal to the federal government.

Paradoxically, the state Australian Labor Party (ALP), which had not supported secession, was swept into power in 1933 and remained there until the narrow victory of the Liberal–Country Party in 1947.

WWII

During WWII the west felt the brunt of war first-hand. The great naval engagement between HMAS *Sydney* and the German auxiliary cruiser *Kormoran* was fought on 19 November 1941 off the coast of WA. The result was the sinking of both ships and the loss of the entire crew (645 personnel) of the *Sydney*.

Broome, Wyndham, Derby and Onslow were bombed by the Japanese in February 1942 and it is believed that the Japanese came ashore and reconnoitred part of the Kimberley. In Broome, 70 people were killed and 16 Royal Dutch Air Force flying boats were destroyed while moored near the old jetty. In Wyndham, the SS *Koolama* was bombed and sunk.

Many military bases were established in the west. Fremantle became an important naval base for Allied operations in the Indian Ocean, and Exmouth Gulf was the centre of Operation Potshot, an advance US submarine refuelling base.

A great number of Italian prisoners of war, captured in North Africa, were allocated to work on farms; many stayed on after the war and their descendants live in WA today.

Post-War to Present

After WWII the west began to prosper, mainly as a result of the exploitation of the state's vast mineral wealth. In 1948 iron ore

---

Edith Dirksey Cowan (1861–1932)

Edith Cowan was born on 2 August 1861 at Glengarry, near Geraldton. A leading social reformer who was passionately interested in women's issues, she was awarded the Order of the British Empire (OBE) in 1920 and in the following year was elected by constituents of West Perth to the Legislative Assembly. In her three-year term she highlighted the need for improved migrant welfare, sex education and infant health centres. She also encouraged women to enter the legal profession through her sponsorship of the Women's Legal Status Act in 1923.

After losing her seat in politics, Edith Cowan continued advocating women's rights until she died on 9 June 1932. Her name lives on at the Edith Cowan University, and her face appears on the $50 note.

was shipped from Yampi Sound and since then WA has not looked back – it is now one of the world's main exporters of iron ore. Mines such as Tom Price, Mt Newman and Goldsworthy flourished in the Pilbara and an elaborate infrastructure of transport and shipping was set up to support this massive growth. Migrants came into the state to bolster the workforce and women took a greater role in all areas of industry. In the Kimberley, the mighty Ord River Irrigation Scheme was established in 1961, bringing fertility to the desert.

State politics of the post-war years has seen three distinct periods of ascendancy by either the ALP or the conservative coalition. The ALP ran the state for six years from 1953 until 1959, when the Liberal & Country League (LCL)–Country Party (CP; called National Country Party from 1975 to 1982, now National Party) coalition came to power.

Except for the three-year interruption of the Tonkin Labor government (1971–74), the LCL–CP coalition held power from 1959 to 1983, under the strong Liberal leaders David Brand and Sir Charles Court. Labor, led by the young and popular Brian Burke, was returned to office in 1983.

During the rapacious 1980s a number of high-flying entrepreneurs added their marks to the Perth city skyline. At this time Fremantle played host to the 1987 America's Cup yacht race, but Australia's defence of the trophy was unsuccessful.

The Labor government of the late 1980s was embroiled in a series of scandals called 'WA Inc'. The term – used loosely to describe a series of titanic collapses involving businessmen and the Labor government – led to a Royal Commission into governmental corruption. The government suffered heavily at the hands of voters in the 1993 election. The conservative Liberal–National Party coalition government, headed by Richard Court, son of former premier Sir Charles Court, took reign and introduced austere economic policies. While the scandals surrounding WA Inc proved painful, they appear to have had little effect on the state's international reputation. A number of key players including Alan Bond and the

late Laurie Connell served prison terms for their indiscretions and in July 1994 former premier Brian Burke was sentenced to two years' gaol for rorting travel expenses.

Today, a larger, far more technologically advanced mineral boom forms the basis of the state's prosperity. As a result, WA is deeply embroiled in the native title debate on Aboriginal land rights because of conflicting mining interests.

Aboriginal Protest, Land Rights & Reconciliation

In May 1946, the first real act of Aboriginal self-determination was enacted in the Pilbara, when 800 Aboriginal workers walked off their stations in the Port Hedland region in protest at their degrading conditions, 'slave wages' and the enforcement of the archaic Native Administration Act.

Led by white prospector Don McLeod and two Aborigines, Clancy McKenna and Dooley Binbin, the strikers congregated in camps. In the atmosphere of post-war security, little news of the protest was leaked to the press and both Binbin and McKenna were arrested for communist subversion. When food coupons were withheld from the protesters they returned to traditional methods of food-gathering.

The protest culminated in a station-to-station march in 1949 and, after protesters were arrested, the Seaman's Union banned the handling of wool from the 'slave stations'. The government conceded to the protesters' demands so that the shipping ban would be lifted (but soon after backed out of the deal). Meanwhile, the strikers had taken up other occupations and never returned to the stations.

Land rights became a prominent issue in June 1966 when a group at Wave Hill station (owned by the British Vestey Corporation) walked off their jobs, requesting that some of their land be returned to them. It wasn't until 1973 that the federal Whitlam Labor government announced that it would buy back two cattle stations in the north-west and return them to the Aborigines. Ironically, it was part of the Wave Hill station which was returned to the traditional Gurindji owners.

In 1992 the High Court handed down the Mabo decision. The result of a claim by Torres Strait Islander Eddie Mabo, it challenged and overturned the established concept of *terra nullius* – that Australia was empty or uninhabited at the time of white settlement. The court's ruling – that Aborigines were the first occupants and had the right to claim land back where continuous association was demonstrated – set off a heated and deeply divided debate on land rights and mining interests within WA. The state government even went as far as passing legislation that conflicted with Commonwealth legislation, though little impact on new resource projects has yet been felt.

In 1993 the federal Labor government introduced the Native Title Act, which formalised the High Court's Mabo ruling. The content of the bill had, somewhat surprisingly, been agreed upon by all the major players involved – miners, farmers, the government and Aborigines. In reality, the act gives Aboriginal people few new rights.

Black & White Western Australia

Like indigenous Australians in the rest of Australia, the 47,000 or so Aborigines who live in Western Australia (WA) are the state's most disadvantaged group. Many live in deplorable conditions, outbreaks of preventable diseases are common and infant mortality rates are higher even than in many Third-World countries.

The issue of racial relations in WA is a vexed one, and racial intolerance is still evident in some parts of the state. Especially (but not exclusively) in the remote north-west, a sort of unofficial apartheid seems to exist, and travellers are bound to be confronted by it. While white people live in the main towns and own most of the businesses, indigenous people live in isolated outlying communities. In some towns, hotels are classified (also unofficially) as 'black' or 'white'; or in some places where there's only one pub, separate bars receive those classifications. Is this really the same country that is focusing so much attention on Aboriginal reconciliation?

Another major political issue in WA is the mandatory sentencing law, introduced by the Court government in 1996, which is considered to discriminate against Aboriginal people. The law provides that third-time property offenders receive a mandatory 12-month gaol sentence. Given the extreme disadvantage which so many indigenous Australian children suffer, many consider that it is difficult for them to avoid participation in criminal acts.

Human rights groups, including the United Nations (UN), have protested the introduction of the law on a number of terms; it infringes upon the independence of the judiciary and forces judges to imprison juvenile offenders for whom gaol sentences should only be a last resort. However, it is the discriminatory nature of the law that has caused the protests, and which was outlined in the UN's report:

The use of mandatory sentencing in an environment where a very high proportion of one racial group, which is in addition both a minority population and economically marginalised, are likely to be incarcerated is…in violation of international human rights standards.

Although WA was the first state to introduce the mandatory sentencing law it was followed soon after by even harsher laws in the Northern Territory which impose gaol sentences on first-time adult offenders and second-time juvenile offenders.

However, it is not all bad news for WA's Aborigines. Indigenous-owned businesses are becoming more prominent throughout the state, especially in the field of tourism, and many people of indigenous descent now take leadership roles on bodies such as shire councils and tourist boards.

We have provided information about indigenous businesses and tours wherever possible throughout this book. To explore Aboriginal WA further, look out for Lonely Planet's *Aboriginal Australia & the Torres Strait Islands*, due for publication in mid-2001.

The application of native title is limited to land which no-one owns or leases, and also to land with which Aboriginal people have continued to have a physical association. The act states that existing ownership or leases extinguish native title, although native title may be revived after mining leases have expired. If land is successfully claimed by Aboriginal people under the act, they will have no veto over developments, including mining.

When the Howard Liberal–National Party coalition government was elected in March 1996 it promised to retain the Native Title Act, but matters were further complicated when the High Court handed down the Wik decision, which established that pastoral leases don't necessarily extinguish native title. This has resulted in some fairly hysterical responses and, especially in WA and Queensland, threatens to undermine the reconciliation process between Aboriginal and non-Aboriginal Australians.

In the face of the Wik decision, which alienated the grass-roots supporters of the National Party, new 'compromise' proposals were introduced. The Labor opposition saw the Native Title Act to be 'gutted' if the government's Wik legislation became law, Aborigines saw it as derailing the reconciliation process, and the National Farmers Federation even found fault with it.

In late 1997 the government proposed legislative amendments to the Native Title Act which further entrenched the pastoralists' position and gave the upper hand to mining companies and the like in the 'development-rampant' west. Thanks largely to independent senator Brian Harradine, the Native Title Amendment Act 1998 is an improvement on the government's intended bill, but it still contains serious negatives for Aboriginal people. These include the removal of the 'right to negotiate' on the way that pastoral leases and reserved lands are used, and the degree to which native title has been extinguished. Aboriginal communities in the west anxiously await the next chapter.

Like the rest of the country, WA is limping slowly towards reconciliation between indigenous and other Australians. Aborigines in WA were not spared the barbaric 'cultural assimilation' policies that were introduced in the late 19th century and continued until the 1970s – in 1904 politician JM Drew told the WA parliament: 'It may appear to be cruel to tear an Aborigine child from its mother, but it is necessary in some cases to be cruel to be kind'. Thousands of WA's Aborigines now count themselves as part of the Stolen Generation, forcibly removed from their families as children. With well over a century of cruelty and discrimination, there is a lot of ground to make up.

GEOGRAPHY

Occupying 2,525,500 sq km, a third of Australia's land mass, WA is the country's largest state. It extends 1621km from the Indian Ocean to the 129th meridian, where the western borders of both SA and the NT begin. It extends 2391km north from the Southern Ocean to the Timor Sea. The most northerly point is Cape Londonderry and the most southerly, Torbay Head.

There's a small coastal strip in the southwest corner of WA; hills rise behind the coast here. Farther north it's dry and relatively barren. Fringing the central west coast is the Great Sandy Desert, an inhospitable region running almost to the sea.

There are interesting variations in the landscape too, such as in the Kimberley, in the extreme north of the state. This is a wild and rugged area, with a convoluted coast and spectacular inland gorges. The Kimberley receives good annual rainfall, but all in the wet (or 'green') season. There are small, remote patches of tropical rainforest here as well.

Farther south is the Pilbara, an area with more magnificent ancient rock and gorge country, and the treasure-trove from which the state derives its vast mineral wealth. The Pilbara has two of the state's most interesting national parks: Karijini, based in the gorges of the Hamersley Range; and Millstream-Chichester, an oasis in the desert. Near Karijini is Mt MeHarry, WA's highest point (1245m). The highest waterfall is King George Falls (80m), the highest town is Tom Price (740m) and the longest river is the Gascoyne (760km).

Christmas & Cocos (Keeling) Islands

Christmas Island

Christmas Island (population 1500) is a rugged mountain, covering 135 sq km, situated 360km south of Java and 2300km north-west of Perth. Part of Australia's Indian Ocean Territories, it was originally settled in 1888 for phosphate mining, which continues today. The island has an exotic blend of Chinese, Malay and Caucasian inhabitants. You will hear Bahasa Malaysian and Mandarin spoken, but English is widely understood.

The port area has excellent snorkelling in the dry season (April to October), and surfing during the wet or 'swell' season (November to March). Steep drop-offs 50m to 200m offshore and huge whale sharks from October to April attract divers from around the world. Temperatures hover around 28°C. Frigate birds and boobies soar on gentle sea breezes, while endemic golden bosun birds with long streamer tail feathers swoop under the wharf where phosphate is loaded.

Christmas Island National Park covers 62% of the island, with tall tropical forests on the plateau (elevation 320m), rare nesting sea birds and soil riddled with crab burrows. Each November/December there is a spectacular breeding migration of red crabs to the sea: They cover roads, the golf course and anything else in their way. Robber crabs (known elsewhere as coconut crabs because they break open coconuts) are common and will check out picnics at Martin Point cliff lookout. There are blowholes along the south coast, and small beaches with coral rubble, rock pools and sand are dotted around the island, reached by forest walks or by boat.

Most of the island's shops and services are situated between Flying Fish Cove and the nearby clifftop area of Settlement. The Christmas Island Visitor Information Centre (☎ 9164 8382, fax 9164 8080, ⓔ cita@christmas.net.au) coordinates accommodation, tours, diving, game-fishing charters and car-hire bookings, and has an excellent Web site (www.christmas.net.au) linking local businesses.

Staff can also advise on the several weekly flights to Jakarta ($450 return). Visa requirements are as for Australia, and Australians should bring their passports.

Accommodation varies from backpacker-style ($18 dorm beds, $45 single rooms) to self-contained apartments and hotel-style suites. A casino-resort was built in 1993, but was changing hands at the time of writing and the casino, bars and entertainment areas were not open. The resort should be fully operational again in late 2000 or early 2001; until it's in full swing, you can stay in the rooms for $140 a night, including breakfast.

There are several Malay and Chinese eating houses, mainland-style cafes and a colonial-style clubhouse on the hill behind the Malay *kampong*. Try roti for breakfast at the *Malay restaurants*, noodles for lunch at the *Chinese Literary Association*, or dine in style at the *Rumah Tinggi* a la carte restaurant.

Off the coast there are a number of large islands and archipelagos: Augustus, Barrow, Bigge, Bernier and Hartog Islands, and the Bonaparte, Buccaneer, Dampier, Houtman Abrolhos and Recherche Archipelagos. There are also numerous peninsulas and capes that jut into the Indian Ocean: Dampier, North West Cape, Peron and Naturaliste.

Christmas & Cocos (Keeling) Islands

A standard fare from Perth (via Learmonth) with National Jet (book through Qantas ☎ 13 1313) costs $731/1462 one way/return. Advance-purchase deals can drop the return price to around $1000. There are flights on Saturday, and sometimes on Wednesday, which do a circle route with the Cocos Islands. In Perth, both Island Bound Holidays (☎ 9381 3644) and Christmas Island Travel (☎ 9481 1200, fax 9481 2005, ℮ info@citravel.com.au) offer packages. To reach some of the more remote parts of the island you need a 4WD. They can be hired from Kiat (☎/fax 9164 8276), which also runs tours – but there is plenty to see walking around Settlement.

Cocos (Keeling) Islands

'Altitude 10 feet', says the sign at the tiny airport. A chain of 27 islands around a clear azure lagoon, the Cocos Islands and Pulu Keeling, 24km to the north, are the islands that inspired Charles Darwin's theory of atoll formation. Surf hums on the outer reef, echoing the mellow lifestyle, and a constant sea breeze keeps temperatures around 23°C to 29°C year-round. White sandy beaches and lots of reef without the resorts…paradise!

First sighted in 1609 by Captain William Keeling (the history is written conveniently on the street signs), Cocos was settled by John Clunies-Ross in 1826. Importing Malay workers, he established a coconut plantation, a shipbuilding business and a dynasty that survives today. The islands were sold to the Australian government in 1978 and now form, with Christmas Island 900km to the east, part of Australia's Indian Ocean Territories. The Cocos Islands are overgrown coconut plantations returning to natural vegetation, with crabs and feral chooks but few birds. In contrast, the uninhabited lone island atoll of Pulu Keeling National Park, which is accessible during good weather in 'the doldrums' from October to March, has retained its native vegetation and is an important sea-bird nesting site for huge numbers of frigate birds, boobies, terns and rails.

Direction Island, also uninhabited and the mooring site for passing yachties during the 'trades' from April to September, is the classic desert island with a perfect protected beach. 'The Rip' is a channel, rich in marine life, between the lagoon and ocean with excellent snorkelling on the turn of the tide. Boat charter to reach 'DI' costs around $20 and charters can also take you deep-sea fishing or to various wild surfing locations. There are annual windsurfing clinics on the lagoon and the diving is truly special, with mantas, turtles, wild dolphins and astounding visibility.

West Island (population 100) hosts the airport, administration and service workers. Accommodation on the island ranges from utilitarian rooms for $95 per night with canteen meals at *The Lodge*, to Bali-style self-catering bungalows at *Cocos Cottages* for $150 per night per double. Social life in this remote community revolves around *the Cocos Club (☎ 9162 6652)* in the cyclone shelter.

West Island is linked by a free ferry with Home Island, where the huge Clunies-Ross home sits abandoned and the Cocos Malay community (population 500) lives. The cemetery and museum are also on Home Island, as well as *Bunga Melati (☎ 9162 7568/7633)*, a Malay restaurant open for dinner on Thursday. The Home Island Malay community is more fundamentalist than that of Christmas Island, so dress modestly to respect Islamic tradition.

For flights to the Cocos Islands see the Christmas Island section earlier. Cocos Islands Tourism Association (☎ 9162 6790, ℮ jenny.freshwater@cocos-tourism.cc) coordinates bookings. Visit its Web site at www.cocos-tourism.cc.

The world's largest west-coast reef, Ningaloo, stretches some 260km south from North West Cape to Coral Bay. It is Australia's closest point to the continental shelf.

Away from the coast, however, most of WA seems a vast empty stretch of Outback: the Nullarbor Plain in the south, the Great Sandy Desert in the north and the Gibson and Great Victoria Deserts in between. There are many interesting features dotted throughout these arid regions to break the monotony, including Mt Augustus, the world's largest 'rock'.

The south-west is different from the bulk of the state. The Mediterranean climate and higher rainfall have made this a much greener place, with large tracts of forest (see Flora later in this chapter) intersected by rivers and streams. The forests only occur where annual rainfall exceeds 500mm, and by far the bulk of forest is jarrah, with nearly 15,000 sq km, followed by the karri, with about 1500 sq km.

There are two interesting mountain ranges which punctuate the rolling, grassy plains: the Porongurup and the Stirling. The Stirling Range rises abruptly more than 1000m above sea level, and stretches east to west for 65km. Prominent peaks include Bluff Knoll, Toolbrunup, Mt Trio, Mondurup and Ellen Peak, all above 800m. The Porongurup Range, 40km south, is distinguishable by its huge, 1100-million-year-old granite domes. Both ranges support unique species of animals and plants.

The coastline in the south is exciting, with numerous rugged headlands, granite boulders, rock shelves and sheltered bays.

GEOLOGY

From Perth you can look to the Darling Range, which is in fact the edge of the Yilgarnia escarpment. Yilgarnia is one of the oldest lands in the world and was formed in the early stages of the Archae period (a subdivision of the Precambrian era), about 2600 million years ago. It was altered for about 1500 million years, covered up in many places and sank below sea level in others. The Archipelago of the Recherche is part of Yilgarnia.

The world's oldest rocks (almost original crust), dated at 4.1 billion years old, can be found north of Yilgarnia. These are the zircon crystals of Mt Narryer, inland from Shark Bay, formed a mere 500 million years after the earth began to coalesce.

To date, WA holds the first tangible proof of when life started on earth. In the Pilbara,

fossilised stromatolites (see the boxed text 'Stromatolites – A Special Sign' in the Central West Coast chapter), found in a layer of siltstone, have been dated at 3.5 billion years old. At sea level, in Shark Bay, stromatolites thrive in the hypersaline waters of Hamelin Pool.

Nearby, the Hamersley Range constitutes the backbone of the Pilbara. The rocks, which form the gorges of Karijini National Park, are more than 2.5 billion years old. They originated as iron- and silica-rich sediment deposits that accumulated on the sea bed. Horizontal compression forced these sediments to buckle and develop cracks, until the whole was elevated to the surface to form dry land.

The Kimberley had its origins in the Proterozoic period more than two billion years ago. Sediments referred to as the Halls Creek Group were laid down and underwent intense folding and faulting. About 150 million years later, the sediments forming the Kimberley Basin were also laid down, remaining remarkably stable in spite of two mobile zones nearby. Approximately 750 and 670 million years ago the region was gripped by two severe glacial epochs.

The most visible geological features were formed in the Devonian era, 375 to 350 million years ago, before mammals or reptiles had evolved. In the Devonian era, a barrier reef grew south-east of Derby where the Canning Basin area was covered by a tropical sea. It is surmised that this reef, 300km of which is exposed, could have extended some 1000km to join with another exposed reef in the Bonaparte Basin near Kununurra.

The limestone reefs – of which Geikie Gorge, Windjana Gorge and Tunnel Creek National Parks are part – rise from 50m to 100m above the river valleys. Obviously the limestone was resilient to the weathering and other geological changes which occurred.

The geological oddity of the Kimberley is the Purnululu (Bungle Bungle) Range. The ancient beehives – gravels and sandstones encased in silica – which make up this massif are 350 million years old. It is believed that rivers flowing south and east from nearby formations washed sand and pebbles into the area. This gradually compacted to form sandstone, which was uplifted over time and gouged out by the wet (monsoonal rains occurring from December and April). The covering of silica (orange in colour) and lichen (green) protected the domes from complete erosion, leaving the curious beehives visible today.

East of Purnululu is the Wolfe Creek meteorite crater, one of the best-preserved craters in the world. It was formed thousands of years ago when a meteor weighing thousands of tonnes hit the earth. The crater floor is 50m below the rim and the outer slopes are 35m high.

CLIMATE

From the tropical savannah in the north (the Kimberley), through the desert and semi-desert of the centre, to the Mediterranean climate of the south-west, WA has a variety of climates. The main influence of topography is a decrease in rainfall the further you get from the coast. The trade winds separate the northern south-east trade winds from the westerlies in the south.

The tropical north has hot, 'sticky', wet summers (December to February) and warm, dry winters (June to August). The climate is characterised by the wet, before which there is an incredible period called the 'build-up'. The horizon is black as ominous clouds roll through the sky and there are occasional flashes of lightning, but no rain falls, until one day there's a deluge and the wet has started. Once the wet begins, the roads are subject to flash flooding at any time.

Occasionally there are tropical cyclones. These usually develop well offshore and produce heavy rain, high winds and the lashing of coastal areas. Port Hedland gets a cyclone about once every two years. Cyclones produced WA's biggest wind gust (267 km/h, Tropical Cyclone Olivia, April 1996) and heaviest rainfall (747mm in one day, in 1975).

The area of WA which could be classified as desert or semidesert is east of a line drawn roughly from Geraldton through Southern Cross to midway between Albany and Esperance, and south of a line drawn

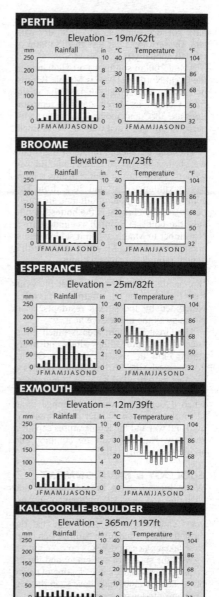

from Broome to Halls Creek. These areas have hot, dry summers and mild, dry winters. (Desert areas get less than 250mm of rainfall annually.)

About 200km south of Port Hedland, on the Great Northern Hwy, is Marble Bar, reputedly the hottest place in Australia, where from October to March, daytime temperatures are 38°C and above. The highest temperature ever recorded was 50.7°C at Eucla (near the SA border).

The Mediterranean climate of the southwest brings hot, dry summers and mild, wet winters. Perth, in the centre of this region, has maximums of around 30°C from December to March, but minimums are rarely below 10°C. February is the hottest month, July the coldest. Rainfall is lightest from November to March, when it seldom rains, and heaviest during May to August. Perth's annual rainfall averages 975mm.

One peculiarity of the local weather is the 'Fremantle Doctor', a wind that blows in from the sea in the late afternoon. It is often welcomed by the state's residents, as it clears away the oppressive heat.

The Great Southern area is much influenced by the prevailing winds and many storms blow in from the Southern Ocean. To the north, the Stirling Range creates a weather pattern all of its own. In late spring to early summer (October to December), when it begins to warm, the range is an ideal place to visit. Winter in this range is cold and wet and the temperatures can drop suddenly. Hail and rain are common and snow occasionally falls.

ECOLOGY & ENVIRONMENT

While humans have been living in, and changing, the physical environment in Australia for at least 50,000 years, it is in the 200 years since European settlement that the most dramatic – and often harmful – changes have taken place, and WA is no exception.

With the spread of settlement and the increase in pastoral use came clearing of native bush. The last 200 years have seen the loss or severe altering of around 66% of all native vegetation in WA's south-western corner and around 30% in the rest of the state.

Land clearing contributes significantly to environmental problems such as soil salinity, degradation of inland waterways, erosion, and greenhouse-gas emissions. Each of these problems contributes to probably the most significant environmental problem in Australia today – loss of biodiversity. Australia has been identified as one of the 12 most biologically diverse countries in the world, due to its large size, many different climatic zones and long period of isolation.

The loss of species goes hand in hand with the loss of habitat. So far, WA's report card doesn't look good – around 30% of mammal, 6% of bird, 2% of reptile, 4% of amphibian and 4% of plant species are either already extinct or severely vulnerable – but the figures for WA are marginally better than those for other Australian states.

In the intensively farmed south-west of WA, especially the Swan Coastal Plain, soil salinity is a major problem. It is caused by the disturbance of natural ecosystems, primarily through land clearing, and the replacement of perennial, deep-rooted, native plants with annual crops, which do not use as much water as native vegetation. The excess water moves off the land as runoff, or into the ground; the ground-water table rises, bringing with it salt stored in the soil. Salinity can kill native vegetation and crops, and can cause erosion, waterlogging and the salinisation of land, rivers and wetlands.

Around 9% of WA's agricultural land is affected by salinity, but without action, this could double in the next 15–25 years.

Problems with greenhouse-gas emissions are not aided by the fact that car use in WA is significantly higher than the Australian average. Sustainable population and resource-usage strategies (for a state population that is expected to increase by one million people in the next 30 years) are also being examined.

Other significant factors that contribute to the loss of biodiversity include the proliferation of introduced plants and animals (and the diseases that they can carry). The European fox is a good example of the latter. Where fox numbers are controlled – through managed poisoning such as used by the Department of Conservation and Land

At Loggerheads over Logging

Trees versus timber: Bring up this subject in the south-west of Western Australia (WA) and you're bound to get a heated response. No-one sits on the fence when it comes to the logging debate.

The jarrah, karri and wandoo forests of the south-west are among the most magnificent sights in WA and they can be counted among the world's most important and beautiful forests. However, since European settlement, these hardwood forests have been slowly but surely whittled away. According to the Conservation Council of WA (CCWA), at the time of European settlement there were around 4,200,000 hectares of old-growth forest. Today it is estimated that there are only 700,000 hectares – or around 16% – of 'ecologically mature and negligibly disturbed' forest remaining.

These figures are alarming in anyone's terms and environmental groups, led by the CCWA and the Western Australian Forestry Alliance, don't want to lose any more. Ideally they'd have *all* the wood production from old-growth forests transferred to plantations.

The flip side of the argument is that timber is a big earner for WA and many towns in the south-west depend upon it. The native-forest-based timber industry employs more than 20,000 people directly and indirectly, and has an annual turnover of more than $850 million. Put simply, reducing the volume of timber felled means job losses and hardship, sometimes for entire communities.

The federal government has been working on a national blueprint for sustainability in forest management, the Regional Forestry Agreement (RFA), for about a decade. The stated aim of the RFA is to conserve 15% of each ecosystem that existed before European arrival, and 60% to 100% of remaining old-growth forest.

However, WA's RFA has had a difficult passage. The original agreement signed by the state and federal governments in May 1999 was dumped by the WA premier two months later, after outcry from environmental groups and the wider community.

The government spin on the RFA as it stands today is that it 'meets all and exceeds many of the nationally agreed targets for biodiversity and old growth protection'. The agreement boasts an additional 150,885 hectares of 'reserve' forest that cannot be logged, bringing the total area of protected forest to 1,047,200 hectares (an increase of 12%), representing two-thirds of old-growth forest in the south-west.

However, environmental groups claim that the Department of Conservation and Land Management (CALM) has deliberately misrepresented the figures and has underestimated the amount of old-growth forest at the time of European settlement, and is now overestimating the area of old-growth forest that remains.

The environmental lobby *has* achieved one of its aims – to separate the conservation and commercial forestry arms of CALM (see Department of Conservation under Ecology & Environment in this chapter) – although it now claims that the newly created Forest Products Commission and ministry will effectively be controlled by the native-forest-logging industry, and that rather than preserving old-growth forest it will in fact perpetuate unsustainable old-growth logging at the expense of the forests and the broader community.

A deadline for the phasing-out of all old-growth logging has been set for 2003.

But with a pro-logging ministry as backup, a lot of trees can be turned into timber in that time. For the forests of the south-west, time is running out.

Management (CALM) in its Western Shield project in WA's south-west – there has been a notable recovery of native fauna and flora.

Tourism plays its part too, with large numbers of visitors putting pressure on fragile natural and cultural heritage areas, in some cases damaging the very thing they have come to see.

Mining has an enormous impact on the environment. At present around 2% of WA is held under mineral exploration. Erosion, soil damage, changes to surface water and ground water, salinisation and acidification are all significant side effects of WA's chief source of income. While mining companies generally comply with prescribed conditions for ecologically sustainable development, the industry is still in its infancy and the damage it has done won't really be known for many decades.

The news is not all bad, however, especially when compared with many other industrialised countries. As WA is a huge, sparsely populated state with a highly urbanised population, large areas are still in good condition, pollution of all kinds is relatively low, recycling is becoming much more widespread and general environmental awareness has risen dramatically.

Department of Conservation

Conservation areas and national parks in WA are managed by CALM. For information call ☎ 9334 0333. Its offices are at Technology Park, Western Precinct, 17 Dick Perry Ave (enter via Hayman Rd or Kent St), Kensington 6151. Its excellent Web site is at www.calm.wa.gov.au.

We have referred to CALM throughout this guide. However, by the time you read this book the department will have been divided into two separate entities: the Department of Conservation, which continues the national park management and conservation role, and a commercial arm, the Forest Products Commission, which will control the forestry, logging and land management areas. The existing offices and contact numbers mentioned throughout this book should remain unchanged for tourism purposes. If in doubt, ask at local tourist offices.

The splitting-up of CALM will be a relief to many environmental groups, as it will eliminate the severe conflict of interest of its dual conservation and commercial/forestry roles. (See the boxed text 'At Loggerheads over Logging' earlier in this chapter.)

Other Conservation Organisations

There are many bodies – from state and federal government right through to local community level – working towards the goal of

Dieback

Many of the national parks along the south coast (and huge areas outside the parks) are infected with dieback, a plant disease caused by the fungus *Phytophthora cinnamomi*. This microscopic fungus lives in the soil and attacks the root systems of plants, causing them to rot. As a result, plants cannot take up water or nutrients through their roots, so they die of 'starvation'.

The fungus is spread by movement of infected soil. You can help prevent its spread by keeping to formed roads and by strictly observing 'no go' road signs in the conservation reserves. Roads and tracks will often be closed in wet weather, when the dieback can be more easily spread. There are footwear cleaning stations in many parks along the south coast; use them. You should also clean mud and soil from your car tyres or bicycle wheels before and after you visit reserves. If in doubt, ask a ranger.

environmental management and sustainable development. These include:

Australian Conservation Foundation (ACF; ☎ 03-9416 1166, fax 9416 0767, ℮ reception@ acfonline.org.au) 340 Gore St, Fitzroy, Victoria 3065. This national body – the largest non-governmental organisation involved in conservation – covers a wide range of issues, including the greenhouse effect and depletion of the ozone layer, the problems of land degradation and the negative effects of logging.
Web site: www.acfonline.org.au

Australian Trust for Conservation Volunteers – WA branch (ATCV; ☎ 9336 6911, fax 9336 6811, ℮ perth@atcv.com.au) 216 Queen Victoria St, North Fremantle 6159. This nonprofit group organises practical conservation projects such as tree-planting, construction of walking tracks and surveys of flora and fauna.
Web site: www.atcv.com.au

Conservation Council of Western Australia (CCWA; ☎ 9420 7266) 2 Delhi St, West Perth 6005. The CCWA is the coordinating body for many of WA's environmental groups.

Environment Centre of WA (☎ 9225 4103) 10 Pier St, Perth 6000. This centre is a resource and information base for both the public and various organisations.

Western Australian Forest Alliance (WAFA; ☎ 9420 7265) 2 Delhi St, West Perth 6005. WAFA campaigns against the destruction of the beautiful native forests in the south-west.

The Wilderness Society WA (☎ 9420 7255, fax 9420 7256, ⓔ wa@wilderness.org.au) 2 Delhi St, West Perth 6005. This organisation is dedicated to the protection of wilderness areas and is involved in issues such as forest management and logging.
Web site: www.wilderness.org.au

FLORA

For information on wildflowers found in WA see the illustrated wildflower special section.

Trees

In WA's south-west, which contains all of the state's forests, there are eucalypts (gum) and other species of tree that you will see nowhere else. In the Kimberley, the curiously shaped boab tree *(Adansonia gregorii)* is a characteristic feature of the landscape (see the boxed text 'Upside-Down Trees' in the Kimberley chapter).

A good reference book is *Key Guide to Australian Trees* by Leonard Cronin. Check a library for Frank Haddon's useful *Environmental Guide to Flora & Fauna: Australia's Outback*, now out of print.

The following species grow only in WA.

Jarrah This majestic hardwood tree *(Eucalyptus marginata)* grows to a height of up to 40m and lives up to 400 years. In coastal areas, poor soils reduce growth to about 15m, and the average height in forests is closer to 30m. The stringy bark has deep vertical grooves and is dark-grey or reddish-brown. The botanical name refers to a thick margin around the leaves.

Karri Another giant tree, karri *(E. diversicolor)* has a pale, smooth bark which changes to the colour of pink in autumn. Reaching upwards of 90m in height, this is the world's third-tallest hardwood tree after Australia's mountain ash *(E. regnans)*. Karri grows in red clay loams wherever there is more than 750mm of rain per year. *'Diversicolor'* refers to the difference between the top and underside of the karri's leaf.

Marri This hardwood tree *(E. calophylla)* is often called red gum, as it oozes drops of red gum from its grey bark. It is different from the jarrah as it has a larger fruit (honkey nut) and its branches are more widespread. In dry areas the marri only grows to about 10m but in forests it can reach up to 60m. It grows widely throughout the south-west and along the Darling Scarp.

Tingle There are three species of this rare and restricted eucalypt (found in a small area near Walpole-Nornalup National Park).

The red tingle *(E. jacksonii)* has a similar look to jarrah except that it is much larger. Its thick trunk has spreading buttresses up to 20m high and the tree is one of the top 10 largest living things on the planet. The 'red' relates to the colour of its timber.

The smaller yellow tingle *(E. guilfoylei)* also has a buttressed base. Identification is difficult, as the flowers and gumnuts are often more than 30m above the ground.

The last of the tingles is the Rates tingle *(E. brevistylis)*, only recently discovered north-east of Walpole. It is not easily distinguished from the red and yellow tingles.

Places where you can get close to the tingles in the Walpole-Nornalup forests include the Tree Top Walk east of Walpole and the aptly named Valley of the Giants.

Wandoo This tree *(E. wandoo)* is one of Australia's dense and durable hardwoods. Commonly referred to as the white gum, wandoo forms a major part of the south-west eucalypt forests. The powder-bark wandoo *(E. accedens)* is found on the hills of the wheatbelt and is distinguished from the common wandoo by the powder on its bark, which rubs off easily.

Tuart The rare and restricted tuart *(E. gomphocephala)*, found between the Hill River and Busselton, is at its best in Tuart National Park. Its height is determined by the salt-laden winds, but it can reach up to 40m. Its presence is an indication of limestone soils.

continued on page 37

WILDFLOWERS OF WESTERN AUSTRALIA

Western Australia (WA) is famous for its beautiful and varied wildflowers – up to 12,000 species can be found within the state's borders – which bloom mainly from August to November.

Many of these wildflowers are known as 'ever-lastings' because the petals stay attached even after the flowers have died. Given a little rain, the flowers seem to spring up almost overnight, and transform vast areas within days.

The jarrah forests in the south-west are particularly rich in wild-flowers. The coastal parks, such as Fitzgerald River and Kalbarri, also put on brilliant displays. Near Perth, the Badgingarra, Tathra, Alexander Morrison, Yanchep and John Forrest National Parks are excellent places to see wildflowers.

Many people will recognise the common names of flowering plants: wattle, gum, feather flower, cone flower, mulla mulla, honey myrtle and mountain bells. With a bit of practice you will soon recognise the names of the genera (those above are *Acacia, Eucalyptus, Verticordia, Isopogon, Ptilotus, Melaleuca* and *Darwinia*). The next step is to identify *Acacia gregorii* as Gregory's Wattle, *Verticordia forrestii* as Forrest's Feather Flower, and so on.

In this section, genera abbreviations are used if it is obvious from the text what the genus is. For example, Stirling Range Banksia, or *Banksia solandri*, becomes *B. solandri*.

Wildflower Guides & Events

Though now out of print, *Flowers and Plants of Western Australia* (Rica Erickson et al) is a valuable resource; check your library. Simon Nevill's *Guide to the Wildflowers of South Western Australia* is one of a number of guides recommended by the Wildflower Society of WA.

The Department of Conservation and Land Management (CALM) produces a number of regional brochures ($6.50) about common wildflowers, and the beautifully illustrated *Wildflower Country* ($19.95), featuring colour photographs of wildflowers across the state.

The Western Australian Tourism Commission's free *Western Australian Wildflower Holiday Guide* has good

WILDFLOWER REGIONS

1 The Kimberley
2 The Pilbara
3 North West Cape
4 The North-West
5 Wildflower Way
6 North of Perth
7 South-East Wheatbelt
8 Around Perth & the South-West
9 Albany Region
10 Stirling & Porongurup Ranges
11 Bremer Bay to Esperance

colour photos and suggested trails. It's available at tourist offices or at www.westernaustralia.net/holiday_exp/nature/wildflowers.shtml.

During the flowering season there are a number of wildflower shows and festivals. The Mullewa Wildflower Show takes place in August. September sees flower shows in Albany, Augusta, Busselton, Kalgoorlie-Boulder, Mingenew, Nannup and Ravensthorpe. Perth's Kings Park has a wildflower festival in October, as does Walpole.

The Wildflower Society of WA's excellent Web site, at www.ozemail .com.au/~wildflowers/, includes lists of recommended books on wildflowers, suggested routes for touring wildflower regions, and details of wildflower shows and exhibitions. The society's Spring Fling takes place in September.

Around Perth & the South-West
September to November
A number of interesting species exist on the Swan Coastal Plain. The Yanchep Rose (Diplolaena angustifolia) is found on sand and limestone; the Rough Daisybush (Olearia rudis) is widespread; the Chenille Honey Myrtle (Melaleuca huegelii) is common along the coast from Geraldton to Augusta; Mangle's Kangaroo Paw (Anigozanthos manglesii), the floral emblem of WA, ranges from Shark Bay to Manjimup; Stirling's Mulla Mulla (Ptilotus stirlingii) and the Snottygobble (Persoonia saccata) grow in sandy woodlands along the coastal plain; and the Vibrant Redcoat (Utricularia menziesii) ranges from Perth to the south coast and as far east as Esperance.

North Dandalup, south of Perth, is a great place to see wildflowers such as colourful peas, Swan River Myrtle (Hypocalymma robustum), Green Kangaroo Paw (Anigozanthos viridis) and Golden Dryandra (D. nobilis). Farther south, near Collie, expect to see the beautiful silky Yellow Banjine (Pimelea sauveolens) and the P. spectabilis, with its large white flowers. Also found here are Blue Lechenaultia (L. biloba) and Spiked Wax Flower (Eriostemon spicatus), which is related to Boronia.

In the Leeuwin-Naturaliste National Park there is an amazing variety of flowering plants, from the Swamp Bottlebrush (Beaufortia sparsa) in Scott National Park to the Common Hovea (H. trisperma) and Yellow Flags (Patersonia xanthina) along Caves Rd. There is also the Flying Duck Orchid (Paracaleana nigrita) in the jarrah forests.

Stirling & Porongurup Ranges
September to November
In the Stirling Range, 1500 species of flowering plants occur and around 60 are endemic. Some 10 species of Darwinia, or Mountain Bells, have been identified. Near Cranbrook you can see the magnificent Cranbrook Bell (D. meeboldii). The lemon-yellow bell (D. collina) is found on Bluff Knoll, the Pink Mountain Bell (D. squarrosa) occurs higher up in the range on the Bluff Knoll Trail and the large red-and-white Mondurup Bell (D. macrostegia) is found on Mondurup Peak.

The Stirling Range Banksia *(B. solandri)*, the stunning Stirling Range Cone Flower *(Isopogon baxteri)* and the Mountain Pea *(Oxylobium atropurpureum)* are also restricted to this range. There are also many Black Gins *(Kingia australis)*, named after the explorer Philip King, near Bluff Knoll; part of the *Xanthorrhoeaceae* family, these are truly beautiful when in flower (any month).

The natural display in the Porongurup Range includes the Tree Hovea *(H. elliptica)*.

Albany Region
June to November

The national parks of the Albany region provide much reward for the keen observer. In West Cape Howe, the coastal heath supports many species of banksias, dryandras and hakeas. The Scarlet Banksia *(B. coccinea)* is common in areas of deep sand, as is Baxter's Banksia *(B. baxteri)*, while the Red Swamp Banksia *(B. occidentalis)* prefers wetter areas. The insect-eating Albany Pitcher Plant *(Cephalotus follicularis)*, the only member of its plant family, is also found in this park.

The five-petalled Sticky Tail-Flower *(Anthocercis viscosa)* is found in William Bay National Park, west of Denmark, and you may be lucky enough to see the Red-Flowering Gum *(E. ficifolia*; see under Flora in the Facts about Western Australia chapter) in bloom along Ficifolia Rd, near Walpole.

North of Albany, on the sandy heaths, the Hidden Feather Flower *(Verticordia habrantha)* blooms from September to November. The Albany Cat's Paw *(Anigozanthos preissii)* grows only within 50km of Albany in sandy jarrah woodlands. A perennial favourite is the Southern Cross *(Xanthosia rotundifolia)*, which is common in sandy soil from Albany to the Stirling Range.

The region is rich in orchids, including the slender Zebra Orchid *(Caladenia cairnsiana)*; the crab-lipped Spider Orchid *(C. plicata)*; the clubbed Spider Orchid *(C. longiclavata)*; the curious Hammer Orchid *(Drakaea elastica)*, one of four species endemic to WA; the King Leek Orchid *(Prasophyllum regium)*; and the Pouched Leek Orchid *(P. gibbosum)*.

Bremer Bay to Esperance
September to November

There is a wealth of flowering plants in this region. North-west of Bremer Bay, near the towns of Ongerup and Gnowangerup, in the open heath under woodland, there are pockets of the tough perennial Herb Pincushions *(Borya nitida)*, the Barrel Cone Flower *(Isopogon trilobus)*, the Sprawling Red Combs *(Grevillea concinna)*, the Ouch Bush *(Daviesia pachyphylla)*, and several varieties of Poison Peas, part of the *Gastrolobium* species.

Along the Jerramungup-Ravensthorpe road is a wide road reserve that is dense with wildflowers. The ubiquitous Bush Cauliflower *(Cassinia aculeata)*, the robust Ashy Hakea *(H. cinerea)* and a host of banksias can be seen along here.

Old Socks Grevillea

RICHARD I'ANSON

Sturt's Desert Pea

RICHARD I'ANSON

Grass Tree

RICHARD I'ANSON

Red Flowering Gum

MITCH REARDON

Common Smokebush

JOHN BANAGAN

RICHARD I'ANSON

Red Kangaroo Paw

RICHARD I'ANSON

Yellow Kangaroo Paw

JOHN BANAGAN

Tall Mulla Mulla

SUSAN STORM

Tinsel Flower

SUSAN STORM

Flame Grevillea

MITCH REARDON

Pincushion Hakea

SUSAN STORM

Blue Lechenaultia

MITCH REARDON

Common Pop-flower

The most coveted flowers in the Fitzgerald River National Park are the strange-looking Royal Hakea (*H. victoria*), the only native plant in WA with variegated leaves; the pink–red Pincushion Hakea (*H. laurina*); the creamy or orange Chittick (*Lambertia inermis*); the striking Scarlet Banksia; the Four-winged Mallee (*Eucalyptus tetraptera*) and the Warty Yate (*E. megacornuta*); the Red or White (or combinations of both) Heath Lechenaultia (*L. tubiflora*); the Silky Triggerplant (*Stylidium pilosum*); the Qualup Bell (*Pimelea physodes*), the only pimelea with a bell-like inflorescence; the Thorny Hovea (*H. acanthoclada*); the Weeping Gum (*E. sepulcharis*), which only grows at the eastern end of the Barrens Range; the Barrens Clawflower (*Calothamnus validus*); the Oak-leafed Dryandra (*D. quercifolia*); Barrens Lechenaultia (*L. superba*); and the beautiful Barrens Regelia (*R. velutina*). Any one of these species is reason enough to turn off the main highway.

In the national parks around Esperance there is a wealth of wild-flowers to be seen. In the Cape Le Grand region, look for thickets of the Showy Banksia (*B. speciosa*) and the spreading shrub of the Teasel Banksia (*B. pulchella*) in the deep sand of the plains. The rocky hills and heaths of Stokes National Park are great places to seek the Bell-fruited Mallee (*Eucalyptus preissiana*). Other flowering plants to look out for include the Nodding Banksia (*B. nutans*), the Southern Plains Banksia (*B. media*), the Shining Honeypot (*Dryandra obtusa*), the Coastal Hakea (*H. clavata*) and the remarkable Crab Claws (*Stylidium macranthum*). The stunning Pink Enamel Orchid (*Elythranthera emarginata*) is found in a number of habitats in the Esperance region.

South-East Wheatbelt
September to November

A lot more than wheat grows in this region. In the Dryandra Wood-land National Park, which is often described as an 'ecological oasis', you will spot many Golden Dryandras, the Zig Zag Grevillea (*G. flexuosa*) and Pink Rainbows (*Drosera menziesii*). Orchids also abound in this forest.

The local tourist offices can usually provide information about flowering plants in their areas. In particular in this region search out the unusual Cricket Ball Hakea (*H. platysperma*), between Coorow and Hyden; the Common Cauliflower (*Verticordia brownii*) towards Lake King; the spectacular King Dryandra (*D. proteoides*) on the ridges between Northam and Narrogin; and Red Bonnets (*Burtonia hendersoni*) near Hyden.

North of Perth
Late July to Late November

The Brand Hwy, north of Perth, is the place to see the Green Kangaroo Paw, Red Kangaroo Paw (*Anigozanthos rufus*), the Open-branched Dryandra (*D. kippistiana*) and many other dryandras.

Coomallo Creek, near Badgingarra National Park, has 200 or more wildflowers in the vicinity: the Black Kangaroo Paw *(Macropidia fuliginosa)*, Yellow Kangaroo Paw *(A. pulcherrimus)*, Scarlet *(Verticordia grandis)* and Painted Feather Flowers *(V. picta)*, the endemic Coomallo Banksia *(B. lanata)* and the Western Australian Christmas Tree *(Nuytsia floribunda)*, one of the few flowering mistletoes in the world (best seen between November and January).

There is an abundance of banksias, including the unusual Propeller Banksia *(B. candolleana)*, around Eneabba. The summer months see the Superb star Flower *(Calytrix superba)* bloom on the open sandy heaths; it has the largest flowers of any *Calytrix*.

Mingenew, on Midlands Rd (State Hwy 116), is a centre of the fledgling wildflower-growing industry. This area has a large variety of wattles, which shade the bright Pink Schoenia *(S. cassiniana)* and a number of everlastings. There are many wildflower drives nearby – keep an eye out for Red Pokers *(Hakea bucculenta)* growing in sand among tall scrub, and prickly Plume Grevillea *(G. annulifera)*, a many-branched shrub which grows on sandy heaths.

Wildflower Way
Late July to Late November

This tourist route starts at Wubin and passes through Perenjori and Morawa before it ends at Mullewa. If the rains come, this road is sandwiched between fields of everlastings, which are at their best for a six-to eight-week period.

The Wildflower Way boasts fields of everlastings *(Helichrysums* and *Helipterums)* stretching off into the distance (just like in the brochures), plus many other varieties of flowering plants.

Other beautiful wildflowers to seek out in this area are the truly magnificent Wreath Lechenaultia *(L. macrantha)*, found between Wubin and Mullewa; Rose Darwinia *(D. purpurea)*, found near granite outcrops around Mullewa; the widespread Native Foxglove *(Pityrodia terminalis)*, a grey-felted perennial herb; Pink Spike Hakea *(H. coriacea)*, found in gravelly soils between Mullewa and Southern Cross; Bottlebrush Grevillea *(G. paradoxa)* growing on heaths; and the Scarlet Honey Myrtle *(Melaleuca fulgens)*, found in gravelly soil among scrub.

If you head towards Geraldton, returning down the coast to Perth, look out for the famous Geraldton Wax *(Chamelaucium uncinatum)*, a longtime favourite in gardens.

The North-West
July to September

The Kalbarri National Park has tremendous displays of wildflowers over a long season – banksias, grevilleas and eucalypts are abundant.

The Shark Bay area and the North West Coastal Hwy from Shark Bay to Carnarvon is a region with a surprising number of flowering plants. Look out for Bright Podolepis *(P. canescans)*; Hairy Mulla

Mulla *(Ptilotus helipteroides)*; Tall mulla mulla *(P. exaltatus)*; Pincushion Mistletoe *(Amyema fitzgeraldii)*; the omnipresent Sturt's Desert Pea *(Clianthus formosus)*; Native Fuchsia *(Eremophila maculata)*; the Shark Bay Poverty Bush *(Eremophila maitlandii)*; and the strange, rare, Sapphire Bulli Bulli *(Tecticornia arborea)*.

North West Cape
April to September
The wildflower display in the Cape Range National Park is dependent on rainfall. The Cape Range Grevillea *(G. varifolia)* is particularly beautiful, as are the Rock Morning Glory *(Ipomoea costata)* and the Yardie Morning Glory *(I. yardiensis)*.

The pretty Yulbah *(Erythrina vespertilio)* is common in the canyons of the range; the leafless Toucan Flower *(Brachysema macrocarpum)* grows in sand or limestone; White Cassia *(C. pruinosa)* occurs on open rocky hillsides; Native Plumbago *(P. zeylanica)*, which grows in shaded parts of gorges, is the only species of plumbago native to Australia; the Green Bird Flower *(Crotalaria cunninghamii)*, which resembles a hummingbird in flight, is found in the coastal dunes; and Mat Mulla Mulla *(Ptilotus axillaris)* grows in open spaces in rocky soil.

One of the most unusual (but aptly named) plants you will see is the cockroach bush *(Cassia notabilis)*. The distinctive yellow pompoms of Gregory's Wattle can be found in sand or limestone country between North West Cape and Lake MacLeod.

The Pilbara
April to October
The best time to see wildflowers in the Pilbara is after the winter rain, when a thin, green blanket of growth spreads across the countryside.

In disturbed soils, the popular Sturt's Desert Pea, Tall Mulla Mulla *(Ptilotus exaltatus)* and the Northern Bluebell *(Trichodesma zeylanicum)* can be seen. Perennials include sennas, native fuchsias, and an abundance of wattles.

In sandy coastal areas, the Dampier Pea *(Swainsonia pterostylis)* and the Coastal Caper *(Capparis spinosa)* are common. The beautiful flowers of the White Dragon Tree *(Sesbania formosa)* are the largest of any native legume in WA; they are seen along rivers on the plains of the upper north-west.

The gorges of the Hamersley Range are home to many flowering plants. The striking mistletoe *(Lysiana casuarinae)* is found on many host plants; the Weeping Mulla Mulla *(Ptilotus calostachyus)* occurs on open plains among spinifex; and the Cadjeput *(Melaleuca leucadendron)*, found in many of the gorges, has terminal white 'bottlebrush-like' flowers.

The Kimberley
April to November
As well as spectacular scenery, the Kimberley has plenty of wildflowers at a time when the pickings are pretty slim in the rest of WA.

Wickham's Grevillea *(G. wickhamii)* is found in the Kimberley. Two species of *Stenocarpus*, with flowers similar to a grevillea, occur in the Kimberley; the Little Wheel Bush *(S. cunninghamii)* grows among sandstone rocks in gorges. Common on rocky sandstone hills are the magnificent Scarlet Gum *(E. Phoenicea)* and the bushy shrub Xanthostemon *(X. paradoxus)*.

Unlike the feather flowers in the south, this species occurs as a tree in the Kimberley. The Tree Feather Flower *(Verticordia cunninghamii)* grows in sand among sandstone rocks and blooms from June to August.

There are nine orchids in the Kimberley and the most common species is *Cymbidium canaliculatum*, seen throughout the region in a number of trees. The waxy flowers of the Native Hoya *(H. australis)* are found where this scrambler clings to sandstone cliffs. The *Melastoma* species, or Native Lasiandra, are attractive shrubs found throughout the tropics, hiding in shady places.

continued from page 29

Red Flowering Gum This pretty gum *(E. ficifolia)*, found on the headland of Point Irwin, between Walpole and Peaceful Bay, is another rare and restricted eucalypt. It has brilliantly coloured flowers, varying from vermilion, crimson, orange and pink. It is a small tree, reaching only 5m, with a short trunk.

FAUNA

In all, WA has 141 native mammal species, two of which are marine mammals: the Australian sea lion and the New Zealand fur seal.

Two of the state's mammals, the numbat and the honey possum, have only been recorded in WA. Australia's most restricted mammal, the Shark Bay mouse *(Pseudomys praeconis)*, is found only on Bernier Island near Shark Bay. Similarly, the western-barred bandicoot *(Perameles bougainville)* and banded hare-wallaby *(Lagostrophus fasciatus)* are now found only on Bernier and nearby Dorre Island.

Marsupials

Marsupials are mammals that raise their young in a pouch, or *marsupium*. They are largely confined to Australia and include kangaroos, wallabies, quokkas, koalas, wombats and possums – as well as others less well known, such as bandicoots and quolls.

The native marsupials most likely to be seen in the wild are wallabies, wallaroos, kangaroos and possums. There are many other marsupial species found in WA, many of them rare and fascinating, such as the rabbit-eared bandicoot or bilby (see the boxed text 'The Bilby' in the Kimberley chapter) and the curious pebble-mound mouse. Unique to the Pilbara, this mouse lives between clumps of spinifex in shallow burrows upon which it heaps a flat mound of pebbles, placed around the burrow entrance to provide insulation and moisture.

Gilbert's potoroo *(Potorous tridactylus gilberti)*, a subspecies of the long-nosed potoroo or kangaroo rat, was recently rediscovered in WA, after being thought extinct for some 100 years.

Kangaroos & Wallabies The extraordinary breeding cycle of the kangaroo is well adapted to Australia's harsh, often unpredictable environment. The young kangaroo, or joey, just millimetres long at birth, claws its way from the uterus unaided to the mother's pouch, where it attaches itself to a nipple. A day or two later, the mother mates again, but the new embryo does not begin to develop until the first joey has left the pouch permanently.

At this point the mother produces two types of milk: one formula to feed the joey at heel, the other for the baby in her pouch. If environmental conditions are right, the mother will then mate again. However, if food or water is scarce, the breeding cycle will be interrupted until conditions improve and the chances of survival are better.

As well as many species of wallaroos and wallabies (some threatened, such as the black-footed rock-wallaby), there are two main species of kangaroos in WA: the western grey *(Macropus fuliginosus)* and the red kangaroo *(Macropus rufus)*.

Quokkas By far the west's most famous example of a wallaby-type marsupial is the quokka *(Setonis brachyurus)*. The quokka is mostly found on Rottnest Island (named by explorer Willem de Vlamingh, who mistook the quokkas for rats), but it also occurs in WA's south-east forests. It is a small, robust wallaby, about a half-metre tall, with a tail about 30cm long. Its fur is grey and brown, with a reddish tinge on the upper side and a pale grey below. It can survive for a long time without water and can reputedly drink sea water.

Possums There is a wide range of possums throughout Australia; these animals have the ability to adapt to all sorts of conditions. Apart from the common ringtail and common brushtail, a number of other species are found in WA, including the scaly-tailed possum *(Wyulda squamicaudata)* and the extremely cute honey possum *(Tarsipes rostratus)*.

The little, arboreal honey possum weighs up to 20gm, is 4cm to 9cm high and has a prehensile tail from 5cm to 10cm long. It uses its long snout and long, brush-tipped tongue to dip into tubular wildflowers such as grevillea or to penetrate the stiff brushes of banksias and bottlebrushes. The honey possum is nomadic, according to the seasonal availability of favoured wildflowers.

Dunnarts These mouse-sized creatures have pointed muzzles, and large ears and eyes. Of the 18 species known, about half are found only in the western half of the continent. These include the very rare long-tailed dunnart *(Sminthopsis longicaudata)* and the sandhill dunnart *(S. psammophila)*.

Dunnarts are common in the south-west of the state and species found there include the fat-tailed *(S. crassicaudata)*, little long-tailed *(S. dolichura)*, Gilbert's *(S. gilberti)*, white-tailed *(S. granulipes)*, grey-bellied *(S. griseoventer)* and common *(S. murina)* dunnart. It is these small innocuous species that suffer most when their habitat is slashed or burnt.

Numbats The beautifully patterned numbat *(Myrmecobius fasciatus)* – a marsupial anteater – is WA's fauna symbol. It is a member of the native cat family, but is vastly different from other members of that family. It has a pointed face and its tongue can extend 10cm beyond the tip of its nose. It is thus ideally suited to search for termites in the fallen wandoo trees of south-west Australia; the species is extinct in the eastern states.

About the size of a rabbit (head and body 30cm and the tail another 20cm), the numbat is easily recognisable by the white transverse stripes across its reddish-brown fur. There is also a dark stripe across the eye from its ear to its mouth. It is endangered because of habitat destruction and predation from foxes.

Wombats Wombats are slow, solid, powerfully built marsupials with broad heads and short, stumpy legs. The common wombat *(Vombatus ursinus)* is not found in WA but the southern hairy-nosed wombat *(Lasiorhinus latifrons)* can be found in the far east of the state around Eucla.

Koalas The koala *(Phascolarctos cinereus)* is distantly related to the wombat and is found along the eastern seaboard. It is not found in the wild in WA (only in special reserves – such as Yanchep National Park).

Monotremes

Platypuses & Echidnas The platypus and the echidna are the only living representatives of the most primitive group of mammals, the monotremes, which lay eggs but also suckle their young.

The amphibious platypus *(Ornithorhynchus anatinus)* has a bill like a duck's, webbed feet and a body like a beaver's. It is not found in the wild in WA.

The short-beaked echidna *(Tachyglossus aculeatus)* is a spiny anteater that hides from predators by digging into the ground and covering itself with dirt, or by rolling itself into a ball and raising its sharp quills.

Eutherians

Dingoes The dingo *(Canis familiaris dingo)* is thought to have arrived in Australia around 6000 years ago, and was domesticated by Aborigines. It differs from the domestic dog in that it howls rather than barks, and breeds once a year rather than twice. It can interbreed with the domestic dog.

After Europeans arrived and Aborigines could no longer hunt freely, dingoes again became 'wild', and by preying on sheep they earned the wrath of graziers. The discovery of dingo bones has been used to verify the radiation of Aboriginal groups from the north-western corner of Australia.

Marine Life

The waters off the WA coast are the habitat of the sea lion, the dugong, 16 species of dolphin and 19 species of whale.

Common Dolphins Found all along the WA coast, the common dolphin *(Delphinus delphis)* favours warm, temperate waters. It is dark-grey to purple-black on its upper body and white on its underside. It is easily recognised by the gold hourglass pattern on its side. The dolphin has a sickle-shaped dorsal fin and a long, slender beak. The single calf is suckled by the mother for one to three years. Adults are from 1.7m to 2.4m long.

Bottlenose Dolphins Also favouring warmer waters, the bottlenose dolphin *(Tursiops truncatus)* is found all along the WA coast. Dark-grey in colour, this dolphin's dorsal fin is also sickle-shaped. The bottlenose dolphin gets its name from having a relatively short beak in which the lower jaw extends beyond the upper jaw. The calf is suckled by the mother for 12 to 18 months. Adults are 2.3m to 4m long. This is the dolphin people come to see at Monkey Mia and Bunbury.

Australian Sea Lions The sea lion seal *(Neophoca cinerea)* is endemic to Australia. It is found in cool, temperate waters and on rocky coastlines such as those on the southwest coast of WA. It has a bulky but streamlined body, a head shaped like a dog's, a blunt snout, front flippers and webbed hind legs. The males are chocolate-brown and the females range from silver-grey to fawn. Males are 1.8m to 2.3m long, females 1.3m to 1.8m.

Dugongs The dugong *(Dugong dugon)*, often known as the 'sea cow', is a herbivorous aquatic mammal found along the northern Australian coast from Shark Bay to the Great Barrier Reef. The Shark Bay population is estimated to be more than 10,000, about 10% of the world's dugong population. It is found in shallow tropical waters and estuaries, where it feeds on sea grasses, supplemented by algae. Its bulky body is grey to bronze on the upperside and lighter beneath, and it has a broad snout; males have a pair of protruding tusks. Dugongs can live for more than 70 years.

Fur Seals Two types of fur seal are found in Australian waters but only one type lives in WA: the New Zealand fur seal *(Arctocephalus forsteri)*. You're likely to see it sunning itself on offshore islands such as those in the Archipelago of the Recherche. The fur seal is smaller than the sea lion and its head has a more pointed snout, with long whiskers. The seal pups congregate in pods and are suckled for about a year. Males grow to between 1.5m and 2.5m, females to between 1.3m and 1.5m.

Southern Right Whales The southern right whale *(Eubalaena australis)* – so called because it was the 'right' whale to kill – was almost hunted to the point of extinction. But since the cessation of whaling it has started to return to Australian coastal waters in increasing numbers and can be seen in the waters of the Great Australian Bight and near Albany.

A baleen whale, it is easily recognised by its strongly down-curved mouth, with long baleen plates that filter water for planktonic krill (a tiny, shrimp-like crustacean). These plates were once used to make corsets. Its head and snout have callosities (barnacle-like protuberances); these are unique to each whale and aid in the identification of

Hunted almost to the point of extinction, the Southern right whale is now increasing in numbers.

individual whales. The southern right whale grows to 18m and travels alone or in small family groups.

Humpback Whales Now a regular visitor to the west and east coasts of Australia, this massive marine mammal *(Megaptera novaeangliae)* is a joy to behold. It breeds in winter in subtropical and tropical waters and in the west you are likely to see it anywhere from Cape Leeuwin to North West Cape, even off the city of Perth, as it migrates northwards from feeding grounds in the polar seas.

The back and sides are grey-black, the belly and throat are black-and-white and the baleen plates are black. The body has a humpback and there are two long flippers which have a row of knobs at the front edges. The young, more than 4m long when born, are weaned at seven months but stay with the mother for two to three years. Adult humpbacks are from 14m to 19m long and live for more than 30 years, mating every two to three years. They are also spectacular jumpers and leapers.

Fish There is a bewildering variety of fish found in WA waters, ranging from minute tropical fish to the world's largest, the whale shark *(Rhiniodon typus)*. Around 1040 of the 1500 or so species are tropical and the remainder either southern temperate (400 species) or freshwater (60 species).

Turtles These are often seen in the waters off the north-west coast of Australia. Four species can be observed coming ashore on islands and beaches to nest: green *(Chelonia mydas)*, loggerhead *(Caretta caretta)*, flatback *(Chelonia depressa)* and hawksbill *(Eretmochelys imbricata)*. All four species are protected; Aborigines, however, whose diet traditionally includes turtle, can hunt them. The flatback is believed to nest only on Australian coasts.

Turtles nest between September and April, although they can be seen in north-west waters throughout the year. Nesting occurs nightly during warmer summer months; the best time to observe this is two hours before

Loggerhead turtle

or after high tide. (For guidelines to watching nesting check with a CALM office.)

Turtles have long lives; they are thought to be about 40–50 years old before they breed. The incubation temperature determines the sex of the hatchlings; outside the temperature range of 24°C to 32°C, no egg development occurs.

Birds
About 510 bird species – of which 380 are breeding species and 130 nonbreeding migratory species – are found in WA. Fourteen species are found only in WA. More than 30 species are threatened; seven of these have been declared in need of special protection.

See also Bird-Watching in the Facts for the Visitor chapter.

Emus The only bird larger than the emu *(Dromaius novaehollandiae)* is the African ostrich, also flightless. The emu is a shaggy-feathered bird with an often curious nature. After the female emu lays the eggs, the male hatches them and raises the young. Emus are common throughout WA.

Black Swans This is the most famous of WA's birds and is very much a state symbol. The slender-necked swan *(Cygnus atratus)* is black except for white flight quills, red eyes and a red beak. It is found in all water habitats, where it builds its bulky nest of sticks, either as a floating island or on a small island. In Northam, on the Avon River, there is a colony of the introduced mute swan *(Cygnus olor)*, which is white with a yellow bill.

Parrots & Cockatoos The noisy pink-and-grey galah *(Cacatua roseicapilla)* is among the most common cockatoos, although the sulphur-crested *(C. galerita)* and pink Major Mitchell *(C. leadbeateri)* cockatoos have to be the noisiest. Other species of cockatoo seen in the state are the little corella *(C. pastinator)*, long-billed black *(Calyptorhyncus baudinii)*, red-tailed black *(C. banksii)* and Carnaby's *(C. latirostris)* cockatoos.

Lorikeets, rosellas and budgerigars are also numerous throughout the state. Parrots are seen just about everywhere, but it is the careful observer who can tell them apart: cockatiels *(Nymphicus hollandicus)* and Bourke's parrot *(Neophema bourkii)* in the arid areas; elegant parrots *(N. elegans)* along the coast; rock parrots *(N. petrophila)* also along the coast, from Esperance to Shark Bay; red-capped parrots *(Purpureicephalus spurius)* in the south-west; regents *(Polytelis anthropeplus)* throughout the goldfields; Alexandra's parrot *(P. alexandrae)* in the extremely arid centre; red-winged parrots *(Aprosmictus erythropterus)* in the Kimberley; blue bonnets *(Northiella haematogaster)* on the Nullarbor; and 28s or Port Lincoln ringnecks *(Barnardius zonarius)* just about everywhere from the Pilbara south.

Raptors Birds that prey on other species have long been a subject of fascination for bird-watchers, and species of all three families of raptors found in Australia can be observed in WA.

The osprey *(Pandion haliaetus)* is found along the coast from the Kimberley to Esperance; several actually nest in Broome. The white-bellied sea eagle *(Haliaeetus leucogaster)* is also found along the coast and you will definitely see it in the Archipelago of the Recherche. The majestic wedge-tailed eagle *(Aquila audax)* is seen throughout the state, often feeding on road kills. The brahminy kite *(Milvus indus)* is seen in north-west mud flats and mangroves.

Kookaburras A member of the kingfisher family, the kookaburra is heard as much as it is seen – you can't miss its loud, cackling laugh, usually at dawn and sunset.

Kookaburras can become quite tame and pay regular visits to friendly households.

In WA, the laughing kookaburra *(Dacelo novaeguineae)* is found in the south-west; in the Kimberley and the coastal centre of the state, the blue-winged kookaburra *(D. leachii)*, unfamiliar in eastern states, can be found.

Reptiles

There are at least 750 known species of Australian reptiles and 439 of these are found in WA. The two main deserts, the Great Sandy and Great Victoria, each support about 75 species of reptile. One of the world's rarest species, the western swamp tortoise, is found in one nature reserve near Perth.

Snakes All of the species of snake found in WA are protected. Many are poisonous, some deadly, but very few are at all aggressive and they'll usually get out of your way before you even realise that they are there. (See also Dangers & Annoyances and Cuts, Bites & Stings under Health in the Facts for the Visitor chapter.)

The best known of the local venomous species is the dugite *(Pseudonaja affinis)*, which is confined to the southernmost part of WA, including the Perth metropolitan area and Rottnest Island. The greenish-brown to greenish-grey dugite prefers sandy areas and places where house mice are plentiful.

One species of blind snake *(Rhamphotyphlops leptosoma)* is known only from the area around Kalbarri. Other venomous snakes found in the west are the desert death adder *(Acanthopus pyrrhus)*, mulga snake *(Pseudechis australis)* and black-striped snake *(Vermicella calonota)*; the latter occurs within a 35km radius of Perth.

Crocodiles There are two types of crocodile in Australia: the extremely dangerous saltwater crocodile *(Crocodylus porosus)*, or 'saltie' as it is known, and the less aggressive freshwater crocodile *(Crocodylus johnstoni)*, or 'freshie'. These living relics existed 200 million years before humans.

Salties are not only confined to salt water. They inhabit estuaries, and, following floods, may be found many kilometres from the coast. They may even be found in fresh water more than 100km inland.

See the boxed text 'Freshies & Salties' in the Kimberley chapter.

Lizards There is a wide variety of lizards in WA, from tiny skinks to prehistoric-looking goannas which can grow up to 2.5m, although most species you'll encounter in WA are much smaller. Goannas can run very fast and when threatened will use their big claws to climb the nearest tree – or perhaps the nearest leg! The 'racing' goanna (known as the 'bungarra') is most often seen.

Blue-tongue lizards, slow-moving and stumpy, are children's favourites and are sometimes kept as pets. Their even slower and stumpier relations, shingle-backs, are common in the Darling Range near Perth.

More fleet-footed are the frilled lizards *(Chlamydosaurus kingii)* and the bizarre and ugly (or beautiful, if you are of the same species) thorny or mountain devil *(Moloch horridus)*. The latter can change colour by a variation of skin pigments to match the desert sand or clay surface.

NATIONAL PARKS & RESERVES
Covering almost 200,000 sq km, WA's more than 70 national parks and marine parks, and countless recreation sites, are administered by CALM. They cover a diverse range of landforms, marine environments and flora and fauna, but they do not cover a large area of this huge state. Rather, they tend to focus on special features; exploration of these parks will reward the traveller with breathtaking scenery, fascinating glimpses of ancient cultures, and objects of interest at almost every turn.

National parks include: Purnululu (Bungle Bungle); Ningaloo Marine Park; Cape Range; Shark Bay Marine Park; Karijini (formerly Hamersley Range National Park); Millstream-Chichester; Nambung; Fitzgerald River; Walpole-Nornalup; Leeuwin-Naturaliste; and Stirling Range. In addition to the national parks, there are 1100 nature reserves and seven marine conservation reserves.

Free pamphlets on all of the main parks, forests and marine reserves are published by CALM; it also sells a number of interesting publications. (See National Parks under Books in the Facts for the Visitor chapter.)

As well as the main office in Perth (see Department of Conservation under Ecology & Environment earlier in this chapter), there are a number of CALM regional offices, listed throughout this book.

National Parks Passes
Of the national parks, 24 require a fee for vehicles (which is often the only way to get into the park): $8 per vehicle, per day ($3 for motorcycles or bus passengers). If you're planning to visit more than one park, get a holiday pass ($20), which allows unlimited entry to the state's national parks for one month. The all-parks annual pass ($45) provides unlimited access for a year. Another option is the local park pass ($15), which allows entry to one park (or a group of local parks, such as Karijini and Millstream-Chichester) for 12 months.

Passes can be purchased from CALM in Perth, and from CALM offices around the state.

GOVERNMENT & POLITICS
One of the six states which, together with the Australian Capital Territory and the NT, make up the Australian Federation, WA is represented vice-regally by a governor who performs official and ceremonial functions pertaining to the Crown. The state contributes 12 senators to the Senate at federal level and a proportional number of members of parliament based on population figures.

The state parliament consists of two parts (a Legislative Council and a Legislative Assembly). The principal minister is called the premier. At the time of writing, Premier Richard Court, is the leader of a coalition of Liberal and National Parties. The main opposition is the ALP.

See also Post-War to Present under History in this chapter.

ECONOMY

The backbone of WA's economy has traditionally been mining and agriculture. However, the 1990s saw new sources of wealth from the expanding technology, manufacturing and service sectors.

Over the past 10 years WA has had the fastest-growing state economy, averaging 5% annually compared with the national average of 2.8%.

In 1997/98, WA's gross state product totalled $61.6 billion and accounted for 11% of the national economy. In 1998/99, WA contributed 23% of Australia's total exports, well above its 10% share of the nation's population base.

While historical economic strengths in agriculture (especially wheat but also forestry and fisheries), mineral commodities and (more recently) oil and gas still dominate the state's exports, WA is taking a more powerful place in the Australian and global economy, developing and exporting a diverse range of goods and services.

The state's growing manufacturing sector contributes around 10% of exports. The products it sells to the world include high-speed ferries, chemicals, mining and rail equipment, communication devices and processed foods and beverages.

Tourism is one of the real growth industries. It is worth around $2.5 billion annually, and more than 10% of the state's workforce is engaged in the industry. Singapore and the UK are the main sources of foreign tourists, although most tourists (around 80%) are from WA or the other states.

POPULATION & PEOPLE

With a population of 1.8 million people, WA accounts for about a tenth of the nation's population. Immigration contributes to the growth (currently around 2%) and diversification of the population, but WA remains a sparsely populated state. There is a large number of British migrants (at 170,000, almost as big as Melbourne's quota), as well as migrants from Ireland, South Africa, New Zealand, Germany, India, Greece, Italy, Poland, the Netherlands and the former Yugoslavia. Its proximity to Asia also means that WA has a sizable Asian population, particularly from Malaysia, Singapore and Vietnam. Perth has more Singaporeans than either Sydney or Melbourne.

Land of the Sandgropers

You will often hear Western Australians colloquially referred to as 'sandgropers'. The actual sandgroper is a subterranean insect known as a cylindrachetid, believed to be a descendant of the grasshopper group. Five species of sandgroper have been found in Australia, one in Papua New Guinea and one separate species in Argentina.

Sandgropers' bodies are perfectly adapted for 'groping' or burrowing in the sandy soils of the Swan Coastal Plain where they are found. They have a swimming motion through sand – propelled with powerful forelegs, their streamlined bodies with middle and hind legs tucked away offer very little resistance.

Like grasshoppers, sandgropers develop from egg to adult with no larval stage. They appear to be vegetarian, although some studies show that at least one species is omnivorous.

Human sandgropers have a diet of Swan Lager and marron, they enjoy sunbathing, footy and surfing, they eat in Freo's cafe strip and they holiday at Rottnest Island. They have yet to perfect the sand-swimming technique.

Around 47,000 Aborigines – about 16% of the nation's total (and roughly the same number as before European colonisation) – are estimated to live in WA.

ARTS

The west has a rich tradition of fine arts, with painting, indigenous art, sculpture and ceramics well represented. Although WA's cultural scene is smaller than those of Sydney/NSW or Melbourne/Victoria, it has a solid artistic and cultural base; the state (particularly Perth) has produced a notable string of contributors in all facets of artistic and cultural endeavour over the years. There is a resident symphony orchestra, an opera, a ballet company, a number of theatre companies, an impressive art gallery, several excellent museums – including the Western Australian Museum (WA Museum) and the Maritime Museum at Fremantle – and literary publishing houses.

The Festival of Perth, Australia's oldest cultural festival, takes place each February, with local and international performers. The Perth Concert Hall is a solid focus for opera and classical music throughout the year. (See Public Holidays & Special Events in the Facts for the Visitor chapter for listings of major festivals around the state.)

The epicentre of fine arts in the west is the Perth Cultural Centre in Northbridge (see the Perth chapter), which includes the Alexander Library, WA Museum, the Art Gallery of Western Australia (AGWA), and the innovative Perth Institute of Contemporary Art (commonly referred to by its acronym, PICA). There are many other galleries in Perth, Fremantle and the south-west region.

Current exhibitions and concerts are listed in the *West Australian* newspaper. They are also listed in the *Gallery Guide*, available from the Art Gallery of WA and private galleries. In country towns, check the local press.

Music

From a pub band in Freo (Fremantle) to a symphony orchestra playing under the stars at a Margaret River winery, to the resonating vibrations of Aboriginal music, all choices of music are available in WA.

Classical The Western Australian Symphony Orchestra (WASO) performs regularly at the Perth Concert Hall and has made many acclaimed recordings. There is also a state youth orchestra.

The Perth Concert Hall has an annual calendar of events which includes the WASO playing classical repertoire, and prominent international performers from chamber groups to pop stars.

The west has also provided a cavalcade of composers including Janet Dobie of Armadale, George Tibbits of Boulder and Jennifer Fowler of Bunbury.

Renowned performers include the saxophonist Peter Clinch, baritones Bruce Martin (a Wagner specialist) and Greg Yurisich, soprano Glenys Fowles and mezzo-soprano Lorna Sydney.

Rock & Pop There's a healthy pop scene in Perth these days, but it wasn't always so. While a lot of good musicians grew up in WA, they inevitably gravitated to Sydney and Melbourne. One such muso was Ronald ('Bon') Scott, who was known for raunchy vocals as the lead singer of AC/DC.

In the 1980s, Dave Faulkner crossed the Nullarbor to Sydney to form the immensely successful Hoodoo Gurus; the guitarist in the Innocent Bystanders became Diesel; and a legend in the west, Dave Warner, crooned the poignant lines of 'I'm Just a Suburban Boy'.

Perth also produced the bands the Dugites, the Scientists, Chad's Tree and The Triffids. The latter band drew rave critical reviews in the UK and France for their countrified rock, showcased in their album *Treeless Plain*.

Contemporary home-grown Perth bands that have enjoyed national success include Jebediah, Ammonia, Sodastream and Eskimo Joe.

There are plenty of venues around Perth where you can see and hear any type of modern music from grunge to covers. You can find out where the action is in *Xpress* magazine, available free from record shops and pubs. (See Entertainment in the Perth chapter for more details.)

Jazz The Avon Valley town of York hosts a jazz festival in September. Jazz lovers have a number of regular venues in Perth (see Entertainment in the Perth chapter).

Aboriginal In the north-west you may have the opportunity to see a contemporary Aboriginal band. The Broome Musicians Aboriginal Corporation was established to promote and develop music among the Aboriginal community and protect musicians from the usual rip-offs associated with the industry. There is a distinctive 'Broome sound' which combines *corroboree* influences, folk music from a number of sources such as Polynesia and Asia, and even Gregorian chant. There has been a succession of bands: the Broome Beats, Tombstone Shadows (aka Crossfire, aka Scrap Metal), Maja, Chocolate Solja, Black Label, Sunburn and Bingurr.

The only major Aboriginal cultural event in WA is the Stompem Festival, held in Broome in October.

Literature

Encompassing the unpolished, rough humour of the early writers from the north-west and goldfields to sophisticated works from a string of modern writers, WA's literary tradition is remarkably fecund.

By far the most prolific of WA's writers was Katharine Susannah Prichard. Though she wasn't born in WA, she settled there in 1916, and wrote extensively on WA themes, often infusing her own communist beliefs into many of her works. *Black Opal* (1921) deals with the independent ownership of mines in the mythical town of Fallen Star Ridge; *Working Bullocks* (1926) is about the timber-getters in the forests of the southwest; *Coonardoo* (1929) examines the taboo subject of black–white sexual relationships; and *The Roaring Nineties* (1946), *Golden Miles* (1948) and *Winged Seeds* (1950) are parts of an enormous socialist realist trilogy about the goldfields.

Henrietta Drake-Brockman, a contemporary of Prichard's, was known mainly for her work *Men without Wives and Other Plays* (1955). Her novels include *Blue North* (1934), set in the pearling town of Broome, and *Sheba Lane* (1936), also set in Broome, when it is no longer a rollicking frontier town.

Respected author Peter Cowan has written a number of collections of short stories *(Drift, The Unploughed Land, The Empty Street, The Tins and Mobiles)* since the end of WWII, most of which have a theme of isolation very much influenced by the WA bush.

Randolph Stow was an accomplished novelist, poet and librettist. His work has deservedly won many awards and his *The Merry-Go-Round in the Sea* (1965), a semi-autobiographical look at life through the eyes of a child in Geraldton, is one of Australia's most popular novels.

Not strictly a novel, but dramatic in its presentation, is Dame Mary Durack's saga of her own family in *Kings in Grass Castles* (1959). The sequel to this monumental work on life in the Kimberley was *Sons in the Saddle* (1983).

One of WA's great modern writers is English-born Elizabeth Jolley, who has won numerous writing awards for her unusual short stories and novels, including the Miles Franklin award for *The Well* (1987). Her most recent works include the 1999 novel *An Accommodating Spouse*, and the short-story collection *Fellow Passengers* (1997).

Jack Davis' *The First-Born and other Poems* (1970) was a watershed in Aboriginal literature. The work was 'discovered' almost by accident after Davis had pinned it on a board outside his office in the Perth Aboriginal Centre. He was later named Aboriginal Writer of the Year (1981) and, in 1985, won the inaugural Sidney Myer Performing Arts Award.

Another outstanding talent is the Aboriginal writer Archie Weller. His *The Day of the Dog*, tracing the fall of the traditional male role in Aboriginal society, garnered great reviews and was highly commended in the 1980 Vogel literary award.

Sally Morgan's autobiography *My Place* charts her Aboriginality and outlines her grandmother's family history. Winner of the inaugural Human Rights and Equal Opportunity Commission Humanitarian award (1987), she also won, in 1988, the WA Week literary award for nonfiction.

Many of the works of Dorothy Hewett (born in Perth in 1923) can be linked to the Great Southern region of the state, including *Windmill Country* (1965), *Rapunzel in Suburbia* (1979) and the plays *The Man from Mukinupin* (1980) and *The Fields of Heaven* (1982).

Author of *Cloudstreet* (1991) and *The Riders* (1995), Tim Winton (born in Perth in 1960) is widely considered to be one of Australia's best contemporary writers. His first novel, *An Open Swimmer*, was joint winner of the Vogel award in 1981 and his second, *Shallows* (1984), won the prestigious Miles Franklin award. Many of Winton's novels feature WA and its landscape, but nowhere is this more evident than in *Land's Edge* (1993), his memoir of a coastal boyhood and a celebration of the WA coast – complete with superb photographs.

Keith McLeod's first novel, *Shore and Shelter* (2000), is set in the south-west of WA, where he was born, and on fishing boats off the coast.

Magabala Books in Broome is the first Aboriginal publishing house in Australia. It aims to preserve Aboriginal culture and history through the written word, and to promote Aboriginal culture to non-Aborigines. Titles include *Lori* by John Wilson and *Don't Go Around the Edges* by Daisy Utemmorah.

Architecture

The most dominating aspect of Perth's architecture is the line of uninspiring skyscrapers that tower above the Swan River. Fortunately, a few fine stone and brick buildings survive (see the Perth chapter) and, not far out of the city, there are gracious Victorian homes. Fremantle's architectural heritage survives thanks to the efforts of residents who fought to preserve it.

The goldfields architecture, often referred to as 'Boom architecture', is the most noticeable aspect of a number of towns in the west. This is most apparent along Kalgoorlie-Boulder's Hannan St (see the boxed text 'Architecture, Kalgoorlie-Boulder Style' in the Southern Outback chapter). The wealth from gold also contributed to the fine architecture seen in Gwalia, Coolgardie and Cue.

There are many examples of vernacular-style homes – those which show ingenious adaptation to the climate and clever use of local, available building materials – in WA. Examples are: Bedamanup Homestead in Gingin; the houses of Yalgoo; the timber-slab-and-stone cottage in West Arthur; Old Blythewood near Pinjarra; the shell-block church in Denham; and the fieldstone buildings of Milligan Homestead near Kellerberrin.

One of the most famous architects in WA was the enigmatic and controversial Monsignor John Hawes (see the boxed text 'Monsignor John Hawes' in the Central West Coast chapter).

Film

The west does not have a large film industry. The Western Australian Film Commission, founded in 1978, produced some good films in the early 1980s, including *Harlequin* and *Roadgames* (neither of which achieved widespread exposure) and the TV series *Falcon Island*. The feminist film *Shame*, starring Deborah Lee-Furness and directed by Steve Jodrell, is set in an isolated WA community and examines attitudes towards rape.

The Film Corporation of WA is a private company which has produced *Runnin' on Empty* (1982), *We of the Never Never* (1982) and *Winds of Jarrah* (1983).

More recent productions which were well received both in Australia and (to a lesser extent) abroad include *Blackfellas*, *Sisterly Love*, *Windrider*, *Fran*, *Under the Lighthouse Dancing* (shot at Rottnest Island) and *Justice*. Most of these films are available for hire from local libraries and good video outlets in WA.

Children's films and TV series of note include *Minty*, *Clowning Around*, *Sweat*, *The Gift* and *Fast Tracks*.

The documentary industry in WA is recognised as a world leader in the genre. *Whalesong*, *Belinda's Baby*, *Diving School*,

Hutan, *The Human Race*, *The Last of the Nomads*, *Dolphins Day* and *The Nature of Healing* are a few of many examples.

The west has given us actors such as Kate Fitzpatrick, Rolf Harris, Alan Cassell, Phillip Ross and Alwyn Kurts (immortalised in TV shows such as *Cop Shop*). The Western Australian Academy of Performing Arts in Perth has some notable alumni making waves both in Australia and internationally. These include: Australian TV's favourite daughter Lisa McCune (of *Blue Heelers* and *Sound of Music* fame); the luminous, talented Frances O'Connor, who has starred in successful films such as *Love and Other Catastrophes* and *Mansfield Park*; and Hugh Jackman, star of the recent Hollywood blockbuster *X-Men*. Heath Ledger, star of *The Patriot* and dubbed 'the next Mel Gibson', grew up in Perth.

Theatre

Theatre is alive and well in the west. The Perth Theatre Company (PTC), Black Swan and Barking Gecko theatre companies reside in Perth. The city also has a number of venues for live theatre, the most striking being the beautiful Edwardian-style His Majesty's Theatre (see the Perth chapter).

A number of playwrights were either born or began their careers in the west. The expatriate Alan Seymour gave us *One Day of the Year* (1962), an examination of generational differences over the course of one Anzac Day. The son of Katharine Susannah Prichard, Ric Throssell, has continued his family's literary tradition, producing a string of satires and plays with serious themes. Dorothy Hewett, known for her poetry, has also written many plays.

The stage adaptation of Tim Winton's novel *Cloudstreet*, a co-production between the Black Swan Theatre and the Belvoir St Theatre, had a highly successful Australian and international tour in 1998–99, receiving rave reviews.

The prolific WA writer Jack Davis has had plays produced throughout Australia and, in 1986, with *The Dreamers*, became the first Aborigine to have a play performed in the UK.

The first Aboriginal stage musical came from Broome. Jimmy Chi's *Bran Nue Dae* has since been produced throughout Australia. *Sistergirl*, a tragicomedy about racial reconciliation, is the first play by WA writer Sally Morgan, and another production that has fared well in Australia.

Painting

In the 1890s there was an influx of people who had formal training as painters, such as FM Williams, AW Bassett, George Pitt Morrison and James WR Linton. The well-known artist Daisy Rossi, whose wildflower and garden paintings were widely exhibited, was prominent during and after WWI.

The 1930s heralded a discernible change in subject matter: Aboriginal portraiture and cityscapes became serious themes. In the late 1930s, Herbert McLintock, as Max Ebert, made an impact with his figurative surrealist compositions; he later joined a group of realists in Sydney and was an official war artist during WWII.

Following WWII, artists branched out from Perth in search of subject matter. Two good interpreters of the Outback were the German Elise Blumann and the late Elizabeth Durack. Blumann painted Aborigines living on the fringe of European society and Durack looked to the familiar Kimberley for many of her ideas.

In 1997 Elizabeth Durack (aged 81) became embroiled in the 'Eddie Burrup' art scandal when she entered her paintings, signed 'Burrup', in an Aboriginal art award. In Australia's highly sensitive and culturally cringing art world her actions caused an earthquake; in the ancient Kimberley they caused no more than a ripple on the surface of Lake Argyle.

Well-known modern WA painters have looked to the local landscape and the special light in the west for their inspiration. Robert Juniper, Guy Grey Smith and George Haynes are three artists to have achieved recent success. While their art would not be considered avant-garde in the eastern states, it nonetheless reflects an inspired interpretation of the aridity and untamed nature of their surroundings. A good place to see the work of Juniper is in the Holy Trinity Church in York, where his designs for stained glass are featured.

Aboriginal Arts

Visual imagery is a fundamental part of Aboriginal life, serving as a connection between past and present, between the supernatural and the earthly, between people and the land. The earliest forms of Aboriginal artistic expression were rock carvings (petroglyphs), body painting and ground designs.

While paintings from the Central Australian Aboriginal communities of the NT and WA are among the more readily identifiable form of contemporary Aboriginal art, there's a huge range of material being produced across Australia, including bark paintings from Arnhem Land, ironwood carving from the Tiwi Islands north of Darwin, batik and woodcarving from Central Australia, didgeridoos and more. A number of Aboriginal artists are now experimenting with printmaking, combining their traditional methods of artistic expression with the techniques of etching, lithography and screen-printing to produce limited editions of images, which can be quite affordable.

Although the art of the more traditional communities differs in style from urban works, a common theme that appears to run through all the works is the strong and ancient connection Aboriginal people have with the land, often mixed with a deep sense of loss occasioned by the horror of the last 200 years. Ultimately, however, the viewer is left with a sense of Aboriginal cultural strength and renewal.

The Art Gallery of WA in Perth has one of the world's best collections of Aboriginal art, while the WA Museum and the Berndt Museum of Anthropology have large collections of artefacts.

Rock Painting Rock art exists in the Kimberley in WA. The art of this region is best known for its images of the Wandjina, a group of ancestor beings who came from the sky and sea and were associated with fertility. They controlled the elements and were responsible for the formation of the country's natural features.

Wandjina images are found painted on rock as well as on more recent, portable art media, with some of the rock images more than 7m long. They generally appear in human form, with large black eyes, a nose but no mouth, a halo around the head (representative of both hair and clouds), and a black oval shape on the chest.

The other significant style of painting found in the Kimberley is that of the so-called Bradshaw figures (named after the first European who saw them). The Bradshaw figures are generally small and seem to depict ethereal beings engaged in ceremony or dance. It is believed that they predate the Wandjina paintings, though little is known about their significance or meaning.

Western Desert Painting Western Desert 'dot' painting partly evolved from 'ground paintings', which formed the centrepiece of dances and songs. While dot paintings may look random and abstract, they usually depict a Dreaming journey, and so can be seen almost as aerial landscape maps. Many paintings feature the tracks of birds, animals and humans. Subjects may be depicted by the imprint they leave in the sand: a simple arc depicts a person (as that is the print left by someone sitting); a *coolamon* (wooden carrying dish) is shown by an oval shape, a digging stick by a single line, a campfire by a circle. Concentric circles usually depict Dreaming sites, or places where ancestors paused in their journeys.

While these symbols are widely used, their meaning within each individual painting is known only by the artist and particular members of their community. In this way sacred stories can be publicly portrayed, as the deeper meaning is not evident to most viewers.

The first permanent image was painted on a school wall at Papunya Tula (in the NT about 250km west of Alice Springs) by a group of Aboriginal elders. The mural spawned an interest among the local Aboriginal community (many of whom were displaced from other areas) in painting permanent images on board and later on canvas, and led to the establishment of

Papunya Tula Pty Ltd, the first Aboriginal cooperative to manage the sale and distribution of the artists' work.

When the Aborigines were allowed to resettle in their tribal homelands in the early 1980s, a number of artists moved from Papunya to Balgo, a remote community on the edge of the Great Sandy Desert in WA, and continued painting in the Western Desert 'style' (see Contemporary Painting below).

Bark Painting An important part of the cultural heritage of Arnhem Land Aboriginal people, bark painting is rarely produced in WA. It's difficult to establish when bark was first used, partly because it is perishable – very old pieces don't exist.

One of the main features of Arnhem Land bark paintings is the use of cross-hatching designs, based on body paintings of the past. The paintings can also be broadly categorised by their regional styles. In the west the tendency is towards naturalistic images and plain backgrounds, while to the east the use of geometric designs is more common.

The art reflects Dreaming themes that vary by region. In eastern Arnhem Land the prominent ancestor beings are the Djangkawu, who travelled the land with elaborate dilly bags (carry bags) and digging sticks (for making waterholes), and the Wagilag Sisters, who are associated with snakes and waterholes. In western Arnhem Land the Rainbow Serpent, Yingarna, is the significant being. The Mimi spirits – who taught the Aborigines to hunt and gather food – are another feature of western Arnhem Land art, both on bark and rock.

Contemporary Painting There's a thriving contemporary art scene in WA. In Broome and Fitzroy Crossing, artists such as Jimmy Pike, Peter Skipper, and 'Jarinyanu' David Downs are popular. Lily Karedada, from Broome, is well known for her Wandjina style.

Contemporary art in the eastern Kimberley also features elements of the works of the desert peoples of Central Australia, a legacy of the forced relocation of people

during the 1970s. The community of Warmun, at Turkey Creek on the Great Northern Hwy, has been particularly active in ensuring that Aboriginal culture through painting and dance remains strong. Some of the best-known artists from this area include Rover Thomas, Queenie McKenzie and Hector Jandany.

Another area of WA where Aboriginal artists are actively producing work is Balgo, on the edge of the Great Sandy Desert. The art from Balgo is characterised by geometric form and the vivid use of colour, as best seen in works by Peter Sunfly (Sandfly) Tjampitjin, Susie Bootja Bootja Napangarti and Donkeyman Lee Tjupurrula.

Artists working outside traditional communities produce work that is both thought-provoking and at times deeply confronting; it often illustrates the terrible injustices of the past 200 years while raising issues about the place of Aboriginal culture and the artist in the modern post-colonial world.

The respected WA writer Sally Morgan is also a nationally recognised artist and printmaker widely exhibited throughout Australia. She was awarded an AM (Member of the Order of Australia) in 1990.

Artefacts & Crafts Objects traditionally made for practical or ceremonial uses, such as weapons and musical instruments, often featured intricate and symbolic decoration. In recent years many communities have also developed nontraditional craft forms that have created employment and income. They include didgeridoos, boomerangs, wooden sculptures, ceremonial shields, and fibre craft such as woven dilly bags, baskets, garments and fishing nets.

Another art form, from the western Kimberley, is the engraved pearl-shell pendants that come from the Broome area. It is believed that the Aboriginal people of the area were using pearl shell for decoration before the arrival of Europeans, but with the establishment of the pearling industry in Broome in the late 19th century the use of pearl shell increased markedly. The highly prized shells were engraved and used for ceremonial purposes, as well as for personal decoration and

Buying Aboriginal Art & Artefacts

One of the best and most evocative reminders of your trip is an Aboriginal work of art or artefact. By buying authentic items you are supporting Aboriginal culture and helping to ensure that traditional skills and designs endure. Unfortunately, much of the so-called Aboriginal art sold as souvenirs is ripped off from Aboriginal people or is just plain fake. Admittedly it is often difficult to tell whether an item is genuine, or whether a design is being used legitimately, but it is worth trying to find out.

The best place to buy artefacts is either directly from the communities that have craft outlets or from galleries and shops that are owned and operated by Aboriginal communities. This way you can be sure that the items are genuine and that the money you spend goes to the right people. There are many Aboriginal artists who get paid very small sums for their work, only to find it being sold for thousands in city galleries.

Didgeridoos are the hot item these days, and you need to decide whether you want a decorative piece or an authentic and functional musical instrument. Many of the didgeridoos sold are not made by Aboriginal people, and there are even stories of backpackers in Darwin earning good money by making or decorating didgeridoos. Do some research and avoid disappointment.

If you're interested in buying a painting, possibly in part for its investment potential, then it's best to purchase the work from a community art centre, Aboriginal-owned gallery or reputable non-Aboriginal-owned gallery. Regardless of its individual aesthetic worth, in most cases a painting purchased without a certificate of authenticity from either a reputable gallery or community art centre will not be easy to resell at a later time, even if the painting is attributed to a well-known artist.

A number of places, especially in the north of the state, sell exquisitely carved emu eggs and boab nuts. Derby is a good place to buy carved boab nuts; inquire at the tourist centre. Bottle-green emu eggs are particularly beautiful; they can be seen in many of the galleries selling traditional Aboriginal crafts.

Places to buy Aboriginal paintings and crafts are: Waringarri Aboriginal Arts in Kununurra; Mangkaja Aboriginal Arts Centre in Fitzroy Crossing; at various places in Broome and Derby; and from outlets in and around Perth, including Creative Native, 32 King St, and Indigenart, 115 Hay St, Subiaco, and 82 High St, Fremantle.

trade – examples of this art have been found as far away as Queensland and SA.

The designs engraved into the shells were usually fairly simple geometric patterns that had little symbolic importance. The practice of pearl-shell engraving has largely died out, although the decorated shells are still highly valued.

RELIGION

A shrinking majority (around 58%) of people in Australia are at least nominally Christian. Most Protestant churches have merged to become the Uniting Church, although the Church of England has remained separate. The Catholic Church is popular (about half of Australian Christians are Catholics), with original Irish adherents boosted by large numbers of Mediterranean immigrants.

Non-Christian minority religions include: Buddhism, Judaism and Islam (the town of Katanning in the wheatbelt of WA has a significant Muslim population made up of Christmas Islanders). Almost 20% of the Australian population describe themselves as having no religion.

LANGUAGE

While English is the main language of Australia, languages other than English are in common use, as you'd expect in a country with such a diverse ethnic mix. The 1996 census found that 240 languages other than English were being spoken in homes, and almost 50 of these were indigenous languages. This amounts to a language other than English being used in 15% of Australian households.

The non-English languages most commonly spoken in Australia are, in order: Italian, Greek, Cantonese, Arabic and Vietnamese. Languages rapidly growing in use are Mandarin, Vietnamese and Cantonese, while those most in decline include Dutch, German, Italian and Greek.

Aboriginal Language

At the time of European settlement, there were around 250 separate Australian Aboriginal languages, comprising about 700 dialects. It is believed that all these languages evolved from a single language family as the Aboriginal people gradually moved out over the entire continent and split into new groups.

There are a number of words, however, that occur right across the continent, such as *jina* (foot) and *mala* (hand), and similarities also exist in the often complex grammatical structures.

Following European settlement the number of Aboriginal languages was drastically reduced. Today, only around 30 are regularly spoken and being taught to children.

Aboriginal Kriol is a new language which has developed since European arrival in Australia. It is spoken across northern Australia and has become the 'native' tongue of many young Aborigines. It contains many English words, but the pronunciation and grammatical usage are along Aboriginal lines, the meaning is often different, and the spelling is phonetic. For example, the English sentence 'He was amazed' becomes 'I bin luk kwesjinmak' in Kriol.

There are a number of generic terms which Aborigines use to describe themselves, and these vary according to the region. The term Murri is used in Queensland, Nyungar or Nyoongah in the south-west of WA, Yolnu in north-eastern Arnhem Land and Koori or Koorie in NSW and Victoria.

Facts for the Visitor

HIGHLIGHTS

It's difficult to select just a few highlights for a state which attracts – and justifies – so many superlative descriptions. Western Australia (WA) is fast becoming one of the great ecotourism destinations of the world, and there is something for everyone here, at any time of the year.

However if we had to name our absolute highlights we'd probably mention the following: the vast expanses of bush rubbing shoulders with the manicured botanical gardens of Kings Park in Perth; the excellent Western Australian Museum and Art Gallery of Western Australia in Perth and the Maritime Museum in Fremantle; the cosmopolitan cafe society of Perth's Subiaco, Northbridge, Leederville and Cottesloe; pedalling, surfing and chilling out on Rottnest Island; watching whales and their young in the Great Australian Bight; enjoying the beaches, wineries and gourmet delights of the Margaret River region; the karri and tingle forests in the south-west; swimming with whale sharks off the coast near Exmouth; exploring the gorges of Kalbarri, Karijini and the Kimberley; understanding the textured, multicultural histories of Broome and Geraldton; and getting a true feeling for Australia's vastness after driving for hours on empty highways.

SUGGESTED ITINERARIES

The distances in WA are huge and should not be underestimated when planning a trip. In two weeks you'd get a good feel for Perth, Fremantle, Rottnest, the Pinnacles and the south-west. A month would allow you to explore farther afield – either south and east to Kalgoorlie, Albany and Esperance, or north to Kalbarri, Monkey Mia, Exmouth and Broome. If you want to see all of the above, six weeks is a reasonable time. Add a couple more weeks for the Pilbara and Kimberley. If you want to do more than scratch the surface of this vast state, three months is the minimum time frame.

PLANNING
When to Go

Any time is a good time to be in WA, but as you'd expect in a state this large, different parts are at their best at different times.

The southern part of the state is most popular during the summer months (December to February), as it's warm enough for swimming and it's great to be outdoors. But in the centre of the state it's too hot to do anything much then, while in the far north, summer is the wet season, when roads get flooded and the heat and humidity can make life pretty uncomfortable. On the other hand, if you want to see the Kimberley green and free of dust, be treated to some spectacular electrical storms and have the best of the fishing while all the other tourists are down south, this is the time to do it.

Spring (September to November) and autumn (March to May) offer the greatest flexibility for a short visit, as you can combine highlights of the whole state while avoiding the extremes of the weather. This is also the best time to see wildflowers, which can be absolutely stunning after rain.

The other major consideration when travelling in WA is school holidays. Families take to the road (and air) en masse at these times and many places are booked out, prices rise and things generally get a bit crazy. Holidays vary somewhat from state to state, but in WA the main holiday period is from late December to late January; the other two-week periods are roughly mid- to late April, mid- to late July, and early to late October.

Maps

The only place in Perth with a good range of maps (including all of the ones that are mentioned here) is the friendly Perth Map Centre (☎ 9322 5733), at 884 Hay St.

Lonely Planet publishes *Australia Road Atlas*, which has 20 maps that together cover the entire state of WA, including a handy city map of Perth.

The Royal Automobile Club of Western Australia (RACWA) publishes a series of useful road maps (approximate scale 1:250,000), including: *Perth City & Suburbs*; *Perth Region*; *Lower South West*; *Geraldton City & Region*; *Kalgoorlie/Boulder City & Region*; *Esperance Region*; and *Perth to Port Hedland*. These maps cost between $3 and $6, and can also be purchased from the RACWA's Web site at www.rac.com.au. Explore Australia/Penguin publishes a very useful map that covers Perth and surrounding suburbs, Fremantle, the south-west and Albany – all on the one map ($4.95).

Two excellent street directories are published by UBD: *Perth* and *Western Australia: Cities and Towns*, with 145 maps of all major and minor towns. These are also available from petrol stations and some bookshops.

The WA Department of Lands Administration produces detailed topographical maps on scales of 1:50,000 and 1:25,000, which are good for bushwalking. The most popular topographical maps for Outback touring are those in the Natmap series (produced by the Australian government), which cost around $8 each and are available in a range of scales.

See the Getting Around chapter for information on maps for cycling.

What to Bring

Anything you might need can be bought in WA: a sunhat; sunscreen; insect repellent; comfortable clothing; boogie board or surfboard; bicycle; tent; sleeping bag; camping supplies; water bottles; and the essentials for a medical kit.

TOURIST OFFICES
Local Tourist Offices

The Western Australian Tourism Commission (WATC) has an office in Perth, at the Western Australian Tourist Centre, in Albert Facey House in Forrest Place, on the corner of Wellington St, opposite the train station. The office is open 8.30 am to 6 pm Monday to Thursday, 8.30 am to 7 pm Friday, 8.30 am to 5 pm Saturday and 10 am to 5 pm Sunday. On weekdays in winter it closes half an hour earlier.

There is a plethora of brochures to weigh you down, but as the office functions as a travel agency as well, the staff seem more intent on selling accommodation than offering advice on what to see and do.

The telephone information line (☎ 1300-361 351, 9483 1111, fax 9481 0190) operates from 7 am to 6 pm Monday to Friday, 8.30 am to 4.30 pm Saturday and 10 am to 5 pm Sunday. Check out the Web site at www.westernaustralia.net.

There are no interstate offices of WATC for general information.

Tourist Offices Abroad

Overseas representatives of the WATC include:

Germany (☎ 89-4376 6250, fax 4376 6159) WATC, Sperberstrasse 23, 81827 Munich
Japan (☎ 03-5214 0797, fax 5214 0799) WATC, Australian Business Centre, New Otani Garden Court Bldg, Level 28F, 4-1 Kioi-cho, Chiyoda-ku, Tokyo 102
Malaysia (☎ 03-232 5996, 232 8300, fax 238 0380) WATC, 4th floor, UBN Tower, Letterbox 51, 10 Jalan P Ramlee, Kuala Lumpur 50250
Singapore (☎ 338 7772, fax 339 7108) WATC, No 05-13 The Adelphi, 1 Coleman St, Singapore 179803
UK (☎ 171-7395 0578, fax 7379 9826) Western Australia House, 115 The Strand, London WC2R OAJ

VISAS & DOCUMENTS
Visas

All visitors to Australia must have a valid passport and a visa to enter the country. Only New Zealand (NZ) nationals are exempt; they receive a 'special category' visa on arrival.

Check the Department of Immigration & Multicultural Affairs (DIMA) Web site at www.immi.gov.au for useful predeparture information on visas, customs and health issues.

Visa application forms are available from Australian diplomatic missions overseas and travel agencies. There are several different types of visas, depending on the reason for your visit.

Tourist Visas Issued by Australian diplomatic missions abroad, tourist visas are valid for stays of three months or up to six months. There is a $60 application fee.

When you apply for a visa, you need to present your passport and a passport photo, provide evidence of 'adequate funds' to support yourself during your stay, and sign an undertaking that you have a valid airline ticket to leave Australia, or sufficient funds to do so.

Electronic Travel Authority Residents of certain countries who require a tourist visa of up to three months can apply for an Electronic Travel Authority (ETA) through participating travel agencies. There are no forms or fees; as the ETA is generated by computer, your travel to Australia can be authorised within a few minutes. Citizens of the UK, USA, Canada, most European and Scandinavian countries, Korea, Malaysia and Singapore can apply for an ETA. Other nationalities will probably be added to the list in the future; check the list at www.immi.gov.au/eta/countries.htm.

Working Holiday Visas Young visitors from the UK, Ireland, Canada, the Netherlands, Germany, Malta, Japan and the Republic of Korea may be eligible for a 'working holiday' visa. 'Young' is loosely interpreted as between 18 and 30 years of age.

A working holiday visa allows a stay of up to 12 months, but the emphasis is on 'incidental' employment (casual rather than permanent); you can't work for longer than three months with any one employer. This visa can be applied for only at Australian diplomatic missions abroad. Citizens of the UK, Canada, Ireland and the Netherlands can apply at any Australian diplomatic mission, while all others must apply in their home country.

Although the number of working holiday visas granted has increased gradually in recent years, it's a good idea to apply as early as possible as there is a limit on the number of visas issued each year. Conditions attached to a working holiday visa include having a return ticket or sufficient funds for a return fare. It is also recommended that unless there is a reciprocal arrangement between Australia and your country of citizenship (see Health Insurance & Medicare under Health later in this chapter), you take out private health insurance. There is an application fee of $150.

See Work later in this chapter for information on work available in WA.

Visa Extensions The maximum stay for visitors to Australia is one year, including extensions. Visa extensions are made through DIMA offices in Australia (☎ 13 1881) and it's best to apply several weeks before your visa expires. There is a non-refundable application fee of $150 (or $170, depending on the length of your stay) – even if they turn down your application they keep your money! Similar conditions as for other visas apply to visa extensions.

If you want to stay longer, the books *Temporary to Permanent Residence in Australia* and *A Practical Guide to Obtaining Permanent Residence in Australia*, both by Adrian Joel, might be useful.

Travel Insurance

A travel insurance policy to cover theft, loss and medical problems is a good idea. Some policies offer lower and higher medical-expense options; the higher ones are chiefly for countries that have extremely high medical costs, such as the USA.

There is a wide variety of policies available, so check the small print. Some policies specifically exclude 'dangerous activities', which can include motorcycling, scuba diving and even bushwalking.

You may prefer a policy which pays doctors or hospitals directly rather than you having to pay on the spot and claim later. If you have to claim later make sure you keep all documentation. Some policies ask you to call back (reverse charges) to a centre in your home country, where an immediate assessment of your problem is made.

Travellers from some countries will be entitled to Australian treatment under Medicare. (See Health Insurance & Medicare under Health later in this chapter.)

Check that the policy covers ambulances or an emergency flight home.

Driving Licence & Permits

You can generally use a foreign driving licence in Australia for up to three months, as long as it is in English (if it's not, a certified translation must be carried). To avoid hassles, consider getting an International Driving Permit and carry both it and your home licence.

Student & Hostel Cards

Carrying a student card entitles you to a wide variety of discounts throughout WA. The most common card is the International Student Identity Card (ISIC), issued by student unions, hostelling organisations and 'alternative-style' travel agencies.

It's also worth bringing a youth hostel membership card – such as those from Hostelling International (HI) or the Youth Hostel Association (YHA). As well as entitling you to discounts, these are valid for membership of the YHA in WA.

Copies

All important documents (passport data page and visa page, credit cards, travel insurance policy, air/bus/train tickets, driving licence etc) should be photocopied before you leave home. Leave one copy with someone at home and keep another with you, separate from the originals.

It's also a good idea to store details of your vital travel documents in Lonely Planet's free, online Travel Vault in case you lose the photocopies or can't be bothered with them. Your password-protected Travel Vault is accessible online anywhere in the world – create it at www.ekno.lonelyplanet.com.

EMBASSIES & CONSULATES
Your Own Embassy

It's important to realise what your own embassy – the embassy of the country of which you are a citizen – can and can't do to help if you get into trouble. Generally speaking, it won't be much help if the trouble you're in is remotely your own fault (even if what you've done is legal in your own country).

In genuine emergencies, you may get some assistance, but only if all other options have been exhausted. For example, if you need to get home urgently, a ticket home is exceedingly unlikely – the embassy would expect you to have insurance. If you have all of your money and documents stolen, it may assist with getting a new passport, but a loan for onward travel is out of the question.

Australian Embassies & Consulates

Australian diplomatic missions abroad include:

Canada (☎ 613-236 0841, fax 236 4376) Suite 710, 50 O'Connor St, Ottawa K1P 6L2; also in Toronto and Vancouver

France (☎ 01 40 59 33 00, fax 40 59 33 10) 4 Rue Jean Rey, Paris, Cedex 15

Germany (☎ 30-880 0880, fax 88 00 88 99) Friedrich St 200, 10117 Berlin

Greece (☎ 01-645 0404) 37 Dimitriou Soutsou, Ambelokpi, Athens 11521

Hong Kong (☎ 2827 8881) 23/F Harbour Centre, 25 Harbour Rd, Wanchai, Hong Kong Island

Indonesia (☎ 21-522 7111, fax 526 1690) Jalan HR Rasuna Said, Kav C15-16, Kuningan, Jakarta 12940; also in Denpasar

Ireland (☎ 01-676 1517) Fitzwilton House, Wilton Terrace, Dublin 2

Italy (☎ 06-85 2721) Via Alessandria 215, Rome 00198; also in Milan

Japan (☎ 03-5232 4111) 2-1-14 Mita, Minato-ku, Tokyo 108; also in Osaka

Malaysia (☎ 03-246 5555, fax 241 5773) 6 Jalan Yap Kwan Seng, Kuala Lumpur 50450

Netherlands (☎ 070-310 8200) Carnegielaan 4, The Hague 2517 KH

New Zealand (☎ 04-473 6411, fax 498 7135) 72–78 Hobson St, Thorndon, Wellington; also in Auckland

Singapore (☎ 836 4100, fax 737 5481) 25 Napier Rd, Singapore 258507

South Africa (☎ 012-342 3740) 292 Orient St, Arcadia, Pretoria 0083

Thailand (☎ 02-287 2680, fax 287 2029) 37 South Sathorn Rd, Bangkok 10120

UK (☎ 020-7379 4334, fax 7465 8217) Australia House, The Strand, London WC2B 4LA; also in Manchester

USA (☎ 202-797 3000, fax 797 3168) 1601 Massachusetts Ave NW, Washington DC 20036; also in Los Angeles, Honolulu, Houston, New York and San Francisco

Foreign Consulates

The principal diplomatic representations to Australia are in Canberra, but about 30 countries are represented in Perth by consular staff or trade representatives, including:

Canada (☎ 9322 7930) 267 St Georges Terrace, Perth 6000

France (☎ 9386 9366) 41 Hampden Rd, Nedlands 6009

Germany (☎ 9325 8851) 16 St Georges Terrace, Perth 6000

Ireland (☎ 9385 8247) 10 Lilika Rd, City Beach 6015

Japan (☎ 9321 7816) 221 St Georges Terrace, Perth 6000

Netherlands (☎ 9381 3539) 77 Hay St, Subiaco 6008

UK (☎ 9221 5400) 77 St Georges Terrace, Perth 6000

USA (☎ 9231 9400) 16 St Georges Terrace, Perth 6000

CUSTOMS

You can bring most articles in duty-free when entering Australia, provided customs is satisfied they are for personal use and that you'll be taking them with you when you leave. There's also the usual duty-free per-person quota of 1125mL of alcohol, 250 cigarettes and dutiable goods up to the value of $400.

With regard to prohibited goods, two areas need particular attention. Number one is illegal drugs – Australian customs can be extremely efficient when it comes to finding them. Unless you want to spend some time in the slammer, don't bring any in with you.

Number two is animal and plant quarantine. You will be asked to declare all goods of animal or vegetable origin: wooden spoons, straw hats, the lot. Authorities are naturally keen to prevent weeds, pests or diseases getting into the country. Fresh food (such as meat or dairy products) and flowers are also prohibited.

There are also restrictions on taking fruit and vegetables between Australian states; in WA there are quarantine stations at the South Australian (SA) and Northern Territory (NT) borders, to avoid the spread of various pests and diseases. Be warned that any meat/vegetable matter will be binned, including your picnic lunch.

Weapons and firearms are either prohibited or require a permit and safety testing. Other restricted goods include products made from protected wildlife species; non-approved telecommunications devices; and live animals.

When you leave the country, don't take any protected flora or fauna with you. Customs comes down hard on smugglers.

MONEY
Currency

The local currency is the Australian dollar, which comprises 100 cents. There are $0.05, $0.10, $0.20, $0.50, $1 and $2 coins, and notes for $5, $10, $20, $50 and $100.

Although the smallest coin in circulation is $0.05, prices are still marked in single cents and then rounded to the nearest $0.05 when you come to pay.

There are no notable restrictions on importing or exporting travellers cheques. Cash amounts in excess of the equivalent of A$5000 must be declared on arrival or departure. You can change foreign currency and travellers cheques at almost any bank.

Unless otherwise stated, all prices given in this book are in Australian dollars.

Exchange Rates

In recent years the Australian dollar has plummeted against the US dollar, and it now seems to hover around the US$0.60 mark – a disaster for Australians travelling overseas but a real bonus for inbound visitors.

country	unit		A$
Canada	C$1	=	1.29
European Union	€1	=	1.69
France	10FF	=	2.58
Germany	DM1	=	0.86
Hong Kong	HK$10	=	2.48
Ireland	IR£1	=	2.14
Japan	¥100	=	1.80
New Zealand	NZ$1	=	0.78
UK	UK£1	=	2.82
USA	US$1	=	1.93

Exchanging Money

Travellers Cheques In our plastic society, travellers cheques are fast going out of fashion, but they are still a good, safe way of carrying money and generally have a better exchange rate than foreign cash in Australia.

American Express (AmEx), Thomas Cook and other well-known international brands of travellers cheques are all widely used in Australia. Have your passport handy when cashing them.

Commissions and charges for changing foreign-currency travellers cheques vary, depending on the bank. Some charge a flat fee, others a percentage commission.

Bringing Australian-dollar travellers cheques is worth considering. These can be exchanged immediately at the cashier's window without being converted from a foreign currency or incurring commissions, fees and fluctuating exchange rates.

ATMs

The ubiquitous automatic teller machines (ATMs) can be used day or night. Most ATMs accept both local and international cash cards and credit cards, although you'll often be charged commission if your account is with another Australian bank or if it is an international transaction. There's a daily limit on how much you can withdraw from your account which varies from bank to bank.

In WA, ATMs are available in all larger towns and increasingly in the smaller ones, although it would be wise to carry plenty of cash when driving long stretches of road between towns.

Most businesses, such as petrol stations, supermarkets and convenience stores, are linked to the EFTPOS system, which allows you to use your bank cash card to pay for services or purchases direct, and sometimes withdraw cash as well.

Credit Cards

Credit cards are widely accepted in Australia and are an alternative to carrying large numbers of travellers cheques. The most common credit cards are Visa, MasterCard, Diners Club and AmEx.

Cash advances from credit cards are available over the counter (with appropriate ID) and from many ATMs, depending on the card.

If you're planning to rent cars in WA, a credit card makes life simpler; many rental companies simply won't rent to you if you don't have a credit card.

Costs

Compared with the USA, Canada and European countries, Australia is cheaper in some ways and more expensive in others. You pay more for clothes, cars and other manufactured items. On the other hand, food is both high in quality and low in cost.

Accommodation is also reasonably priced, with good-value options for all budgets. Transport and fuel will be the biggest costs in any trip to WA, because of the state's size.

A mid-range traveller might spend about $140 to $160 a day for B&B accommodation, car hire, a restaurant meal, and fuel; two people travelling together will spend a little less per person. Budget travellers could get by on $30 to $40 a day for hostel accommodation and meals but will need to factor in transport costs.

The GST

A Goods and Services Tax (GST) was introduced in Australia on 1 July 2000. This means that a 10% tax is added to all manufactured goods (not basic food or primary products) and to services ranging from getting your hair cut to staying in a hotel. Shelf prices include any applicable GST.

The GST has a number of ramifications for travellers. While international air/sea travel to/from Australia is GST-free, as is domestic air travel when purchased outside Australia by nonresidents, accommodation, transport and dining out are subject to the 10% increase. **Note that most prices quoted in this book do not include the GST.** However, prices advertised in Australia will include the tax.

Nonresidents are entitled to a refund of any GST paid on new or second-hand goods from any one supplier (with a total minimum value of $300) within 28 days of departure from Australia. Call the Australian Taxation Office inquiry line (☎ 13 2861) for details.

Tipping

Hardly anyone tips in WA, except in the odd posh restaurant in Perth. If you feel that way inclined, 10% of the bill is the usual amount.

POST & COMMUNICATIONS
Post

Postal services in Australia are relatively efficient and reasonably cheap. Most post offices are open from 9 am to 5 pm Monday to Friday, but you can often get stamps at other times (including Saturday) from post office agencies (operated from newsagencies) or from Australia Post shops, found in large cities.

It costs $0.45 to send a standard letter or postcard within Australia. Australia Post has divided international destinations into two: Asia-Pacific and Rest of the World. Airmail letters cost $1/1.50 respectively. The cost of sending a postcard or aerogram is the same to any country: $1/0.80 respectively.

Parcels weighing up to 20kg can be sent by post. By sea mail (only available for Europe and the USA), a 1/2kg parcel costs $14/26. Air mail is considerably more expensive and the only option to all other destinations. A 1/2kg parcel sent by economy air to NZ costs $12/22; to other Asian-Pacific destinations it costs $14/26.

All post offices hold mail for visitors and the Perth GPO (general post office) has a busy poste restante. You can also have mail sent to you at the American Express office in Perth if you have an AmEx card or travellers cheques.

Telephone

The Australian telecommunications industry is deregulated and there are a number of providers offering various services. Private phones are serviced by two main players, Telstra and Optus, with newer companies entering the market (and providing the most competition). These include Vodafone, One.Tel, Unidial, Global One and AAPT. They operate predominantly in the area of mobiles and pay phones, but some (such as One.Tel) also offer cheaper local calls.

Pay Phones & Phonecards There's a wide variety of local and international phonecards. Both Telstra and Optus have phonecards with a variety of face values (available from post offices and newsagents).

Lonely Planet's eKno Communication Card is aimed specifically at independent travellers and provides budget international calls, a range of messaging services, free email and travel information. You can join online at www.ekno.lonelyplanet.com, or by phone from anywhere in Australia by dialling ☎ 1800-674 100. Once you have joined, to use eKno from WA, dial ☎ 1800-114 478 and follow the prompts.

From WA eKno offers especially good rates for international calls to the UK and USA, but is less economical than other cards for calls to Europe or Asia. For local calls, you're better off with a local card.

Local Calls From most pay phones, local calls cost $0.40 for an unlimited amount of time, while local calls from private telephones generally cost $0.25. Calls to mobile phones are charged at higher rates.

Long-Distance Calls Although the whole of WA shares a single area code (08), once you call outside of the immediate area or town, it is likely you are making a long-distance (STD) call.

It's possible to make long-distance calls from virtually any pay phone, although rates are more expensive than from a private phone. Long-distance calls are cheaper during off-peak hours (basically outside normal business hours), and different service providers have different charges.

International Calls From most pay phones you can also make International Subscriber Dialling (ISD) calls. The international dialling code will vary, depending on which provider you are using.

International calls from Australia are among the cheapest you'll find anywhere, and there are often specials that bring rates down even further.

The Country Direct service gives callers in Australia direct access to operators in nearly 60 countries, to make reverse-charge (collect) or credit-card calls. For a full list of the countries hooked into this system, check any *White Pages* telephone directory.

Toll-Free & Other Calls Many businesses and some government departments operate a toll-free service from around the country with a prefix of 1800. Other companies have numbers beginning with 13 or 1300 which are charged at the rate of a local call. However, these numbers may not always be accessible from certain areas – you'll have to call to find out. From mobile phones these numbers are charged at the normal mobile rate.

Numbers starting with 190 are usually recorded information services, provided by private companies. They are expensive – from $0.35 to $5 or more per minute (more from mobile phones and pay phones).

Mobile & Satellite Phones Mobile phone coverage is good in Perth, but hopeless in the rest of WA. Once you've moved more than a few kilometres outside the main centres in the south or north-west, mobile phone coverage is nonexistent.

Satellite phones have universal coverage at considerable cost: Rental will set you back some $20 per day, before you even pay for the calls.

Fax
Just about all small towns in WA have some sort of fax service, usually in a newsagent or Telecentre.

Email & Internet Access
You can get online easily in WA. Cyber-cafes are popping up in all the larger towns, and, thanks to a government initiative, most rural communities – even tiny towns – now have a local Telecentre (indicated throughout this book), which provides Internet and email, fax and photocopying facilities. Internet access at these rural Telecentres costs around $10 an hour. Most hostels in Perth and many in the rest of the state have computers for Internet access.

If you're travelling with your computer and want to surf the Internet, even just to access your email, you can set up a short-term account with a local service provider. However, choose carefully, and sign up with a company that has the most access nodes in the areas where you plan to travel. Because of WA's size, it is likely that for at least some part of your travels you'll have to pay for a long-distance call to log on.

EFTel (☎ 9322 6230) has a growing network of access nodes around WA, and can provide short-term accounts. Check out its Web site at www.eftel.com. Telstra Big Pond (☎ 1800-804 282) has access nodes in Bunbury, Geraldton, Kalgoorlie-Boulder and Rockingham as well as Perth. Its Web site is at www.bigpond.com.

Keep in mind that your PC-card modem may not work in Australia. The safest option is to buy a reputable 'global' modem before you leave home, or buy a local PC-card modem once you get to Australia. For more information on travelling with a portable computer, see www.teleadapt.com or www.warrior.com.

Australia uses RJ-45 telephone plugs and Telstra EXI-160 four-pin plugs, available from electronics shops. Check the compatibility of your equipment with Australia's power supply. A universal AC adaptor will enable you to plug the computer in anywhere without frying the innards (see Electricity later in this chapter).

INTERNET RESOURCES
The World Wide Web is a rich resource for travellers. You can research your trip, hunt down bargain air fares, book hotels, check on weather conditions or chat with locals and other travellers about the best places to visit (or avoid!).

There's no better place to start your Web explorations than the Lonely Planet Web site (www.lonelyplanet.com). Here you'll find succinct summaries on travelling to most places on earth, postcards from other travellers and the Thorn Tree bulletin board, where you can ask questions before you travel or dispense advice when you get back. You can also find travel news and updates to many of our most popular guidebooks, and the subWWWay section links you to the most useful travel resources elsewhere on the Web.

The Web site for WA's lifestyle magazine *Scoop*, at www.scoop.com.au, is an excellent source of entertainment listings, although its information mainly relates to Perth. For up-to-date news and features, there's the *West Australian* newspaper's Web site at www.thewest.com.au. For pre-planning transport, you can check out Westrail's timetables and fares at www.westrail.wa.gov.au; for Greyhound Pioneer buses, look up www.greyhound.com.au.

The Aussie Index, a useful list of Australian companies, educational institutions and government departments that maintain Web sites can be found at www.aussie.com.au.

BOOKS
Guidebooks

Lonely Planet publishes *Australia*, as well as state and city guides.

The informative *The Kimberley: Horizons of Stone* (1992) by Alisdair McGregor and Quentin Chester is recommended, as is Australian Geographic's *The Kimberley* (1990) by David McGonigal, which includes a touring map of the region.

Lonely Planet's *Bushwalking in Australia* describes 35 walks of varying lengths and difficulty all over the country, including several in WA. If you are planning a fair amount of Outback driving, Lonely Planet's *Outback Australia* is the book to get. If you're having trouble with the vernacular, then the *Australia phrasebook* might help.

History

A Short History of Australia by Manning Clark is a succinct, fascinating and readable history of Australia. Robert Hughes' bestseller *The Fatal Shore*, a colourful and detailed historical account of convict transportation, has a brief section on this era in WA. Geoffrey Blainey's *The Tyranny of Distance* is a captivating narrative of white settlement and his *The Rush that Never Ended* covers some of the WA goldfields history.

Finding Australia by Russel Ward traces the period from the first Aboriginal arrivals up to 1821. It's strong on Aborigines, women and the full story of foreign exploration.

The most comprehensive history of WA is the 836-page *A New History of Western Australia* (1981), edited by CT Stannage. It has nearly 20 contributors and includes excellent coverage of the clash of white and Aboriginal cultures, colonisation, education, religion, sport, unionism and party politics. Shorter, but now dated, is Frank Crowley's *A Short History of Western Australia* (revised edition 1969).

Important historical biographies include: *Alexander Forrest: His Life and Times* (1958) by GC Bolton; R Duffield's *Rogue Bull: The Story of Lang Hancock, King of the Pilbara* (1979); Mary Durack's three family sagas *Kings in Grass Castles* (1959), *Sons in the Saddle* (1983) and *To Be Heirs Forever* (1976) (see also Literature in the Facts about Western Australia chapter); *Thomas Peel of Swan River* (1965) by A Hasluck; *Bishop Salvado: Founder of New Norcia* (1943) by JT McMahon; and *The Chief: CY O'Connor* (1978) by M Tauman. Short biographies can be found in the *Dictionary of West Australians 1829–1914* (1979, three volumes) compiled by R Erickson.

The best of the autobiographies is AB Facey's *A Fortunate Life* (1981). This microcosm of life in post-Federation WA is Albert Facey's account of his misfortunes in what was the extraordinary life of a seemingly ordinary person (see the boxed text 'Albert Facey' in the Midlands chapter).

Good historical accounts of Perth are: *The Beginning: European Discovery and Early Settlement of Swan River, Western Australia* (1979) by RT Appleyard and T Manford; and the Perth chapters in *The Origins of Australia's Capital Cities* (1989) edited by Pamela Statham. For Fremantle's history, see *The Western Gateway* (1971) by JK Ewers.

Australian Aboriginal Culture

There are many good books that examine Aboriginal culture and sacred places in Aboriginal history. The best coverage is given in Josephine Flood's *Archaeology of the Dreamtime* (1983) and *Riches of Ancient Australia* (1993).

The excellent *Sacred Places in Australia* (1991), a photo-essay by James Cowan and Colin Beard, looks at the sacred areas of the Pilbara, Depuch Island, the Kimberley and Purnululu. More specific to WA are *Thalu Sites of the West Pilbara* (1990) by David Daniel, and *Devil's Lair: A Study in Prehistory* (1984) by Charles Dortch.

The local Aboriginal language is covered in *A Nyoongar Wordlist from the South-West of Western Australia* (1992) edited by Peter Bindon and Ross Chadwick.

For an understanding of Aboriginal art, RM and CH Berndt's *Aboriginal Australian Art* (1988) describes the art in its own traditional settings and tells how to 'read' what is painted, carved or etched. IM Crawford's *The Art of the Wandjina* (1968) describes the fascinating paintings of the Kimberley. Also focusing on the region is *Painting the Country: Contemporary Aboriginal Art from the Kimberley Region* (1989).

Many modern writings focus on the theme of Aboriginal alienation in white society. One account is *Outback Ghettos* by Patty O'Grady, which deals with the separation of Aboriginal children from their natural parents. Another is *Encounters in Place: Outsiders and Aboriginal Australians 1606–1985* by DJ Mulvaney.

The two-volume *Encyclopedia of Aboriginal Australia* edited by David Horton is an excellent comprehensive and inclusive history of Australia.

Fiction & Drama

From the unpolished humour of the early writers from the north-west and goldfields to sophisticated works by internationally renowned contemporary writers, WA has a rich literary tradition. (See Literature and Theatre in the Facts about Western Australia chapter.)

National Parks

The WA national parks custodian, Department of Conservation and Land Management (CALM), provides free pamphlets on all of the main parks, marine reserves and forests, and a range of small booklets and pocket guides (starting from around $6.50 each). These include: *Discovering Valley of the Giants*; *Discovering Shark Bay Marine Park and Monkey Mia*; and *From Range to Reef* (Cape Range and Ningaloo). In addition it has a number of larger publications for sale, such as *Wild Places*, *Quiet Places* (south-west; $21.95), *North-West Bound* (Shark Bay to Wyndham; $21.95), *Broome and Beyond* ($49.95) and *Lookouts of the Karri Country* ($14.95).

The excellent and informative quarterly *Landscope: WA's Conservation, Forests & Wildlife Magazine* ($6.50 single issue; $27 12-month subscription) is also produced by CALM. The magazine has comprehensive articles and often focuses on one area, eg, Shark Bay.

These publications can be purchased from CALM's head office in Perth, (☎ 9334 0333), at Technology Park, Western Precinct, 17 Dick Perry Ave (enter via Hayman Rd or Kent St), Kensington 6151. The full list of available publications can be viewed on CALM's excellent Web site (www.calm.wa.gov.au) and can also be purchased online.

NEWSPAPERS & MAGAZINES

The *West Australian* and the *Australian* are available each morning from Monday to Saturday. The Saturday issue of the *West Australian* has a supplement, the *West Magazine*. The *Sunday Times* is available on Sunday.

Some smaller towns have their own newspapers which focus on local news and events, including *Kalgoorlie Miner*, *Albany Advertiser*, *North-West Telegraph* and *Kimberley Echo*.

International newspapers are available in Perth at the Plaza Newsagency, Plaza Arcade (off Hay St Mall), as well as from Library & Information Services of Western Australia (LISWA), in the Alexander Library Building in James St. Interstate newspapers such as Melbourne's *Age* are usually available in the afternoon of the day of publication.

Weekly newspapers and magazines are widely available. These include Australian editions of *Time* and the national news magazine the *Bulletin*, which incorporates an edition of the US *Newsweek*. The British newspapers *Daily Express*, the *Guardian* and the *Independent* have weekly digest editions – popular in Perth because of its large number of British expats.

Scoop is a quarterly lifestyle magazine, good for keeping up with news on museums, restaurants and other hot spots in and around Perth.

RADIO & TV

Unfortunately, WA has probably the worst radio coverage of all the states of Australia, due, most likely, to its small listener base in the country. Perth, however, is well served with both commercial and non-commercial radio and the Australian Broadcasting Corporation (ABC) does its best in the country.

The ABC's stations are Regional 6WF (720 AM), Radio National 6RN (810 AM), ABC Classical (97.7 FM) and ABC Newsradio (585 AM), which broadcasts continuous news and current affairs. The popular youth station Triple J FM can be found on 99.3 FM. SBS (96.9 FM) has multicultural programs, including many foreign-language broadcasts. These stations have clear reception in Perth, although it can get a bit crackly in country areas.

There are plenty of commercial radio stations (again, the reception is better in Perth than elsewhere) including the rock-and-roll stations Triple M (96.1 FM) and PMFM (92.9 FM) and The Mix (94.5 FM), which plays easy-listening music.

Some Aboriginal communities have their own radio stations and make the best of minimal resources. Examples include Wangki Yupurnanupurru Radio (WYRS) in Fitzroy Crossing and Radio Goolari in Broome.

Perth has five TV stations. The three commercial networks are Channels 7, 9 and 10. The ABC (Channel 2) is government-funded and supposedly free of bias, as is the multicultural broadcaster SBS (Channel 28). The most comprehensive world news coverage is on SBS at 6.30 pm.

Country stations generally receive two TV stations: the ABC and a local commercial network, Golden West Network. A lot of places are too remote to get good reception unless they have good antennae or satellite dishes. In the country, head to the pub to watch cable TV.

The *West Australian* newspaper usually carries a TV and radio program guide.

VIDEO SYSTEMS

Overseas visitors thinking of purchasing videos should remember that Australia uses the Phase Alternative Line (PAL) system, which isn't compatible with other standards unless converted.

PHOTOGRAPHY & VIDEO

Australian film prices are in line with those in the rest of the Western world. A roll of 36-exposure Kodachrome 64 or Fujichrome 100 slide film costs around $26 including developing.

There are plenty of well-stocked camera shops in the main centres and standards of camera service are high. Developing standards are also high; many places offer one-hour developing of print film.

In the arid areas of WA you will have to allow for the exceptional intensity of the light. Best results in the Outback regions are obtained early in the morning and late in the afternoon. As the sun gets higher, colours appear washed out. You must also allow for the intensity of reflected light when taking shots of Ningaloo Reef or at other coastal locations. In the Outback, allow for temperature extremes, especially in summer, and do your best to keep film as cool as possible, particularly after exposure. Other film and camera hazards are dust in the Outback and humidity in the tropical region of the Kimberley.

Lonely Planet's *Travel Photography: A Guide to Taking Better Pictures*, written by internationally renowned travel photographer Richard I'Anson, is designed to take on the road.

As in any country, politeness goes a long way when taking photographs; ask before taking pictures of people. Note that many Aboriginal people do not like to be photographed, even from a distance.

TIME

Australia is divided into three time zones: the Western Standard Time zone (GMT/ UTC plus eight hours) covers WA; Central Standard Time (plus 9.5 hours) covers the NT, SA and parts of WA's Central Desert and Nullarbor regions near the border; and Eastern Standard Time (plus 10 hours) covers Tasmania, Victoria, New South Wales and Queensland. When it's noon in WA, it's 1.30 pm in the NT and SA, and 2 pm in the rest of the country.

Daylight saving time – for which clocks are put forward an hour – operates in most states during summer and for a month or so either side. However, things can get pretty confusing as neither WA nor Queensland adopt daylight saving time, and it starts a month earlier and finishes a month later in Tasmania.

This time difference isn't really a problem in the south where the Nullarbor provides a good distance buffer but it is in the north, in East Kimberley, where a mere border crossing changes the time significantly.

In winter, when it's noon in Perth, it is 5 am in London, 6 am in Paris, 1 pm in Tokyo and 4 pm in Auckland the same day, 9 pm in Los Angeles the evening before, and midnight in New York the night before.

ELECTRICITY

Voltage is 220–240V and the plugs are three-pin, but not the same as British three-pin plugs. Users of electric shavers or hairdriers should note that, apart from in upmarket hotels, it's difficult to find converters to take either US flat two-pin plugs or the European round two-pin plugs, so bring them with you. Adapters for British plugs can be found in good hardware shops, chemists and travel agencies.

WEIGHTS & MEASURES

Australia uses the metric system. Petrol and milk are sold by the litre, apples and potatoes by the kilogram, distance is measured by the metre or kilometre, and speed limits are in kilometres per hour (km/h).

See the conversion table at the back of this book.

LAUNDRY

Most accommodation in WA (including hostels) will have a small laundry. In the main towns, and many smaller ones, there are laundrettes. It will cost about $6 to wash and dry one load.

HEALTH

The heat in the north and desert areas of WA is probably the main hazard that you are likely to encounter while travelling in the state; with the heat come problems such as heatstroke, dehydration and sunburn.

No vaccinations are required, but if you are coming to Australia from a country that is infected with yellow fever you will need proof of vaccination.

If you require particular medication take an adequate supply, as it may not be available, and make sure you know the generic (not just the brand) name. If you wear glasses take an extra pair, as well as your prescription.

Medical care in Australia is good and only moderately expensive. A typical visit to the doctor costs around $40. If you have an immediate health problem, telephone or visit the casualty section at the nearest public hospital, or in the Outback make contact with the Royal Flying Doctor Service.

As doctors are few and far between outside of the south-west of WA, consider bringing a basic medical kit: aspirin or paracetamol (acetaminophen in the US) – for pain or fever; antihistamine (eg, Benadryl), useful as a decongestant for colds and allergies, to ease the itch from insect bites or stings, and to help prevent motion sickness; antiseptic such as povidone-iodine (eg, Betadine) – for cuts and grazes; calamine lotion or aluminium sulphate spray (eg, Stingose) – to ease irritation from bites or stings; bandages and Band-Aids; scissors, tweezers and a thermometer; lip balm; insect repellent; and sunscreen.

Lonely Planet's pocket guide *Healthy Travel: Australia, New Zealand & the Pacific* is packed with useful information including pretrip planning, emergency first aid and what to do if you become ill while travelling.

Health Insurance & Medicare

Don't leave home without a travel insurance policy that has good medical coverage (see Travel Insurance under Visas & Documents earlier in this chapter).

Under reciprocal arrangements, residents of the UK, NZ, the Netherlands, Sweden, Finland, Malta and Italy are entitled to free or subsidised medical treatment under Medicare, Australia's compulsory national health insurance scheme. To enrol you need to show your passport and health-care card or certificate from you own country, after which you are given a Medicare card.

A Medicare card entitles you to free, necessary public hospital treatment. While residents of the Republic of Ireland cannot get a Medicare card, they can present their passport at a public hospital and be given free necessary treatment.

Visits to a private doctor are also claimable under Medicare, although you usually have to pay the bill first and then make a claim yourself from Medicare. You also need to find out how much the doctor's consultation fee is, as Medicare only covers you for a certain amount and you will need to pay the balance. Clinics that advertise 'bulk billing' are the easiest to use as they charge Medicare direct. Call Medicare on ☎ 13 2011 for more information.

Environmental Hazards

Heat Exhaustion Dehydration and salt deficiency can cause heat exhaustion. Take time to acclimatise to high temperatures, drink sufficient fluids and do not do anything too physically demanding.

Symptoms of salt deficiency include headaches, fatigue, lethargy, giddiness and muscle cramps. Although salt tablets may help, adding extra salt to your food will be more effective.

Heatstroke This serious, occasionally fatal condition can occur if the body's heat-regulating mechanism breaks down and the body temperature rises to dangerous levels. Long, continuous periods of exposure to high temperatures, and insufficient fluids can leave you vulnerable to heatstroke.

The symptoms are: feeling unwell, not sweating very much (or at all) and a high body temperature (39°C to 41°C or 102°F to 106°F). Where sweating has ceased, the skin becomes flushed and red. Severe, throbbing headaches and lack of coordination will also occur, and the sufferer may be confused or aggressive. Eventually the victim will become delirious or convulse. Hospitalisation is essential, but in the interim get victims out of the sun, remove their clothing, cover them with a wet sheet or towel and then fan them continually. Give fluids if they are conscious.

Dehydration In hot climates make sure you drink enough – don't rely on feeling thirsty to indicate when you should drink. Not needing to urinate or small amounts of very dark yellow urine is a danger sign.

Always carry plenty of water with you on long trips – up to 20 litres if you intend going off-road. Excessive sweating can lead to loss of salt and therefore muscle cramping. Salt tablets are not a good idea as a preventative.

Prickly Heat This itchy rash is caused by excessive perspiration trapped under the skin. It usually strikes people who have just arrived in a hot climate. Keeping cool, bathing often, drying the skin and using a mild talcum or prickly heat powder, or resorting to air-conditioning, may help.

Sunburn In the tropics, in the desert or at high altitude you can get sunburnt surprisingly quickly, even through cloud cover. Use a sunscreen, a hat, and a barrier cream for your nose and lips. Calamine lotion or a commercial after-sun preparation are good for mild sunburn. Protect your eyes with good-quality sunglasses, particularly if you will be near water, sand or snow.

Fungal Infections Occurring more commonly in hot weather, fungal infections are usually found on the scalp, between the toes (athlete's foot) or fingers, in the groin and on the body (ringworm). You get ringworm (which is a fungal infection, not a worm) from infected animals or other people. Moisture encourages these infections.

Haunting landscape in Nambung NP

A welcoming oasis, Millstream-Chichester NP

PETER PTSCHELINZEW

PETER PTSCHELINZEW

Ancestral shadows: Wandjina figures, Gibb River, East Kimberley

MITCH REARDON

Junction of the Red, Weano, Joffre and Hancock Gorges from Oxers Lookout, Karijini NP

The historic town hall, Kalgoorlie-Boulder

Japanese cemetery, Broome

Clear blue waters and a relaxed atmosphere – Broome is the destination of many travellers.

To prevent fungal infections wear loose, comfortable clothing, avoid artificial fibres, wash frequently and dry yourself carefully. If you do get an infection, wash the infected area at least daily with a disinfectant or medicated soap and water, and rinse and dry well. Apply an antifungal cream or powder like tolnaftate. Try to expose the infected area to air or sunlight as much as possible and wash all towels and underwear in hot water, change them often and let them dry in the sun.

Infectious Diseases

Hepatitis A common disease worldwide, hepatitis is a general term for inflammation of the liver. There are several different viruses that cause hepatitis, and they differ in the way that they are transmitted. The symptoms are similar in all forms of the illness; they include fever, chills, headache, fatigue, feelings of weakness and aches and pains, followed by loss of appetite, nausea, vomiting, abdominal pain, dark urine, light-coloured faeces, jaundiced (yellow) skin and yellowing of the whites of the eyes. People who have had hepatitis should avoid alcohol for some time after the illness, as the liver needs time to recover.

Hepatitis A is transmitted by contaminated food and drinking water. You should seek medical advice, but there is not much you can do apart from resting, drinking lots of fluids, eating lightly and avoiding fatty foods. Hepatitis E is transmitted in the same way as hepatitis A and it can be particularly serious in pregnant women.

There are almost 300 million chronic carriers of hepatitis B in the world. It is spread through contact with infected blood, blood products or body fluids, eg, through sexual contact, unsterilised needles and blood transfusions, or contact with blood via small breaks in the skin. Other risk situations include having a shave, tattooing and body-piercing with contaminated equipment. The symptoms of hepatitis B may be more severe than type A and the disease can lead to long-term problems such as chronic liver damage, liver cancer or a long-term carrier status. Hepatitis C and D are spread in the same way as hepatitis B and can also lead to long-term complications.

There are vaccines against hepatitis A and B, but there are currently no vaccines against the other types of hepatitis. Following the basic rules about food and water (hepatitis A and E) and avoiding risk situations (hepatitis B, C and D) are important preventative measures.

HIV & AIDS Infection with HIV (human immunodeficiency virus) may lead to AIDS (acquired immune deficiency syndrome), which is a fatal disease. Any exposure to blood, blood products or body fluids may put the individual at risk. The disease is often transmitted through sexual contact or dirty needles – vaccinations, acupuncture, tattooing and body-piercing can be potentially as dangerous as intravenous drug use. HIV/AIDS can also be spread through infected blood transfusions. If you do need an injection, ask to see the syringe unwrapped in front of you, or take a needle and syringe pack with you.

Fear of being infected with HIV should never preclude you from seeking treatment for serious medical conditions.

Sexually Transmitted Diseases Both hepatitis B and HIV/AIDS can be transmitted through sexual contact (see the relevant sections earlier for more details). Other STDs include gonorrhoea, herpes and syphilis; sores, blisters or rashes around the genitals, and discharges or pain on urinating are common symptoms. In some STDs, such as wart virus or chlamydia, symptoms may be less marked or not observed at all, especially in women. Chlamydia infection can cause infertility in both men and women before any symptoms are noticed. Syphilis symptoms eventually disappear completely but the disease continues and can cause severe problems in later years. While abstinence from sexual contact is the only 100%-effective prevention, using condoms is also effective. The treatment of gonorrhoea and syphilis is with antibiotics. The different sexually transmitted diseases each require specific antibiotics.

Cuts, Bites & Stings

Insect Bites & Stings Bee and wasp stings are usually painful rather than dangerous. However, in people who are allergic to them, severe breathing difficulties may occur and require urgent medical care. Calamine lotion or Stingose spray will give relief and ice packs will reduce the pain and swelling. There are some spiders with dangerous bites but antivenins are usually available.

Jellyfish Stings Avoid contact with these sea creatures with stinging tentacles – seek local advice. The box jellyfish found in inshore waters around northern Australia during the summer months is potentially fatal, but stings from most jellyfish are simply rather painful. Dousing in vinegar will deactivate any stingers which have not 'fired'. Calamine lotion, analgesics and antihistamines may reduce the reaction and relieve the pain.

Snake Bites Generally, snake bites do not cause instantaneous death and antivenins are usually available. Immediately wrap the bitten limb tightly, as you would for a sprained ankle, and then attach a splint to immobilise it. Keep the victim still and seek medical help, if possible with the dead snake for identification. Don't attempt to catch the snake if there is a possibility of being bitten again. Tourniquets and sucking out the poison are now comprehensively discredited.

Cuts & Scratches Wash well and treat any cut with an antiseptic such as povidone-iodine. Where possible avoid bandages and Band-Aids, which can keep wounds wet. Coral cuts are notoriously slow to heal and if they are not adequately cleaned small pieces of coral can become embedded in the wound. Severe pain, throbbing, redness, fever or generally feeling unwell suggest infection and the need for antibiotics promptly as coral cuts may result in serious infections.

Women's Health

Antibiotics, synthetic underwear, sweating and contraceptive pills can lead to fungal vaginal infections, especially if travelling in hot climates. Characterised by a rash, itch and discharge, fungal infections can be treated with a vinegar or lemon-juice douche, or with yoghurt. Nystatin, miconazole or clotrimazole pessaries or vaginal cream are the usual treatment. Maintaining good personal hygiene and wearing loose-fitting clothing and cotton underwear may help prevent these infections.

Sexually transmitted diseases are a major cause of vaginal problems. Symptoms include a smelly discharge, painful intercourse and sometimes a burning sensation when urinating. Medical attention should be sought and male sexual partners must also be treated. (For more details see Sexually Transmitted Diseases under Infectious Diseases earlier in this chapter.) Besides abstinence, the best preventative is to practise safe sex using condoms.

TOILETS

There are public toilets in most towns – you'll soon discover that some are better than others. Travel in WA usually means it's a long distance between 'long drops', so you'll have to use the great outdoors at some stage. A roll of toilet paper is a must if you're travelling by car.

In the desert leave your stool on the surface – it will dry, desiccate and eventually blow away. In other places, dig a hole, 20cm deep and at least 100m from a watercourse. Use toilet paper sparingly. Cover the waste with soil and a rock.

WOMEN TRAVELLERS

Although WA is generally a safe place for women travellers, you should try to avoid walking alone late at night in any of the major towns.

While you rarely feel actually threatened as a female traveller alone, you can feel very conspicuous – particularly outside wildflower season in some of the inland north-west towns. Stepping into some pubs alone in any town can also draw some long, unsmiling stares from male patrons. Be warned that hotels with the word 'Skimpy' written on a board outside have lingerie-clad female bar staff inside.

Female hitchers should exercise care at all times (see Hitching in the Getting Around chapter).

Useful women's organisations, all of which are based in Perth, are:

Sexual Assault Resource Centre (SARC;
☎ 1800-199 888, 9340 1828) 24-hour crisis line
**Health Information Resource Service for
Women** (☎ 1800-651 100, 9340 1100) King
Edward Memorial Hospital for Women, Bagot
Rd, Subiaco 6008
Women's Information Service (☎ 1800-199
174, 9264 1900) 141 St Georges Terrace, Perth
6000
Women's Refuge Group of WA (☎ 9420 7264)
24-hour crisis line; (☎ 9325 7716) multicultural
service

GAY & LESBIAN TRAVELLERS

There are active and proud gay and lesbian communities in WA, but they are mainly based in Perth. Farther afield, perhaps with the exception of 'anything-goes' Kalgoorlie-Boulder, homophobia rears its ugly head and attitudes towards gays and lesbians are definitely less tolerant.

Perth Pride takes place in October, as does the annual Reclaim-the-Night march. The state holds its Gay Olympics in November. The best way to hone in on gay community news, events and action is through the free *Westside Observer (WSO)* newspaper or its excellent Web site (www.wso.com.au), which has news and a long list of links to useful organisations and groups. Also check out the monthly lesbian magazines *Grapevine* and *Women Out West*.

Useful organisations include:

AIDS Council of Western Australia (☎ 9429
9900, 9429 9944) 664 Murray St, West Perth
6005
Gay & Lesbian Counselling Service of WA
(fax 9486 9855) 2 Delhi St, West Perth 6005;
(☎ 9420 7201) counselling line, 7.30 to 10.30
pm daily
Hedland Gay Info Line (☎ 9172 2925)
Lesbian & Gay Pride WA (☎/fax 9227 1767,
e pride@pridewa.asn.au) PO Box 30, North
Perth 6906
Web site: www.pridewa.asn.au
Perth Outdoors Group (☎ 9472 5947) PO Box
47, Northbridge 6865

Gay and Lesbian Tourism Australia (www.galta.com.au) promotes gay and lesbian travel. It's not a booking office but it has a lot of useful information on gay-friendly operators in all states.

DISABLED TRAVELLERS

Reliable information is the key ingredient for travellers with a disability. Nationally, the best source is the National Information Communication and Recreation Network (Nican; TTY 1800-806 769, ☎/TTY 02-6285 3713, fax 6285 3714, e nican@spirit.com.au), PO Box 407, Curtin, ACT 2605. This is an Australia-wide directory that provides information on access issues, accessible accommodation places, sporting and recreational activities, transport and specialist tour operators.

People with Disabilities WA (PWDWA; ☎ 1800-193 331, 9386 6477, fax 9386 6705, e info@pwdwa.org), 37 Hampden Rd, Nedlands 6009, is a good starting point in WA. Its TTY number is 9386 6451. PWDWA has an excellent Web site at www.pwdwa.org, which has heaps of useful information including an up-to-date listing of the major disability service providers in the state. The PWDWA staff are well informed and helpful.

The office of the Australian Council for the Rehabilitation of the Disabled (Acrod; ☎ 9242 5544, TTY 9242 3800, fax 9242 5044, e acrodwa@acrod.org.au), PO Box 1428, Osborne Park 6916, produces information sheets for disabled travellers, including lists of state-level organisations, specialist travel agencies, wheelchair and equipment hire, and access guides. Acrod can also help with specific queries by post; staff will be grateful if you send a stamped, self-addressed envelope.

Other useful organisations are:

Blind Association (☎ 9311 8202) 16 Sunbury
Rd, Victoria Park 6100
Deaf Society of WA (☎ 9443 2677, TTY 13
2544/9441 2655, fax 9444 3592) 16 Brentham
St, Leederville
Paraplegic-Quadriplegic Association of WA
(☎ 9381 0111, fax 9382 3687) 10 Selby St,
Shenton Park 6008

The Australian Tourist Commission publishes *Travel in Australia for People with Disabilities*, which contains travel tips and contact addresses of organisations on a state-by-state basis. The WATC should have copies (see Tourist Offices earlier in this chapter for contact details).

SENIOR TRAVELLERS

Travellers over the age of 60 get good discounts on all forms of travel within WA and reduced admission to most forms of entertainment, such as museums and cinemas.

You can get information on available services from the state government's general inquiry line (☎ 9346 5111). A full list of services for seniors appears in the Perth *White Pages*, on the 'Age Page'.

TRAVEL WITH CHILDREN

Travel with your children if you have them. The kilometres will be made more interesting, but no easier, by their presence. Remember: There are huge distances between points of interest and it is hard to convince a kid that the Great Sandy Desert is more than sand. Get a copy of Lonely Planet's *Travel with Children* by Maureen Wheeler for more tips.

In Perth, Little Hugger Hire (☎ 0419-197 242) rents all sorts of baby kit – car seats, cots, booster seats, prams and strollers – at reasonable rates.

All the main car-hire companies can install child safety seats in their vehicles, but you have to book in advance. Many taxis also have child seats, but again, it's wise to book ahead.

USEFUL ORGANISATIONS
National Trust

The National Trust is dedicated to preserving historic buildings and artefacts, as well as important natural features, in all parts of Australia. It owns and manages a large number of properties, most of which are open to the public. Annual membership costs $49 for adults, $35 concession and $68 for families.

In Perth the National Trust (☎ 9321 6088, fax 9324 1571) is at Old Observatory, 4 Havelock St, West Perth 6005.

DANGERS & ANNOYANCES
Animal Hazards

There are a few unique and sometimes dangerous creatures in WA, although it's unlikely that you'll come across any of them, particularly if you stick to the cities.

Snakes The best-known danger in the Outback, and the one that captures the imagination of visitors, is snakes. There are many venomous snakes but few that are aggressive, and unless you have the bad fortune to stand on one it's unlikely you'll be bitten. Some snakes, however, will attack if alarmed, and sea snakes can also be dangerous.

To minimise your chances of being bitten, always wear boots, socks and long trousers when walking through undergrowth. Don't put your hands into holes and crevices, and be careful when collecting firewood.

See under Cuts, Bites & Stings in the Health section in this chapter for how to treat snake bites.

Spiders & Insects Avoid spiders, as there are a couple of really nasty ones. The redback is the most common poisonous spider in WA. If you're bitten, seek medical attention immediately.

Leeches are common, but while they will suck your blood, they're not dangerous and are easily removed by the application of salt or heat.

Box Jellyfish & Other Sea Hazards

Also known as the sea wasp or 'stinger', the nasty box jellyfish is found in the northwest for six months of the year (mainly in October to April) and its sting can be fatal. The stinging tentacles spread several metres out from the sea wasp's body; by the time you see it you're likely to have been stung. Stay out of the sea when the sea wasps are around – the locals are ignoring that lovely water for an excellent reason.

If someone is stung, they will probably run out of the sea screaming and collapse on the beach, with weals on their body as though they've been whipped. Douse the stings with vinegar (if you're in stinger

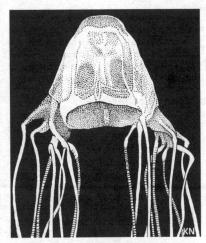
The sting of the box jellyfish can be fatal.

country you should carry it with you), do not try to remove the tentacles from the skin, and treat as for snake bite. Be prepared to resuscitate the victim, who may stop breathing.

When reef-walking you must always wear shoes to protect your feet against coral cuts which can become infected quickly. There are stonefish – venomous fish that look like a flat rock on the sea bed – throughout the tropical waters of WA. Also watch out for the scorpion fish, which has venomous spines.

Crocodiles Up in the north-west of WA, saltwater crocodiles can be a real danger (see the boxed text 'Freshies & Salties' in the Kimberley chapter). Before diving into that inviting, cool water be careful to find out if it's croc-free. There are some local rules to remember: Don't launch your boat or collect water from the same spot all the time; don't throw fish guts or old bait into the water; and camp well away from the banks.

Flies & Mosquitoes For four to six months of the year you'll have to cope with the bane of the Australian outdoors – flies and mosquitoes.

The flies are not too bad in towns and cities; it's in the country that they start to get out of hand, and the further 'out' you get the worse the flies seem to be. Flies are a real problem in north-west Australia and are responsible for much of the conjunctivitis and trachoma found in the Kimberley. Try hard to prevent flies from getting near the eyes of infants and young children. Repellents such as Aerogard, Rid and Bushmen's go some way to deterring flies, but don't let any of this stuff get near children's eyes.

Mosquitoes can also be a problem, especially in the warmer tropical and subtropical areas. Mosquitoes in the Kimberley are responsible for the transmission of a number of diseases such as Ross River virus and Australian encephalitis. Cover up bare skin and wear a mosquito repellent if you go outside at dusk.

On the Road
Common driving hazards in WA include poor road surfaces (especially in outback regions), extreme weather conditions, and long distances. (See Car in the Getting Around chapter.)

Cyclones
These are a feature of the weather pattern of the north-west and the northern coastal areas. A cyclone is a circular rotating storm of tropical origin in which the mean wind speed exceeds 63km/h (gale force). Speeds of 100km/h are common and a speed of 248km/h was recorded at Onslow in 1975. Some winds can extend up to 200km from the centre or 'eye' of the cyclone. Heavy rain falls as the system decays, which it does 24 to 48 hours after hitting land, and flooding often occurs. The cyclone season in the west is officially 1 November to 30 April.

Cyclones are erratic, so it is important to listen to ABC radio for information – the best option is a battery-powered radio, as power supplies may be cut. For the Bureau of Meteorology's Tropical Cyclone Information line call ☎ 1300-659 210. The WA Severe Weather Warning recorded information line is ☎ 1900-155 349. The Bureau of Meteorology issues 'watch' messages, indicating that there could be gales within 48 hours, and 'warning' messages where there could be gales within 24 hours. The Bureau of Meteorology provides a free pamphlet, *Surviving Cyclones*, available from the bureau in all states (see the *White Pages*) or from its Web site (www.bom.gov.au).

There are three cyclone warning stages issued by the State Emergency Services: blue – cyclone may affect the area within 48 hours; yellow – cyclone moving closer and inevitable within 12 hours; red – cyclone is imminent.

The all clear is sounded when the cyclone has passed, but there may still be wind and heavy rain. If you have any doubts, seek local advice.

Bushfires

Bushfires happen every year in Australia. Don't be the mug who starts one. In hot, dry, windy weather, be extremely careful with any naked flame – cigarette butts thrown out of car windows have started many a fire. On a total fire ban day (listen to the radio or watch the billboards on country roads) it is forbidden to use a camping stove in the open. The locals will happily dob you in if you break the law, and the penalties are severe.

If you're unfortunate enough to find yourself driving through a bushfire, stay inside your car and try to park off the road in an open space, away from trees, until the danger has passed. Lie on the floor under the dashboard, covering yourself with a wool blanket if possible. The front of the fire should pass quickly, and you will be much safer than if you were out in the open.

Bushwalkers should take local advice before setting out. On a day of total fire ban, don't go – delay your trip until the weather has changed. Chances are that it will be so unpleasantly hot and windy, you'll be better off in an air-conditioned pub sipping a cool beer anyway.

If you're out in the bush and you see smoke, even from a great distance, take it seriously. Go to the nearest open space, downhill if possible. A forested ridge is the most dangerous place to be. Bushfires move extremely quickly and can change direction suddenly with the wind.

Having said all that, more bushwalkers die of cold than in bushfires! Even in summer, temperatures can drop below freezing at night in the mountains of WA's south-west.

Ocean Beaches

Be aware that many surf beaches can be dangerous places to swim if you are not used to the conditions. Undertows (or rips) are the main problem, but a number of people are paralysed each year by diving into waves in shallow water and hitting a sand bar – check first.

Many popular beaches are patrolled by surf lifesavers, and patrolled areas are designated with flags. If you swim between the flags assistance should arrive quickly if you get into trouble; raise your arm if you need help. Outside the flags and on unpatrolled beaches you are on your own.

If you find yourself being carried out by a rip, the main thing to try to do is just stay afloat; don't panic and don't ever try to swim against the rip. In most cases the current will stop within a couple of hundred metres of the shore, and you can then swim parallel to the shore for a short way to get out of the rip, and then make your way back to the shore.

On the south coast, freak 'king waves' from the Southern Ocean can sometimes break on the shore with little or no warning, dragging people out to sea. In populated areas there are warning signs; in other areas, be extremely careful.

EMERGENCY

In the case of a life-threatening emergency call ☎ 000. This call is free from any phone, and the operator will connect you to either the police, ambulance or fire brigade. Local emergency numbers can be found in the Perth *White Pages*. Otherwise you can call the police on ☎ 9222 1111 in Perth.

In case of an emergency in remote areas, if you're near a phone, call the Royal Flying Doctor Service (RFDS) on ☎ 1800-625 800. From satellite phones call ☎ 9417 6364. In remote areas a number of travellers will be equipped with a RFDS emergency radio, which can be operated at any time in the event of an emergency. Otherwise, the radios are monitored from 7 to 9 am Monday to Friday and from 8.30 to 10 am on weekends. There are two frequencies: Kalgoorlie-Boulder (VJQ) RFDS, which covers a zone as far north as Meekatharra, is at 5360 kHz; and in the north-west, Port Hedland (VKL) RFDS is at 5300 kHz.

There is an interpreter service available on ☎ 13 1450.

LEGAL MATTERS

There is not much to worry about in WA, just a few simple rules. Don't buy illegal drugs such as marijuana; don't drink and drive; don't smoke cigarettes where they are forbidden; don't litter (sensitive Aussies rightly hate it); don't whip your clothes off on a beach where most people are fully clothed for swimming (there are plenty of beaches where you can bare it all); don't light any fire on a total fire ban day; and don't bring fruit or vegetables across the SA and NT borders.

If you do breach this simple set of rules and are apprehended, you are allowed to contact a legal representative. Although local consulates will do what they can when their nationals call for help, this may not be much if you've broken the law.

BUSINESS HOURS

Most shops close at 5 or 5.30 pm weekdays, and either noon or 5 pm Saturday. In some places Sunday trading is starting to catch on, but it's currently limited to central Perth and suburban areas such as Subiaco, Northbridge and Fremantle. In the larger towns there is one late-shopping night each week when the doors stay open until 9 pm. In central Perth it's Friday; in the suburbs it's Thursday.

Banks open from 9.30 am to 4 pm Monday to Thursday, and until 5 pm on Friday.

There are exceptions to WA's opening hours and all sorts of places – milk bars, convenience stores, supermarkets, delicatessens and bookshops – stay open late and on weekends.

PUBLIC HOLIDAYS & SPECIAL EVENTS
Public Holidays

The main national and WA public holidays are:

New Year's Day 1 January
Australia Day 26 January
Labour Day (WA) March – second Monday
Easter March/April – Good Friday, Easter
    Sunday & Easter Monday
ANZAC Day 25 April
Foundation Day June – first Monday
Queen's Birthday September – last Monday
Christmas Day 25 December
Boxing Day 26 December

Special Events

Perth has a number of special events including the huge Perth International Arts Festival from late January to mid-February. One of the oldest cultural festivals in Australia, this always features a rich mix of Australian and international performing arts at venues throughout the city. For details, check out the Web site at www.festival.uwa.edu.au.

Migrants have added a number of festivals to the calendar, including the Perth Italian Festival in September; an Oktoberfest in, of course, October; and the Japanese-style Shinju Matsuri (Pearl) Festival in Broome in August. There are exhibitions of indigenous art and cultural performances in Perth during National Aboriginal & Islander Day Observance Committee (Naidoc) week in July.

Check out the www.westernaustralia.net and www.events.tourism.wa.gov.au Web sites, which list some (but not all) of the events taking place throughout the state.

Outside Perth, WA's major annual festivals and events include the following (for more information see the relevant chapters):

January

Ledge Point–Lancelin Sailboard Classic This annual 24km race is an important event on the world windsurfing calendar.

Fremantle Sardine Festival This one-day food festival includes street parades and stalls on Fremantle's Esplanade.

February

Leeuwin Estate Concert (Margaret River) Each year, the magnificent grounds of the Leeuwin Estate winery host leading international performers.

March

Vintage on Avon Vintage sports cars take to the streets of Northam for this annual car rally.

Kalgoorlie Gold Panning Championships Get your gold pan and go for gold.

April

Broome Easter Dragon Boat Regatta Local paddlers meet annually for this carnival. For two days the town entertains the racers.

June

Port Hedland Black Rock Stakes In this annual wheelbarrow race for charity, teams push barrows full of iron ore over a 120km course.

Broome Fringe Arts Festival Local artists highlight 'fringe arts' during this festival, which features markets, art installations, workshops and Aboriginal art exhibitions.

Kununurra Mardi Gras This local festival features arts and music.

July

National Aboriginal & Islander Day Observance Committee (Naidoc) week Indigenous art exhibitions and performances take place in and around Perth and throughout WA during Naidoc week.

August

Avon Descent Power boats, kayaks and canoes race down the Avon River from Northam in this annual event.

Karratha FeNaCLNG Festival This local festival includes exhibitions and performances.

Broome Shinju-Matsuri (Festival of the Pearl) Broome commemorates its early pearling years and the town's multicultural heritage annually.

Broome Opera Under the Stars World-class opera singers come to sing under clear Kimberley night skies.

September

Royal Perth Show This is the west's biggest agriculture, food and wine show.

York Jazz Festival Jazz aficionados flock to the historic Avon Valley town of York for concerts, busking and jamming.

Kalgoorlie-Boulder Racing Round There's lots of boozing during this week of horse racing.

October

City of Perth Awesome Children's Festival There's plenty of activities during this contemporary arts festival for kids.

Perth Wildflower Festival Kings Park and the Botanic Garden are the focal point of displays, workshops and guided walks during this floral festival.

Toodyay Folk Festival Hippies let down their hair at this longstanding folk music festival.

Broome Stompen Ground This Aboriginal cultural festival features bands and food.

Festival of Geraldton The town of Geraldton celebrates with dragon boat races, parades and parties.

November

Perth Food and Wine Fair The west showcases its best for gourmets and gourmands.

Festival of Fremantle Fremantle comes alive with exhibitions and performances.

Margaret River Surf Classic Surfers from all over the world hit Margaret River's waves.

Manjimup Timber Festival This local festival takes place in the heart of karri country.

Broome Mango Festival Broome celebrates the mango harvest, with mango-tasting, mardi gras and the Great Chefs of Broome Cook-off.

Margaret River Wine Region Festival This 10-day festival titillates the tastebuds with the best of the south-west's wine, food, art, music and outdoor adventures.

ACTIVITIES

A huge range of activities exist and there's something for everyone in WA. Many operators are based in Perth and travel to the site of the particular activity, such as the south-west or the south coast.

Bushwalking

There are some great bushwalks in this state, ranging from short trips in the forests of the south-west to the long Bibbulmun Track (see the boxed text later in this chapter) or untracked coastal walks. Many involve substantial climbs and the traversing of picturesque ranges.

The beauty of WA is that the walks are in vastly different environments. There is the tropical Kimberley; the dry Pilbara with its magnificent gorges; Kalbarri and the Murchison River; the Darling Range near Perth; and the great variety of the coastline and forests of the south-west.

For bushwalkers who like to have something high to climb, there is Mt Augustus, twice the size of Uluru (Ayers Rock); Pyramid Hill in the Pilbara with its stunning views; the precipitous peaks of the Stirling and Porongurup Ranges; and Peak Charles, Mt Ragged and Frenchmans Peak near Esperance.

There is a surfeit of spectacular coastline punctuated by interesting walks. Of particular interest are the walks in the Fitzgerald River, William Bay, Leeuwin-Naturaliste, Walpole-Nornalup and D'Entrecasteaux National Parks. It is not unusual to see humpback whales at sea and wildflowers cascading down coastal tracks.

The Bibbulmun Track

Western Australia's only true long-distance walking trail, the Bibbulmun Track stretches from Kalamunda in the Darling Range (about 20km east of Perth) through virtually unbroken natural environment to Albany on the south coast.

The 963km track is named after an Aboriginal language group, known as the Bibbulmun, who inhabited some of the areas on the south coast through which the track passes. It was first conceived in the 1970s, and is modelled on the 3450km Appalachian Trail in the USA.

The first stages of the track were officially opened in 1979, as part of the celebrations of 150 years of European settlement. A project to upgrade and transform the Bibbulmun Track into one of the world's greatest long-distance walking trails began in October 1993 and was completed in 1998.

To walk from end to end takes about eight weeks. The trail meanders through the full gamut of the south-west's landscape, including jarrah and marri forests, wandoo flats carpeted with wildflowers, and rugged granite outcrops. The track passes through (or close to) the towns of Dwellingup, Balingup, Pemberton and Northcliffe. On the south coast, walkers traverse coastal heath country, spectacular cliffs, headlands and beaches, as well as the towns of Walpole and Denmark.

Highlights include climbing Mt Cooke, the highest peak (548m) in the Darling Range; walking through the magnificent tingle forests of the Valley of the Giants near Walpole; and along the rugged south coast.

About 5000 walkers use the track each year, although most are on it for only two or three days. There are a number of sections at the northern end of the track which are ideal for short walks of two to four days, with good transport connections from each end.

The route is clearly marked by signs with gold waugals (mythical snakes). There are 47 purpose-built camp sites spaced between 10km and 20km apart. They are among the best on the long trails of Australia, and include three-walled, timber sleeping shelters with space for eight to 12 people, large-capacity rainwater tanks, bush toilets, picnic tables, fireplaces and tent sites.

The shelters can be used free of charge, on a first-come first-served basis. The northern section of the trail is especially popular, so walkers are advised not to depend on space being available.

Most of the original track has now been realigned to avoid main roads and logging operations, and hundreds of kilometres of purpose-built walking trail have been created. Originally the Bibbulmun Track finished in Walpole, but it has since been extended by 180km along the south coast to Albany.

The best time for walking is from late winter into spring (August to October), when the weather is mild but sunny and the wildflowers magnificent, and in autumn (late March to May). In summer, when it's hot and dry, walkers need to carry plenty of water and walk early in the morning or later in the afternoon, to avoid the heat of the day.

For more information contact the Department of Conservation and Land Management (CALM; ☎ 9334 0265, @ bibtrack@calm.wa.gov.au), Technology Park, Western Precinct, 17 Dick Perry Ave (enter via Hayman Rd or Kent St), Kensington 6151. CALM publishes and sells a series of maps and trail notes which are essential for walkers. There's heaps of introductory information on CALM's Web site at www.calm.wa.gov.au/tourism/bibbulmun.

The CALM Web site (www.calm.wa .gov.au) has lists and descriptions of many national park trails. You can also pick up brochures from CALM offices. There are a number of bushwalking clubs in WA. The umbrella organisation is the Federation of Western Australian Bushwalkers (☎ 9362 1614) in Perth. Check out the Web site at www.bushwalking.org.au/wapage.html.

There are a number of suppliers in Perth who can provide bushwalking equipment and information, including:

Mountain Designs (☎ 9322 4774, e mtdesign@ iinet.net.au) 862 Hay St, Perth 6000; (☎ 9335 1431) Queensgate Centre, William St, Fremantle 6160
Paddy Pallin (☎ 9321 2666) 884 Hay St, Perth 6000
Snowgum (☎ 9321 5259) 581 Murray St, West Perth 6005

Books Suitable bushwalking books, all published by CALM, are: *Beating About the Bush: Discover the National Parks and Forests near Perth* (1986) by Andrew Cribb; *Family Walks in Perth Outdoors*; *Perth Outdoors: A Guide to Natural Recreation Areas In and Around Perth* (1992); and the recently revised *Guide to the Bibbulmun Bushwalking Track*, which covers the 600km-plus walk from Perth to the south-west corner of the state (see the boxed text 'The Bibbulmun Track' in this chapter).

Lonely Planet's *Walking in Australia* guide describes a number of walks in WA, mainly in the south-west and on the south coast. These include the northernmost section of the Cape to Cape Walk in Leeuwin-Naturaliste National Park; the Stirling Range Ridge Walk in the Stirling Range National Park as well as two shorter walks, Bluff Knoll and Toolbrunup Peak; West Cape Howe National Park – the walks from Lowlands Beach to Cosy Corner; and the Walpole to Peaceful Bay trail in Walpole-Nornalup National Park.

Australia's excellent *Wild* magazine sometimes features articles covering bushwalks in WA.

Bird-Watching

This state is one of the best places in Australia for bird-watching because of the variety of species and the ease with which you can observe them. The state is a birdwatcher's delight, so much so that two of the four official Birds Australia observatories are in WA – at Eyre and Broome.

The Birds Australia WA Group (☎ 9383 7749, fax 9387 8412) is at 71 Oceanic Dr, Floreat 6014.

Useful books to aid identification of species include: *Field Guide to the Birds of Australia* (1989) by K Simpson and N Day; *Field Guide to the Birds of Western Australia* (1985) by GM Storr and RE Johnstone; and *The Slater Field Guide to Australian Birds* (1990) by Peter Slater et al.

Cycling

This is a very popular activity in WA. The distances may be great but the terrain is not especially hilly.

In Perth, Bikewest (☎ 9320 9301), at 441 Murray St, has heaps of information about cycling in the state, including maps. The Bicycle Transportation Alliance (☎ 9420 7210), 2 Delhi St, West Perth 6005, is an advocacy group with an excellent Web site for cyclists (sunsite.anu.edu.au/wa/bta) which has useful links.

For cycling in the north of the state, Bob Craine's *Cycling Northern Australia* is worth a look – it's available from Bicycle New South Wales' mail-order bookshop (☎ 02-9283 5200, fax 9283 5246), PO Box 272, Sydney, NSW 2000, and some tourist offices.

See Bicycle in the Getting Around chapter.

Horse & Camel Trekking

Enabling explorers and settlers to make inroads into the inhospitable interior, horses and camels were the animal pioneers of this country. Today, there are many places in WA where you can go horse and camel trekking.

Local tourist offices are the best places to get details of companies running treks, which range from a leisurely camel ride along Cable Beach near Broome to an overnight or moonlight horse ride in Kalbarri

A leisurely camel ride is one of the best ways to see Cable Beach near Broome

National Park. The more adventurous could contemplate an overnight trip south of Wyndham in the rugged East Kimberley. The Canning Stock Route, by camel, even looms as a possibility!

A number of operators also offer horse riding and trekking in the south-west of the state.

Rock-Climbing

It is widely thought that WA has the greatest remaining areas of unclimbed rock. Most activity has been concentrated in the south-west of the state, close to Perth, but the Pilbara, North West Cape and the Kimberley have endless climbing possibilities.

In the south-west corner of the state are Churchmans Brook and Mountain Quarry near Perth, the sea cliffs of Willyabrup, West Cape Howe and the Gap, the Stirling and Porongurup Ranges, and Peak Charles. Canyoning and abseiling, necessary skills of the exploratory climber, are popular activities in their own right, especially in the Karijini gorges and Murchison gorges near Kalbarri.

Experienced climbers should always check with local CALM officials as to where climbing is permitted. Inexperienced climbers should only climb with a qualified guide. Adventure Out (☎ 9472 3919) conducts instructional courses for beginners near Perth and in the south-west.

See the boxed text 'Go South for Adventure' in the South Coast chapter.

Caving

Adventure caving is vastly different to tours through electrically lit 'commercial' caves, and involves specialist knowledge and skill. Many caves are in the Leeuwin-Naturaliste karst system and a number, such as Brides and Dingo's, have to be accessed using ropes. Cape Range National Park of North West Cape has a number of unexplored caves (although human moles are rapidly drifting north and underground).

Adventure Out (☎ 9472 3919) operates adventure discovery trips to the Margaret River region which include abseiling, climbing and caving.

Surfing

The WA coast is a mecca for surfers. The south-west, and the Margaret River area in particular, are well known throughout the world (see the boxed text 'Surfing the South-West' in the South-West chapter). Around

Bunbury, Geraldton, Kalbarri, Carnarvon and Albany there is also good surfing. Chances are that if you are here with your board, then we don't have to tell you where to go.

Nat Young's *Surfing & Sailboard Guide to Australia* and the coffee-table publication *Atlas of Australian Surfing* cover the west-coast beaches.

Scuba Diving & Snorkelling

There's more than 6000km of coastline in WA. Good diving areas include the large stretch of coast from Esperance to Geraldton, and between Carnarvon and Exmouth. You can also get out to the islands and reefs in small boats.

The more popular diving spots include Esperance, Bremer Bay, Albany, Denmark, Windy Harbour, Margaret River, Busselton, Rottnest Island, Shoalwater Islands Marine Park (near Rockingham), Bunbury, Lancelin, Houtman Abrolhos Islands (near Geraldton), Carnarvon and North West Cape (Exmouth, Coral Bay, Ningaloo Reef).

Perhaps the most spectacular underwater experience would be diving (or snorkelling) alongside the world's largest fish, the whale shark, or swimming with the graceful manta rays. This is possible off Ningaloo Reef and Exmouth (see Exmouth and the boxed text 'The Biggest Fish in the World' in the Coral Coast & the Pilbara chapter). There is a strong possibility you will also see green and loggerhead turtles, dolphins, dugongs and humpback whales, depending on when you visit.

Watching Marine Mammals

Although commercial operators will happily take you to spot marine mammals such as humpback whales and bottlenose dolphins, you can often glimpse them purely by chance. There are few other accessible places in the world where spotting such a variety of marine mammals is so easy.

Humpback whales are commonly seen, anywhere from Cape Leeuwin north to Dampier, even between Perth and Rottnest Island. The southern right whale can be seen in numbers off the Great Australian Bight, near Albany and by Cape Leeuwin.

Bottlenose dolphins attracts thousands of tourists to Monkey Mia on Shark Bay, and to Rockingham and Bunbury south of Perth. Common dolphins are likely to be seen on boat trips in places like the Archipelago of the Recherche.

Other marine mammals include the Australian sea lion at Carnac Island (opposite Perth); any one of the 10,000 dugongs that frequent Shark Bay; and NZ fur seals basking along the southern coastline.

See Fauna in the Facts about Western Australia chapter for more information about common marine mammals.

Sailing

The America's Cup yachting trophy was brought home to WA for a brief period from 1983 to 1987 when *Australia II* triumphed over the US yacht *Liberty*. There are a number of opportunities to learn basic or advanced sailing, or just go for a sail, in and around Perth and Fremantle. The Swan River is a great place to begin and there is another school at Sorrento at Hillary's Boat Harbour. Fun catamarans are available for hire at a number of southern and northern beaches.

Fremantle is one of the six world legs in the Whitbread Around-the-World Yacht Race, concluding the arduous 'bash' across the Southern Ocean from Cape Town.

Fishing

The coastal regions of WA offer some of the best fishing in the world. Some of the more popular areas include Rottnest Island, Albany, Geraldton and the Houtman Abrolhos Islands, Mackerel Islands, Shark Bay, Carnarvon and the coastline to the north, the North West Cape and Broome.

Licences are required if you intend to catch marron and rock lobsters, if you use a fishing net and for freshwater angling. Costs range from $15 to $25, and an annual licence covering everything costs $60. They are available from Fisheries Western Australia (☎ 9482 7333), in the SGIO Atrium, 168–70 St Georges Terrace, Perth 6000, or its country offices. The department publishes fishing guides, including one for the environmentally sensitive Ningaloo Reef.

Canoeing & Kayaking

There is ample scope to paddle a canoe or kayak in WA.

The most famous river is the Avon, which is 'descended' by a rabble of powered and unpowered craft in Northam's annual Avon Descent, held in August. The Amateur Canoe Association of WA (☎ 9387 5756) can provide details of the state's many good canoeing and kayaking rivers.

The WA Ministry of Sport & Recreation (☎ 9387 9700) publishes a series of free *Canoeing Guides*; the one on *Avon River: Northam to Toodyay* is particularly useful.

Sea kayaking has a good following in the west, but it requires skill and should only be undertaken with good equipment and the necessary training. In the northwest, the tidal changes are huge and there are dangers from crocodiles and sharks. Perhaps the best trip is along Ningaloo Reef with Sea Kayak Wilderness Adventures (☎ 1800-625 688).

White-Water Rafting

White-water rafting is not as popular in the west as it is in the eastern states. However, in summer the Collie River is suitable for two-person rafts; and in winter the Murray River, about a 90-minute drive south of Perth, can be tackled in seven-person rafts. The Murchison River (after heavy rain) can also provide rafting possibilities.

From Perth, white-water rafting trips are available with Adventure Out (☎ 9472 3919).

Windsurfing

This is immensely popular, especially at Perth's city beaches. On windy days Scarborough and Cottesloe become ablaze with multicoloured sails, and wave riders leaping over intimidating, incoming breakers.

Beaches in the south-west, such as Mandurah, Rockingham, Busselton, Dunsborough and Bunbury, are also popular. So are northern beaches: Seabird, Lancelin (probably the sailboard mecca), Ledge Point and Geraldton. In January each year there is an ocean race from Ledge Point to Lancelin.

For more information contact the tourist offices in the towns mentioned here.

LANGUAGE COURSES

If English isn't your first language and you want to study it, places specialising in teaching English include: the Edith Cowan University International English Centre (☎ 9442 1402, fax 9442 1451), Goldsworthy Rd, Claremont 6010; and the Phoenix English Language Academy (☎ 9227 5538, fax 9227 5540), 223 Vincent St, North Perth 6006.

WORK

If you come to Australia on a tourist visa, you're not allowed to work. Although you might find casual labour in the fruit-picking or tourism industries, if you're illegal the work will not be well paid and if you're caught breaching your visa conditions you can be expelled from the country.

With a working holiday visa (see Visas & Documents earlier in this chapter) there are many possibilities for temporary work, such as bar work, factory work, fruit-picking, nannying, working as a station hand and collecting for charities. People with computer or secretarial skills should have little difficulty finding work in Perth and major towns. Nurses are also in demand by agencies.

Apples and pears are harvested in the Donnybrook and Manjimup areas of the southwest from February to April. Grape-picking takes place in Margaret River, Albany, Mt Barker and Manjimup from February to March. Bananas are harvested year-round in Carnarvon, and from April to December in Kununurra. There is also vegetable-picking in Kununurra from May to November, and tourism jobs from May to December. September to November is the time for flower-harvesting in the Midlands; you might also find some crop-seeding work from April to June. The Esperance lobster industry is busy from November to May and prawn trawlers are busy off Carnarvon from March to June.

Try the classifieds section of the *West Australian* under Situations Vacant, especially on Saturday and Wednesday. Also check local newspapers for jobs vacant. For employment agencies see the *Yellow Pages*. The various backpacker magazines and hostels are good sources of information – some local employers even advertise on their notice boards.

Centrelink (☎ 13 2850), the government's employment and welfare department, has offices in Perth and most of WA's larger towns. Seasonal jobs such as fruit-picking are often listed there. Centrelink's Web site is at www.centrelink.gov.au. Call the Australian Taxation Office on ☎ 13 1020 or check out its Web site (www.ato.gov.au) for information on tax requirements.

Workabout Australia by Barry Brebner gives a comprehensive state-by-state breakdown of seasonal work opportunities.

ACCOMMODATION

The WATC produces the free guide *Western Australia Accommodation Listing*, available from all tourist offices, covering Perth and most towns.

Another source of accommodation listings is the RACWA's comprehensive and reliable annual directory. It's updated annually, so prices are current. There are two books: one for the north of the state ($5) and the other for the south ($7); if you buy both, it's $10. Both books include Perth. They can be purchased only at RACWA offices (see Car in the Getting Around chapter).

Camping & Caravan Parks

If you want to get around WA cheaply, then camping's the way to go; it costs from around $10 to $16 for two per night.

Caravan parks in WA are generally well kept, conveniently located and excellent value. Many of them also have on-site vans which you can rent for the night (from around $30 a night). These give you all the comfort of a caravan without the inconvenience of towing one. On-site cabins – with their own bathroom and toilet – are also widely available (from around $40 to $50 for two). In most large towns, camping grounds are situated well away from the centre so you really need your own transport to get to them.

Camping in the bush, either in national parks (around $8 for two) or in the open, can be the highlight of a visit to WA. Nights spent around a campfire under the stars, sleeping in a swag, will be nothing short of unforgettable.

Hostels

You'll find hostels all over the state, with more official hostels and backpacker hostels popping up all the time. The WA Youth Hostel Association (YHA; ☎ 9227 5122, fax 9227 5123, ⓔ enquiries@yhawa.com.au) main office is at 236 William St, Northbridge 6003. The helpful staff give out all sorts of information and make bookings for tours and accommodation. Pick up the giveaway booklet *Backpackers Guide to WA*, available there and at hostels around the state.

YHA Hostels Providing basic accommodation, in small dormitories or twin rooms, YHA hostels charge from $15 a night. There are communal kitchen and lounge areas and laundry facilities. Some hostels are permanently full and as a result have a maximum-stay period.

Australian YHA hostels are part of Hostelling International (HI), so if you're already a member of the YHA in your own country, you can use the Australian hostels. To become a full YHA member in Australia costs $49 a year. You can join at any youth hostel. The annual *YHA Australia Accommodation & Discounts Guide*, available from any YHA office in Australia and from some YHA offices overseas, lists all YHA hostels around Australia, with useful maps showing how to find them. It also highlights hostels with disabled access.

You must have a regulation sleeping sheet or bed linen (it can usually be rented).

Backpacker Hostels In recent years the number of backpacker hostels in WA has increased dramatically – Perth has more per capita than any other capital city in Australia, with varying standards.

Some hostels are purpose-built as backpacker hostels; these are usually the best places in terms of facilities; former hotels/motels can often be gloomy and run-down. If you want peace and quiet, avoid the places that actively promote themselves as 'party' hostels.

Prices at backpacker hostels are generally in line with YHA hostels, typically $12 to $18. One practice that many people find objectionable in independent hostels (it never happens in YHAs) is the 'vetting' of Australians, designed to keep unwanted customers out.

One backpacker organisation you can join to receive a discount card ($29, valid for 12 months) is VIP Backpackers Resorts (☎ 07-3395 6111, fax 3395 6222, ℮ backpack@ backpackers.com.au), PO Box 600, Cannon Hill, Qld 4170. The card qualifies members for discounts on accommodation and other services, such as transport. Check out the Web site at www.backpackers.com.au.

Guesthouses & B&Bs

These are the fastest-growing segment of the accommodation market. New places are opening all the time, and the network of accommodation alternatives throughout the state includes everything from rambling old guesthouses, upmarket country homes and romantic escapes, to a simple bedroom in a family home. Many of these places are listed throughout this book. Tariffs cover a wide range, but are typically in the $50 to $120 (per double) bracket and include a full breakfast.

Hotels & Pubs

Hotels in WA are generally older places, while motels are newer. Not all hotels have rooms to rent, although many still do. A 'private hotel', as opposed to a 'licensed hotel', provides accommodation and does not serve alcohol.

The old hotels in some older towns and historic centres such as Kalgoorlie-Boulder can be magnificent. Though the rooms may be old-fashioned and unexciting, the hotel facade and entrance area will often be quite extravagant. In the Outback, the old hotels are often places of real character. The single rooms are often a bargain for lone travellers, as they really are single rooms, relics of the days when single men travelled the country looking for work.

Another good thing about hotels (guesthouses and private hotels, too) is that the big breakfasts usually served there are generally excellent. Most hotel rooms cost around $30 to $60.

Motels

If you've got transport and want a modern, utilitarian place with your own bathroom and other facilities, then you're moving into the motel bracket. Motels are everywhere, but they're usually away from city centres. Prices are usually for a double room, with no discounts for singles. In motels, the rooms are almost always doubles. You'll find motel rooms from about $60. Most motels provide tea-/coffee-making facilities and a small fridge, at the least.

Farm & Station Stays

One of the best ways to come to grips with Australian life is to spend a few days on a farm (known as 'stations' in the Outback, where they are greater in size and characterised by their red dust). The Gascoyne, Pilbara and Murchison areas of WA are popular areas for station stays. A few travellers get actively involved in daily activities, but most use farm and station stays as rural B&B.

Most farms and stations provide comfortable accommodation in the main homestead (B&B-style, with dinner often included in the price) or in self-contained cottages on the property. In some cases, budget accommodation is available in outbuildings or former shearers' quarters. Some stations also allow caravans and campers for a reasonable site fee, but they do not have the facilities of caravan parks.

The WATC's free brochure *Farms, Stations and Country Retreats* lists station stays available in the state; prices are pretty reasonable.

Chalets

In the south-west in particular you'll find very comfortable self-contained cottages, often in a medium-sized development, which will be referred to as chalets. These can sleep from two to 10 people (depending on the size and configuration of bedrooms) and can range from being comfortable and functional to absolute luxury with all modcons, video, CD player and the like. Most of these have warming potbelly stoves for heating – essential in winter.

Serviced Apartments

Mostly found in cities, serviced apartments tend to be upmarket and often cater to business travellers. Linen is included and the apartments are serviced every few days (sometimes daily). Newer-style serviced apartments can be more comfortable – and more economical – than mid-range hotels.

Check out the classifieds in the *West Australian* on Wednesday and Saturday.

Other Accommodation

Renting a room, holiday flat or house can be an economical accommodation option, particularly if you wish to base yourself in an area for any length of time.

Holiday flats are found in holiday areas, and are much like motel rooms but usually with a kitchen or cooking facilities, cooking utensils, cutlery and crockery, so you can fix your own food. They are not serviced like motels – you make your own bed and do your own dishes. In some holiday flats you have to provide your own sheets and bedding, or pay a charge for linen hire.

Holiday flats are often – but not always – rented on a weekly basis. They can be a bargain for more than two people. A two-bedroom holiday flat is about 1.5 times the cost of a comparable single-bedroom unit.

The WATC produces a comprehensive guide, updated annually, of self-catering accommodation. Tourist offices in every region have lists of self-catering options. Many local estate agents also handle holiday accommodation and short-term rentals.

In Perth, if you want to rent a flat or a room for an extended period of time, check out the classifieds in the *West Australian* on Wednesday and Saturday.

FOOD

Culinary delights can be one of the real highlights of travelling in Australia. Since the Chinese brought sweet-and-sour to the goldfields, migrants to this country – Greek, Yugoslav, Italian, Lebanese and others – have influenced the country's cuisine, to create the culinary melting pot of Australia today.

There's an excellent variety of cuisines and a range of local specialities on offer in Perth, Fremantle, a few south-western towns such as Margaret River and Albany, and Broome. Elsewhere, the choice may not be so great, and you'll have to go for pub meals (typically grilled steaks, fried fish, and pasta) or fairly average Chinese.

Note that there are strict antismoking laws in restaurants and pubs in WA.

Australian Food

Although there is no real definition of 'Australian cuisine', there is certainly a great deal of excellent Australian food to try. There's been a rise in popularity of exotic local and 'bush' foods, like kangaroo or emu, and for the adventurous these dishes offer something completely different. The good news about Australian food is the range and quality of ingredients. There is a fine market-garden industry in WA, so nearly all the produce is grown in the state. The meat and poultry is also top quality.

A superb range of seafood is a highlight: fish like spangled emperor, coral trout, many species of cod, groper, pink schnapper, King George whiting, sand whiting and the esteemed barramundi, or superb lobsters and other crustaceans like Exmouth Gulf prawns.

Unique to the south-west of the state are delicious marron or freshwater crayfish. The French settlers named the crustacean after the large edible chestnut, which has a dark exterior, sweet taste and white flesh.

Cafes and restaurants in Perth and the main towns serve 'Modern Australian' food, which borrows heavily from a wide range of foreign cuisines, but has a definite local flavour. You might find an Asian-

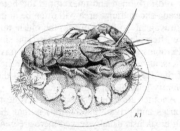

Deliciously sweet marron features on many restaurant menus in WA.

inspired curry on the menu with European-or Mediterranean-inspired dishes. Although most menus tend to be heavy on the meat and fish choices, vegetarians won't have too much trouble, and there are some excellent vegetarian restaurants in the state.

Fast Food

You'll find the usual big-name fast-food outlets all over the state. Chicken Treat is a WA chain that does quite good chicken dishes. Australians love fish and chips just as much as the British.

For something a little bit healthier, most delis can put together a good sandwich, roll or focaccia. Otherwise try the Australian favourite, the ubiquitous meat pie – usually steak and gravy in a pastry case, sometimes with vegetables added or with chicken instead of beef. These can vary in quality; Mrs McGregor's is a good commercial brand, widely available throughout WA.

Unless you're particularly partial to deep-fried food, steer clear of the dreary roadhouses that punctuate the nothingness between towns. They were designed to serve fuel and the food sometimes tastes as if it has been cooked in it. Generally, the only thing worth eating at these places is the 'truckies' breakfast'.

Pub Grub

In the evening the best bargain meals can be found in pubs. Look for 'counter meals', so called because they used to be eaten at the bar counter. A few places are still like that, although most are now more like restaurants.

The food is simple: seafood or meat with chips, usually with a help-yourself salad bar. 'Surf 'n' turf' – fish and steak in the same dish – is a quintessentially Australian pub meal. The quality is usually good and the prices reasonable – around $10 to $20 for a huge main meal. One catch is the strict hours. The evening meal time may be just 6 to 7.30 or 8 pm.

Self-Catering

There are fresh produce markets in most of the larger towns. Fremantle's markets are among the most famous (see the Perth chapter). On either side of large drives, stock up with fresh produce from supermarkets in towns.

Remember that if you are crossing into WA from SA or NT, you'll have to dump all of your fresh fruit and vegetables because of quarantine regulations.

DRINKS
Nonalcoholic Drinks

Australians knock back cola and flavoured milk like there's no tomorrow and there are also excellent mineral waters.

Although WA hasn't quite got the hang of coffee like Melbourne or Sydney has, coffee snobs will be happy in Perth, Fremantle, Margaret River, Albany and Broome, but will probably be hanging out for a good espresso fix everywhere else. Most places – even small towns – do have cappuccino machines; the problem is, not many people seem to know how to use them.

In the Outback, unless you like instant coffee, you might be better off drinking tea.

Alcoholic Drinks

Beer Foster's, Carlton Draught, Tooheys, XXXX and Victoria Bitter (VB) are all well-known Australian beers.

The Swan Brewery, the west's biggest producer of beer, has two major brands: Swan and Emu. Swan comes as Draught, Gold and Lager; Emu comes as Export and Bitter. The Swan Brewery in Canning Vale has a free tour (see the Perth chapter) and it throws in a couple of free beers.

Another smaller brewery, Matilda Bay, in North Fremantle, produces boutique beer which is popular in all states. The beers are Redback (including a light version), Fremantle Bitter and Matilda Bay Pils and Bitter. There are many boutique breweries in various pubs; two drops worth a mention are the Perth Brass Monkey's Stout and Fremantle's Sail & Anchor Seven Sea Real Ale. Guinness is occasionally found on draught in Irish-style pubs such as Rosie O'Grady's and The Bog in Perth.

Australian beer is always served ice-cold and has a higher alcohol content than British or American beers. Standard beer is generally around 5% alcohol, although most breweries now produce light beers, with an alcohol content of between 2% and 3.5%. People who drive under the influence of alcohol risk a heavy fine and the loss of their licence (see Car in the Getting Around chapter).

Wine As WA has the perfect climate for producing wine, there are some superb wine-growing areas. Best known are the Swan Valley, the Margaret River region and the Great Southern area around Mt Barker. (See the special section 'Wineries of Western Australia'.)

All over WA you'll find restaurants advertising that they're BYO, which stands for 'Bring Your Own' and means that they're not licensed to sell alcohol, but you are permitted to bring your own with you (for a small corkage fee).

ENTERTAINMENT

Perth is the epicentre of the state's cultural attractions. On Friday nights in Northbridge, Subiaco and Leederville (and increasingly around King St in central Perth) crowds spill out of bars and restaurants, rage in the nightclubs and swamp the many cafes along the streets. There's a mix of suited business types, the hip and fashionable designer mob, gays, lesbians, straights, and the ultracasual (dare we say sloppy?) backpacker crowd.

The regional centres have one or two pubs where those in the know hang out. Just ask someone at the tourist office where you should go. In most smaller towns in WA there is only one watering hole, but Hannan St, the main drag of Kalgoorlie-Boulder, is choked with pubs, as befits a frontier mining town.

Pubs

Many pubs in Perth, Fremantle and large towns have live music, so these are great places for catching live bands. There are comprehensive listings in newspapers, particularly on Friday and Saturday, and in the entertainment magazine *Xpress*.

In country towns ask the locals, or look out for bills advertising forthcoming bands.

Nightclubs

While there's no shortage of clubs, they are confined to Perth and larger towns. They range from the exclusive 'members-only' variety to barn-sized discos where anyone who wants to spend the money is welcome. Admission ranges from $6 to $12.

Some places have dress standards, but it is generally left to the discretion of the beefy bouncers or 'door bitches' at the door; if they don't like the look of you, bad luck. The upmarket nightclubs attract an older, more sophisticated and affluent crowd, and generally have stricter dress codes, smarter decor and higher prices.

Theatre & Dance

Most performances take place in Perth and Fremantle but occasionally shows will travel to towns like Bunbury, Albany and Kalgoorlie- Boulder – and sometimes even as far afield as Broome.

Opera & Classical Music

The West Australian Symphony Orchestra (WASO; ☎ 9326 0000) and the West Australian Opera (☎ 9321 5869) perform regularly at the Perth Concert Hall. Check out the WASO Web site at www.waso.com.au.

Leeuwin Estate Winery near Margaret River in the state's south-west puts on an annual concert which attracts thousands of visitors (see the special section 'Wineries of Western Australia').

Cinemas

The big operators such as Greater Union and Hoyts have cinemas scattered across Perth and Fremantle. Seeing a new-release mainstream film costs around $13 ($8 for children under 15) in the big cities, less in country areas. Local newspapers usually list the cinema's program.

You will also find 'art-house' cinemas in Perth, screening independent and foreign-language films and reruns of classics and cult movies.

There are still a few drive-ins around the state; these are an atmospheric way to take in starry Kimberley skies and a film simultaneously.

SPECTATOR SPORTS

Residents of WA are keen sports lovers and enthusiastically support their local or state teams in national competitions.

Ticket agencies in WA include BOCS Ticketing (☎ 9484 1133) and Red Tickets (☎ 1800-199 991, 13 6100).

Australian Rules Football

The unique game of Australian Rules Football (or Aussie Rules) is the west's most popular spectator sport. Though most of the season takes place during winter months, with finals in September/October, preseason competition sees some matches played as early as March.

The Perth-based West Coast Eagles is one of the top teams in the Australian Football League, having won the premiership twice since entering the national competition in 1987. The other WA team in the AFL is Fremantle Dockers. AFL matches are played regularly at Subiaco Oval (☎ 9484 1222 for ticket sales) and at Fremantle (☎ 9430 8975). For up-to-date recorded information, call the Footy Info Line on ☎ 1900-997 005.

There is also a Western Australian Rules Football competition for teams in and around Perth. Most country towns have teams that compete in regional divisions within the WA Country Football League. Ask at the local pub; you'll have no trouble finding out what, where and when.

Cricket

The WA state cricket team has also had its fair share of success in the national competition. Interstate games are played at the Western Australia Cricket Association oval, known colloquially as 'the WACA' (☎ 9265 7222).

Some of the world's greatest cricketers have come out of WA. They include the pace bowlers Graham McKenzie and Dennis Lillee and the swing bowlers Bob Massie and Terry Alderman.

At least one of the test matches of an international cricket series (or a one-day game of that competition) is usually played in Perth, keeping interested eastern TV viewers glued to their sets until late. Games are played at the WACA, which is close to the

centre of the city. The cricket season generally takes up where footy leaves off, with major test matches played during summer months.

Basketball

There are both women's and men's teams – the Perth Breakers and the Perth Wildcats respectively – from WA in the national competition. Games are played at the Perth Entertainment Centre (☎ 9484 1222) during the winter months. For match details, contact Basketball WA (☎ 9284 0555).

Other Sports

Both men's and women's teams compete in the National Hockey League (NHL). Details can be obtained from the WA Hockey Association (☎ 9451 3688).

The men's team Western Heelers participates in the International Baseball League Australia, and has held the national crown.

Horse racing is held regularly at Perth's Ascot and Belmont Park racetracks. Contact the WA Turf Club (☎ 9277 0777) for details of forthcoming race meetings.

Motor racing is held on Sundays from March to October at Wanneroo Park Raceway, Pinjar Rd, Wanneroo. Throughout spring and summer, speedcar and motorcycle races are held on Friday night at the Royal Agricultural Showground at Claremont.

SHOPPING

You probably won't be coming to WA to shop, although you'll find plenty of interesting items which can encourage you to part with your money – everything from kitsch 'Australiana' to stunning Aboriginal art, from precious metals to delicious wines.

There is good shopping in Perth, especially in the centre of town and in groovy 'cafe society' suburbs such as Subiaco and Claremont (see under Shopping in the Perth chapter). In country towns and remote areas the choice is often more limited.

Aboriginal Art

A piece of original art can be both a special souvenir and a great investment, but take care when purchasing Aboriginal artworks that you are buying an authentic work. (See the boxed text 'Buying Aboriginal Art & Artefacts' in the Facts about Western Australia chapter.)

Australiana

A rather vague cultural term, 'Australiana' refers to collections of 'souvenirs' – tea towels, ashtrays, polystyrene 'stubby holders' (beer-can coolers) and T-shirts to name a few. It's those things you buy as gifts, supposedly representative of Aussie culture. Most of them are tacky, and are usually not even made in Australia. Buy at your peril.

The seeds of many native plants (such as kangaroo paw) are on sale all over the place – but check whether you can take them home.

Wine & Food

What better way to remember your trip than with a Margaret River chardonnay or a shiraz from the Great Southern? (See the special section 'Wineries of Western Australia' for descriptions of the best wines from each area.)

Bush tucker – things like tinned witchetty grubs or honey ants – might not really take your fancy but can be good as a novelty gift. Customs regulations allowing, cheese from the Margaret River Cheese Company will probably please a wider audience.

Gold, Diamonds, Pearls & Opals

The main street of Kalgoorlie-Boulder has plenty of jewellery shops where you can buy earrings, bracelets and pendants that incorporate gold nuggets (which have sometimes

been tumbled to give a slightly polished appearance or are attached in a raw state). They are relatively inexpensive – but make sure that the fittings are of good quality.

World-famous Argyle diamonds are mined south of Kununurra. Pink diamonds can be purchased from outlets in Kununurra including Nina's Jewellery and Kimberley Fine Diamonds, and in jewellery and other shops in Perth.

Broome pearls, reputed to be the best, are cultured from the beautiful silver-lipped oyster; they are probably the most expensive in the world. There are many pearl galleries in Broome.

The opal is Australia's national gemstone and you'll find plenty of jewellery made with it.

Handcrafts

Many of the handcrafts for sale feature local motifs such as wildflower designs or dried-and-dyed wildflower arrangements.

One favourite handcraft is carved and turned timbers from the giant forests; tables made of timber burls (unusual circular growths which occur on tree trunks), turned wooden bowls and exquisite hand carvings depicting whales and dolphins. The timbers used for these items include local jarrah, the rare curly jarrah, sheoak, WA blackbutt, wandoo, karri, marri, coastal banksia and the grass tree.

Herb products – ranging from pillows to essential oils to chutneys – make great gifts. They are available from cottage industries in the south-west, in places such as Walpole and Balingup.

Getting There & Away

AIR – INTERNATIONAL
Airports & Airlines

The only international airport in Western Australia (WA) is in Perth. Qantas Airways operates direct flights between Perth and Singapore, Tokyo, Denpasar (Bali), Jakarta and Johannesburg. South African Airways flies direct between Perth and Johannesburg. The other major Australian carrier, Ansett Australia, flies direct between Perth and Denpasar. Singapore Airlines, Malaysia Airlines, Thai Airways International and Garuda Indonesia all have direct flights from Perth to their home countries.

Many travellers fly to the east coast of Australia, then take domestic flights to Perth. The gateways of Sydney and Melbourne provide far more possibilities for flights out of Australia to the rest of the world than Perth does.

Buying Tickets

Buying air tickets these days is like shopping for a car, a stereo or a camera. Rule number one to remember if you are looking for a cheap ticket is to go to an agent, rather than directly to the airline. The airline can usually only quote the regular fare. An agent, on the other hand, can offer all sorts of special deals, particularly on competitive routes.

Ideally, airlines would like every seat occupied on all of their flights, with every passenger paying the highest fare possible. Fortunately for travellers, life usually isn't like that and airlines would rather carry a half-price passenger than have an empty seat. When faced with the problem of too many empty seats, they will either let agents sell them at cut prices, or make one-off special offers on particular routes – keep an eye on the travel advertisements in newspapers.

Round-the-world tickets can be a good option for getting to Perth, either after entering Australia from the eastern states or using the city as the first port of call.

Travellers with Special Needs

Most international airlines can cater for passengers with special needs: travellers with disabilities, people with young children and even children travelling alone. Travellers with special dietary needs and preferences (vegetarian, kosher etc) can request appropriate meals, with advance notice; remind the airline of your request when you confirm your booking, again when you check in, and on each leg of your journey. If you are travelling in a wheelchair, most international airports can provide an escort from the check-in desk to the plane where needed, and ramps, lifts, toilets and phones are generally available.

Airlines usually allow babies up to two years of age to fly for 10% of the adult fare, although a few may allow them to travel free of charge. Reputable international airlines usually provide nappies (diapers), tissues, talcum powder and all the other

Warning

The information in this chapter is particularly vulnerable to change: Prices for international travel are volatile, routes are introduced and cancelled, schedules change, special deals come and go, and rules and visa requirements are amended. Airlines and governments seem to take a perverse pleasure in making price structures and regulations as complicated as possible. You should check with the airline or a travel agent to make sure you understand how a fare (and ticket you may buy) works. In addition, the travel industry is highly competitive and there are many lurks and perks.

The upshot of this is that you should get opinions, quotes and advice from as many airlines and travel agents as possible before you part with your hard-earned cash. Details given in this chapter should be regarded as pointers and are not a substitute for your own careful, up-to-date research.

paraphernalia needed to keep babies clean, dry and half-happy. For children between the ages of two and 12, the fare on international flights is usually 50% of the regular fare, and 67% of a discounted fare.

Departure Tax

There is a $30 departure tax for flights leaving Australia. This is usually paid at the time of purchasing the ticket.

The USA & Canada

There are various connections across the Pacific from Los Angeles, San Francisco and Vancouver to Australia, including direct flights and flights via New Zealand (NZ), island-hopping routes and more circuitous Pacific-rim routes via nations in Asia. In most cases you will need to purchase an additional fare to WA, as the usual gateway is the east coast.

All of these routes to Australia are covered by the two major airline alliances: One World, which includes Qantas, American Airlines, British Airways, Cathay Pacific Airways, Air Pacific and US Airways; and Star Alliance, which includes Ansett Australia, United Airlines, Air Canada, Air New Zealand, All Nippon Airways and Thai Airways International. In both cases, you might get ticketed by one airline but then find that your flight is a code-share with another, ie, that you are flying on the aircraft of one of the alliance partners.

Discount-travel agencies in the USA and Canada are known as consolidators. Discount fares in Canada tend to be about 10% higher than those sold in the USA. Ticket Planet is a leading ticket consolidator in the USA and is recommended. Visit its Web site at www.ticketplanet.com.

To find good fares to Australia check the travel ads in the weekly travel sections of papers such as the *Los Angeles Times*, *San Francisco Examiner*, *New York Times* or Canada's *Globe & Mail*, *Toronto Star* and *Vancouver Sun*.

In the USA the student travel operators are good agents for discounted tickets. Council Travel's head office (☎ 800-226 8624) is at 205 E 42nd St, New York, NY

10017; call for the location of the office nearest you or visit the Web site at www.ciee.org. STA Travel (☎ 800-781 4040) has offices in Boston, Chicago, Miami, New York, Philadelphia, San Francisco and other major cities. Call the toll-free 800 number for office locations or visit the Web site at www.statravel.com.

Travel CUTS/Voyages Campus (☎ 1800-667 2887) is Canada's national student travel agency and has offices in all major cities. Its Web address is www.travelcuts.com.

The straightforward return excursion fare with United Airlines from the USA west coast to Melbourne/Sydney ranges from US$1000 to US$1800, depending on the season. To Perth it is a little more expensive and it's not a direct flight – from US$1500 with United (via Melbourne) in low season, rising to as much as US$2500 or more for a high-season return. Return fares from the east coast of the USA are more expensive (and it's a long trip). Check United's Web site at www.united.com.

As open-jaw fares are calculated as half the return fare to the arrival city plus half the return fare to the departure city, they are cheaper than a USA-WA return, but around US$250 to US$300 more expensive than a USA-Sydney return.

New Zealand

The *New Zealand Herald* has a travel section in which travel agencies advertise fares. Flight Centre (☎ 09-309 6171) has a large central office in Auckland at National Bank Towers (corner Queen and Darby Sts) and many branches throughout the country. STA Travel (☎ 09-309 0458) has its main office at 10 High St, Auckland, and has other offices in Auckland as well as in Hamilton, Palmerston North, Wellington, Christchurch and Dunedin. The Web address is www.sta.travel.com.au.

Qantas, Ansett and Air New Zealand operate trans-Tasman flights linking Auckland, Wellington and Christchurch in NZ with most major Australian gateway cities. Another flight, about the same distance, will be required to reach Perth, entailing more time and expense.

Air Travel Glossary

Cancellation Penalties If you have to cancel or change a discounted ticket, there are often heavy penalties involved; insurance can sometimes be taken out against these penalties. Some airlines impose penalties on regular tickets as well, particularly against 'no-show' passengers.

Courier Fares Businesses often need to send urgent documents or freight securely and quickly. Courier companies hire people to accompany the package through customs and, in return, offer a discount ticket which is sometimes a phenomenal bargain. However, you may have to surrender all your baggage allowance and take only carry-on luggage.

Full Fares Airlines traditionally offer 1st class (coded F), business class (coded J) and economy class (coded Y) tickets. These days there are so many promotional and discounted fares available that few passengers pay full economy fare.

Lost Tickets If you lose your airline ticket an airline will usually treat it like a travellers cheque and, after inquiries, issue you with another one. Legally, however, an airline is entitled to treat it like cash and if you lose it then it's gone forever. Take good care of your tickets.

Onward Tickets An entry requirement for many countries is that you have a ticket out of the country. If you're unsure of your next move, the easiest solution is to buy the cheapest onward ticket to a neighbouring country or a ticket from a reliable airline which can later be refunded if you do not use it.

Open-Jaw Tickets These are return tickets where you fly out to one place but return from another. If available, this can save you backtracking to your arrival point.

Overbooking Since every flight has some passengers who fail to show up, airlines often book more passengers than they have seats. Usually excess passengers make up for the no-shows, but occasionally somebody gets 'bumped' onto the next available flight. Guess who it is most likely to be? The passengers who check in late.

Promotional Fares These are officially discounted fares, available from travel agencies or direct from the airline.

Reconfirmation If you don't reconfirm your flight at least 72 hours prior to departure, the airline may delete your name from the passenger list. Ring to find out if your airline requires reconfirmation.

Restrictions Discounted tickets often have various restrictions on them – such as needing to be paid for in advance and incurring a penalty to be altered. Others are restrictions on the minimum and maximum period you must be away.

Round-the-World Tickets RTW tickets give you a limited period (usually a year) in which to circumnavigate the globe. You can go anywhere the carrying airlines go, as long as you don't backtrack. The number of stopovers or total number of separate flights is decided before you set off and they usually cost a bit more than a basic return flight.

Transferred Tickets Airline tickets cannot be transferred from one person to another. Travellers sometimes try to sell the return half of their ticket, but officials can ask you to prove that you are the person named on the ticket. On an international flight tickets are compared with passports.

Travel Periods Ticket prices vary with the time of year. There is a low (off-peak) season and a high (peak) season, and often a low-shoulder season and a high-shoulder season as well. Usually the fare depends on your outward flight – if you depart in the high season and return in the low season, you pay the high-season fare.

From Auckland to Perth fares with both Qantas and Air New Zealand are around NZ$980 return (low season) and NZ$1085 (high season).

At the time of writing, the Air New Zealand–owned Freedom Air, a new budget airline connecting NZ and Australia, was operating six direct flights per week from Hamilton, Palmerston North and Dunedin to Australia's eastern seaboard. Examples of return fares include: from Hamilton or Palmerston North to Sydney NZ$419, and to Melbourne or Brisbane NZ$439; and Dunedin-Sydney NZ$449. Check out the Web site at www.freedomair.com.au.

The UK

Airline ticket discounters are known as 'bucket shops' in the UK. Despite the somewhat disreputable name, there is nothing under-the-counter about them. Discount air travel is big business in London. Advertisements for many travel agencies appear in the travel pages of the weekend broadsheets, such as the *Independent* on Saturday and the *Sunday Times*. Look out for the free magazines, such as *TNT*, which are widely available in London – start by looking outside the main train and Underground stations.

Popular travel agencies in the UK include STA Travel (☎ 020-7361 6144), which has an office at 86 Old Brompton Rd, London SW7 3LQ, and other offices in London and Manchester. Visit the Web site at www.statravel.co.uk. Usit Campus (☎ 0870-240 1010), at 52 Grosvenor Gardens, London SW1WOAG, has branches throughout the UK. The Web site is at www.usitcampus.com. Both of these agencies sell tickets to all travellers but cater especially to young people and students. Charter flights can work out as a cheaper alternative to scheduled flights, especially if you do not qualify for the under-26 and student discounts.

Other recommended travel agencies include: Trailfinders (☎ 020-7938 3939), at 194 Kensington High St, London W8 7RG; Bridge the World (☎ 020-7734 7447), at 4 Regent St, London W1R 6BH; and Flightbookers (☎ 020-7757 2000), at 178 Tottenham Court Rd, London W1P 9HL.

Low-season (March to June) fares to Perth from London start at around £409 with Singapore or Malaysia Airlines, £530 with Qantas and £650 with British Airways. In high season fares can pretty much double along this route. British Airways charges £1029 return over the Christmas period. Open-jaw tickets work out slightly more expensive, as you pay the sum of two single fares and flying into the east coast is more expensive than flying into WA.

From Perth to London you can expect to pay around A$1909 return (low season) rising to A$2569 (high season) with Qantas, with stops in Asia on the way.

Continental Europe

Continental operators such as Lauda Air, Alitalia, Olympic Airways and KLM-Royal Dutch Airlines fly to the eastern states, so you'll have to get a domestic ticket to WA. Qantas has direct flights to Perth from Frankfurt, Paris and Rome via Singapore and/or Bangkok.

There are many travel agencies across Europe that have ties with STA Travel, where cheap air tickets can be purchased and STA-issued tickets can be altered (usually for a US$25 fee). In major cities such outlets include: Voyages Wasteels (☎ 0 803 88 70 04 – this number can only be dialled from within France, fax 01 43 25 46 25), at 11 rue Dupuytren, 756006 Paris; STA Travel (☎ 030-31 10 950, fax 31 30 948), at Goethestrasse 73, 10625 Berlin; Viaggi Wasteels (☎ 06-445 66 79, fax 06-445 66 85), at Via Milazzo 8/C, Rome 00185; and ISYTS (☎ 01-322 1267, fax 323 3767), at 11 Nikis St, Upper Floor, Syntagma Square, Athens.

From Paris, return fares to Perth range from 7200FF to 7600FF. The Paris-Sydney return fare is slightly cheaper at 6400FF to 6950FF. Several agencies offer open-jaw tickets between the east and west coasts. Good agencies to try in Paris are Austral (☎ 01 45 61 47 25), at 122, rue La Boétie, 75008, and Nouvelles Frontières (☎ 08 03 33 33 33), at 5 Ave de l'Opéra, 75001. Check the latter's Web site at www.nouvelles-frontieres.fr.

The return excursion fare from Rome to Perth with Qantas ranges from around L2,000,000 to L2,500,000, depending on the season.

From Perth to Frankfurt, Paris and Rome, Qantas fares are A$1909 return (low season) rising to A$2569 (high season).

Africa

South African Airways has four direct flights per week between Johannesburg and Perth. The excursion fare from Johannesburg to Perth is R7120 (R8260 to Sydney). Buying the ticket in Australia costs A$1699 (ex-Perth) and A$1900 (ex-Sydney). Qantas also flies direct between Johannesburg and Perth (continuing to Sydney).

A cheaper alternative from East Africa might be to fly from Nairobi to India or Pakistan and on to South-East Asia, then connect from there to Australia.

Asia

Although most Asian countries now offer fairly competitive deals on air fares, Bangkok, Singapore and Hong Kong are still the best places to shop around for discount tickets.

In Bangkok, STA Travel (☎ 02-236 0262), 33/70 Surawong Rd, is a reliable agency. In Singapore, STA Travel (☎ 737 7188), at 35a Cuppage Rd, Cuppage Terrace, offers competitive discount fares for Asian destinations and beyond.

Hong Kong has a number of excellent and reliable travel agencies and some not-so-reliable ones. Many travellers use the Hong Kong Student Travel Bureau (☎ 2730 3269), on the 8th floor at Star House, Tsimshatsui.

Typical fares to WA from Asia include: Bangkok-Perth 24,760B; Hong Kong–Perth around HK$6000; and Singapore-Perth around S$850.

From Australia, some typical mid-season return fares from the west coast include: Singapore A$906; Kuala Lumpur A$1008; Denpasar A$906; Bangkok A$1022; Hong Kong A$1115; and Tokyo A$1680.

Asian operators through Perth are Garuda Indonesia (which often has some of the cheapest deals), Thai Airways International, Cathay Pacific Airways, Malaysia Airlines, Singapore Airlines, Qantas and Ansett (to Denpasar).

AIR – DOMESTIC

The major domestic carriers are Ansett Australia (☎ 13 1300), which also flies some international routes, and Qantas (☎ 13 1313), which is also the international flag carrier. Both fly between Perth and the other capital cities, and both have subsidiaries that fly smaller planes on shorter intra- and interstate routes. Check out the Web sites at www .ansett com.au and www.qantas.com.au.

Qantas operates from other interstate cities and tourist destinations to Perth but does not offer a service within the state. Ansett's subsidiaries SkyWest Airlines, Maroomba Airlines and Skippers Aviation operate throughout WA.

At the time of writing, new 'low-cost, no-frills' domestic carriers Virgin Blue (☎ 13 6789) and Impulse Airlines (☎ 13 1381) were operating flights only on the eastern seaboard, but either or both may in time extend their services to Perth. Check the Web sites at www.virginblue.com.au and www.impulseairlines.com.au.

All airports and domestic flights are non-smoking.

Fares

Few people pay full fare on domestic travel, as the airlines offer a wide range of discounts. These come and go and there are regular special fares, so keep your eyes open.

Regular one-way and return domestic fares are the same on Qantas and Ansett. Full economy one-way fares between Perth and other parts of Australia include: Darwin $750; Melbourne $743; Adelaide $648; Sydney $807; Uluru $590; and Brisbane $838.

Advance-purchase deals provide the cheapest air fares. Some advance-purchase fares offer up to 33% discount off one-way fares and up to 50% or more off return fares. You have to book one to four weeks ahead, and you often have to stay away for at least one Saturday night. There are restrictions on changing flights and you can lose up to 100% of the ticket price if you cancel, although you can buy health-related cancellation insurance.

A 21-day advance-purchase Sydney-Perth return ticket costs $713. Fares from/to other destinations include: Darwin $818; Melbourne $678; Adelaide $590; Uluru $601; and Brisbane $846.

Full-time students get 25% off the regular economy fare when producing student ID or an International Student Identity Card (ISIC), but you can usually find fares discounted by more than that.

There are also special deals available only to foreign visitors (in possession of an outbound ticket). If booked in Australia these fares offer a 40% discount off a full-fare economy ticket. They can also be booked from overseas (which usually works out a bit cheaper).

Air Passes

With so much discounting these days, air passes do not represent the value they once did, so shop around.

Ansett still has its Kangaroo Airpass, which gives you two options: 6000km with two or three stopovers for $1020 ($784 for children); and 10,000km with three to seven stopovers for $1612 ($1236 for children). There are a number of restrictions on these tickets, but they can be a good deal if you want to see a lot of country in a short time. You do not need to start and finish at the same place. One of the stops must be at a noncapital-city destination and be for at least four nights. All sectors must be booked when you purchase the ticket, although these can be changed without penalty (unless the ticket needs rewriting). Refunds are available before travel commences, but not after you start using the ticket.

LAND

The south-west of WA is isolated from the rest of Australia; interstate travel therefore entails a major journey. The nearest state capital to Perth is Adelaide, 2650km away by the shortest road route. To Melbourne it's at least 3380km, Darwin is around 4020km and Sydney 3900km away. In spite of the vast distances, you can still drive across the Nullarbor Plain from the eastern states to Perth and then all the way up the Indian Ocean coast and through the Kimberley to Darwin on sealed roads.

Bus

You might find special deals with one of the student travel agencies or through a hostel, but generally speaking Greyhound Pioneer Australia (☎ 13 2030) has a monopoly on coach travel between the eastern states and Perth as it is the only company that covers the long Adelaide-Perth leg.

With Greyhound Pioneer, major interstate routes/fares (one way) from Perth are:

destination	fare (A$)	distance (km)
Sydney via Nullarbor	310	4475
Melbourne via Nullarbor	257	3565
Adelaide via Nullarbor	209	2780
Darwin via north-west	459	4460
Darwin via Centre	504	5835

These are straight-through fares; there are no stopovers allowed.

If you're planning to travel around Australia, check out Greyhound's excellent Aussie Passes deals – but make sure you get enough time and stopovers. Greyhound's 'Best of the West' ticket allows you to travel from Adelaide to Perth, Perth to Darwin via the coastal highway and return to Adelaide through the Centre; the cost is $1064 but the fare does not allow backtracking.

The Greyhound Aussie Kilometre Pass is purchased in kilometre blocks, starting at 2000km ($233), in 1000-kilometre blocks up to 20,000km ($1664); 5000km costs $476, 8000km $713, 10,000km $8811, and 15,000km $1264. You can get off at any point on the scheduled route and have unlimited stopovers within the life of the pass. Backtracking is also allowed.

There are also 'day passes', which allow travel on a set number of days during a specified period. There are no restrictions on where you can travel, and passes range from $565/844 for seven/15 days of travel in a month, up to $1113 for 21 days of travel in two months.

Building the Transcontinental Railway

The promise of a transcontinental railway link helped lure gold-rich Western Australia into the Australian Commonwealth in 1901.

Port Augusta (South Australia) and Kalgoorlie were the existing state railheads in 1907 and, that year, surveyors were sent out to map a line between those towns. In 1911 the Commonwealth government legislated to fund north–south *(The Ghan)* and east–west *(Indian Pacific)* routes across the continent; 90 years later the former has not been completed.

The first soil was turned in Port Augusta in 1912 and, for five years, two self-contained gangs – a total of 3000 workers – inched towards each other. They endured sandstorms, swarms of blowflies and intense heat as they laid 2.5 million sleepers and 140,000 tonnes of rail.

There was no opening celebration as planned, as Australia was embroiled in WWI. The first transcontinental train pulled out of Port Augusta at 9.32 pm on 22 October 1917, heralding the start of the 'desert railway from Hell to Hallelujah'. It arrived in Kalgoorlie on 24 October at 2.50 pm, 1682km and almost 43 hours later.

Australian students get a 25% discount and ISIC card holders and Youth Hostel Association (YHA) members get discounts of 10% with Greyhound Pioneer and other companies.

Check out the Greyhound Pioneer Web site at www.greyhound.com.au.

Train

There is only one interstate rail link: the famous *Indian Pacific* transcontinental train journey, run by Great Southern Railway (☎ 13 2147). Along with *The Ghan* to Alice Springs, the 4352km *Indian Pacific* run is one of Australia's great train journeys – a 65-hour trip between the Pacific Ocean on one side of the continent and the Indian Ocean on the other. Travelling this way, you see Australia at ground level and by the end of the journey you really appreciate the immensity of the country (or, alternatively, you are bored stiff).

From Sydney, you cross New South Wales to Broken Hill, then continue on to Adelaide and across the Nullarbor Plain. From Port Augusta to Kalgoorlie-Boulder, the seemingly endless crossing of the virtually uninhabited Centre takes well over 24 hours, including the 'long straight' on the Nullarbor – at 478km this is the longest straight stretch of train line in the world. Unlike the trans-Nullarbor road, which runs south of the Nullarbor along the coast of the

Great Australian Bight, the train line crosses the actual plain. From Kalgoorlie-Boulder, it's a straight run into Perth.

Classes, Reservations & Costs There are three different classes of travel on the *Indian Pacific*: coach class – basically a recliner lounge chair, with shared shower and toilet facilities; holiday class, comprising day cabins that convert to twin sleepers, with shared shower and toilet facilities; and 1st class, which has larger en suite day-and-night sleeper accommodation. With 1st-class fares, all meals on board are included and served in the restaurant car; passengers also have access to a luxurious lounge car and bar (complete with piano). For holiday- and coach-class passengers, meals are not included but can be purchased: in the holiday-class cafe/restaurant car for that class and in the buffet car for coach class.

To Perth from Sydney, one-way fares are: $459 coach class; $1071 holiday class; and $1717 1st class ($230/718/1151 for children). Students with ISIC cards pay $367/857/1374. You can also do part of the journey, from Sydney to Broken Hill, or from Adelaide to Perth, for example. For the latter, fares are $283/690/1222.

The rail distance from Sydney to Perth is 3961km. If you want to break the journey, you have to buy 'sector' fares, which work out to be a bit more expensive than the through fare. The 1st-class berths get booked up, especially in wildflower season, so advance bookings are a good idea.

Cars can be transported between Perth and Sydney/Adelaide ($679/522). This makes a good option for those not wishing to drive across the Nullarbor Plain in both directions.

Check out the *Indian Pacific* Web site at www.gsr.com.au/theindianpacific/.

Car, Motorcycle & Bicycle

The two entry points into WA from the eastern states are at Kununurra (Victoria Hwy), near the Northern Territory (NT) border, and Eucla (Eyre Hwy), close to the border with South Australia (SA).

Distances to eastern state capitals are: Adelaide 2650km; Brisbane 4290km; Darwin 4020km; Melbourne 3380km; and Sydney 4020km.

See under Car in the Getting Around chapter for details of road rules, driving conditions and information on buying and renting vehicles.

Hitching

Hitching is never entirely safe – we don't recommend it. Hitching to or from WA across the Nullarbor is definitely not advisable, as waits of several days are not uncommon.

People looking for travelling companions for the long car journeys to WA from Sydney, Melbourne, Adelaide or Darwin often leave notices on boards in hostels and backpacker accommodation. Ask around.

ORGANISED TOURS

Amesz Adventure Tours (☎ 1800-999 204, 9250 4888) runs a variety of 4WD camping tours starting or finishing in WA. Tours include: a nine-day Alice Springs–Perth tour ($1073) via the Great Central (Warburton) Rd, Uluru, the Great Western Desert, Kalgoorlie-Boulder and Wave Rock; a 37-day 'Western Half Explorer' tour ($3735) in the NT and WA, starting and finishing in Perth and travelling via the central west coast, the Pilbara and the Kimberley to Darwin, Kakadu, Alice Springs, Uluru and the Gibson Desert; and a 17-day Emu Junction–Birdsville–Cooper Creek tour ($2305), departing from Perth and passing through SA and Queensland.

Travelabout (☎ 1800-621 200, 9244 1200) has several 4WD tours, including a Broome-Darwin 'Tropical Summer' tour ($1195) via Gibb River Rd, Kununurra and Katherine, and a six-day Perth–Alice Springs tour ($599) via the goldfields, Great Victoria Desert and Uluru.

Getting Around

AIR

Western Australia (WA) is so vast (and at times and in places, so empty) that unless you have unlimited time you will probably have to fly at some point.

Deregulation has made little difference to flying within WA. Ansett Australia, with its WA subsidiaries SkyWest, Maroomba Airlines and Skippers Aviation, controls most traffic. Ansett has a comprehensive network of flights connecting Perth with WA's regional centres. The frequency of some flights seems ridiculous given the state's small population – until you realise how many mining projects are based there; in WA, large companies use aircraft to shuttle workers from Perth to the Outback.

Ansett Australia (☎ 13 1300) operates regular services from Perth to the following

destinations: Kalgoorlie-Boulder, Derby, Geraldton, Learmonth (for Exmouth), Port Hedland, Newman, Carnarvon, Karratha, Broome and Kununurra. These are linked with interstate flights to Darwin, Sydney, Adelaide, Melbourne, Uluru, Alice Springs, Cairns and Townsville.

SkyWest Airlines operates services from Perth to the following destinations: Albany, Carnarvon, Esperance, Kalgoorlie-Boulder, Laverton, Learmonth, Leinster, Leonora, Geraldton, Denham (for Monkey Mia), Meekatharra and Wiluna. All reservations are handled through Ansett.

Specialising in charter flights to remote mining towns, Skippers Aviation (☎ 9478 3044) also operates regular services to Leonora, Laverton, Meekatharra and Wiluna, as well as a service between Broome and Derby. For reservations and information contact Ansett.

There are also flights to the Australian protectorates the Cocos (Keeling) Islands and Christmas Island, in the Indian Ocean. These depart from Perth and operate via Learmonth. They are run by National Jets, a Qantas Airways subsidiary (☎ 13 1313); fares are $731/1462 one way/return.

There are other smaller operators within the state. Western Airlines (☎ 1800-998 097, 9277 4022) operates services from Perth to Kalbarri, Useless Loop and Denham (Monkey Mia). There is a regular service to Rottnest Island with Rottnest Air-Taxi (☎ 1800-500 006, 9292 5027). The south-west is serviced by Maroomba Airlines (☎ 9478 3850), which has scheduled services between Perth and Margaret River (via Busselton), and Perth and Mt Magnet.

Check out the Web sites at www.ansett .com.au and www.qantas.com.au.

Airport Taxes

Small, regional airports in WA tend to charge hefty airport taxes, which must be paid when you purchase your ticket. Taxes for return flights include: $13.20 (Esperance); $22

WESTERN AUSTRALIA AIR FARES

All fares in Australian dollars
One-way economy air fares

DARWIN
422 195
286
Kununurra
Broome 138 Derby
225 1185
293
Karratha
Port Hedland
Learmonth (Exmouth)
598 750
Newman
371
460 599 724
378
Carnarvon 460
Monkey Mia
Useless Loop
90 306
253 Kalbarri
Geraldton
287
192
731 141 242
To Cocos Islands
731 PERTH 217
120 160 Esperance
To Christmas Island
Margaret River Albany
Meekatharra
Wiluna
Laverton

See Enlargement

Meekatharra
Wiluna
310 345
Mt Magnet Leinster
227 291 Laverton
Leonora 337
To Perth 286

(Broome, Kununurra, Derby); and $34.76 for Kalgoorlie-Boulder. The highest tax ($37.40) is at Albany airport. If you only fly one way, the tax is halved. There are no airport taxes for Perth.

BUS

Bus travel is generally the cheapest way from A to B; the main problem is finding the best deal. A great many travellers see WA by bus because it's one of the best ways to come to grips with the state's size and its variety of terrain, and because the bus lines have more comprehensive route networks than the limited railway system. All buses look pretty similar and are equipped with air-con, toilets and videos.

The only national bus line operating in WA is Greyhound Pioneer Australia (☎ 13 2030). As well as travelling interstate, it has departures from Perth to Dongara–Port Denison ($37), Geraldton ($39), Northam ($53), Kalbarri ($80), Kalgoorlie-Boulder ($104), Monkey Mia ($136), Meekatharra ($137), Newman ($170), Port Hedland ($190), Exmouth ($204), Broome ($271), Derby ($315) and Kununurra ($429).

Greyhound Pioneer buses also run from Perth along the coast to Darwin ($459) and to Adelaide/Melbourne via Kalgoorlie-Boulder and the Eyre Hwy ($209/257). Greyhound Pioneer offers the most extensive service in the state, with an interconnecting service that would allow almost a loop trip, such as Perth to Kalbarri, Monkey Mia, Exmouth, Broome, and return via the inland route. (A return fare is double, less 5%.) The Greyhound Pioneer terminal in Perth is at 250 Great Eastern Hwy, Ascot, near the airport. Check out the Web site at www.greyhound.com.au.

The largest operator in the mid-west and south-west is Westrail (☎ 1800-099 150, 13 1053, 9326 2222), its buses run in conjunction with limited rail services. Westrail services York, Geraldton, Kalbarri, Esperance, Bunbury, Kalgoorlie-Boulder, Margaret River, Augusta, Pemberton, Mukinbudin, Hyden, Albany and Meekatharra. Reservations are necessary for all Westrail bus/train services. All Westrail bus services from/to Perth start/finish at the East Perth train station. Check out Westrail's Web site at www.westrail.wa.gov.au.

Concession-card holders (WA pensioners, seniors, unemployed/low-income earners and students) can get a fare reduction on Westrail. Children aged 15 and under travel for half fare. The free luggage allowance is 50kg (two items) and bicycles (suitably packed) and surfboards can only be carried if room permits.

Integrity Coach Lines (☎ 1800-226 339, 9226 1339) has services between Perth and Carnarvon via the central west coast, with some services continuing to Exmouth. Northbound services depart daily except Saturday (the Sunday and Thursday services continue to Exmouth). Southbound services depart Carnarvon daily except Sunday (Monday and Friday services originate from Exmouth).

Perth Goldfields 5 Star Express (☎ 1800-620 440) does the Perth-Laverton run via the Great Eastern Hwy and Kalgoorlie-Boulder. One-way fares from Perth include: Leinster $121; Leonora $110; Kalgoorlie-Boulder $80; and Merredin $39.

South West Coach Lines (☎ 9324 2333 Perth, 9791 1955 Bunbury) runs services from Transperth City Busport in Wellington St, to Bunbury ($16), with connections to: Margaret River and Augusta; Collie; Donnybrook, Balingup, Bridgetown and Manjimup; Busselton and Nannup.

Popular with backpackers is the Easyrider (☎ 9226 0307), which offers 'jump-on, jump-off' transport (ex-Perth), which allows you to get on and off the bus at designated stops en route within a certain time frame. Easyrider's 'Down South' bus runs from Perth to 13 towns in the south-west, including Mandurah, Bunbury, Margaret River, Walpole, Denmark and Albany. Tickets cost $185 and are valid for three months; there are two/four departures each week in winter/summer. The 'Up North' tour departs on Thursday and takes in Lancelin, Cervantes, Jurien, Geraldton, Kalbarri, Monkey Mia, Carnarvon, Coral Bay and Exmouth. Tickets are valid for six months and cost $328. While accommodation is not included in the price, national park entry fees are.

TRAIN

The state's internal rail network, operated by Westrail (☎ 1800-099 150, 13 1053, 9326 2222), is limited to services between Perth and Kalgoorlie-Boulder (the *Prospector*, which departs from the East Perth terminal); Perth and Northam (the *Avon Link*, which also departs from the East Perth terminal); and Perth and Bunbury in the south (the *Australind*, which departs from the Perth train station on Wellington St). There are connections with Westrail's more extensive bus service (see Bus earlier in this chapter). Check out the useful Westrail Web site at www.westrail.wa.gov.au.

For information on the *Indian Pacific* and the transcontinental railway, see Train in the Getting There & Away chapter.

CAR

There is no doubt that travelling by car is the best option in WA, as it gives you the freedom to explore off the beaten track. With several people travelling together, costs are reasonable and, provided that you don't have any major mechanical problems, the benefits are many.

Many budget travellers choose to buy a vehicle and are often looking for people to share costs for all or part of the journey. Ask around or look for notices at hostels and backpacker accommodation.

It's worth carrying a few useful spare parts if you're travelling on highways in the Kimberley, Pilbara or remote south-eastern parts of the state. A broken fan belt can be a real nuisance if the next petrol station is 200km away.

Self Drive Tours Within WA lists 15 or so of the state's most popular drives; it's free from the Western Australian Tourist Centre (WATC; ☎ 1300-361 351, 9483 1111, fax 9481 0190) in Wellington St, Perth, opposite the train station. Gregory's *Touring Guides* cover the Great Southern, south-east and goldfields, Mandurah and Murray and northern agricultural regions.

In WA, petrol prices vary enormously from place to place. In a trip from Kununurra to Perth, expect a price variation of $0.30 or $0.40 per litre for diesel or petrol, with prices decreasing as you get closer to major centres and increasing on lonely stretches of road.

In the Outback, the price of petrol can soar and some outback petrol stations are not above exploiting the monopoly they have, especially those located along the Eyre Hwy and those between Kununurra and Geraldton, where fuel-transport costs feature heavily in the equation.

Fuel prices were increasing alarmingly at the time of writing, but in general expect to pay around $1 per litre and up. If you're travelling in a 4WD, long-range fuel tanks assist in making large savings on fuel costs.

Along the coastal route, the Eyre Hwy and the Great Northern Hwy, fuel supplies are widely spaced. There is usually round-the-clock availability, but it should be noted that roadhouses are under no obligation to stay open for 24 hours a day, so always be prepared to have to drive further.

Road Rules

Driving in WA holds few surprises. Cars are driven on the left-hand side of the road (as they are in the rest of Australia). The speed limit in urban areas is generally 60km/h, unless signposted otherwise. The state speed limit in WA is 110km/h, applicable to all roads in nonbuilt-up areas, unless otherwise indicated.

The police have radar speed traps and speed cameras and are very fond of using them in carefully hidden locations – don't exceed the speed limit as the boys and girls in blue may be waiting for you.

Seat belts are compulsory – you'll be fined if you don't use them. Children must be strapped into an approved safety seat. Talking on a hand-held mobile phone while driving is illegal.

Drink-driving is a serious problem in WA, especially in country areas. Random breath tests are used in an effort to reduce the road toll. If you're caught driving with a blood–alcohol level of more than 0.05% – or 0.08% in the Northern Territory (NT) – be prepared for a hefty fine, a court appearance and the loss of your licence.

Although foreign licences are acceptable in Australia for genuine visitors (for up to three months, as long as it is in English – if it's not, make sure you carry a certified translation), an International Driving Permit is preferred.

Main Roads Western Australia produces a number of useful publications, many of which are available online at www.mrwa.wa.gov.au.

Road Conditions

This vast state is not crisscrossed by multi-lane highways; there's not enough traffic and the distances are simply too great to justify them.

On all of the main routes, roads are well surfaced and have two lanes. You don't have to get very far off the beaten track, however, to find yourself on unsealed roads, and anybody who sets out to see the state in reasonable detail will have to expect to do some dirt-road travelling. A 2WD car can cope with a limited amount of this, but if you want to do some serious exploration, then you'd better plan on having a 4WD and a winch.

Driving on unsealed roads requires special care – a car will perform differently when braking and turning on dirt. Under no circumstances should you exceed 80km/h on dirt roads; if you go faster you will not have enough time to respond to a sharp turn, stock on the road or an unmarked gate or cattle grid. So take it easy. Take time to see the sights and don't try to break the land speed record!

Travelling by car within WA means sometimes having to pass road trains. These articulated trucks and their loads can be up to 53.5m long, 2.5m wide and travel at around 100km/h. Overtaking them is a tricky process; at times you will have to drive off the bitumen to get past. Exercise caution – and remember that it is much harder for the driver of the larger road train to control their vehicle than it is for you to control your car.

Hazards Contact the Royal Automobile Club of Western Australia (RACWA; ☎ 9421 4444) for general information and advice before embarking on any long-distance car travel in WA.

Some of the more common hazards to be aware of when driving in the state include the following:

Animals Cattle, emus and kangaroos are common hazards on country roads, and a collision is likely to kill the animal and cause serious damage to your vehicle. Kangaroos are most active around dawn and dusk, and they travel in groups. If you see one hopping across the road in front of you, slow right down – its friends are probably just behind it. It's important to keep a safe distance behind the vehicle in front, in case it hits an animal or has to slow down suddenly.

If an animal runs out in front of you, brake if you can, but don't swerve unless it is safe to do so. You're likely to survive a collision with an emu better than a collision with a tree.

Floods It's important to note that when it rains, some roads in WA flood. Flooding is a real problem up north because of cyclonic storms. Exercise extreme caution at the frequent yellow 'Floodway' signs. If you come to a stretch of water and you're not sure of the depth or what could lie beneath it, pull up at the side of the road and walk through it (if you're not in a saltwater crocodile area – for example, the Pentecost River crossing on the Gibb River Rd). Even on major highways, if it has been raining you can sometimes be driving through 30cm or more of water for hundreds of metres at a time.

For statewide road-condition reports, call ☎ 1800-800 009 and follow the prompts for information about the area in which you are driving. This information is updated daily (and more frequently if necessary).

Road Distances

One thing you have to adjust to in WA is the vast distances. The truth is that many places of interest are a bloody long way from Perth. There are rest areas, where tired drivers can revive. Ask for maps from the RACWA that indicate free coffee stops and rest areas.

See the Road Distances from Perth table for some examples of the distances from Perth to regional centres.

Road Distances from Perth

destination	km	route	km
Albany	406	**North West Coastal Highway**	
Augusta	324	Cataby Roadhouse	164
Broome (inland/coast)	2230/2357	Dongara–Port Denison	362
Bunbury	181	Geraldton	427
Carnarvon	904	Billabong Roadhouse	657
Cervantes	247	Overlander Roadhouse	705
Coral Bay	1132	Carnarvon	904
Cue	651	Minilya Roadhouse	1035
Dampier	1557	Nanutarra Roadhouse	1263
Denham	834	Karratha	1537
Derby (inland/coast)	2383/2500		
Esperance	731		
Eucla	1429	**Great Northern Highway**	**km**
Exmouth	1263	Wubin	273
Fitzroy Crossing (inland/coast)	2558/2675	Meekatharra	765
Geraldton	427	Kumarina	1022
Hyden	339	Auski Roadhouse	1374
Kalbarri	592	Port Hedland	1638
Kalgoorlie-Boulder	595	Sandfire Roadhouse	1910
Karratha	1537	Roebuck Roadhouse	2196
Lake Argyle	3276	Willare Roadhouse	2326
Manjimup	303	Fitzroy Crossing	2558
Marble Bar	1476	Halls Creek	2846
Margaret River	278	Warmun (Turkey Creek)	3009
Monkey Mia	859	Kununurra	3206
Mount Barker	359		
Newman	1186		
Onslow	1389	**Eyre Highway (Nullarbor)**	**km**
Pemberton	335	Norseman	721
Port Hedland (inland/coast)	1638/1765	Balladonia	911
Roebourne	1563	Caiguna	1092
Southern Cross	369	Mundrabilla	1364
Tom Price (inland/coast)	1458/1556	(WA/SA) Border Village	1441
Walpole	422	Ceduna	1938
Wyndham (inland/coast)	3216/3333	Adelaide	2651

Outback Travel

If you really want to see outback WA, there are lots of unsealed roads where the official recommendation is that you report to the police before you leave one end, and again when you arrive at the other. That way, if you fail to turn up at the other end they can organise search parties (there are at least a couple of stories each year of motorists being stranded for weeks).

Nevertheless, many of these tracks are now better kept and you don't need a 4WD or fancy expedition equipment to tackle them. You do, however, need to be carefully prepared and to carry important spare parts. Backtracking 500km to pick

Driving through Aboriginal Land

If you are planning to drive on roads in the Outback that pass through Aboriginal reserves, it is essential to have the required transit permits. Applications can be made in person, by mail or by fax, but in all cases they take some time to be processed and you should allow a minimum of three weeks.

Permits are issued free of charge, but you have to complete an official application form (which the offices below can send you), or you can download it from www.aad.wa.gov.au/aalform.html. In your letter of application you should indicate your intended route, the date of your journey, the make and registration number of your vehicle and the number and names of the people travelling with you.

Applications should be made to the Aboriginal Lands Trust (☎ 9235 8000, fax 9235 8093), 197 St Georges Terrace, Perth 6000, for travel through Aboriginal reserves in Western Australia (WA). For travel in the Northern Territory (NT), apply to the Central Land Council (☎ 08-8951 6320, fax 8953 4345), 33 Stuart Hwy, Alice Springs, NT 0871.

Aboriginal Lands Trust Reserves WA produces the booklet *Permit Information*, which includes conditions of entry/transit through Aboriginal land and some simple rules to follow. It should be noted that you should not take photographs/videos without permission, nor purchase any artwork or artefacts except from an approved agency. Additional approval needs to be granted for hunting or fishing on Aboriginal land.

up a replacement for a minor component that's malfunctioning, or, much worse, to arrange a tow, is unlikely to be easy.

You will need to carry a fair amount of water in case of disaster; around 20L per person, stored in more than one container, is sensible. Food is less important – space may be better allocated to an extra spare tyre.

The state automobile associations (see Automobile Associations later in this chapter) can advise on preparation, and supply maps and track notes. Most tracks have an ideal time of year: In the Centre it's not wise to attempt the tough tracks during the heat of summer (December to February) when the dust can be severe, chances of mechanical trouble are much greater and water will be scarce; a breakdown under these conditions will be more dangerous. Similarly, in the north, travelling during the wet season may be impossible due to flooding and mud.

If you do run into trouble in the back of beyond, stay with your car. It's easier to spot a car than a human from the air, and you wouldn't be able to carry your 20 litres of water very far anyway.

Make sure you practise gate etiquette. The rule is quite simple: Leave it as you found it. Farm owners can be understandably irate if you neglect to do this.

Some of the favourite outback tracks in the west follow.

Great Central Road & Gunbarrel Highway These two routes run west from Yulara past the Aboriginal settlements of Docker River and Warburton, then into WA. For 300km, near the Giles Meteorological Station, the Gunbarrel Hwy and the Great Central Rd run on the same route.

The road divides at Warburton, from where you can take the Great Central Rd (also known as Warburton Rd) to Laverton, down to Kalgoorlie-Boulder and on to Perth. A well-prepared conventional vehicle can complete this route, although ground clearance can be a problem and the area is very remote. Weather conditions can render the road impassable to 2WD vehicles. From Yulara to Warburton is 567km. It's another 568km from there to Laverton on the Great Central Rd. It's then 361km on sealed road to Kalgoorlie-Boulder.

Alternatively, you can follow the old Gunbarrel Hwy north of Warburton through the Gibson Desert to Wiluna, eventually joining up with the Great Northern Hwy. This is a much rougher trip, requiring 4WD.

Both routes pass through Aboriginal land, and you must get permission to enter in advance (see the boxed text 'Driving through Aboriginal Land').

The RACWA produces a good map and leaflet: *Perth–Alice Springs via Gunbarrel Highway or Great Central Road* ($2.50).

Tanami Track Turning off the Stuart Hwy just north of Alice Springs, the Tanami Track goes north-west across the Tanami Desert to Halls Creek in WA. It's a popular short cut for people travelling between the Centre and the Kimberley. The road has been extensively improved in recent years and conventional vehicles are OK, although there are occasional sandy stretches on the WA section.

Be warned that Rabbit Flat Roadhouse, in the middle of the desert, is open Friday to Monday only.

Canning Stock Route This old stock trail runs south-west from Halls Creek to Wiluna in WA. It crosses both the Great Sandy and Gibson Deserts, and since the track has not been maintained for more than 30 years, it's a route to be taken seriously. You should only travel in a well-equipped party, and careful navigation is required.

Two good books on the route are Ronele and Eric Gard's *Canning Stock Route: A Traveller's Guide for a Journey through History* (1990) and the *Australian Geographic Book of the Canning Stock Route* (1992).

Gibb River Road The short cut between Derby and Kununurra; this runs through the heart of the spectacular Kimberley region in northern WA. Although badly corrugated in places, the road can be negotiated with care by conventional vehicles in the dry season. The trip is 720km, compared with about 920km via the bitumen Northern Hwy.

For more information see Gibb River Road in The Kimberley chapter.

Rental

There are many places in the state where you'll have to choose between an organised tour and a rented vehicle because there is no public transport and the distances are too great for walking or even bicycles.

The three major car-hire companies are Budget, Hertz and Avis; all have offices in regional centres including Kalgoorlie-Boulder, Albany, Broome, Geraldton, Carnarvon, Exmouth and Kununurra. The larger companies allow airport collection/drop-off (sometimes with a surcharge), but some of the smaller car-hire companies also allow this.

One-way car rentals are generally not available into or out of the NT or WA. Even the big-name car-hire companies don't like you driving their cars only one way. That means, if you hire a car in Perth, you have to drive it back to Perth or pay an enormous drop-off fee to have it transported back from wherever you leave it (one Perth-based company quoted $750 to drop a car in Kununurra).

The WATC in Perth (☎ 1300-361 351, 9483 1111, fax 9481 0190) often has good deals on car hire and can arrange bookings for you. The following is a selection of some of the many car-hire outfits in Perth:

Avis Rent A Car (☎ 13 6333, 9325 7677) 46 Hill St, Perth 6000
Bayswater Car Rental (☎ 9325 1000) 160 Adelaide Terrace, Perth 6000
Budget Rent A Car (☎ 13 2727, 1300-362 848, 9322 1100) 1960 Hay St, Perth 6000
City Centre Rentals (☎ 1800-806 1419, 322 1887) 41 Milligan St, Perth 6000
Hertz (☎ 1800-550 067, 13 3039, 9321 7777) 39 Milligan St, Perth 6000
Perth Rent-A-Car (☎ 9225 5855) 229 Adelaide Terrace, Perth 6000
Thrifty Car Rental (☎ 1300-367 227, 13 1286, 9464 7444) 198 Adelaide Terrace, Perth 6000

Unlimited-kilometre rates (with the larger rental companies) are generally around $59 a day for a small Class A car (eg, Ford Festiva, Mazda 121, Nissan Micro); about $69 a day for a Class C medium car (eg, Holden Mondeo, Toyota Camry); $79 a day for a big Class D car (eg, Holden Commodore, Ford Falcon); and about $89 for a luxury, Class E car (eg, Holden Statesman or Ford Fairlane). Prices can jump in periods of high demand (eg, school holidays), when you should book well in advance.

The smaller rental companies often have good deals on not-so-new cars for rentals of a week or more. Bayswater Car Rental charges from $14 a day for a two-year-old car, including 100km free. Perth Rent-a-Car charges $30 per day for a small manual car for rentals of a week or more.

Note that most car rental companies do include insurance in the price but in the event of an accident the hirer is still liable for a sometimes-hefty excess. Most offer excess-reduction insurance on top of the rental rate.

All companies offer lower rates for hiring vehicles for a week or more. Membership of state automobile associations can also help secure a good deal. You'll have to be at least 21 to hire a car, and for some car rental companies the minimum age is 25.

There's a plethora of smaller car-hire companies, which are often markedly cheaper than the majors, but make sure you are fully aware of free-kilometre allowances: WA is a huge state and you are bound to have the odometer working overtime.

4WDs A 4WD enables you to get off the beaten track and see some great wilderness and outback regions (such as the Kimberley and Purnululu National Park).

Hiring something small like a Toyota RAV or Suzuki Vitara costs from $70 to $85 per day; for a Toyota Landcruiser or Nissan Patrol you're looking at anything from $90 to $110, depending on how long you keep the vehicle. Prices should include insurance and some free kilometres (typically 150km per day; extra kilometres are about $0.25 each). Check the insurance conditions carefully, especially excess; they can be onerous. Some companies, such as Hertz, have excess-reduction insurance (around $19 a day); others don't and in the event of a collision, you'll be up for an excess of $2500.

A few places to check are:

Hertz Bus & 4WD Rentals (☎ 9451 1244) 130 Welshpool Rd, Welshpool 6106
Osborne Rentals (☎ 1800-999 206, 9464 7777) 130 Hector St W, Osborne Park 6017
South Perth Four Wheel Drive Rentals (☎ 9362 5444) 80 Canning Hwy, Victoria Park 6100

Camper Vans Britz Australia (☎ 1800-331 454, 9478 3488), at 469 Great Eastern Hwy, Redcliffe 6104, hires out fully equipped 4WD vehicles fitted out as camper vans. These have proved extremely popular in WA in recent years, but they are not cheap at $230 per day for a three-sleeper in high season, with unlimited kilometres.

Insurance is $28 per day with a $2200 bond excess or $44 per day otherwise. In low season vehicle rates can start at $120; there are discounts for hires of more than 21 days. Britz Australia has offices in all the mainland capitals, so one-way rentals are also possible (although a $200 fee applies). Check out the Web site at www.britz.com.

Other companies that hire out camper vans are: Camperworld (☎ 9478 2755), at 501 Great Eastern Hwy, Redcliffe 6104; and Camperent WA (☎ 9364 5529), at 708 Canning Hwy, Applecross 6153.

Purchase

Although Australian cars are relatively cheap to purchase, if you're buying a second-hand vehicle, reliability is all-important. Breaking down in the Outback are very inconvenient (and dangerous) – the nearest mechanic can be a long way down the road! Shopping around for a used car involves much the same rules as anywhere in the western world, but with a few local variations.

For any given car you'll probably get it cheaper by buying privately through newspaper ads (try Saturday's *West Australian)* rather than through a car dealer. Buying through a dealer does give the advantage of some sort of guarantee, but a guarantee is not much use if you're buying a car in Perth and intend setting off for Sydney the next week. Used-car guarantee requirements vary from state to state – check with the RACWA.

There's much discussion among travellers about the best place to buy used cars. Popular theories exist that you can buy a car in Sydney or Melbourne, drive it to Darwin or Perth and sell it there for a profit. Or is it vice versa? It's quite possible that prices do vary, but don't count on turning it to your advantage. Check the notice boards in hostels and backpacker accommodation; you might score a bargain.

Remember that in Australia, third-party personal-injury insurance is included in the vehicle registration cost. This ensures that every registered vehicle carries at least minimum insurance. You're wise to extend that minimum to third-party property insurance as well.

When you come to buy or sell a car, there are usually some local regulations to be complied with. In WA a car has to have a compulsory safety check and obtain a Road Worthiness Certificate (RWC) before it can be registered in the new owner's name – usually the seller will indicate whether the car already has a RWC. Stamp duty has to be paid when you buy a car; as this is based on the purchase price, it's not unknown for the buyer and the seller to agree privately to understate the price. It's much easier to sell a car in the state in which it's registered, as it will have to be re-registered in other states. Although it may be possible to sell a car without re-registering it, you're likely to get a lower price for it.

One way of getting around the hassles of buying and selling a vehicle privately is to enter into a buy-back arrangement with a car or motorcycle dealer. However, some dealers frequently find ways of knocking down the price when you return the vehicle, even if a price has been agreed on in writing – usually by pointing out expensive repairs that they claim will be required to gain the dreaded RWC needed to transfer the registration.

The cars on offer have often been driven around Australia a number of times, usually with haphazard or minimal servicing, and are generally pretty tired. The main advantage of these schemes is tha you don't have to worry about being able to sell the vehicle quickly at the end of your trip, and can usually arrange insurance, which short-term visitors may find hard to get.

One local possibility is Deals on Wheels (☎ 9493 3155), 1844 Albany Hwy, Maddington 6109. As an example, in 2000 it was selling a 1982 Corolla for $2000, a 1989/90 Nissan Pulsar or 1983 VW Combivan for $5000, and a 1993 Ford Falcon for $8000.

It buys vehicles back (although there is no guarantee that it will) for around half the purchase price, 'depending on the condition'.

Automobile Associations

The Royal Automobile Club of Western Australia (RACWA; ☎ 9421 4444) is at 228 Adelaide Terrace in Perth. It can advise you of local regulations, give general guidelines about buying a car and, most importantly, for a fee ($90 to $110) will check over a used car and report on its condition before you agree to purchase it. The RACWA also offers car insurance to its members, and membership can get you discounts on car rentals and some motel accommodation. Road-travel specialists in bordering states are:

Royal Automobile Association of South Australia (RAA; ☎ 08-8202 4500) 41 Hindmarsh Square, Adelaide 5000
Web site: www.raa.net
Automobile Association of the Northern Territory (AANT; ☎ 08-8981 3837) 81 Smith St, Darwin 0800

MOTORCYCLE

Motorcycles are a popular way of getting around. The climate is just about ideal for biking much of the year, and the many small trails from the road into the bush often lead to perfect spots to spend the night in the world's largest camping ground.

The long, open roads of Australia are really made for large-capacity machines, but that doesn't stop enterprising individuals tackling the length and breadth of the continent on 250cc trail bikes. Doing it on a small bike is not impossible, just tedious at times.

If you bring your own motorcycle into Australia you'll need a *carnet de passage*, and when you try to sell it you'll get less than the market price because of restrictive registration requirements (not so severe in WA). Shipping from just about anywhere is expensive.

Australian newspapers and the local bike press have extensive classified-advertising sections where, if you know a bit about bikes, $2500 gets you something that will easily take you around the country. The main drawback is that you'll have to sell it afterwards – and bikes are more difficult to offload than cars.

An easier option is a buy-back arrangement with a large motorcycle dealer in a major city. Basic negotiating skills allied with a fat wad of cash (say, $8000) should secure an excellent second-hand bike with a written guarantee that the dealer will buy it back in good condition minus, say, $1500, after your four-month, around-Australia trip.

You'll need a rider's licence and a helmet. A fuel range of 350km will cover fuel stops up the inland route and on Hwy 1 along the coast. Beware of dehydration in the dry, hot air – force yourself to drink plenty of water, even if you don't feel thirsty.

The 'roo bars' (outsize bumpers) you'll see on interstate trucks and many outback cars should be a warning to avoid riding at night, dusk and dawn because of the native animals, cattle and sheep that stray onto the roads at these times.

Many roadhouses offer showers free of charge or for a nominal fee. They're meant for truck drivers, but other people often use them too.

It's worth carrying some spares, tools and the workshop manual for your bike even if you don't know how to use them because someone else often will. If you do know, you'll probably have a fair idea of what to take. If you don't, consult an expert (eg, the person who sells or rents the motorcycle to you) to ensure that you're equipped for most mechanical emergencies.

Make sure you carry water everywhere, stored in good-quality carriers – at least 2L on major roads in WA and much more than that off the beaten track. In 1993 a foreign motorcyclist headed off to do the Great Central Rd with a couple of cheap plastic containers of water, which subsequently leaked. A major search ensued and the rider was lucky to be found alive.

If something does go hopelessly wrong in the Outback, park your bike where it's clearly visible and observe the cardinal rule: Don't leave your vehicle.

Big Boyz Toyz Hire (☎ 9244 4293), at 4 Wotan St, Innaloo, runs motorcycling tours to the Pinnacles Desert, Kalgoorlie-Boulder and the south-west, and does long-term hire of good-quality road and trail bikes.

BICYCLE

Whether you're hiring a bike to cycle around Rottnest Island, planning a day or two riding around the Margaret River wineries or attempting a trans-Nullarbor marathon, WA is a great place for cycling.

Perth has a growing network of bike tracks, and in country areas you'll find thousands of kilometres of good, virtually traffic-free roads. Especially appealing is that in many areas you'll ride a very long way without encountering a hill.

Cycling has always been popular here, and not only as a sport: Some shearers would ride for huge distances between jobs, rather than use less-reliable horses. It's rare to find a town that doesn't have a shop stocking at least basic bike parts.

If you're coming specifically to cycle, it makes sense to bring your own bike. Check with your airline for costs and the degree of dismantling/packing required. Within WA you can load your bike onto a bus to skip the boring bits. Check with bus companies about how the bike needs to be secured, and book ahead to ensure that you and your bike can travel on the same vehicle.

Dehydration is no joke and can be life-threatening. No matter how fit you are, water is still vital. It can get very hot in summer, and you should take things slowly until you're used to the heat. Cycling in 35°C-plus temperatures isn't too bad if you wear a hat and plenty of sunscreen, and drink *lots* of water.

Of course, you don't have to follow the larger roads and visit towns. It's possible to fill your mountain bike's panniers with muesli, head out into the bush, and not see anyone for weeks – or ever again: Outback travel is very risky if not properly planned. Water is the main problem in the 'dead heart', and you can't rely on it where there aren't settlements. That tank marked on your map may be dry or the water in it may be unfit for drinking, and those station buildings probably blew away years ago.

That little creek marked with a dotted blue line? Forget it – the only time it has water is when the country's flooded for hundreds of kilometres.

Always check with locals or police if you're heading into remote areas and notify the police if you're about to do something particularly adventurous.

Bicycle helmets are compulsory in all Australian states and territories.

In Perth, Bikewest (☎ 9320 9301), at 441 Murray St, has information on cycling in the state, including maps. The Bicycle Transportation Alliance (☎ 9420 7210), at 2 Delhi St, West Perth 6005, is an advocacy group which has an excellent Web site for cyclists (sunsite.anu.edu.au/wa/bta), with useful links.

Maps & Books

The RACWA regional tour planner maps (approximate scale 1:250,000) are best for road touring in relatively well-inhabited areas. They are available at petrol stations and tourist offices. Some areas are covered by larger-scale tourist maps, which usually also include town maps.

For travelling in the Outback, Natmap topographic maps ($7.70 each), published by Auslig, are available in a range of scales. Try the Perth Map Centre (☎ 9322 5733), at 884 Hay St.

In Perth, Bikewest's excellent 1:30,000 *Perth Bike Map* series ($3.95) is invaluable for getting around Perth and Fremantle. Bikewest's free *Ride Around the Rivers* booklet has maps and ride descriptions for more than 60km of cycling around Perth's Swan and Canning Rivers.

Lonely Planet's *Cycling Australia* is due for publication at the same time as this guide and contains more detail on cycling in WA.

HITCHING

Hitching is never entirely safe anywhere, and we don't recommend it. Travellers who do decide to hitch should understand that they are taking a potentially serious risk. People who hitch will be safer if they don't travel alone and if they let someone know where they are planning to go.

If you must hitch in WA, do it in pairs. Ideally, the pair should comprise one male and one female – two guys hitching together can expect long waits. It is not advisable for women to hitch alone, or even in pairs.

If you're visiting from abroad, a nice prominent flag on your pack will help, and a sign indicating your destination can also be useful. University and hostel notice boards are good places to look for hitching partners. Remember not to stand on the road.

BOAT

Transperth (☎ 13 6213) has a ferry service from Perth's city centre to South Perth and there are a number of operators who travel from Fremantle, Hillary's Boat Harbour and Perth to Rottnest Island. See Getting Around in the Perth chapter and Getting There & Away under Rottnest Island in the Around Perth chapter.

LOCAL TRANSPORT

Perth's central public transport organisation, Transperth (☎ 13 6213), operates buses, trains and ferries. There are two free Central Area Transit (CAT) bus services in Perth's city centre; using the two, you can get to most sights in the inner city. The red CAT runs east–west and the blue CAT operates north–south. See Getting Around in the Perth chapter for other local transport options.

Outside Perth local transport is limited, although some of the larger country towns, such as Kalgoorlie-Boulder, have limited local bus services.

Taxi

Taxis are available in most of the larger towns, where locals are heavily reliant on them as a means of beating the booze buses and police patrols. Taxis are a good means of getting around and, shared among a few people, costs are reasonable.

ORGANISED TOURS

There are dozens of tours through WA to suit all tastes and budgets; most originate from Perth. The 'adventure' tours include 4WD safaris – some of these go to places that you simply couldn't get to on your

Tours on Aboriginal Land

Tours that incorporate aspects of Aboriginal life and culture provide the best opportunity for travellers to make meaningful contact with Aboriginal people. In the Kimberley there are a number of options run by Aboriginal communities, including Lombadina and Kooljaman (see Dampier Peninsula in the Kimberley chapter for more information).

In one of the first attempts in Australia to balance the needs of local people with the demands of tourism, the Purnululu Aboriginal Corporation and the Department of Conservation and Land Management (CALM) jointly manage the Purnululu National Park. At Turkey Creek, near Purnululu, the Daiwul Gidja Cultural Centre (☎ 9168 7580) has half- and full-day tours led by local Aboriginal people.

In the Pilbara, Aborigines have worked closely with CALM in establishing a cultural centre in the Karijini National Park and an information centre about the Yinjibarndi people's culture in Millstream-Chichester National Park.

own without large amounts of expensive equipment.

The WATC (☎ 1300-361 351) in Perth has a huge range of brochures, as does the nearby Traveller's Club Tour & Information Centre (☎ 9226 0660), at 499 Wellington St, which specialises in budget travel. Both can book tours on your behalf, as can travel agencies.

The tours listed here are only a selection of what is available. Full prices are quoted, but students and Youth Hostel Association (YHA) members get 5% to 10% discounts.

AAT Kings Australian Tours (☎ 1800-334 009, 03-9274 7422) AAT Kings offers bus trips for a less adventurous crowd, including: a nine-day trip from Broome to Darwin via Halls Creek, the Bungle Bungle Range and Emma Gorge ($2495, including accommodation); and a 'western wildflowers' five-day trip, including Monkey Mia, New Norcia, Kalgoorlie-Boulder, Esperance, Albany and Margaret River ($3485, including accommodation).

Active Safaris (☎ 1800-222 848, 9450 7776) This small but highly recommended operator runs a four-day Monkey Mia 4WD safari that includes the Pinnacles Desert and Kalbarri, and two-/four-day tours to the south-west, including Margaret River and Walpole.

Australian Adventure Travel (☎ 1800-621 625, 9248 2355) This outfit offers tours of the Kimberley, departing from Broome and taking in Bell Gorge, Mitchell Plateau and Mitchell Falls, Kununurra and the Bungle Bungle Range ($2250, 15 days); and the Karijini National Park and Hamersley Range tour ($550, four days).

Redback Safaris (☎ 9275 6204) This operator offers daily day 4WD tours to the Pinnacles Desert, Cervantes and Lancelin, including sandsurfing ($78); four-day Pinnacles Desert, Kalbarri gorges and Monkey Mia tours ($350); and a five-day Esperance, Wave Rock, Albany and the south-west tour ($490).

Snappy Gum Safaris (☎1800-094 811, 9185 1278) This Karratha-based company has two-/three-day tours of Karijini National Park ($235/320), departing from Karratha and Dampier, and a tour of the Pilbara region ($650).

Travelabout Outback Adventures (☎ 9244 1200) Travelabout runs a huge range of bus and 4WD tours, including: 11-day 4WD tour from Broome to Darwin, including the Gibb River Rd and the Bungle Bungle Range ($1535); 24-day West Coast Explorer tour from Perth to Darwin via Monkey Mia, Coral Bay, Broome, Windjana Gorge and the Bungle Bungle Range ($2859); 11-day Ningaloo Reef and Karijini tour via Kalbarri, Monkey Mia, Exmouth and De Grey River ($1535); a five-day tour from Perth to Exmouth via Kalbarri, Monkey Mia and Coral Bay ($549); and a four-day Monkey Mia-Kalbarri-Pinnacles tour ($410).

West Coast Explorer (☎ 1800-651 210, 9418 8835) West Coast Explorer offers 4WD adventure tours from Perth via Broome and the Kimberley to Darwin in both the wet ($1750, 16 days) and dry seasons ($1990, 18 days); and tours of the south-west, including Margaret River, Walpole and the Stirling Range ($690, eight days); $390, four days).

Western Travel Bug (☎ 1800-627 488, 9204 4600) This operator runs six-day 'eco-activity' bus tours to the south-west and to Esperance and Wave Rock/Hyden ($555). Two-/four-day tours also available.

Perth

pop 1.38 million

Claimed to be the sunniest state capital in Australia, Perth is a vibrant and modern city, pleasantly situated on the Swan and Canning Rivers, with the cerulean Indian Ocean to the west and the ancient Darling Range to the east. Perth is the most isolated capital city in the world, and is closer to Singapore than it is to Sydney.

The city centre has more than its fair share of concrete and glass skyscrapers dominating the skyline. Not all of them are magnificent feats of architecture, but there is no better representation of the prosperity that Perth and Western Australia (WA) have enjoyed thanks to the valuable minerals that lie beneath its vast surface. The city's domineering edifices hide a handful of lovely 19th-century buildings and facades, which remain from Perth's early days as the Swan River Colony.

But what you notice more than its skyline is Perth's picturesque riverside setting, the well-manicured lawns along the riverbanks and the magnificent bushland and Botanic Garden of Kings Park, all right next to the city centre. The city's stunning natural environment is enhanced by the beaches of the Indian Ocean, hillside hideaways and the historic port of Fremantle. The Swan River is fringed with affluent suburbs with leafy streets and twee names such as Peppermint Grove, Applecross, Floreat, Maylands and Cottesloe, as well as cosmopolitan enclaves of cafes, restaurants and designer boutiques.

Of WA's 1.8 million people, almost 80% live in and around Perth, and a fair number of them are intent on enjoying the type of easy-going lifestyle that this city and its climate fosters. Indeed, Perthites exhibit a tunnel-visioned and self-conscious quest for 'lifestyle' – good food and wine, open-air restaurants, groovy nightclubs, designer clothes and a wealth of cultural events – despite, or perhaps in spite of, the city's isolation.

HIGHLIGHTS

- Walking or cycling through the large tract of natural bushland and in the Botanic Garden at Kings Park

- Checking out the magnificent artworks – particularly the superb paintings and graphic art of indigenous artists – at the Art Gallery of Western Australia

- Delving into the deep at the spectacular Underwater World aquarium and taking a whale-watching trip from Hillary's Boat Harbour

- Swimming and body-surfing at any of the city's many fine beaches

- Marvelling at 'Megamouth', meteorites found in the Outback, and a 25m whale skeleton – just three of the exhibits at the excellent Western Australian Museum

- Watching a game of cricket at 'the WACA' or Australian Rules Football at Subiaco or Fremantle Oval

- Enjoying yum cha at one of Northbridge's famous Chinese restaurants

- Taking tea at the Indiana Tea House at Cottesloe Beach as the sun sets over the Indian Ocean

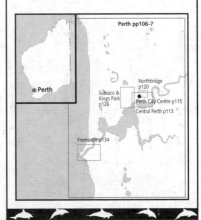

Perth pp106-7

Northbridge p120

Perth

Subiaco & Kings Park p126

Perth City Centre p115

Central Perth p113

Fremantle p134

PERTH

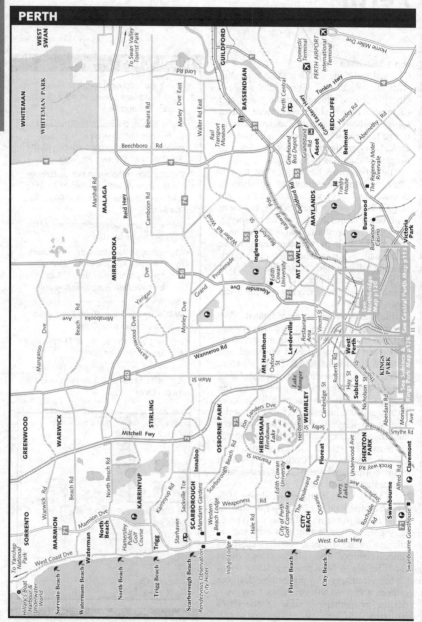

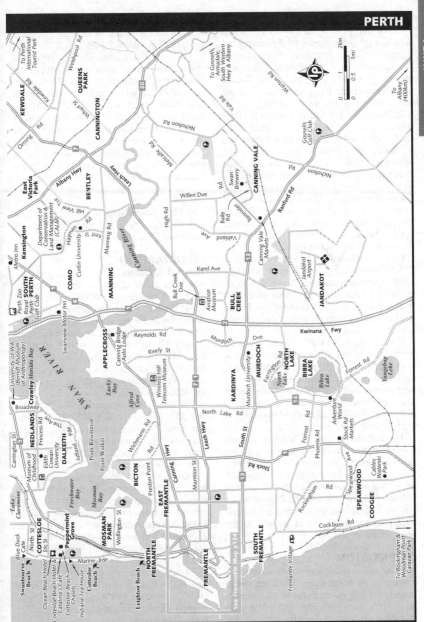

PERTH

HISTORY

The site that is now the city of Perth had been occupied by groups of the Aboriginal Nyungar tribe for thousands of years before the first Europeans settled there. The tribe's ancestors can be traced back some 40,000 years (evidenced by discoveries of stone implements near the Swan Bridge).

In December 1696 three ships in the fleet commanded by Willem de Vlamingh anchored off what is now Rottnest Island. On 5 January 1697 a well-armed party landed near present-day Cottesloe Beach, then marched eastward to a river near Freshwater Bay. They tried to contact some of the Nyungar to inquire about survivors of the *Ridderschap van Hollant*, lost in 1694, but they were unsuccessful. They sailed north, but not before de Vlamingh had bestowed the name 'Swan' on the river.

Perth was founded in 1829 as the Swan River Colony, but it grew very slowly until 1850, when convicts were brought in to alleviate a labour shortage. Many of Perth's fine buildings, such as Government House and Perth Town Hall, were built using convict labour.

Even then, Perth's development lagged behind that of cities in the eastern colonies until the discovery of gold in the mid-1880s increased the population fourfold over the next decade and initiated a building boom. Many of these 19th-century buildings have disappeared amid concrete and buildings of questionable architectural taste.

The mineral wealth of WA has undeniably contributed to Perth's growth, sparking further construction in the outer suburbs. The city's squeaky-clean, nouveau-riche image has been tainted by scandals such as WA Inc (see Post-War to the Present under History in the Facts about Western Australia chapter), but it all seems to add to the town's frontier image.

ORIENTATION

The city centre is fairly compact, situated on a sweep of the Swan River. The river, which borders the city centre to the south and east, links Perth to its port, Fremantle. The main shopping precinct in the city is along the Hay St and Murray St Malls and the arcades that run between them. St Georges Terrace is the hub of the financial district.

The train line bounds the city centre on the northern side. Immediately north of the train line is Northbridge, a popular restaurant and entertainment enclave with hostels and other cheap accommodation. At the western end, Perth rises to the pleasant Kings Park, which overlooks the city and Swan River, then farther on to cosmopolitan Subiaco. Farther again to the west, suburbs extend as far as Scarborough and Cottesloe Beaches on the Indian Ocean.

Maps

The Perth Map Centre (☎ 9322 5733), at 884 Hay St, has a full range of maps of Perth and WA, as well as travel guides.

INFORMATION
Tourist Offices

The head office of the Western Australian Tourism Commission (WATC) is in Perth, at the Western Australian Tourist Centre, in Albert Facey House in Forrest Place, on the corner of Wellington St, opposite the train station. The office is open from 8.30 am to 6 pm Monday to Thursday, 8.30 am to 7 pm Friday, 8.30 am to 5 pm Saturday, and 10 am to 5 pm Sunday. On weekdays in winter the office closes half an hour earlier.

The telephone information line (☎ 1300-361 351, 9483 1111, fax 9481 0190) operates from 7 am to 6 pm Monday to Friday, 8.30 am to 4.30 pm Saturday, and 10 am to 5 pm Sunday. Check out the Web site at www.westernaustralia.net.

The WATC produces a wide range of maps and brochures on Perth and WA, and runs an accommodation and tours booking service. Guides to Perth, including *Hello Perth & Fremantle*, *What's On in Perth & Fremantle* and *West Coast Visitor's Guide*, are free from most tourist offices, hostels and hotels.

Though not strictly a tourist office, the Traveller's Club Tour & Information Centre (☎ 9226 0660) at 499 Wellington St, Perth, is great for tour information, especially for budget travellers.

Money

Currency-exchange facilities at Perth airport and city banks are open from 9.30 am to 4 pm Monday to Thursday (until 5 pm Friday). Foreign banks include BNP (☎ 9221 3011) and Chase Manhattan (☎ 9225 4099). Most large stores, petrol stations and supermarkets accept credit cards (such as AmEx, Bankcard, Diners Club, MasterCard and Visa) and use the Eftpos system.

Post & Communications

Perth's general post office (GPO) is located in Forrest Place, which runs between Wellington St and the Murray St Mall. There are phones for international calls in the GPO foyer. The GPO provides post office service from 8 am to 6 pm weekdays, and 9 am to noon Saturday. Telephone ☎ 13 1318 to be automatically connected to the post office nearest to where you are calling from.

See Post & Communications in the Facts for the Visitor chapter for more information.

Email & Internet Access Most hostels in Perth have computer terminals for email and Internet access. Many of the more upmarket hotels now have dedicated modem/data ports in guest rooms. Internet access is usually available free at public and university libraries (see both Libraries and Universities later in this section), but you might have to book or queue up to use the terminals.

There are also plenty of Internet cafes, including Net.Chat (☎ 9228 2011), at 196a William St, Northbridge, and Traveller's Club Tour & Information Centre (☎ 9226 0660), at 499 Wellington St, Perth.

Travel Agencies

STA Travel has several branches in Perth and its suburbs, including: 127 William St, city; 100 James St, Northbridge; 93 Rokeby Rd, Subiaco; and 53 Market St, Fremantle. Call ☎ 13 1776 for the nearest location, or check the Web site at www.statravel.com.au.

The Youth Hostel Association (YHA; ☎ 9227 5122, fax 9227 5123, e yhawa@ yhawa.com.au) membership and travel centre is at 236 William St, Northbridge 6003.

The staff here will hunt around for the best travel bargains.

Traveller's Club Tour & Information Centre (☎ 9226 0660), at 499 Wellington St, Perth, caters for budget travellers. It has heaps of information about tours geared for backpackers and offers free Internet access to its clients (those who book tours through them), or you can use its computers for a reasonable cost. Traveller's Club can also help with discounted car hire.

Bookshops

Some good city bookshops include Angus & Robertson, at 625 Hay St, and Dymocks, in the Hay St Mall. Both have extensive travel sections including a full range of Lonely Planet titles. All Foreign Languages, at 101 William St, specialises in travel, foreign-language guides, dictionaries and phrasebooks, and also has an extensive range of maps. Down to Earth, at 790 Hay St, specialises in travel, gay and lesbian, metaphysical and New Age books. At 806 Hay St, Boffins Bookshop's range includes travel, photography and architecture.

Libraries

Library & Information Services of Western Australia (LISWA; ☎ 9427 3111), in the Alexander Library Building in James St, Northbridge, is WA's state library; it has many major daily newspapers, including foreign titles. The Perth City Council library (☎ 9461 3581) is at 573 Hay St.

Most local councils run a public library. Look up the name of the suburb/area and then under 'Local Council' in the *White Pages* telephone directory. The Subiaco library (☎ 9381 5088) is at 237 Rokeby Rd.

Universities

There are five main universities in and around Perth. There are also several colleges of Tertiary and Further Education (TAFE) listed under 'TAFE' in the *White Pages*.

Curtin University (☎ 9266 9266) Kent St,
Bentley 6102
Web site: www.curtin.edu.au

Edith Cowan University (☎ 9273 8333)
Pearson St, Churchlands 6018 (campuses also at Mt Lawley, Claremont, Joondalup and Bunbury)
Web site: www.ecu.edu.au
Murdoch University (☎ 9360 6000) South St, Murdoch 6150
Web site: www.murdoch.edu.au
University of Western Australia (☎ 9380 3838) Stirling Hwy, Nedlands 6009
University of Notre Dame (☎ 9239 5555)
19 Mouat St, Fremantle 6160
Web site: www.nd.edu.au

Laundry

Most hostels have laundry facilities. Serviced apartments and holiday flats usually provide washing machines in the apartment or flat, or have coin-operated, communal laundries. There is a laundrette on the corner of Bennett and Wellington Sts in East Perth.

Medical Services

The Travellers Medical & Vaccination Centre (☎ 9321 1977), The Capita Centre, 5 Mill St, Perth, provides vaccinations (and international certificates) and medical advice. Hospitals close to the centre are the Royal Perth (☎ 9224 2244) in Victoria Square, and King Edward Memorial Hospital for Women (☎ 9340 2222) in Bagot Rd, Subiaco. For emergency dental work, contact the Perth Dental Hospital (☎ 9220 5777), at 196 Goderich St, East Perth.

Emergency

In the case of a life-threatening emergency call ☎ 000. This call is free from any phone, and the operator will connect you to either the police, ambulance or fire brigade. Local emergency numbers can be found in the Perth *White Pages*. Otherwise you can call the police on ☎ 9222 1111 in Perth.

KINGS PARK

There are superb views across Perth and the river from this 4-sq-km park, the lungs of the city centre. Kings Park includes the 17-hectare **Botanic Garden**, which contains more than 2000 different plant species from WA, and a section of natural bushland as it was before white settlement. In spring there's a cultivated display of WA's famed wildflowers.

Free guided walks of Kings Park and the Botanic Garden are available all year. These depart at 10 am and 2 pm most days (call ☎ 9480 3659 for information and bookings). The park also has a number of bike tracks; bikes can be rented from Koala Bike Hire (☎ 9321 3061) at the western side of the main car park ($4 per hour, $15 a day). An information centre, next to the car park, is open from 9.30 am to 4 pm daily. The park also has a restaurant with a pleasant coffee shop.

To get there, catch the red Central Area Transit (CAT) bus to the entrance of Kings Park or walk up Mount St from the city, then cross the freeway overpass.

HISTORIC BUILDINGS

There are a few architectural remnants of yesteryear, but you need the archaeological tenacity and guile of Indiana Jones to find them. Our 'Perth Walking Tour' (see the boxed text) should help.

PERTH CULTURAL CENTRE

Just north of the city centre, across the train line and bounded by Roe, Francis, Beaufort and William Sts, the Perth Cultural Centre includes the state museum, art gallery and state library, and Perth's institute of contemporary arts.

Western Australian Museum

This museum (☎ 9427 2700) includes an excellent gallery of Aboriginal culture, a marine gallery with a 25m blue-whale skeleton, vintage cars, a gallery of dinosaur casts and a good collection of meteorites, the largest of which is the Mundrabilla specimen, which weighs 11 tonnes. In the courtyard, set in its own preservative bath, is 'Megamouth', one of the largest species of shark. Only about five of these benign creatures have ever been captured – this one beached itself near Mandurah.

The museum complex also includes Perth's original **prison**, built in 1856 and used until 1888 – a favourite spot for hangings in the past. There is a good cafe on the

Perth Walking Tour

The civic mothers and fathers haven't been kind to central Perth – charming old buildings have been bulldozed and replaced with giant concrete and glass towers. This tourh commences at the Western Australian Tourism Commission's tourist office in Forrest Place, and traces some remnants of old Perth.

Pass the general post office (GPO) and proceed through one of the arcades to the Hay St Mall. Turn left and look out for **London Court** on your right. Between Hay St and St Georges Terrace, the narrow, touristy London Court looks very Tudor English, but it only dates from 1937. At one end of this shopping court St George and the dragon pop out to do battle above the clock each quarter of an hour, while at the other end knights joust on horseback.

Turn left at the end of the court and follow St Georges Terrace to Barrack St. Recognisable by their patterned brick, the **Central Government Buildings** on the corner of Barrack St and St Georges Terrace were built between 1874 and 1902 (at one stage they housed the GPO). Uphill on Barrack St, on the corner of Hay St, is **Perth Town Hall** (1867–70).

Head back the way you came, to St Georges Terrace, then turn left, passing the 1888 **St Georges Cathedral**, constructed from local stone and jarrah. On the corner of Pier St is the **Deanery**, built in 1859 and restored after a public appeal in 1980, and one of the few cottage-style houses that have survived from colonial days; it's not open to the public. Across St Georges Terrace are the Stirling Gardens. The old **courthouse**, next to the **Supreme Court**, is also here. One of the oldest buildings in Perth, it was built in Georgian style in 1836. A little farther along is **Government House**, a Gothic-looking fantasy built between 1859 and 1864.

Follow St Georges Terrace to Hill St (St Georges Terrace becomes Adelaide Terrace at Victoria Ave). Turn left and head up to Hay St. On the right (entrance on Hay St) is the **Perth Mint** (see Perth Mint later in this chapter for more information). Continuing up to Goderich St and left to Victoria Square you'll find **St Marys Cathedral** (1863) and a grassed area that's popular with office workers at lunch time. Follow Murray St, on the far side of the square, west to William St. Turn left into William St and head to St Georges Terrace. On the corner of St Georges Terrace is the grand and once-extravagant **Palace Hotel** (1895), now a banking chamber. Turn right into St Georges Terrace and head down to King St – on your left, at No 139, is the **Old Perth Boys' School** (1854), which is now a National Trust gift shop.

At King St turn right and follow it to Hay St. On the corner is the restored **His Majesty's Theatre** (1904); there are free foyer tours of the 'Maj' from 10 am to 4 pm daily, and backstage tours at 10.30 am Thursday ($10). Return to St Georges Terrace and turn right. Walk a short distance to the **Cloisters** (1858), on the right, noted for its beautiful brickwork. Originally a school, it is now part of a modern office development.

The distinctive **Barracks Archway**, at the western end of St Georges Terrace, is all that remains of a barracks built in 1863 to house the pensioner guards of the British army – discharged soldiers who guarded convicts.

On the far side of the Mitchell Fwy is **Parliament House**. Tours of the Parliament buildings can be arranged on weekdays through the parliamentary information officer (☎ 9222 7222) – you will of course get a more extensive tour when parliament is not in session.

Take the red Central Area Transit (CAT) bus from Harvest Terrace to return to the city centre. Fit walkers may wish to proceed to **Kings Park**.

ground floor of the gaol building, as well as an excellent children's discovery centre (which runs programs in school holidays). The museum is open from 9.30 am to 5 pm daily. Admission is free.

Art Gallery of Western Australia

The Art Gallery of Western Australia, founded in 1895, houses the state's pre-eminent art collection. There's a strong emphasis here on the heritage of WA and

Aboriginal art. A visit to the gallery is a must on any Perth itinerary.

On display are early depictions of the Swan River Colony and the eastern-state settlements by colonial artists, early to mid-20th-century views of the developing city by WA's modern movement, watercolours of wildflowers, and works by post-WWII migrant artists as well as modern and contemporary Australian masters such as Fred Williams, Arthur Boyd and John Olsen.

The international collection features work by artists including Niki de St Phalle and Lucian Freud, while the decorative arts are represented by superbly crafted early WA furniture made from local woods and materials.

But it is the indigenous art that is the real highlight of the gallery: stunning bark paintings by Arnhem Land artists, which demonstrate a figurative tradition stretching back in an unbroken line to images many thousands of years old; the so-called 'dot' paintings by Western Desert artists, which express powerful Dreamtime traditions; and the eye-catching, almost graphic works by Kimberley artists such as Rover Thomas and Jimmy Pike, from Turkey Creek, who used a limited range of natural-coloured pigments (blacks, whites and browns). Urban Aboriginal artists, including writer, painter and printmaker Sally Morgan, are also represented.

The gallery also has a changing program of temporary exhibitions. It is open from 10 am to 5 pm daily. Admission is free (except for special exhibitions).

Perth Institute of Contemporary Arts

Commonly referred to by its acronym, PICA, the Perth Institute of Contemporary Arts (☎ 9227 6144) promotes the creation, presentation and discussion of new and experimental art, with an emphasis on nontraditional media such as video, sound and performance. There is a changing program of temporary exhibitions.

PICA is open 11 am to 8 pm Tuesday to Sunday. Admission is free. On the ground floor is a groovy cafe, Fuel.

PERTH MINT

The mint (☎ 9421 7223), on the corner of Hill and Hay Sts, originally opened in 1899. It is now open for public tours. A variety of coins are on display, including a 1kg gold nugget coin (a numismatist's delight). You are allowed to touch an 11.3kg gold bar worth about $200,000.

Visitors can mint their own coins and watch gold pours, which are held on the hour from 10 am to 3 pm weekdays and 10 am to noon weekends. The mint is open from 9 am to 4 pm weekdays, and 9 am to 1 pm weekends. Admission is $6/4 adults/children.

PERTH ZOO

In South Perth, across the river from the city, Perth's popular zoo is set in attractive gardens at 20 Labouchere Rd.

It has a number of interesting collections, including a nocturnal house (open from noon to 3 pm daily), an Australian wildlife park, a numbat display, and an interesting conservation discovery centre.

The zoo (☎ 9367 7988) is open from 10 am to 5.30 pm daily. Admission is $8/3/25 adults/children/families. You can reach the zoo by taking the ferry across the river from the Barrack St jetty.

UNDERWATER WORLD

One place deserving of special mention is Underwater World, north of the city, at Hillary's Boat Harbour, Sorrento Quay.

This is definitely not your run-of-the-mill aquarium. There is a fantastic 98m underwater tunnel aquarium displaying some 2500 examples of 200 marine species, including sharks and stingrays.

The seals are fed at 10.30 am and 1.30 and 4 pm, and the sharks get their dinner at 11 am and 2 pm. There are also interactive displays inside, such as a touch pool, microworld and an audio-visual theatre.

Underwater World (☎ 9447 7500) is open from 9 am to 5 pm daily. Admission is $16.50/9/42 adults/children/families. To get there, take the Joondalup train to Warwick Interchange; transfer to bus No 423 and get off at Sorrento.

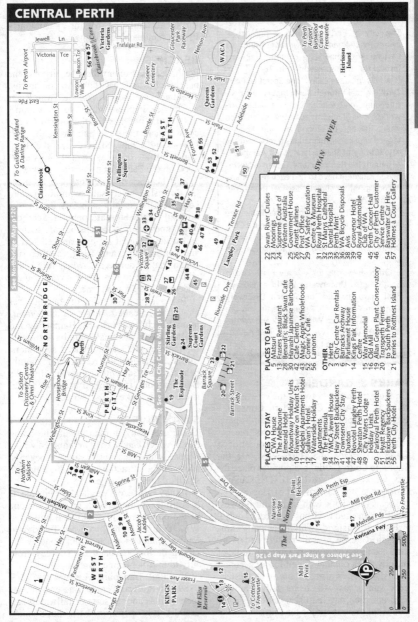

CENTRAL PERTH

PLACES TO STAY
1 CWA House
4 The Melbourne
8 Emerald Hotel
9 Mountway Holiday Units
10 Riverview on Mount St
12 Aarons Apartments Hotel
17 Sullivan's Hotel
17 Waterside Holiday
Apartments
18 The Peninsula
26 YMCA Jewell House
37 Hay Street Backpackers
41 Novotel Langley Perth
48 Sheraton Perth Hotel
49 City Waters Lodge
Holiday Units
50 Parkroyal Perth Hotel
51 Hyatt Regency
53 Exclusive Backpackers
55 Perth City Hotel
44 Duxton

PLACES TO EAT
5 Matsuri
13 Frasers Restaurant
28 Benardi's; Black Swan Cafe
30 Hayashi Japanese Barbecue
42 Gie Ciento
43 Magic Apple Wholefoods
52 Connie's Cafe
56 Lamonts

OTHER
22 Swan River Cruises
23 Moorings
24 Supreme Court of
Western Australia
25 Government House
26 Qantas Airlines
27 Post Office
29 WA Safety Education
Centre & Museum
31 Royal Perth Hospital
32 St Mary's Cathedral
33 Dental Hospital
35 Perth Mint
36 WA Bicycle Disposals
38 Avis
39 Grosvenor Hotel
40 Royal Automobile
Club of WA
45 Perth Concert Hall
46 City of Perth Customer
Service Centre
54 Bayswater Car Hire
57 Holmes à Court Gallery
2 Hertz
3 City Centre Car Rentals
6 Barracks Archway
7 Parliament House
14 Kings Park Information
Centre
15 War Memorial
16 Old Mill
19 Allan Green Plant Conservatory
20 Transperth Ferries
to South Perth
21 Ferries to Rottnest Island

Perth for Kids

The City of Perth organises a number of events for children. The **Awesome Children's Festival** in October is a contemporary-arts festival for children aged five to 16.

A new initiative called **'The Secret of Point Zero'** is a trail through Perth that is part treasure hunt, part interaction with public artworks. It is aimed specifically at children under the age of nine. There are 12 sites tagged with colourful markers throughout the city, starting at the Barrack St jetty and continuing to the Perth Cultural Centre in Northbridge. Children have to find each marker and decode its information to discover the 'secret' of Point Zero.

Maps and trail booklets are available free from the City of Perth Customer Service Centre (27 St Georges Terrace), the Art Gallery of Western Australia, and the information desk at the state library.

Other diversions for kids are **Perth Zoo** in South Perth, **Underwater World** at Hillary's Boat Harbour, and the **Scitech Discovery Centre** in West Perth. Around Perth, you can visit the **Caversham Wildlife Park** and **Whiteman Park** (both in West Swan), and **Adventure World** at Bibra Lake.

PARKS & GARDENS

On the Esplanade, between the city and the river, is the **Allan Green Plant Conservatory**. It has both a tropical and semitropical environment display. Admission is free.

Also close to the city, on the corner of St Georges Terrace and Barrack St, are the **Supreme Court Gardens**, a popular place for city workers to have lunch. The **Queens Gardens**, at the eastern end of Hay St, is a pleasant little park with lakes and bridges; get there on a red CAT bus (weekdays only).

Heirisson Island, which basically supports the Causeway at the eastern end of the city, is a tiny nature reserve in the middle of the city and a popular circuit for joggers and cyclists. There's a small colony of western grey kangaroos, which are fed at around 7.30 am each day (call ☎ 0419-861 737 if you want to be there for feeding).

Lake Monger, in Wembley, is a hang-out for local feathered friends, particularly Perth's famous black swans.

BEACHES

Perth residents claim that the city has the best beaches and surf of any Australian city. There are calm beaches on the Swan River at Crawley, Peppermint Grove and Como.

The surf beaches on the Indian Ocean coast, where there are patrols by the Surf Lifesaving Club (SLSC), are the best. Watch out for rips (see Dangers & Annoyances in the Facts for the Visitor chapter).

Surf beaches include **Port** near Fremantle; **Cottesloe**, a very safe swimming beach; **Leighton**; the usually safe **City Beach**; the normally safe **Floreat**; popular **Scarborough**, known for its beachside cafe society, and which is great for experienced surfers and sailboarders; and **Trigg**, another surf beach that is dangerous when rough and which is prone to rips. Perth's very popular nude beach is **Swanbourne**.

To the north lies a string of good beaches along the so-called Sunset Coast. **Watermans Beach**, **North Beach**, **Hamersley** and **Mettams Pool** are small, safe bays suitable for families and inexperienced swimmers. **Burns** and **Mullaloo** are both safe family beaches and **Sorrento**, south of Hillary's Boat Harbour, is patrolled because the onshore winds make the surf rough.

SWAN RIVER

There are many attractions up the Swan River, which can be easily combined with a winery tour of the Swan Valley vineyards. Most of the attractions listed here have a small admission charge.

Tranby House, on Maylands Peninsula, is beautifully restored. Built in 1839, it's one of the oldest and finest colonial houses in WA. It's open from 2 to 5 pm Tuesday to Saturday, and 11 am to 5 pm Sunday. It's closed during June and on Tuesday from July to mid-September.

The **Rail Transport Museum** (☎ 9279 7189), on Railway Parade, Bassendean, has locomotives and all sorts of railway memorabilia. It is open from 1 to 5 pm Sunday.

PERTH CITY CENTRE

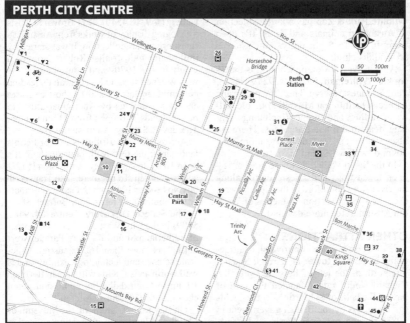

PERTH CITY CENTRE

PLACES TO STAY

3   West End Apartment Hotel
11 Rydges Perth; CBD
14 Parmelia Hilton;
    The Globe
25 Wentworth Plaza Hotel
27 Royal Hotel
30 Globe Backpackers
34 Grand Central Backpackers
38 Sebel of Perth
39 Criterion Hotel

PLACES TO EAT

1   Fast Eddy's
2   Katong Singapore;
    Taj Tandoor
4   Millioncino
6   Matsuri Takeaway

9   barre
19 Metro Food Court
21 Java Juice
23 No 44 King St
24 Mezzonine
33 Ann's Malaysian
36 Jaws Sushi Tempura

OTHER

5   Bikewest
7   Perth Map Centre
8   Post Office
10 His Majesty's Theatre
12 Cloisters
13 Travellers Medical &
    Vaccination Centre
15 Transperth City Busport
16 Old Perth Boys' School

17 Qantas/British Airways
18 Malaysia Airlines
20 Thomas Cook
22 Creative Native
26 Wellington St Bus Station
28 STA Travel
29 Traveller's Club Tour &
    Information Centre
31 WATC
32 General Post Office
35 Cinecentre
37 Cinema City
40 Perth Town Hall
41 National Australia Bank
42 Central Government Buildings
43 St Georges Cathedral
44 Playhouse Theatre
45 Deanery

Guildford has a number of historic buildings; the **Old Courthouse, Gaol and Museum** in Meadow St, is open from 2 to 5 pm Sunday. **Woodbridge House** in Ford St, Midland, is a beautifully furnished 1885 colonial mansion overlooking the river. It's open from 1 to 4 pm Monday to Saturday (closed Wednesday), and 11 am to 5 pm Sunday.

In Arthur St, West Swan, **Caversham Wildlife Park & Zoo** has a large collection of Australian animals and birds. It's open from 10 am to 5 pm daily. Admission is $5/2 adults/children.

Also in West Swan, on Lord St, is the 26 sq km **Whiteman Park** (☎ 9249 2446), Perth's biggest reserve. There are picnic and barbecue facilities at Mussell Pool, old railway buildings and engines (including a vintage steam train) and tram rides. There are also craft shops and displays, more than 30km of walkways, and bike paths.

In the Swan Valley, there are vineyards – open for tastings and sales – dotted along the river from Guildford to the Upper Swan. (See the special section 'Wineries of Western Australia' for more details.)

OTHER ATTRACTIONS

One of Perth's more controversial 'attractions' is the **bell tower** at Barrack Square, just north of the jetty. The state's premier, Richard Court, rather fancied the idea of having the bells of St Martin's-in-the-Fields (given to WA by the British government in 1988) ringing out over Perth, so he fast-tracked a controversial project to build a bell tower to house them, using more than $6 million of taxpayers' money.

In the Social Sciences Building of the University of WA, off Hackett Dr in Nedlands, is the excellent **Berndt Museum of Anthropology** (☎ 9380 2854), which houses one of Australia's finest collections of traditional and contemporary Australian Aboriginal art and artefacts. It combines material from Arnhem Land in the Northern Territory and the south-west, desert and Kimberley regions of WA. The museum is open from 2 to 4.30 pm Monday and Wednesday, and 10 am to 2 pm Friday. Admission is free.

The **WA Fire Safety Education Centre and Museum** (☎ 9323 9468), on the corner of Irwin and Murray Sts, has displays on fire safety and firefighting equipment. The limestone building became the headquarters of the Perth City Fire Brigade in 1901. It is open from 10 am to 3 pm weekdays. Admission is free.

In East Perth, the small **Holmes à Court Gallery** (☎ 9218 4540), at 11 Brown St, hosts a changing display of works from Australia's finest private art collection. It was started by millionaire industrialist Robert Holmes à Court in the 1970s and continued by his widow Janet. It includes Australia's leading contemporary artists and the best canvases and bark paintings by Aboriginal artists in private hands. It is open from 11 am to 6 pm Tuesday to Sunday. Admission is free.

Across Narrows Bridge is one of Perth's landmarks: the **Old Mill**, built in 1835. It's open 10 am to 4 pm daily. Admission is $2/1 adults/children. To get there, take Transperth bus Nos 108 or 109 from St Georges Terrace, or the South Perth ferry from Barrack St.

The **Scitech Discovery Centre** (☎ 9481 5789) in the City West centre, on the corner of Sutherland St and Railway Parade, West Perth, has more than 160 hands-on, large-scale science and technology exhibits and is well worth a visit. Kids will love it. It's open 10 am to 5 pm daily, but admission is not cheap: $11/7/30 adults/children/families.

On Bay Rd in Claremont, the **Museum of Childhood** houses an interesting collection of memorabilia. It is open from 10 am to 4 pm weekdays. Admission is $3/2 adults/children.

Across the Canning River towards Jandakot Airport, on Bull Creek Dr, the excellent **Aviation Museum** has a large collection of aviation relics. It is open daily. Admission is $5/2 adults/children.

Adventure World, 15km south of Perth at 179 Progress Dr, Bibra Lake, is a large amusement park. It's open from 10 am to 5 pm daily October to April.

Tumbulgum Farm (☎ 9525 5888), 6km south of Armadale on the South Western Hwy, is a display farm where children (and adults) can feed the animals and milk the cows. There are farm shows (including whip-cracking and sheepdog-working) and Aboriginal culture shows throughout the day. It is open from 9.30 am to 5 pm daily. Admission is $8/4 adults/children.

On Mills Rd East, near Gosnells, you can ride a miniature railway through **Cohunu Koala Park** (☎ 9390 6090) while watching native animals in natural surroundings. There are also plenty of waterbirds and a large, walk-in aviary. Open from 10 am to 5.30 pm daily, the park's about a 35-minute drive from Perth. Admission is hefty: $17/8/42 adults/children/families.

GOLF

There are several world-class public golf courses in and around Perth, taking advantage of the availability of space to good effect. Good courses include the 36-hole City of Perth Golf Complex (☎ 9484 2500) in Floreat; the Lake Claremont Public Golf Course (☎ 9384 2887); the 18-hole Hamersley Public Golf Course (☎ 9447 7137), in Karrinyup; the Fremantle Municipal Golf Course (☎ 9430 2316); and the Burswood Park Golf Course (☎ 9362 7576).

Upmarket courses include Vines Resort (☎ 9297 0222) in the Swan Valley, a 30-minute drive from Perth; and the Joondalup Country Club (☎ 9400 8811), about 30 minutes north of Perth.

WATER SPORTS

Perth thrives on aquatic sports. At **Cables Waterski Park** (☎ 9418 6888), on Troode St in Spearwood (just off Rockingham Rd, south of Perth), a boatless cable system pulls skiers through the water. Admission is $3, and an hour's water-skiing costs $16.

Windsurfing is very popular both on the Swan River and on the Sunset Coast beaches north of Perth; you can hire boards from Pelican Point Windsurfing (☎ 9386 1830) on Hackett Dr at Crawley. **Sailing**, for those who prefer bigger craft, is also popular. This can range from Funcats on the Swan River in South Perth to yachting on the Indian Ocean. Funcat Hire (☎ 0408-926 003), on Coode St, South Perth, can provide the former; and Viking Sailing School (☎ 9401 7491), at 64 Dampier Ave, Mullaloo, and Sailaway Sailing School and Yacht Charter (☎ 9457 6480), in Ferndale, the latter.

Surfing and **diving** are two other water pursuits, and the Sunset Coast and Rottnest Island are good spots. For diving info call Diving Ventures (☎ 9421 1052) in Perth, the Perth Diving Academy (☎ 9430 6300) in

Fremantle, Malibu Diving Centre (☎ 9527 9211) in Rockingham, or Dolphin Scuba Diving (☎ 9353 2488) in Welshpool.

Rivergods (☎ 9324 2662), 862 Hay St, organises **white-water rafting** in both summer (on the Collie River) and winter (on the Avon River), **sea kayaking** to Seal and Penguin Islands off the Rockingham coast, and **Canadian canoeing** on the Blackwood River. Prices for trips depend on duration and the type of equipment used.

WHALE-WATCHING

Whale-watching is possible out of Perth from September to December. The trip with Mills Charters (☎ 9401 0833), which runs its tours in conjunction with Underwater World, is very informative. The search is for the humpback whale, as it returns to Antarctic waters after wintering in the waters of northwest Australia. The trip leaves from Hillary's Boat Harbour and costs $25/20 weekends/weekdays (children $15/10). Other operators are Oceanic Cruises (☎ 9430 5127) in Fremantle, and Boat Torque (☎ 9246 1039) at Hillary's Boat Harbour.

ORGANISED TOURS

The WATC produces a huge range of brochures on tours in and around Perth, and the tourist office can book them.

Land-Based Tours

Half-day city tours of Perth and Fremantle cost about $30, and for around $60 you can get tours to the Swan Valley wineries, Underwater World and the Sunset Coast beaches north of Perth.

A favourite is the tour of the operating **Swan Brewery**, 25 Baile Rd, Canning Vale. Tour times vary, and bookings are essential; for details, call ☎ 9350 0651.

Other day tours, to places including the Avon Valley, Mandurah, New Norcia and the south coast, cost from $50 to $100, depending on the tour and the operator. Some of the larger operators include Outstanding Tours (☎ 9368 4949), Planet Perth tours (☎ 9276 5295), Feature Tours (☎ 9479 4131), Australian Pinnacle Tours (☎ 9221 5411) and Gold 'n' Valley Tours (☎ 9401 1505).

For day tours to Rottnest Island, see the Around Perth chapter. See also Organised Tours in the Getting Around chapter.

Cruises

Companies that run cruises from the Barrack St jetty include Captain Cook Cruises (☎ 9325 3341) and Boat Torque (☎ 9221 5844). Tours include scenic cruises of the Swan River, winery visits, trips to Fremantle, and lunch and dinner cruises. Captain Cook's half-day cruises up the Swan River cost $24/12 adults/children.

Air

Preston Helicopters (☎ 9414 1000) runs 'flightseeing' tours over Perth ($40), Fremantle ($75) and the coastal beaches ($125).

SPECIAL EVENTS

Every year for several weeks in February the Perth International Arts Festival offers entertainment in the form of music, drama, dance and film. World-class Australian and international performers are big features.

The Claisebrook Carnival is held in April and includes family entertainment in the form of dragon-boat races, tug-of-war championships and performing arts. In early June, West Week is held to celebrate WA's foundation – there are historical recreations, arts and crafts events, concerts and sporting events.

The Royal Perth Show takes place in September. In October wildflowers as well as not-so-wild flowers are the centrepiece of Flower Art, part of the Perth Wildflower Festival. Perth Pride also takes place in October, as does the annual Reclaim-the-Night march.

In November gourmets and gourmands enjoy the Perth Food and Wine Fair, and gays and lesbians compete in WA's Gay Olympics.

Check out the WATC's Web site at www.westernaustralia.net for more events.

PLACES TO STAY

Perth has accommodation for all tastes and pockets. There are numerous caravan parks scattered around the metropolitan area. The main area for budget beds is Northbridge, while hotels, motels, holiday flats and serviced apartments of all standards are spread throughout Perth.

Camping & Caravan Parks

Perth, like many other large cities, is not well endowed with camp sites convenient to the city centre. There are, however, many caravan parks in the suburbs. The WATC has a full list. Prices quoted in this section are for two people.

Perth International Tourist Park (☎ 9453 6677, 186 Hale Rd, Forrestfield), 18km east of the city centre, is one of the better caravan parks. It has tent sites for $18 and cabins for $65 to $79.

Starhaven Caravan Park (☎ 9341 1770, 18 Pearl Parade, Scarborough), on the beach 14km north-west of the city, has tent sites for $16, on-site vans for $40 and holiday units for $65.

Well positioned for the Swan Valley wineries and access to the Perth Hills is *Swan Valley Tourist Park (☎ 9274 2828, 6581 West Swan Rd, Guildford)*, 19km north-east of town. It has tent/powered sites for $14/16, on-site vans from $35 and holiday units for $45.

Closest to the city centre is *Perth Central Caravan Park (☎ 9277 1704, 34 Central Ave, Redcliffe)*, 8km east of the city. It has tent/powered sites for $16/20 and on-site vans from $30.

Hostels

There are many hostels in Perth – probably more than the city can support. As a result, competition is fierce, and most places offer reduced rates for longer stays. Some hostels are good, others need lots of improvement. Most hostels provide pickups from airport terminals, by prior arrangement. Australian travellers should be aware that some Perth hostels practise discrimination by refusing accommodation to those who don't have an international passport, ostensibly to reduce the possibility of the hostel being used as a rooming house by unsavoury locals.

City Centre East of Victoria Square, the well-run *YMCA Jewell House (☎ 9325 8488, ⓔ jewellhouse@bigpond.com, 180*

Goderich St) has more than 200 rooms, which are comfortable and clean even though a little worn; singles/doubles cost $34/44 and weekly rates are six times the daily rate. It has 24-hour reception, off-street parking and free baggage storage.

The *Country Women's Association (CWA) House (☎ 9321 6081, 1174 Hay St, West Perth)* has comfortable singles/doubles with bathrooms for $55/65, including a light breakfast. Some rooms have good city views.

The *Hay Street Backpackers (☎ 9221 9880, 268 Hay St, East Perth)* is good value, with good facilities, a pool, dorm beds for $15, and double rooms for $40, but like all hostels in the city area, it is away from the action of Northbridge and Leederville.

Not far away is the not-so-exclusive *Exclusive Backpackers (☎ 9325 2852, 158 Adelaide Terrace)*. The restored building in which it's located is in need of a cleanup. Dorm beds in crowded six-person rooms cost $15; more spacious are the single ($30) and double ($40) rooms.

Closer to the city centre is the *Townsend City Stay (☎ 9325 4143, ℮ info@townsend .wa.edu.au, 240 Adelaide Terrace)*, basically student accommodation that also accepts travellers. Simple singles cost $30 per night (or $125 per week); there are good communal areas and Internet access.

Close to the train station (read noisy) and Northbridge is the *Globe Backpackers (☎ 9321 4080, ℮ globe@iinet.net.au, 497 Wellington St)*. Dorm beds cost $16, while singles/doubles cost $27/42. Farther along Wellington St is the *Grand Central Backpackers (☎ 9421 1123, ℮ grandcentralbp@ hotmail.com, 379 Wellington St)*, where dorm beds cost $16, singles/doubles $32/45 and en suite doubles $50. This is a lively, rambling place with a good atmosphere and its own Internet cafe.

Northbridge There are two official YHA hostels in Northbridge, and literally dozens of backpacker lodges. The large, central *Britannia YHA (☎ 9328 6121, 253 William St)* has dorm beds for $16 and double rooms for $50 (non-YHA members pay $3 more). The best rooms (some of which are singles) are

at the back on the verandah; rooms near the hallways can be noisy. Around the corner, the *Northbridge YHA (☎ 9328 7794, 42–46 Francis St)* is popular with travellers for its homely feel. This ageing but renovated former guesthouse has good facilities including Internet access. Dorm beds cost $16, double rooms $45. The staff can help you find work and they run a daily bus to the beach.

One of the most popular hostels in Perth and one which gets consistently good reviews from travellers is *Witch's Hat (☎ 9228 4228, 148 Palmerston St)*, named for its wonderful Edwardian turret. There is a well-equipped kitchen (with a cappuccino machine and juicer!), good barbecue and TV areas, and a spa, as well as a resident dog called Winnie. A dorm bed costs $16; twin and double rooms cost $43.

Another top place, brand new at the time of writing and well equipped with its own pool, is the spacious *Nomads Underground Backpackers (☎ 9228 3755, 268 Newcastle St)*. The staff are friendly, there are several computers for Internet access, and it has a licensed bar – it's a real find. Dorm beds cost $16; double rooms cost $50.

The *Coolibah Lodge (☎ 9328 9958, 194 Brisbane St)* is in two clean (and joined) renovated colonial houses in a quiet street at the quieter northern end of Northbridge, next to the Northbridge Hotel. It has good common spaces, including a pleasant courtyard and a barbecue area. This is a nice place (it even has a bar licence). Dorm beds cost $16, standard double rooms cost $40 and deluxe doubles with fridge cost $42 (non-VIP members pay $1 or $2 more). Don't come here if you hate cats – there are several and they have the run of the place.

Spinner's Backpackers (☎ 9328 9468, 342 Newcastle St) has a comfortable lounge and good kitchen facilities. Dorm beds cost from $15 per night and double rooms cost $36. In the same street is *Ozi Inn (☎ 9328 1222, 282 Newcastle St)*, a large, renovated house with all the necessary facilities, and friendly staff. Beds in air-con dorms cost $15; double rooms cost $38. Nearby, there is an overflow place for longer-term (perhaps noisier) patrons working in the city.

The **Shiralee** (☎ 9227 7448, 107 Brisbane St), in a former house, has been described by travellers as 'one of the best' backpacker hostels in Australia – quite a claim. It has pleasant recreation areas and all facilities are clean and shipshape. Dorm beds cost $17; air-con twin and double rooms cost $42.

Tucked away next to the Buddhist Centre, the small **Backpack City & Surf** (☎ 9227 1234, 41 Money St), is an unusual place, with a large central corridor with tables, and dorms (with windows to the corridor only) off to the side. It is cheap though – $14 for dorm beds.

Another good alternative is the **North Lodge** (☎ 9227 7588, 225 Beaufort St), in a renovated historic house. It's clean, friendly and has all the usual facilities. Beds in comfortable dorm rooms cost $13, or $15 in 'upmarket' dorms (for four, with fridge and TV); a self-contained flat for two costs $45.

Scarborough This area is a good alternative to Northbridge, being close to the surf, but you could be at any beach resort, not necessarily in Perth. To get there, take bus No 400 from the Transperth City Busport.

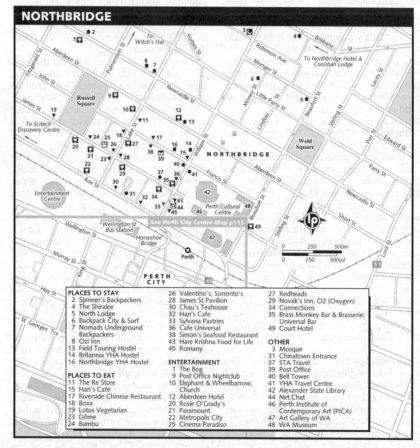

NORTHBRIDGE

See Perth City Centre Map p115

PLACES TO STAY
2 Spinner's Backpackers
4 The Shiralee
5 North Lodge
6 Backpack City & Surf
7 Nomads Underground Backpackers
8 Ozi Inn
13 Field Touring Hostel
14 Britannia YHA Hostel
16 Northbridge YHA Hostel

PLACES TO EAT
11 The Re Store
15 Han's Cafe
17 Riverside Chinese Restaurant
18 Boxx
19 Lotus Vegetarian
23 Dôme
24 Bambu

26 Valentino's; Sorrento's
28 James St Pavilion
30 Chau's Teahouse
32 Han's Cafe
33 Sylvana Pastries
36 Cafe Universal
38 Simon's Seafood Restaurant
43 Hare Krishna Food for Life
45 Romany

ENTERTAINMENT
1 The Bog
9 Post Office Nightclub
10 Elephant & Wheelbarrow; Church
12 Aberdeen Hotel
20 Rosie O'Grady's
21 Paramount
22 Metropolis City
25 Cinema Paradiso

27 Redheads
29 Novak's Inn; O2 (Oxygen)
34 Connections
35 Brass Monkey Bar & Brasserie; Universal Bar
49 Court Hotel

OTHER
3 Mosque
31 Chinatown Entrance
37 STA Travel
39 Post Office
40 Bell Tower
41 YHA Travel Centre
42 Alexander State Library
44 Net.Chat
46 Perth Institute of Contemporary Art (PICA)
47 Art Gallery of WA
48 WA Museum

The best backpacker-style accommodation is at the relaxed *Western Beach Lodge* (☎ *9245 1624, 6 Westborough St)*. A converted home, it is compact, clean and airy; rates are $13 for beds in dorms and $30 for doubles. The friendly owner treats guests like family and will arrange airport and bus/train station pickups for guests.

Indigo Lodge (☎ 9341 6655), on the West Coast Hwy (on the corner of Brighton Rd), has dorm beds for $13, single rooms for $22, and twins and doubles for $36. *Mandarin Gardens (☎ 9341 5431, 20–28 Wheatcroft St)* has dorm beds for $14. This hostel is 500m walk to popular Scarborough Beach, has a pool and sizable recreational areas. It also has self-contained rooms from $55 and two-bedroom apartments for $90.

A few kilometres south at Swanbourne, *Swanbourne Guesthouse (☎ 9383 1981, e ralphh@wantree.com.au, 5 Myera St)*, in a quiet residential street off Alfred Rd, has excellent singles/doubles with bathroom for $55/95; breakfast is included and there are cooking and laundry facilities for guests. It's private and quiet and particularly friendly to gay travellers.

Hotels

City Centre There are a number of old-fashioned hotels around the city centre. The *Criterion Hotel (☎ 9325 5155, 560 Hay St)*, a refurbished Art-Deco building, has friendly staff and clean renovated singles/doubles for $80/120, including breakfast.

The *Royal Hotel (☎ 9324 1510)*, on the corner of Wellington and William Sts, is recommended by travellers, but being opposite the bus and train stations, it can get pretty noisy. No-frills rooms cost $55/65 with shared bathroom or $65/80 with private bathroom. The same management runs the *Wentworth Plaza Hotel (☎ 9481 1000, 300 Murray St)* around the corner, which has rooms from $60/70 (shared bathroom) to $85/105. The carpet in the foyer is enough to make you dizzy.

Sullivan's Hotel (☎ 9321 8022, 166 Mounts Bay Rd), about 2km from the centre and next to Kings Park, is a very popular family-run place with comfortable

doubles from $89. It has a pool, restaurant and off-street parking and is on the CAT bus route. It gets consistently good reviews from travellers.

If you want something upmarket, you won't be disappointed with what's available in the city centre. Most of these hotels have modem data ports in rooms and prices usually include breakfast.

The newly revamped *Parmelia Hilton (☎ 9215 2000, 14 Mill St)*, at the eastern end of the city centre near the Cloisters, has doubles from $220 (rack rates) including breakfast; weekend specials start at $140. A bonus is its excellent cafe/restaurant The Globe (see Places to Eat later in this chapter).

The groovy *Rydges Perth (☎ 9263 1800, 815 Hay St)*, on the corner of King St, is one of Perth's newest boutique hotels. The decor is the epitome of chic, and the hotel, together with the downstairs restaurant CBD (see Places to Eat later in this chapter) attracts a very hip crowd. There are fabulous artworks (predominantly WA artists) throughout.

On the corner of Hay and Milligan Sts, *The Melbourne (☎ 9320 3333)* is a lovely century-old heritage building where rather twee (albeit comfortable) singles/doubles (all with modem data ports) cost $100/120, including breakfast. Be sure to ask for a room leading onto the building's superb iron-lacework balcony.

One of Perth's newest city hotels, and a good mid-range choice, is the well-positioned *Perth City Hotel (☎ 9220 7000, e info@ perthcityhotel.com.au, 200 Hay St)*. None of the rooms has a great outlook, but they are modern and very clean, with free in-house movies. Doubles start at $75 per night.

Novotel Langley Perth (☎ 9221 1200, 221 Adelaide Terrace), on the corner of Hill St, has doubles from $179, some with great river views. Rooms here are comfortable, if a little innocuous.

Located in the heart of the shopping and theatre area, but with a personal touch (including a complimentary Rolls Royce to take you to the beach each morning) is the *Sebel of Perth (☎ 9325 7655, 37 Pier St)*, which has spacious, well-appointed doubles from around $140.

The **Duxton** (☎ 9261 8000, 1 St Georges Terrace, e duxton@global.net.au), housed in a converted office block overlooking the Supreme Court Gardens, is in a good spot for the central business district. It has huge, comfortable bedrooms, a pleasant outdoor pool area and a good gym. Standard rates for deluxe double rooms are $200 per night; weekend packages start at $140.

The **Sheraton Perth Hotel** (☎ 9224 7777, e sheraton_perth@sheraton.com, 207 Adelaide Terrace) offers typical hotel-chain five-star luxury, including room service, outdoor pool and gym. While the official rack rate for double rooms is $240, there are regular specials, including weekend packages for $165 per night.

One of the city's most attractive boutique hotels is the **Parkroyal Perth** (☎ 9325 3811, 54 Terrace Rd), tastefully renovated under the philosophy that less is more. Standard doubles, nicely decorated and including gorgeous linen and bathrobes in each room, start at $280 (rack rate) but there are often weekend specials (from $165); some rooms have Swan River views, for which you pay a $30 surcharge. There's a good gym and a timber-decked lap pool.

At the top of the luxury scale is the **Hyatt Regency** (☎ 9225 1245, e hyatt@hyp.com .au, 99 Adelaide Terrace), in an airy, star-shaped atrium, which has pricey rooms of the five-star variety from around $205, often with good special deals on weekends and in low season.

Northbridge, Cottesloe & Scarborough

In Northbridge, the **Court Hotel** (☎ 9328 5292, 50 Beaufort St) is a gay-friendly place with a predominantly (but not exclusively) gay clientele; B&B singles/doubles cost $35/50; en suite doubles cost $80.

In Cottesloe, the **Cottesloe Beach Hotel** (☎ 9383 1100, 104 Marine Parade) is a renovated Art-Deco place right on Cottesloe Beach on the corner of John St. Spacious beachfront doubles with fridge, TV and tea- and coffee-making facilities cost $90; standard singles/doubles cost $60/80.

The **Rendezvous Observation City Hotel** (☎ 9245 1000), on The Esplanade in Scar-

borough, is a bit of an eyesore, but the rooms have great views, particularly of the sunset. Its size (more than 300 rooms) is matched by its prices; doubles cost from $195 to $285, and suites from $500 to $1200.

Motels

Motels serve a purpose – to break your road journey – and their rooms are generally functional rather than luxurious. There are plenty of motels in and around Perth; facilities are more or less the same in each – only the location and the proximity to a major traffic thoroughfare might sway your choice. A motel can be a good option if you're just passing through or if other places are booked out.

The **Murray Lodge Motel** (☎ 9321 7441, 718 Murray St, West Perth), next to Shenton Park, is an economical place; singles/doubles cost $58/66. The **Kings Park Motel** (☎ 9381 3488, 225 Thomas St, Subiaco) has single/doubles from $75/80 and some self-contained rooms ($10 extra).

In Applecross the **Canning Bridge Auto Lodge** (☎ 9364 2511, 891 Canning Hwy) has rooms starting at $55 for two people. Along the Swan River are the **Swanview Motor Inn** (☎ 9367 5755, 1 Preston St, Como), with rooms for $58; the **Metro Inn** (☎ 9367 6122, 61 Canning Hwy, South Perth), where rooms start at $88 a double; and the **Regency Motel** (☎ 9362 3000, 61–69 Great Eastern Hwy, Rivervale), with single/double rooms starting at $62/68.

Other Accommodation

Perth and the surrounding suburbs have an abundance of self-contained holiday flats and serviced apartments, many of which are listed in the *Western Australia Accommodation & Tours Listing* available from the WATC. These are ideal for a longer stay or for those wanting to self-cater; they usually have full cooking facilities, washing machine (or laundry access), iron and ironing board.

Well positioned in the city is the very tasteful and comfortable **West End Apartment Hotel** (☎ 9480 3888, 451 Murray St). Self-contained one-bedroom apartments usually cost $190, but there are weekend specials from $99 per night. Less luxurious, the *City Waters Lodge Holiday Units* (☎ *9325 1566,* e *perth@citywaters.com.au, 118 Terrace Rd)*, down by the river, are good value, with cooking facilities, bathroom, TV and laundry. Rates are $73/78 singles/doubles, with discounts for stays of more than a week. Family units sleeping five cost $108.

In West Perth, the *Emerald Hotel* (☎ *9481 0866, 24 Mount St)*, between the city and Kings Park, with magnificent views over the city and river, has serviced apartments (for two people) from $103 ($116 for a deluxe room). Nearby, across the overpass, are the *Mountway Holiday Units* (☎ *9321 8307, 36 Mount St)*, where basic one-bedroom units cost $57. In the same vicinity is the newly refurbished *Riverview on Mount Street* (☎ *9321 8963,* e *manager@riverview .com.au, 42 Mount St)*, with standard studios for $75 and plush riverview suites for $85.

The *Adelphi Apartments Hotel* (☎ *9322 4666, 130a Mounts Bay Rd)* has basic self-contained units sleeping two/four people for $80/116. Renovated units cost $100/140.

Across the bridge, in the leafy residential area of South Perth (well connected by ferries), the friendly *Waterside Holiday Apartments* (☎ *9474 4474,* e *waterside@ assuredhospitality.com.au, 29 Melville Parade)* has very comfortable one- and two-bedroom apartments with every possible mod con from $125 per night (seasonal discounts available) – great for a longer stay. Nearby, with great views of the river and the city skyline, *The Peninsula* (☎ *9368 6688,* e *reception@thepeninsula.net, 53 South Perth Esplanade)* has very attractive apartments from $105/125 in low/high season, with discounts for stays of more than a week.

Also in South Perth, *Drake's Apartments* (☎ *9367 5077, 2 Scenic Crescent)* has the novel idea of renting out self-contained units with cars. Prices start at $100 per day for a one-bedroom apartment and small aircon car.

The *Cottesloe Beach Chalets* (☎ *9383 5000, 6 John St)*, behind the Cottesloe Beach Hotel, are economical, sleeping five people. Rates are $135 in low season, rising to $180 (December to April).

PLACES TO EAT

Perth is a great place to dine out, with bounteous local produce, wines and beers. All tastes and budgets are easily satisfied.

City Centre

The city centre is a particularly good place for lunches and light meals. Fast-food junkies will be well satisfied if they head for the grease strip on the east side of William St between Murray and Hay Sts.

The *Metro Food Court*, downstairs in the Hay St Mall, near the corner of William St, has Chinese, Indonesian, Thai, Italian and many other types of food. It is open from 8 am to 7 pm Monday to Wednesday, and 8 am to 9 pm Thursday to Saturday.

The *Carillon Arcade Food Hall*, in the Carillon Arcade on Hay St Mall, is slightly more upmarket than the Metro Food Court and has the same international flavour, with Italian, Middle Eastern and Chinese food from $6 to $10. It also has sandwich shops, a seafood stall and fast-food outlets. It is open until around 8 pm daily (9 pm Friday, 6 pm Sunday).

At the other end of the food spectrum, *Magic Apple Wholefoods* (*445 Hay St)* does delicious pitta sandwiches, cakes and fresh juice 'cures'. The busy *Benardi's* (*528 Hay St)* has gourmet sandwiches ($3.60 to $4.90), quiches, home-made soups, and healthy salads. Next door, the licensed *Black Swan Cafe* (*514 Hay St)* does good salads ($4.50 to $9), pasta, and meat dishes such as Cajun chicken salad ($12.50).

Ann's Malaysian, at the northern end of Barrack St, is a good place for a quick $6 noodle meal or takeaway. If sushi is your thing, head for the *Jaws Sushi Tempura* in the Cinema City Arcade between Hay and Murray Sts (near Barrack St). Small, colour-coded plates ($1.50 to $4) of sushi and sashimi rumble around on a conveyor belt; you eat what you want and pay at the end. There's also a tempura bar. There is a second outlet in Forrest Place.

Dinner for two at the good-value *Hayashi Japanese Barbecue* (☎ *9325 6009, 107 Pier St)*, specialising in teppanyaki, tempura and sushi, costs around $35.

The eternally popular *No 44 King Street* (☎ *9321 4476, 44 King St*) bakes and sells its own bread, has a fabulous wine list and a changing daily menu that always includes delicious goat's cheese, roasted capsicum and olive pizza ($14). Opposite, *Mezzonine* (☎ *9481 1148, 49 King St*), one of the most happening eateries in Perth, is open 24 hours Friday and Saturday and from 6.30 am to 11.30 pm other days, serving snacks, light and heavier meals. There are tables outside on the pavement and an open area upstairs. Try the lamb cutlets with mustard and macadamia stuffing ($21.50).

There are good, reasonably priced eateries (wall-to-wall with tailored suits at lunch times on weekdays) farther east of the malls on Adelaide Terrace, including *Cafe Cilento (254 Adelaide Terrace)*, which has breakfast specials, and *Connie's Cafe (156 Adelaide Terrace)*, where focaccia costs $6.

There's a string of places towards the western (Kings Park) end of the city centre, including the highly recommended *Katong Singapore (446 Murray St)*, which has a cavernous dining room, satay vegetables ($8) and barbecue pork chow mein ($7).

Next door, the reasonable Indian *Taj Tandoor* serves Kashmiri dam aloo ($11) and chicken vindaloo for $9. A few doors up, *Fast Eddy's (454 Murray St)*, on the corner of Milligan St, is open 24 hours a day and has good breakfasts, grills, burgers and ice cream; spare ribs cost $15.45. Across the road, the elegant *Millioncino* (☎ *9480 3884, 451 Murray St)* does Italian specialities such as risotto ($9.80) and baked eggplant and capsicum ($11.80), and has $14/19 lunch/dinner specials.

The Globe (☎ *9327 7421, Parmelia Hilton, 14 Mill St)* is a trendy restaurant with both a varied snack menu and a more formal and extensive 'fine dining' menu. It has an atmosphere of understated elegance.

At His Majesty's Theatre, *barre (825 Hay St)* is the theatre's original bar and features an impressive wooden mirrored counter. It's a good place for a light lunch or snack. Focaccia costs $8, pasta $12 and chicken breast with sauteed vegetables $16. Nearby, *Matsuri (900 Hay St)* does great takeaway Japanese food. The sushi and roll lunch box costs $4.50.

CBD (☎ *9263 1859, Rydges Perth, 815 Hay St)* has a fabulous Modern Australian menu, which includes dishes such as lamb cutlets with red lentils ($16.50), spiced chicken pizza ($13.50), and kangaroo fillets with Swiss chard, shallots and glazed baby leeks ($13.50).

If you're feeling thirsty, head straight for *Java Juice (810 Hay St)*, near the corner of King St, the *best* place for juices, smoothies and fruity concoctions in the whole state!

Down at the Barrack St jetty, on Barrack Square, is *Moorings (☎ 9325 4575)*, a good place for coffee or a light meal in an atmospheric setting.

In the affluent area of East Perth is one of Perth's best new restaurants, *Lamonts* (☎ *9202 1566, 11 Brown St)*, on the boardwalk next to the Holmes à Court Gallery. Delicious starters include warm Kervella goat's cheese with sourdough crumb and greens, and salmon on salad of seaweed and spring onion with orange vinaigrette (both $14.50). Main courses include Swan Valley marron ($23.50) and loin of lamb served with grilled eggplant, roasted peppers, yoghurt and spinach ($25).

Northbridge

North of the city centre, the area bounded by William, Lake, Newcastle and Roe Sts is full of ethnic restaurants to suit all tastes and budgets. William St (and the streets that run perpendicular to and west of it) is the hub. The best approach is to cruise around and follow your nose.

Sylvana Pastries (☎ 9328 6691, 197 William St), a comfortable Lebanese coffee bar, has an amazing selection of sticky Middle Eastern cakes. Across the road, *Romany* (☎ *9328 8042, 188 William St)* is one of the city's long-running Italian eateries. A few doors down, the vegetarian *Hare Krishna Food for Life (200 William St)* has cheap meals daily (and extra-cheap $2 meals from 4 to 6 pm Tuesday). The *Cafe Universal (221 William St)* is a mellow spot for a reviving cappuccino, with good music and tasty snacks. *Simon's Seafood (☎ 9227*

9055, 73 Francis St) is a restaurant renowned for its top-quality fish. The poor crays and marrons in tanks in the window probably don't realise they'll be tonight's dinner.

Boxx, on the corner of Lake and Francis Sts, is good for novelty value, with meals served not on plates but in a carton (takeaway style). The menu includes tempura vegetables with jasmine rice, lamb rogan josh and gado gado Indonesian-style salad (all $7.90). Diagonally opposite, **The Re Store** *(72–74 Lake St)* is a gourmet deli selling lots of treats; it also does excellent sandwiches. Nearby, **Valentino's** *(27 Lake St)*, painted in electric blue, has a good-value special on coffee and cake for $4.90. Next door, **Sorrento's** *(☎ 9328 7461, 158 James St)* is a large, traditional Italian eatery serving the usual pizza and pasta. Opposite, **Dôme** *(149 James St)* is a French-style cafe, part of a chain. Smoked-salmon salad costs $12.50 and Provencal tart $17.50. There's a good breakfast menu.

Bambu *(☎ 9228 1016, 182 James St)*, opposite the Russell Square park, serves great fusion food such as prawn nori rolls ($9), chicken tom yum soup ($6) and warm emu salad ($15). On the other side of the park, **Lotus Vegetarian** *(☎ 9228 2882, 220 James St)* does good buffet lunches and dinners for $10.90 to $15.90.

Yum cha and dim sum are extraordinarily popular in Perth, most people heading to Chinatown in Northbridge. The entrance to Chinatown is on Roe St, west of the train station. Wandering around this area, you're bound to find a place that takes your fancy or smells you can't resist. Two of the most popular places here are **Chau's Teahouse** *(☎ 9328 9438, 26 Roe St)*, by the entrance to Chinatown, which is noisy and crowded from 11.30 am Sunday, and the **Riverside Chinese Restaurant** *(☎ 9328 1688, 74 Francis St)*, which has queues tailing down the street – as well as great dim sum for next-to-nothing prices. **Han's Cafe** *(38 Roe St)* does good cheap rice and noodle dishes ($5.50 to $8). There's another outlet on the corner of William and Francis Sts.

Beyond Forbes St is the **City Fresh Food Co**, the place for self-caterers to buy healthy fruit and vegetables. The large **James St Pavilion**, on the corner of Lake and James Sts, is a good-value food hall, with Thai, Japanese, Italian, Indian, vegetarian and Chinese food.

Leederville

The areas of Oxford St between Vincent and Melrose Sts, and Newcastle St, in the suburb of Leederville, north-west of the city centre, have earned popularity with the Perth cappuccino set, and the enclave is fast becoming a chic alternative to the hustle and bustle of Northbridge.

The cuisines of the world are represented in an eclectic collection of eateries. **Cosmos Kebabs** *(129 Oxford St)*, open daily until late, does souvlaki and kebabs ($5 to $6) that fall just the right side of fast food. **Cino to Go** *(136 Oxford St)* does good coffee and fabulous focaccia ($7.90 to $8.90), including the Commesso (gourmet sausage, caramelised onions and chilli jam) and Di Vinci (roast pumpkin, mushrooms, grilled peppers and fetta). Nearby, **Oxford 130** *(130 Oxford St)* does all-day breakfasts, sandwiches and destroy-your-waistline cakes (including lime brulee tart). Ignore the slightly imperious staff. **Banzai Sushi & Noodle Bar** *(741 Newcastle St)* has a good lunch special of miso soup, vegetarian rolls and salad for $9.50.

Perch upoon a leather stool at a long communal bench at **Fourteen-7** *(☎ 9443 7372, 147 Oxford St)*, where the Asian-inspired menu ranges from chilli salt squid ($11.50) and chicken laksa ($14.50) to red curry of duck with snake beans ($19.50).

Subiaco

This enclave, known as 'Subi', has a number of eateries, mostly on (or just off) Rokeby Rd. Some of Perth's trendiest and most upmarket restaurants are found here.

Cappuccino hunters will find their target at **The Merchant Tea & Coffee Company** *(162 Rokeby Rd)*, near the post office, which has 40 varieties of tea and coffee any way you want. Opposite, **Food** *(151a Rokeby Rd)* has excellent sandwiches made with Turkish bread, a short daily menu including

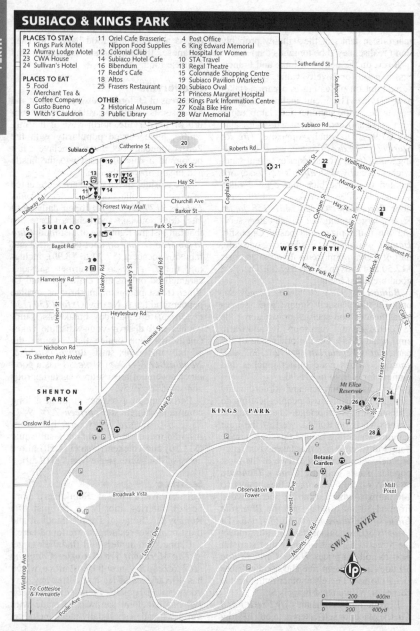

SUBIACO & KINGS PARK

PLACES TO STAY
1 Kings Park Motel
22 Murray Lodge Motel
23 CWA House
24 Sullivan's Hotel

PLACES TO EAT
5 Food
7 Merchant Tea & Coffee Company
8 Gusto Bueno
9 Witch's Cauldron

11 Oriel Cafe Brasserie; Nippon Food Supplies
12 Colonial Club
14 Subiaco Hotel Cafe
16 Bibendum
17 Redd's Cafe
18 Altos
25 Frasers Restaurant

OTHER
2 Historical Museum
3 Public Library

4 Post Office
6 King Edward Memorial Hospital for Women
10 STA Travel
13 Regal Theatre
15 Colonnade Shopping Centre
19 Subiaco Pavilion (Markets)
20 Subiaco Oval
21 Princess Margaret Hospital
26 Kings Park Information Centre
27 Koala Bike Hire
28 War Memorial

a wok-tossed noodle dish ($6.90), and gourmet treats for the pantry. A few doors down, **Gusto Bueno** *(147 Rokeby Rd)* is another good place for sandwiches and rolls.

Witch's Cauldron *(☎ 9381 2508, 89 Rokeby Rd)* has been in Subiaco forever (well, for 30 years) and is famous for its sizzling garlic prawns ($14). The **Oriel Cafe Brasserie** *(☎ 9382 1886, 483 Hay St)*, a Subiaco favourite, is open 24 hours a day and serves Modern Australian and Mediterranean dishes. The shady terrace lends itself to hanging out.

If you want Indian food but your friend wants pumpkin soup, head for the **Colonial Club Cafe** *(☎ 9381 2099, 67 Rokeby Rd)*, on the corner of Hay St; it has an eclectic menu divided into five 'continents' – whether you're after shepherd's pie, Caesar salad or toasted nan bread and beef curry, chances are you'll be satisfied. It's open 10 am to midnight daily.

Between the Colonial Club and Oriel on Hay St, **Nippon Food Supplies** is a good Japanese takeaway where you can grab a quick nori or California roll.

Wood-panelled, dimly lit **Altos** *(☎ 9382 3292, 424 Hay St)* has style written all over it and brings a touch of New York to Perth. The Art-Deco theme continues down to the posters on the wall and the individual table lamps. This is a good spot for late-night dining – last orders are taken at 11 pm. Pink-peppercorn-crusted salmon with caramelised grapefruit is a signature dish; mains cost around $20. A few doors down, **Redd's Cafe** *(420 Hay St)* is good for breakfast, coffees and light meals.

Around the corner, in the ritzy Colonnade shopping centre, is **Bibendum** *(☎ 9382 3292, 388 Hay St)*, which has separate cafe and restaurant areas (the latter with a gorgeous courtyard filled with potted olive trees). The menu features dishes such as sea-scallop ravioli and duck leg confit; starters cost $12, mains $22. If you want to go the whole hog, there's a five-course degustation menu for $65. The cafe offers (more affordable) stir-fries and curries.

Subiaco Hotel Cafe *(☎ 9381 1028, 465 Hay St)* is an award-winning pub dining room with an attractive courtyard. It serves comfort food like bangers-and-mash, and more adventurous fare such as whiting saltimbocca served with spinach risotto.

In Kings Park, **Frasers** *(☎ 9481 7100)*, on Fraser Ave, is a perennial Perth favourite. It has great city and river views and excellent Modern Australian cuisine (specialising in seafood). The wine list features more than 400 labels. Main courses cost around $25.

Cottesloe

As well as a plethora of beachside cafes, Cottesloe has a number of top eateries.

A trip to this beachside suburb would not be complete without a meal, or at least a cup of tea, at **Indiana Tea House** *(☎ 9385 5005, 99 Marine Parade)*. It's like stepping back to the Raj, with wicker chairs, ceiling fans, leadlight windows, Indian weavings, and great tea. You can gaze over the Indian Ocean (divine at sunset) as you enjoy the varied and exotic flavours of India and Asia, such as steamed pork dumplings or the Raffles plate for two ($21.50) featuring onion bhaji, pi pa prawns, chicken tikka and spring rolls. Bookings are essential for meals.

Catalina's Cafe *(☎ 9383 3344, 104 Marine Parade)*, at the Cottesloe Beach Hotel, is modelled on a 1930s luxury ocean liner and features a mural mirroring the hotel's original Art-Deco foyer. It's a light and airy place, with an Australian-Italian-inspired menu featuring upmarket fish and chips ($13.70), five varieties of pasta ($12.70 to $16.70) and mains such as veal cutlet ($21.70) and vegetarian polenta ($15.20).

The **Blue Duck Cafe** *(☎ 9385 2499, 151 Marine Parade)* is another Cottesloe favourite. Many locals come here strictly for the wood-fired pizza – said to be excellent. This is the favourite hang-out of former business tycoon and local resident Alan Bond, who had one of his first meals here after being released from prison. This place is popular, so you might need to book.

ENTERTAINMENT

Perth has plenty of pubs, discos and nightclubs. *Xpress*, a weekly music mag available free at record shops, cafes and other outlets, has a gig guide. Another free rag, good for clubs and venues listings, is *Hype*. See the *West Australian* newspaper for listings of mainstream theatre, cinema and nightclubs. The free local newspaper *Perth Weekly* is another good source of local news and gig listings.

The Perth lifestyle magazine *Scoop* has a very useful Web site at www.scoop.com.au. Although the magazine is published only quarterly, the online listings are updated weekly and you'll find everything from opera to exhibitions to dance to festivals to sports to children's activities.

Northbridge, Leederville and Subiaco are the places to go after dark, especially on weekends, when the city centre remains dead despite efforts to revitalise it.

Pubs & Live Music

Cover bands, original music, comedy, DJs and karaoke – Perth's pubs have something for everyone.

Popular pubs (most with live music on weekends) in Northbridge include the *Brass Monkey Bar & Brasserie (209 William St)*, on the corner of James St; *Novak's Inn (147 James St)*; the *Elephant & Wheelbarrow (53 Lake St)*, a heaving, new, English-style pub with a beer garden facing the street; *Rosie O'Grady's (205 James St)*, which has Irish bands most nights of the week; *The Bog (☎ 9228 0900, 361 Newcastle St)*, Perth's most happening Irish pub (open until 6 am); and the 'Deen', the *Aberdeen Hotel (84 Aberdeen St)*, which has bands most nights and 'backpackers night' on Monday.

The *Universal Bar*, on William St next to the Brass Monkey, is a trendy, open-fronted bar, with regular jazz sessions.

The *Leederville Hotel* on Oxford St in Leederville has a legendary Sunday afternoon session. On Tuesday and Thursday many backpackers will be found at the *hipe-club*, behind the Leederville Village, enjoying free entry, a complimentary drink and lining up for hours for a sausage. The club provides a free bus back to local hostels.

The Sunday blast at the *Cottesloe Beach Hotel (104 Marine Parade)* goes off in the large beer garden, but the sunset view from

the bar of the *Ocean Beach Hotel* (the 'OBH'), near North Cottesloe Beach, is much better.

Perth has the usual pub-rock circuit, with cover charges depending on the gig. Popular venues include the *Grosvenor Hotel (339 Hay St)*, where live music is belted out Wednesday to Sunday; the *Indi Bar & Bistro (23 Hastings St, Scarborough)*; the *Junction (309 Great Eastern Hwy, Midland)*; the *Civic (981 Beaufort St, Inglewood)*; the *Inglewood Hotel (803 Beaufort St, Inglewood)*; and the *Babylon Hotel (901 Albany Hwy, East Victoria Park)*, which also serves good pizza. Check the gig guides to see what's on.

Jazz

There are a number of regular venues in Perth for jazz lovers. The Perth Jazz Society meets every Monday night at the Hyde Park Hotel in Bulwer St, Perth, to play swing and modern jazz. The Jazz Club of WA (which plays traditional jazz and Dixieland) meets at the same place on Tuesday night. In Fremantle there's the Fremantle Jazz Club.

For information on current gigs, call the Jazz Coordination Association (☎ 9439 1504) or the recorded information Jazz Line (☎ 9357 2807).

Nightclubs

Perth has plenty of places where you can dance into the wee small hours, but as in many big cities, clubs come and go. What's fashionable one month might not be the next, so check the gig guides in *Xpress* and on the *Scoop* Web site.

The *New Loft Nightclub (104 Murray St)*, in the city centre, has a variety of styles, including retro on Sunday night.

The majority of late-night venues are in Northbridge. Hard-core dance clubs include the *Church (69 Lake St)*, *Redheads (44 Lake St)*, just across the road, and *O2 (Oxygen) (139 James St)*. The *Post Office (133 Aberdeen St)* handles a slightly older crowd with aplomb (especially at the over-30s session on Thursday), but is also popular with backpackers and has free entry from 8 to 11 pm Wednesday, with a meal thrown in.

A glittering Perth skyline, viewed from Kings Park.

Tranby House on Maylands Peninsula

Cafe culture, Perth style

Cottesloe Beach, Perth

His Majesty's Theatre in Perth opened in 1904.

Art Gallery of Western Australia, Perth

A sunset surf on Cottesloe Beach

The Georgian-style Customs House, Fremantle

Fremantle Arts Centre

St Johns Anglican Church, built in 1882

Perth's Old Mill, built in 1835

Maritime Museum, on Fremantle's waterfront

Old Fremantle Prison

Architectural detail, Fremantle

Another backpacker favourite is the *hip-e-club* (☎ 9227 8899, 663 Newcastle St, Leederville), on the corner of Oxford St. If you come early on Tuesday or Thursday you get free entry and a free meal.

Some of the best new venues are the smaller, more intimate clubs. *Paramount* (☎ 9228 1344, 163 James St) is hugely popular – dancers on podiums at the front signal that you've found the place. *Metropolis City* (☎ 9228 0500, 146 Roe St, Northbridge) is the original big-city nightclub and concert venue, but its popularity is waning. When the bands finish, the nightclub/disco takes over.

Theatres
Popular theatres include *His Majesty's Theatre* (☎ 9265 0900, 825 Hay St), on the corner of King St, and the *Regal Theatre (474 Hay St, Subiaco)*.

Other theatre venues include the *Effie Crump Theatre* (☎ 9227 7226, 81 Brisbane Rd, Northbridge); the *Playhouse* (☎ 9231 2377, 3 Pier St); and the *Stirling Theatre* (☎ 9349 6044), on Cedric St, Stirling. You can enjoy the work of a local playwright or an internationally renowned production.

Theatre programs are listed daily in the *West Australian* newspaper.

Classical Music
The *Perth Concert Hall* (☎ 9484 1133, 55 St Georges Terrace), home to the Western Australian Symphony Orchestra (WASO), and the large *Entertainment Centre* (☎ 9484 1222), on Wellington St, are venues for concerts and recitals by local and international performers. There are free concerts under the stars in the Supreme Court and Queens Gardens and in Kings Park during the Perth International Festival.

Comedy
Perth has a lively comedy scene, although those that survive the smoke, late nights and audience abuse generally gravitate to stand-up heaven in Melbourne. Some pubs double as music and comedy venues. Check the listings press. Otherwise, see an international act at the *Burswood Casino* on the Great Eastern Hwy in Burswood.

Gay & Lesbian Venues
The *Court Hotel (50 Beaufort St)* has live music, drag shows and gay-friendly accommodation. *Connections (81 James St)* is popular for dance music and floor shows. *O2 (Oxygen) (139 James St)* has trade on Thursday night, and *Rainbow Connection Cafe (615 Beaufort St, Mt Lawley)* is a happening venue, with drag cabarets on Friday and Saturday.

Check the *Westside Observer (WSO)*, available from the above-mentioned places, for more venues and activities.

Cinemas
The *Cinema Paradiso (☎ 9227 1771, 166 James St, Northbridge)*, the *Luna (☎ 9444 4056, 155 Oxford St, Leederville)*, and the *Astor (☎ 9370 1777, 659 Beaufort St, Mt Lawley)* usually have quality art-house films. All of the Hollywood favourites are shown in the Hoyts, Greater Union and Village suburban cinemas and at the Hoyts complexes at *Cinema City (☎ 9325 2377)*, in Hay St, and *Cinecentre (☎ 9325 4992, 139 Murray St)* in central Perth; budget night is Tuesday. In summer, *Kings Park* hosts an open-air cinema.

Programs and session times are listed daily in the *West Australian*.

Casino
Perth's glitzy *Burswood Casino (☎ 9362 7777)*, on the Great Eastern Hwy at Burswood, is built on an artificial island. It is open all day, every day. Its setup seems pretty similar to other Australian casinos, with the usual gaming tables (roulette and blackjack), a two-up 'shed', Keno, poker machines and extensive off-course betting. Burswood Casino also hosts a cavalcade of prominent local and international entertainers throughout the year.

SPECTATOR SPORTS
Perthites flock to watch Australian Rules Football at Subiaco Oval and in Fremantle during winter, cricket at the Western Australia Cricket Association oval ('the WACA') in summer, and basketball at the Perth Entertainment Centre.

See Spectator Sports in the Facts for the Visitor chapter for more information.

SHOPPING

King St in central Perth has an interesting array of shops and galleries. Creative Native, at 32 King St, is an art/crafts gallery devoted solely to Aboriginal artists. It sells a lot of quality stuff as well as a few tacky souvenirs. Around Forrest Place are the main department stores, Myer and Aherns, as well as shopping arcades of varying quality. For camping and climbing equipment, there's Paddy Pallin, at 884 Hay St, and, across the road at No 862, Mountain Designs.

Subiaco is a good place to shop. The Colonnade centre, at 388 Hay St, has a range of Australian and international designer stores. There's a Nike factory outlet at 440 Hay St and Empire Homewares at No 120. At 115 Hay St, Indigenart sells original Aboriginal paintings on bark, canvas and paper. Around in Rokeby Rd you'll find some interesting book/gift/homewares stores.

Claremont's ritzy Bayview Terrace shopping centre features fashion stores such as Sportsgirl and Witchery, as well as Dymocks bookshop, and Plantation Colonial Trading Co, which sells eclectic homewares and furniture (fancy a stone Buddha?). Nearby, St Quentin Ave is also popular with shoppers.

Cottesloe's Napoleon St features a few unusual homewares shops, including Ma Cuisine and Plane Tree Farm (luxury linens and towels), and several boutiques.

Markets

There are many lively markets around Perth that are ideal if you're into browsing and buying. The Subiaco Pavilion, on the corner of Roberts and Rokeby Rds near Subiaco train station, is open Thursday to Sunday. The Wanneroo Markets, north of Perth at Prindiville Dr, Wangara, has a variety of stalls and a food hall; it's open weekends.

Other markets include the historic Fremantle Markets (see under Fremantle later in this chapter); the weekend Stock Rd Markets, on the corner of Stock Rd and Spearwood Ave in Bibra Lake; Gosnells Railway Markets, on the corner of Albany Hwy and Fremantle Rd, open Thursday to Sunday; and the Canning Vale Markets, on the corner of Ranford and Bannister Rds, open every Sunday.

GETTING THERE & AWAY
Air

Both Qantas Airways (☎ 13 1313) and Ansett Australia (☎ 13 1300) operate regular flights between Perth and other Australian state capitals.

Ansett and its subsidiaries operate regular services between Perth and Kalgoorlie-Boulder, Geraldton, Carnarvon, Derby, Learmonth (for Exmouth), Newman, Karratha, Port Hedland, Broome, Kununurra, Albany, Esperance, Laverton, Leinster, Leonora, Denham (for Monkey Mia), Meekatharra and Wiluna.

Check out the Web sites at www.ansett.com.au and www.qantas.com.au.

See also under Air in both the Getting There & Away and Getting Around chapters.

Bus

Greyhound Pioneer Australia (☎ 13 2030) runs regular bus services between Perth and Dongara–Port Denison ($37), Geraldton ($39), Kalbarri ($80), Monkey Mia ($136), Port Hedland ($190), Exmouth ($204), Broome ($271), Derby ($315), Kununurra ($429), Meekatharra ($137), Newman ($170), Northam ($53) and Kalgoorlie-Boulder ($104). Being a national company, Greyhound Pioneer also operates services from Perth to Darwin ($459), Adelaide ($209) and Melbourne ($257).

The Greyhound Pioneer terminal in Perth is at 250 Great Eastern Hwy, Ascot, near the airport. Check out the Web site at www.greyhound.com.au.

Westrail (☎ 1800-099 150, 13 1053, 9326 2222) buses operate in the south-west and mid-west, connecting Perth with Geraldton, Kalbarri, Esperance, Bunbury, Kalgoorlie-Boulder, York, Margaret River, Augusta, Pemberton, Mukinbudin, Hyden, Albany and Meekatharra. All Westrail bus services from/to Perth start/finish at the bus terminal at East Perth train station. Check out Westrail's Web site at www.westrail.wa.gov.au.

Another operator is South West Coach Lines (☎ 9324 2333), which offers services between Perth and Bunbury, Margaret River, Augusta, Donnybrook, Balingup, Bridgetown, Collie, Manjimup, Busselton and Nannup.

Other operators run services between Perth and regional centres across the state (see under Bus in the Getting Around chapter).

Train
The state's internal rail network, operated by Westrail (☎ 1800-099 150, 13 1053, 9326 2222), is limited to services between Perth and Kalgoorlie-Boulder (the *Prospector*, which departs from the East Perth terminal); Perth and Northam (the *Avon Link*, which also departs from the East Perth terminal); and Perth and Bunbury in the south (the *Australind*, which departs from the Perth train station on Wellington St). There are connections with Westrail's more extensive bus service. See under Bus earlier in this chapter for details or check out Westrail's Web site at www.westrail.wa.gov.au.

There is only one interstate rail link: the famous *Indian Pacific* transcontinental train journey, run by Great Southern Railway (☎ 13 2147). To Perth from Sydney, one-way fares are $459 coach class, $1071 holiday class and $1717 first class, with discounts for children and students. Between Adelaide and Perth, fares are $283/690/1222.

See under Train in the Getting There & Away chapter for more information.

Boat
Transperth (☎ 13 6213) runs ferries from Perth to South Perth and there are a number of operators which run regular boat services between Perth and Rottnest Island.

Oceanic Cruises (☎ 9325 1191, 9430 5127) runs Seacats (four daily, five on Friday) between Perth's Barrack St jetty and Rottnest Island. It costs $47/14 for adults/children (same-day return).

The Rottnest Shuttle, operated by Boat Torque (☎ 9430 5844, 9221 5844) leaves from Perth's Barrack St jetty, with same-day returns from Perth/Fremantle costing $45/35 adults/children.

See Getting There & Away under Rottnest Island in the Around Perth chapter for more information on services from Perth and Fremantle to Rottnest Island.

GETTING AROUND
Perth's central public transport organisation, Transperth (☎ 13 6213), operates buses, trains and ferries. There are Transperth information offices at the Perth train station in Wellington St and at the Transperth City Busport on Mounts Bay Rd.

Transperth provides advice about getting around Perth and produces a system map and timetables. Its offices are open from 7.30 am to 5.30 pm weekdays. Check out the Web site at www.transperth.wa.gov.au.

To/From the Airport
The domestic and international terminals of Perth's airport are 10km and 13km east of Perth respectively. Taxi fares to the city are around $16 and $20 from the domestic and international terminals respectively.

The privately run airport shuttle (☎ 9479 4131) provides transport to the city centre, hotels and hostels. It claims to meet all incoming domestic and international flights, but travellers have reported that sometimes it doesn't turn up – if this occurs late at night, a taxi is the best option.

The shuttle costs $8.80/15.40 one way/return from the domestic terminal and $11/19 from the international terminal. From terminal to terminal costs $5.50/4 adults/children. The shuttle also runs to the Greyhound Bus Depot in Redcliffe ($7.70). To the airport terminals from the city, there are scheduled runs every hour or so from 3 am to 10 pm. Bookings are essential (24 hours ahead if possible).

Alternatively, you can get into the city for $2.50 on Transperth bus Nos 200, 201, 202, 208 and 209 to St Georges Terrace. They depart from the domestic terminal every hour or so (more frequently at peak times) from around 5.30 am to 10 pm weekdays, 7 am to 11 pm Saturday and 9 am to 6.44 pm Sunday.

There are no Transperth buses servicing the international terminal.

Bus

There are two free Central Area Transit (CAT) services in the city centre. The buses are state-of-the-art and there are computer readouts (and audio) at the stops telling you when the next bus is due. Using the two services, you can get to most sights in the inner city.

The red CAT operates east–west from Outram St, West Perth, to the WACA in East Perth. The service runs every five minutes from 6.50 am to 6.20 pm weekdays. A 45-minute service operates from 10 am to 6.15 pm weekends. The blue CAT operates north–south from the river to Northbridge, roughly in the centre of the red CAT route. Services run every eight minutes from 6.50 am to 6.20 pm weekdays. A modified version of the blue CAT runs every 12 minutes on weekends – from 6 pm to 1 am Friday, 8.30 am to 1 am Saturday, and 10 am to 5 pm Sunday.

On regular Transperth (☎ 13 6213) buses, a short ride of one zone costs $1.70, two zones $2.50 and three zones $3.30. Zone 1 includes the city centre and the inner suburbs (including Subiaco and Claremont), and Zone 2 extends all the way to Fremantle, 20km from the city centre. A Multi-Rider ticket gives 10 journeys for the price of eight or nine. A DayRider day ticket costs $6.50. A MaxiRider ticket ($6.50) allows weekend travel for two adults and up to five children anywhere on all Transperth trains, buses and ferries.

The City Explorer Tram (☎ 9322 2006) is actually a bus (which looks like an old tram) that takes you around some of Perth's main attractions (such as the city, Kings Park, Barrack St jetty and the Burswood Casino) in 1½ hours. It costs $12/6 adults/children and departs from 565 Hay St (near Barrack St) at least six times daily. You can break your journey at any stop and pick up the subsequent tram.

Train

Transperth (☎ 13 6213) operates the Fastrak suburban train lines to Armadale, Fremantle, Midland and the northern suburb of Joondalup from around 5.20 am to midnight weekdays, with reduced services on weekends. During the day, some of the Joondalup trains continue to Armadale and some Fremantle trains run through to Midland.

All trains leave from Perth station on Wellington St. Your rail ticket can also be used on Transperth buses and ferries within the ticket's area of validity. Fares are calculated according to the same zone system as for buses.

Ferry

Transperth ferries (☎ 13 6213) cross the river from the Barrack St jetty in the city to the Mends St jetty in South Perth every 30 minutes (more frequently at peak times) from 6.45 am to 7.15 pm ($1; one zone). Take this ferry to get to the zoo.

Car & Motorcycle

Driving in the city centre takes a little bit of getting used to, as some streets are one way and many street signs are not prominent.

In the city you will have no trouble getting fuel from 7 am to 9 pm on Monday to Saturday but on Sunday some fuel outlets work on a rostering basis.

Rental Budget (☎ 13 2727), Avis (☎ 9325 7677), Hertz (☎ 9321 7777) and Thrifty (☎ 9464 7444) all have offices in Perth, along with local firms mentioned in the Getting Around chapter.

Taxi

Perth has a good system of metered taxi cabs and there are ranks throughout the city and in nearby Fremantle. The two main companies are Swan Taxis (☎ 13 1388) and Black & White (☎ 9333 3333). A taxi service for the disabled can be booked on ☎ 9333 3377.

Bicycle

Cycling is an excellent way to explore Perth. There are bicycle routes along the Swan River, running all the way to Fremantle, and along the Indian Ocean coast.

You can buy a bike from the WA Bicycle Disposal Centre (☎ 9325 1176), at 293 Hay St in East Perth, knowing you'll get a guaranteed buy-back price after a certain time.

About Bike Hire (☎ 9221 2665), in the No 4 car park on Riverside Dr near Narrows Bridge, also rents out cycles, for about $15 per day.

Bikewest (☎ 9320 9301), at 441 Murray St, produces some excellent maps and booklets for cyclists, including the *Perth Bike Map* series. The main map, *Perth/ Fremantle-Stirling*, covers most of the city; four other maps cover outer areas. Each map costs $5.95; they're available from most tourist information centres, bike shops and some bookshops, and from Bikewest.

Bikewest's free *Ride Around the Rivers* booklet includes maps and ride descriptions for more than 60km of cycling around Perth's Swan and Canning Rivers. It's available from Bikewest.

The cyclists advocacy group Bicycle Transportation Alliance (☎ 9420 7210), at 2 Delhi St, West Perth 6005, has an excellent Web site, sunsite.anu.edu.au/wa/bta, which includes practical information as well as some useful links.

Fremantle

pop 25,000
Fremantle (known as 'Freo' to the locals), Perth's port, lies at the mouth of the Swan River, 19km south-west of the city centre. Over the years, Perth has sprawled to engulf Fremantle, which is now more a suburb of the city than a town in its own right.

Despite recent development, Fremantle has a wholly different feel than gleaming, skyscraper-riddled Perth. It's a place with a real sense of history and it has an extremely pleasant, relaxed atmosphere.

The town has a number of interesting old buildings, some excellent museums and galleries, lively produce and craft markets, and a diverse range of pubs, cafes and restaurants.

History
This region was settled many thousands of years ago by the Nyungar people. Several trails joined on the south side of the Swan River at the hub of intertribal trading routes;

here was a natural bridge almost spanning the Swan. Aboriginal groups quickly came to occupy various parts of the area, known to them as Munjaree.

Fremantle's modern, European history began when the ship HMS *Challenger* landed here in 1829. The ship's captain, Charles Howe Fremantle, took possession of 'the whole of the west coast in the name of King George IV'.

Like Perth, the settlement made little progress until convict labour was taken on. These hard-worked labourers constructed most of the town's earliest buildings; some of them are now among the oldest and most treasured in WA.

As a port, Fremantle was abysmal, until the brilliant engineer CY O'Connor (see the boxed text 'Where Water is Like Gold!' in The Southern Outback chapter) created an artificial harbour in the 1890s.

In 1987 the city of Fremantle was the site of the unsuccessful defence of what was, for a brief period, one of Australia's most prized possessions – the America's Cup yachting trophy. Preparations for the influx of tourists transformed Fremantle into a more modern, colourful and expensive city.

Information
There are two privately run tourist offices. The main one (☎ 9431 7878) is located in the Fremantle Town Hall in Kings Square; it offers a wide range of maps and brochures, tour information and assistance with accommodation bookings. It is open from 9 am to 5 pm Monday to Saturday, and noon to 4.30 pm Sunday.

A smaller tourist office is located on The Esplanade Reserve, opposite the Esplanade Hotel. It is open from 9.30 am to 4.30 pm weekdays and has information about tours and transport.

You can get information about the state's national parks at CALM's WA Naturally shop (☎ 9430 8600), at 47 Henry St (on the corner of Croke St); it is open from 10 am to 5.30 pm daily except Tuesday.

The local newspapers *Fremantle Gazette* and *Fremantle Herald* have news, information and listings; both are free and available

PERTH

FREMANTLE

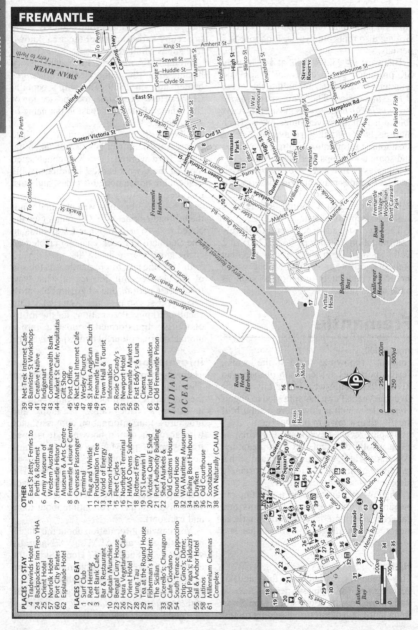

PLACES TO STAY
4 Tradewinds Hotel
24 Backpackers Inn Freo YHA
25 Norfolk Hotel
57 Port City Pirates
60 Orient Hotel
62 Esplanade Hotel

PLACES TO EAT
1 Surf Club
2 Red Herring
3 Left Bank Cafe,
    Bar & Restaurant
10 Captain Munchies
23 Bengal Curry House
26 Hara Vegetarian Cafe
27 Orient Hotel
28 Vung Tau
29 Tea at the Round House
31 Fisherman's Kitchen;
    The Sicilian
33 Cicerello's; Chunagon
50 Cafe Giordano
54 South Terrace Cappuccino
    Strip; Gino's Dome;
    Old Papa's; Falduzzi's
55 Sail & Anchor Hotel
58 Latinos
61 Millennium Cinemas
    Complex

OTHER
5 East St Jetty; Ferries to
    Perth & Rottnest
6 WA Maritime Museum of
    Western Australia
7 Fremantle History
    Museum & Arts Centre
8 Fremantle Leisure Centre
9 Overseas Passenger
    Terminal
11 Flag and Whistle
12 Proclamation Tree
13 World of Energy
14 Samson House
15 Fleet Cycles
16 Northport Terminal
17 HMAS Ovens Submarine
18 Rottnest Ferry
19 STS Leeuwin II
20 Victoria Quay E Shed
21 Port Authority Building
22 Shed Markets &
    Old Customs House
30 Round House
34 WA Maritime Museum
35 Fishing Boat Harbour
36 Dayrfkkat
37 Scootabout
38 WA Naturally (CALM)
39 Net Trek Internet Cafe
40 Bannister St Workshops
41 Creative Native
42 Indigenart
43 Commonwealth Bank
44 Market St Cafe; Moulitatas
    Gift Shop
45 Post Office
46 Net.Chat Internet Cafe
47 Wesley Church
48 St Johns Anglican Church
49 Fremantle Tram
51 Town Hall & Tourist
    Information
52 Rosie O'Grady's
53 Newport Hotel
56 Fremantle Markets
59 Fast Eddy's & Luna
    Cinema
63 Tourist Information
64 Old Fremantle Prison

widely in Fremantle. The City of Fremantle also publishes a free monthly newspaper called *Freo*.

Fremantle's post office (☎ 13 1318) is at 13 Market St.

Email & Internet Access All of the hostels mentioned under Places to Stay in this section have Internet access. Net Trek (☎ 9336 4900), at 8 Bannister St Mall, also has access, for $4 per hour. It is open from 9 am to 6 pm weekdays. Net.Chat (☎ 9433 2011), in Wesley Way Arcade off Market St and opposite the post office, charges $4 per hour from 8 to 11 am and 8 to 11 pm, and slightly more from 11 am to 8 pm.

HISTORY MUSEUM & ARTS CENTRE

The Fremantle History Museum (☎ 9430 7966), housed in an impressive building on the corner of Ord and Finnerty Sts, was originally constructed by convict labourers as a lunatic asylum in the 1860s. It houses a fine collection, including exhibits on Fremantle's early social history and sections on Aboriginal history, the colonisation of WA, and the early whaling industry. There is a focus on the diverse nationalities that make up the town's population. The museum is open from 10.30 am to 4.30 pm Sunday to Friday, and 1 to 5 pm Saturday. Admission is by donation.

The Fremantle Arts Centre (☎ 9432 9555) occupies one wing of the building and has a changing program of exhibitions. There is also a craft shop and bookshop. It is open from 9.30 am to 5 pm daily. Admission is free.

MARITIME MUSEUM

Don't miss the Western Australian Maritime Museum (☎ 9431 8444), on Cliff St near the waterfront – it is Fremantle's highlight.

The museum, in a building constructed in 1852 as a commissariat store, has a display on WA's maritime history, with particular emphasis on the history, recovery and restoration of the famous wreck *Batavia*, other Dutch merchant ships and some more recent wrecks.

At one end of the *Batavia* gallery is a huge stone façade intended for an entrance to Batavia Castle. It was being carried by the *Batavia* when it sank. The dominant feature of the gallery, however, is the reconstruction of a part of the hull of the ship from recovered timbers, which you can view from ground level as well as from a mezzanine floor above.

Another interesting exhibit here is the original de Vlamingh plate. When navigator Willem de Vlamingh retrieved Dutch explorer Dirk Hartog's inscribed plate from Hartog Island (see The Europeans under History in the Facts about Western Australia chapter), he replaced it with another. Hartog's plate is preserved in a museum in the Netherlands.

Other exhibits include coins and corroded artefacts from the many ships that went aground along the coast of WA. This rather intriguing, not-to-be-missed museum is open from 9.30 am to 5 pm daily. Admission is by donation.

THE DUYFKEN

Bobbing in Fishing Boat Harbour opposite the Esplanade Reserve is an exact replica of the *Duyfken* (Little Dove), a Dutch *jacht* (scout ship) for the Moluccan Fleet, which made the first recorded voyage to Australia in 1606. It was built in Fremantle, which has become something of a centre for building replica boats – the replica of James Cook's *Endeavour* was also built here.

The *Duyfken*, known to have reached Cape York Peninsula with about 20 crew, is very small for a sailing ship but it's worth a poke around if you're interested in maritime history. It's open from 9.30 am to 4.30 pm daily. Admission is $5/3 adults/children.

FREMANTLE MARKETS

The colourful Fremantle Markets (☎ 9335 2515), at the corner of South Terrace and Henderson St, is a prime attraction in Fremantle. Originally opened in 1897, it was reopened in 1975 and draws crowds looking for anything from hand-decorated overalls to essential oils, and fruit and vegetables to jewellery and antiques; there is also a great tavern bar where buskers often perform. Fremantle Markets is open 9 am to 9 pm Friday, 9 am to 5 pm Saturday, and 10 am to 5 pm Sunday. Late Sunday afternoon is the time to buy fruit and vegetables, which are sold off cheap before closing time.

ROUND HOUSE

On Arthur Head, at the western end of High St near the Maritime Museum, is the Round House. Built in 1831, it's the oldest public building in WA. It was originally a local prison (in the days before convicts were brought into WA) and was the site of the colony's first hanging.

Later, the building was used for holding Aborigines before they were taken away to Rottnest Island. To the Nyungar people, the Round House is a sacred site because of the number of their people killed while incarcerated here. One local remarked ironically that, although WA was initially settled as a penal colony, the first thing the authorities did was to build a prison using convict labour to house local Aborigines.

Incidentally, the tunnel underneath the Round House was cut by a whaling company in 1837 for access to Bathers Bay. The Round House shop and information office is housed in one of the nearby pilots' cottages. The building is open from 10 am to 5 pm daily. Admission is free. The site provides good views of Fremantle, especially historic High St.

CONVICT-ERA BUILDINGS

Many other buildings in Fremantle date from the period after 1850, when convict labour was introduced. They include the **Old Fremantle Prison** (☎ 9430 7177), at 1 The Terrace, one of the unlucky convicts' first building tasks. To a certain extent, the prison, with its 5m-high walls, dominates modern Fremantle. It operated as a prison from 1855 until 1991.

The prison is open from 10 am to 6 pm daily. Admission is $10/5 adults/children. The best time to visit is at 7.30 pm on Wednesday and Friday for candlelight tours; these also cost $10 – bookings are essential.

Beside the prison gates, at No 16 The Terrace, is a **museum** on the convict era in WA. The entrance for both the prison and the museum is on The Terrace.

SUSAN STORM

Built in 1831, the Round House in Fremantle is the oldest public building in WA.

The **Army Museum of WA** (☎ 9335 2077), on Burt St, has a display of army memorabilia dating from colonial times to WWII. It is housed in the former Artillery Barracks, built in 1910, where soldiers stayed before they embarked on ships bound for European wars. It is open from 12.30 to 4.30 pm Wednesday, Saturday and Sunday. Admission is $3/1 adults/children.

LATER LANDMARKS

Fremantle boomed during the WA gold rush and many buildings were constructed during, or shortly before, this period. **Samson House** is a well-preserved 1888 colonial home in Ellen St. Tours of the house are run by volunteer guides. Samson House is open from 1 to 5 pm on Thursday and Sunday. The fine **St Johns Anglican Church** (1882), on the corner of Adelaide and Queen Sts, contains a large stained-glass window.

Other buildings of the boom era include **Fremantle Town Hall** (1887) in Kings Square; the former **German consulate building** (1902), at 5 Mouat St; the **Fremantle Train Station** (1907); and the Georgian-style **Customs House** on the corner of Cliff and Phillimore Sts. The **Victoria Grandstand** of Fremantle Oval (1897) is a good example of the once-popular timber-and-iron pavilion, complete with lacework and towers.

The **water trough**, in the park in front of the station, has a memorial to two men who died of thirst on an outback expedition.

The **Proclamation Tree**, near the corner of Adelaide and Edwards Sts, is a Moreton Bay fig, planted in 1890.

VICTORIA QUAY DOCKS

The Victoria Quay Docks are on Fremantle Harbour, just to the west of the city centre. From the observation tower on top of the **Port Authority Building** (☎ 9430 4911), on Cliff St, you can enjoy a panoramic view of Fremantle Harbour. Guided tours leave the foyer at 1.30 pm weekdays.

The training ship STS *Leeuwin II*, a 55m, three-masted barquentine, is based at B Berth, Victoria Dock (☎ 9430 4105). This ship has half- and full-day trips in spring and summer. Half-day tours include light refreshment and full-day tours include a full smorgasbord lunch and morning tea. Half-/full-day trips cost $55/99 for adults and $30/50 for children. In the winter months there are longer trips up the northwest coast; they cost from $1650/990 adults/students for 10 days.

Also at Victoria Quay is the submarine **HMAS *Ovens***. The vessel was part of the Australian Navy's fleet from 1969 to 1997. It is open from 11 am to 4.30 pm Friday and Saturday, and 10 am to 4 pm Sunday. Admission is $8.80/3.30 adults/children.

The **historic boats museum** at Victoria Quay was undergoing a major overhaul at the time of writing. Ask at the Maritime Museum for an update.

Nearby is the restored warehouse known as **E Shed**, housing an international food court. The **E Shed Markets**, open from 10 am to 9 pm Friday, and 9 am to 5 pm weekends, boasts more than 100 stalls selling everything from fruit and vegetables to clever craft work to knick-knacks that you never knew you needed.

OTHER ATTRACTIONS

Fremantle is well endowed with parks, which include popular **Esplanade Reserve**, beside picturesque Fishing Boat Harbour off Marine Terrace.

World of Energy, at 12 Parry St, has some entertaining, educational displays tracing the development of gas and electricity. It is open 9 am to 5 pm Monday to Saturday, and 1 to 5 pm Sunday. Admission is free.

The city is a popular centre for craft workers of all kinds and one of the best places to find them is at the imaginative **Bannister St Craftworks**.

For Aboriginal art, head for **Indigenart**, at 82 High St, or **Creative Native**, opposite.

ACTIVITIES

The **Fremantle Leisure Centre** (☎ 9432 9533), at 10 Shuffrey St, has a full-sized pool, gymnasium, spa and saunas; pool entry is $3.50. You can party on the water with **Fremantle Yacht Charters** (☎ 9335 3844), which runs two-day sailing safaris to Rottnest Island, sleeping on the yacht and snorkelling in secluded bays, returning the following afternoon. All meals, snorkelling equipment and pickup at Fremantle train station are included in the price ($169). Fremantle Yacht Charters also does day sailing trips to Rottnest Island ($95), with a gourmet lunch and champagne.

ORGANISED TOURS

The Fremantle Tram (☎ 9339 8719) is in fact a bus that looks like an old-fashioned trolley car. It does tours ($8, 45 minutes) of historical Fremantle or the four harbours. It leaves from the town hall at Fremantle every hour on the hour from 10 am to 4 pm.

PLACES TO STAY

The *Fremantle Village Caravan Park* (☎ 9430 4866, 1 Cockburn St), on the corner of Rockingham Rd, has noisy sites and chalets (courtesy of its proximity to a very busy road). Powered sites cost $19 per night, mobile homes $55 and chalets $75. The *Woodman Point Caravan Park* (☎ 9434 1433), on Cockburn Rd 10km south of Fremantle, is well set up, with a pool and playground, but it also suffers from vehicle noise. Tent and caravan sites cost $18 for two, and chalets cost $55 to $85 a double.

Backpackers Inn Freo YHA (☎ 9431 7065, 11 Pakenham St) is arguably the best backpacker accommodation in the whole Perth area. It has a huge indoor recreation area, good kitchen facilities, clean bathrooms and comfortable rooms. It is run by the gorgeous Gary, who has overseen the renovation of two old buildings. Dorm beds cost $14, single rooms $20, twins and doubles $34 ($44 with air-con) and en suite double rooms $55. Non-YHA/HI members pay a few dollars more. Triples and family rooms are also available.

In a terrific location, equidistant between The Esplanade and South Terrace, *Port City Pirates* (☎ 9335 6635, [e] freopirates@ hotmail.com, 5 Essex St) is in a building that was originally the second pub built in Fremantle. At the time of writing it had recently come under new, competent management, which was enthusiastically improving and cleaning up the place. There are several

computers for Internet access, and a good outdoor recreation area. Dorm beds cost $17 and double rooms cost $45.

The *Norfolk Hotel* (☎ 9335 5405, 47 South Terrace), diagonally opposite the Fremantle Markets, has good-value singles/doubles for $40/60, doubles with en suite from $75 and family rooms from $90. The hotel has arguably the best beer garden in Perth. The stunning *Orient Hotel* (☎ 9336 2455, 39 High St), on the corner of Henry St, has won awards for its tasteful and sympathetic renovation. Single/double rooms cost $30/50. There is also a good restaurant/cafe.

The rambling *Tradewinds Hotel* (☎ 9339 8188, 66 Canning Hwy) in East Fremantle has purpose-built accommodation tacked onto a lovely century-old pub building. Standard doubles cost from $135; family rooms cost $160. Rooms with views of the river cost more. There's a pool in the private courtyard.

The ritziest hotel in town is the huge, four-star *Esplanade Hotel* (☎ 1800-998 201, 9432 4000, 46 Marine Terrace), on the corner of Essex St. Very comfortable double rooms start at $237, but ask about special packages. There are two heated swimming pools, spa and gym facilities.

B&B accommodation is a popular alternative in Fremantle; prices range from $50 to $100 for doubles. The tourist office has listings and can provide assistance with bookings.

Near South Beach, in South Fremantle, *Painted Fish* (☎ 9335 4886, [e] paintedfish@ optusnet.com.au, 37 Hulbert St) is a charming B&B-style place (without the breakfast) in a garden of sunflowers. It is full of personal touches (fun, decorative furniture, iron bedsteads, and lots of painted fish). Doubles with shared facilities (including kitchen) cost $55, or you can take the whole place (six people) for a bargain $110.

PLACES TO EAT

A highlight of Fremantle is the diverse range of cafes, restaurants, food halls and taverns. Many a traveller's afternoon has been whiled away sipping beer or drinking coffee and watching life go by from kerbside tables.

There's a concentration of places on South Terrace and another enclave at the western end of town near Fishing Boat Harbour.

South Terrace, Kings Square & Market Street

There are numerous cafes and restaurants in Fremantle's 'cappuccino strip', along South Terrace, all of which can be crowded on weekends if the weather is fine. Cruise the strip and take your pick.

Gino's (1 South Terrace), once a tailor's shop, is the type of place where you come for a quick coffee and end up spending the whole afternoon. The comforting menu here includes grilled calamari, lasagne and veal cutlets. A few doors down, *Dôme (13 South Terrace)* and *Old Papa's (17 South Terrace)* are both perennially popular for having leisurely breakfasts and watching the passing parade. The eggs Benedict ($9.50) at Dôme are filling and spot on, and its coffee would satisfy any coffee snob. *Falduzzi's (5 Bannister St)* has a reputation for making the best pizzas in Fremantle.

The historic *Sail & Anchor Hotel (64 South Terrace)*, built in 1854, has been impressively restored to recall much of its former glory. It specialises in locally brewed Matilda Bay beers; there's a brasserie serving snacks and meals on the 1st floor.

Just off South Terrace is the *Millennium Cinema Complex (25 Collie St)*, which has a variety of eateries including two cafes; *Into the Fryer*, a fish and chips joint, with special $6 deals and $4 children's menus; and a Japanese restaurant, *Kyo Sushi*, where you perch on stools and grab what takes your fancy from the conveyor belt.

If it's vast quantities of grease you're after, head for *Fast Eddy's (13 Essex St)*, not far from South Terrace. It also does good value breakfasts with bottomless cappuccinos.

Cafe Giordano, on Kings Square next to the town hall and tourist office, is an unsophisticated and unpretentious cafe serving coffee and toasted sandwiches. In the same area, the groovy *Market St Cafe*, next to the post office, does all-day breakfasts and heartier fare such as Philadelphia cheese steak ($5.50) and vegetarian focaccia ($6.80).

West End & Harbour

Vegetarians will be happy at *Hara Cafe (33 High St)* near the Orient Hotel, which has a variety of tasty dishes to eat in or take away. For Vietnamese fare, you could do worse than *Vung Tau (19 High St)*, which has spicy beef in a curry stew for $6.90 and fish in oyster sauce for $7.20. Next to the Round House, *Tea at the Round House* is open for breakfast, lunch and afternoon tea. It's worth a stop for the home-baked muffins and scones alone.

In the old fire station building, *Bengal Indian Curry House (18 Phillimore St)* does decent Indian and has good curry lunch specials.

There are a couple of converted wharf buildings down at Fishing Boat Harbour, with several places to eat. One contains the popular *Cicerello's*, on Mews Rd, which has been serving up top-notch fish and chips since 1903. Nearby, *Chunagon (46 Mews Rd)* is Fremantle's largest Japanese restaurant and offers the usual tempura, teriyaki, sashimi and sushi, as well as setprice crayfish menus.

In the adjacent wharf building are various low-budget eateries popular with families, including the *Fisherman's Kitchen* and *The Sicilian (47 Mews Rd)* – a huge plate of fish and chips and a mountain of salad at The Sicilian costs around $15.

East Fremantle

The renovated *E Shed* at Victoria Quay Docks has a variety of places to satisfy your hunger, including a large food court.

Captain Munchies (2 Beach St), a van parked (permanently) opposite the Flag and Whistle pub, will satisfy any urgent pangs of hunger – 24 hours a day. It has a phone and Internet lounge behind it.

The hip and groovy head under the Queen Victoria St and Stirling Hwy bridges. The *Left Bank Cafe, Bar & Restaurant (☎ 9319 1116, 15 Riverside Rd)*, an Edwardian riverside inn up from the East St jetty, is patronised by a lively young crowd in the downstairs cafe and bar. The restaurant upstairs has a more formal menu featuring dishes such as char-grilled kangaroo on parsnip mash (around $17). Try to get a table on the balcony.

Farther along Riverside Rd is the **Red Herring** *(☎ 9339 1611, 26 Riverside Rd)*, regarded as one of the best restaurants in WA. It does lunch and dinner daily as well as buffet breakfasts on weekends. The menu is long on fish and seafood, reflecting what's freshest at the market, and staples such as mustard-crusted sirloin of beef and Moroccan spiced chicken. Quality comes at a price: main courses cost $21.50 to $40.

ENTERTAINMENT

Fremantle buzzes at night. There are many venues in town with music and/or dancing.

The home of the 'big gig' is the much-lauded **Metropolis** *(52 South Terrace)*. At the **Newport Hotel** *(2 South Terrace)* there are live bands playing on most evenings. Down the road at the **Seaview Tavern** *(282 South Terrace)* you can listen to live acoustic music on Wednesday, Friday and Saturday.

The **Railway** *(44 Tydeman St)*, in North Fremantle, has regular live jazz on Saturday afternoon.

A large variety of talent performs regularly at the **Fly by Night Musicians Club** *(☎ 9430 5976)*, on Queen St, which specialises in ethnic and 'World' music. Tickets cost around $10 to $15.

Rosie O'Grady's *(23 William St)* is an Irish pub where you can hear live music (washed down with Guinness) three or four nights per week.

Latinos Restaurant *(☎ 9430 7797, 92 South Terrace)*, opposite the markets, has a live South American band from 8 pm Friday and Saturday (and Latino dance lessons at other times of the week). There's a good food menu if you want to make a night of it.

The **Flag and Whistle** *(☎ 9433 2055, 4 Beach St)*, on the corner of Parry St, has a 'word of mouth' session on Tuesday night for potential comedians to strut their stuff, and a reggae night on Sunday.

SHOPPING

Fremantle is not really a shopper's paradise, but some great and interesting bargains can always be found at the eclectic Fremantle Markets *(☎ 9335 2515)*, at the corner of South Terrace and Henderson St. Here you'll find pretty placemats, knitwear, hand-decorated overalls, pot plants, hand-made jewellery, antiques and bric-a-brac, and essential oils, among other things.

The best place in Fremantle for buying Aboriginal art (including some interesting etchings and lithographs by indigenous artists) is Indigenart, at 82 High St.

Moulitatas, at 25 Market St between the Market St Cafe and the post office, is a gift shop selling fun photo frames, vases and other objects.

GETTING THERE & AWAY

The Transperth *(☎ 13 6213)* train between Perth and Fremantle runs every 15 minutes or so throughout the day; tickets cost around $2.50.

There are countless buses between the Transperth City Busport (among other stops in Perth) and Fremantle. These include bus Nos 111, 106, 881, 103 and 158. Some buses travel via the Canning Hwy; others go via Mounts Bay Rd and the Stirling Hwy.

Ferries run from Perth's Barrack St jetty to Fremantle's East St jetty ($7 one way, $14 return) at 8.45 and 10 am and 12.30, 2 and 5.45 pm daily. They depart Fremantle for Perth at 11.30 am and 1.20, 3.15 and 5.30 pm. Call Oceanic Cruises *(☎ 9325 1191)* for information. The same group also runs a 'scenic' cruise from Perth, with commentary and complimentary tea and coffee ($9 one way, $14 return).

Captain Cook Cruises also operates cruises between Perth and Fremantle ($13 one way), departing Perth's Barrack St jetty at 9.45 am and 2 pm, and Fremantle's East St jetty at 11 am and 3.15 pm, with wine-tasting on the Fremantle-Perth journey.

The Fremantle airport shuttle *(☎ 9383 4115, fax 9383 4763)* departs Fremantle for the airport at 7, 8.45 and 10.45 am and 1.45, 3.45 and 9.30 pm in summer, and at 7.45, 9.45 and 11.45 am and 1.45, 3.45 and 10.30 pm in winter.

From the airport to Fremantle departures are approximately every two hours from 8 am to 10.30 pm (9 am to 11.30 pm in winter).

The price of $12 (domestic terminal) and $15 (international terminal) includes drop-off/pickup at your accommodation. It is advisable to book in advance for airport pickup/drop-off.

GETTING AROUND

You can see most of the sights of Fremantle on foot. The Fremantle Clipper Service is a free jump-on, jump-off bus that runs every 15 minutes from the train station in a loop around Fremantle, to Victoria Quay, the Maritime Museum, the markets, Samson House, the History Museum and the Arts Centre. It operates from 10 am to 6 pm. At the time of writing the service was only operating at weekends but local authorities had announced that it would soon run daily. Ask at the tourist office for an update.

Driving around is easy enough (once you master the one-way traffic system) but parking can be difficult. There are city car parks all around the centre of town, where you can leave your car for the whole day; these cost between $0.80 and $1 per hour. There are also plenty of ticket/meter parking spots, but these work out more expensive than the larger car parks.

Bicycles are available for hire from Fleet Cycles (☎ 9430 5414) at 66 Adelaide St. They cost from $20 per day, with discounts for longer-term rentals.

Scooters can be rented from Scootabout (☎ 9336 3471) at 37 Cliff St. Helmets are included in the rental charge of $15 for the first hour, $5 for each successive hour. You must be over the age of 18 and a credit card or cash bond is requested.

Around Perth

There's a wealth of attractions and activities around Perth, including the picturesque Perth Hills and Avon Valley, the traffic-free holiday resort of Rottnest Island, and the beaches along the coast north of the capital. Most of these places are only an hour or two away from Perth's city centre.

Rottnest Island

pop 400

'Rotto', as Rottnest Island is known by the locals, is a sandy island about 19km off the coast of Fremantle. It's 11km long, 5km wide and is extremely popular with Perth residents and visitors. Crystal-clear water offers excellent swimming and some of the southernmost coral in the world; a number of shipwrecks make for great snorkelling and diving. The island's beaches range from secluded coves to longer expanses of sand and surf (The Basin is the most popular, while Parakeet Bay is the place for skinny-dipping). The island is virtually traffic-free; most people hire bikes or bring their own.

History

There are signs of Aboriginal occupation dating from 7000 years ago, when a hill on a coastal plain became the island after being cut off by rising seas. However, the island was uninhabited when Europeans arrived.

Dutch explorer Willem de Vlamingh claimed discovery of Rottnest Island in 1696. He named it *Rotte-nest* ('rat's nest') because of the numerous king-size 'rats' (quokkas) he saw there, but the Aboriginal Nyungar tribe knew it as Wadjemup.

The Rottnest settlement was originally established in 1838 as a prison for Aborigines from the mainland – the early colonists had trouble imposing their ideas of private ownership on the nomadic Aborigines. Although there were no new prisoners after 1903, the existing prisoners had to serve out their sentences until 1920.

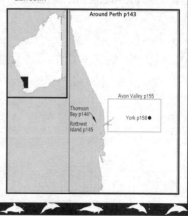

The island soon became an escape for Perth society. Only in the last 30 years, however, has it really developed as a popular day trip.

The island is a sacred site to the Nyungar because hundreds of their people died there; the buildings of the original prison settlement that held them are among the oldest in Western Australia (WA).

Orientation

The island's largest settlement is Thomson Bay; ferries arrive at the main ferry jetty

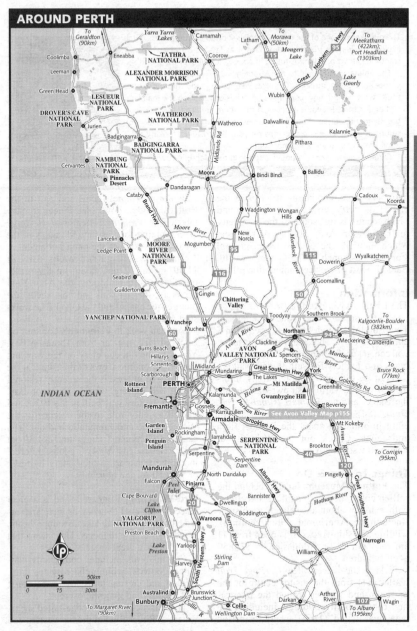

AROUND PERTH

To Geraldton (90km)

Yarra Yarra Lakes

Carnamah

Latham

To Morawa (50km)

Mongers Lake

To Meekatharra (422km); Port Headland (1303km)

Coolimba

Eneabba

TATHRA NATIONAL PARK

Coorow

Great Northern Hwy

Leeman

ALEXANDER MORRISON NATIONAL PARK

Lake Goorly

Green Head

Wubin

Wubin

LESUEUR NATIONAL PARK

DROVER'S CAVE NATIONAL PARK

Jurien

WATHEROO NATIONAL PARK

Watheroo

Dalwallinu

Kalannie

Badgingarra

Midlands Rd

Pithara

Ballidu

BADGINGARRA NATIONAL PARK

Cervantes

NAMBUNG NATIONAL PARK

Pinnacles Desert

Moora

Bindi Bindi

Ballidu

Cadoux

Koorda

Cataby

Dandaragan

Waddington

Wongan Hills

Brand Hwy

Moore River

Lancelin

MOORE RIVER NATIONAL PARK

Mogumber

New Norcia

Mortlock River

Dowerin

Wyalkatchem

Ledge Point

Seabird

Guilderton

Gingin

CHITTERING VALLEY

Toodyay

Southern Brook

Goomalling

To Kalgoorlie-Boulder (382km)

YANCHEP NATIONAL PARK

Yanchep

Muchea

Avon River

Northam

Clackline

Meckering

Cunderdin

Burns Beach

Hillarys

Sorrento

Scarborough

Midland

Mundaring

AVON VALLEY NATIONAL PARK

Spencers Brook

Mortlock River

To Bruce Rock (77km)

Great Southern Hwy

York

Goldfields Rd

Quairading

Rottnest Island

PERTH

Kalamunda

Helena R

Mt Matilda

Greenhills

INDIAN OCEAN

Fremantle

Gosnells

Karragullen

Gwambygine Hill

Darling River

Beverley

See Avon Valley Map p155

Armadale

Brookton Hwy

Mt Kokeby

Garden Island

Rockingham

Jarrahdale

SERPENTINE NATIONAL PARK

Brookton

Avon River

To Corrigin (95km)

Penguin Island

Serpentine

Serpentine Dam

Mandurah

North Dandalup

Albany Hwy

Pingelly

Great Southern Hwy

Falcon

Pinjarra

Peel Inlet

Dwellingup

Bannister

Hotham River

Cape Bouvard

Lake Clifton

YALGORUP NATIONAL PARK

Waroona

Boddington

Preston Beach

Murray River

Lake Preston

Yarloop

Stirling Dam

Williams

Narrogin

Harvey

South Western Hwy

Australind

Brunswick Junction

Darkan

Arthur River

Wagin

Bunbury

Collie R

Collie

Wellington Dam

To Albany (195km)

To Margaret River (90km)

0 25 50km

0 15 30mi

Quokkas

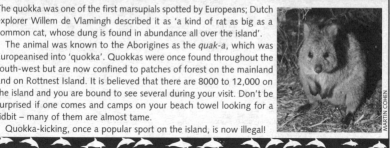

The quokka was one of the first marsupials spotted by Europeans; Dutch explorer Willem de Vlamingh described it as 'a kind of rat as big as a common cat, whose dung is found in abundance all over the island'.

The animal was known to the Aborigines as the *quak-a*, which was Europeanised into 'quokka'. Quokkas were once found throughout the south-west but are now confined to patches of forest on the mainland and on Rottnest Island. It is believed that there are 8000 to 12,000 on the island and you are bound to see several during your visit. Don't be surprised if one comes and camps on your beach towel looking for a tidbit – many of them are almost tame.

Quokka-kicking, once a popular sport on the island, is now illegal!

MARTIN COHEN

here. The accommodation office is at the end of the ferry jetty. An information and visitor centre is just south of the ferry jetty on Henderson Ave. The shopping area, which includes the post office, a general store, and a branch of the Commonwealth Bank, is west of the accommodation office.

Information

The island's visitor centre (☎ 9372 9752), just to the south of the main ferry jetty at Thomson Bay as you arrive, is open from 8 am to 5 pm daily. There, and at the museum, you can get useful publications, such as trail maps and leaflets for self-guided walking tours of the old settlement buildings, information on the various shipwrecks around the island, and the *Rottnest Island Bicycle Guide* ($4). The latter includes heaps of extra information about the island's flora and fauna. Check out the Web site at www.rottnest.wa.gov.au.

Things to See & Do

The **Rottnest Museum**, located behind the settlement's shopping mall, is excellent, with exhibits about the island, its history (including Aboriginal incarceration), wildlife and shipwrecks. It is open from 11 am to 4 pm daily. Admission is $2/0.50 adults/children.

Pick up the *Vincent Way Heritage Trail* leaflet ($1) from the visitor centre or the museum, and wander around the interesting, **convict-built buildings**, including the octagonal 'Quod' (1864), where the prison

cells are now hotel rooms and part of the Rottnest Lodge hotel (see Places to Stay later). The *Vlamingh Memorial Heritage Trail* walking-tour leaflet ($1) takes in the areas just outside of the main settlement.

There are free **guided walks** daily at 11.30 am and 2 pm, taking in the settlement's historic buildings, the Aboriginal cemetery, the sea wall and boat sheds, the picturesque chapel and the Quod. The walks start at the visitor centre.

You can walk to **Vlamingh's Lookout** on Lookout Hill, not far from Thomson Bay. You pass the old cemetery on the way and there's panoramic views of the island at the top. Also of interest is the recently restored **Oliver Hill Battery**, west of Thomson Bay. This gun battery was built in the 1930s and played a major role in the defence of the WA coastline and Fremantle harbour. You can do a 'Guns and Tunnels' tour at 1.30 pm daily. Tickets cost $9/4.50 adults/children, including transport to the battery by train, or $2/0.50 for the tour only.

Bird-Watching Rottnest Island is a great place for the avid twitcher, as there are varied habitats: coast, salt lakes, swamps, heath, woodlands and settlements. This means that you will see a great range of species.

Coastal birds include: cormorants; bartailed godwits; whimbrels; roseate, fairy, bridled and crested terns; oyster-catchers; reef herons; and majestic ospreys.

There is a colony of wedge-tailed shearwaters at Radar Reef at the far western end of the island and, at Phillip Point at the opposite end of the island, fairy terns nest on the sand. Parakeet Bay takes its name from the rock parrot, seen at many places on the coast feeding on sandfly larvae. Osprey can be seen along the southern coast from Strickland Bay to West End.

In the salt lakes you can see black swans, white-faced herons, red-necked avocets, ruddy turnstones, caspian terns, grey-tailed tattlers, stints and sandpipers. Even in Garden Lake, next to the village, you can see red-necked avocets, plovers and ruddy turnstones. Caspian terns breed near Government House Lake.

Ducks and teals are found in the swamps, and turtledoves, welcome swallows and red-capped robins in the woodlands.

In the settled areas are a great number of introduced birds such as the peafowl and natives such as the sacred kingfisher and rainbow bee-eater.

Majestic ospreys can be seen along Rottnest Island's southern coast.

AROUND PERTH

For more information, get *The Birdlife of Rottnest Island* by Denis Saunders and Perry de Rebeira ($14.95) from the visitor centre.

Rottnest Underwater The glass-bottom boat *Underwater Explorer* does up to five 'Reef and Wreck' tours daily, departing from the main ferry jetty at Thomson Bay. This fabulous 45-minute trip costs $16/10/45 adults/children/families. One of the daily tours is also a snorkelling tour ($20/12 adults/children; snorkelling gear hire $5),

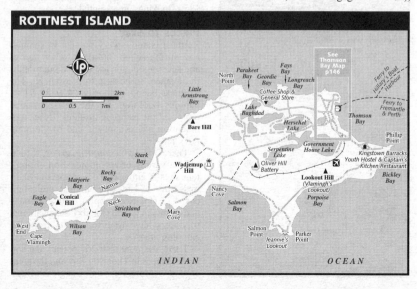

where you can get even closer to the reefs and shipwrecks. Contact Boat Torque Cruises (☎ 9221 5844) or the visitor centre to book in advance.

Some of Rottnest Island's shipwrecks are accessible to snorkellers, but getting to them requires a boat. Marker plaques around the island tell the sad tales of how and when the ships sank. The visitor centre sells copies of the useful *Rottnest Island Snorkellers' Guide* ($5), which covers 20 bays around the island.

Snorkelling and diving equipment, surfboards, boogie boards and fishing gear and

boats can be hired from Rottnest Malibu Diving (☎ 9292 5111), at Thomson Bay near the main ferry jetty. Two boat dives with all equipment provided (and including lunch) costs $110. Snuba Australia (☎ 9292 5919), at Pinky Beach, runs shallow-water diving, where you are connected to an inflatable raft and an oxygen supply through tubes and can dive down to 6m. No previous diving experience is necessary.

Organised Tours

A two-hour bus tour around the island ($12/6 adults/children) departs at 11.15 am and 1.15 pm daily; it's wise to book in high season. The tour visits the island's main **lighthouse**, on Bathurst Point, built in 1895 and which is visible 60km out to sea.

Rottnest Island Aquatic Adventures (☎/fax 9434 2737, 0419-863 602) runs day tours from Perth, with courtesy pickup in the CBD and transfer to the boat departure point in Fremantle. The itinerary includes viewing whales, dolphins and sea lions (seasonal), snorkelling at two different reefs/shipwrecks, barbecue lunch on board, beach walks and more snorkelling, at a cost of $135. (You can also hop on the boat at Thomson Bay for $85.) Bookings are essential.

Places to Stay

Rottnest Island is very popular in summer and during school holidays, when ferries and accommodation are booked out months in advance, so be sure to plan ahead. The Rottnest Island Authority (☎ 9432 9111) handles bookings for the self-contained units and the camping grounds; its accommodation office is at the end of the main ferry jetty.

There are two *camping areas*, which offer a variety of accommodation options: tent sites at either cost $5 per person (mattress hire is $4 for three nights) and cabins cost $22 (for two people), $30 (for four), and from $34 to $58 (for six). Be aware that travellers have reported thefts from the camping areas.

There are more than 250 houses and cottages for rent in Thomson Bay and the areas around Geordie, Fays and Longreach Bays.

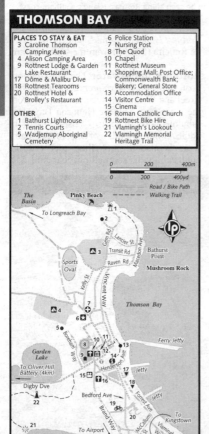

THOMSON BAY

PLACES TO STAY & EAT
3 Caroline Thomson Camping Area
4 Alison Camping Area
9 Rottnest Lodge & Garden Lake Restaurant
17 Dôme & Malibu Dive
18 Rottnest Tearooms
20 Rottnest Hotel & Brolley's Restaurant

OTHER
1 Bathurst Lighthouse
2 Tennis Courts
5 Wadjemup Aboriginal Cemetery
6 Police Station
7 Nursing Post
8 The Quod
10 Chapel
11 Rottnest Museum
12 Shopping Mall; Post Office; Commonwealth Bank; Bakery; General Store
13 Accommodation Office
14 Visitor Centre
15 Cinema
16 Roman Catholic Church
19 Rottnest Bike Hire
21 Vlamingh's Lookout
22 Vlamingh Memorial Heritage Trail

These range from refurbished villas and basic units to renovated older cottages and smart oceanfront units sleeping from four to eight people. Prices range from $124 to $203 per night for a four-bed unit/villa/cottage, and $231 to $379 for three nights. Linen, TVs, fans and microwaves can be hired at additional cost.

The **Kingstown Barracks Youth Hostel** (☎ 9372 9780), 1.2km from the ferry jetty, is housed in an old barracks built in 1936. Dorm beds cost from $16 for YHA/VIP members, $19 nonmembers (doubles cost $38/44 members/nonmembers). Linen can be hired and bookings are essential for the hostel (the office is open from 8 am to 5 pm Saturday to Thursday, 8 am to 8 pm Friday). This place has more than the appearance of an army barracks – part of the complex is often shared with school groups staying here on environmental awareness courses. Be warned that at busy times hot water for the showers is not always on tap. The kitchen facilities are adequate (there's also a cheap canteen-style restaurant) and the salvation is the communal lounge with its potbelly stove.

There are a couple of good places at the other end of the scale. The central core of the **Rottnest Hotel** (☎ 9292 5011), on Bedford Ave, was once the governor's mansion. All of the motel rooms have an en suite but the place is probably due for a facelift, and is expensive for the standard provided. B&B singles/doubles range from $85/100 (courtside rooms) and $100/120 (bayside rooms) low season, to $130/165 (courtside rooms) and $160/185 (bayside rooms) high season.

More upmarket and better value is the **Rottnest Lodge** (☎ 9292 5161), on Kitson St, which is based on the former Quod and boys reformatory school. These days it is far more inviting; there is a cafe, restaurant and private pool (the only one on the island). All rooms have en suite bathrooms and are decorated with cheery fabrics. The units range in price from quad rooms (sleeping six) for $184/280 during low/high season, to luxury lakeside rooms (sleeping three) for $150/240 low/high season.

Places to Eat

Just south of the main ferry jetty, **Dôme** is a pleasant licensed cafe (part of the successful chain throughout Perth), with great views over Thomson Bay. It does top-notch breakfasts, and gourmet focaccia, salads and pasta for lunch and dinner, as well as coffee and cakes anytime. Nearby, **Rottnest Tearooms** has good-value burgers and fish, fancy salads, a daily wok special ($12.50) and a decent selection of wine by the bottle or glass. There's also an above-average children's menu. Make sure you get a table on the verandah.

Brolley's Restaurant, in the Rottnest Hotel (☎ 9292 5011), serves average fare and meals heavily decorated with parsley garnish. At the Rottnest Lodge, the licensed **Garden Lake Restaurant** (☎ 9292 5161) has tables in the attractive courtyard.

Your best bet for a quick fix might be the sandwiches or gourmet pies fresh from the oven at the **bakery** in Thomson Bay's shopping mall, where there's also a well-stocked **general store**.

New at the time of writing was **Captain's Kitchen**, a canteen-style restaurant at the youth hostel. Open for breakfast, lunch and dinner, it offers great-value $6 meals (if you buy your ticket from the hostel office, $7 at the kitchen otherwise). Dinners feature a meat dish and a vegetarian option; lunch is a buffet.

Geordie Bay has a **coffee shop**, open during summer and school holidays. There is also a **general store** there.

Getting There & Away

There are regular ferry services to/from Rottnest Island, with additional services on weekends. The Rottnest Express (☎ 9335 6406) departs from the C Shed at Victoria Quay in Fremantle at 7.30, 9.30 and 11.15 am and 3.30 pm daily; fares are $34/10 adults/children for a same-day return, $39/14 for an extended stay. There is an additional trip at 6.45 pm on Friday. The return ferry leaves Rottnest Island at 8.30 and 10.30 am, noon and 4.30 pm.

Oceanic Cruises (☎ 9325 1191, 9430 5127) runs Seacats to Rottnest Island from

AROUND PERTH

Perth's Barrack St jetty and from the East St jetty in Fremantle. It costs $47/14 adults/children (same-day return) from Perth, $34/10 from Fremantle. There are four runs daily, with an extra trip on Friday at 6.15 pm from Perth, 7.15 pm from Fremantle. The return ferry leaves Rottnest Island at 9.30 and 10.45 am and 3.15 and 5 pm.

Boat Torque's (☎ 9430 5844, 9221 5844) Rottnest Shuttle leaves from the Barrack St jetty in Perth and from the Northport ferry terminal at the Emma Place jetty in North Fremantle. Same-day returns from Perth/Fremantle cost $45/35 adults/children. Boat Torque also runs the speedy, luxurious *Star Flyte* ferry twice daily from Hillary's Boat Harbour at Sorrento, north of Perth. A day return costs $45, extended returns $50.

Rottnest Air-Taxi (☎ 1800-500 006, 9292 5027) has a special same-day return fare starting at $120, and extended return for $220. This price is for a four-seater plane (three passengers) so can be a good deal.

Getting Around
Bicycles are the time-honoured way of getting around the island. The number of motor vehicles here is strictly limited, so cycling is a real pleasure. Furthermore, the island is just big enough (and with enough hills) to make a day's ride good exercise.

You can bring your own bike over on the ferry ($5) or rent one from Rottnest Bike Hire (☎ 9292 5105) in Thomson Bay. Adults' bikes cost $15 to $25 per day (depending on the number of gears). Children's bikes cost $10 to $18. The rate decreases for longer rentals. A refundable deposit of $25 is required and helmets (which must be worn) and locks (bicycles are often stolen) are provided.

There are two bus services. A free shuttle runs between the main accommodation areas on the island, departing from the accommodation office at the end of the main ferry jetty roughly every 20 minutes throughout the day, hourly after 6 pm. The Bayseeker is a jump-on, jump-off service that does a loop around the island. Day passes for unlimited travel are $5/2 adults/children.

South of Perth

The coast south of Perth appears softer than the often harsh landscape to the north. This is another popular resort area for residents of Perth, many of whom have holiday houses along this stretch of coast.

ROCKINGHAM
pop 66,000
Rockingham, 47km south of Perth, was founded in 1872 as a port, but in time that function was taken over by Fremantle. There's nothing especially fantastic about the town itself, although the beaches in the area are good. Rockingham is popular with people who want to swim with dolphins and look at fairy penguins and sea lions.

The well-organised Rockingham tourist office (☎ 9592 3464), at 43 Kent St, is open from 9 am to 5 pm weekdays, and 10 am to 4 pm weekends.

Things to See & Do
There are a couple of **wineries** in the region. Pick up information at the tourist office. Children will enjoy **Marapana Wildlife World**, on Paganoni Rd, Karnup, between Rockingham and Mandurah. It's open 9 am to 5 pm daily.

Worshippers of the industrial revolution can visit the **Kwinana power station**, WA's second largest after Muja (see Collie under Around Bunbury in The South-West chapter). Tours operate daily; call ☎ 9411 2440.

Close to Rockingham is **Penguin Island**, home to a colony of fairy penguins from late March to December, and **Seal Island**, with a colony of sea lions. Both islands are off-limits during the breeding season from June to August. Rockingham Sea Tours (☎ 9528 2004) operates tours to the islands daily ($7.50/4.50 adults/children).

Sea Kayak Tours (☎ 9259 0749) runs kayaking tours to Seal and Penguin Islands for $95 including all equipment. Rockingham Dolphin Cruises (☎ 0418-958 678) has daily tours to swim with bottlenose dolphins; the $130 cost includes wet suits. Courtesy bus services are available from Perth. If you only want to watch the dolphins, Dolphin Watch (☎ 0409-090 011) has daily tours.

The naval base of **Garden Island** is nearby and open during daylight hours, but it can be reached only by private boat. There are pleasant beaches, picnic and barbecue areas. Shy tammar wallabies can sometimes be seen on the bush fringes.

Places to Stay

The tourist office has a list of all accommodation options, including self-contained holiday flats.

There are several caravan parks in and around Rockingham, all with similar prices. The *Cee & See* (☎ 9527 1297), on the corner of Rockingham and Governor Rds, is on the beachfront, close to shops, and has barbecues. Tent/powered sites cost $11/16 per night for two people.

Down near the seafront, the *Rockingham Hotel* (☎ 9592 1828, 26 Kent St) has renovated singles/doubles for $35/50. *Leisure Inn* (☎ 9527 7777, 1 Simpson Ave), on the corner of Read St, is probably the nicer of the motels, with singles/doubles for $60/70.

Palm Beach B&B (☎ 9592 4444, 42 Thorpe St), off Patterson St, is run by a friendly Scottish couple and has spotless, comfortable singles/doubles for $55/80.

Places to Eat

Food is not Rockingham's strong point, but there are plenty of places to refuel. *Wok Wok*, on the Boardwalk, Railway Terrace, is a noodle bar down by the seafront and is about as good as it gets in not-so-rocky Rockingham. The place is painted in a kaleidoscope of vibrant colours and does good laksas ($9.50 to $11.50), noodle stir-fries and rice dishes – eat in or takeaway.

Capricci (7a Rockingham Rd) does passable pasta and Italian standards. *Rockingham Beach Seafood*, on Rockingham Beach Rd near Railway Terrace, is good for quick, easy fish and chips. The full gamut of takeaways is available along the foreshore.

Getting There & Away

You can get to Rockingham on Transperth bus No 866 from Perth's City Busport.

From Fremantle take bus No 920 from the train station.

MANDURAH
pop 29,000
Situated on the calm Mandurah Estuary, this is yet another popular beach resort and dormitory suburb, 75km south of Perth. The name comes from the Aboriginal *mandjar* ('meeting place'). Dolphins are often seen in the estuary, and the waterways in the area are noted for good fishing, prawning (March and April) and crabbing.

The well-equipped, helpful tourist office (☎ 9550 3999) is right on the estuary at Mandurah Terrace, on the Boardwalk. It is open from 9 am to 5.30 pm weekdays, and 9 am to 5 pm weekends.

Things to See & Do

Prolific birdlife can be seen on **Peel Inlet** and the narrow coastal salt lakes, **Clifton** and **Preston**, 20km to the south.

Full-day and short wildlife cruises are available on the MV *Peel Princess* (☎ 9535 3324) from the jetty in town (lunch cruise $34/17 adults/children, departs 10 am daily; one-hour canals and estuary tour $8/5, departs 10.30 and 11.30 am, and 1.30 and 3 pm).

You can 'do' dolphins with *Peel Supercat* cruises (☎ 9535 6591) at 11 am and 1 and 2.30 pm daily. Adults/children pay $10/5; boats depart from the Boardwalk jetty.

If you want to swim with the dolphins, Dolphin Encounters (☎ 0407-090 284), which is licensed by the Department of Conservation and Land Management (CALM), has 2½-hour cruises for $95.

If you want to go it alone, motorised dinghies can be hired from Mandurah Boat Hire (☎ 9535 5877), starting at $25 an hour; crab nets and bait can be supplied.

Things to see in town include the restored, limestone **Hall's Cottage** (open 1 to 4 pm Sunday), built in the 1830s, and the **Parrots of Bellawood Park** (☎ 9535 6732), on Pinjarra Rd about 11km south-east of Mandurah, which is open 10 am to 4 pm Thursday to Monday. Admission is $5/2.50 adults/children.

AROUND PERTH

There is no shortage of activities here, especially during holidays, and the options available for kids – including horse, boat, camel, sailboard, jet ski, yacht and cycle rides – will render parents penniless!

Places to Stay

Mandurah is one of those places close to a major city that becomes congested with holiday-makers at certain times of the year. The tourist office has a list of all of the accommodation options.

There is a string of caravan parks around town. *Settlers Estuary (☎ 9534 2121, 25 Olive Rd, Falcon)*, outside of town overlooking the estuary, is a 10-minute walk from ocean beaches. Tent/powered sites cost $14/16 and on-site vans cost $40 for two people.

The *Roof Top Inn (☎ 9586 8897, 113 Mandurah Terrace)* is a new backpacker hostel that was just about to open at the time of writing. Call for prices. *Mandurah Holiday Village (☎ 9535 4633, 124 Mandurah Terrace)* has cosy units with all the necessary facilities, starting at $85.

The top-notch *Atrium Resort (☎ 9535 6633, 65 Ormsby Terrace)* has all the facilities you could want, including in-house movies and indoor and outdoor pools, plus an affiliation with a nearby golf club. Doubles cost $95 midweek, $117 weekends.

Good B&B options around Mandurah include *Peel Manor House (☎ 9524 2838)*, on Fletcher Rd, Baldivis, a neo-Georgian mansion country retreat set in pleasant gardens just north of town. Standard doubles cost $120, spa rooms $185.

If you really want to get on the water why not rent a houseboat? *Dolphin Houseboat Holidays (☎ 9535 9898)*, Dolphin Pool, Mandurah Ocean Marina, has six-berth boats for $550 to $800 for two weekend nights in high season. Larger boats are also available.

Places to Eat

The ubiquitous *Dôme*, on Mandurah Terrace next to the tourist office, does excellent coffee, cakes and tasty sandwiches, pasta, salad and seafood, including a local speciality, quenelles of Mandurah crab with salt bread ($14.50). Most tables have wonderful panoramas of the estuary.

Mezzo Cafe (11 Halls Head Rd) overlooks Doddi's Beach and does healthy stone-grilled dishes.

Outlaws (149 Mandurah Terrace) does Mexican food and has a special $13.50 'feeding frenzy' on Monday and Tuesday evening.

If you want something creamy and cold to eat, head for the **Great Australian Ice Creamery** *(47 Mandurah Terrace)*. The name says it all.

Getting There & Away

To get to Mandurah, catch the Transperth express bus No 107 from the City Busport in Perth. From Fremantle bus No 126 to Rockingham connects with bus No 168, which continues to Mandurah.

Westrail (☎ 1800-099 150, 13 1053, 9326 2222) also operates a number of bus services that pass through Mandurah and stop at all the towns between Mandurah and Bunbury.

SOUTH WESTERN HIGHWAY

From Armadale, 29km south of Perth, the South Western Hwy skirts the Darling Range then heads south to Bunbury via Pinjarra and Harvey. Westrail (☎ 1800-099 150, 13 1053, 9326 2222) runs services that stop at all towns along the South Western Hwy in this section.

Serpentine & Jarrahdale

The peaceful area of forest running between Serpentine and Jarrahdale, some 50km from Perth, includes the Serpentine National Park. On Falls Rd, at the base of the park, are the **Serpentine Falls**; entry is $8 per car. There are walking tracks and picnic areas near the Serpentine Dam.

Established in 1871, Jarrahdale is an old mill town. There is a 7km **walking trail** from Jarrahdale to the South Western Hwy; it follows part of the old Rockingham-Jarrahdale timber railway. The town's **old post office**, built in 1880, serves as a tourist office (☎ 9525 5352); it's open from 10 am to 4 pm weekends and public holidays.

Places to Stay & Eat The *Serpentine Park Home Village* (☎ 9525 2528), on the South Western Hwy, near Serpentine Falls, is a caravan park with powered sites for $16 for two people.

At Jarrahdale, the *Jarrahdale Holiday Carriages* (☎ 9525 5780, 324 Jarrahdale Rd) offers accommodation in converted train carriages for $60 a double ($100 for two nights), with shared facilities. There's a similar operation at Whitby Falls: *Whitby Falls Railway Carriage Accommodation* (☎ 9525 5256, 101 Kiernan St, Mundijong) charges from $80 a double, including breakfast. Be warned: The carriages can get a bit cold! You can get good meals at the *Whitby Falls Coach House Restaurant*.

North Dandalup & Dwellingup

These towns, respectively 71km and 97km south of Perth, are jumping-off points for the nearby forests. **Old Whittaker's Mill**, off Scarp Rd near North Dandalup, is a great spot for bushwalking and camping.

Destroyed by fire in 1961, Dwellingup has been rebuilt and is now a busy timber town. It is the terminus for the popular Hotham Valley Tourist Railway (see Pinjarra later in this chapter). The Bibbulmun Track (see the boxed text in the Facts for the Visitor chapter) passes Dwellingup, some 500m to the east. Here, at Nanga Mill and Pool, is a night stopover for walkers on the track.

Dwellingup Adventures (☎ 9538 1127) runs canoeing day trips and overnight trips from Dwellingup, supplying all equipment. A 10km trip in a single-person kayak costs from $40 for a day, from $80 overnight.

The **Forest Heritage Centre** (☎ 9538 1395), on Acacia St, is a rammed-earth building in the shape of three leaves; the centre interprets the forest. There's a woodwork gallery and three well-labelled trails leading off from the centre, each of which takes about 20 minutes to walk. One of these is an Aboriginal biodiversity trail illustrating plants used by indigenous people for medicinal purposes; another leads to a reconstructed timber-getter's hut. The centre is open from 10 am to about 5 pm daily. Admission is $5/2/10 adults/children/families.

The best places to stay and eat in the area are at Serpentine and Pinjarra.

Pinjarra

Pinjarra, 86km south of Perth, has a number of old buildings picturesquely sited on the banks of the Murray River.

The Pinjarra tourist office (☎ 9531 1438) is in the historic building **Edenvale**, on the corner of George and Henry Sts. Behind the historic mud-brick post office is a pleasant picnic area and a wobbly **suspension bridge** that will test most people's coordination! **St John's Church**, built in 1861 from mud bricks, is beside the original 1862 **schoolhouse**. Picturesque **Cooper's Mill**, on Culeenup Island and only accessible by boat, was the first in the Murray region.

About 4km from the town is the **Old Blythewood Homestead**, an 1859 colonial farm that is now owned and operated by the National Trust.

Steam trains run from Pinjarra to Dwellingup (departing 11 am), through blooming wildflowers and jarrah forests, most Wednesdays and Saturdays from May to October. The cost is $21.50/13 adults/children return. Hotham Valley Tourist Railway (☎ 9221 4444) operates this and many other services throughout the winter months. Call for details and a timetable.

Places to Stay & Eat The *Pinjarra Caravan Park* (☎ 9531 1374, 95 Pinjarra Rd), 2km west of Pinjarra, has tent/powered sites for $12/14 for two people, and on-site vans/cabins from $35/45. The *Pinjarra Motel* (☎ 9531 1811, 131 South Western Hwy), just south of town, has singles/doubles for $55/65 including breakfast, and family rooms for $95. The motel has a nice pool.

The *Heritage Tearooms*, in the same building as the tourist office, serves light meals such as sandwiches and quiches for around $7.50.

Waroona, Yarloop & Harvey

Originally called Drakesbrook, Waroona is another popular holiday spot, 112km south of Perth. It is ideally situated, with Lakes Preston and Clifton to the west and the forests to the east. Following Preston Beach Rd from Waroona you come to **Yalgorup National Park**, which has bushwalking trails through the tuart trees. Trail leaflets are available from the Waroona tourist office (☎ 9733 1506) on the corner of Millar St and the South Western Hwy, which also has details on other activities in the area – from horse riding to water-skiing.

Some 13km south of Waroona is Yarloop, where there are restored engineering workshops dating from the steam and horse-drawn eras.

Inland from the south-west coast is the town of Harvey, in a bushwalking area of green hills to the north of Bunbury. There are a few historic buildings in town; outside there are dam systems (Harvey Weir and Stirling Dam) and some beautiful waterfalls nearby. The Harvey Districts tourist office (☎ 9729 1122) is on the South Western Hwy. Behind the tourist office is **Stirling's Cottage**, modelled on a cottage built on the site in the 1880s, which was for a short time the home of May Gibbs, author of the children's classic *Snugglepot & Cuddlepie*. The cottage is set in a pretty garden and there's a lovely, short river walk – great for a leg-stretch if nothing else.

Places to Stay & Eat There is a range of accommodation in this region. In Waroona, campers can head to the *Waroona Caravan Village (☎ 9733 1518, 311 Logue St)*, which has tent/powered sites for $10/12.

The charming *Drakesbrook Guesthouse (☎ 9733 1245, 111 South Western Hwy)* has B&B for $60 a double, including complimentary Devonshire tea on arrival. The *Tea Garden Cottage (136 South Western Hwy)* is a good place, with a shady garden for snacks and light lunches. The toasted sandwiches ($4.50) are the best in the south-west.

In Yarloop, the 1890 timber *Old Mill Guest House (☎ 9733 5264, 113 Railway Parade)* looks quaint from the outside, but inside the mostly single rooms with shared bathrooms are pretty basic. However, at $15 a night, who's complaining?

In Harvey, the *Rainbow Caravan Park (☎ 9729 2239, 199 King St)* has tent/powered

sites for $7/15 and on-site vans for $30 for two people. The *Wagon Wheels Motel (☎ 9729 1408)*, on Uduc Rd, has singles/doubles for $50/60 and a decent restaurant. *Stirling's Cottage*, behind the tourist office on the South Western Hwy, is good for snacks and light lunches.

Darling Range

The Darling Range – more commonly known as the Perth Hills – is popular for picnics, barbecues and bushwalks. There are also excellent lookouts from where you can see Perth and farther down the coast. Araluen Botanic Park with its constructed waterfalls, Mundaring Weir and Gardens, Gooseberry Hill and Kalamunda National Parks, and Lake Leschenaultia are all places of interest.

One fascinating aspect of the Darling Range is its geological diversity – in the range you can explore evidence of the break-up of Gondwanaland (formerly one of two ancient supercontinents). *The Hills Forest* is a good, free pamphlet produced by CALM.

KALAMUNDA

The township of Kalamunda is about a 30-minute drive east from Perth, on the crest of the Darling Range. The area had its beginnings as a timber settlement in the 1860s, but the clean air and magnificent bush later attracted Perth and Fremantle residents – and more recently British migrants – to this forest getaway, now very much an outer suburb of Perth. From Kalamunda, there are fine views over Perth to the coast.

The quaint **Stirk's Cottage** (1881) is built of mud brick and shingle. Just north of Kalamunda, off Gooseberry Hill Rd, **Gooseberry Hill National Park**, with the amazing Zig-Zag Scenic Drive, is well worth the trip for spectacular views of the city. At **Kalamunda National Park** you can walk, rest and picnic in beautiful surroundings. There are also a number of wineries (Hainault Vineyard and Darlington Estate), plant nurseries and arts-and-craft places nearby.

South of Kalamunda, just off Brookton Hwy, is **Araluen Botanic Park** (☎ 9496 1171), a real gem; get to it from Croydon Rd, Roleystone.

Originally constructed in the 1920s by the Australian Youth League as a bush retreat the park was neglected for many years and became overgrown. But in recent years, the almost-'archaeological' excavations have revealed elaborate garden terraces, waterfalls and an ornamental pool, all surrounded by many species of tall trees. There are barbecues and a restaurant.

The best time to visit is in spring when the tulips are in flower. Araluen Botanic Park is open from 9 am to 6 pm daily. Entry is $3/1 adults/children (higher in tulip season).

Places to Stay & Eat

The *Kalamunda Hotel* (☎ *9257 1084, 43 Railway Rd*) has no-frills doubles for $50. Numerous B&Bs are tucked away in the hills and valleys. At *Villa du Lac* (☎ *9293 3906, 58 Betti Rd*), a pleasant family home, B&B costs $30 to $40 per person. Another good option is *Whistlepipe Cottage* (☎ *9291 9872, 195 Orange Valley Rd*), set in a shady garden. B&B costs $45/80 singles/doubles.

If you are after coffee and a snack then try *Coffee Time*, on Central Court, Kalamunda, or *Village Coffee Shoppe*, on Haynes St. *Thai on the Hill* (☎ *9293 4312, 2 Haynes St)*, on the corner of Railway Rd, does good, spicy food and takeaway. Locals recommend *Chalet Rigi* (☎ *9293 1261)*, on Mundaring Weir Rd, five minutes out of Kalamunda. For light lunches and afternoon teas surrounded by flowers, head for the *Rose Heritage Tea Rooms*, at Melville Nursery, Masonmill Rd, Carmel, a short drive south-east.

Getting There & Away

Transperth has about six different bus routes serving Kalamunda. Bus Nos 300 and 302 depart from Perth's City Busport, travelling via Maida Vale and the Great Eastern Hwy. Bus Nos 305 and 292 go to Kalamunda via Wattle Grove and Lesmurdie. Taking one route out and the other back makes for an interesting circular tour.

MUNDARING
pop 1900

Mundaring, in the ranges only 35km east from Perth, is the site of the Mundaring Weir – a dam built some 100 years ago to supply water to the goldfields more than 500km to the east. The reservoir has an attractive setting and there are walking tracks nearby.

The Mundaring tourist office (☎ 9295 0202), at The Old School on Great Eastern Hwy, is open from 10 am to 4 pm Monday to Saturday, 10am to 1 pm Sunday. Pick up a copy of the useful brochure, *Mundaring: The Essential Guide to the Heart of the Hills* ($2).

The **CY O'Connor Museum** (☎ 9295 2455), in the old pumping house at the weir, has exhibits about the water pipeline to the goldfields – in its time one of the world's most amazing engineering feats (see the boxed text 'Where Water is Like Gold!' in The Southern Outback chapter). At the time of writing the museum was about to close for an extended period for refurbishment and improvements. Ask at the tourist office for an update.

North of the Great Eastern Hwy, near the village of Chidlow, is the beautiful, freshwater **Lake Leschenaultia**, ideal for picnics, bushwalking and swimming. Entry is $7 per car.

The 16-sq-km **John Forrest National Park**, near Mundaring, was the state's first national park. It has protected areas of jarrah and marri trees, native fauna, waterfalls and a pool. Entry is $8/3 cars/motorcycles.

Places to Stay & Eat

The *Djaril Mari YHA Hostel* (☎ *9295 1809)*, on Mundaring Weir Rd, close to the weir, 8km south of town, is a little more upmarket than regular hostels. It is popular with Bibbulmun Track bushwalkers and school/scout groups, so book ahead. Beds in four- or six-bed rooms cost $14/17 YHA members/nonmembers. Staff will prepare a hot meal on request. You can also pitch a tent in the hostel grounds for $10 per person and have full use of the hostel facilities. Nearby, the *Mundaring Weir Hotel* (☎ *9295 1106)*, on Mundaring

Weir Rd, is exceedingly popular with Perth escapees. Its heritage-style self-contained units, grouped around a lovely pool and terraced garden, cost from $70 per night. Weekend rates are higher but dinner is included.

The historic *Mahogany Inn (☎ 9295 1118, 4260 Great Eastern Hwy, Mahogany Creek)* dates from 1842. Its comfortable singles/doubles cost $70/120, including continental breakfast.

If you're looking for a gourmet, luxury retreat, head for the multi-award-winning *Loose Box (☎ 9295 1787, e loosebox@ ozemail.com.au, 6825 Great Eastern Hwy)*. The restaurant here has long been regarded as one of Australia's best, and chef Alain René Fabrègues is so good that he's been prevented from entering any more cooking competitions! Stunning, spacious cottages with delectable furnishings have been built in the restaurant's grounds. Quality comes at a price – from $220 a double, with midweek dinner packages available – but if you want a treat, it is worth the splurge.

A good place to stop for a light lunch or snack near the weir is *Lavender Garden & Tea Rooms*, on Mundaring Weir Rd, which has shady tables in a unique bush setting peppered with lavender bushes. The menu features lavender-flavoured cakes, lavender tea and more familiar staples such as home-made soup with lavender bread ($7) and Ploughman's lunch ($11.50). The gardens are planted with 20 different varieties of lavender.

WALYUNGA NATIONAL PARK

The Avon River cuts a narrow gorge through the Darling Range at Walyunga National Park in Upper Swan. This 18-sq-km park is off the Great Northern Hwy, 40km north-east of Perth. There are walking tracks along the river and it's a popular picnic spot.

The **bushwalks** include a 5.2km return walk to Syd's Rapids as well as a 1.2km Aboriginal Heritage Trail. Perhaps the best trail is the 10.6km Echidna Loop, which has tremendous views over the Swan and Avon Valleys. For information call CALM in Mundaring (☎ 9295 1955).

The park has one of the largest known camp sites of the Nyungar people; the camp site was still in use last century. The area may well have been occupied by Aborigines for more than 6000 years.

Avon Valley

The green and lush Avon Valley looks very English (in spring at least, when it's rich in wildflowers) and proved a delight to home-sick early settlers. In early 1830 food short-ages forced Governor Stirling to dispatch Ensign Dale to search the Darling Range for arable land – soon after, he 'discovered' the Avon Valley. In fact, what he found was the upper reaches of the Swan River that flows through Perth, but it was presumed that they were two separate rivers. They are in fact the same river, but it changes name from the Swan to the Avon as it crosses the Great Northern Hwy. The valley was first settled in 1830, only a year after Perth was founded, so there are many historic buildings in the area. The picturesque Avon River is very popular with canoeing enthusiasts.

Getting There & Away

Northam and Toodyay are connected to Perth by Westrail trains from the East Perth terminal; there are two services on Monday, Wednesday and Friday and one service on other days. Fares from Perth to Toodyay are $9.70/19.40 one way/return, to Northam $11.40/22.80.

You can get to York on the Westrail bus, which runs once daily (except Saturday) via Mundaring and Northam; the cost from Perth is $9.70.

The best way to see the valley is by car as this allows you the flexibility to make stops and detours along the way.

TOODYAY
pop 800

This charming, small town is only 85km north-east of Perth. It has numerous old classified buildings, many of them built by convicts. Toodyay was declared an historic town by the National Trust in 1980.

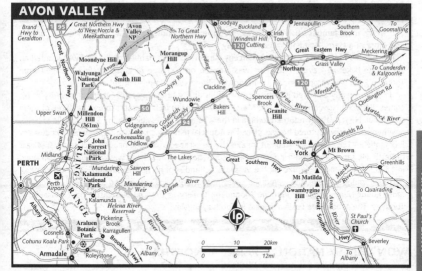

AVON VALLEY

The town was originally known by the name Newcastle – Toodyay (pronounced '2J'), from the Aboriginal word *duidgee* ('place of plenty'), was applied in 1910.

A big folk-music festival is held ion Toodyay during the Queen's Birthday long weekend (September/October).

Things to See & Do

The local tourist office (☎ 9574 2435) is in **Connor's Mill**, Stirling Terrace, which still houses a working flour mill. It's open from 9 am to 5 pm Monday to Saturday, and 10 am to 5 pm Sunday. Admission to the mill is $2.50/2 adults/children.

The **Old Newcastle Gaol Museum**, on Clinton St, was built in the 1860s. The Moondyne Gallery inside the museum tells the story of bushranger Joseph Bolitho Johns (see the boxed text 'Moondyne Joe' in this chapter). Admission is $3/2 adults/children. Also in town is the historic **St Stephen's Church**, built in 1862.

Coorinja, the oldest inland **winery** in WA, is located some 5km from Toodyay. It began operating in the 1870s, and now specialises in fortified wines, particularly port. It is open Monday to Saturday.

Places to Stay & Eat

There are three similarly priced caravan parks in Toodyay. The best is **Hoddywell** (☎ 9574 2410, 330 Clackline Rd, Hoddy's Well), where there is also an archery park. Powered sites cost $12 and camping costs $4 per person.

Motel-style rooms at the **Freemasons Hotel** (☎ 9574 2201, 125 Stirling Terrace) cost $65/75 singles/doubles.

The Toodyay tourist office has a list of recommended B&Bs, including **Pecan Hill Guesthouse** (☎ 9574 2636), on Beaufort St, which has single/double rooms for $55/75 midweek and $65/85 weekends.

Also recommended is the **Ipswich View** (☎ 9574 4038, 45 Folewood Rd), which has similar prices as the Pecan Hill Guesthouse. It can also provide an evening meal ($20) on request.

There are a few eating places on Stirling Terrace, including a bakery, **Wendouree Tearooms** and **Stirling House Cafe** (for light lunches and afternoon teas).

Connor's Restaurant, behind the tourist office, is the best place in town for meals, and is popular with day-trippers. Both of the town's **pubs** do good counter meals.

Moondyne Joe

The west's most famous bushranger was Joseph Bolitho Johns, known as Moondyne Joe, but he was more of a Harry Houdini than a Ned Kelly.

Transported to Western Australia for larceny, he arrived in Fremantle in 1853 and was granted an immediate ticket-of-leave. In 1861 he was arrested on a charge of horse-stealing, escaped from Toodyay gaol, was recaptured, and sentenced to three years' imprisonment.

He subsequently achieved infamy because of his ability to escape rather than the severity of his crimes. Between November 1865 and March 1867 he made four attempts to escape, three of them successful. He repeatedly returned to hide in the wild and inaccessible Darling Range while at large.

When eventually captured he was placed in a special reinforced cell with triple-barred windows in Fremantle. In 1867 when allowed out for exercise he escaped again and headed back to the hills east of Perth. He served more time in Fremantle prison when recaptured and was conditionally pardoned in 1873. After release he worked in the Vasse district and kept his nose clean until his death in 1900.

He is reputed to have discovered the caves near Margaret River, named after him. To find out more about Moondyne Joe, visit the Moondyne Gallery at the Old Newcastle Gaol Museum in Toodyay. The Moondyne Festival is held in Toodyay in May.

AVON VALLEY NATIONAL PARK

This national park is 45km from Midland and access is along Toodyay and Morangup Roads. Features of the park are the granite outcrops, transitional forests and diverse fauna. The Avon River flows through the centre of the park in winter and spring, but is usually dry at other times.

The Avon Valley National Park is the northern limit of the jarrah forests, and the jarrah and marri are mixed with wandoo woodland. The two species of wandoo *(Eucalyptus wandoo* and *E. accedens)* grow in the heavy, clay soils; deep-rooted jarrah grows on the well-drained higher slopes; and the marri grows farther down the slopes in moist, deep soil.

Many bird species make use of the diverse habitats in this forest – species seen are rainbow bee-eaters, honeyeaters, kingfishers and rufous treecreepers. Animals and reptiles live in the understorey: Honey possums and western pygmy-possums hide among the dead leaves, and skinks and geckos are everywhere. Predators such as foxes and cats are a real problem and CALM is trying to eradicate them.

There are *camp sites* – a small charge is payable – with basic facilities such as pit toilets and barbecues; contact the ranger (☎ 9574 2540). Entry for cars is $8.

NORTHAM
pop 7500

Northam, the major town of the Avon Valley, is a busy farming centre on the railway line to Kalgoorlie-Boulder. The line from Perth once ended here and miners had to make the rest of the weary trek to the goldfields by road.

Northam is a likable country town, with some fine heritage buildings that have been proudly restored. It is packed on the first weekend in August every year for the start of the gruelling 133km Avon Descent for powerboats, kayaks and canoes.

The Avon Valley tourist office (☎ 9622 2100) is located on the banks of the Avon River at 2 Grey St. Open from 9 am to 5 pm daily, it is run by friendly, knowledgeable staff and has information about Northam and the entire Avon Valley. You can also book train and bus travel here. There are showers and toilets for weary travellers passing through.

Things to See & Do

The 1836 **Morby Cottage** served as Northam's first church and school, and it now houses a museum, open from 10.30 am to 4 pm Sunday. Admission is $2. The **old train station**, listed by the National Trust, has been restored and turned into a museum;

it is open from 10 am to 4 pm Sunday and admission is $2. Also of interest in town is the colony of **white swans** on the Avon River, descendants of birds introduced from England in the early 20th century.

Annual events in Northam include the **Vintage on Avon** vintage sports car rally held on the last weekend in March, and the Avon River Festival and Descent in late July/early August.

Hot-air ballooning over the Avon Valley is a memorable experience. From March to November, Windward Balloon Adventures (☎ 9621 2000) has early-morning flights for $190 per person.

Places to Stay
The *Northam Caravan Park* (☎ 9622 1620), on the Great Eastern Hwy, has really picked up in the past few years and has new on-site vans and very helpful staff. Vans cost from $25 to $45 (with en suite) per night; tent/powered sites cost $5/12 per person.

The *Colonial Tavern* (☎ 9622 1074, 197 Duke St), on the corner of Morrell St, was built in 1907. Its spotlessly clean rooms are a bargain at $25 per person.

The aptly named *Northam Motel* (☎ 9622 1755, 13 John St) is the only motel in town. Clean singles/doubles cost $55/65; some rooms have been refurbished.

The friendly *Shamrock Hotel* (☎ 9622 1092, 112 Fitzgerald St) is the best place in town, with elegant en suite double/triple rooms for $99/119 and spa rooms for $125 to $155. It's a shame all country towns don't have accommodation of this quality.

The White Swans of Northam

White swans were originally introduced to Western Australia in 1896 by British colonists. The story goes that the birds were brought to Northam by the town's mayor, Oscar Bernard. The swans made their home on the Avon River, which, by chance, provided a perfect habitat and breeding ground for them, with its small islands and thickly covered riverbanks.

The swans are protected by a local warden, and are fed daily near the suspension bridge.

An excellent out-of-town B&B highly recommended by readers is the rustic *Stackallan Homestead* (☎ 9622 7206, Lot 1005 Henty Place) on the southern edge of town, which is homely and comfortable and has doubles from $105.

Places to Eat
At the tourist office, *Cafe Fiume (1 Grey St)* has a superb outlook over the Avon River. Good traditional Italian cooking and seriously wicked cakes are on offer from 9 am to 5 pm and for dinner on Friday.

Gates Cafe (112 Fitzgerald St), at the Shamrock Hotel, does excellent breakfasts, and a new take on counter meals, with an inventive, Mediterranean-style menu that includes veal saltimbocca ($17), seafood crepes ($12) and prawn risotto ($16).

For a steak bigger than your plate, and, according to the locals, top quality and value, head for *End of the Road Steakhouse (☎ 9623 2273)*, on Goomaling Rd. Bookings are advisable.

If you're craving some MSG, head for *Mann Wah Chinese*, on Fitzgerald St, which has main courses from $12 to $15.

Northam's best-kept secret (until now) is the restaurant at the *Colonial Tavern (☎ 9622 1074, 197 Duke St)*, where Erica, the proprietor, whips up a storm in the kitchen – dinner only.

YORK
pop 2800
The oldest inland town in WA, York is 97km from Perth. York was first settled in 1831, only two years after the Swan River Colony. The settlers here saw similarities in the Avon Valley to their native Yorkshire, so Governor Stirling bestowed the name York on the region's first town.

Convicts were introduced to the region in 1851 and contributed to the development of the district; the ticket-of-leave hiring depot was not closed until 1872, four years after transportation to WA had ceased.

During the gold rush, York prospered as a commercial centre, equipping miners who were travelling overland to Southern Cross and beyond.

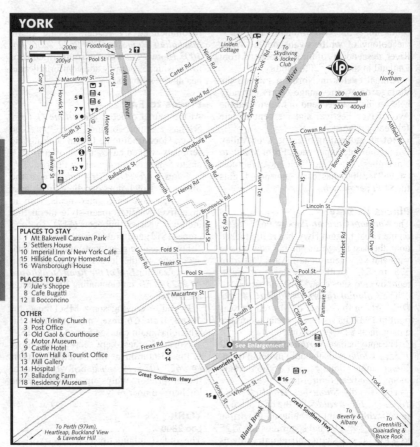

YORK

Footbridge

Pool St
Macartney St
Grey St
Howick St
Low St
South St
Monger St
Avon Tce
Railway St
Balladong St

Avon River

PLACES TO STAY
1 Mt Bakewell Caravan Park
5 Settlers House
10 Imperial Inn & New York Cafe
15 Hillside Country Homestead
16 Wansborough House

PLACES TO EAT
7 Jule's Shoppe
8 Cafe Bugatti
12 Il Bocconcino

OTHER
2 Holy Trinity Church
3 Post Office
4 Old Gaol & Courthouse
6 Motor Museum
9 Castle Hotel
11 Town Hall & Tourist Office
13 Mill Gallery
14 Hospital
17 Balladong Farm
18 Residency Museum

To Linden Cottage
To Skydiving & Jockey Club
To Northam

Carter Rd
Ninth Rd
Bland Rd
Spencers Brook – York Rd
Avon River
Cowan Rd
Atfield Rd
Osnaburg Rd
Newcastle St
Bouverie St
Northam Rd
Pioneer Dve
Tenth Rd
Avon Tce
Lincoln St
Herbet Rd
Eleventh Rd
Henry Rd
Brunswick Rd
Alfred St
Grey St
Ulster Rd
Ford St
Fraser St
Pool St
Pool St
Suburban Rd
Panmure Rd
Macartney St
Clifford St
South St
Frews Rd
14
See Enlargement
18
Henrietta St
17
Great Southern Hwy
16
15
Forrest St
Wheeler St
Bland Brook
Great Southern Hwy
York Rd

To Perth (97km),
Heartleap, Buckland View
& Lavender Hill

To Beverly & Albany
To Greenhills, Quairading & Bruce Rock

A stroll down York's main street, with its restored old buildings, is a real step back in time. In fact, the many intact colonial and Victorian buildings have earned York the National Trust classification of 'historic town'. This is the most atmospheric spot to base yourself for spending a short break in the Avon Valley.

Most of the activity happens along Avon Terrace, very much the focal point of York. The tourist office (☎ 9641 1301) is in the old town hall on Avon Terrace.

South-east of York, also on the Avon River, is **Beverley**, founded in 1838 and named after a town in Yorkshire. It isn't worth a detour, although it is noted for its small **aeronautical museum** (☎ 9646 1555) and a couple of good examples of Art-Deco architecture. You can try your hand at **gliding** there, courtesy of the Beverley Soaring Society (☎ 9646 1015, Friday to Sunday only).

Things to See & Do

There are many fine, old buildings. The old **town hall**, the **Castle Hotel** (built in 1853), the old **police station**, and the **Old Gaol & Courthouse** and **Settlers House** are all places of interest. The old gaol and court-house includes a main law court, the old courtroom, prison cell block and exercise yard, troopers cottage and stables with a carriage display.

The **Residency**, on Brook St, was built in the 1850s. It now houses a museum of York's history, with fascinating exhibits ranging from an antique egg rack and butter churn to old medical instruments, furniture and photos of York through the ages. It is open from 1 to 3 pm Tuesday to Thursday, and 1 to 5 pm weekends. Admission is $2.

The **Holy Trinity Church**, on Pool St by the Avon River, was completed in 1854. It contains glass designed by the WA artist Robert Juniper (see Painting under Arts in the Facts about Western Australia chapter) and a rare pipe organ with eight bells. The **suspension bridge** across the Avon was built in 1906.

York's classy **Motor Museum**, on Avon Terrace, is a must for vintage-car enthusiasts. The cars range from an 1894 Peugeot to the Saudi Williams driven by Alan Jones, the 1980 Formula One world champion. The museum is open from 9 am to 5 pm daily. Admission is $7/2 adults/children.

The **Mill Gallery**, housed in a converted flour mill on Henrietta St, exhibits and sells art, craft and jarrah furniture by local artisans. It is open from 10 am to 5 pm daily.

Historic **Balladong Farm**, established in the 1830s, houses a museum focusing on the lives of early pioneering families. Admission is free, but the place is a bit of a mess. Equidistant between York and Beverley is **Gwambygine Park**, where there is a viewing tower over a permanent pool on the Avon River. It's a good spot for picnicking and barbecues.

York has earned a reputation as the state's **skydiving** centre; the drop zone is about 3km from town. The Perth-based Skydive Express (☎ 1800-355 833, 9444 4199) does tandem jumps for $220.

York is a festival town. It has the Antique and Collectors fair at Easter, the Daffodil Festival in mid-August and a Jazz Festival in September. The agricultural show is held in September.

Places to Stay

The *Mt Bakewell Caravan Park* (☎ 9641 1421), on Eighth Rd, has powered sites for $15 and on-site vans for $34.

The *Imperial Inn* (☎ 9641 1010, 83 Avon Terrace) offers quaint budget singles/doubles with shared facilities for $30/70. If you stay two nights the third is free. The historic *Settlers House* (☎ 9641 1096, 125 Avon Terrace) was originally a staging post and guesthouse for goldfields travellers and once housed WA's first provincial newspaper. The historic part of the building is like a step back in time; accommodation is in modern motel-style rooms out the back, and priced from $59/69 singles/doubles.

There are a number of quality B&Bs and farmstays in the region; inquire at the tourist office. *Hillside Country Homestead* (☎ 9641 1065), on Forrest St, is highly recommended. It has rooms in the Edwardian home, and rammed-earth units starting at $60 for doubles, including a hearty country breakfast. *Wansborough House* (☎ 9641 2887, 22 Avon Terrace), just over Bland Brook on the road to Beverley, offers B&B in a secluded setting for a similar price.

Greenhills Inn (☎ 9641 4095), on Greenhills Rd, Greenhills, 22km east of York, is a beautifully restored homestead offering comfortable and welcoming B&B singles/doubles from $55/95. Take York Rd towards Quairading, then follow the signs to Greenhills.

Places to Eat

All of the eateries are along Avon Terrace. *Jule's Shoppe (121 Avon Terrace)* does hearty sandwiches, exquisite pasties and some great Lebanese shish kebabs with either meat or vegetable patties ($6). *Cafe Bugatti*, across the road, serves mediocre Italian food (spaghetti and lasagne for $8.50).

Il Bocconcino, next to the town hall, serves distinctly un-Italian fare such as a smoked-salmon open sandwich ($8.50) and pumpkin and roasted capsicum soup ($5.50).

The *New York Cafe* at the Imperial Inn has a menu that includes fish and chips, New York burgers ($10.50) and Mexican tacos ($11.50).

North Coast

The windswept coast north of Perth, along State Hwy 60 through Yanchep National Park to Lancelin, has great scenery, with long sand dunes, but it quickly becomes the inhospitable terrain that deterred early visitors. Although the beaches here look inviting, the reality is that they are usually pretty windy – better for water sports than sun-worshipping.

Getting There & Away

Having your own wheels is your best bet for travelling this part of the coast. Otherwise, you can take a Transperth train from Perth to Joondalup, followed by bus No 490 as far as Two Rocks.

Lancelin Lodge YHA (see Places to Stay & Eat under Ledge Point & Lancelin in this chapter) operates Catch-a-Bus (☎ 9655 2020), which picks up in Perth on Monday, Wednesday and Friday and runs to Lancelin for $20 one way (sailboards are $5 extra). Staff might drop you off at Seabird or Ledge Point on request.

Lancelin is the first stop on Easyrider's (☎ 9226 0307) 'Up North' tour. It departs on Thursday from Perth (see under Bus in the Getting Around chapter).

YANCHEP

The first break in Perth's northward urban sprawl is Yanchep, 51km north of Perth, at the end of the Swan Coastal Plain. The name comes from the Aboriginal *yanget*, after the bulrushes at the edge of the lakes in the area.

Yanchep National Park (☎ 9561 1004) has natural bushland with tuart forests, some fine caves and Loch McNess. Entry to the park is $8 per car. The visitor centre is open from 9 am to 5 pm daily. The park features fauna such as the honey possum, grey kangaroo, bandicoots, reptiles and a host of water birds. The koala, which is not indigenous to the west, can also be seen here in a special large enclosure. The limestone **Crystal Cave** is open daily. Entry is $5/2 adults/children.

There are plenty of bushwalking trails. A guide was being prepared at the time of writing; ask about it at the visitor centre. The 28km **Yaberoo Budjara Aboriginal Heritage Trail** follows a chain of lakes used by the Yaberoo people.

Yanchep Sun City at Two Rocks is a major **marina**, with a shopping complex. You can go **horse riding** at The Stables Yanchep (☎ 9561 1606).

Places to Stay & Eat

Accommodation isn't plentiful in Yanchep. Comfortable motel-style singles/double at the *Yanchep Lagoon Lodge Guest House* (☎ 9561 1033, 11 Nautical Court) cost $50/90. *Club Capricorn* (☎ 9561 1106), on Two Rocks Rd, is a rambling resort with beachfront and sports facilities; doubles start at $123 per night and two-bedroom family chalets cost $110 to $130. You can also camp here; tent/powered sites for two people cost $12/16.

Two Rocks Harbour View Apartments (☎ 9561 1469) has good-value family-sized apartments overlooking the marina. Apartments for two/four people cost $70/80, plus $5 for each extra person.

The shopping centre at the Two Rocks Marina has a *mini-market* and some *takeaway food outlets*.

GUILDERTON & SEABIRD

Some 43km north of Yanchep, Guilderton, a popular holiday resort, is at the mouth of the Moore River. The *Vergulde Draeck*, part of the Dutch East India Company fleet, ran aground near here in 1656. There is good fishing both in the Moore River and in the ocean. The *Guilderton Caravan Park* (☎ 9577 1021) has tent/powered sites for $13/15 for two people and chalets for four for $65. The Moore River Roadhouse at the edge of town also has houses for rent from $60 to $120 a night.

Seabird, 36km north of Guilderton, is a quaint fishing village. It also has the *Seabird Caravan Park* (☎ 9577 1038) close to a safe swimming area. Cabins and on-site vans are available.

Crystal-clear water, shipwrecks and coral – Rottnest Island is ideal for snorkeling.

30,000-year-old limestone pillars in the Pinnacles Desert

Stands of giant karri trees in Western Australia's beautiful south-west

Pretty Lake Cave – Leeuwin-Naturaliste NP

Enjoying a drink at Prevelly Park beach

The lighthouse at Cape Naturaliste

LEDGE POINT & LANCELIN

Ledge Point, 115km from Perth, is another fishing town and is a very popular holiday spot for Perth families. It is the starting point for the 24km Ledge Point–Lancelin Sailboard Classic, an important event on the world windsurfing calendar, held each January.

The coast road (State Hwy 60) ends at Lancelin, a small fishing port 14km north of Ledge Point, but coastal tracks continue north and may be passable with a 4WD. Lancelin was possibly named after PF Lancelin, a French scientific writer, by the 1801 French expedition (which passed here in *Le Géographe* and *Le Naturaliste*). Tourism information can be obtained from Lancelin Information & Business Directory (☎ 9655 1920), at 67 Gingin Rd near the jetty, from 9 am to 5 pm daily.

For those keen to learn **windsurfing**, there is Werner's Hot Spot (☎ 9655 1553, e windslanc@hotmail.com); hire of beginners' boards costs $20 per hour, advanced boards $50 per day. You'll usually find Werner at the windsurfing beach.

The dazzling white dunes behind Lancelin are popular for sandboarding. Lancelin Surf Sports (☎ 9655 1441), at 127 Gingin Rd, rents out sandboards and boogie boards ($10 for two hours, $20 per day). Big Foot Bus Adventure (☎ 9655 2550) has a huge 4WD vehicle that climbs the dunes and takes you to spectacular scenery you'd otherwise have trouble getting to. Tours (including sandboarding) cost $28, with YHA discounts.

Fishing, boating, diving and swimming are options for those who have yet to stand up on a windsurfer. Lancelin Dive and Charter (☎ 0417-965 063) does diving, fishing and dolphin-watching trips. You can find out about these and other tourist activities from Lancelin Tourist Information (☎ 9655 1155), at 102 Gingin Rd, open from 10 am to 4 pm daily.

The Lancelin Telecentre, at 127 Gingin Rd, above the surf shop is open for cheap Internet access from 10 am to 6 pm weekdays, and 10 am to 1 pm Saturday.

Places to Stay & Eat

There is a plethora of accommodation but booking is strongly advised during holiday periods. The *Ledge Point Caravan Park* (☎ 9655 1066) has powered sites/on-site vans for $15/48 for two people.

The *Lancelin Caravan Park* (☎ 9655 1056), near the windsurfing beach, has tent/powered sites for $8/10 per person, and on-site vans for $20.

The tidy, purpose-built *Lancelin Lodge YHA* (☎ 9655 2020, 10 Hopkins St) is run by two travellers, Trish and Trevor, who have included many of the features they would have liked to have seen in accommodation while they were on the road (such as a fully equipped kitchen and the cleanest bathrooms in the west). A comfortable dorm bed costs $15 ($14 YHA members) and neat doubles cost $40 ($50 high season). There's even a lock-up garage for storing windsurfers.

The *Lancelin Inn Hotel Motel* (☎ 9655 1005, 1 North St) has en suite singles/doubles/triples for $65/75/85. *Coastal Real Estate* (☎ 9655 1305, 127 Gingin Rd) rents out houses and units in the area (some sleeping up to 12) from $100 to $150. They are open daily.

The colourful *El Troppo (141 Gingin Rd)* is a popular spot where multilingual, multitalented Werner (of windsurfing fame) whips up Modern Australian dishes with an emphasis on seafood. *Finny's Pizza*, in the same street, does decent pizzas for $12 to $15. *Offshore Cafe*, on The Point, has fish and chips, and vegetarian selections. The *Endeavour Tavern* near the jetty is a good place for a drink.

The South-West

The beautiful south-west region of Western Australia (WA) has a spectacular coastline, rugged ranges, magnificent national parks and the greenest, most fertile areas in the state – a great contrast to the dry and barren country found in much of the rest of WA. Here you will find great patches of forest, famous surfing beaches, opportunities for watching whales and dolphins, prosperous farms, the Margaret River wineries, and more of the state's beautiful wildflowers.

Not surprisingly, the south-west region is one of the state's most favourite holiday destinations. It is particularly popular with Perth residents for short breaks and during long weekends.

In this chapter, the south-west includes the coast from Bunbury to Augusta, taking in a number of wineries, and the 'tall trees' hinterland (Southern Forests) to the east. The main towns of the south-west region are Bunbury, Busselton, Margaret River, Augusta, Manjimup and Pemberton.

Getting There & Away

Westrail (☎ 13 1053, 1800-099 150) runs daily bus services from Perth to Bunbury ($18 one way), Busselton ($21.30), Yallingup ($24.50), Margaret River ($24.50), and to Augusta ($29.10).

Westrail's *Australind* train service links Perth with Bunbury ($18). The journey takes around two hours; the bus takes just over two hours.

South West Coach Lines (in Perth ☎ 9324 2333; in Bunbury ☎ 9791 1955; in Busselton ☎ 9754 1666) also services the region and has regular services from Perth to Bunbury ($16, three times daily), Busselton ($20, three times daily), Dunsborough ($22, twice daily), Margaret River ($23, twice daily) and Augusta ($28, twice daily), and Monday to Friday services to Collie ($20), Donnybrook ($20), Bridgetown ($23), Manjimup ($27), Nannup ($24) and Balingup ($23).

The Easyrider (☎ 9226 0307) jump-on, jump-off bus service runs from Perth to 13

HIGHLIGHTS

• Watching the dolphins' spontaneous visits to Koombana Beach, Bunbury

• Enjoying premium wine and fabulous food at the wineries of the Margaret River region

• Exploring the labyrinthine limestone caves between the capes – especially stunning Lake Cave and the beautiful Jewel and Ngilgi Caves

• Climbing to the top of Cape Leeuwin lighthouse, where the Southern and Indian Oceans meet

• Surfing a left-hander off the coast at Yallingup

• Climbing the Gloucester, Bicentennial and Diamond karri trees near the timber town of Pemberton

• Driving through the karri forest of Shannon National Park

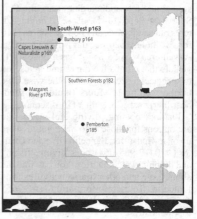

The South-West p163

Bunbury p164

Capes Leeuwin & Naturaliste p169

Southern Forests p182

Margaret River p176

Pemberton p185

towns in the south-west, including Mandurah, Bunbury, Margaret River, Walpole, Denmark and Albany. Tickets cost $185 and are valid for three months; there are two departures each week during winter, four each week in summer.

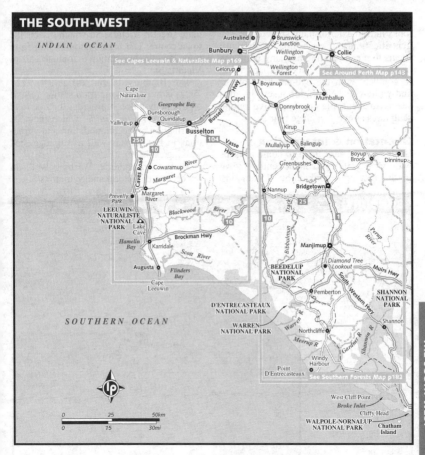

THE SOUTH-WEST

INDIAN OCEAN

See Capes Leeuwin & Naturaliste Map p169

See Around Perth Map p143

Australind
Brunswick Junction
Bunbury
Wellington Dam
Collie
Gelorup
Wellington Forest
Boyanup
Cape Naturaliste
Geographe Bay
Capel
Mumballup
Dunsborough
Quindalup
Donnybrook
Yallingup
Busselton
Kirup
Cowaramup
Margaret River
Mullalyup
Balingup
Boyup Brook
Dinninup
Greenbushes
Prevelly Park
Margaret River
Nannup
Bridgetown
LEEUWIN-NATURALISTE NATIONAL PARK
Lake Cave
Blackwood River
Brockman Hwy
Hamelin Bay
Karridale
Scott River
Manjimup
Perup River
Augusta
Flinders Bay
BEEDELUP NATIONAL PARK
Diamond Tree Lookout
Muirs Hwy
SHANNON NATIONAL PARK
Cape Leeuwin
SOUTHERN OCEAN
D'ENTRECASTEAUX NATIONAL PARK
Pemberton
Shannon
WARREN NATIONAL PARK
Northcliffe
Meerup R
Gardner R
Point D'Entrecasteaux
Windy Harbour
See Southern Forests Map p182
West Cliff Point
Broke Inlet
Cliffy Head
WALPOLE-NORNALUP NATIONAL PARK
Chatham Island

0   25   50km
0   15   30mi

THE SOUTH-WEST

Bunbury Region

BUNBURY

pop 22,000

Bunbury, WA's third-largest town and the fastest-growing city in Australia, is a port and industrial town as well as a holiday resort. Some 184km south of Perth, this pleasant place is worth a short stop on your way to the south-west. Some science boffins actually identified the region as being the 'most comfortable climatic environment for human existence'.

The town lies at the western end of Leschenault Inlet, which Nicolas Baudin, commander of *Le Géographe*, named after his botanist Leschenault de la Tour in 1803. In 1836 James Stirling sailed south from the Swan River Colony, met Henry William Bunbury, commander of the military detachment in Pinjarra, at Port Leschenault and renamed the port Bunbury, supposedly for the young officer's efforts in trekking overland to meet him. However, the reason was more likely to replace French place names with English ones.

Visitors to Bunbury might think the town looks like an exterior-paint showroom: The gentrification and expansion of Bunbury seems to mean painting as many buildings as possible in vivid colours – perhaps trying to compete with the eye-catching black-and-white-checked lighthouse. It also seems to mean placing attractive public sculptures at every vantage point.

Orientation & Information

Bunbury is an easy town to come to grips with. Most facilities are in the centre of town in the rectangle formed by Wittenoom, Clifton, Blair and Stirling Sts. Bunbury's main street is Victoria St, which bisects the town centre. The train station is 3km from town, and the bus station is a block east of Victoria St.

The Bunbury tourist office (☎ 9721 7922) is in the historic train station (1904) on Carmody Place. It provides the free *Port of Bunbury Visitor Guide*, which includes information on accommodation and attractions in Bunbury as well as on suggested walking trails.

There's a laundrette, Washing Well, on the corner of Victoria and Symmons Sts.

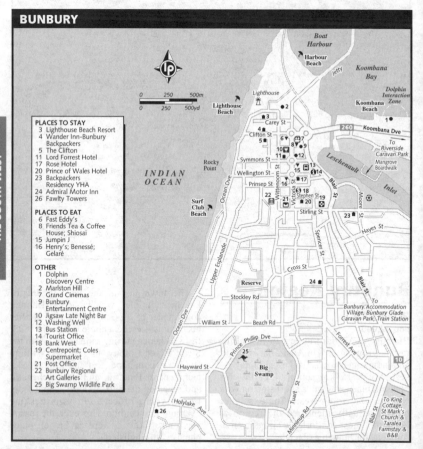

BUNBURY

PLACES TO STAY
3 Lighthouse Beach Resort
4 Wander Inn-Bunbury Backpackers
5 The Clifton
11 Lord Forrest Hotel
17 Rose Hotel
20 Prince of Wales Hotel
23 Backpackers Residency YHA
24 Admiral Motor Inn
26 Fawlty Towers

PLACES TO EAT
6 Fast Eddy's
8 Friends Tea & Coffee House; Shiosai
15 Jumpin J
16 Henry's; Benessé; Gelaré

OTHER
1 Dolphin Discovery Centre
2 Marlston Hill
7 Grand Cinemas
9 Bunbury Entertainment Centre
10 Jigsaw Late Night Bar
12 Washing Well
13 Bus Station
14 Tourist Office
18 Bank West
19 Centrepoint; Coles Supermarket
21 Post Office
22 Bunbury Regional Art Galleries
25 Big Swamp Wildlife Park

THE SOUTH-WEST

Things to See & Do

The town's historic buildings include **King Cottage**, in Forrest Ave, which now houses a museum; the **Rose Hotel**, in Victoria St; and **St Mark's Church** (1842), on the corner of Charterhouse and Flynn Rds. **Bunbury Regional Art Galleries**, in Wittenoom St, is in a restored 1897 convent.

The **Mangrove Boardwalk** (enter off Koombana Dr) is definitely worth a wander (it's free). These mangroves are the most southerly located in WA, and are rich in bird life, with over 70 species. Informative panels provide information about the ecosystems of the mangroves.

Big Swamp Wildlife Park (☎ 9721 8380), on Prince Phillip Dr, has rare white kangaroos, possums and aviary-kept parrots, the latter of which you can hand feed. It is open from 10 am to 5 pm daily and entry is $3/2 for adults/kids.

Dolphins Bunbury's Dolphin Discovery Centre (☎ 9791 3088) on Koombana Beach was set up in 1989, and wild dolphins started to interact with the public in early 1990. Three pods of about 100 bottlenose dolphins regularly feed in the inner harbour. They enter the harbour several times a day (less frequently in winter) and sometimes come in as early as 6 am; a flag is hoisted when the dolphins are in the harbour. You're not allowed to touch the dolphins, but you can snorkel alongside them, which you can't do at Monkey Mia. According to reader Richard Clarke, this experience is 'more natural' than at Monkey Mia.

Dolphin cruises depart at 9.30 and 11 am and 2 pm daily ($18); there are also daily 'swims' with the dolphins, which cost $70 (booking one day in advance is essential).

Places to Stay

There are six caravan parks in and outside of town – the tourist office has a list. Those in town include **Bunbury Accommodation Village** (☎ 9795 7100) on Washington Ave, which has tent/powered sites for $16/19 for two people in high season and chalets starting at $80. Outside town, the **Riverside Caravan Park** (☎ 9725 1234, 5 Pratt Rd,

Eaton) has powered sites for $18 and chalets starting at $65.

The efficiently run and friendly **Wander Inn – Bunbury Backpackers** (☎ 9721 3242, ⓔ wanderinnbp@yahoo.com, 16 Clifton St) is close to both the town centre and the ocean. It costs $16 for a dorm bed, $38 for a double or twin. Its adventure tours and eco-safaris, such as trips to the forests, waterfalls and wildflowers around Wellington Dam, are especially popular with backpackers.

Backpackers Residency YHA (☎ 9791 2621, 55 Stirling St) is in a historic residence. Good dorm beds in this clean hostel are $17 ($14 for members), doubles are $44 ($35) and a family room is $62. It does pick-ups from the bus and train stations by arrangement.

You can take your luck at two of the pubs in town: **Prince of Wales Hotel** (☎ 9721 2016, 41 Stephen St) has B&B singles/doubles for $30/50 (shared bathroom); the **Rose Hotel** (☎ 9721 4533), on the corner of Victoria and Wellington Sts, is a lavishly restored place, but the rooms, $69/79 with breakfast, are somewhat rough and ready.

The big hotel in town is **Lord Forrest Hotel** (☎ 9721 9966, 20 Symmons St). It has an atrium surrounding a pool, restaurants, a gym and a sauna. Singles/doubles start at $120/140. At the top of Marlston Hill on Carey St, with fabulous views, is the **Lighthouse Beach Resort** (☎ 9721 1311), which was undergoing improvements at the time of writing. It has 'budget' rooms for $55/65 singles/doubles, climbing to $150 for an ocean-front executive spa suite. Also in the upmarket category, **The Clifton** (☎ 9721 4300, 2 Molloy St) offers luxurious accommodation with all the trimmings. Deluxe doubles are $99 and executive spa suites are $170.

Overlooking the Indian Ocean is the courageously named **Fawlty Towers** (☎ 9721 2427, 205 Ocean Dr). Despite connotations it is extremely popular, with singles/doubles/triples for $59/69/79. There are several other similarly priced motels nearby on Ocean Dr. Closer to the town centre is **Admiral Motor Inn** (☎ 9721 7322, Spencer St) where singles/doubles are $79/95. It has a pool.

Taralea Farmstay and B&B (☎ *9728 1252, Ford Rd, Dardanup)* is on the banks of the Preston River 12km south of Bunbury; B&B doubles are a very reasonable $60.

Places to Eat

The bulk of the town's better eateries are in Victoria St – Bunbury's 'cappuccino strip'.

Henry's (97 Victoria St) does bruschetta, burgers and quiche as well as tempting coffee and cakes. Next door, the ice-cream cafe *Gelaré (95 Victoria St)* will satisfy any sweet cravings, with waffles and ice cream or ice-cream sundaes. In the same group of cafes, *Benessé (93 Victoria St)* does a tasty satay chicken and cheese bagel ($5.50). Opposite, *Jumpin J (62 Victoria St)* has an eclectic decor, with guitars and football jerseys on the walls, and its menus are written on old LP records. Reef and beef (prawns in garlic sauce served on top of an eye fillet steak) is $19.50 and a Thai chicken salad is $8.90.

Friends Tea & Coffee House, in the Grand Cinema Complex, Victoria St, does sandwiches and light meals and has a good selection of cakes. It's a popular place for breakfast. *Shiosai*, also in the Grand Cinema Complex, does good Japanese. Teriyaki beef and chicken is $8.50; California rolls are $4.50.

If the midnight munchies take hold, try *Fast Eddy's*, on the corner of Victoria and Clifton Sts, which is open 24 hours a day.

Various pubs do counter meals. Try the *Rose Hotel*, on the corner of Victoria and Wellington Sts, which also has nine beers on tap, or the *Prince of Wales (41 Stephen St)*.

Entertainment

Grand Cinemas, on the corner of Victoria and Clifton Sts, has four cinemas, each showing current-release movies.

Bunbury Entertainment Centre, on Blair St, attracts local and overseas acts, and is the region's main cultural centre. It hosts regular performances of theatre, classical music and ballet.

The pubs sometimes have live music – ask at the tourist office or look for the posters plastered around town. There's also the *Jigsaw Late Night Bar (43 Victoria St)*.

Getting Around

Bunbury City Transit (☎ 9791 1955) covers the region around the city as far north as Australind and south to Gelorup. You can get a bus from the tourist office to the train station for free.

AROUND BUNBURY
Australind
pop 800

Australind, another holiday resort, is a pleasant 11km drive north of Bunbury. The town takes its name from an 1840s plan to make it a port for trade with India. The plan never worked but the strange name (from 'Australia-India') remains.

The tiny **St Nicholas Church** (1860), on Paris Rd, is just 4m by 7m, and is said to be the smallest church in Australia. **Henton Cottage**, built from local materials in 1842, has arts and crafts for sale. There is a wonderful scenic drive between Australind and Binningup along **Leschenault Inlet**, a good place to net blue manna crabs.

Places to Stay The *Leschenault Inlet Caravan Park* (☎ *9797 1095, 5 Cathedral Ave)* has powered sites for $13 and on-site vans for $25. *Leschenault B&B* (☎ *9797 1352, 14 Old Coast Rd)* is in a family home overlooking the inlet, and has B&B singles/doubles for $35/65. *Settler's Guest House* (☎ *9725 9661, 7 Watermass Place, Settlers Estate)* is a purpose-built B&B, complete with indoor spa and a games room; singles/doubles cost $60/90.

Collie

Collie, the state's only coal town and with a regional population of 10,000, is about 50km east of Bunbury (202km south of Perth). The Collie tourist office (☎ 9734 2051) is at 156 Throssell St.

Collie has an interesting replica of a coal mine, a **historical museum** and a **steam locomotive museum**. There is some pleasant bushwalking country around the town and plenty of wildflowers in season.

The **Wellington Forest**, near Wellington Dam and Collie, offers a great number of 'natural' recreational activities. Walking tracks include the 900km-plus Bibbulmun Track; the two-day 24km Lennard Circuit; the four-hour Wellington Mills and Sika Circuits; and the 2½-hour lookout loop, close to Honeymoon Pool. About 300 species of wildflowers grow in the Wellington Forest, some unique to the area.

The **Muja power station** is the state's non-nuclear answer to Three Mile Island; free tours of the complex are available at 11 am Sunday to Friday – book at the tourist office. Far more interesting would be a **rafting** descent of the rapids of the Collie River. The Perth-based company Rivergods (☎ 9324 2662) runs rafting trips in the area.

Places to Stay The *Mr Marron Holiday Village* (☎ 9734 2507), on Porter St, has tent/powered sites for $12/14 and on-site vans for $30 for two people. There are a number of hotels offering accommodation, including the *Colliefields Hotel* (☎ 9734 2052, 91 Throssell St), which has very basic singles/doubles for $15/30 and the *Victoria Hotel* (☎ 9734 1138, 119 Throssell St) with better singles/doubles for $40/60. The new *Best Western Banksia Motel* (☎ 9734 5655) rises above the average standard in Collie, offering satellite TV, barbecue and pool. Doubles are $90.

Donnybrook

South of Bunbury, and on the fringe of the forest region, is Donnybrook, the centre of a vegetable- and fruit-growing area. It was named by five Irish settlers in 1842 because it reminded them of their home, a suburb of Dublin. Apple-picking work is available in season – apparently that's most of the year.

The Donnybrook tourist office (☎ 9731 1720) is in the old stationmaster's residence, opposite the Railway Hotel. It can provide information on farmstays in the area.

If you are planning to work as a fruit picker, it pays to join the Harvester Club (☎ 9731 2400) on South Western Hwy, next to the Railway Hotel. The club will help you find work when it's available, and membership ($25) guarantees discounts on accommodation and transportation to/from work. The office is also an Internet cafe.

Places to Stay & Eat Unless you're fruit picking you probably won't want (or need) to stay in Donnybrook.

Of the three hostels, only two are worth staying at: *Brook Lodge* (☎ 9731 1520, 3 Bridge St) is a well-regarded backpacker hostel with kitchen and laundry facilities. The rolling green lawn around the house is a perfect place to relax (or do yoga) in the afternoon sun after a hard day picking fruit. Dorm accommodation is $80 per week, twins and doubles $180 per week. *Workstay Cottages* (☎ 9731 1384, 11 Collins St) are converted houses in the road parallel to the South Western Hwy on the other side of the railway line. Dorm rooms are $85 per week, doubles $170 to $180. They are set up for couples more than singles.

On South Western Hwy, *Donnybrook Motorlodge* (☎ 9731 1499) has singles/doubles for $48/65. The tourist office has a list of B&B operators in and around town.

The *Railway Hotel* offers half-decent counter meals. Built in 1862 as a coach inn, the delightful *Anchor & Hope* (☎ 9731 1395, 2 South Western Hwy) is now a cafe and restaurant. Open Friday to Wednesday, it serves light lunches and dinners as well as indulgent Devonshire teas.

Balingup

About 65km south of Bunbury is the arts-and-crafts village of Balingup. You can get tourist information (including a list of the accommodation options) from the **Old Cheese Factory** craft centre (☎ 9764 1018) on Nannup Rd, which sells pottery and foodstuffs made by locals. It is open daily. Other craft places include Village Pedlars for home crafts.

About 6km north of Balingup, in Mulla-lyup, is the historic 1864 **Blackwood Inn**, an old stage-coach post classified by the National Trust. (See Places to Stay & Eat.)

Places to Stay & Eat One of the nicest places to stay is *Blackwood Inn* (☎ 9764 1138) on the South Western Hwy at Mulla-lyup. This former coach house has spacious suites with open fires. B&B costs $90 for singles, and from $120 for standard doubles

THE SOUTH-WEST

to $240 for double spa suites; no children under 18 years. The inn has a classy (though expensive) a la carte *restaurant*.

Woodlands (☎ *9764 1272*), on Russell Rd, Balingup, on the Mullalyup side of the village, is a self-contained cottage attached to a farmhouse in a peaceful, pretty setting. In apple season you'll probably be given armfuls of the sweetest apples you've ever tasted. Doubles are $90, extras about $10 per person.

In the post office building in Brockman St, **Balingup Backpackers** (☎ *9764 1049)* has beds in dorms for $15/20 midweek/weekends. It is popular with people walking the Bibbulmun Track.

Almost opposite the Old Cheese Factory and up a steep hill – the highest point in the south-west – is **Balingup Heights** (☎ *9764 1283,* e *sconcept@highway1.com.au, Lot 6 Nannup Rd)*. Its secluded, self-contained cabins in a truly magnificent setting with everything you could want (including toasty potbelly stove and gas barbecue) are $110 to $120 (for two to four people). Midweek specials are offered at $170 for two nights (a two-night stay is preferred).

For light lunches, try the **Old Cheese Factory Garden Cafe** or grab a pie from the **Balingup Bakehouse**, located on the South Western Hwy.

Naturaliste to Leeuwin

The capes region (Naturaliste to Leeuwin) is easily defined: to the north-east are the holiday resorts of Busselton and Dunsborough; in the north-west corner is Cape Naturaliste and the surf of Yallingup; the south-west corner has Cape Leeuwin, several interesting caves, and remote Augusta at the confluence of two oceans, the Indian and Southern; and the regional centre is the laid-back town of Margaret River.

The region is known for its picturesque wineries (see the special section 'Wineries of Western Australia'), great surfing beaches (see the boxed text 'Surfing the South-West'

later in this chapter) and labyrinthine caves. Arts and crafts places are everywhere and there are accommodation options for all travellers. Mapanew's quarterly *Map and Guide to the South West Capes*, and Cape Naturaliste Tourism Association's *The South West & Great Southern Holiday Planner*, are handy free brochures.

Caves Rd, the **old coast road** between Busselton, Margaret River and Augusta, is a good alternative to the direct road, which runs slightly inland. The coast here has real variety – cliff faces, long beaches pounded by rolling surf, and calm, sheltered bays.

You can walk the 140km track between Cape Naturaliste and Cape Leeuwin, passing though heathland, forest and sand dunes. Most Cape-to-Cape walkers take five days. For information, call Friends of the Cape to Cape Track (☎ 9755 5607) or contact the Margaret River tourist office.

Getting There & Around

Both South West Coach Lines and Westrail have daily services from Perth or Bunbury to Busselton, Dunsborough, Margaret River and Augusta. The journey from Perth to Margaret River takes about five hours. See the Getting There & Away section at the start of this chapter.

To get the best out of this region, your own wheels are essential as transport between smaller centres is virtually nonexistent.

Geographe Bay Coachlines (☎ 9754 2026) has day tours from Busselton to Cape Naturaliste and Cape Leeuwin, the caves, Augusta and Margaret River, depending on the time of year.

BUSSELTON
pop 11,000

Busselton, 230km south of Perth on the shores of Geographe Bay, is a popular holiday resort, especially with parents in the hunt for diversions for their frenetic kids. During holidays the population increases fourfold, accommodation is fully booked, and the beaches and restaurants are crowded. At this time Busselton represents the worst habitat of the peripatetic species *Holidayus australii*.

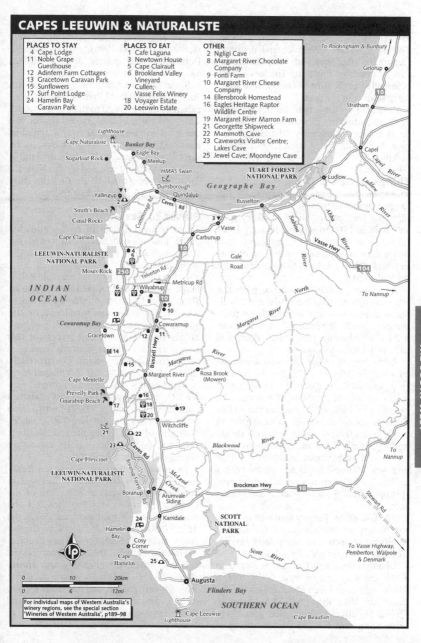

CAPES LEEUWIN & NATURALISTE

PLACES TO STAY
4 Cape Lodge
11 Noble Grape
    Guesthouse
12 Adinfern Farm Cottages
13 Gracetown Caravan Park
15 Sunflowers
17 Surf Point Lodge
24 Hamelin Bay
    Caravan Park

PLACES TO EAT
1 Cafe Laguna
5 Newtown House
5 Cape Clairault
6 Brookland Valley
    Vineyard
7 Cullen;
    Vasse Felix Winery
18 Voyager Estate
20 Leeuwin Estate

OTHER
2 Ngligi Cave
8 Margaret River Chocolate
    Company
9 Fonti Farm
10 Margaret River Cheese
    Company
14 Ellensbrook Homestead
16 Eagles Heritage Raptor
    Wildlife Centre
19 Margaret River Marron Farm
21 Georgette Shipwreck
22 Mammoth Cave
23 Caveworks Visitor Centre;
    Lakes Cave
25 Jewel Cave; Moondyne Cave

To Rockingham & Bunbury

Gelorup

Stratham

Lighthouse
Cape Naturaliste
Bunker Bay
Sugarloaf Rock
Eagle Bay
Meelup
HMAS Swan
Dunsborough
Quindalup
Yallingup
Caves Rd
Smith's Beach
Canal Rocks
Cape Clairault

Capel

Capel River

TUART FOREST
NATIONAL PARK

Geographe Bay
Busselton
Ludlow

Ludlow River

Abba River

Sabina River

Vasse
Carbunup

Vasse Hwy

Vasse River

LEEUWIN-NATURALISTE
NATIONAL PARK
Moses Rock

Gale
Road

*INDIAN
OCEAN*

Yelverton Rd
Metricup Rd
Wilyabrup

North

Margaret River

To Nannup

Cowaramup Bay
Gracetown

Bussell Hwy

Cowaramup

Margaret River

Cape Mentelle

Margaret River
Rosa Brook
(Mowen)

River

Prevelly Park
Gnarabup Beach

Witchcliffe

To
Nannup

Georgette Shipwreck

Blackwood River

Cape Freycinet

Caves Rd

Boranup Forest Rd

LEEUWIN-NATURALISTE
NATIONAL PARK
Boranup

McLeod Creek

Arumvale
Siding

Brockman Hwy

Stewart Rd

Karridale

SCOTT
NATIONAL
PARK

Hamelin
Bay
Cosy
Corner

Scott River

To Vasse Highway,
Pemberton, Walpole
& Denmark

Cape
Hamelin

Augusta

Flinders Bay

0   10   20km
0   6   12mi

For individual maps of Western Australia's
winery regions, see the special section
'Wineries of Western Australia', p189–98

SOUTHERN OCEAN
Lighthouse
Cape Leeuwin
Cape Beaufort

THE SOUTH-WEST

In 1801 a French sailor named Vasse was lost at sea in Geographe Bay during a storm. The names Vasse (the river and district), Geographe (the bay) and Naturaliste (the cape) come from this time. The town itself is named after the Bussell family, who were early settlers in the area.

Bussleton's reliable tourist office (☎ 9752 1288, e info@bsn.downsouth.com.au) is on the corner of Causeway Rd and Peel Terrace. The South West Coach Lines depot is in Albert St.

Things to See & Do

The town has a 2km jetty, reputedly the **longest timber jetty in Australia** and a popular spot for fishing. The first 175m jetty was built in 1865 to service the busy local timber trade. A skeleton railway was placed on the jetty to facilitate the transport of timber and other produce to and from the docked ships.

As bigger vessels visited the port, the jetty was extended further into the sea, with the final extension in 1960 bringing it to its present length. It remained in active use until 1973 when the port of Busselton was officially closed to shipping

A fair section of the jetty was destroyed by Cyclone Alby in 1978, but the repairs/reconstruction (funded by the $2 admission price) are almost complete. If you can't be bothered to walk all the way to the end (a pleasant 45-minute stroll) you can ride the jetty train on the hour between 10 am and 4 pm daily ($6/4 adults/children).

The **old courthouse** has been restored and now houses a small arts centre with a gallery, coffee shop and artists' workshops; it is open from 9 am to 5 pm. Admission is free.

The **Old Butter Factory Museum** exhibits the history of Busselton and the Bussell family; it is open 2 to 5 pm daily (except Tuesday); entry is $3/2 for adults/kids.

Diving is popular in Geographe Bay, both under the jetty and on Four Mile Reef, a 40km limestone ledge about 6.5km off the coast. The Dive Shed (☎ 9754 1615), at 21 Queen St, offers accompanied jetty dives with equipment for $55 (double dive) or

$25 (night/day single dive). It also rents equipment, as does the Naturaliste Dive Academy (☎ 9752 2096), at 103 Queen St. Both offer accompanied dives to HMAS *Swan* (see the Dunsborough section).

Some 7km east of the town, the 20-sq-km **Tuart Forest National Park** is the only considerable natural stand of tuart in the world. Tuart has hard, coarse-grained timber and can grow extremely large over a period of about 500 years. **Wonnerup House**, in the tuart forest, is a colonial-style house built in 1859 and lovingly restored by the National Trust; it's open from 10 am to 4 pm daily and entry is $4/2 for adults/children.

Places to Stay

There is a great deal of accommodation along this popular stretch of coast; the tourist office has a full list and can assist with bookings.

In the centre of town, near the old courthouse and the jetty, is *Kookaburra Caravan Park (☎ 9752 1516, 66 Marine Terrace)* which has powered sites for $15.50, on-site vans and cabins for $30 to $35, and park homes starting at $60 (all prices for two people). Most of the caravan parks are west of the town centre towards Dunsborough. *Acacia (☎ 9755 4034, Lot 100 Bussell Hwy)* is one of the best-value places. Powered sites are $22, on-site vans $63 and self-contained cottages/chalets start at $85/91 for two. Also on Bussell Hwy, the *Amblin (☎ 9755 4079)*, 6km west of town, is popular and has shady sites and good barbecues. Its prices are slightly higher than Acacia's.

Dorm beds at the small *Busselton Backpackers (☎ 9754 2763, 14 Peel Terrace)*, in converted units, start at $16. One of the cheapest places to stay (but possibly the noisiest given its roadside location) is the *Motel Busselton (☎ 9752 1908, 90 Bussell Hwy)* which has B&B for $35 per double.

Halfway between the beachfront and the centre of town, *Geographe Guest House (☎ 9752 1451, 28 West St)* is in an old house with a lovely garden, and has B&B for $60 to $75. Those who do not like lace and frills, steer clear! There are many more B&Bs; check with the tourist office.

There is a string of holiday resorts along the Bussell Hwy west of Busselton. They all have similar features: self-contained apartments and villas of varying sizes and luxury levels, some with pools and tennis courts. Most have beach frontage and some of the newer, ritzier places also have cafes, bars and restaurants. The *Abbey Beach Resort* (☎ *9755 4600, 595 Bussell Hwy*) has motel-style doubles starting at $92, small self-contained units (for two people) for $159, and luxury apartments sleeping two/four for $176/252. The *Broadwater Resort* (☎ *9754 1633*), on the corner of Bussell Hwy and Holgate Rd, has one-bedroom units for $156, rising to $268 for a three-bedroom villa; there's a games room, international food hall and a kid's beach club. The *Amalfi Resort* (☎ *9754 3311, 13 Earnshaw Rd*), west of Busselton, was the new kid on the block at the time of writing; it has interesting villa-style accommodation from $135 (deluxe villa) to $235 (premier villa).

For a touch of history set amid gorgeous gardens, head for *Newton House* (☎ *9755 4485, 737 Bussell Hwy, Vasse*), an early settler residence which has lovely guesthouse doubles (including breakfast) for $125. Booking is essential as there are only four rooms. It has a great restaurant.

Places to Eat
A Lump of Rump Steakhouse (☎ *9752 1872*), on Queen St behind the Commercial Hotel, is a BYO place that reputedly serves Busselton's best steaks, but it also has seafood and vegetarian dishes. *Grand River Chinese Restaurant* (*53 Queen St*) can cater for any leanings towards Chinese nosh.

Geographe Bayview Resort Restaurant has a three-course dinner special for $16 on Wednesday and Sunday. The *Esplanade Hotel* (☎ *9752 1078, 167 Marine Terrace*) does good pub lunches and dinners. A local favourite is the *Equinox Cafe*, on the beachfront in Queen St, which does light meals and dinners (with mains about $15).

Historic *Newton House* (☎ *9755 4485, 737 Bussell Hwy*) at Vasse, just after the turn-off to Margaret River, is set amid green lawns and lovely gardens of herbs and lavender. The BYO restaurant here has a reputation for offering the best food in the region (we cannot disagree). The menu lists everything from seafood to venison and duck, and some good vegetarian dishes and excellent pizzas. A full meal created with top-quality local produce costs around $25 per person, and morning/afternoon tea is an indulgent treat. You can also buy fabulous home-made preserves and chutneys.

If you're after grease, you won't have to look too far: there are your regular fast-food chains and various hamburger/pizza joints in Queen St and on the Bussell Hwy.

DUNSBOROUGH
Dunsborough, just west of Busselton, is a pleasant coastal town that is dependent on tourism. Like Busselton, its beaches suit families as the water is shallow.

The helpful tourist office (☎ 9755 3299) is in the Dunsborough Park shopping centre on Seymour Boulevard.

Things to See & Do
North-west of Dunsborough, the Naturaliste road leads to excellent beaches such as **Meelup**, **Eagle Bay** and **Bunker Bay**, some fine coastal lookouts and the tip of **Cape Naturaliste**, which has a lighthouse and some walking trails. The lighthouse was built in 1903, and is open from 9.30 am to 4 pm Tuesday to Sunday. Admission is as steep as the steps inside it: $10/2.50 for adults/children.

In season you can see humpback whales, southern right whales and dolphins from the lookouts over Geographe Bay. The southern-most nesting colony of the red-tailed tropicbird is at scenic **Sugarloaf Rock**. (See the boxed text 'The Bird Has Flown – Too Far South' in this chapter.)

There is some excellent **diving** in Geographe Bay (see also Bussleton, earlier in this chapter). In 1997 a decommissioned Navy destroyer, HMAS Swan, was sunk purposely for divers. Marine life has moved quickly to colonise the wreck, located 2.5km off Dunsborough. Diving Ventures (☎ 9756 8848), at 26 Dunn Bay Rd, offers two accompanied dives with all equipment

THE SOUTH-WEST

The Bird Has Flown – Too Far South

Keen bird-watchers will marvel at the sight of the red-tailed tropicbird (Phaethon rubricauda) soaring happily in the sea breezes above Sugarloaf Rock, south of Cape Naturaliste. The section of beaches between Capes Naturaliste and Leeuwin is anything but the tropics; nevertheless, this stretch of coast is home to the most southerly breeding colony of red-tailed tropicbirds in Australia.

The tropicbird is distinguished by its two long red tail streamers – almost twice its body length. It has a bill like a tern's and, from a distance, could easily be mistaken for a Caspian tern. You'll have fun watching through binoculars as the inhabitants of this small breeding colony soar, glide, dive then swim with their disproportionately long tail feathers cocked up. They are ungainly on land and have to descend almost to the spot where they wish to nest.

for $135. Cape Dive (☎ 9756 8778), at 222 Naturaliste Terrace, also does accompanied dives in this area.

You can go horse riding through the farms and countryside around Dunsborough. Mirravale Riding School (☎ 9755 2180) is halfway between Dunsborough and Yallingup on Biddles Rd.

Places to Stay

There's only one caravan park, **Dunsborough Lakes Hotel & Caravan Park** (☎ 9756 8300, 2 Commonage Rd) with powered tent sites starting at $20 for two people and on-site vans at $50. Cabins and chalets are also available. It's not paradise and you'd do better if you head to Yallingup.

Nomads Dunsborough Inn and Backpacker (☎ 9756 7277) is in the centre of town on Dunn Bay Rd, close to the shops and beach. Dorm beds are $18 to $20; twins are $22.50 per person. There's Internet access here, and a shuttle bus runs to the surf beaches. In Quindalup is the **Three Pines Resort YHA** (☎ 9755 3107, 285 Geographe Bay Rd), on the beachfront. Dorm

accommodation costs $18 ($16 for YHA members); twins/doubles cost $22.50 per person (nonmembers). Readers report that the rooms can get noisy at night. This hostel hires out bicycles and canoes.

Dunsborough Farm Cottages and Railway Carriages (☎ 9755 3865, Lot 6 Commonage Rd) has spacious cottages that sleep up to four people for $120 and recycled train carriages that sleep two for $100. All have private bathrooms.

Family-oriented beach resorts in Dunsborough include **Dunsborough Bay Village Resort** (☎ 9755 3397), on Dunn Bay Rd, which has fully equipped cottages starting at $155/195 for two/four people; facilities include TV, in-house movies and potbelly stoves. Opposite the beach at Quindalup, the **Bayshore Resort** (☎ 9756 8353, 374 Geographe Bay Rd), has well-furnished self-contained units. Villas (some with spas) sleeping up to eight cost $130 per night for a double (linen included), and $15 per extra person.

The quality self-contained, rammed-earth villas of **Whaler's Cove** (☎ 9755 3699, Lot 3 Lecaille Court) can sleep up to six people and cost from $145 to $195. Whaler's gets glowing reports from all who stay here. **Mercure Inn Dunsborough** (☎ 9755 3200), on the corner of Caves Rd and Seymour Boulevard, has motel-style doubles ranging from $140 to $160.

The tourist office has an extensive list of private homes for rent.

Places to Eat

Adrian's Seafood Grill (☎ 9756 7777), near the tourist office, serves only WA seafood and fish and is licensed. **Galley Cafe** (26 Dunn Bay Rd), opposite the hostel, has theme nights. **Bay Cottage** (☎ 9755 3554, Lot 28 Dunn Bay Rd), near the centre of town, offers upmarket dining Tuesday to Saturday evenings. At the Radisson Resort on Caves Rd, **Toby's Restaurant** (☎ 9756 8777) is licensed; it has a two-course dinner special for $20 in low season. **Simmo's Ice-creamery** (Commonage Rd) has 26 flavours of home-made ice cream (based on secret Irish recipes) as well as tasty waffles. The minigolf and children's playground make it popular with younger travellers.

There are several winery restaurants in the area. See under Places to Eat in the Yallingup section.

YALLINGUP

Yallingup, surrounded by a spectacular coastline and some fine beaches, is a mecca for surfers (see the boxed text 'Surfing the South-West' later in this chapter). At Yallingup and Smith's Beach there are a number of **walking trails**.

Near Yallingup is the mystical **Ngilgi Cave** (see the boxed text 'Cave to Cave from Cape to Cape'). The **Canal Rocks**, a series of rocky outcrops forming a natural canal, are off Caves Rd just outside of Leeuwin-Naturaliste National Park.

Places to Stay

Yallingup Beach Caravan Park (☎ 9755 2164), right on the beachfront in Valley Rd, has tent/powered sites for $12/14 as well as pristine new cabins (sleeping four people) for $120.

Caves Caravan Park (☎ 9755 2196), on the corner of Caves and Yallingup Beach Rds, is a little more expensive than other parks but it is probably the best in the south-west. Each site (tent, campervan or caravan) has its own toilet/shower block. Camp sites are $27 for up to eight people, van sites are $45, cabins are $58 and chalets (with TV, video, CD player and heating) are $90 to $120.

Caves House Yallingup (☎ 9755 2131), on Caves Rd, was established in 1903 and is one of those old-world lodges with ocean views and an English garden. Double rooms in the 1930s guesthouse cost $80 (with shared bathroom) to $120 (en suite). En suite garden rooms are available for $125 to $155, and refurbished winery rooms, complete with Jacuzzi, cost $150 per night.

Canal Rocks Beach Resort (☎ 9755 2116), on Smiths Beach Rd, has a variety of accommodation: basic on-site vans (sleeping six, no bathroom) are $100; cottages (for up to six people, with bathroom and TV) are $135; two-/three-bedroom luxury beachfront apartments with spa, TV, video and CD player are $210/240.

Top of the range is *Cape Lodge* (☎ 9755 6311), on Caves Rd, which has luxury suites set among manicured gardens and natural forest. The place is described as 'simple unadulterated luxury' – perfect for a romantic getaway. Doubles start at $175 a night, including gourmet breakfast. There's also an upmarket restaurant here.

There's a variety of holiday homes and cottages available; inquire at the Dunsborough or Margaret River-Augusta tourist offices.

Places to Eat

From Dawson Dr, *Cafe Laguna* (☎ 9755 2133) overlooks the beach; it is open for breakfast, lunch and dinner. The menu here combines Asian and Modern Australian cuisines. *Fisherman's Hut* (☎ 9756 8564, Lot 21 Caves Rd) serves good-value fish and seafood as well as meat and vegetable dishes. It's very child-friendly; there's a separate menu for kids, and a play area.

Gourmets should head for the fabulous winery restaurants around Yallingup. At Brookland Valley's vineyard, on Caves Rd at Willyabrup (south of Yallingup), *Flutes Cafe* (☎ 9755 6250) has one of the loveliest restaurant settings in the region, if not the country, overlooking a dam where ducks hang out happily. The food here is excellent. In busy periods there is often a set two-/three-course menu for $35/45.

Cape Clairault (☎ 9755 6225), on Henry Rd, Willyabrup, produces superb food – both full meals and gourmet platters to complement the wines – in a contemporary building of timber and corrugated iron amid vineyards and eucalypts. Prices are reasonable for the quality of the food which is among the region's best. A superb three-course meal with wine will cost up to $65. The menu changes seasonally but includes dishes such as yabby-tail noodles, nori rolls, Moroccan beef curry and fish. The desserts are of the to-die-for variety.

Although the waiting staff can be somewhat supercilious, the elegant restaurant at *Vasse Felix* (☎ 9755 5242), on the corner of Caves and Harman's South Rds between

THE SOUTH-WEST

Cave to Cave from Cape to Cape

Limestone caves (perhaps 350) are dotted throughout the Leeuwin-Naturaliste Ridge between the capes. These include Jewel Cave (the most spectacular), Lake Cave (the prettiest), Mammoth Cave and the Moondyne Adventure Cave.

The first stop on any caving tour should be at the Caveworks visitor centre (☎ 9757 7411), on Caves Rd around 25km from Margaret River. There are excellent screen displays about caves and cave conservation, an authentic model cave and a 'cave crawl' experience. There are also displays on fossils found in the area. The staff at Caveworks are enthusiastic and knowledgeable and are happy to answer questions.

The limestone formations are reflected in the still waters of an underground stream in the **Lake Cave**, entered from Caveworks. Creative lighting effects enhance the forms of the stalactites and stalagmites. The vegetated entrance to this cave is spectacular and includes a karri tree with a girth of 7m. Lake Cave is the deepest of all the caves open to the public. There are over 300 steps down (a 72m drop) to the entrance.

Mammoth Cave, 21km south of Margaret River, boasts a fossilised jawbone of *Zygomaturus trilobus*, a giant wombat-like creature, that can be touched. Other fossil remains have revealed a great deal about prehistoric fauna of the south-west region. This cave has partial wheelchair access, and there's an easy bushwalk (20 minutes) nearby.

Jewel Cave, 8km north of Augusta, was discovered in 1957 and is consideredto be the most spectacular cave in the area. One of its most impressive features is a 5.9m straw stalactite, so far the longest seen in a 'commercial' cave. Fossil remains of a Tasmanian tiger *(thylacine)*, believed to be 25,000 years old, have been discovered in the cave.

Moondyne Cave, near Jewel Cave, is the adventure cave. It is unlit and an experienced guide takes visitors on a two-hour 'passive' adventure. Overalls and hard hats are provided. This is getting closer to the real caving experience.

Lake Cave and Jewel Cave can be visited only by guided tour. These depart at 9.30, 10.30 and 11.30 am and 12.30, 1.30, 2.30 and 3.30 pm. There are often extra tours put on in busy holiday periods. Mammoth Cave is open for self-guided tours (with CD audio commentary) from 9 am to 4 pm daily.

Single cave tickets cost $14/5.50/37 for adults/children/families, and include entry to Caveworks. Three-cave passes (which can be used over several days) cost $33/13/92.

Moondyne Cave can be visited at 2 pm daily, but bookings are essential. Tickets for tours of Moondyne cost $27.50/19 adults/children (minimum age is 10). There are sometimes extra tours in peak holiday season.

You can book other guided cave adventures ($70/95 for half/full-day) through Caveworks. These are run by well-trained, locally based adventure groups.

Near Yallingup is the mystical **Ngilgi Cave**, which was discovered, or rather stumbled upon, in 1899. Formations include the white 'Mother of Pearl Shawl' and the equally beautiful 'Arab's Tent' and 'Oriental Shawl'. The cave (off Caves Rd) is open from 9.30 am to 4.30 pm (last entry 3.30 pm; $13/5 for adults/children) daily; in school holidays and on long weekends the caves close at 5 pm (last entry 4 pm). Entry is on the half hour; tours are semiguided with guides available to answer questions.

Yallingup and Margaret River, is often booked out. The menu features Modern Australian dishes and the top-notch chefs are matched by the prices. Be sure to taste the delicious Vasse Felix drops.

Nearby, *Cullen Wines* (☎ 9755 5277), on Caves Rd, Cowaramup, has a pleasant, low-key (and reasonably priced) cafe overlooking the vines. It offers good-value salads, seafood, meat and vegetarian dishes and yummy cakes.

MARGARET RIVER

The attractive town of Margaret River (AKA Margie's or Margaret's) is a popular holiday spot due to its proximity to the fine surf of Margaret River Mouth, Gnarabup, Suicides and Redgate, and to the swimming beaches at Prevelly and Gracetown. It is also close to some of the best wineries in Australia (see the special section 'Wineries of Western Australia') as well as some very pleasant rural scenery.

Extremely popular with people from Perth, Margaret River gets very busy at Easter and Christmas when you should book weeks, if not months, ahead. It also gets busy during the annual food and wine bash in November, surf competitions in March/April and at the time of the famous Leeuwin Estate Concerts in February, at which renowned entertainers such as Diana Ross, Shirley Bassey, Ray Charles, Tom Jones and Michael Crawford have performed.

Information

The Margaret River–Augusta tourist office (☎ 9757 2911), on the corner of the Bussell Hwy and Tunbridge St, has a wad of information on the area, including a good vineyard map ($3).

There are several banks with ATMs on the Bussell Hwy in the centre of town including a National Australia Bank and Challenge/Westpac. You can get online at Cybercorner Cafe at 2/72 Willmott Ave.

Bikes can be rented by the hour ($7) or day ($20) from the Gull service station on Bussell Hwy.

Things to See & Do

Wine tasting is the most popular activity in the area. See the special section 'Wineries of Western Australia'.

The National Trust property, **Ellensbrook Homestead** (1857), the first home of the Bussell family, is 8km north-west of town. It has a fascinating history and a visit is an absolute must.

Pioneer settlers Alfred and Ellen Bussell founded the property in 1857. The homestead they built expanded over the years as the farm became more prosperous. The local Nyungar people led the Bussells to this sheltered but isolated site, which had a good supply of fresh water.

Three generations of the Bussell family lived at Ellensbrook, from its founding until the 1960s; a few pieces of original furniture and farm equipment remain. Between 1899 and 1917, Edith Bussell, who farmed the property on her own for many years, established an Aboriginal mission here. Ellensbrook is open from 10 am to 4 pm Saturday

A visit to historic Ellensbrook Homestead, near Margaret River, is an absolute must.

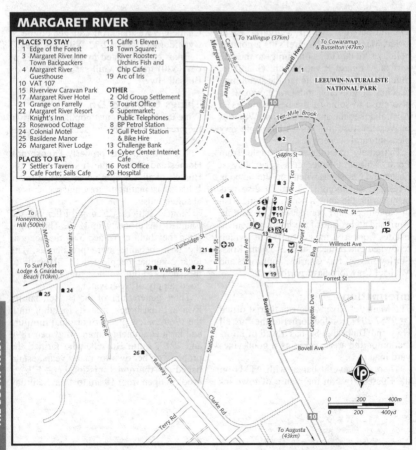

MARGARET RIVER

PLACES TO STAY
1 Edge of the Forest
3 Margaret River Inne
  Town Backpackers
4 Margaret River
  Guesthouse
10 VAT 107
15 Riverview Caravan Park
17 Margaret River Hotel
21 Grange on Farrelly
22 Margaret River Resort
  Knight's Inn
23 Rosewood Cottage
24 Colonial Motel
25 Basildene Manor
26 Margaret River Lodge

PLACES TO EAT
7 Settler's Tavern
9 Cafe Forte; Sails Cafe

11 Caffe 1 Eleven
18 Town Square;
  River Rooster;
  Urchins Fish and
  Chip Cafe
19 Arc of Iris

OTHER
2 Old Group Settlement
5 Tourist Office
6 Supermarket;
  Public Telephones
8 BP Petrol Station
12 Gull Petrol Station
  & Bike Hire
13 Challenge Bank
14 Cyber Center Internet
  Cafe
16 Post Office
20 Hospital

To Yallingup (37km)
To Cowaramup & Busselton (47km)
LEEUWIN-NATURALISTE NATIONAL PARK
Ten-Mile Brook
To Honeymoon Hill (500m)
To Surf Point Lodge & Gnarabup Beach (10km)
To Augusta (43km)

THE SOUTH-WEST

to Wednesday (closed June/July); admission is $4 (free to National Trust members).

There are a number of potteries, art galleries and craft workshops both in town and off Caves Rd. **Eagles Heritage Raptor Wildlife Centre**, 5km south of Margaret River on Boodjidup Rd, rehabilitates between 200 and 300 birds of prey each year. There are free-flight displays and a 1km bird-of-prey bushwalk. It is open from 10 am to 5 pm daily and costs $7/3 for adults/children.

The **Margaret River Marron Farm**, off Wickham Rd, Witchcliffe (7km south of Margaret River), is an interesting place to learn about the breeding of WA's native freshwater crayfish. They were dubbed 'marron' (French for 'sweet chestnut') by early French settlers because of their dark exterior shell casing a sweet, white flesh. The farm is open from 10 am to 4 pm daily; self-guided tours cost $2. The licensed cafe serves light meals featuring delicious marron.

Also worth a visit are the **Margaret River Cheese Company** and **Fonti Farm**, whose cheeses and yogurt are distributed throughout WA. Fonti is part of Margaret River Cheese Company – you can watch the cheese being made. They are about 1km apart on Bussell Hwy at Cowaramup. Chocoholics should head straight for **Margaret River Chocolate Company**, on Harman's Mill Rd, where the European-trained chocolatier works wonders with silky-smooth imported chocolate and local ingredients. The chocolate fudge sauce is indescribably indulgent. It is open 10 am to 5 pm daily.

Not far from Margaret River there are several **caves** that can be visited. (See the boxed text 'Cave to Cave from Cape to Cape' earlier in this chapter.)

The **Old Group Settlement**, on the banks of the Margaret River just north of town, is worth a wander. It is home to historic buildings and displays (admission is free).

Organised Tours

One fascinating tour, highly recommended by readers, is the search for forest secrets with Cave & Canoe Bushtucker Tours at Prevelly Park (☎ 9757 9084). This combines walking and canoeing up the Margaret River, aspects of Aboriginal culture, uses of flora, tasting of bush tucker (smoked kangaroo and emu, quandongs, damper and bardie grub pate) and ends with a descent into an adventure cave. The three-hour exploration costs $30/15 for adults/children and is worth every cent.

For the more adventurous, Adventure in Margaret River (☎ 9757 2104) offers full-/half-day abseiling, climbing and caving trips for $95/65. Milesaway Tours (☎ 9754 2929) does canoe adventure trips for $65 and also offers two-/three-day trips for $195/295. Outdoor Discoveries (☎ 0407-084 945) offers canoeing, rock-climbing, caving, abseiling and bushwalking tours. Full-/half-day abseiling and rock-climbing tours cost $80/60, and canoeing tours cost around $30.

Boranup Eco Walks (☎ 9757 7576) does interpretive bushwalks ($15), 'wild walks' off the beaten track ($10) and night walks ($12), all of which take place in the area south-west of Margaret River. Margaret River Horse-Back Tours (☎ 9757 3339), on Rosa Brook Rd about 4km from Margaret River, has scenic rides in the area.

Various outfits do tours of the wineries. Bushtucker (☎ 9757 9084) does a four-hour 'Wine, Food and Forest Adventure' tour in a 4WD for $40. Milesaway Tours (☎ 9754 2929) offers a full-day Wine & Dine tour (including lunch) for $65 and half-day wineries tours for $40. Margaret River Tour Co (☎ 0419-917 166) has similarly structured and priced tours and combined wineries/sightseeing tours.

For something totally indulgent you can take a chauffeured Rolls Royce around the vineyards (including private barrel tastings and a progressive lunch) with The Margaret River Lady (☎ 9757 1212).

Places to Stay

The tourist office can help find and book accommodation, but it cannot work miracles so it is advisable to book well in advance, especially around Easter and Christmas.

Surfing the South-West

Known colloquially to surfers as 'Yal's' and 'Margaret's' (when viewed from far-off Perth), the beaches between Capes Naturaliste and Leeuwin offer powerful reef breaks, mainly left-handers (the direction you take after catching a wave). The surf at Margaret's has been described by surfing supremo Nat Young as 'epic', and by world surfing champ Mark Richards as 'one of the world's finest'.

The better locations include Rocky Point (short left-hander), the Farm and Bone Yards (right-hander), Three Bears (Papa, Mama and Baby, of course), Yallingup (breaks left and right), Injidup Car Park and Injidup Point (right-hand tube on a heavy swell; left-hander), Guillotine/Gallows (right-hander), South Point (popular break), Left-Handers (the name says it all) and Margaret River (with Southside or 'Suicides').

You can get a copy of the Down South Surfing Guide leaflet, free from the Dunsborough and Busselton tourist offices, which indicates wave size, wind direction and swell size.

Former WA champion Josh Palmateer gives surfing lessons in the area. Call ☎ 9757 3850 or ☎ 0418-958 264 for information.

Camping The *Gracetown Caravan Park* (☎ 9755 5301), on the corner of Caves and Cowaramup Bay Rds, is probably the best of several camping grounds in the area. It is about 10km north of Margaret River and about 3km inland from the coast. On-site vans cost $30 and park cabins $40 for two people. *Riverview Caravan Park* (☎ 9757 2270, 8–10 Willmott Ave), in town by the river, has tent/powered sites for $15/16 for two people (tent dwellers may have to pitch their tents on unlevel ground) and comfortable cabins starting at $55 ($45 in winter).

Hostels Backpacker-style options include the *Margaret River Lodge* (☎ 9757 9532, ℮ info@mrlodge.com.au, 220 Railway Terrace), about 1.5km south-west of the town centre. It's clean and modern with all the facilities (and it doesn't mind families); dorm beds cost $16, and en suite rooms sleeping two to eight cost $55 to $180.

The friendly *Margaret River Inne Town Backpackers* (☎ 9757 3698, 93 Bussell Hwy), in a converted house in the centre of town, has dorm beds for $14, twins and doubles for $32 and a triple room for $39. There's Internet access.

One of the nicest hostels you could hope to stay in is the beachside *Surf Point Lodge* (☎ 9757 1777), on Riedle Dr at Gnarabup Beach, 10km from Margaret River. Purpose-built by travellers for travellers, it has a large, fully equipped kitchen and many recreation areas – surfers will love the theme. Dorm beds in four-/eight-bed rooms cost $19, twins and doubles cost $47 and en suite rooms cost $62.

Guesthouses & B&Bs You can't get more central than the *Margaret River Hotel* (☎ 9757 2655), on the Bussell Hwy. It's an attractive 1936 heritage building with singles/doubles for $85/95 and one deluxe spa suite for $160. Opposite the hospital on Farrelly St, *Grange on Farrelly* (☎ 9757 3177), also known as the 1885 Inn, has comfortable motel doubles for $120. Nearby, the *Margaret River Resort Knight's Inn* (☎ 9757 0000, 40 Wallcliffe Rd) has doubles with spa baths for $155 to $210.

Pretty *Rosewood Cottage* (☎ 9757 2845, 54 Wallcliffe Rd) is almost drowning in flowers. B&B singles/doubles start at $70/80. The *Margaret River Guesthouse* (☎ 9757 2349), on Valley Rd, has singles with shared/private bathrooms for $50/70 and doubles for $65/85. The modern, purple building *VAT 107* (☎ 9758 8877, 107 Bussell Hwy) is a restaurant downstairs and has equally modern motel-style bedrooms upstairs for $160 to $200.

Edge of the Forest (☎ 9757 2351, 25 Bussell Hwy) is just north of Margaret River opposite Carters Rd. Its motel-style units really are at the edge of the forest and are good value at $75 a double, with breakfast included. In Cowaramup, the *Noble Grape Guesthouse* (☎ 9755 5538, Lot 18 Bussell Hwy) is a modern guesthouse that has been built in colonial style. It's set amid pretty gardens, and.has B&B for $77/99 singles/doubles. It has a laundry for guest use.

Probably the best place of all if you want luxury and privacy is *Honeymoon Hill* (☎ 9357 3124, Lot 30 Illawarra Ave), just outside town off Wallcliffe Rd. It has huge, comfortable double rooms with TV, video, kitchenette and bathrooms with the biggest showers imaginable for $180. It also has nice personal touches, such as interesting contemporary books and a delicious cooked breakfast delivered to your room in a basket. It is open Thursday to Sunday only and bookings are essential. Another superb spot is *Basildene Manor* (☎ 9757 3140, Lot 100 Wallcliffe Rd), a historic home converted into a luxury hotel and set among manicured gardens. B&B doubles start at $181.50, rising to $269.50 for a lakeview suite. Special low-season packages offer good value for stays of two nights or more.

Chalets Families will find *Sunflowers* (☎ 9757 3343), on Caves Rd near the corner of Carters Rd, north-west of Margaret River, convenient. Well-equipped self-contained chalets (one of which sleeps up to 11 people) start at $75 for a double, $95 for four. The 'zoo' with 100 farm animals, numerous walking trails and enclosed playground has plenty of distractions for children.

In Cowaramup *Adinfern Farm Cottages* (☎ 9755 5272), on the Bussell Hwy, has self-contained rammed-earth cottages ($60/90 singles/doubles), and some cottages sleeping up to six.

Places to Eat

You won't starve in Margaret River. There are several cafes in the centre of town on Bussell Hwy, including *Sails Cafe* and *Cafe Forte*, both perennial favourites good for light meals, cake and coffee.

Caffe 1 Eleven (111 Bussell Hwy) does excellent breakfasts (muesli $4.50, cooked breakfast from $5.50 to $11) and good lunches (lentil, chicken or fish burgers for $6, warm salads for $8.50, Turkish bread stacks with chicken or smoked salmon for $8.50). It is open for dinner on Friday to Sunday only. Its cakes are worth breaking the diet for.

VAT 107 (☎ 9758 8877, 107 Bussell Hwy) is a trendy new addition to the main drag but its hypermodern architecture looks strangely out of place. The cooking is contemporary but homely. Be warned: portions are huge and desserts are dangerous.

The *Arc of Iris (☎ 9757 3112, 151 Bussell Hwy)* is popular with locals and always busy. It's eclectic, lively and a throwback to the hippy generation. None of the chairs, tables or glasses match but who cares when the food is this good and this cheap. Creamy, thick fish chowder costs $7, Thai salad costs $14 and Hokkien noodles with tofu, chicken or beef cost $12 to $14. Make sure you book and make sure you save room for the world's most divine creme caramel ($6).

The *Margaret River Hotel (☎ 9757 2655)*, on Bussell Hwy, has well-priced cafe-style counter meals including Greek salad, pumpkin ravioli ($12) and chargrilled chicken breast ($10.50). *Settler's Tavern (☎ 9757 2398, 114 Bussell Hwy)*, near the supermarket, has good counter meals and live music on weekends.

There are several fast-food joints in the Town Square complex including *River Rooster* barbecue chicken and the trendy and popular *Urchins Fish and Chip Cafe*,

which does great Thai fish cakes ($2.50 for three) and fish and chips.

Winery restaurants located just out of Margaret River include the no-expense-spared complex at *Voyager Estate (☎ 9385 3133)*, on Gnarawary Rd, which has a large restaurant serving lunch and dinner, and the excellent eatery at *Leeuwin Estate (☎ 9757 6253)*, on Stevens Rd, where divine dishes include marinated grilled mushrooms, marron, and veal shank on mash. Expect to part with about $50 a head for a memorable meal. The green lawns rolling gently down to the bush form a natural amphitheatre – the site of the annual alfresco concerts – and are inviting for an afternoon snooze to sleep off your lunch. It is open for lunch daily and for dinner on Saturday. For anyone interested in food and wine this is an essential stop on the Margaret River itinerary. Leeuwin's wines are world class – its Chardonnay is ranked as one of the world's best (see the special section 'Wineries of Western Australia' for more information on Margaret River wineries) – and paintings by famous Australian artists used for their wine labels adorn the walls.

AUGUSTA

A popular holiday resort, Augusta is 5km north of Cape Leeuwin where the Indian Ocean meets the Southern Ocean. The cape is the most south-westerly point in Australia. Cape Leeuwin **lighthouse** (open from 9 am to 4 pm daily, $4) has magnificent views of the rugged coastline. Not far away is a salt-encrusted **waterwheel** that was built in 1895.

Cape Leeuwin took its name from a Dutch ship which passed here in 1622. The **Matthew Flinders memorial**, between Groper Bay and Point Matthew on the Leeuwin Rd, commemorates Flinders' mapping of the Australian coast, which commenced at the cape on 6 December 1801.

Augusta Historical Museum, also on Blackwood Ave, has interesting exhibits relating to local history, the surrounding environment, whales, the Leeuwin lighthouse and shipwrecks off the coast; it is open from 10 am to noon and 2 to 4 pm daily ($2).

Augusta's tourist office (☎ 9758 0166), on the corner of Blackwood Ave and Ellis St, is open 9 am to 5 pm daily. It has a range of brochures including a free walking and cycling trail guide.

Leeuwin Souvenirs, at 70 Blackwood Ave, hires out bikes. For a taxi call Augusta Taxis (☎ 0417-914 694).

There are some good beaches between Augusta and Margaret River, including **Hamelin Bay** and **Cosy Corner**.

Organised Tours

Whale-watching is good from Cape Leeuwin between June and September. Naturaliste Charters (☎ 9755 2276) has three-hour trips ($38/22 for adults/children) to see southern right and humpback whales, bottlenose dolphins, a colony of New Zealand fur seals on Flinders Island and, occasionally, pygmy blue whales.

There are more sedate cruises ($14/7/35 adults/children/families) up the Blackwood River from the Ellis St jetty on the *Miss Flinders*. Call ☎ 9758 1944 or the tourist office for departure times and bookings.

Places to Stay

Doonbanks Caravan Park (☎ 9758 1517), on Blackwood Ave, is the most central. It has tent/powered sites for $12/14 and on-site vans from $25 to $45 for two people. Other caravan parks in the area include the nicely positioned *Flinders Bay* (☎ 9758 1380), on Albany Terrace right on the beach, which has tent/powered sites for $12/15 for two people. It closes from May until September.

Hamelin Bay Caravan Park (☎ 9758 5540), 8km west of Karridale, has powered sites for $13 to $20, on-site vans for $30 to $38 and park cabins for $36 to $50 for two people. Prices vary according to the season. Fishing and swimming at the lovely beach are popular pastimes.

There are basic *camp sites* in the Leeuwin-Naturaliste National Park, including sites on Boranup Dr, Point Rd and Conto's Field, near Lake Cave; camping costs $5 per person. The ranger comes around late evening or early morning.

The Federation-style *Baywatch Manor Resort* (☎ 9758 1290, 88 Blackwood Ave) offers good budget accommodation and is fully equipped for disabled travellers. Dorm beds cost $17 and double and twin rooms cost $60 for two people (linen included).

The riverfront *Augusta Hotel* (☎ 9758 1944), on Blackwood Ave, has doubles starting at $65 and self-contained units. There's a restaurant and free in-house videos. The *Georgiana Molloy Motel* (☎ 9758 1255, 84 Blackwood Ave) has comfortable rooms (and family rooms) with kitchenettes and TV starting at $68 a double.

Some of the self-contained holiday flats have reasonable rates but they may have minimum-booking periods in peak season; inquire at the tourist office.

Places to Eat

The *Augusta Hotel*, on Blackwood Ave, does decent counter meals. For an Asian fix head to the *August(a) Moon Chinese Restaurant*, on Ellis St in the Matthew Flinders shopping centre. The *Augusta Bakery and Cafe (121 Blackwood Ave)* is known for its pizzas, buns and home-baked pies. *Cosy's Corner, on* Blackwood Ave, has breakfasts and tasty focaccia for $6. The *Gull Rock Cafe*, on Blackwood Ave at the Gull petrol station opposite the bakery, is new in town and recommended.

Down on Albany Terrace, you can watch the Blackwood River meet the waters of Flinders Bay while drinking coffee and eating pasta at what claims to be the 'last cafe before Antarctica', the *Colourpatch*.

Southern Forests

A visit to the forests of the south-west is a must for any traveller to WA. Interspersed between the forests are many interesting towns, a variety of attractions and a host of things to do. The forests are magnificent – towering jarrah, marri and karri trees protect the natural, vibrant undergrowth. Unfortunately, parts of these forests are being increasingly threatened by logging. (See the boxed text 'At Loggerheads over Logging' under Ecology & Environment in the Facts about Western Australia chapter.)

The area of 'tall trees' lies between the Vasse Hwy (State Hwy 10) and the South Western Hwy, and includes the timber towns of Bridgetown, Manjimup, Nannup, Pemberton and Northcliffe.

Getting There & Away

Westrail (☎ 13 1053, 1800-099 150 from interstate) has daily buses from Perth (the East Perth terminus) to Pemberton, via Bunbury, Donnybrook and Manjimup; the trip takes about five hours. On most days you can also take Westrail's Australind train from Perth (Wellington St station) to Bunbury, connecting with the same bus service. The fare is $30.60 one way, regardless of which form of transport you use.

There's a daily bus service from Albany to Pemberton ($22.90, three hours). The Pemberton-Albany bus goes via the Northcliffe turn-off, but you will need your own transport to get to Windy Harbour.

BRIDGETOWN

pop 4000

Bridgetown, a quiet country town on the Blackwood River and centre of the Blackwood Valley, is in an area of karri forests and farmland. It has some old buildings, including **Bridgedale House**, which was built of mud and clay by the area's first settler in 1862 and has been restored by the National Trust; it is open from 10 am to 2 pm Friday to Sunday ($3).

There is a local history display as well as a captivating **jigsaw collection** in the tourist office (☎ 9761 1740) on Hampton St (open 9 am to 5 pm daily). The staff are enthusiastic, so you'll have no trouble fitting the pieces together.

Bridgetown Telecentre next to the old gaol in Hampton St has Internet access.

Interesting features of the Blackwood Valley are the burrawangs (grass trees) and large granite boulders. There's a panoramic view over the town from **Sutton's Lookout** off Phillips St. About 10km north of Bridgetown on the South Western Hwy is **Greenbushes**, once a tin-mining centre.

The small town of **Boyup Brook**, 31km north-east of Bridgetown, is notable for its eclectic attractions: the Haddleton flora reserve features banksias, orchids and a rare boronia; a large butterfly and beetle display (which was once the collection of a local entomologist) is located at the tourist office; and there is the unique Harvey Dickson country-music centre. Nearby is **Norlup Pool**, with glacial rock formations, and to the north **Wilga**, an old timber mill with vintage engines.

Places to Stay & Eat

The *Bridgetown Caravan Park (☎ 9761 1053)*, on the South Western Hwy, has tent/powered sites for $12/14 and on-site vans starting at $28 for two people.

Hampton House (☎ 9761 2526, 26 Hampton St) has comfortable beds (with doonas) and tasty breakfasts at $40/70 for singles/doubles. The *Bridgetown Country Cottages (☎ 9761 1370, 419 Mattamattup St)*, 2km east of Bridgetown, dubs itself 'a country retreat with a hint of Tuscany': You decide for yourself. Two-bedroom cottages here cost $65. There's also a swimming pool. *Glenlynn Cottages (☎ 9761 1196)*, on a working farm on Press Rd at Glenlynn, 6km south of Bridgetown, has cottages at similar prices.

Two upmarket B&Bs in town, both charging from $120 a double, are *Aislinn House (☎ 9761 1816)*, at Ford House, Eadle Terrace, which boasts spa baths, fresh flowers and fluffy bathrobes; and *Woodlands of Bridgetown (☎ 9761 1106)*, on the South Western Hwy. Ask at the tourist office about other B&Bs and self-catering cottages.

The Cidery (43 Gifford Rd) brews its own cider (alcoholic and nonalcoholic) and has apple juice, good light lunches daily and dinners Friday to Sunday. There's also a display on the town's apple history. It's definitely worth a visit. For snacks and takeaways in Hampton St, try the *Pottery* (also known as Pip's) or the *1896 Cafe*, which does the best coffee in town. For a splurge, try the BYO *Le Chef (☎ 9761 4445)*, on Tweed Rd.

SOUTHERN FORESTS

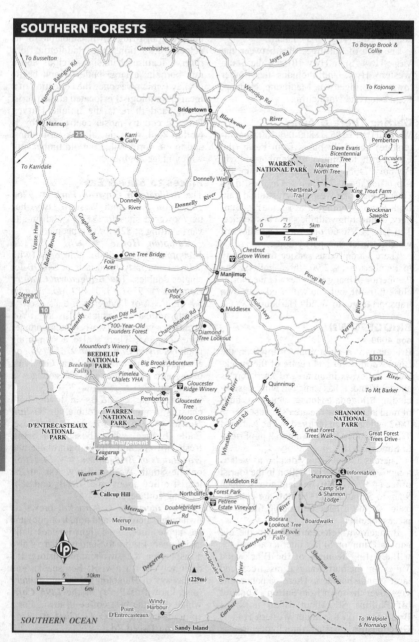

To Busselton

To Boyup Brook & Collie

Greenbushes

Nannup-Balingup Rd

Jayes Rd

Winroup Rd

Bridgetown

Blackwood

River

To Kojonup

Nannup

25

Karri Gully

Pemberton

Cascades

To Karridale

WARREN NATIONAL PARK

Dave Evans Bicentennial Tree

Donnelly Well

Marianne North Tree

King Trout Farm

Donnelly River

Donnelly River

Graphite Rd

Heartbreak Trail

Brockman Sawpits

0   2.5   5km
0   1.5   3mi

Barlee Brook

Vasse Hwy

One Tree Bridge

Four Aces

Chestnut Grove Wines

Manjimup

Perup Rd

Stewart Rd

10

Donnelly River

Fonty's Pool

Seven Day Rd

100-Year-Old Founders Forest

Channybearup Rd

Middlesex

Muirs Hwy

Perup River

Perup River

Diamond Tree Lookout

Mountford's Winery

BEEDELUP NATIONAL PARK

Big Brook Arboretum

102

Tone River

Beedelup Falls

Pimelea Chalets YHA

Pemberton

Gloucester Ridge Winery

Gloucester Tree

Quinninup

To Mt Barker

SHANNON NATIONAL PARK

D'ENTRECASTEAUX NATIONAL PARK

WARREN NATIONAL PARK

Moon Crossing

Warren River

Wheatley Coast Rd

South Western Hwy

Great Forest Trees Walk

Great Forest Trees Drive

See Enlargement

Yeagarup Lake

Warren R

Middleton Rd

Shannon

Information

Callup Hill

Meerup

Northcliffe

Forest Park

Petrene Estate Vineyard

Camp Site & Shannon Lodge

Meerup Dunes

Doublebridges Rd

River

Boorara Lookout Tree

Lane Poole Falls

Boardwalks

Doggerup

Creek

Canterbury

Chesapeake Rd

Shannon River

(229m)

River

Gardner

Windy Harbour

Point D'Entrecasteaux

0   5   10km
0   3   6mi

SOUTHERN OCEAN

Sandy Island

To Walpole & Nornalup

THE SOUTH-WEST

NANNUP
pop 1100
In the heart of the south-west's forests and farmland, Nannup (with a population of 550 rednecks, 550 alternatives), around 50km west of Bridgetown, is a quiet, historical town in a picturesque setting.

It is home to the extremely rare **Nannup tiger**, which is sighted so rarely that it has become almost mythical. The most recent sighting by a Department of Conservation & Land Management (CALM) officer, in the late 1990s, indicates that the species is does still exist.

The tourist office (☎ 9756 1211) at the 1922 police station in Brockman St, is open from 9 am to 5 pm daily and produces an excellent free booklet that points out places of interest around town and details scenic drives through forests and along the Blackwood River Rd.

Things to See & Do
Nannup's fine old buildings and numerous craft shops will keep you busy. Garden lovers should head to **Blythe Gardens** ($1), opposite the tourist office. Once a paddock, the gardens have been lovingly transformed into a floral wonderland mixing native and exotic plants.

There are free tours of the Sotico timber mill at 9.30 am every Monday, Wednesday and Friday (wear covered shoes).

The Blackwood River begins in the salt-lake system to the east of Wagin and Katanning. It then flows for more than 400km through forests and farmland and near many towns before emptying into the ocean east of Augusta, and is a good river to **canoe**.

The river is most suited to Canadian-style canoes, which can be hired in Nannup, Boyup Brook and Bridgetown. The best time to paddle the river is in late winter and early spring, when the water levels are up. Leaflets on canoeing areas are available from the tourist office (which can also help with canoe tour bookings).

Blackwood Forest Canoeing (☎ 9756 1252) charges $17.50 per person for a half-day canoeing trip including all equipment and basic stroke instruction.

Places to Stay & Eat
Nannup Caravan Park (☎ 9756 1211), on Brockman St, offers powered sites/on-site vans for $10/14 for doubles.

The rustic ***Black Cockatoo*** (☎ 9756 1035, 27 Grange Rd) backpacker lodge is the place to 'kick back and mellow out' (their words, not ours). Dorm beds here cost $15. Ask about the possibility of an 'ecostay', where you will work your butt off doing gardening or tidying up and you may get a free bed in return.

Nannup has a great number of B&Bs, farmstays and bush cottages; the tourist office can assist with bookings. ***Bee's Place*** (☎ 9756 1408), situated on Thomas Rd, about 3km out of Nannup on the road to Augusta, is highly recommended, with B&B for $35 per person in a mud-brick home (shared bathrooms). The friendly owner can provide evening meals made from organic produce by arrangement, and also provides a babysitting service.

In town, ***Argyll Cottage*** (☎ 9756 3023, 121 Warren Rd) is equipped for disabled travellers; B&B with full cooked breakfast costs $80 for doubles.

Redgum Hill (☎ 9756 2056), on Balingup Rd, is one of the nicest places to stay in the area. It has B&B in a beautiful homestead for $80/120 for singles/doubles and self-contained cottages for $85 to $99 (for two people). However, it is not child-friendly.

The Lodge (☎ 9756 1276), on Grange Rd, is also upmarket; it is furnished with antiques. B&B costs $120 for doubles.

The Good Food Shop, on Warren Rd, sells all the usual health foods and serves light lunches, cakes and slices. Next door, the ***Nannup Hotel*** dishes out less healthy counter meals. The ***Blackwood Cafe***, also on Warren Rd, has good light meals such as quiche, soup and sandwiches.

MANJIMUP
pop 4650
Manjimup is the commercial centre of the south-west, a major agricultural centre noted for apple growing and reviled by greenies for its wood chipping.

The **Timber Park Complex**, on the corner of Rose and Edwards Sts, includes various museums, old buildings and the Manjimup tourist office (☎ 9771 1831), open from 9 am to 5 pm daily. The tourist office, built in 1986, is almost an attraction in its own right. The sixteen-sided mud-brick building features supports of jarrah and karri.

There is a picturesque route from Nannup to Manjimup via the back roads rather than via Bridgetown. Ask the tourist offices in either town for directions.

Things to See & Do
Some 22km down Graphite Rd, **One Tree Bridge**, or what's left of it after floods in 1966, was constructed from a single karri log carefully felled to span the width of the river. The **Four Aces**, 1.6km from One Tree Bridge, are four superb karri trees, believed to be more than 300 years old, in a straight line. There's a 1½-hour bushwalking trail from the Four Aces to One Tree Bridge and back. **Fonty's Pool**, a great spot to cool off, is 10km south-west of town along Seven Day Rd.

Nine kilometres south of town, along the South Western Hwy, is the **Diamond Tree Lookout**. You're allowed to climb this 51m karri (not for the faint-hearted or vertigo sufferers); there's a nature trail nearby.

Manjimup is one of Australia's newest successful wine regions. Wineries in the area are worth a visit (the tourist office has details). **Chestnut Grove Wines** (☎ 9772 4255) has both award-winning wine *and* olive oil.

Perup, 50km east of Manjimup, is the centre of a 400-sq-km forest, which has populations of rare mammals, including the numbat, tammar wallaby and southern brown bandicoot. The Pemberton Hiking Company (☎ 9776 1559) organises overnight tours there (bookings essential) – most of the animals are nocturnal.

Places to Stay & Eat
The best of Manjimup's three caravan parks is *Fonty's Pool* (☎ 9771 2105), on Seven Day Rd, which has powered sites for $14, on-site vans for $30, park cabins for $40 and two-bedroom cottages for $50. All prices are for two people.

A basic backpacker hostel, the *Barracks* (☎ 9771 1154, 8 Muir St), caters for apple pickers in season, when it's hard to get a bed ($15). *Kingsley Motel* (☎ 9771 1177, 1 Chopping St) also has facilities for disabled travellers. *Manjimup Country Guesthouse* (☎ 9777 1213), on Southern St, is one of the best places to stay. B&B costs $60/70 for singles/doubles with shared bathroom, or $95 an en suite double. You can also get massages and aromatherapy facials.

Glenoran Valley Guesthouse (☎ 9772 1382), on Hodgsons Rd 17km out of Manjimup off Graphite Rd, is a delightful rammed-earth guesthouse. Not all rooms have private bathrooms. B&B doubles start at $90. About 15km out of town on the road to Pemberton (at the Vasse Hwy turn-off) is the idiosyncratic *Warren Grange Farmstay* (☎ 9772 3527, RMB 240), where accommodation ranges from en suite doubles ($65) down to a caravan ($20).

If you fancy some marron, head for the *Blue Marron Restaurant* (☎ 9776 1330), on Channybearup Rd at the Eagles Springs Marron Farm. You can be guaranteed they are fresh! It is closed on Friday. The nicest place to eat, *Graphiti Cafe* (☎ 9772 1283), on Graphite Rd at One Tree Bridge, is 20km out of town and surrounded by karri forests. Warming potato and pumpkin soup costs $5.50 and mains such as oriental chicken noodle salad and Greek lamb and veggie kebabs cost around $11. *Deja Vu Cafe*, on Giblett St, does coffees and cakes and has Internet access. *Manjimup Hotel*, on Giblett St, does good-value counter meals. There are a couple of large *supermarkets* in town to pick up self-catering supplies.

PEMBERTON
pop 1200
Deep in the karri forests is the delightful town of Pemberton. The child-friendly, well-organised Karri Visitor Centre (☎ 9776 1133) in Brockman St incorporates the tourist office, pioneer museum and karri forest discovery centre (the kids will love the frog and the possum). The Pemberton Telecentre has Internet access and is next door to the tourist office.

THE SOUTH-WEST

Things to See & Do

Pemberton has some interesting **craft shops** specialising in handcrafted timber products.

The **Big Brook Arboretum** features 'big' trees from all over the world and from the eastern states. Pretty **Pemberton Swimming Pool**, surrounded by karri trees, is ideal on a hot day.

A **trout hatchery** supplies fish for the state's rivers. The tourist office can provide details for all these attractions.

Also of interest in the area are a series of waterfalls and shallow, rocky pools known as the **Cascades** (spectacular when the water level is high); the **Founders Forest**, over 100 years old, which was once a wheat field; and **Warren National Park**, 11km south of Pemberton and home to the tallest karri, which are almost 90m high. There are two great forest drives in the park: the **Heartbreak Trail** (16km) and the **Maidenbush Trail**. Both pass through 400-year-old karri stands.

Pemberton also has a burgeoning **wine industry**, with reds attracting favourable comparison to those from Burgundy in France. Ask at the visitor centre for the free leaflet *Wineries & Vineyards of the Pemberton Wine Region*.

If you're feeling fit, make the scary 60m climb to the top of the **Gloucester Tree**, 3km east of town, for magnificent views. This is not for the faint-hearted! National Parks entry ($8 per car) applies; follow the signs from town. The tree was named after the Duke of Gloucester, who visited in 1946.

The **Dave Evans Bicentennial Tree**, at 68m the tallest of the 'climbing trees', is in Warren National Park, 11km south of Pemberton. It's tree-house cage weighs two tonnes and can sway up to 1.5m in either direction in strong winds. Don't say you haven't been warned.

Pemberton Tramway The scenic Pemberton Tramway (☎ 9776 1322), one of the

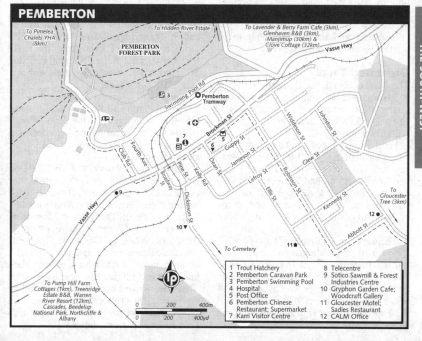

PEMBERTON

To Pimelea Chalets YHA (8km)
To Hidden River Estate
To Lavender & Berry Farm Cafe (3km); Glenhaven B&B (3km); Manjimup (30km) & Clove Cottage (32km)
Vasse Hwy
PEMBERTON FOREST PARK
Swimming Pool Rd
Pemberton Tramway
Brockman St
Widdeson St
Johnston St
Fourth Ave
Club Rd
Broadway
Pine St
Dean St
Cuppy St
Jamieson St
Glew St
Robinson St
Kelly Rd
Dickinson St
Lefroy St
Ellis St
Kennedy St
Vasse Hwy
To Gloucester Tree (3km)
Abbott St
To Cemetery
To Pump Hill Farm Cottages (1km), Treenridge Estate B&B, Warren River Resort (12km), Cascades, Beedelup National Park, Northcliffe & Albany

1 Trout Hatchery	8 Telecentre
2 Pemberton Caravan Park	9 Sotico Sawmill & Forest
3 Pemberton Swimming Pool	Industries Centre
4 Hospital	10 Gryphon Garden Cafe;
5 Post Office	Woodcraft Gallery
6 Pemberton Chinese	11 Gloucester Motel;
Restaurant; Supermarket	Sadies Restaurant
7 Karri Visitor Centre	12 CALM Office

0   200   400m
0   200   400yd

THE SOUTH-WEST

area's main attractions, was built between 1929 and 1933. It was part of a planned line between Bunbury and Albany and was in use for passengers and goods until 1986.

Trams leave Pemberton train station for Warren River at 10.45 am and 2 pm daily ($13/6.50 for adults/children), and for Northcliffe ($29/14.50) at 10.15 am on Tuesday, Thursday and Saturday.

The route travels through lush karri and marri forests with occasional photo stops; a commentary is also provided. The trip is incredibly noisy and only worthwhile if you don't have a car.

Beedelup National Park This enchanting forest park should not be missed. There is a short but scenic walk that crosses **Beedelup Brook** near **Beedelup Falls**; the bridge was built from a karri log.

For the keen bird-watcher there are numerous species to be found flitting in and around the tall trees. One of the most striking, the red-winged fairy wren, is seen in the undergrowth of the forests. CALM publishes booklets on birds in the area.

Beedelup National Park is about 15km west of Pemberton on Vasse Hwy.

Organised Tours

The Pemberton Hiking Company (☎ 9776 1559) organises half-/full-day walks through virgin forest, clear rivers and sand dunes. It can also plan longer hikes, night hikes and wildflower walks.

Pemberton Discovery Tours (☎ 9776 1133) has half-day 4WD tours to the Warren and D'Entrecasteaux National Parks and other parks around Pemberton. It also does full-day tours to the mouth of the Warren River at Yeagarup Dunes, and to the eastern end of the Warren River at Callcup Dunes.

There are Forest Discovery Tours (☎ 9771 2915) at 10.30 am Monday to Saturday, departing from the Forest Industries Centre (part of the Sotico Sawmill) in Brockman St. Free guided tours of the **Sotico Sawmill** leave from the centre at 9.30 and 11 am and 1.30 pm Monday to Thursday and 9.30 and 11 am Friday.

Places to Stay

You can *camp* in Warren National Park and in some areas of the Pemberton Forest. Call the Pemberton CALM office (☎ 9776 1207) for details. Less atmospheric, the *Pemberton Caravan Park (☎ 9776 1300)*, on Swimming Pool Rd, has powered sites for $14 and on-site vans/cabins for $55/65 for two people.

Pimelea Chalets YHA (☎ 9776 1153), in a beautiful forest location at Pimelea, 9km from Pemberton, has dorm beds for $14 a night and twins/doubles for $35/38 (non-members pay $3 more). Some readers have reported having problems getting transport to this hostel.

In town, the *Gloucester Motel (☎ 9776 1266)*, on Ellis St, has tidy singles/doubles for $50/65.

Scottish hospitality at its best is on display at *Glenhaven B&B (☎ 9776 0028)*, on Browns Rd near Lavender & Berry Farm. The cooked breakfast will keep you going for hours, and there's complimentary afternoon tea and evening sherry. Singles/doubles cost $65/90. Luxury B&B can be had at *Treenridge Estate B&B (☎ 9776 1131)*, a winery on Packer Rd off the Vasse Hwy between the Warren National Park and Treenbrook State Forest. Doubles with spa cost $110, twins $85.

Pump Hill Farm Cottages (☎ 9776 1379), on Pump Hill Rd, is good for those travelling with children; the farm animals will amuse them for hours. Two-bedroom cottages start at $85 a double ($15/5 for extra adults/children).

Warren River Resort (☎ 9776 1400), on Northcliffe Rd 8km from Pemberton, has comfortable rammed-earth cottages situated in karri forest. Prices start at $100 a double.

An angler's delight is about 32km from Pemberton at *Clover Cottage (☎ 9773 1262)*, on Wheatley Coast Rd. The self-contained limestone cottages complete with potbelly stoves, TV, video and electric blankets start at $120 for two people. Also on offer here is freshwater fishing (including fly fishing) in private lakes stocked with brown and rainbow trout. Note that children under 12 are not allowed.

For more information on the plethora of farmstays, cottages and B&Bs, inquire at the Karri Visitor Centre, which has a free accommodation booking service.

Places to Eat

The town, for its size, has many places to eat; some have local trout and marron on their menus.

Gryphon's Garden Cafe, on Dickinson St, has a pleasant setting and is attached to Woodcraft Gallery, a fantastic arts-and-crafts gallery. It does hearty breakfasts, snacks and lunches throughout the day (it's closed on Thursday) and has daily blackboard specials.

Sadies Restaurant, on Ellis St at the Gloucester Motel, has excellent smorgasbords featuring trout and marron.

If you feel like Chinese food try the rather unimaginatively named *Pemberton Chinese Restaurant (3 Dean St)* next to the supermarket. *The Lavender & Berry Farm Cafe*, on Browns Rd just out of town, has good light meals and delicious berry and lavender ice cream.

Hidden River Estate (☎ 9776 1437), on Mullineaux Rd, is a delightful winery and cafe off the Golf Links Rd. A warming bowl of delicious soup costs only $5.50 and the menu includes other interesting dishes – all the tastier when washed down with a glass of Hidden River Chardonnay or cabernet sauvignon.

NORTHCLIFFE

pop 800

Northcliffe, 32km south of Pemberton, has a **pioneer museum** and a **forest park** close to town with good walks through stands of grand karri, marri and jarrah trees – a brochure and map of the trails is available from the tourist office (☎ 9776 7203), by the museum on Wheatley Coast Rd.

The popular and picturesque **Lane Poole Falls** are 19km south-east of Northcliffe; the 2.5km track to the falls leaves from the 50m Boorara lookout tree.

Windy Harbour, on the coast 29km south of Northcliffe, has prefabricated shacks and a sheltered beach, although, true to its name, it is very blustery. The cliffs of the magnificent **D'Entrecasteaux National Park** can be accessed from here.

Places to Stay & Eat

Round-Tuit Holiday Park (☎ 9776 7276), on Muirillup Rd, charges $5 per person for camping, $15 for a powered site and $40 for on-site vans. It also offers B&B for $40/60 for singles/doubles.

The *Northcliffe Hotel (☎ 9776 7089)*, on Wheatley Coast Rd, is the only pub in town. It offers good budget singles/doubles for $30/45 and basic backpacker beds with shared facilities for $15.

In the centre of this thriving metropolis, *Traveller's Rest (☎ 9776 6060)*, on Wheatley Coast Rd, has B&B singles/doubles for $45/79. Out of town, *Meerup Springs Farm (☎ 9776 7216)*, on Double Bridges Rd, has self-contained cabins with log fires from $75.

The *Northcliffe Hotel* does good counter meals and *King Karri* next door is also recommended. *Petrene Estate Vineyard (☎ 9776 7145)*, on Muirillup Rd 2km from town, serves delicious snacks and light meals.

At Windy Harbour the only place to stay is the *camping area (☎ 9776 8398)*, where tent sites cost $5 per person.

SHANNON NATIONAL PARK

This 535-sq-km national park is on the South Western Hwy, 53km south of Manjimup. Virtually all of the Shannon River catchment is included in the park. The Shannon was once the site of WA's biggest timber mill (it closed in 1968). Exotic plants, including deciduous trees from the northern hemisphere, are today the only reminders of the old town.

The 48km **Great Forest Trees Drive** is well worth doing. For information on the park's history and ecology pick up a copy of *The Great Forest Trees Drive* ($12.95), a detailed map and guidebook, published by CALM and available from its Pemberton office. Information is also provided by radio on the drive: Just tune your car radio to 100FM when you see the signs.

THE SOUTH-WEST

The drive is split in two by the highway. In the north you can hike the 8km-return **Great Forest Trees Walk**, crossing the Shannon River at one point; in the south boardwalks give access to stands of giant karri at **Snake Gully** and **Big Tree Grove**.

There is also a 3.5km walk to the Shannon Dam and a 5.5km circuit to Mokare's Rock, where there is a boardwalk and great views. There is a fine *camping* area in the spot where the original timber-milling town used to be, and some small huts equipped with potbelly stoves.

The self-contained *Shannon Lodge* is available for groups (of up to six people). For information and bookings contact CALM in Pemberton (☎ 9776 1207) or Walpole (☎ 9840 1027).

The wine industry in Western Australia (WA) is a mere drop in the vat of a burgeoning worldwide wine industry. Figures current for the year 2000 show that by volume WA accounts for just 3% of Australia's total national wine production, but what the state's wine industry lacks in size, it makes up for in quality and variety. It accounts for a disproportionate amount of the premium end of the market – none of the wine produced in WA is destined for the cask.

That doesn't mean that all WA wine is expensive. Generally, you pay for what you get in quality, but there is plenty of good-priced, very drinkable wine, from the historic Swan Valley on the doorstep of the state's capital, Perth, to the rolling southern hills of Margaret River, Mt Barker and Pemberton.

The best way to appreciate the industry, and maybe pick up a bargain, is to visit the regions, enjoy the scenery, meet the owners and wine makers and sample their wines.

The main wine regions boast other significant tourist assets: the Swan Valley is just 20km from the heart of Perth and can be enjoyed as a day trip; the Great Southern region, centred on Mt Barker, about 350km south of Perth, has the most spectacular coastal and mountain scenery in the state; Margaret River, a thriving artistic hub about 300km south of Perth, has world-renowned surf beaches; and Pemberton, sandwiched between the other two southern regions, is in tall-timber country, with its unique karri and jarrah forests.

MARGARET RIVER

An intriguing mix of the ostentatious and the modest, this best known of WA's wine regions has flourished, with wealthy investors from outside the district pushing its reputation to the world market.

The first vines in the region were planted in the mid-1960s, and rapid industry growth occurred in the 1980s and 1990s. Chardonnay and cabernet sauvignon have been the most successful varieties, but others, including semillon and shiraz, also thrive.

The region is home to about 60 wine producers and most offer cellar sales and tasting. Many have gone to great lengths to make their mark on the countryside. They are big, bold and impressive, but, to some eyes, a little over the top. Voyager Estate, 8km south of Margaret River on Stevens Rd, flies the biggest Australian flag you'll see above its manicured white-walled gardens and large paved car park. Just up the road, the celebrated Leeuwin Estate has an impressive restaurant, spacious wine-sales area and lush gardens. Leeuwin knows how to put on the ritz; its annual outdoor concert is one of WA's major social occasions, drawing the cream of Perth society to hear big names such as Dame Kiri Te Kanawa, Ray Charles and Michael Crawford perform under the stars.

There are many tiny, owner-operated wineries, such as the quaint *Woody Nook* (☎ 9755 7547), on Metricup Rd off the Bussell Hwy

Title page: Perfect partners: The best way to appreciate WA's many excellent wines. (Photo by John Hay.)

MARGARET RIVER WINERIES

WINERY	OPEN
1 Woody Nook	Daily 11-3.30
2 Brookland Valley	Daily 11-4
3 Pierro Wines;	Daily 10-5
Cullen Wines;	Daily 10-4
Evans & Tate;	Daily 10.30-4.30
Ashbrook Estate Wines;	Daily 11-5
Vasse Felix;	Daily 10-5
Gralyn Estate Winery	Daily 10.30-4.30
4 Juniper Estate;	Daily 10-5
Howard Park Wines	Daily 10-5
5 Chateau Xanadu	Daily 10-5
6 Voyager Estate	Daily 11-5
7 Redgate	Daily 10-5
8 Leeuwin Estate	Daily 10-4.30
9 Serventy Organic Wines	Daily 10-4

about 20km north of the town of Margaret River, and no-nonsense **Ashbrook Estate Wines** (☎ 9755 6262), tucked away at the end of a long gravel driveway on a cattle property, on Harmans Rd South. Some of the small operators are located in converted buildings on farms, with wine sometimes a sideline to other farming practices.

The choice can be bewildering, but several companies offer organised day or half-day tours, taking in a selection of the best wineries and usually including lunch at one of them. This allows you to get on with some serious tasting without worrying about whether you're fit to drive.

The Margaret River tourist office (☎ 9757 2911), on the Bussell Hwy in the town of Margaret River, handles bookings. Check out the Web site at www.margaretriverwa.com.

If you want to do the driving yourself but you're not sure where to start, the Margaret River Regional Wine Centre (☎ 9755 5501), at 9 Bussell Hwy in Cowaramup, about 10km north of Margaret River, can help. The centre is run by wine buffs, who can provide useful information and devise an itinerary so you don't miss any highlights. It also offers tastings of local wines and is licensed, so you can buy there if you don't have time to visit individual cellars.

The oldest vines in the region are in the Willyabrup Valley, 10km to 15km north of Margaret River, and this is where the highest concentration of vineyards remains.

The self-drive visitor is spoilt for choice, with many worthy spots to try, from the big and flashy, such as **Howard Park Wines** (☎ 9755 9988), on Miamup Rd, to the more modest and cosy, such as **Juniper Estate** (☎ 9755 9000), a newcomer on Harmans Rd South.

Highlights of the Margaret River wineries include two of the district's original and most successful vineyards: **Vasse Felix** (☎ 9755 5242) and **Cullen Wines** (☎ 9755 5277), both on Caves Rd. Each produces outstanding cabernet sauvignon and Vasse Felix's semillon is as good as you will find. Others on Caves Rd include **Brookland Valley** (☎ 9755 6250), **Pierro Wines** (☎ 9755 6220) and **Evans & Tate** (☎ 9755 6244); all three offer quality wines in beautiful settings. Brookland Valley is a regional showpiece, with well-kept grounds, the highly regarded **Flutes Cafe** and a gallery.

Vineyards are also clustered to the south-west of Margaret River, notably **Leeuwin Estate** (☎ 9757 6253), on Stevens Rd, which has a range of outstanding wines, including what is widely regarded as Australia's best chardonnay. Winery tours are available. Near neighbours **Voyager Estate** (☎ 9757 6354) and **Chateau Xanadu** (☎ 9757 2581), on Boodjidup Rd, also make excellent chardonnay.

Chateau Xanadu is worth a visit to see its charming stone cellar, with its many artistic features. The wines are very good too, especially the cabernet sauvignon and chardonnay. **Redgate Wines** (☎ 9757 6208), on the corner of Boodjidup and Caves Rds, is one of the district's older producers and has a wide and creditable range.

Serventy Organic Wines (☎ 9757 7534), on Rocky Rd, south-east of Margaret River, boasts entirely organically grown grapes in its wines. **Gralyn Estate Winery** (☎ 9755 6245), on Caves Rd, sells only through the cellar door and, unlike most local producers, has a selection of fortified wines.

GREAT SOUTHERN

The first plantings in the Great Southern were made in the late 1960s, but the region developed slowly for 25 years. That changed dramatically in the latter part of the 1990s, with major vineyards going in at Mt Barker and farther north-west along the Frankland River. The Great Southern is now the biggest producer of grapes in WA, with riesling and shiraz its trademark varieties.

Plantagenet Wines (☎ 9851 2150), on the Albany Hwy in central Mt Barker, was one of the first to establish vines and was the first winery in the area in the mid-1970s. It produces a big range, but among the best are riesling, cabernet sauvignon, shiraz and pinot noir. Plantagenet's winery building is a rustic converted apple-packing shed, a reminder of the area's horticultural history.

The greatest concentration of wineries in Mt Barker is west of town on Muirs Hwy. About 10km from Mt Barker is **Goundrey** (☎ 9851 1777), a great building of concrete and glass that stands out from the farmland. Goundrey is the biggest and most modern winery in Mt Barker, with its broad range of wines highlighted by shiraz, pinot noir, riesling, unwooded chardonnay and cabernet–merlot blend. The big, glass-fronted tasting area is built to accommodate a coach load. Winery tours take place at 11.30 am and 3 pm daily.

Nearby cellars, including **Pattersons** (☎ 9851 2063) and **Galafrey Wines** (☎ 9851 2022), offer a cosier, more personal approach, especially Galafrey, on Quangellup Rd (try the riesling). Pattersons, on scenic St Werburghs Rd, makes fine pinot noir and chardonnay.

Other small producers worth visiting in Mt Barker are **Gilberts** (☎ 9851 4028), 20km north of town on the Albany Hwy, and **Chatsfield** (☎ 9851 1704), 10km south on O'Neill Rd. Gilberts has some of the best riesling in the region, and Chatsfield's best variety is shiraz.

COURTESY OF VOYAGER ESTATE

Voyager Estate, 8km south of Margaret River, with manicured white-walled gardens

JOHN HAY

Wine grapes

COURTESY OF VOYAGER ESTATE

Voyager Estate curlicue

JOHN HAY

Gloucester Ridge vineyard, near Pemberton

The impressive Salitage Winery and restaurant

A bountiful harvest

Fresh from the garden

Lunch menu, Cullen Wines

Flutes Cafe at the Brookland Valley winery is named for the pipe-playing Pan.

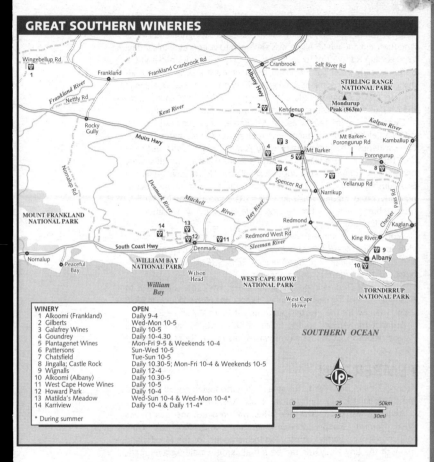

GREAT SOUTHERN WINERIES

WINERY	OPEN
1 Alkoomi (Frankland)	Daily 9-4
2 Gilberts	Wed-Mon 10-5
3 Galafrey Wines	Daily 10-5
4 Goundrey	Daily 10-4.30
5 Plantagenet Wines	Mon-Fri 9-5 & Weekends 10-4
6 Pattersons	Sun-Wed 10-5
7 Chatsfield	Tue-Sun 10-5
8 Jingalla; Castle Rock	Daily 10.30-5; Mon-Fri 10-4 & Weekends 10-5
9 Wignalls	Daily 12-4
10 Alkoomi (Albany)	Daily 10.30-5
11 West Cape Howe Wines	Daily 10-5
12 Howard Park	Daily 10-4
13 Matilda's Meadow	Wed-Sun 10-4 & Wed-Mon 10-4*
14 Karriview	Daily 10-4 & Daily 11-4*

* During summer

East of Mt Barker, the ancient rock formations and tall karri trees of the Porongurup Range form the setting for one of the smallest and most spectacular wine districts in Australia. There's a handful of producers open to the public, with *Jingalla* (☎ 9853 1023), on Bolganup Rd, and *Castle Rock* (☎ 9853 1035), on Porongurup Rd, well worth breaking the scenic drive.

The southern coastal city of Albany, 50km south-east of Mt Barker, is home to one of the state's best producers of pinot noir. *Wignalls* (☎ 9841 2848), about 10km from the city centre on Chester Pass Rd, has won numerous awards for this distinctive variety.

Alkoomi (☎ 9855 2229) is based near Frankland, some 130km to the north-west of Mt Barker, but it has a cellar in Albany (☎ 9841 2027), on Stirling Terrace, for those not keen to make the trip to what must be one of the world's most remote wine regions. Alkoomi has a consistently good range of wines, especially riesling, shiraz, cabernet sauvignon and Frankland River red and white. Alkoomi is also open to visitors at Frankland on Wingebellup Rd, west of town. It was the only cellar-sales outlet in the district in early 2000 but Frankland has undergone a surge in wine industry growth, with some of the biggest vineyards in the state planted in the late 1990s. More operations will be open to the public soon, so call the Mt Barker tourist office (☎ 9851 1163) for updated information.

Denmark, 55km south-west of Mt Barker near the south coast, offers a delightful mix of tall trees, green pastures and charming boutique wineries. The biggest is *Howard Park* (☎ 9848 2345) on Scotsdale Rd. This is the original Howard Park base, but a second winery opened in Margaret River in 2000. A small range is available under the premium Howard Park label, with the riesling and cabernet merlot regularly rated among Australia's best. The second label, Madfish, offers a bigger line-up of more affordable wines, many available only at the cellar door.

Scotsdale Rd is home to several other vineyards that are worth a visit, including *Matilda's Meadow* (☎ 9848 1951), which has wines and cafe-style meals, and *Karriview* (☎ 9840 9381), which produces outstanding chardonnay and pinot noir.

Just east of Denmark, on the South Coast Hwy (the main road to Albany), is one of the newest wineries, *West Cape Howe Wines* (☎ 9848 2959), named for the nearby southernmost tip of WA.

Contact the Albany tourist office (☎ 9841 1088), on Proudlove Parade near York St, for details of wine tours in the Great Southern.

PEMBERTON

Around 335km from Perth, the small Pemberton wine region lies amid the spectacular karri country of the south-west of WA.

Although less developed than other wine regions, the area shows great promise as a producer of chardonnay and pinot noir. Wine tourism makes a perfect companion to the beauty of the forests, and many of the tiny vineyards can be found along winding gravel roads between stands of karri and attractive farmland.

Salitage Winery (☎ 9776 1771), an impressive winery and restaurant on the Vasse Hwy a few kilometres east of Pemberton, is the biggest and best known of the locals, with chardonnay and pinot noir worth sampling. There is a free winery tour at 11 am daily.

Other highlights of the area are *Gloucester Ridge* (☎ 9776 1035), on the edge of Pemberton township (top chardonnay and an award-winning restaurant); *Donnelly River Wines* (☎ 9776 2052), 30km west on the Vasse Hwy, whose pinot noir and chardonnay are very good; and *Black George Wines* (☎ 9772 3569), a little off the main road, on Black Georges Rd. Its pretty rural setting and adjacent alpaca farm are worth a look.

Producers open by appointment only include: *Picardy Winery* (☎ 9776 0036), 11km east of Pemberton on the Vasse Hwy; *Smithbrook* (☎ 9772

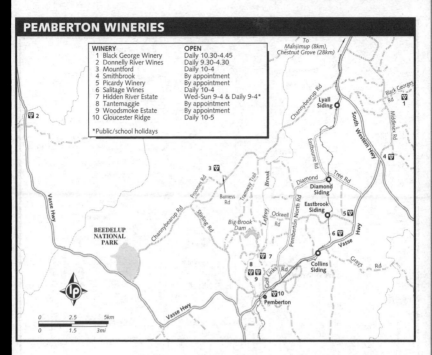

PEMBERTON WINERIES

WINERY	OPEN
1 Black George Winery	Daily 10.30-4.45
2 Donnelly River Wines	Daily 9.30-4.30
3 Mountford	Daily 10-4
4 Smithbrook	By appointment
5 Picardy Winery	By appointment
6 Salitage Wines	Daily 10-4
7 Hidden River Estate	Wed-Sun 9-4 & Daily 9-4*
8 Tantemaggie	By appointment
9 Woodsmoke Estate	By appointment
10 Gloucester Ridge	Daily 10-5

*Public/school holidays

3557), a picturesque vineyard overlooking superb karri forest, off Middlesex Rd 15km from Pemberton; **Woodsmoke Estate** (☎/fax 9776 0225), a boutique vineyard on Kemp Rd, 3km from Pemberton; and, close by, **Tantemaggie** (☎ 9776 1164), the largest family owned and operated vineyard in the region.

Nearby, **Hidden River Estate** (☎ 9776 1437) sells local boutique wines and simple, freshly prepared meals, and welcomes families. **Mountford** (☎/fax 9776 1345), off Channybearup Rd, is an award-winning winery and art gallery, housed in a building made of mud brick and timber. It also sells cider and scrumpy.

Chestnut Grove (☎ 9848 2959), 20km east of Manjimup on Perup Rd, on the fringe of the Pemberton region, is remote from the other producers but its wine is top-class, especially the verdelho, which has won several awards.

The Pemberton tourist office (☎ 9776 1133), on Brockman St, has a small but useful brochure and regional map.

SWAN VALLEY

The Swan Valley is the heart of WA's wine industry, where history and tradition survive. Vines were planted on the outskirts of the young Swan River Colony at Perth as early as the 1830s; many of them were planted

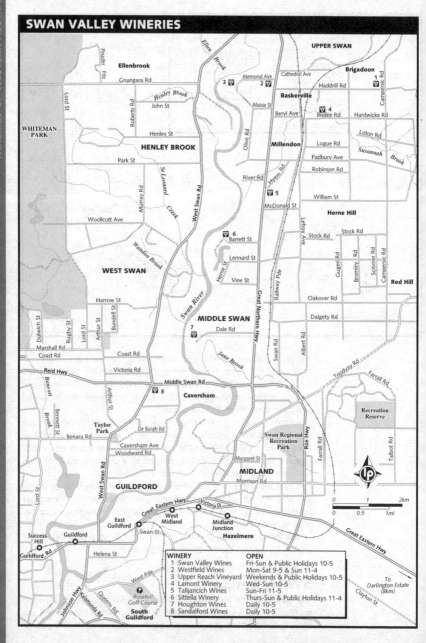

SWAN VALLEY WINERIES

WINERY	OPEN
1 Swan Valley Wines	Fri-Sun & Public Holidays 10-5
2 Westfield Wines	Mon-Sat 9-5 & Sun 11-4
3 Upper Reach Vineyard	Weekends & Public Holidays 10-5
4 Lamont Winery	Wed-Sun 10-5
5 Talijancich Wines	Sun-Fri 11-5
6 Sittella Winery	Thurs-Sun & Public Holidays 11-4
7 Houghton Wines	Daily 10-5
8 Sandalford Wines	Daily 10-5

by European migrants keen to maintain their traditions. Today the vines are tended by the descendants of those migrants and many others.

The majority of the 30 commercial wine makers in the valley are small family concerns. This allows them to approach their wine making in an individual way, offering a unique experience to the visitor, with many wines confined to cellar-door sales.

The style of wines grown here varies considerably from the cooler southern areas. The summer heat in the Swan Valley allows for greater ripening and is perfect for producing fine fortified wines. Most of the small cellars offer some gems in red or white liqueur, port and tokay.

White-wine varieties that thrive in the valley include verdelho, chenin blanc and chardonnay, with shiraz one of the best reds.

The wineries are clustered around the Swan River within 25km of Perth. There are several options for visitors who want someone else to do the driving, including river cruises that take in several cellars. The Swan Valley Tourism Council (☎ 9250 4400), at 508 Great Northern Hwy in Middle Swan, has details.

The Swan Valley is home to two of the state's biggest and oldest wineries: *Houghton Wines* (☎ 9274 9540), on Dale Rd in Middle Swan, and *Sandalford Wines* (☎ 9374 9300), on West Swan Rd in Caversham. Both combine high-class wines with historic, expansive, visitor-friendly cellar outlets.

Houghton's white burgundy is one of Australia's best-value and most popular white wines, but there is quality right through this winery's big range. It produces award-winning riesling, shiraz and cabernet sauvignon, much from its extensive vineyards in the state's south. It is one of the most popular wine venues in the valley, with broad grassed areas, a cafe and an art gallery.

Sandalford also has vineyards in the south, but the Swan Valley is its public focus. In 2000 Sandalford completed a major redevelopment of its Caversham base and now has one of the most attractive venues for wine visitors, including a new tasting area, popular restaurant, private tasting room and theatrette. There is also a viewing platform to watch work in the winery.

Of the smaller businesses, *Talijancich Wines* (☎ 9296 4289) is a must-see. On Hyem Rd just off the Great Northern Hwy, its fortified liqueur muscats are a treat. Talijancich is also renowned for its aged verdelho. *Lamont Winery* (☎ 9296 4485), on Bisdee Rd, Millendon, is a little farther off the main road but it has a wide selection of wines at reasonable prices, a top-notch restaurant and a gallery of fine art and craft produced locally.

Other places worth a visit include third-generation wine makers *Westfield Wines* (☎ 9296 4356), on Memorial Ave in Baskerville, whose chardonnay should be tried; *Swan Valley Wines* (☎ 9296 1501), on Haddrill Rd, Baskerville, which has top chenin blanc; and the relative newcomers *Sittella Winery* (☎ 9296 2600), on Barrett St in Herne Hill, and *Upper Reach Vineyard* (☎ 9296 0078), on Memorial Ave in Baskerville.

The wine country surrounding Perth extends into the Perth Hills to the east and south, with several vineyards worth seeking out. One of the best of these is **Darlington Estate** (☎ 9299 6268), around 15km from Caversham, and set amid the hillside jarrah forest on Nelson Rd at Darlington, 5km off the Great Eastern Hwy. Darlington Estate also has a well-regarded restaurant.

TASTING

Most wine producers offer free tasting at their cellar door, so you can try before you buy, but some choose to restrict their tasting list and charge a small fee to try some of the higher-priced wines. Others have a flat charge to taste. This can be up to $5 but is refundable if you buy something. Usually the fee is posted clearly on the tasting list, so you don't get caught out.

It's OK to spit. Cellar-sales areas always provide a spittoon or two, so feel free to use them. All those small sips add up if you keep swallowing and can quickly put you over the legal limit for blood–alcohol content when you're driving. If you're new to the spitting caper, it's best not to try to aim from too far away. Things can get messy if you miss!

FESTIVALS

Where there's a wine industry, there's a festival, and WA's wine regions have their fair share of celebrations, including the following:

Leeuwin Estate Concert (☎ 9757 6253) Held in the grounds of Leeuwin Estate winery in Margaret River in February each year, this is a highlight on the WA social calendar.

Taste of the Valley (☎ 9250 4400) This series of wine and food functions in the Swan Valley takes place throughout April each year.

Spring in the Valley (☎ 9250 4400) The Swan Valley's major festival, featuring the region's wine, food and art, is held on the second weekend in October each year.

Great Southern Wine Festival (☎ 9851 1163) Incorporating the Mt Barker Wine Show, this series of wine and food functions is held over a weekend in late October.

Margaret River Wine Festival (☎ 9757 2911) Held over the third week in November, this festival features a range of food, wine, art and music events.

Craig McKeough

South Coast

To the east of Capes Naturaliste and Leeuwin and the karri forests is the vast area of the south coast, sometimes referred to as 'the Great Southern'. This includes the coastline from Walpole in the west to Cape Arid, east of Esperance. The scenery is magnificent and the main road often hugs the coastline.

This region has some of the state's best coastal parks: D'Entrecasteaux, Walpole-Nornalup, William Bay, West Cape Howe, Fitzgerald River and Cape Le Grand. The towns throughout this area all have their own distinctive characters; they include Denmark, 'old' Albany and Esperance. Some excellent wines hail from this part of the world (see the special section 'Wineries of Western Australia').

Inland, north of Albany, are two of the best mountain parks in Australia – the 'ecological islands' of the Stirling Range, which rise abruptly 1000m above the surrounding plains, and the karri forest and ancient granite spires of the Porongurup Range.

Getting There & Away

SkyWest Airlines (☎ 13 1300) flies twice daily from Perth to Albany (☎ 9841 6655) as well as several times a day from Perth to Esperance (see the Western Australia Air Fares map in the Getting Around chapter).

Westrail (☎ 1800-099 150, 13 1053, 9326 2222) has a daily Perth-Albany service ($35.10) via Williams, Kojonup and Mt Barker ($30.60, for the Stirling Range), which takes six hours. A longer route goes via Northam and Wagin ($35.10, about eight hours). You can also travel by train to Bunbury then by coach from Bunbury to Albany ($44.70 through fare).

There's a direct coach from Perth to Denmark on Friday ($39.30, eight hours); on other days of the week you have to take the train to Bunbury and connect with the coach ($41.50, about eight hours). Both services also stop at Walpole ($36.70).

Westrail operates a bus service three times a week from Kalgoorlie-Boulder to

HIGHLIGHTS

- Walking among (and above) the giant tingle trees in the Valley of the Giants, Walpole-Nornalup National Park

- Exploring the beautiful, rugged Stirling Range and the ancient Porongurup Range

- Whale-watching in King George Sound near Albany

- Tasting the Great Southern's best wine

- Driving or walking through the biosphere reserve of the Fitzgerald River National Park with its unique flora

- Visiting Cape Le Grand National Park, with its stunning views from the top of Frenchman Peak, and the solitude of Lucky Bay

- Relaxing in historic Albany, an easy distance from the Natural Bridge, the Gap and Two People's Bay

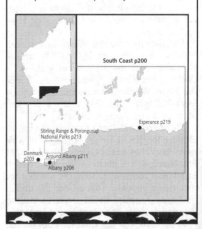

South Coast p200

Esperance p219

Stirling Range & Porongurup National Parks p213

Denmark p203

Around Albany p211

Albany p206

Esperance ($33.50), an Esperance-Albany service ($45.90) and a 10-hour service from Perth to Esperance ($52.60) that runs via Jerramungup (on Monday), Lake Grace (Wednesday, Thursday, Friday and Sunday) and Hyden (Tuesday).

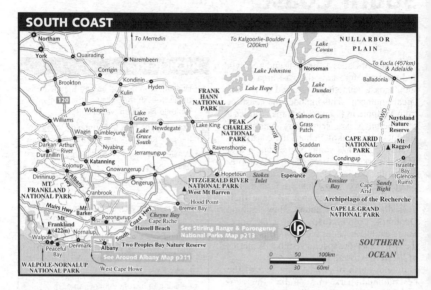

SOUTH COAST

WALPOLE & NORNALUP

The South Western Hwy almost meets the coast at the twin inlets of Walpole and Nornalup, then becomes the South Coast Hwy east of here.

The heavily forested Walpole-Nornalup National Park covers 180 sq km around Nornalup Inlet and the town of Walpole; it contains beaches, rugged coastline, inlets, the Nuyts Wilderness area and the magnificent Valley of the Giants. It's a pleasant place to spend a couple of days.

There are a number of scenic drives, including the Knoll Drive 3km east of Walpole; the Valley of the Giants Rd; and to **Mt Frankland**, 29km north of Walpole. At Mt Frankland you can climb to the summit for panoramic views or walk around the trail at its base. Opposite Knoll Drive is Hilltop Rd, which leads to a **giant tingle tree**; this road continues to the **Circular Pool** on the Frankland River, a popular canoeing spot.

About 13km west of Walpole via Crystal Springs is a 4WD road to Mandalay Beach, where the *Mandalay*, a Norwegian barque, was wrecked in 1911. It seems to appear out of the sands every 10 years as the sea washes the sand away.

Parrot Jungle, off the South Coast Hwy at Bow Bridge, is an aviary that has a host of native birds, including rainbow lorikeets, Major Mitchell and black cockatoos, western and eastern king parrots and rose-breasted cockatoos, as well as exotic birds such as Amazon rainforest macaws.

The helpful and informative Walpole tourist office (☎ 9840 1111) is at the Pioneer Cottage on South Coast Hwy. Its free *Walpole, Nornalup, Peaceful Bay Visitor Guide* tells you everything you need to know. It also carries other interesting local guides and distributes free Department of Conservation and Land Management (CALM) leaflets outlining walks in and around Walpole, including the Hilltop Giant Tingle Tree Trail (40 minutes) and a section of the Bibbulmun Track (which passes through Walpole) to Coalmine Beach (two hours). You can hire canoes from Tree Top Canoe Hire (☎ 9840 1272).

The CALM office (☎ 9840 1027), also on the South Coast Hwy, can provide plenty of information about the Walpole-Nornalup National Park, including the protected and relatively inaccessible Nuyts Wilderness, and bushwalking and camping in the area.

Valley of the Giants Tree Top Walk

The Tree Top Walk has become Walpole's main *raison d'être*, and it is not hard to see why. A 600m-long ramp rises from the floor of the valley, allowing visitors to get up high into the canopy of the giant tingle trees. You really are walking 'through' the tree tops. At its highest point the ramp is 40m above the ground and the views below and above are simply stunning. It's on a gentle incline so it's easy to walk, and it is even accessible by wheelchair.

The ramp is an engineering feat in itself. Reader Helen Tapping's description that 'it looks quite safe – but it doesn't half wobble' is an understatement, and vertigo sufferers might have a few problems with it. It has been so successful as a tourist attraction that a delegation of Walpole locals involved with its planning and construction was recently invited to the USA to assist with plans for a similar structure in the redwood forests of the west coast.

A boardwalk at ground level, the **Ancient Empire**, meanders around and through the base of veteran red tingles, some of which are 16m in circumference, including one that soars to 46m.

Four species of rare eucalypts grow in the Valley of the Giants area: inland are the red, yellow and Rates tingle, and closer to the coast is the red flowering gum (see Flora in the Facts about Western Australia chapter for more information). Pleasant, shady and ferny paths lead through the forests, which are frequented by bushwalkers.

The Valley of the Giants (☎ 9840 8263) is open from 9 am to 4.15 pm daily (extended to 8 am to 5.15 pm in the Christmas school holidays). Entry to the Tree Top Walk is $5/2 for adults/children. The Ancient Empire walk is free.

Wilderness Cruise

A trip to Walpole would not be complete without a WOW Wilderness Cruise (☎ 9840 1036) through the Walpole and Nornalup Inlets and the river systems. Knowledgeable and enthusiastic Gary Muir – who is a cross between a scientific encyclopaedia, a history book and an entertainer – brings this magnificent landscape and its ecology to life with anecdotes of the Aborigines in the area, early settlers, salmon fishers and shipwrecked pirates. The 2½-hour trips (book at the tourist office) run at 10 am daily (also 2 pm in school-holiday periods); snacks (including Gary's mum's home-made cake) are included in the $25/15 adults/children ticket.

Places to Stay

There are a number of *camp sites* in the Walpole-Nornalup National Park, including

---

Go South for Adventure

The south coast is a popular destination for adventure-sports enthusiasts, who come here for the paragliding, rock-climbing, abseiling or challenging bushwalking.

Most operators work on a seasonal basis, as there is not enough traffic for companies to be set up year-round, but there are often groups heading down from Perth. Contact local tourist offices or the Traveller's Club Tour & Information Centre (☎ 9226 0660), at 499 Wellington St, Perth, for an update on who's offering what and when.

The Great Southern is the hub of the Western Australia (WA) climbing scene, with West Cape Howe, Torndirrup, Porongurup and the Stirling Range National Parks. West Cape Howe is remote climbing territory where a group of three should be the minimum. The area has multipitch climbs on granite sea cliffs. Torndirrup National Park includes the Gap, Natural Bridge and Amphitheatre granite climbing areas. Bluff Knoll in the Stirling Range is the closest that WA gets to offering a real mountaineering experience and has been the scene of many 'epics'. Climbs can be up to 350m long, involving a dozen or more pitches and as many hours to complete.

Those who'd prefer to fly above the Great Southern should contact the Australian Paragliding Academy (☎ 0418-954 176), which is based in Albany.

tent sites at Crystal Springs and huts at both Fernhook Falls and at Mt Frankland. Contact the CALM office (☎ 9840 1027) for bookings and prices.

Coalmine Beach (☎ 9840 1026), on Knoll Dr, has tent/powered sites for \$14.50/16.50 for two people, and cabins from \$50 to \$90. The new ***Walpole Backpackers*** (☎ 9840 1244), on the corner of Pier St and Park Ave, has dorm beds (\$15), doubles (\$38) and family rooms (\$50) and is run by enthusiastic managers. ***Tingle All Over*** (☎ 9840 1041), on Nockolds St, has budget accommodation with shared bathrooms, kitchen and lounge for \$25/40 singles/doubles.

The best B&B in town is ***The Ridgeway*** (☎ 9840 1036), on Walpole St overlooking Walpole Inlet, which is a bargain at \$35/70 for singles/doubles. ***Dolphin House*** (☎ 9840 1304, 41 Latham Ave) is also good value at \$45/88 for singles/doubles. It can provide evening meals on request.

The ***Tree Top Walk Motel & Restaurant*** (☎ 1800-420 777, 9840 1444), on Nockolds St, is pretty pricey as motels go, at \$109 for a double (no single rate), but the rooms are very comfortable, with free in-house movies. Down a notch (both price and quality) is the ***Walpole Hotel-Motel*** (☎ 9840 1023), on the South Coast Hwy.

There are also many farmstays and cottages in the area; inquire at the tourist office. You can rent a houseboat with ***Houseboat Holidays*** (☎ 9840 1310), on Boronia Ave, but you'll have to book months ahead.

Places to Eat

By day there's plenty of choice, with at least three *cafes* along the South Coast Hwy. In Nornalup, the ***Nornalup Tea Rooms*** does tasty home-made soups (\$7.50), sandwiches and a daily pasta special (\$10). The food is excellent. Also good for light lunches, coffee and cakes is the ***Thurlby Herb Farm***, on Gardiner Rd 14km north of Walpole, which also makes and sells herb pillows, olive-oil soaps and delicious jams and chutneys.

At night, you might find a cafe open (up to 7 pm only). Otherwise go for a counter meal at the ***Walpole Hotel-Motel***, on the South Coast Hwy, or a more formal (more expensive, but good) meal at the ***Tree Top Walk Motel & Restaurant*** (☎ 9840 1444), on Nockolds St. Self-caterers can grab supplies at the ***supermarket***, on Nockolds St.

PEACEFUL BAY

Some 24km east of Walpole, Peaceful Bay is an archetypal, get-away-from-it-all place. This is a beach area for those keen on fishing and swimming. There is a *caravan park* (☎ 9840 8060) with powered sites/on-site vans starting at \$14/30 for two people, and ***Peaceful Bay Chalets*** (☎ 9840 8169), on Peppermint Way, with units starting at \$50 for two people.

DENMARK
pop 3500

Denmark, or Koorabup ('place of the black swan'), 55km west of Albany, was established to supply timber for the goldfields. The area was once settled by Aborigines, and 3000-year-old fish traps have been found in Wilson Inlet.

Today it is a popular holiday spot with a good selection of restaurants, wineries and accommodation. Fishing, sailing and surfing are popular pastimes and there are some fine beaches in the area (especially Ocean Beach for surfing). It is also a good base for trips into the karri forests.

Walpole and Denmark fight over which town 'owns' the Tree Top Walk (see under Walpole & Nornalup earlier). Walpole wins on proximity but the Valley of the Giants actually falls within Denmark shire.

The 17-sq-km William Bay National Park west of Denmark has coastal dunes, granite boulders, heathland and mature karri forest.

Information

The friendly Denmark tourist office (☎ 9848 2055), housed in an old church on Strickland St, has Heritage Trail brochures, including brochures on the Mokare Trail (a 3km trail along the Denmark River) and the Wilson Inlet Trail (a 6km trail starting at the river mouth). It sells a *Discover Denmark* information package (\$2) complete with maps, attractions, accommodation and restaurant listings.

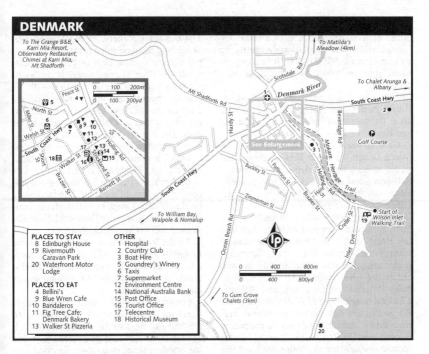

DENMARK

To The Grange B&B,
Karri Mia Resort,
Observatory Restaurant,
Chimes at Karri Mia,
Mt Shadforth

To Matilda's
Meadow (4km)

To Chalet Arunga &
Albany

Scotsdale Rd

Denmark River

South Coast Hwy

Mt Shadforth Rd

Hardy St

Beveridge Rd

Golf Course

See Enlargement

Mokare Rd

Heritage

Buckley St

Patterson St

Hollings Rd

Haig Rd

Brazier St

Trail

To William Bay,
Walpole & Nornalup

Ocean Beach Rd

Zimmerman St

Creilin St

Inlet Dve

Start of
Wilson Inlet
Walking Trail

19

To Gum Grove
Chalets (3km)

20

Peace St

North St

Miller St

Welsh St

South Coast Hwy

Short St

Brazier St

Walker St

Strickland St

Barnett St

Hollings Rd

South Coast Hwy

0   100   200m
0   100   200yd

0   400   800m
0   400   800yd

PLACES TO STAY
8 Edinburgh House
19 Rivermouth
   Caravan Park
20 Waterfront Motor
   Lodge

PLACES TO EAT
4 Bellini's
9 Blue Wren Cafe
10 Bandaleros
11 Fig Tree Cafe;
   Denmark Bakery
13 Walker St Pizzeria

OTHER
1 Hospital
2 Country Club
3 Boat Hire
5 Goundrey's Winery
6 Taxis
7 Supermarket
12 Environment Centre
14 National Australia Bank
15 Post Office
16 Tourist Office
17 Telecentre
18 Historical Museum

For Internet access head to the Denmark Telecentre, next to the tourist office in Strickland St.

The Environment Centre (☎ 9848 1644), on Strickland St, has an extensive library and bookshop.

Things to See & Do

There are fine views from **Mt Shadforth Lookout**, while the **William Bay National Park**, 15km west of Denmark, has fine coastal scenery. There are also scenic spots such as Greens Pool, Elephant Rocks, Madfish Bay, Tower Hill and Waterfall Beach.

Sandpiper Cruises (☎ 9848 1734) runs two-hour sightseeing tours of the Wilson Inlet and Denmark River departing from Town Jetty at Berridge Park at 10 am all year (also 2 pm December to May). Tickets cost $13/7 adults/children. George and Adrea Endacott (☎ 9848 2604) run 4WD day tours to West Cape Howe National Park ($63) and to the Valley of the Giants ($68).

Tours include morning tea and lunch. Book at the tourist office.

Denmark Southern Wonders organises winery tours ($35) and Tree Top Walk tours ($35), and a variety of canoe adventures: a river paddle from 9 to 11 am Wednesday ($20/12 adults/children), a 'sun-up' canoe at 7.30 am Saturday ($35/18), and a 'sundowner' at 3.30 pm Sunday ($35/18).

Places to Stay

None of Denmark's four caravan parks can be classified as fabulous. The closest to town is the *Rivermouth Caravan Park* (☎ 9848 1262), on Inlet Dr 1km south of the town centre; tent sites cost $11 and on-site vans start at $30 for two people.

The *Waterfront Motor Lodge* (☎ 9848 1147, 63 Inlet Dr) has dorm beds from $15, refurbished motel rooms from $55 (for two people), and two-storey, rustic, self-contained apartments. *Edinburgh House* (☎ 1800-671 477, 9848 1477, 31 South Coast Hwy), in the centre of town, is a funny old guest-house from another era, with a huge TV lounge and clean single/double/family en suite rooms for $55/80/100. It is a convenient spot for those without their own transport.

There are many varieties of farmstays, B&Bs, chalets and cottages in the Denmark area; the tourist office keeps a current list and has a free booking service.

Gum Grove Chalets (☎ *9848 1378)*, on Ocean Beach Rd about 3km south of Denmark, is recommended by many readers. Self-contained units with TV and potbelly stove cost from $50 to $85 for two people. Larger chalets sleep up to nine.

The Grange (☎ *9848 2319)*, on Mt Shadforth Rd about 4km east of town, has luxury B&B for $70 per person. The cooked 'farmhouse' breakfast, complimentary nightcaps, chocolates and freshly brewed coffee are nice touches. At Torbay, about halfway between Denmark and Albany, *Chalet Arunga* (☎ *9845 1025)*, on Hunwick Rd South, is a self-contained 'retreat' surrounded by farmland and close to the beach. Rooms cost $180 (doubles) or $240 (for four people). Gourmet continental breakfast provisions are provided.

Two top-of-the-range choices are *Chimes at Karri Mia* (☎ *9848 2255)* and *Karri Mia Resort* (☎ *9848 2233)*, both on Mt Shadforth Rd. They are separate enterprises on the same land, with magnificent views over Denmark and Wilson Inlet. The former is an architect-designed luxury guesthouse, tastefully decorated with Indonesian antiques. Its rooms have spas (fragrant bubble baths and candles are provided), some have double showers and there's complimentary nibbles throughout the day. A gym and beauty salon complete the five-star offering. Double rooms cost $154 to $253 (champagne gourmet breakfast included) depending on the view, the size of your bed and the number of bubbles in your bath. Karri Mia Resort comprises 10 tastefully decorated and fully equipped (CD, video, electric blankets included) self-contained bungalows sleeping up to six people for $140 to $195.

Places to Eat

The *Denmark Bakery*, on Fig Tree Square, Strickland St, won third prize in a national pie-making competition in 1997 and standards have not slipped since. It makes its sausage rolls ($2) even tastier with by adding cheese, ham and tomato, and the chicken pies ($2) are great. Get in early, as the beef pies (especially) just walk out the door. The *Fig Tree Cafe*, next to the bakery, does OK coffee (you can't ask for miracles) and has a good choice of toasted sandwiches, light meals and cakes.

Bellini's, on Holling Rd, has a great balcony with views of the river. The food could be classified as Greek even though the name is Italian, but you are in Denmark, Australia. A meal will set you back about $25.

All the locals eat at the *Waterfront Motor Lodge* (☎ *9848 1147, 63 Inlet Dr)*, which has a lovely outlook over the inlet. The food is good, too. It gets packed to bursting so you might need to book.

For an enchilada fix head to *Bandaleros Mexican Restaurant* (☎ *9848 2188, 16 Holling Rd)* next to the Denmark Hotel. It does authentic, reasonably priced food and has good vegetarian options. Seafood burritos cost $15. If you're after pizza, look no further than *Walker St Pizzeria*, on the corner of Walker and Strickland Sts, open from 5 pm daily for eat-in or takeaway pizzas.

Matilda's Meadow, on Hamilton Rd, is a pretty winery about 4km north of Denmark. You can taste its range of wines as an aperitif and then move into the restaurant for a meal of good country cooking. There's a bit of 1960s music memorabilia as the manager is Keith Potger from the Seekers.

The aptly named *Observatory* (☎ *9848 2600)*, on Mt Shadforth Rd at Karri Mia Resort, has views and food to die for. Try a light lunch of delicious roasted capsicum, caramelised onion and brie tartlet ($12.50), or dinner of Spanish paella ($18.50) or local marron with goat's cheese tortelli in burnt-butter sauce ($15.50). It has a good Great Southern wine list – all local labels.

For self-caterers, there's a *supermarket* on the corner of South Coast Hwy and Strickland St.

ALBANY

pop 26,000

Albany is the commercial centre of the southern region and the oldest European settlement in the state. It was established in 1826, three years before Perth. The area was previously occupied by Aborigines and there is much evidence of their earlier presence, especially around Oyster Harbour.

Albany's excellent harbour, on King George Sound, made it a thriving whaling port. Whales are still very much a part of the Albany experience, but instead of being brutally harpooned for their oil they are now hunted down for less-traumatic photo opportunities.

Later Albany was a coaling station for British ships bound for the east coast. During WWI it was the gathering point for troop transport ships of the 1st Australian Imperial Force (AIF) before they sailed for Egypt and the Gallipoli campaign.

The coastline around Albany features some of Australia's most rugged and spectacular scenery. There are a number of pristine beaches in the area where you don't have to compete for sand space – try the misnamed Misery Beach, or Ledge Bay and Nanarup Beaches.

The Bibbulmun Track (see the boxed text under Activities in the Facts for the Visitor chapter) ends at Albany, just outside the tourist office. Some of the log books of the end-to-end walkers are kept in the tourist office – have a read.

Information

The informative and helpful Albany tourist office (☎ 1800-644 088, 9841 1088) is in the old train station on Proudlove Parade. It's open from 8.15 am to 5.30 pm weekdays, 9 am to 5 pm weekends. Pick up an information pack ($1), which includes a good town map and information on local attractions.

The post office is at 218 York St. Most of the banks, all of which have ATMs, are on York St. The CALM office (☎ 9842 4500) is at 120 Albany Hwy.

For Internet access, go to Yak Bar (☎ 9842 9399), at 38 Stirling Terrace. The nearby Albany Rods and Tackle hires out fishing gear and can provide you with all the local information you'll need. Southcoast Diving Supplies (☎ 9841 7176), at 84b Serpentine Rd, can do the same for divers.

Old Buildings

Albany has some fine old colonial buildings. **Stirling Terrace** is noted for its Victorian shopfronts. The informative **Albany Residency Museum**, opposite the Old Gaol, was originally built in the 1850s as the home of the resident magistrate. It is open from 10 am to 5 pm daily; admission is by donation. Displays include seafaring subjects, flora and fauna and Aboriginal artefacts. Housed in another building is 'Sea & Touch', a great hands-on experience for both children and adults that focuses on the marine and animal world (eg, sea urchins, possum fur, bones). There is also a leather artisan's workshop which has an array of saddlery tools and machines.

Next to the museum is a full-scale **replica** of the brig *Amity*, the ship that carried Albany's founding party (including commandant Major Edmund Lockyear, his captain, soldiers, convict tradesmen, a surgeon and livestock) to the area from Sydney in 1826. It is open from 9 am to 5 pm daily (admission is $2/0.50 adults/children).

The **Old Gaol**, built in 1851, was originally intended as a hiring depot for ticket-of-leave convicts. Most were in private employment by 1855 so it was closed until 1872, when it was extended and reopened as a civil gaol. Now a folk museum, it is open from 10 am to 4.15 pm daily. Admission is $3.50/2, and this includes entry to the 1832 wattle-and-daub **Patrick Taylor Cottage**.

The National Trust–owned **Old Farm at Strawberry Hill**, 2km from town, is one of the oldest farms in the state, established in 1827 as the government farm for Albany. The homestead features antiques and artefacts that belonged to the farm's original owner, and beautiful gardens. It is open from 10 am to 5 pm daily (admission $3/2).

The restored **old post office**, built in 1870, now houses Albany's Inter-Colonial Museum. It has an interesting collection of

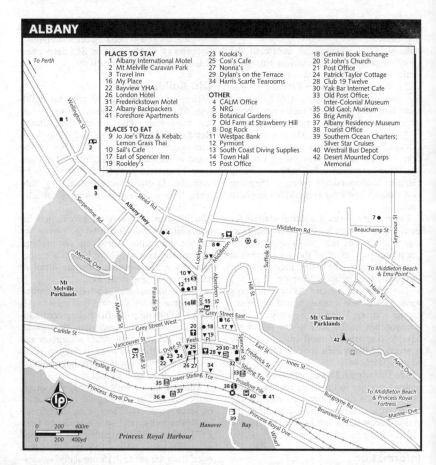

ALBANY

PLACES TO STAY
1 Albany International Motel
2 Mt Melville Caravan Park
3 Travel Inn
16 My Place
22 Bayview YHA
26 London Hotel
31 Frederickstown Motel
32 Albany Backpackers
41 Foreshore Apartments

PLACES TO EAT
9 Jo Joe's Pizza & Kebab;
    Lemon Grass Thai
10 Sail's Cafe
17 Earl of Spencer Inn
19 Rookley's

23 Kooka's
25 Cosi's Cafe
27 Nonna's
29 Dylan's on the Terrace
34 Harris Scarfe Tearooms

OTHER
4 CALM Office
5 NRG
6 Botanical Gardens
7 Old Farm at Strawberry Hill
8 Dog Rock
11 Westpac Bank
12 Pyrmont
13 South Coast Diving Supplies
14 Town Hall
15 Post Office

18 Gemini Book Exchange
20 St John's Church
21 Post Office
24 Patrick Taylor Cottage
28 Club 19 Twelve
30 Yak Bar Internet Cafe
33 Old Post Office;
    Inter-Colonial Museum
35 Old Gaol; Museum
36 Brig Amity
37 Albany Residency Museum
38 Tourist Office
39 Southern Ocean Charters;
    Silver Star Cruises
40 Westrail Bus Depot
42 Desert Mounted Corps
    Memorial

communications equipment from WA's past; it is open daily and admission is free.

Other historic buildings in town include the **train station**, **St John's Anglican Church** and the **courthouse**. A guided walking-tour brochure of colonial buildings is available from the tourist office.

Views & Walks

There are fine views over the coast and inland from the twin peaks, **Mt Clarence** and **Mt Melville**, which overlook the town. On top of Mt Clarence is the Desert Mounted Corps Memorial, originally erected in Port

Said as a memorial to the events of WWI. It was brought here when the Suez crisis in 1956 made colonial reminders less than popular in Egypt.

To climb Mt Clarence follow the track accessible from the end of Grey St East; turn left, take the first turn on the right and follow the path by the water tanks. The walk is tough but the views make it worthwhile; take a picnic and enjoy a well-earned rest at the top. By car, take Apex Dr.

There are also panoramic views from the lookout tower on Mt Melville; the turn-off to the tower is off Serpentine Rd.

A coastal trail and boardwalk runs from Middleton Beach to the Pilot Station (from where you can follow Princess Royal Dr back into town). The walk takes about an hour. This trail is part of a project for 35km of walking paths to link Oyster Harbour, Middleton Bay, Albany town and French-man Bay.

Other Attractions

As Albany was a strategic port, its vulnerability to attack loomed as a potential threat to Australia's security. The **Princess Royal Fortress**, on Mt Adelaide, was built in 1893. The restored buildings, gun emplacements and fine views make it well worth a visit. Particularly poignant are the photos of the troop transports on their way to Gallipoli. The fortress is open from 7.30 am to 5 pm daily. Admission is $3/2/7 adults/children/families.

On Middleton Rd is Albany's most bizarre sight: **Dog Rock** is a painted boulder that looks like a dog's head.

Whale-Watching

The whale-watching season is from July to mid-October – southern right and hump-back whales can be observed near the bays and coves of King George Sound. Silver Star Cruises (☎ 9842 9876) and Spinners Charters (☎ 9841 7151) operate whale-watching cruises. Ask at the tourist office about any other charters.

Organised Tours

The *Silver Star* leaves the town jetty at 9.30 am daily for a 2½-hour cruise around King George Sound. The cruise costs $25/16 adults/children. In whale season these tours become whale-watching expeditions, and an extra tour at 1 pm is sometimes run.

Southern Ocean Charters (☎ 9844 3615) has a 15m catamaran, *Big Day Out*. In whale season there are departures from the town jetty at 9.30 am and 1 and 3.30 pm. Tickets cost $25/16/70 for adults/children/families.

Spinners Charters (☎ 9841 7151) runs deep-sea fishing trips, scenic cruises and whale-watching tours. It operates from the Emu Point jetty.

Escape Tours (☎ 9841 2865) operates from the tourist office and has land-based half-/full-day tours around Albany (to the Stirling Range, Tree Top Walk, Plantagenet Wines and Porongurup Range, among other destinations) for $36/72. Albany Taxi Tours (☎ 9844 4444) charges $25 per hour for tours (a maximum of four passengers). Ask the tourist office for information on these and others.

Albany Wine Tours has half-/full-day winery tours ($40/70) to Denmark, Mt Barker and the Porongurup Range (no need to worry about driving with a few glasses of wine in you).

Places to Stay

Camping & Caravan Parks There are caravan parks aplenty in and around Albany. The closest are *Mt Melville Caravan Park (☎ 9841 4616)*, on the corner of Lion and Wellington Sts, 1km north of town, and the spotless *Middleton Beach Caravan Park (☎ 9841 3593)*, on Middleton Rd 3km east of town and right on the beach. Both have tent/powered sites for around $14/18 and tidy park cabins starting at $45 for two people. *Frenchman Bay Caravan Park (☎ 9844 4015)*, on Frenchman Bay Rd, is similarly priced and well positioned for the Torndirrup National Park and Whaleworld Museum (see under Around Albany later in this chapter). The tourist office has a list of other places.

Hostels An excellent option is *Albany Backpackers (☎ 9841 8848)*, on the corner of Spencer St and Stirling Terrace, which has extras such as free coffee and cake each afternoon, bike hire and in-house 4WD tours. Dorm beds cost $17; double/twin rooms cost $42 for the first night and $38 for additional nights. There is also limited free email access.

The rambling *Bayview YHA (☎ 9842 3388, 49 Duke St)* is 400m from the centre; dorm beds cost $14, single rooms cost $20 (available winter only) and twins/doubles cost $34 (nonmembers pay $3 extra). There are also surfboards, bicycles and kites for hire here.

B&Bs, Hotels & Motels Albany also has a number of reasonably priced guesthouses and B&Bs; the tourist office has a full list and can help with bookings.

Centrally located is the *Frederickstown Motel* (☎ 9841 1600), on the corner of Frederick and Spencer Sts, which has singles/doubles with harbour views starting at $82/92. The revamped *London Hotel* (☎ 9841 1048), on Stirling Terrace near York St, has singles/doubles with shared bathrooms starting at $25/40 or with en suite starting at $35/60. It also has dorm beds for $15 per person.

There are several motels on the Albany Hwy, good as a last resort if you can't find anything better in town or if you arrive late at night. Most were built in the 1960s and 1970s and haven't seen a renovator since. The *Albany International* (☎ 9841 7399, 270 Albany Hwy) has a restaurant, in-house movies, tennis court and heated pool. Rooms cost from $83 (single or double) and triples cost $93. At the *Travel Inn* (☎ 9841 4144, 191 Albany Hwy) deluxe singles/doubles cost $98/105 and spa rooms cost $115/130. The *Quality Inn Motel* (☎ 9841 1177, 369 Albany Hwy) has doubles from $68 to $85. There's a bar and in-house movies.

Down at Middleton Beach, the *Discovery Inn* (☎ 9842 5535, 9 Middleton Rd) is a real bargain at $37.50/59.50 for singles/doubles in clean, comfortable rooms with shared bathrooms. The price includes breakfast. In the same area, *Terrace Cottage* (☎ 9842 9901, 36 Marine Terrace), 100m from the beach, has comfortable singles/doubles for $45/70. Upmarket at Middleton Beach is the *Esplanade Hotel* (☎ 9842 1711), on the corner of Adelaide Crescent and Flinders Parade. Deluxe rooms cost from $144 to $210 depending on the view. There are also self-contained apartments starting at $130 per night for two people.

Farther along the coast towards Emu Point, *B&B by the Sea* (☎ 9844 1135), on Griffiths St, has en suite double rooms for $80 including breakfast. Another Emu Point choice is the *Emu Point Motel* (☎ 9844 1001), on the corner of Mermaid Ave and Medcalf Parade, which has singles/doubles for $64/69.

Other Accommodation Friendly Margaret from Scotland runs *My Place* (☎ 9842 3242, 47–61 Grey St East), in the centre of town, where comfortable self-contained rooms with kitchenette and en suite start at $75 (a studio for two people) and rise to $85/110 for a one-/two-bedroom unit.

Foreshore Apartments (☎ 9842 8800, 81–89 Proudlove Parade), near the tourist office, dubs itself 'executive apartments'. One-/two-bedroom apartments cost $110/170, although prices jump to $135/210 during school holidays and on long weekends.

There are a number of possibilities at Middleton Beach, including the extremely popular (read 'book early') *Pelicans* (☎ 9841 7500, 3 Golf Links Rd), which offers self-contained budget units for $65 and standard/deluxe units (sleeping up to four) for $75/85. The prices quoted are for two people; each extra person costs $10.

Top of the range at Middleton Beach is the Mediterranean-inspired *Balneaire* (☎ 1800-625 877, 9842 2877, 27 Adelaide Crescent). Extremely comfortable, pretty two-bedroom apartments with all the trimmings cost $180.

The town's grandest accommodation is the *Castlereagh Luxury Boutique Villas* (☎ 9842 0500, 9 Flinders Parade), on the corner of Barnett St at Middleton Beach. Tastefully decorated two-bedroom apartments with fully equipped kitchen and everything that opens and shuts cost from $150 for two people and $25 for each extra person.

Cello's of Churchlane (☎ 9844 3370), on Churchlane Rd off the Hassell Hwy about 15 minutes' drive out of town, has a magnificent restaurant (see Places to Eat) and a couple of self-contained chalets. You would be forgiven for thinking you've died and gone to heaven: The setting, above the beautiful Kalgan River, is paradisiacal. Self-contained chalets sleeping up to six are a bargain at $90 a double for the first night then $45 a double for every extra night. Extra people are charged at $40 per couple per night.

For movable accommodation try *Albany Houseboat Holidays* (☎ 9844 8726, 107 The Esplanade, Lower King).

This is just a small selection of available accommodation; the Albany tourist office has more details.

Places to Eat

Kooka's Restaurant (☎ 9841 5889, 204 Stirling Terrace), in a restored old house, has long been regarded as the best restaurant in town. The food is excellent; the restaurant has (not surprisingly) won numerous awards. Kooka's lamb curry served with potato nan and cardamom rice ($19) is nothing short of divine, and the share-or-despair desserts ($7.50) include rich puddings of the sticky-date or bread-and-butter variety. Expect to pay about $38 for a three-course meal. At the time of writing it was about to change hands; let's hope it maintains its high standards.

At **Rookley's** (36 Peel Place), a gourmet deli on the corner of York St, you can sit at alfresco tables and watch Albany walk by. The best coffee in town is complemented by fabulous food – gourmet pies such as spinach and fetta or sweet potato and olive ($5), 'Mediterranean' rolls and focaccia ($5.50 to $9), the world's most delicious date slice ($1.50) and cakes that make you drool ($5). Similarly tasty food at similar prices is served at **Sail's Cafe** (7 Albany Hwy), near the corner of York St next to the Westpac bank. It also has outdoor tables.

Other long-standing and ever-popular cafes in town include **Cosi's Cafe**, on Peels Place, which serves good breakfasts, coffee, cakes and light lunches, and **Dylan's on the Terrace** (82 Stirling Terrace), which has a good range of light meals including hamburgers and pancakes at reasonable prices. It is open late most nights and early for breakfast, and has a takeaway section.

If you fancy pasta, **Nonna's** (135 York St) might hit the spot. The menu lists Italian-inspired dishes and there are good specials on coffee and cake. Readers have recommended the **Harris Scarfe Tearooms**, on Lower Stirling Terrace, for its great-value bottomless cups of coffee and tea.

For pub counter meals head to the **Earl of Spencer Historic Inn**, on the corner of Earl and Spencer Sts, or the **London Hotel**, on Stirling Terrace, which also has daily roasts.

Lemon Grass Thai (370 Middleton Rd) has a good range of Thai food (including vegetarian meals) to take away. It also does home deliveries. **Jo Joe's Pizza & Kebab** (362 Middleton Rd) near Dog Rock is a great place for late-night souvlaki or felafel. Its lamb gyros with sour cream and garlic ($6.20), filled with fresh, tasty ingredients, was better than any this writer had recently eaten in the Ionian islands.

The **Yak Bar Internet Cafe** (38 Stirling Terrace), near Albany Backpackers, does good food and snacks for cybersurfers and has $12.50 all-you-can-eat curry specials on Friday and Saturday. It's open from 9 am until late daily.

At Middleton Beach, **Matt's on Flinders** (9 Flinders Parade) is a swanky new place attached to the Castlereagh apartments. Lots of money has been invested here with chef and waiting staff imported from Perth. The coffee is OK, the cakes tempting and the meals inventive and at the upper end of reasonably priced.

It is the setting more than the food which attracts diners to Emu Point. Restaurants in the vicinity of the view include **Emu Point Cafe** and the Japanese **Gosyu-Ya**; both are BYO and located on Mermaid Ave.

Out of town, head for the delightful **Cello's of Churchlane** (☎ 9844 3370), on Churchlane Rd off the Hassell Hwy. This is Albany's other gourmet success story, with relaxed country dining in a beautiful house and not enough wall space to hang all the awards it has received. An added attraction (not that you need it with this view or this food) is that everything – from the paintings to the antique furniture to the tableware and decorative knick-knacks – is for sale.

Entertainment

The *Albany Advertiser*, published Tuesday, Thursday and Saturday, has information on events in and around town.

There are a couple of clubs to entertain dedicated revellers: the evergreen **Club 19 Twelve** (120 York St) and **NRG** (338 Middleton Rd). There are sometimes bands at the **Earl of Spencer Historic Inn**, although new management seems to be cooling to the idea.

Albany's *Town Hall Theatre* has regular shows and there are also *cinemas* on the Albany Hwy.

Getting Around

Love's (☎ 9841 1211) runs bus services around town weekdays and on Saturday morning. Buses will take you along Albany Hwy from Peels Place to the roundabout; others go to Spencer Park, Middleton Beach, Emu Point and Bayonet Head (Thursday only). The tourist office has timetables.

Albany Car Rentals (☎ 9841 7077), at 386 Albany Hwy, has cars priced from $40 per day (100km free). Avis (☎ 9842 2833) and Budget (☎ 9841 7799) have offices in town. The Bayview YHA also does car rentals starting at $35 a day. Call ☎ 0408-746 599.

You can rent bicycles from Rainbow Coast Bikes on Albany Hwy and from Albany Backpackers on Stirling Terrace. Emu Beach Caravan Park (☎ 9844 1147) also rents out bikes.

Get Reel Boat Hire (☎ 9844 1597) rents out 5.2m Bayrunner boats for $150 a day or $700 a week, and can also set you up with rods and lines. Emu Point Boat Hire (☎ 9844 7896) can provide paddle boats, 'surfcats', canoes and motorised dinghies.

AROUND ALBANY

South of Albany, off Frenchman Bay Rd, is a stunning stretch of coastline that includes the Gap and Natural Bridge, rugged natural rock formations surrounded by pounding seas; the Blowholes, especially interesting in heavy seas when spray is blown with great force through the surrounding rock; the rock-climbing areas of Peak Head and West Cape Howe National Park; steep, rocky coves such as Jimmy Newhills Harbour and Salmon Holes, popular with surfers but considered quite dangerous; and Frenchman Bay, which has a caravan park, a fine swimming beach and a grassed, shady barbecue area. This is a dangerous coastline so beware of freakish, large waves.

Whaleworld Museum

The Whaleworld Museum, at Frenchman Bay 21km from Albany, is based at Cheyne Beach Whaling Station (which ceased operations in November 1978). There's a rusting *Cheynes IV* whale chaser and station equipment (such as whale-oil tanks – a 40-tonne whale would provide seven tonnes of oil) to inspect outside.

The museum screens a gore-spattered film about whaling operations and displays harpoons, whaleboat models and scrimshaw (etchings on whalebone).

Whaleworld Museum is open from 9 am to 5 pm daily. Admission is $8/6 for adults/children. There are free guided tours on the hour. The museum also has a superb collection of paintings of marine mammals by noted US artist Richard Ellis.

National Parks & Reserves

There are a number of excellent natural areas near Albany. From west to east along the coast you can explore many different habitats and see a wide variety of coastal scenery.

West Cape Howe National Park, 30km west of Albany, is a 35-sq-km playground for naturalists, bushwalkers, rock climbers and anglers. Inland, there are areas of coastal heath, lakes and swamp, and karri forest. With the exception of the road to Shelley Beach, access is restricted to 4WD and walkers.

Torndirrup National Park includes two very popular attractions, the Natural Bridge and the Gap, as well as the Blowholes, the beach at Jimmy Newhills Harbour, and Bald Head. The views are spectacular. Whales are frequently seen from the cliffs and the park's varied vegetation provides habitats for many native animals and reptiles.

Keen walkers can tackle the hard 10km-return bushwalk (more than six hours) over Isthmus Hill to Bald Head, at the eastern edge of the Torndirrup National Park.

Some 20km east of Albany, **Two Peoples Bay** is a 46-sq-km nature reserve which has a good swimming beach, scenic coastline and a small colony of the noisy scrub bird (once thought to be extinct – see the boxed text 'Noisy Scrub Bird' in this chapter). There is a 2km heritage trail called 'Baie des Deux Peuples'.

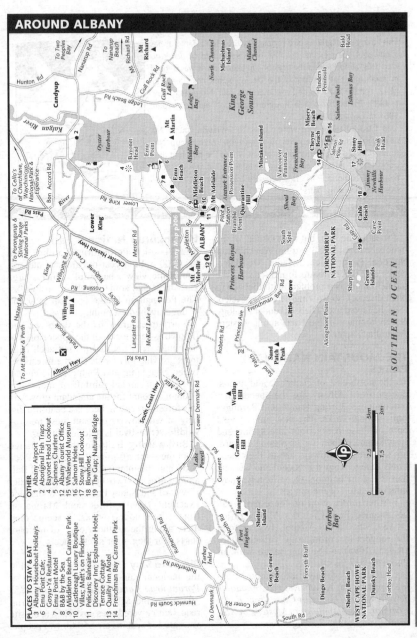

AROUND ALBANY

PLACES TO STAY & EAT
3 Albany Houseboat Holidays
6 Emu Point Cafe;
  Gosyu-Ya Restaurant
7 Emu Point Motel
8 B&B by the Sea
9 Middleton Beach Caravan Park
10 Castlereagh Luxury Boutique
  Villas; Matt's on Flinders
11 Pelicans; Balneaire;
  Discovery Inn; Esplanade Hotel;
  Terrace Cottage
13 Quality Inn Motel
14 Frenchman Bay Caravan Park

OTHER
1 Albany Airport
2 Aboriginal Fish Traps
4 Bayonet Head Lookout
5 Spinners Charters
12 Albany Tourist Office
15 Whaleworld Museum
16 Salmon Holes
17 Stony Hill Lookout
18 Blowholes
19 The Gap; Natural Bridge

SOUTH COAST

Noisy Scrub Bird

This little, near-flightless bird certainly lives up to its name. It has a powerful, ear-piercing call. The noisy scrub bird (*Atrichornus clamosus*) almost joined the thylacine in extinction. It was sighted in jarrah forest at the foot of the Darling Scarp, near Perth, in 1842, and the last recorded specimen was collected near Torbay in 1889. The bird was then thought extinct until rediscovered in 1961 at Two Peoples Bay.

In 1983 breeding pairs were moved to similar habitats in Mt Manypeaks Nature Reserve (now part of Waychinicup National Park) to regenerate populations where the bird had died out. In 1987 another colony was established at the Walpole-Nornalup National Park. It is believed that there are now well over 100 breeding pairs.

Probably the best, but least visited, of the national parks, is the 39-sq-km **Waychinicup National Park**, which includes Mt Manypeaks and other granite formations. At the moment there is a problem with dieback (a plant disease), so walking here is restricted. (See the boxed text 'Dieback' under Ecology & Environment in the Facts about Western Australia chapter.)

THE MOUNTAIN NATIONAL PARKS

To the north-east of Denmark and almost due north of Albany are the spectacular, mountainous Stirling Range and Porongurup National Parks. The best time to visit both of these parks is in late spring and early summer when it is beginning to warm up and the wildflowers are at their best. From June to August it is cold and wet and hail is not uncommon. Occasionally, snow falls on the top of the ranges.

Further information on these parks can be obtained from CALM's Albany office (☎ 9842 4500), 120 Albany Hwy, or from the rangers at Porongurup National Park (☎ 9853 1095) and Stirling Range National Park (☎ 9827 9230).

CALM produces two informative booklets covering this region: *Rugged Mountains Jewelled Sea: The South Coast from Eucla to Albany* and *Mountains of Mystery: A Natural History of the Stirling Ranges.*

Porongurup National Park

The 24-sq-km Porongurup National Park has 1100-million-year-old granite outcrops, panoramic views, beautiful scenery, large karri trees and some excellent bushwalks. The Porongurup Range is 12km long and 670m at its highest point.

Karri trees grow in the deep red soil (known as karri loam) of the upper slopes of the range. It is unusual to find such large trees growing this far east of the forests between Manjimup and Walpole; the correct soil and an annual rainfall of more than 700mm account for the abundant growth in this forest. In season there is a beautiful display of wildflowers beneath these trees. A **wildflower festival** is held in October.

Bushwalking trails in the park range from the short, 10-minute Tree in the Rock stroll and the intermediate Castle and Balancing Rocks (two hours) to the harder Hayward and Nancy Peaks (four hours) and excellent Devil's Slide and Marmabup Rock (three hours) walks. A scenic 6km drive along the northern edge of the park starts near the ranger's residence.

Places to Stay There is no camping within the national park but you can camp at *Porongurup Range Tourist Park* (☎ 9853 1057), on the Mt Barker to Porongurup road. Tent/powered sites cost $14/16, on-site vans are $35, cabins are $50 for two people.

STIRLING RANGE & PORONGURUP NATIONAL PARKS

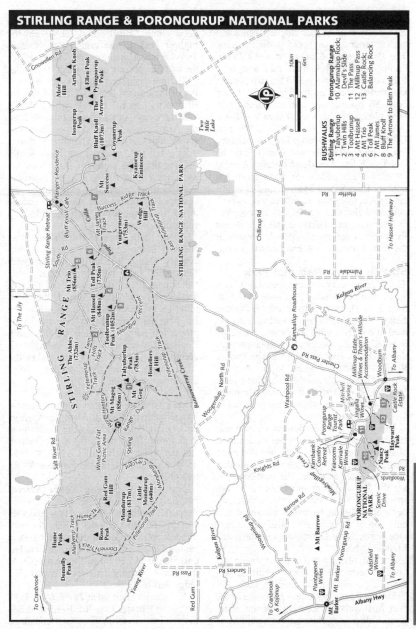

BUSHWALKS

Stirling Range
1 Talyuberlup
2 Twin Hills
3 Toolbrunup
4 Mt Hassell
5 Mt Trio
6 Toll Peak
7 Mt James
8 Bluff Knoll
9 The Arrows to Ellen Peak

Porongurup Range
10 Marmabup Rock;
   Devil's Slide
11 The Pass
12 Millinup Pass
13 Castle Rock;
   Balancing Rock

Arthur's Knob
Moir Hill
Ellen Peak
The Pyungorup Peak
Isongerup Peak
The Arrows
Bluff Knoll (1073m)
Coyanerup Peak
Two Mile Lake
Ranger's Residence
Kyanorup Eminence
Mt Success
Stirling Range Retreat
Bluff Knoll Cafe
Success Ridge Track
Colla
Mt James Track
East Pillenorup Track
Wedge Hill
Yungermere (753m)
STIRLING RANGE NATIONAL PARK
To The Lily
Mt Trio (856m)
Toll Peak (735m)
South Rd
Mt Hassell (848m)
Toolbrunup Peak (1052m)
Moingup Crescent
Bonnarrup Creek
STIRLING RANGE
The Abbey (752m)
Twin Hills Track
Yetemerup Track
Talyuberlup Peak (783m)
Hostellers Hill
Pillenorup Track
Chillinup Rd
Pfeiffer Rd
Palmdale Rd
Kambalup Roadhouse
Kalgan River
Chester Pass Rd
Washpool Rd
To Hassell Highway
To Albany
White Gum Flat Picnic Area
Mt Trio Hatton
Mt Magog (856m)
Mt Gog
Stirling Range Dve
Red Gum Hill
Mondurup Peak (817m)
Little Mondurup (640m)
Mondurup Track
Pillenorup Track
Knights Rd
Mindelup Creek
Barrow Rd
Hume Peak
Ross Peak
Donnelly Peak
Madyerip Track
Hume Tk
Donnelly Track
Salt River Rd
To Cranbrook
Young River
Kalgan River
Pass Rd
Sanders Rd
Red Gum
Mt Barrow
Woogenellup North Rd
Woogenellup Rd
To Cranbrook & Kojonup
Plantagenet Wines
Mt Barker
Chatsfield Wines
Albany Hwy
To Albany
PORONGURUP NATIONAL PARK
Scenic Drive
Woodlands Rd
Nancy Peak
Hayward Peak
Porongurup Range Tourist Park
Karribank Country Retreat
Tearooms
Karrivalle Wines
Jingalla Wines
Mitchell Spring
Millinup Estate Wines & Thorn's Hillside Accommodation
Woodburn
To Albany
Castle Rock Estate
Castle Rock
Mt Barker-Barker-Porongurup Rd

SOUTH COAST

The Mt Barker tourist office (see under Mt Barker later in this chapter) can assist with accommodation bookings for this area. The *Porongurup Chalets* (☎ 9853 1034), on the corner of Bolganup and Porongurup Rds, costs from $60 to $70 for two people; the chalets sleep up to six people. Linen costs $5 per person. For accommodation with plenty of character, *Thorn's Hillside Accommodation* (☎ 9853 1105), at Millinup Estate Wines, Porongurup Rd, has a charming pioneer cottage as well as self-contained wooden chalets. *Karribank Country Retreat* (☎ 9853 1022), on Main St, Porongurup, has doubles from $75 to $137 (breakfast is $10 per person, linen hire $5.50), as well as self-contained chalets for $106 for four people.

Farmstays and B&Bs in the region cost from $60 to $80 for two people; inquire at the tourist offices in Albany or Mt Barker.

Stirling Range National Park

This 1156-sq-km national park consists of a single chain of peaks, 10km wide and 65km long. Running most of its length are isolated peaks, which tower above broad valleys covered in prickly shrubs and heath. The range is noted for its spectacular colour changes through blues, reds and purples. The Stirling Range was first visited in 1832 by explorer Ensign Dale in search of grains. Three years later, Surveyor-General Roe named the range after Captain James Stirling, first governor of the Swan River Colony.

Due to the combination of altitude and climate there's a large number of localised plants in the range. It is estimated that more than 1500 species of plants occur naturally, 60 of which are endemic. The most beautiful are the Darwinias or mountain bells. Ten species of these mountain bells, which only occur above 300m, have been identified, and only one of them occurs outside the range. One particularly beautiful example is the Mondurup bell.

The Talyuberlup bell, with its finger-like buds, is restricted to a few localities; you can see it on the Mt Talyuberlup walk.

Stirling Range National Park is one of the best **bushwalking** locations in the state. Keen walkers can choose from a number of high points: Toolbrunup (for views and a good climb), Bluff Knoll (at 1073m the highest peak in the range), Mt Hassell, Talyuberlup, Mondurup and Toll Peak (for the wildflowers) are popular half-day walks.

The most challenging walks are a crossing of the eastern sector of the range from Bluff Knoll to Ellen Peak, which should take three days, or the shorter traverse from the Arrows to Ellen Peak, for which you should allow two days. The latter option is a loop but the former, from Bluff Knoll, will require a car shuttle. For track details see Lonely Planet's *Walking in Australia*. Walkers must be suitably experienced and equipped as the range is subject to sudden drops in temperature, driving rain and sometimes snow.

About 12km north of Bluff Knoll is an anomaly in the landscape – a replica 16th-century Dutch windmill complete with functioning sails, built by an enterprising Dutchman, Pleun Hinzert. At the time of writing you could still get inside the windmill (it is used as a restaurant, known as The Lily) but plans are afoot to have it doing its proper job, namely working as a flour mill. Replica 16th-century Dutch cottages sit comfortably next to it, which makes the Australian bush look like something out of a Rembrandt etching.

Places to Stay You can camp in Stirling Range National Park at *Moingup Springs* on Chester Pass Rd, near the Toolbrunup Peak turn-off, but the facilities are limited; call the Albany office of CALM (☎ 9842 4500) for details. Tent sites here cost $8 for two people.

The well-run *Stirling Range Retreat* (☎ 9827 9229), on Chester Pass Rd, is on the park's northern boundary. Powered sites cost $17.60, on-site vans $33/35 for two/three people, self-contained rammed-earth cabins $71.50 for two people, and chalets cost $93.50/115.50 for two/three people. At the time of writing a six-room backpacker lodge was being built.

You can stay and eat at *The Lily* (☎ 9827 9205), on Chester Pass Rd, Borden, inside the replica windmill. Cosy self-contained apartments cost $89 a double for the first night and $79 a double for subsequent nights, which includes a breakfast basket. Even if you're not staying, a visit for lunch in the windmill is a must: it serves the most delicious soup in WA ($5.50) and this may be your only chance to eat real Dutch apple cake ($6.50). It is open daily for lunches and snacks and for dinners some evenings (booking advisable).

MT BARKER
pop 4500

Mt Barker, 55km north-east of Denmark, 64km south of the Stirling Range and 20km west of the Porongurup Range, is very much the centre of the mountain national parks region. The very helpful tourist office (☎ 9851 1163), in the restored train station at 622 Albany Hwy, is open from 9 am to 5 pm weekdays, 9 am to 3 pm Saturday, and 10 am to 3 pm Sunday.

Things to See & Do

The town has been settled since the 1830s and the old convict-built **police station and gaol** of 1868 has been preserved as a museum.

South-west of Mt Barker, on the Egerton-Warburton estate is **St Werburgh's Chapel**, built between 1872 and 1873. The wrought-iron chancel screen and altar rail were shaped on the property. You can get a panoramic view of the area from the **Mt Barker Lookout**, 5km south of town.

The town is home to a **banksia farm**, which features every species and subspecies of banksia. Admission is $5.

The region has a good reputation for wine making, and there are more than a dozen **wineries** with cellar sales and tastings within a few kilometres of town (see under Great Southern in the 'Wineries of Western Australia' special section).

Kendenup, 16km north of Mt Barker, was the site of WA's first gold discovery, although this was considerably overshadowed by the later and much larger finds in the Kalgoorlie-Boulder area. Also north of Mt Barker is Cranbrook, an access point to the Stirling Range National Park.

Places to Stay & Eat

The Mt Barker *caravan park* (☎ 9851 1691), on Albany Hwy, has tent/powered sites for $11/14 and on-site vans/park homes for $25/40.

Chill Out Backpackers (☎ 9851 2798, 79 Hassell St) offers dorm beds or doubles for $15. The *Plantagenet Hotel Motel* (☎ 9851 1008, 9 Lowood Rd) has singles/doubles from $25/40 (in the older hotel section) and en suite motel units for $35/50. It serves good counter meals. The *Mt Barker Hotel* (☎ 9851 1477, 39 Lowood Rd) has basic single/twin rooms with shared facilities for $25/45. If you want to sample country air try the quaint 1869 stone cottage *Abbeyholme B&B* (☎ 9851 1101), on Old Albany Hwy. B&B doubles cost $85 and self-contained units cost $110 for two people.

Two places on Lowood Rd, *Gene's Kitchen* and *Lockwood's Bread Shop*, have home-style meals.

ALBANY TO ESPERANCE

From Albany, the South Coast Hwy runs north-east along the coast before turning inland to skirt the Fitzgerald River National Park and finishing in Esperance. The distance is 476km.

Jerramungup

Jerramungup, 182km north-east of Albany, is not much more than a road junction with a service station, a handful of houses and a tourist office (☎ 9835 1022) of sorts, with limited information (there's not much to see here so it doesn't really matter). **Ongerup**, a small wheat-belt town 41km west of Jerramungup, has an annual wildflower show in September/October with hundreds of local species on show. The Ongerup-Needilup district (within a 40km radius of Ongerup) has more than 1300 recorded species, ranging from the 30m salmon gum to small 25mm trigger plants. Two excellent nature reserves are Cawallelup, 19km to the south, and Vaux's Lake, 19km north.

Places to Stay Jerramungup's *caravan park* (☎ 9835 1174) has powered sites for $15. The *Jerramungup Farmstay B&B*

SOUTH COAST

(☎ 9835 1002) is on a 30-sq-km sheep and wheat property 2km south of town; singles/doubles cost $40/60. Similarly priced is the highly recommended *Fitzgerald River National Park B&B* (☎ 9835 5026), on Quiss Rd, Jerramungup, on the park's western boundary. There's a *caravan park* (☎ 9828 2090) and a *hotel* (☎ 9828 2001) in Ongerup.

Bremer Bay
pop 200
This fishing and holiday hamlet, 61km from the South Coast Hwy, sits at the western end of the Great Australian Bight. The BP petrol station (☎ 9837 4093), on Gnombup Terrace, acts as the information office.

From July to November, Bremer Bay is a good spot to observe **southern right whales**, which enter many bays in the area to give birth to their calves. Sometimes they are as close as 6m from the shore, and can be seen from many vantage points on the coastline – Point Ann in Fitzgerald River National Park and Dillon Bay are good observation points.

Places to Stay The *caravan park* (☎ 9837 4018) has powered sites for $14 and park cabins from $40. The *Bremer Bay Hotel* (☎ 9837 4133) has singles/doubles for $65/75.

A nice place to stay within Fitzgerald River National Park is the historic 1858 *Quaalup Homestead* (☎ 9837 4124), on Gairdner Rd. It has camping ($5 per person), caravans ($29 for two people), double motel-type rooms ($45) and self-contained chalets ($55, up to four people).

Ravensthorpe
pop 400
The small town of Ravensthorpe was once the centre of the Phillips River goldfield; later, copper was also mined here. These days the area is dependent on farming, although new nickel mines in the vicinity are expected to have an ongoing economic effect. Every September a wildflower show is held in town.

The tourist office (☎ 9838 1277), located in the Going Bush Craft Shop in Morgans St, provides a detailed visitor map and more information on the region than you could ever need, including several scenic drives and guides to wildflowers and birds.

The remains of a disused government smelter and the Cattlin Creek Mine (copper) are near town. West of town is the **WA standard time meridian**, indicated by a boulder with a plaque on it, and – as readers David and Beth Williams poetically noted – 'a rubbish bin in front of it, which rather ruins the romance of time'.

Places to Stay & Eat The *caravan park* (☎ 9838 1050), on Elston St, has powered sites for $14 and on-site vans for $20 for two people. The *Palace Hotel* (☎ 9838 1005), on Morgans St and classified by the National Trust, has singles/doubles with shared facilities for $20/30 and en suite motel units for $45/60. Counter meals at its restaurant are your best bet for food.

Chambejo Farmstay (☎ 9835 7015), on the South Coast Hwy 34km west of town, has a self-contained cottage for $40 for two people or single B&B for $30. About 50km east of Ravensthorpe is the *McArthur Park Angora Stud* (☎ 9839 6040), on the South Coast Hwy, a working farm with friendly owners and comfortable B&B accommodation for $35. Evening meals cost $15. At Munglinup, 90km east of Ravensthorpe, is the *Singing Winds* (☎ 9075 1018), which caters to long-distance cyclists and provides B&B plus dinner (and a cut lunch on request) for $35.

Hopetoun
pop 300
There are fine beaches and bays around Hopetoun, which is also the eastern gateway to the Fitzgerald River National Park (see that section later in this chapter). Due to its natural delights and proximity to the park, Hopetoun has been tipped as one of the next 'big' tourist destinations. There's a bit of work to do yet, so don't hold your breath.

For tourist information, try Cafe Barnacles in Veal St, although information is limited to a map and leaflets.

Dunns Swamp, about 5km north of town is an ideal spot for picnicking, bushwalking and bird-watching. West of town is the landlocked **Culham Inlet**, great for fishing (especially for black bream), and east of town is the very scenic **Southern Ocean East Drive**, which features beaches and the Jerdacuttup Lakes.

The **world's longest fence** – the 1822km-long rabbit-proof fence – enters the sea in the south at Starvation Bay, east of Hopetoun and 40km south of the South Coast Hwy. It starts at Eighty Mile Beach on the Indian Ocean, north of Port Hedland. The fence was built during the height of the rabbit plague between 1901 and 1907. However, the story goes that the naughty bunnies beat the fence builders to the west side so the erection of the barrier was a bit of a joke.

Bunnies beat the builders to the other side of the 1822-km 'rabbit-proof' fence.

Places to Stay & Eat The *caravan park* (☎ *9838 3096*), on Spence St, is in a gorgeous position on the beach. Tent/powered sites cost $11/13 and on-site vans start at $30 for two people. The historic *Port Hotel* (☎ *9838 3053*), in a fabulous location on Veal St, is just waiting to be snapped up by a canny developer. Single/double rooms here cost $30/40 (backpackers pay $15 per person). The *Hopetoun Motel & Chalet Village* (☎ *9838 3219*), on the corner of Canning and Veal Sts, has motel rooms for $65 and self-contained units for $75.

The *Old Jetty Restaurant* at the pub serves counter meals. *Cafe Barnacles* (☎ *9838 3228*), on Veal St, is the other spot to eat.

Fitzgerald River National Park

This 3300-sq-km park is one of two places in the state with a Unesco Biosphere rating and is one of the most fascinating places to explore in the whole of WA. The park has a very beautiful coastline (some of the beaches have dangerous rips), sand plains, the rugged Barrens mountain range and deep, wide river valleys.

The **bushwalking** is excellent and the wilderness route from Fitzgerald Beach to West Beach is recommended – there is no trail and no water but camping is permitted (you will need to plan water drops yourself at the end of access roads). Although it is one of the least affected areas in south WA for dieback, you should still take precautions to ensure it remains so. If roads are closed (as indicated by signs) you should respect this. Clean your shoes before each walk and wash the undercarriage and tyres of your vehicle to discourage the spread of the fungus. You should also register with the ranger on Quiss Rd, Jerramungup (☎ 9835 5043); Murray Rd (☎ 9837 1022), just north of Bremer Bay, or at East Mt Barren (☎ 9838 3060).

Shorter walks in the park are East Mt Barren (three hours), West Mt Barren (two hours) and Point Ann (one hour).

Wildflowers are most abundant in spring but there are flowers in bloom throughout the year. This park is botanically significant in Australia, with 20% of WA's described species. The park contains half the orchids in WA (more than 80 species; 70 of these occur nowhere else); 22 mammal species, including honey possums, dibblers – highly endangered with only a few hundred left – and tammar wallabies; 200 species of birds including the endangered ground parrot and western bristlebird; 41 reptile and 12 frog species; and 1700 species of plants. Many of the plant species are yet to be named by botanists. To top off the list of superlatives, this is the home of the spectacular royal hakea and Quaalup bell, and **southern right whales** can be seen offshore from July to September.

The main entry point to the park is from Hopetoun via the Culham Inlet causeway.

However in January 2000 the causeway (built at vast expense in 1996) was washed away and at the time of writing it was not clear when it would be rebuilt. The other entry points are from Bremer Bay or from the South Coast Hwy along Devils Creek, Quiss and Hamersley Rds.

There are *camp sites* at Four Mile Beach, Hamersley Inlet, Whale Bone Beach, Quoin Head, Fitzgerald Inlet and St Mary Inlet.

Mary Anne Haven (☎ 9838 3022) organises scenic 4WD tours of the park.

ESPERANCE
pop 12,000

Esperance, on the coast 200km south of Norseman, was named in 1792 when the *Recherche* and *L'Espérance* sailed into the bay to shelter from a storm. Although the first settlers came to the area in 1863, it was during the gold rush in the 1890s that the town really became established as a port. When the gold fever subsided, Esperance went into a state of suspended animation until after WWII.

In the 1950s it was discovered that adding missing trace elements to the soil around Esperance restored fertility, and since then the town has rapidly become an agricultural centre. It has deservedly become a popular resort due to its temperate climate, stunning coastal scenery, blue waters, good fishing and dazzling, sandy beaches. The seas offshore are studded with the many islands of the Archipelago of the Recherche.

Distinctive Norfolk Island pines line the delightful foreshore, which is marred only by the docks area. Esperance is Australia's major iron-ore export gateway; minerals are stockpiled on the docks in rather unsightly green tin sheds.

Information

The helpful Esperance tourist office (☎ 9071 2330), on Dempster St in the museum village, is open from 9 am to 5 pm daily. The office has information about tours along the coast and to the islands, and you can pore over the extensive pamphlet collection. The post office is on the corner of Andrew and Dempster Sts.

The Village Cafe in the museum park has Internet access, as does the Top End Cafe in Dempster St.

Things to See & Do

The **Esperance Municipal Museum** consists of various old buildings, including a gallery, smithy's forge, cafe and craft shop. The museum is on James St between the Esplanade and Dempster St. It contains a Skylab display – when the USA's Skylab crashed to earth in 1979, it made its fiery re-entry right over Esperance. It is open from 10.30 am to 6 pm on Monday, Wednesday, Thursday and Friday and 9 am to noon on Saturday.

The 36km **Great Ocean Drive** includes spectacular vistas from Observatory Point and the Rotary Lookout on Wireless Hill; Twilight Bay and Picnic Cove, popular swimming spots; and the Pink Lake, stained by a salt-tolerant algae called *Dunalella salina*.

There are about 100 small islands in the **Archipelago of the Recherche**. Colonies of seals, penguins and a wide variety of waterbirds live on the islands. **Woody Island** is a wildlife sanctuary.

Kids will enjoy **Telegraph Farm**, 21km west of town on the South Coast Hwy. This commercial protea farm has a host of animals including buffalo, camels, deer and birds. It is open 10 am to 5 pm Thursday to Monday with tours ($6/3 adults/children) at 10.30 am and 1.30 and 3 pm.

Organised Tours

The McKenzies (☎ 9071 5757) power catamaran *Seabreeze* regularly tours Esperance Bay (Bay of Isles). These very pleasant cruises provide a chance to see New Zealand fur seals, Australian sea lions, sea eagles, Cape Barren geese, common dolphins and a host of other wildlife, but they don't come cheap ($45/18 adults/children). McKenzies also operates the daily ferry to Woody Island in January ($28/14).

Vacation Country Tours (☎ 9071 2227) has a town-and-coast coach tour for $28 and a Cape Le Grand tour for $45. More adventurous is Aussie Bight Expeditions (☎ 9071 7778), which has 4WD safaris to secluded beaches and bays and to the national parks.

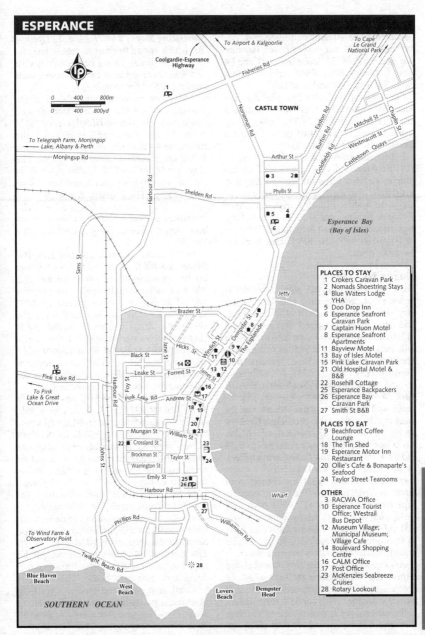

ESPERANCE

PLACES TO STAY
1 Crokers Caravan Park
2 Nomads Shoestring Stays
4 Blue Waters Lodge YHA
5 Doo Drop Inn
6 Esperance Seafront Caravan Park
7 Captain Huon Motel
8 Esperance Seafront Apartments
11 Bayview Motel
13 Bay of Isles Motel
15 Pink Lake Caravan Park
21 Old Hospital Motel & B&B
22 Rosehill Cottage
25 Esperance Backpackers
26 Esperance Bay Caravan Park
27 Smith St B&B

PLACES TO EAT
9 Beachfront Coffee Lounge
18 The Tin Shed
19 Esperance Motor Inn Restaurant
20 Ollie's Cafe & Bonaparte's Seafood
24 Taylor Street Tearooms

OTHER
3 RACWA Office
10 Esperance Tourist Office; Westrail Bus Depot
12 Museum Village; Municipal Museum; Village Cafe
14 Boulevard Shopping Centre
16 CALM Office
17 Post Office
23 McKenzies Seabreeze Cruises
28 Rotary Lookout

SOUTH COAST

Half-day tours to Mt Ridley or Cape Le Grand cost $58/40 adults/children and full-day tours ($132 one price) cover Israelite Bay and the Point Malcolm area or Cape Le Grand, Lucky Bay, Cape Arid National Park, Yokinup Bay and Arid Bay.

For a bit of fun, you can take a three-wheeled motorbike tour with Southern Edge Trike Tours (☎ 9071 4684) along Great Ocean Drive ($60) or to Cape Le Grand National Park ($110).

Esperance Diving & Fishing (☎ 9071 5111) conducts dive charters and diving courses (it also hires out equipment) and has regular fishing charters. Advance booking is advisable. Full-day trips for either diving or fishing cost $120. For the fishing trips all tackle and bait is included. Drewies (☎ 0419-868 589) also has fishing trips for the same price.

Places to Stay

There are seven caravan parks around Esperance that provide camp sites and on-site vans and cabins; the tourist office has a list. The rates for tent/powered sites are around $13/16 and on-site vans cost $28 to $42; en suite park cabins start at $45 for two people. The most central are the *Esperance Bay Caravan Park* (☎ 9071 2237, 162 Dempster St) and the *Esperance Seafront Caravan Park* (☎ 9071 1251), on the corner of Goldfields and Norseman Rds. Others not far away are the well-kept and efficient *Crokers* (☎ 9071 4100, 629 Harbour Rd), which also has larger self-contained chalets ($49 to $69) and a pool, and the *Pink Lake Caravan Park* (☎ 9071 2424), on Pink Lake Rd.

Backpackers are spoilt for choice, with three well-run options. The large, popular *Blue Waters Lodge YHA* (☎ 9071 1040, 299 Goldfields Rd) is on the beachfront about 1.5km from the centre. Dorm beds cost from $14; rooms cost from $30. It has a nice breakfast area with views over the water.

Also good value is the tidy, comfortable *Esperance Backpackers* (☎ 9071 4724, 14 Emily St), which has dorm beds for $16 and twin and double rooms for $37. It runs tours to the national parks with 'scurfing' (surfing the sand hills) included. It also hires out

bikes. Newest kid on the block is *Nomads Shoestring Stays* (☎ 9071 3396, 23 Daphne St), which has an Internet lounge, a spa and free use of bikes. Dorm beds/doubles cost $15/40. There are also two-bedroom units starting at $80 for four.

There are numerous motels in town. Though none are spectacular, some are well positioned. The *Bay of Isles Motel* (☎ 9071 3999, 32 The Esplanade) is probably the nicest, with a pool bar and in-house movies. It has single/double rooms for $75/92. The *Bayview* (☎ 9071 1533, 31 Dempster St) is central to everything and charges a reasonable $55/65. The *Captain Huon* (☎ 9071 2383, 5 The Esplanade) has spacious self-contained units complete with lace curtains and ocean views. Singles/doubles cost $65/75.

In the centre of town, The *Old Hospital Motel and B&B* (☎ 9071 3587, 1a William St) has motel-style units with kitchenette, TV and video. Single/double rooms cost $65/80. It also has a more interesting B&B section in an older building, which was the site of the first Esperance hospital. B&B singles/doubles start at $60/80. Other B&Bs include *Smith St Bed & Breakfast* (☎ 9071 1815, 2 Smith St), in an old stone house at the end of the Esplanade overlooking the harbour. B&B costs $60 a double.

A good choice is the Spanish-style *Doo Drop Inn* (☎ 9071 5043, 3 Norseman Rd), run by people who have travelled and know the B&B trade. It does B&B for $35 per person. The same management also has some self-contained cottages. Just out of town, country hospitality is offered at the *Rosehill Cottage* (☎ 9071 5050, 30 Crossland St), with B&B singles/doubles for $55/75; evening meals can be arranged.

The best accommodation option in town by far is the well-positioned *Esperance Seafront Apartments* (☎ 9072 0044, 15–16 The Esplanade). Most people would be happy to have these tastefully furnished and decorated units as a home. The kitchens have all mod cons, and there's a washing machine, a gas barbecue and spacious living areas. One-/two-bedroom units cost $99/130 in low season, rising to $130/160 in high season. There are also three-bedroom units sleeping six to eight people for $160/220.

Check with the tourist office for more accommodation options.

Places to Eat

Surprisingly for a seaside town with plenty of accommodation, there aren't many good eateries. If you're after fast food, cruise Dempster St.

The best place to eat, either for a light lunch or a more substantial dinner (or just a calorific cake) is the attractive *Taylor Street Tearooms*, by the jetty. There's a good choice of salads, burgers, grills and pastas. Get a table on the grass or on the attractive covered terrace.

Another smart place is *Bonaparte's Seafood* (☎ 9071 7727, upstairs 51 The Esplanade), good for a splurge, although the menu is fairly old-fashioned: it includes seafood chowder ($8.50), Thai-style Moreton Bay bugs ($25) and bouillabaisse for two ($42).

Directly below is *Ollies Cafe*, which will appeal to the more thrifty. You can get breakfasts, burgers and light meals.

The *Beachfront Coffee Lounge* (19 The Esplanade) does decent coffee and toasted sandwiches ($3.50 to $4.50), and burgers for $4.50. The *Village Cafe*, on Dempster St in the museum enclave, is good for afternoon and morning teas and has Internet access.

The *Esperance Motor Inn* (14 Andrew St) is famous for its $6 counter-meal specials. One day it's meat, another it's fish. Nearby, *The Tin Shed* (☎ 9071 2172, 22 Andrew St) is a brightly painted and decorated BYO restaurant in the centre of town with basic pastas ($14), salads ($8.50 to $12.50) and fish and chips ($14).

Self-caterers are well catered for at the *Woolworth supermarket*, on Forrest St in the Boulevard Shopping Centre.

Getting Around

There is a taxi rank by the post office. You can order a taxi by calling ☎ 9071 1782. Hire bicycles from the Blue Waters Lodge YHA ($15 a day; see Places to Stay earlier in this section).

For car rentals try Avis (☎ 9071 3998), on the corner of Norseman and Harbour Rds, or Budget (☎ 9071 2775), in Lalor Dr. If you want to hire a 4WD, call Esperance 4x4 (☎ 9071 1874).

NATIONAL PARKS

There are four national parks in the Esperance region. The closest and most popular is **Cape Le Grand**, which extends 60km east of Esperance. The park has spectacular coastal scenery, some good white-sand beaches and excellent walking tracks. There are fine views across the park from Frenchman Peak, at the western end of the park, and good fishing, camping and swimming at Lucky Bay and Le Grand Beach. Make the effort to climb Frenchman Peak (a 3km uphill walk) as the views from the top and through the 'eye' (the huge open cave at the top), especially during the late afternoon, are superb. Within the park, just over 6km east of Cape Le Grand is **Rossiter Bay**. This is where explorers Edward John Eyre and the Aborigine Wylie, during their epic overland crossing in 1841, fortuitously met Captain Rossiter of the French whaler *Mississippi*, on which the pair spent two weeks resting.

Farther east, at the start of the Great Australian Bight and on the fringes of the Nullarbor Plain, is the coastal **Cape Arid National Park**. It is a rugged and isolated park with abundant flora and fauna, good bushwalking, great beaches and camp sites. Whales, seals and Cape Barren geese are seen regularly from here.

Most of the park is accessible by 4WD only, although the Poison Creek and Thomas River sites are accessible in normal vehicles. Sites such as Mt Ragged require 4WD. For the hardy, there is a tough walk to the top (3km return, three hours).

Mt Ragged and the Russell Range were islands during the late Eocene period (40 million years ago) and there are wave-cut platforms on their upper slopes. The world's most primitive species of ant was found thriving near Mt Ragged in 1930. Good information on the national park is in the CALM pamphlet *Cape Arid & Eucla*.

For those travelling east across the Nullarbor, there is a good 4WD route north-east of Esperance to Balladonia on the Eyre Hwy (heavy rain can close this road, so check before setting out). From Esperance, head out on Fisheries Rd, and when Grewer Rd comes in on the right, turn left. This becomes Balladonia Rd, and allows you to traverse part of the Cape Arid National Park and takes you past Mt Ragged. Take plenty of fuel and water.

Other national parks in the area include the **Stokes National Park**, 90km west of Esperance, with an inlet, long beaches and rocky headlands backed by sand dunes and low hills; and the **Peak Charles National Park**, 130km to the north. Close to Esperance is the **Monjingup Reserve**, on Telegraph Rd (off the South Coast Hwy); it has a boardwalk across the lake, interpretive displays and excellent bird-watching. For information about these national parks, contact CALM (☎ 9071 3733) in Dempster St, Esperance.

If you are going into the national parks, take plenty of water as there is little or no fresh water in most of these areas. Also, be wary of spreading dieback; get information about its prevention from park rangers.

Places to Stay & Eat

There are limited-facility **camp sites** at Le Grand Beach and Lucky Bay in Cape Le Grand National Park (☎ 9075 9072; $10 for two people); on the shores of the inlet at Stokes (☎ 9076 8541; $10 for two people); in Peak Charles (☎ 9071 3733), although there are no facilities; and at Seal Creek, Jorndee Creek and Thomas River at Cape Arid (☎ 9075 0055). Apply for permits with the ranger at the park entrances.

The **Orleans Bay Caravan Park** (☎ 9075 0033), near the eastern end of Cape Le Grand, is a good, friendly place to stay. Its tent/powered sites cost $13.50/16 for two people, cabins $35 for two people and chalets $60 for four.

If you are heading into the national parks, make sure you stock up with supplies from the supermarkets in Esperance. Just before the turn off to Cape Le Grand is **Merivale Farm**, on Merivale Rd, known for its cakes and tempting tortes.

The Southern Outback

East beyond the expansive wheatbelt lies a huge region of semidesert and desert, the southern Outback. Towns are few and far between, the distances are great and much of the attraction is found in the isolation of this frontier. The goldfields includes the mining towns of Kalgoorlie-Boulder, Kambalda and Norseman and the many ghost towns in between, which appear and, just as quickly, fade into the spinifex. East of the goldfields is the famed Nullarbor Plain and the sealed Eyre Hwy to the eastern states.

Eastern Goldfields

Some 50 years after its establishment in 1829, the Western Australia (WA) colony was still going nowhere, so the government in Perth was delighted when gold was found at Southern Cross in 1887. That first strike petered out quickly, but following more discoveries WA profited from the gold boom for the rest of the century. Gold put WA on the map and finally gave it the population to make it viable in its own right, rather than just a distant offshoot of the eastern colonies.

The major strikes were made in 1892 at Coolgardie and nearby Kalgoorlie, but in the whole goldfields area Kalgoorlie, now known as Kalgoorlie-Boulder, is the only large town left. Coolgardie's period of prosperity lasted only until 1905, and many other gold towns went from nothing to populations of 10,000, then back to nothing, in just 10 years. Nevertheless, the towns capitalised on their prosperity while it lasted, as the many magnificent public buildings grandly attest.

Life on the early goldfields was terribly hard. This area of WA is extremely dry – rainfall is erratic and never great. Even the little rain that does fall quickly disappears into the porous soil. Many early gold seekers, driven more by enthusiasm than by common sense, died of thirst while seeking the elusive metal. Others succumbed to diseases that broke out periodically in the unhygienic

HIGHLIGHTS

- Checking out the modern frontier town of Kalgoorlie-Boulder, with its golden-age architecture, two-up, raucous pubs and enormous mining operations
- Exploring the old ghost towns of the goldfields
- Driving 4WDs along the Canning Stock Route, Gunbarrel Hwy and Great Central (Warburton) Rd
- Travelling the Eyre Hwy, Australia's greatest sealed-road adventure, from Perth to Adelaide
- Bird-watching at the renowned Eyre Bird Observatory and walking along the lonely Great Australian Bight
- Visiting remote Eucla, with its sand hills and slowly disappearing telegraph station

The Southern Outback p224

Kalgoorlie-Boulder p227

shantytowns. The supply of water to the goldfields by pipeline in 1903 was a major breakthrough (see the boxed text 'Where Water is Like Gold!' in this chapter) and ensured the continuation of mining.

Today, Kalgoorlie-Boulder is the main goldfields centre and mines still operate there. Elsewhere, a string of fascinating

THE SOUTHERN OUTBACK

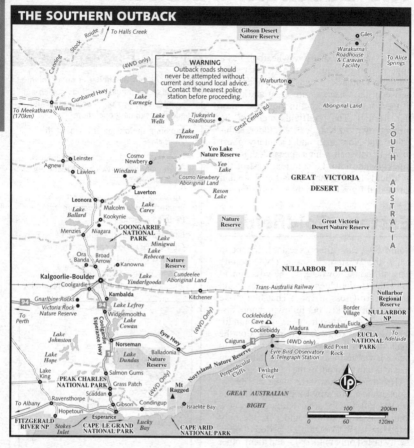

ghost and near–ghost towns, which are often surrounded by carpets of wildflowers, make visiting WA's gold country a must.

COOLGARDIE
pop 1000

Coolgardie is a popular pause in the long journey across the Nullarbor Plain. A reef of gold was discovered here in 1892 by the prospector Arthur Bayley and his mate Bill Ford, and called 'Bayley's Reward'. By the end of the 19th century the population of Coolgardie had boomed to 15,000, there were two stock exchanges, six newspapers,

more than 20 hotels and three breweries. You only have to glance at the huge town hall, courthouse and post-office building to appreciate the size that Coolgardie once was. The gold then petered out and the town withered away quickly. During the boom of the 1990s, when world gold prices went up and mines were reopened, the population grew to around 2000, but has since declined.

The helpful tourist office (☎ 9026 6090), in the Warden's Court in Bayley St, is open from 9 am to 5 pm daily. The post office is just across from the BP petrol station, on Hunt St, which has an ATM.

Rainbow over Bluff Knoll, the highest peak in the Stirling Range NP, south coast

Hoping for a feed – Emu Point, Albany

Dawn breaks at Twilight Bay, Esperance

Great Ocean Drive, Esperance

Surf-fishing off Twilight Bay, Esperance

The unforgettable desert-type landscape of the Nullarbor Plain

Rugged coastline, Great Australian Bight

Mazza's store near Leonora, goldfields region

Balanced rock near Kookynie

Sand dunes are gradually engulfing the remains of the telegraph station at Eucla.

Things to See & Do

The **Goldfields Exhibition**, in the same building as the tourist office, is open from 9 am to 5 pm daily and has a fascinating display of goldfields memorabilia. You can even find out about former US President Herbert Hoover's days on the WA goldfields. It's worth the $3.30/1.10 entry fee for adults/children, which includes a film.

The **train station** in Woodward St also operates as a museum (admission is by donation); you can learn the incredible story of the Varischetti mine rescue. In 1907, an Italian miner named Varischetti was trapped 300m underground by floodwater and was rescued by divers 10 days later.

One kilometre west of Coolgardie is the **town cemetery**, which includes many old graves, such as those of explorer Ernest Giles (1835–97) and several Afghan camel drivers. Due to the unsanitary conditions and violence on the goldfields, it's said that 'one half of the population buried the other half'. The old **pioneer cemetery**, used from 1892 to 1894, is near the old oval at the end of Forrest St.

Warden Finnerty's Residence was built for Coolgardie's first mining warden and magistrate, John Michael Finnerty. The house, restored by the National Trust, is open 9 am to 4 pm Tuesday to Saturday, 10 am to noon Sunday. Admission is $2. Nearby is the lightning-dissected Gaol Tree, complete with leg irons.

At the **Camel Farm** (☎ 9026 6159), 3km west of town on the Great Eastern Hwy, you can take camel rides or organise longer camel treks; it is open daily.

About 30km south of Coolgardie, on Rock Rd, is **Gnarlbine Rocks**, an important watering point for the early prospectors. **Victoria Rock Nature Reserve**, with primitive camping, is a farther 18km south.

Places to Stay & Eat

Coolgardie Caravan Park (☎ 9026 6009, 99 Bayley St) has excellent tent/powered sites for $10/14 and on-site vans for $30. Parents travelling with kids will appreciate the playground.

There are a couple of historic hotels in Bayley St with long, shady verandahs. The

Railway Lodge (☎ 9026 6238) has singles/doubles for $25/35, and the *Denver City Hotel* (☎ 9026 6031) has rooms for $25/45. The *Coolgardie Motel* (☎ 9026 6080, 49 Bayley St) has good rooms for $55/65.

Both pubs do good *counter meals*, and the Coolgardie Motel also has a *restaurant*. There are a couple of *roadhouses* on Bayley St that do meals.

Getting There & Away

Perth Goldfields Express (☎ 9021 2954) runs from Perth to Coolgardie (continuing to Kalgoorlie-Boulder) Tuesday to Friday, and Sunday. From Kalgoorlie-Boulder via Coolgardie to Perth, buses run daily Monday to Friday. One-way fares are $72. Greyhound Pioneer Australia buses pass through Coolgardie on their Perth to Adelaide runs; the one-way Perth to Coolgardie fare is $102.30.

The *Prospector*, from Perth to Kalgoorlie-Boulder, stops at Bonnie Vale train station, 14km away, every day except Saturday; the one-way Perth–Bonnie Vale fare is $47.

For bookings call the Coolgardie tourist office or Westrail (☎ 13 1053).

KALGOORLIE-BOULDER
pop 33,000

Kalgoorlie-Boulder ('Kal' to the locals), some 600km from Perth, is a real surprise – it's a prosperous, humming metropolis and the state's second-largest town, with wide streets and well-preserved historic buildings (see the boxed text 'Architecture, Kalgoorlie-Boulder Style' in this chapter). The longest-lasting and most successful of WA's gold towns, it rose to prominence much later than Coolgardie. Today, it's the centre for ongoing mining in this part of WA.

Kalgoorlie-Boulder represents Australia's raw edge, and has the feel of a US 'Wild West' frontier town. Several brothels and a huge number of pubs (at one stage there were 93 of them, and the amount of alcohol consumed here is twice the state average) attest to the city's function, unchanged since the 19th century, as a prosperous mining centre. Don't be surprised if the female bar staff appear somewhat deshabille in underwear, suspenders and high heels – it might be a 'skimpy' night.

A few decent restaurants cater for the town's more sophisticated residents, but it's probably easier to find a gold nugget here than a good cup of coffee.

Come September, the town is packed to bursting with visitors from all over the state and further afield for the annual Kalgoorlie-Boulder Racing Round. Everyone gets frocked up and very drunk to watch horses race around the red dirt in Kalgoorlie-Boulder, Broad Arrow and other towns.

History

In 1893 Paddy Hannan, a prospector, set out from Coolgardie for another gold strike with a couple of Irish mates but stopped at the site of Kalgoorlie. He found enough gold lying on the surface to spark another rush.

As in so many places, the surface gold soon dried up, but at Kalgoorlie the miners went deeper and more and more gold was found. These weren't the storybook chunky nuggets of solid gold – Kalgoorlie's gold had to be extracted from the rocks by a costly and complex process of grinding, roasting and chemical action – but there was plenty of it.

Kalgoorlie quickly reached fabled heights of prosperity. The magnificent, enormous public buildings, erected at the turn of the 19th century, are evidence of its fabulous wealth. After WWI, however, increasing production costs and static gold prices led to Kalgoorlie's slow but steady decline.

In 1934 there were bitter race riots in twin towns Kalgoorlie and Boulder. On 29 and 30 January that year, mobs of disgruntled Australians roamed the streets, angrily setting fire to foreign-owned businesses and shooting at anyone deemed to be a foreigner. They were supposedly upset at preference being given by shift bosses to workers of southern-European descent. The disturbance had died down by the time police reinforcements and volunteers arrived by train from Perth.

With the substantial increase in gold prices since the mid-1970s, mining of lower-grade deposits has become economical and Kalgoorlie-Boulder is again the largest producer of gold in Australia. Large mining conglomerates have been at the forefront of new open-cut mining operations in the Golden Mile, the mines east of Kalgoorlie-Boulder, which is probably the wealthiest gold-mining locale for its size in the world.

Where Water is Like Gold!

With the discovery of gold it became clear to the Western Australia government that the large-scale extraction of the metal, the state's most important industry, was unlikely to continue in the Kalgoorlie goldfields without a reliable water supply. Stop-gap measures, like huge condensation plants that produced distilled water from salt lakes, or bores that pumped brackish water from beneath the earth, provided temporary relief.

In 1898, however, the engineer CY O'Connor proposed a stunning solution: he would build a reservoir near Perth and construct a 556km pipeline to Kalgoorlie. This was well before the era of long oil pipelines, and his idea was opposed violently in Parliament and regarded by some to be impossible, especially as the water had to go uphill all the way (Kalgoorlie is 400m higher than Perth). Nevertheless, the project was approved and the pipeline laid at breakneck speed.

In 1903 water started to pour into Kalgoorlie's newly constructed reservoir – a modified version of the same system still operates today. For O'Connor, however, there was no happy ending: Long delays and continual criticism by those of lesser vision resulted in his suicide in 1902, less than a year before his scheme proved operational.

In mid-2000 the nickel-mining company Anaconda announced the discovery of a huge inland body of water beneath the Great Victoria Desert – good news for the goldfields. Tests conducted on the water found it to be slightly saline, but reverse-osmosis treatment will make it fit for human consumption. Once tapped, the water will be used mainly for gold and nickel processing.

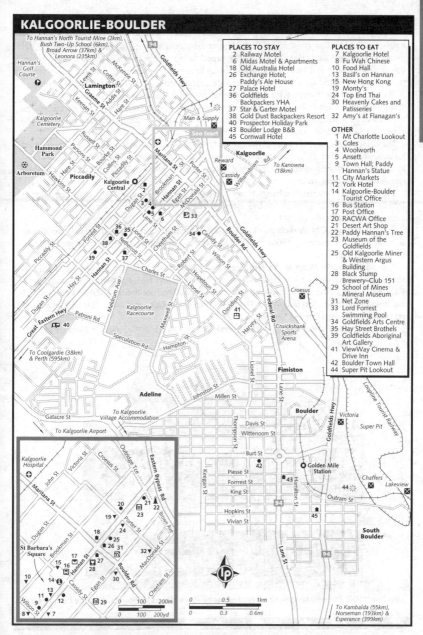

KALGOORLIE-BOULDER

PLACES TO STAY
2 Railway Motel
6 Midas Motel & Apartments
18 Old Australia Hotel
26 Exchange Hotel;
 Paddy's Ale House
27 Palace Hotel
36 Goldfields
 Backpackers YHA
37 Star & Garter Motel
38 Gold Dust Backpackers Resort
40 Prospector Holiday Park
43 Boulder Lodge B&B
45 Cornwall Hotel

PLACES TO EAT
7 Kalgoorlie Hotel
8 Fu Wah Chinese
10 Food Hall
13 Basil's on Hannan
15 New Hong Kong
19 Monty's
24 Top End Thai
30 Heavenly Cakes and
 Patisseries
32 Amy's at Flanagan's

OTHER
1 Mt Charlotte Lookout
3 Coles
4 Woolworth
5 Ansett
9 Town Hall; Paddy
 Hannan's Statue
11 City Markets
12 York Hotel
14 Kalgoorlie-Boulder
 Tourist Office
16 Bus Station
17 Post Office
20 RACWA Office
21 Desert Art Shop
22 Paddy Hannan's Tree
23 Museum of the
 Goldfields
25 Old Kalgoorlie Miner
 & Western Argus
 Building
28 Black Stump
 Brewery–Club 151
29 School of Mines
 Mineral Museum
31 Net Zone
33 Lord Forrest
 Swimming Pool
34 Goldfields Arts Centre
35 Hay Street Brothels
39 Goldfields Aboriginal
 Art Gallery
41 ViewWay Cinema &
 Drive Inn
42 Boulder Town Hall
44 Super Pit Lookout

Architecture, Kalgoorlie-Boulder Style

Kalgoorlie-Boulder boasts an eclectic collection of architectural styles, and nowhere is this better demonstrated than along Hannan St. You can expect to see curious blends of Victorian gold-boom, Edwardian, Moorish and Art Nouveau styles, which have melded to produce a bizarre mix of ornate facades, colonnaded footpaths, recessed verandahs, stuccoed walls and general overstatement.

The facade of the **York Hotel** is one of Hannan St's most elaborate, with arches, bay windows, stucco and brick decoration, a pair of silver cupolas and a huge French-style square dome. The hotel's interior features a beautiful carved staircase. The hotel was built in 1900 and played host to many stage shows that came through Kalgoorlie.

The **Palace Hotel**, on the corner of Hannan and Maritana Sts, was designed to be the town's most luxurious hotel; all of its furnishings were brought in from Melbourne. The Palace was built from locally quarried stone and was the first hotel to have electric lighting. Former US president Herbert Hoover was a regular visitor.

The much-photographed **Exchange Hotel** is one of Kalgoorlie-Boulder's most attractive pubs; its facade features an array of decorative elements, two-storey verandahs, a corner tower and a corrugated, galvanised-iron roof.

The single-storey **City Markets** building (272–280 Hannan St) has a triple-arched gateway topped by twin turrets. In the early 1900s the central covered courtyard was the home of greengrocers, butchers and fruiterers.

The old *Kalgoorlie Miner* & *Western Argus* building (125–127 Hannan St) was the first three-storey building in town. It was built in 1900; the upper storeys feature elaborate classical details. Kalgoorlie's first newspaper, the *Western Argus*, was published for the first time in 1894, only 17 months after gold was first discovered. The first edition of the *Kalgoorlie Miner* (the only local paper remaining today) appeared in September 1895.

The tourist office sells a useful booklet *Hannan Street Kalgoorlie: Our Golden Heritage* ($4.50).

Built in 1900, the ornate York Hotel hosted many stage shows during Kalgoorlie's boom years.

Gone are most of the old mine headframes and corrugated-iron homes. Mining, pastoral development and a busy tourist trade ensure Kalgoorlie-Boulder's continuing importance as an Outback centre.

The town can get very hot in December and January; overall the cool winter months are the best time to visit. From late August to the end of September, however, the town is packed because of wildflower tours and the local horse-racing round, and accommodation of any type can be difficult to find.

Orientation

Although Kalgoorlie sprang up close to Paddy Hannan's original find, the mining emphasis soon shifted a few kilometres away to the Golden Mile and the satellite town of Boulder developed to service this area. The two towns amalgamated in August 1989 into the City of Kalgoorlie-Boulder.

The town centre (Kalgoorlie) is a grid of broad, tree-lined streets. The main street (Hannan St), flanked by imposing public buildings (see the boxed text), is wide enough to turn a camel train – a necessity in turn-of-the-century goldfield towns. You'll find most of the town's hotels, restaurants and offices on or close to Hannan St.

Information

There's a helpful tourist office (☎ 9021 1966) on the corner of Hannan St and St Barbara's Square. It can provide a good, free town map and gives friendly advice. It also has a number of other area maps for sale. The office is open from 8.30 am to 5 pm weekdays and 9 am to 5 pm weekends.

The long-distance bus station is on Hannan St (outside the tourist office). The Kalgoorlie Central train station is on the corner of Wilson and Forrest Sts.

The town's post office is at 204 Hannan St. Net Zone is an Internet cafe on Maritana St. There's an office of the Royal Automobile Club of Western Australia (RACWA; ☎ 9021 1511) on the corner of Porter and Hannan Sts.

The daily newspaper is the *Kalgoorlie Miner*. There are laundrettes in McDonald St and in Boulder Rd.

Hannan's North Tourist Mine

One of Kalgoorlie-Boulder's biggest attractions, Hannan's North Tourist Mine (☎ 9091 4074) is just off Goldfields Hwy. Located on the site of Paddy Hannan's original lease, it was a working mine until 1952. After languishing in obscurity for 40 years it was transformed into an excellent educational display of heritage buildings, miners' camps, headframes and mining equipment. A guided tour takes you more than 30m underground. The original supports of the 'step mine' are clearly visible, and modern equipment is demonstrated, with ear-blasting noise.

The admission fee ($15/7.50/38 for adults/children/families) is a bargain and covers the underground tour, an audiovisual display, a tour of the surface workings, a gold 'pour' and panning. More than 550 grams of gold are placed in the prospecting ponds each year, so you might strike it lucky. Underground tours are at 9.30 and 11 am and 12.30, 2 and 3.15 pm daily (more frequently during peak season), and the complex is open from 9.30 am to 4.30 pm. Enclosed shoes must be worn underground.

A miner's hall-of-fame museum was in the planning at the time of writing. Check with the mine or with the tourist office.

Loopline Tourist Railway

The 'Rattler' makes an hour-long trip around the Golden Mile at 10 am daily. It also goes at 11.45 am, according to demand, on Sunday and public holidays. It leaves from Boulder's Golden Mile train station, passing the old mining works. The cost is $9/6 for adults/children. For more information call ☎ 9093 3055.

In the early part of the 20th century, the Loopline was the most important urban transport for Kalgoorlie and Boulder, and the Golden Mile station was once the busiest in WA.

Museum of the Goldfields

The impressive Ivanhoe mine headframe at the northern end of Hannan St marks the entrance to this excellent museum. It is open from 10 am to 4.30 pm daily (admission is by 'gold coin' donation) and has a wide range of exhibits including an underground gold vault and historic photographs. A lift takes you to a viewing point on the headframe, where you can look out over the city and mines and down into delightfully untidy backyards. The tiny **British Arms Hotel** (the narrowest hotel in Australia) is part of the museum.

Other Attractions

The **Mt Charlotte Lookout** and the town's reservoir are a few hundred metres from the north-eastern end of Hannan St, off the Goldfields Hwy (also known as the Eastern Bypass Rd). The view over the town is good, but there's little to see of the reservoir,

which is covered to limit evaporation. This reservoir is the culmination of the genius of engineer CY O'Connor (see the boxed text 'Where Water is Like Gold' earlier in this chapter) – the water in it took 10 days to get here from Mundaring Weir outside Perth.

The **School of Mines Mineral Museum**, on the corner of Egan and Cassidy Sts, has a geology display including replicas of big nuggets discovered in the area. It's open from 8.30 am to 12.30 pm weekdays.

Along Hannan St, you'll find the imposing **town hall** and the equally impressive **post office**. There's an art gallery upstairs in the decorative town hall, while outside is a replica of a statue of Paddy Hannan holding

Bush Two-Up

Two-up is a frenetic, uniquely Australian gambling game that can be traced back to the country's early convicts. It involves two pennies, which are tossed into the air from a wooden paddle, landing either heads or tails up (large white crosses denote tails). The game is controlled by a ring keeper, who selects 'spinners' who toss the coins in the centre of the ring. The coins have to spin or the ring keeper will 'bar'em' and the result will be void. The spinners bet with the ring keeper for a two heads–up (two-up) result; if they win they pay the ring keeper a 10% 'boxer' or commission. At the same time, the ring keeper makes bets with other participants who bet for a tails result. If the spinner 'ones'em' (one head, one tail) they keep spinning until a result occurs. If they 'tail'em', they lose their money and forfeit the right to spin again. If they 'heads'em' they win and can either pass or spin again.

Amid the gamblers' yelps, a lot of money seems to change hands. The Bush Two-Up is open from about 4.30 pm until after dark.

Come in spinner: Punters hope for a two heads–up result at Kalgoorlie-Boulder's two-up school.

a water bag. The original is inside the town hall, safe from nocturnal painters.

North-west of Hannan St in Hay St is one of Kalgoorlie-Boulder's most notorious 'attractions'. Although it's quietly ignored in the tourist brochures, the town has a block-long strip of **brothels**. A blind eye has been turned to them for so long that it has become an accepted and historical part of the town. At the time of writing, the newest and swankiest of the brothels, Langtree's 181, was about to start daytime tours ($20) of its elaborate, if tasteless, premises for curious tourists. Ask at the tourist office for details.

Kalgoorlie-Boulder also has a legal **two-up school** in a corrugated-iron amphitheatre 6km north of town, off the Goldfields Hwy. Follow the signs from Hannan St, then look for the sign on the right that says '2UP'. The patrons are mostly locals, and a lot of money changes hands. It opens from about 4.30 pm daily. (See the boxed text.)

On Outridge Terrace is **Paddy Hannan's tree**, marking the spot where the first gold strike was made.

Hammond Park, in the west of Kalgoorlie-Boulder, is a small fauna reserve with a miniature Bavarian castle. It's open from 9 am to 5 pm daily.

The **Goldfields War Museum**, in Burt St, has a collection of war memorabilia and military vehicles. Boulder's **Golden Mile train station** was built in 1897.

The **Super Pit** lookout, just off the Goldfields Hwy, near Boulder, is open from 6 am to 7 pm daily. The view from the lookout is awesome and the big trucks at the bottom of the huge hole look like kids' toys.

The **Goatcher Theatre Curtain** in the 1907 Boulder Town Hall has recently been restored. The Neapolitan scene was painted by Englishman Philip W. Goatcher, one of the great scenic artists of the Victorian era. The curtain is dropped from 10 am to noon Wednesdays.

Organised Tours

The tourist office has information on tours, including wildflower tours in spring, and can book most of them. Goldrush Tours (☎ 9021 2954) offers tours of Kalgoorlie-Boulder

($40/20 adults/children), Coolgardie and nearby ghost towns. Kalgoorlie Adventure Bus (☎ 0412-110 001) does similar tours.

Geoff Stokes (☎ 9093 3745) runs Aboriginal bush tours ($70), plus camping trips ($150). There's also an expensive gold-prospecting tour ($280 full day) for avid fossickers with Cranston's Gold Tours (☎ 9021 6747), and a gold-detecting tour with 4 Wheel Drive Tours (☎ 0419-915 670) for $125/80 full/half day.

You can see Kalgoorlie-Boulder and the Golden Mile mining operations from the air with Goldfields Air Services (☎ 9093 2116) and AAA Charters (☎ 9021 6980). Prices start at $25.

Places to Stay

Camping & Caravan Parks The tourist office has a list of caravan parks. The *Kalgoorlie Accommodation Village (☎ 9039 4800)*, on Burt St about 6km from the centre of Kalgoorlie, has powered sites for $18, chalets for $65 and self-contained 'resort units' for $85.

The chalets and units here have recently received an extensive and expensive makeover. There's a swimming pool and a children's playground and is fully equipped for disabled travellers.

The *Prospector Holiday Park (☎ 9021 2524)*, on the corner of Great Eastern Hwy and Ochiltree St, is closest to the city centre. It has tent/powered sites for $17/18 and standard/en suite cabins for $56/66. The park has a pool, a grassed area for campers and one of the best campers' kitchens in the state.

Hostels Opposite Kalgoorlie-Boulder's red-light action (and partly located in a former brothel itself) is *Goldfields Backpackers YHA (☎ 9091 1482, 166 Hay St)*. It has a pool, a fully equipped kitchen, Internet access, air-conditioning and a comfy TV lounge. Dorm beds (with comforts such as linen, mirrors and towel racks) cost $16 and doubles cost $36.

Gold Dust Backpackers Resort (☎ 9091 3737, 192 Hay St) is very similar to Goldfields in facilities; beds in dorms are a bargain $12, singles cost $25 and twins/doubles cost $34. There is free tea and coffee and free use of the hostel's bicycles.

B&Bs B&B accommodation is growing in popularity here. *Boulder Lodge (☎ 9093 2094, 50–55 Piesse St)* is about 100 years old, with comfortable single/double rooms for $65/85, including a cooked breakfast. Evening meals (by prior arrangement) cost $10. The tourist office has a list of other B&B operators.

Hotels & Motels There are several pleasantly old-fashioned hotels in the centre of town, including the *Palace Hotel (☎ 9021 2788)*, on the corner of Maritana and Hannan Sts, which has single/double rooms with en suite for $40/60. The *Exchange Hotel (☎ 9021 2833)*, on Hannan St, has rooms starting at $35/50 and is well placed in the heart of town.

The superbly renovated *Old Australia (☎ 9021 1320)*, on the corner of Maritana and Hannan Sts, has beautiful iron lacework and offers B&B singles/twins for $55/85 (en suite rooms cost $90/105). It also has several self-contained units. The wide 1st-floor verandah is perfect for a bit of people-watching.

The *Cornwall Hotel (☎ 9093 2510, 25 Hopkins St)* in Boulder has singles/doubles with shared facilities for $55/65, including continental breakfast. It is close to the Super Pit and the Loopline railway.

There is no shortage of good-quality motels. The *Midas Motel & Apartments (☎ 9021 3088, 409 Hannan St)* has standard rooms for $95/110 and superior rooms for $115/135. The *Star & Garter (☎ 9026 3399, 497 Hannan St)* is well priced, with basic rooms for $65/75.

Perhaps the nicest accommodation in town is the new *Railway Motel (☎ 9088 0000, 51 Forrest St)*, built on the site of the old hotel of the same name, opposite the train station. Standard/deluxe double rooms here cost $115/135.

There are also self-contained apartments (sleeping up to four people) around town for $110. Weekend rates can be lower.

Places to Eat

The tourist office produces a leaflet on restaurants in town – a good place to start.

Monty's, on the corner of Hannan and Porter Sts, is open 24 hours a day for grills, salads and sandwiches. The tasty Caesar salad ($18.50) and chicken and avocado salad ($12.50) are excellent. The attractive *Basil's on Hannan (268 Hannan St)* is good for pasta, sandwiches and coffees. *Heavenly Cakes and Patisseries (2 Boulder Rd)* is a bakery-cum-coffee shop, where the cakes here are indeed heavenly and much better than the rather average coffee. It also does toasted sandwiches and focaccia ($7.50 to $8) and lasagne with salad for $9.

There are plenty of pubs, restaurants and cafes, particularly along Hannan St. Counter meals cost around $12 to $20. At the time of writing the *Star and Garter (497 Hannan St)* was considered the best. It has a good range of meat, seafood and chicken dishes (from $12 to $18) and an all-you-can-eat vegetable and salad bar. The portions are so large it's almost off-putting, but, hey, miners have big appetites. At the *Palace*, on the corner of Hannan and Maritana Sts, you can get Mediterranean-style food with main courses for around $21. *Paddy's Ale House (135 Hannan St)*, at the Exchange Hotel, has an overflowing hot and cold buffet (around $15 a head) and great fish and chips that comes to the table on a plate but also wrapped in butcher's paper. The truckies breakfast will set you up for the day – if not the week.

If you want Chinese, head for *New Hong Kong (248 Hannan St)*, in St Barbara's Square opposite the tourist office, or *Fu Wah Chinese*, on Wilson St, where you can bring your own (BYO) alcohol. If Thai takes your fancy there's the BYO *Top End Thai (71 Hannan St)*, which has chilli chicken ($17), delicious beef satays ($12) and vegetables in oyster sauce ($10) as well as other fish, chicken and beef curries.

For a bit of a splurge and desserts that have locals drooling, try the licensed *Amy's at Flanagans (☎ 9021 1749, 1 McDonald St)*. The crocodile fritters and the sticky date pudding have achieved cult status; bookings are recommended. Another great place for a tasty meal is the **Kalgoorlie Hotel**, on the corner of Hannan and Wilson Sts, where tables are arranged on the wide 1st-floor balcony and the food is fabulous. It has excellent wood-fired pizzas and great meat-based or vegetarian mains.

There is a **food hall** in Brookman St, open from 11.30 am to 2.30 pm and from 5 to 9 pm. It serves everything from lamb chops to chop suey. Self-caterers will have no trouble, with two huge **supermarkets**: **Coles**, on Brookman St, and **Woolworth**, in Hannan St.

Entertainment

Visiting artists perform regularly at the **Goldfields Arts Centre**, on Cassidy St. In the same complex is the Goldfields Art Gallery, with local and travelling exhibitions.

The town's nightlife tends to revolve around the pubs, some of which have late-night licences. The **Palace Hotel**, on the corner of Hannan and Maritana Sts, the **Exchange Hotel** *(135 Hannan St)* and **The Black Stump Brewery – Club 151** *(151 Hannan St)*, next door to the Palace Hotel, are the places to hang out.

For movies, head to the **ViewWay Cinema and Drive Inn**, on Oswald St.

Shopping

The Goldfields Aboriginal Art Gallery on Dugan St, and the Desert Art shop, next to the Museum of the Goldfields, have crafts for sale. Kalgoorlie-Boulder is a good place to buy gold nuggets fashioned into relatively inexpensive jewellery – shop along Hannan St.

Getting There & Away

Air Ansett Australia has flights from Perth to Kalgoorlie-Boulder and return daily (except Sunday). The Ansett office is at 314 Hannan St. SkyWest Airlines has at least one direct flight daily, with good deals for weekend advance-purchase fares. To contact SkyWest and Ansett, call ☎ 13 1300.

Bus Perth Goldfields Express (☎ 1800-620 440, 9021 2954) has a Perth to Kalgoorlie-Boulder service ($72 one way) Tuesday to Friday and Sunday. On Wednesday, Friday and Sunday this bus continues to Leonora ($40 from Kalgoorlie-Boulder) and Laverton ($60). The return journey to Perth runs from Laverton and Leonora on Sunday, Wednesday and Friday. Two other services run from Kalgoorlie-Boulder to Perth on Tuesday and Thursday.

Greyhound Pioneer (☎ 13 2030) buses pass through Kalgoorlie en route from Perth to Sydney, Melbourne and Adelaide. The one-way fare to Perth is $103.40, and to Adelaide is $229.90.

Westrail (☎ 13 1053, 1800-099 150) runs a bus at least three times a week to Esperance ($33.50, 5½ hours) via Norseman ($18). There are daily Westrail services between Perth and Kalgoorlie-Boulder (see under Bus in the Getting Around chapter for more information).

Train Westrail's *Prospector* from Perth ($49.30 one way, 7½ hours) runs daily. In Perth, you can book seats at the Western Australian Tourism Commission's office in Forrest Place or at the Westrail terminal (☎ 13 1053, 1800-099 150). It's wise to book, as this service is fairly popular, particularly in the tourist season. Book at the station or tourist office if travelling from Kalgoorlie-Boulder to Perth.

The *Indian Pacific* and *Trans-Australian* trains also go through Kalgoorlie-Boulder twice a week.

Getting Around

Between Kalgoorlie and Boulder, there's a regular bus service from about 8 am to 6 pm with Goldenlines (☎ 9021 2655). The tourist office has timetables. There are also daily buses from/to Kambalda and Coolgardie (during school term only).

If you want to explore farther afield, you'll have to drive, hitch or take a tour as public transport is limited. A taxi to the airport costs around $10.

You can rent cars from Hertz (☎ 9093 2211), Budget (☎ 9093 2300), Avis (☎ 9021 1722) and Halfpenny Hire (☎ 9021 1804).

Ask at the tourist office if you want to hire a bicycle.

NORTH OF KALGOORLIE-BOULDER

The road north is surfaced from Kalgoorlie-Boulder to the three 'Ls' – the mining towns of Laverton (367km north-east), Leinster (372km north) and Leonora (237km north). Off the main road, however, traffic is virtually nonexistent and rain can quickly close unsealed roads. There are several towns of interest along the way – including Kanowna, Broad Arrow, Ora Banda, Menzies and Kookynie. Beyond Leinster, remote Wiluna is a true Outback town.

Getting There & Away

There are flights from Perth to Laverton (four per week), Leinster (daily except Saturday), Leonora (weekdays) and Wiluna (three a week). These are operated by Sky-West Airlines or Skipper's Aviation; booking is through Ansett Australia (☎ 13 1300).

Goldfields Express (☎ 9021 2954) has a service from Perth to Leonora ($100) and Laverton ($110) via Kalgoorlie on Wednesday, Friday and Sunday. The bus heads to Perth from these towns on Monday, Wednesday and Friday.

Kanowna

This is the most fascinating of the goldfields ghost towns in terms of history. It is just 18km from Kalgoorlie-Boulder along a dirt road. In 1905 Kanowna had a population of 12,000, 16 hotels, two breweries, many churches and an hourly train service to Kalgoorlie. Today, the population is zero, and apart from the train station platform and the odd pile of rubble, nothing remains.

Kanowna is now the starting point, each September, for the Balzano barrow race – during which teams push a miner's barrow to Kalgoorlie-Boulder.

Broad Arrow & Ora Banda

Broad Arrow was featured in *The Nickel Queen*, the first full-length feature film made in WA. It is a shadow of its former self – at the beginning of the 20th century it had a population of 2400; now there's just one pub and a couple of derelict-looking houses. The pub hasn't changed much over the past 100 years and is worth a stop, if only to see miners from the north revving up for a few days off in Kalgoorlie-Boulder.

Ora Banda, 28km west of the Goldfields Hwy (turn off at Broad Arrow), has shrunk from a population of 2000 to less than 50. The *Ora Banda Historic Inn (☎ 9024 2059)*, built in 1911, represents the closest thing to civilisation; doubles with private bathroom cost $60, and singles with shared bathroom cost $50. Bar staff at the pub say all there is to do here is 'get drunk and have sex'.

Menzies & Kookynie

Menzies, around 132km north of Kalgoorlie-Boulder, is another typical goldfields town. It has about 230 people today, compared with 10,000 in 1905. Many early buildings remain, including the train station with its 120m platform (1898), and the imposing town hall (1896) with its clockless clock tower. The ship bringing the clock from England, the SS *Orizaba*, sank south of Rottnest Island.

There are no rivers in the area and the surrounding countryside is mostly flat with eucalypts, salmon gum and blackbutt trees.

Kookynie is a small ghost town, 69km south-east of Leonora, surrounded by old mine workings and tailings. There is also a small museum with a collection of photographs and antique bottles. About 10km from Kookynie is the **Niagara Dam**, built with cement carried from Coolgardie by a caravan of 400 camels.

The 500-sq-km **Goongarrie National Park**, which includes large areas of mulga, prolific birdlife of the arid region and wildflowers in season, is worth a visit, especially in spring, is t. The park is reached by way of a reasonable road south-east of Menzies.

Places to Stay & Eat The *Menzies Hotel (☎ 9024 2043, 22 Shenton St)* has rooms for $35 per person, or $55 with dinner and breakfast. Meals can also be obtained from the *Caltex Roadhouse*.

In Kookynie unwind with a beer (and barbecue) in the beer garden of the *Grand Hotel (☎ 9031 3010)*, built in 1894, which has big verandahs and spacious rooms. Singles/doubles cost $35/55.

Leonora

pop 2600

Named after the wife of a WA governor, Leonora is 237km north of Kalgoorlie-Boulder. It serves as the railhead for the nickel from Windarra and Leinster. Climb to the summit of **Mt Leonora** to get a great view of the town or wander down to the **cenotaph** to see the restored 1927 hearse.

Leonora's tourist office (☎ 9037 6176), in the shire offices on Tower St, is open from 8.30 am to 5 pm weekdays.

In adjoining Gwalia (a ghost town), the Sons of Gwalia Goldmine, the largest in WA outside Kalgoorlie-Boulder, closed in 1963 and much of the town shut down. The increase in gold prices in the 1990s led this and other mines in the area to reopen. In the late 1890s, the Gwalia mine was managed by Herbert Hoover, who later became president of the USA.

The Gwalia Historical Society is housed in the 1898 **mine office** and is open daily. Also of interest are the restored State Hotel, Patronis Guesthouse and the mine manager's house. The *Historic Gwalia Heritage Trail* pamphlet describes the places of interest on a fascinating 1km walk around the town.

Places to Stay Tent/powered sites at the *Leonora Caravan Park* (☎ 9037 6568), on Rochester St, cost $12/15 for two people. The *Leonora Motor Inn* (☎ 9037 6444), on Tower St, is the most comfortable place to stay. It has singles/doubles for $75/85. The *Whitehouse Hotel* (☎ 9037 6030), also on Tower St, is more basic, with singles only, for $35. The *Central Hotel* (☎ 9037 6042), on Tower St, has single/double rooms starting at $45/55.

Laverton

From Leonora you can turn north-east to Laverton, some 360 km north of Kalgoorlie-Boulder, where the surfaced road ends. There are many abandoned mines in the area.

Laverton marks the start of the Great Central (Warburton) Rd. From here, it is a mere 1132km to Uluru and 1710km to Alice Springs (see Great Central Road following for more information about this route).

The *Desert Pea Caravan Park* (☎ 9031 1072), on Weld Ave, has tent/powered sites starting at $10/12. Single/double rooms at the *Desert Inn Motel Hotel* (☎ 9031 1188, 2 Laver St) cost $50/70 and motel units cost $55/75.

Laverton Downs Station (☎ 9037 5998) is 25km north-east of Laverton and offers B&B plus dinner starting at $60 per person.

Great Central Road

For those interested in a genuine outback experience, the unsealed Great Central Rd (also known as Warburton Rd), which runs from Laverton to Yulara (a tourist development near Uluru) via the Cosmo Newbery Aboriginal Land and Warburton, provides a rich scenery of red sand, spinifex, mulga and desert oaks.

The road, while sandy in places, is suitable for conventional vehicles, although a 4WD would give a much smoother ride. Although this road is often mistakenly called the Gunbarrel Hwy, the genuine article actually runs some distance to the north, and is very rough and only partially maintained.

You should take precautions relevant to travel in such an isolated area – tell someone (shire office or local police) of your travel plans and take adequate supplies of water, petrol, food and spare parts.

The route passes through various pockets of Aboriginal land; permission to enter these areas must be obtained in advance from the Aboriginal Lands Trust in Perth (☎ 9235 8000, ℮ alt@aad.gov.au). Permits can take several weeks (or longer) to be granted.

The RACWA publishes a very good map of the route ($2.50, available from tourist offices in WA, including the tourist office in Kalgoorlie-Boulder). Petrol is available at Laverton, Warburton (where basic supplies are also available) and Yulara. In an emergency, you may be able to get fuel at the Docker River settlement.

The longest stretch of road without fuel is between Laverton and **Warburton** (570km). *Warburton Roadhouse & Caravan Facility* (☎ 8956 7656) has accommodation (camping and self-catering), fuel and food supplies. Tent sites cost $6 per person, single/double cabins start at $35/70. The Warburton township is an Aboriginal community on private land and not open to the public.

At **Giles**, 231km north-east of Warburton and 105km west of the Northern Territory border, there is a meteorological station which has a friendly 'Visitors Welcome' sign and a bar – it is well worth a visit. *Warakurna Roadhouse & Caravan Facility* (**☎** *8956 7344*) has accommodation, fuel and food supplies, and also arranges tours to the meteorological station.

Don't even consider travelling on this route from November to March, when there's extremely hot temperatures in this region. (See Car in the Getting Around chapter for more details.)

For nearly 300km west from Giles, the Great Central Rd and Gunbarrel Hwy run on the same route. Taking the old Gunbarrel Hwy (to the north of the Great Central Rd) to Wiluna is a rough, serious trip through lots of sand dunes; it's only passable in a 4WD.

Leinster

North-west of Leonora, the road is surfaced to Leinster, another modern nickel-mining centre, with a population of around 1000. **Agnew**, 23km west of Leinster, is an old gold town that has all but disappeared. The old brick gaol at **Lawlers**, 25km south-east of Leinster on the Agnew-Leonora Rd, is all that is left of that township.

From Leinster, it's 170km north to Wiluna and another 180km west to Meekatharra. From there, the surfaced Great Northern Hwy runs 765km south-west to Perth or 860km north to Port Hedland.

If you're driving through this area and need somewhere to stay in Leinster, the best option is the *Leinster Lodge Motel* (**☎** *9037 9040)*, on the corner of Mansbridge and Agnew Rds, which has double rooms for $80.

Wiluna

The remote town of Wiluna marks the end of civilisation eastwards until Alice Springs. As the local shire puts it: 'Wiluna is a dusty Outback town that hasn't got a lot of creature comforts. What Wiluna has got is friendly people and a real bush atmosphere'.

When gold was mined in the district, Wiluna was a prosperous town. Today, it's an administrative centre with a mainly Aboriginal population. You can obtain tourist information from the shire office (**☎** *9981 7010*) in Scotia St.

About 11km east of town is the Desert Gold **orange orchard**, proof that the desert can bloom.

Wiluna is also the starting or finishing point of two of Australia's greatest driving adventures – the **Canning Stock Route** and the **Gunbarrel Hwy**. (See Outback Travel under Car in the Getting Around chapter.)

The Canning Stock Route runs south-west from Halls Creek to Wiluna, crossing the Great Sandy and Gibson Deserts. As the track has not been maintained for more than 30 years it's a route to be taken seriously. If you intend to travel on this route get the *Australian Geographic Book of the Canning Stock Route* (1992), which has all the maps and information you'll require.

Places to Stay & Eat Most visitors come in a 4WD and head to the *Wiluna Club Hotel* (**☎** *9981 7012*), on Wotton St, which has basic rooms with shared facilities for $45 and double motel units for $100. It also runs the *caravan park*; powered sites cost $25 for two people.

You can get counter meals at the *Wiluna Club Hotel*, which also has a licensed restaurant. Provisions for the inevitable long journeys (whichever way you leave town) are available from stores on Wotton St.

SOUTH OF KALGOORLIE-BOULDER
Kambalda
pop 5000

Kambalda died as a gold-mining town in 1906, but nickel was discovered here in 1966, and today it is a major mining centre, with a population of 5000. Kambalda is split into two parts, East and West, about 4km apart. East Kambalda was the original centre, but when nickel was found in an area due for housing expansion, the mining company simply built another town away from the nickel deposits.

The tourist office (☎ 9027 1446), on Emu Rocks Rd (the road to Norseman) in Kambalda West, provides a map of the area.

Kambalda is on the shores of Lake Lefroy, a large saltpan and a popular spot for land sailing on summer Sundays. The first land sailors were prospectors who mounted wheels on a 5m sailing boat. The yachts can travel at 100km/h across the smooth salt lake. The view from **Red Hill Lookout**, in Kambalda East, is well worth checking out.

Widgiemooltha

Widgiemooltha, or 'Widgie', just off the Coolgardie Esperance Hwy, is good for a stop at breakfast time. The '*roadhouse*' truckies breakfast – a stomach-bursting three sausages, several slices of bacon, two or three eggs and three pieces of toast – is famous!

Norseman

pop 2500

To most people, Norseman is just a crossroads where you turn east for the trans-Nullarbor Eyre Hwy journey, south to Esperance along the Coolgardie Esperance Hwy or north to Coolgardie and Perth. The town, however, also has gold mines, some of which are in operation.

The tourist office (☎ 9039 1071), at 68 Roberts St, next to a park (with good public showers), is open from 9 am to 5 pm daily. The **Historical & Geological Collection** in the old School of Mines has items from the gold-rush days; it's open 10 am to 1 pm daily except Thursday and Sunday ($2/1 adults/children).

You can get an excellent view of the town and surrounding salt lakes from the **Beacon Hill Mararoa Lookout**, past the mountainous tailings. The tailings, one of which contains 4.2 million tonnes of rock, are the result of 40 years of gold mining.

The graffiti-covered **Dundas Rocks** are huge boulders 22km south of Norseman. Also worth a look are the views at sunrise and sunset of the dry, expansive and spectacular **Lake Cowan**, north of Norseman.

South of Norseman, halfway along the road to Esperance, is the small township of **Salmon Gums** (population 50), named after

the gumtrees, prevalent in the area, which acquire a seasonal rich-pink bark in late summer and autumn.

See the Kalgoorlie-Boulder Getting There & Away section for information on buses to Norseman and beyond.

Places to Stay & Eat The tidy *Gateway Caravan Park* (*☎ 9039 1500*), on Prinsep St, has tent/powered sites for $14/17, and on-site vans/cabins for $25/42 for two. *Lodge 101* (*☎ 9039 1541, 101 Prinsep St*) does B&B in rooms with shared facilities for $25 per person and has backpacker beds for $15.

The *Norseman Hotel* (*☎ 9039 1023*), on Roberts St in the centre of town, has single/double rooms with shared facilities for $25/40. The *Railway Hotel* (*☎ 9039 1115*), on Roberts St, has en suite motel units for $45 a double. The *Norseman Eyre Motel* (*☎ 9039 1130*), also on Roberts St, has similar rooms and prices.

Norseman is not a gourmet's paradise. The pubs do counter meals, and the BP and Ampol *roadhouses* have eat-in or takeaway pies, sandwiches and coffees. Cafes include the *Rainbow Drive Cafe*, on Roberts St, and the *Norseman Deli*, on Prinsep St. *Topic Caterers Dining Room*, on Phoenix Rd, usually feeds the miners, but it has a $10 all-you-can-eat buffet in the evenings.

Eyre Highway

It's a little more than 2700km between Perth and Adelaide, not much less than the distance from London to Moscow. The long and sometimes lonely Eyre Hwy crosses the southern edge of the vast and legendary Nullarbor Plain. Nullarbor is bad Latin for 'no trees', but there is actually only a small stretch where you see none at all: The road is flanked by vegetation most of the way, as this coastal fringe receives regular rain, especially in winter.

The road across the Nullarbor Plain takes its name from John Eyre, the explorer who made the first east-west crossing in 1841. It was a superhuman effort that took five months of hardship and resulted in the death of Eyre's companion, John Baxter. In 1877 a telegraph line was laid across the Nullarbor, roughly delineating the route the first road would take.

Later in the century, miners on their way to the goldfields followed the same telegraph line route across the empty plain. In 1896 the first bicycle crossing was made and in 1912 the first car was driven across, but in the next 12 years only three more cars managed to traverse the continent.

In 1941 WWII inspired the building of a transcontinental highway, just as it had the Alice Springs to Darwin route. It was a rough-and-ready track when completed, and in the 1950s only a few vehicles a day made the crossing. In the 1960s the traffic flow increased to more than 30 vehicles a day and in 1969 the WA government surfaced the road as far as the South Australia (SA) border. Finally, in 1976, the last stretch from the SA border was surfaced and now the Nullarbor crossing is a much easier drive, but still a long one.

The surfaced road runs close to the coast on the SA side. The Nullarbor region ends dramatically on the coast of the Great Australian Bight, at cliffs that drop steeply into the ocean. It's easy to see why this was a seafarer's nightmare, for a ship driven onto the coast would quickly be pounded to pieces against the cliffs, and climbing them would be a near impossibility.

From Norseman, where the Eyre Hwy begins, it's about 730km to the WA/SA border, near Eucla, and almost 500km farther to Ceduna (from an Aboriginal word meaning 'a place to sit down and rest') in SA. From Ceduna, it's still another 783km to Adelaide via Port Augusta.

A good alternative route to the Eyre Hwy for travellers coming from the south coast is the 4WD-only Balladonia Rd, between Esperance and Balladonia. For more information, see under National Parks in The South Coast chapter.

North of the Eyre Hwy, the Trans-Australia Railway runs across the Nullarbor Plain. One stretch of the railway runs dead straight for 478km – the longest piece of straight railway line in the world.

Information

At the western end of the highway, there's a tourist office (☎ 9039 1071) in Norseman (see under Norseman earlier). The first tourist office at the eastern end in SA is at Ceduna (☎ 1800-639 413), in Poynton St.

All of the roadhouses along the route have stacks of pamphlets relating to tourist sights and towns in the area.

Books & Maps A number of helpful publications cover the Nullarbor. One of the most comprehensive is the free *The Nullarbor: Australia's Great Road Journey*, available from tourist offices throughout WA and SA.

Crossing the Nullarbor

Car Although the Nullarbor is no longer a torture trail where cars get shaken to bits by potholes and corrugations or where you're going to die of thirst waiting for help to turn up if you break down, it's still wise to prepare well.

The longest distance between fuel stops is about 200km, so make sure you've got plenty of petrol and a basic spare-parts kit. It's essential that your vehicle is in good shape and has good tyres.

The cost of fuel varies greatly: it's cheaper in major cities and towns and ridiculously expensive in tiny places in the Outback, where you have no choice but to fill up.

Carry some drinking water (at least 4L per person for short stretches; 20L if you're travelling long distances in the Outback) just in case you do have to sit it out by the road on a hot summer day. Remember, there are limited freshwater facilities between Norseman and Ceduna.

There are no banking facilities between Norseman and Ceduna so take plenty of cash. However, all roadhouses, except at Mundrabilla, have Eftpos and take major credit cards.

Take it easy on the Nullarbor – plenty of people try to set speed records and plenty more have messed up their cars when they've run into kangaroos at night. There are many rest areas – make use of them!

For more driving information see under Car in the Getting Around chapter.

Bus & Train As the Eyre Hwy is the most important transcontinental route, there are daily scheduled bus services all the way from Perth to Adelaide with Greyhound. There is also a rail option – one of the world's great train journeys (see under Train in the Getting There & Away chapter).

Bicycle The Nullarbor Plain is a real challenge to cyclists. They are attracted by the barrenness and distance, certainly not by the interesting scenery. As you drive across you see many cyclists, at all times of the year, lifting their water bottles to their parched mouths or sheltering from the sun.

Excellent equipment is needed and adequate water supplies must be carried. The cyclist should also know where all the water tanks are located. Adequate protection (hats, lotions etc) from the sun should be used even in cloudy weather. The prevailing wind for most of the journey is west to east, the most preferable direction to be pedalling.

For more cycling information, see under Bicycle in the Getting Around chapter.

Pedal Power

Spare a thought for the first cyclist to cross the Nullarbor. Arthur Richardson set off from Coolgardie on 24 November 1896 with a small kit and water bag. Thirty-one days later he arrived in Adelaide having followed the telegraph line, on the way encountering hot winds, '100 in the shade' and 40km of sand hills west of Madura station.

MW

Norseman to Cocklebiddy

From Norseman, the first settlement you reach is **Balladonia**, 191km to the east. Kids will enjoy a stop here and some fun on the shady playground. The *Balladonia Hotel Motel* (☎ 9039 3453) has singles/doubles starting at $58/68; its dusty caravan facility has tent/powered sites for $10/14.

The small cultural heritage **museum** in Balladonia has displays on subjects such as Afghan camel drivers, Aboriginal settlement and the crash landing of the US National Aeronautics & Space Administration Skylab in the 1970s. As travellers David and Beth Williams noted, 'the cappuccino, like the petrol, is expensive'.

After Balladonia, near the ruins of the old telegraph station, you may see remains of stone fences built to enclose stock. Clay saltpans are also visible in the area.

The road from Balladonia to Cocklebiddy, some 210km, is a lonely section. To the town of Caiguna, it includes one of the world's longest stretches of straight road – 145km, the so-called 90 Mile Straight.

Caiguna, over 370km from Norseman, has a broken-down playground, a single functioning petrol pump and generally looks like it's falling to pieces. The *John Baxter Motel* (☎ 9039 3459) has rooms for $50/65 and a caravan facility with tent/powered sites starting at $8/15 for two people. Some 10km south of Caiguna is the memorial to John Baxter, Eyre's companion on his crossing of the Nullarbor.

At **Cocklebiddy** are the stone ruins of an Aboriginal mission. There's a decent playground for kids and shaded picnic tables. **Cocklebiddy Cave** is the largest of the Nullarbor caves (see the boxed text 'Under the Nullarbor' in this chapter). In 1984 a team of French explorers set a record here for the deepest cave-dive in the world.

The *Wedgetail Inn Hotel Motel* (☎ 9039 3462) has expensive fuel, tent/powered sites for $9/15, budget singles/doubles for $40/48 and motel rooms for $60/70.

With a 4WD, you can travel south of Cocklebiddy to **Twilight Cove**, where there are 75m-high limestone cliffs, or to Birds Australia's *Eyre Bird Observatory*

Under the Nullarbor

Beneath the uninhabited and barren landscape of the Nullarbor Plain lies a wealth of interest. The Nullarbor is an ancient limestone sea bed, up to 300m thick in places. About 20 million years ago shells and marine organisms began to settle and some three million years ago the bed was gently raised, forming a huge plateau 700km long and up to 300km wide.

Within this raised plateau is Australia's largest network of caves, formed over the millennia as rain seeped through cracks in the surface limestone. The caves vary in size from shallow depressions to elaborate, deep caves with immense chambers. About 50 of the caves begin via passages in large sinkholes or dolines; others can be accessed only through narrow, vertical blowholes.

The most accessible of the caves is Cocklebiddy Cave, 12km north of the Eyre Hwy. It has one of the longest underwater passages known in the world. The Mullamullang Cave east of Cocklebiddy is the most extensive cave network known in Australia and contains superb mineral formations known as the Salt Cellars.

West of Eucla are the Weebubbie, Pannikin Plains and Abrakurrie Caves. Both the Weebubbie Cave and Pannikin Plains Cave have been off limits for the past decade as they are so unstable. The Abrakurrie Cave contains the largest chamber of the Nullarbor caves, 180m long and 45m wide and with a 40m-high ceiling; it is reached by a steeply sloping passage from the sinkhole entrance.

More caves exist on the South Australia (SA) side of the border. The best known is Koonalda, which is entered through a huge sinkhole. This cave contains a large main chamber, 70m below the surface, which has a 45m-high domed ceiling. Aborigines quarried flint from this cave over 20,000 years ago and they left unexplained incisions on the main entrance passage.

As these caves can be unstable and are not staffed, you should *never* enter any of them without an experienced guide and proper safety gear. Many lives have been lost and the vertical access to a number of the caves requires highly specialised equipment. Safety at such sites can never be fully guaranteed, as the cave environs are continually changing.

Those keen to venture underground should contact the Esperance office of the Department of Conservation & Land Management (CALM; ☎ 9071 3733) or the SA National Parks & Wildlife Service in Ceduna (☎ 08-8625 3144) for more information.

Expert, accredited Cave Diving Association of Australia cave divers are permitted to visit and dive in some caves. However divers still have to get authorisation from CALM and must follow its strict guidelines. CALM will not give its approval to dive in any cave if the participants don't have the necessary expertise and accreditation.

(☎ 9039 3450). The observatory, some 50km from Cocklebiddy, was established in 1977, and is housed in the Eyre Telegraph Station, an 1897 stone building in Nuytsland Nature Reserve. It offers full board for $77, dropping to $66 for two to four nights and $55 a night thereafter. Birds Australia and YHA members get a $5 a night discount. There are also discounts for groups of four or more.

Surrounded by mallee scrubland and looking up to spectacular roving sand dunes (which separate the buildings from the sea), this is the perfect getaway for nature lovers to study a wide range of desert flora and fauna. From the buildings there is a 1km walk, via the dunes, to the beach and the lonely Great Australian Bight.

You can reach the observatory only by 4WD transport. If you are staying here, the observatory managers will pick you up from the observatory car park, 14km off the Eyre Highway.

Cocklebiddy to Eucla

The journey between Cocklebiddy and Eucla is around 270km. Some 83km east of Cocklebiddy is **Madura**, close to the hills of the Hampton Tablelands. At one time, horses were bred here for the Indian army. You get good views over the plains from the road.

The ruins of the **Old Madura Homestead**, several kilometres west of the new homestead by a dirt track, have some old machinery and other equipment. Caves in the area include the large **Mullamullang Caves**, north-west of Madura, with three lakes and many side passages.

The ***Madura Pass Oasis Inn*** (☎ 9039 3464) has rooms from $52 to $86 for two people, good tent/powered sites starting at $12/15, and a pool.

The **Mundrabilla Roadhouse** is on the lower coastal plain, with the Hampton Tablelands as a backdrop.

Mundrabilla has a *caravan park* and the ***Mundrabilla Motor Hotel*** (☎ 9039 3465), with rooms starting at $55. From Mundrabilla it's about 65km to Eucla.

Eucla & Beyond

Just before the SA border is Eucla, which has picturesque ruins of an old **telegraph repeater and weather station**, first opened in 1877. The telegraph line now runs along the railway line, far to the north. The telegraph station, 5km from the Eucla roadhouse, is gradually being engulfed by the sand dunes. You can also inspect a historic jetty, which is visible from the top of the dunes. The dunes around Eucla are a truly spectacular sight.

The 33-sq-km **Eucla National Park** is only a 10-minute drive from the town. It features the Delisser Sandhills and the high limestone Wilson Bluff. The mallee scrub and heath of the park is typical of the coastal vegetation in this region.

At Eucla, many people have their photo taken with the international sign pinpointing distances to many parts of the world; it's near a ferroconcrete sperm whale, a species seldom seen in these parts. Another popular photo stop is at the **Travellers' Cross**. This is atop the escarpment which overlooks the ruins of old Eucla.

Eucla is the border town and an important stop-off. The ***Eucla Motor Hotel*** (☎ 9039 3468) has doubles for $75, basic singles/doubles for $20/35 and tent/powered sites for $12/15.

At **Border Village**, 13km from Eucla, connoisseurs of kitsch will appreciate the 5m-high fibreglass kangaroo. Remember to set your watch forward 1½ hours when you get to the border – or 2½ hours if daylight-saving time is operating in SA.

The ***WA-SA Border Village*** (☎ 9039 3474) has sites starting at $12/15, cabins starting at $35 a double and motel units starting at $65.

From Border Village, it's a spectacular 200km coastal drive to the **Nullarbor Roadhouse**, and about 300km farther to **Ceduna**, passing the **Yalata Aboriginal Reserve**, **Nundroo** and **Penong** along the way.

For more information on the Eyre Hwy and exploring Nullarbor National Park, see Lonely Planet's *South Australia* and *Outback Australia*.

The Midlands

On any extended road journey in Western Australia (WA), you're likely to pass through some part of the Midlands region, which extends from the coast near Kalbarri National Park, east to the Murchison Valley and south to the wheatbelt towns some 300km or so south of the Great Eastern Hwy.

Compared with other parts of the state, there is little to attract the traveller here. However, there are some exceptions: the haunting Pinnacles Desert; the fascinating Benedictine mission town of New Norcia; the gold towns in the Murchison Valley for the dilapidated remains of a once-booming era; the carpets of wildflowers that appear in late winter and spring; and the much-photographed Wave Rock, near Hyden.

Pick up the free Western Australian Tourism Commission (WATC) brochure *The Golden Heartlands*, available from all tourist offices in the area, from the WATC in Perth and from most other tourist offices in the state.

The Wheatbelt

East of the Darling Range, stretching north from the Albany coastal region to beyond the Great Eastern Hwy, is the WA wheatbelt. This area is noted for its unusual rock formations (the best known of these being Wave Rock) and for its many ancient Aboriginal rock carvings and *namma* (water holes).

Some towns that are considered to be part of the wheatbelt have been covered in other chapters of this book, where they are part of a distinct and well-known route north or east. For ease of description, the wheatbelt has here been divided into three areas: north-eastern wheatbelt; Great Eastern Hwy; and central and southern regions. The Department of Conservation & Land Management (CALM) produces the informative *Voices of the Bush – A Wheatbelt Heritage*, available from CALM offices.

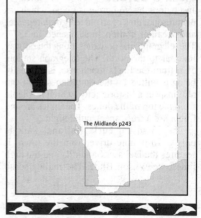

The Midlands p243

NORTH-EASTERN WHEATBELT

This vast area is north of the Great Eastern Hwy and east of the Great Northern Hwy. It begins at the towns of Goomalling and Wongan Hills and stretches over 200km east to Mukinbudin. Between towns are vast expanses of boring yellow paddocks (fields) of wheat and sheep. Occasionally you can also see from the road where salt-pans encroach on areas of pasture and bush as the land loses its battle against salinity.

Facilities in each town in this region are similar. There's generally a basic caravan

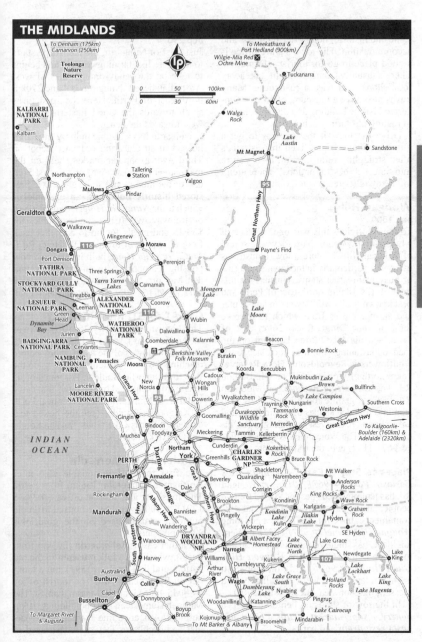

THE MIDLANDS

park and an old-fashioned (and often handsome and historic) hotel offering meals and accommodation. The town's shire office is a good place to go for tourist information. There's usually some form of takeaway food shop, or at least a roadhouse. Many towns also have a museum, often in a converted historic building and doing a big line in rusting old farm machinery.

Drive out to visit these towns to get a glimpse of how life is lived in Australia's often struggling rural interior, or if you're into 'unusual rock formations'. There aren't too many other reasons to go there.

Wongan Hills
pop 1000

To the Aborigines this was once a place of whispering *(wongan)*. Nowadays the sound of Wongan Hills is more a low, industrious murmur – particularly in the town's neat row of busy main-street shops (unusual for this region). It's 184km north-east of Perth and best known for its wildflowers in late winter and spring. Places from which to observe these include **Dingo Rock**, 26km east of town, and the **Mt O'Brien Lookout** on the road to Piawaning. Another good place to see wildflowers is **Reynoldson's Flora Reserve**, 15km north of Wongan Hills on Old Ballidu Rd. The **Gathercole Reserve**, on Moonijin Rd, features granite rocks sculpted by erosion into rounded shapes up to 2m high, and **Lake Ninan**, 10km west on Calingiri Rd, attracts birds. The Wongan Hills tourist office (☎ 9671 1157) is in the train station.

Places to Stay & Eat The *Wongan Hills Caravan Park (☎ 9671 1015)*, on Wongan Rd, has tent/powered sites for $10/15 for two people, on-site vans starting at $30 and self-contained cabins for $65. The handsome *Wongan Hills Hotel (☎ 9671 1022)*, on Fenton Place, has singles/doubles for $35/50 and motel units for $60/70. The *Wongan Hills Guest House (☎ 9671 1015)*, on Moore St, is in a relatively modern building with a pleasant outdoor area. B&B costs $30/50.

In the row of shops on Fenton Place is a *bakery*, a *supermarket*, a *cafe*, a *pizza and pasta restaurant* and banks.

Nungarin
pop 290

Just west of Nungarin, the landscape starts to look less like farming country and begins to take on the sandy-orange hues of west Australian desert. Nungarin is some 270km north-east of Perth. Here the road turns south towards the Great Eastern Hwy, or west towards the coast.

Nungarin has a sizable **military museum**, housed in an old army ordnance depot on Third Ave; a popular **market**, held on the main street (Railway Ave) on the first Sunday of the month; and some attractively restored **historic buildings**, an example of which is the *Nungarin Hotel (☎ 9046 5084)*, on Railway Ave. It has singles/doubles for $30/45 and meals for up to $13. Set back from the centre of town on Old Hotel Rd is *McCorry's Old Hotel*, built in 1911 and now housing tearooms, with an inviting verandah. McCorry's also runs the town's *caravan park (☎ 9046 5006)*, also on Old Hotel Rd.

GREAT EASTERN HIGHWAY

This highway (State Hwy 94; also known as the Golden Way), starts in Perth and passes through the towns of the Avon Valley before reaching the many agricultural towns on the way to Kalgoorlie-Boulder. For much of its length it is paralleled by the pipes that carry water from Mundaring Reservoir near Perth to Kalgoorlie-Boulder (see the boxed text 'Where Water is Like Gold!' in The Southern Outback chapter).

Cunderdin to Merredin

The first town of reasonable size after Northam is **Cunderdin**, 156km from Perth. The museum and tourist office (☎ 9635 1291), at 100 Forrest St, is housed in an old pumping station used on the goldfields water pipeline.

Farther east is **Kellerberrin** (203km from Perth), which has a **folk museum** in the old agricultural hall (built in 1897) and a lookout on **Kellerberrin Hill**. The tourist office (☎ 9045 4006) is at 110 Massingham St. The **Milligan Homestead** and outbuildings, 10km north of town, are a fine example of vernacular architecture as they are constructed of local fieldstone. Like many towns in the area, a great attraction is the profusion of **wildflowers** in spring. Two of the best places to see them are the Durakoppin Wildlife Sanctuary, 27km to the north, and Charles Gardner National Park, about 15km south of Tammin.

Merredin, the largest centre in the wheatbelt (population 3500), is 260km east of Perth on the Kalgoorlie-Boulder train line and the Great Eastern Hwy. It has a tourist office (☎ 9041 1666) on Barrack St. The train station, built in 1893, has been turned into a charming **museum** with a vintage 1897 locomotive and an old signal box with 95 signal-switching levers. **Mangowine Homestead**, 65km north of Merredin, has been restored by the National Trust.

There are interesting **rock formations** around Merredin, including Kangaroo Rock, 17km to the south-east; Burracoppin Rock, to the north; and Sandford Rocks, 11km east of Westonia. Look for the signs to these places in town.

Places to Stay & Eat Cunderdin has a *caravan park (☎ 9635 1258)*, on Olympic Ave, which has on-site vans for $30 for two people. *Cunderdin Hotel Motel (☎ 9635 1104)*, on Main St, has singles/doubles for $50/70. This pub serves good meals, including a hearty Sunday roast.

In Kellerberrin there's a *caravan park (☎ 9045 4066)* with tent/powered sites for $7/10 for two people. The *Shell Roadhouse Motel (☎ 9045 4007)* has rooms for $40/50 and does meals. There are also a couple of cafes in town.

Merredin has a variety of accommodation. Just off the Great Eastern Hwy, *Merredin Caravan Park (☎ 9041 1535, 2 Oats St)* has tent/powered sites for $8/14 for two people and on-site vans for $30. The *Merredin Motel (☎ 9041 1886, 10 Gamenya Ave)* has singles/doubles starting at $50/55. *Potts Motor Inn (☎ 9041 1755)*, on the Great Eastern Hwy at the Kalgoorlie-Boulder end of town, has rooms for $63/73.

The *Commercial Hotel*, on Barrack St, and the Merredin Motel are the best places for meals.

Southern Cross
pop 2200

Southern Cross was the first gold-rush town on the WA goldfields, although the gold quickly gave out and the big rush soon moved east to Coolgardie and Kalgoorlie. Like the town itself, the streets of Southern Cross are named after the stars and constellations. The **Yilgarn History Museum**, in the old courthouse, has local displays; stretch your legs and take in a bit of history at the same time. If you follow the continuation of Antares St south for 3km, you will see a couple of active **open-cut mines**.

Situated 368km east of Perth, this is really the end of the wheatbelt and the start of the desert; when travelling by train the change of landscape is very noticeable. In the spring, the sandy plains around Southern Cross are carpeted with **wildflowers**.

Places to Stay & Eat The *Southern Cross Caravan Park (☎ 9049 1212)*, on Coolgardie Rd, has powered sites for $12 for two people, and on-site vans from $20 to $25 for two people.

On Antares St, the nicely renovated *Palace Hotel (☎ 9049 1555)*, has lovely stained-glass windows. Singles/doubles with shared bathrooms cost $50/60; basic backpacker singles are $20. The restaurant here is the best place in town for a meal. The *Southern Cross Motel (☎ 9049 1144)*, on Canopus St, has rooms for $65/75.

CENTRAL & SOUTHERN REGIONS

This is the area south of the Great Eastern Hwy and east of the Albany Hwy (State Hwy 30). It stretches from Brookton and Pingelly out to Hyden and Wave Rock in the north, and from Kojonup to Grace and King Lakes in the south. The considered highlight is Wave Rock, but you've got to drive about 200km south of the Great Eastern Hwy to get to it and there's nothing else there, so you'd want to be keen on rock formations.

This region also features wildflowers in season, the magnificent Dryandra Woodland National Park and the homestead of author Albert Facey.

THE MIDLANDS

Pingelly

Pingelly is 160km south-east of Perth. Its name comes from the Aboriginal word for the area, 'Pingecullin'. **Historic buildings** in the town include the courthouse, which is now the museum.

Boyagin Rock Reserve, 26km north-west of the town, is an important remnant of natural bush on the edge of the wheatbelt.

Located in town, the *Pingelly Roadhouse/Motel* (☎ 9887 1015) has single/double rooms for $45/65 and also does meals. *Tianco Emu Farmstays* (☎ 9887 1375), outside town, has B&B for $45 per person. The *Exchange Tavern*, on Pasture St, serves decent counter meals.

Dryandra Woodland National Park

This 280-sq-km national park (☎ 9881 1113) is a remnant of the open eucalypt woodlands that once covered much of the wheatbelt but were cleared for agriculture. The woodlands are predominantly wandoo, powderbark and brown mallet and the plateaus have pockets of jarrah associated with *kwongan* (heath and shrublands).

At least 20 species of native mammal have been found in the park, including the state's faunal emblem, the numbat. The small kangaroo-like woylie (also known as the brush-tailed bettong) and tammar (a wallaby) are other ground-dwelling mammals found here. It is a fine bird-watching area, with over 100 species (including mallee fowl), and in spring there are many wildflowers.

There is a good 5km walk, the **Ochre Trail**, which has an ochre pit once quarried by the local Nyungar people. The ochre was valued for body decoration and rock art. There is also a 25km **radio drive trail** (tune to 100 FM).

Dryandra Woodland National Park is 165km south-east of Perth and 20km northwest of Narrogin, and is accessible from the Narrogin-Wandering Rd. Camping in the forest itself is not allowed, but you can stay in rustic cottages at the *Lions Dryandra Village* (☎ 9884 5231), in the park, for about $12 per person.

Narrogin

This town, 189km south-east of Perth, is an agricultural centre in the heart of WA's richest farming land. The **Old Courthouse**, in Egerton St, houses a museum and Narrogin's information centre (☎ 9881 2064).

Albert Facey

A great 'battler' story is Albert Barnett Facey's autobiography *A Fortunate Life*, which won the New South Wales Premier's Award for nonfiction in 1981.

Facey was born in Maidstone, Victoria, in 1894 and grew up in the Coolgardie goldfields and outback Western Australia (WA). His father died before he was two and his mother deserted him (and his sister and two brothers). The family was subsequently raised by his grandmother. He started work at eight and was variously employed doing station work, railway work, droving and even boxing in an itinerant troupe.

He returned to Perth in 1915 after fighting in WWI and sustaining injury at Gallipoli (his brother Joseph was killed there). Facey married, joined the WA Tramways, then became a farmer as part of the soldier settlement scheme near Wickepin. After the war he learned to read and write and he eventually compiled the notes that formed the basis of his best-selling autobiography.

The Depression and his injuries forced him to return to Perth in 1934. He rejoined the tramways and became active in the union. Three of his sons went off to fight in WWII and one was killed when Singapore fell. Facey died in Perth in 1982.

A Fortunate Life is a marvellous heart-wrenching story, giving an historic glimpse of the lives of ordinary Australians from the turn of the 19th century to the 1970s. The story subsequently has been dramatised and made into a TV series.

It is open from 9.30 am to 4.30 pm weekdays and from 9 am to noon Saturday. The tourist office has excellent pamphlets outlining various heritage trails in and around the town.

The **Albert Facey Homestead** (☎ 9882 7040), 39km east of Narrogin and just south of Wickepin, is worth a visit, especially if you have read Albert Facey's popular book *A Fortunate Life* (see the boxed text). The 86km self-drive Albert Facey Heritage Trail begins at the homestead and visits many of the places around Wickepin mentioned in the book. The homestead has a rambling collection of Facey memorabilia and is open daily.

Places to Stay Accommodation options in Narrogin include the *Narrogin Caravan Park* (☎ 9881 1260), on Williams Rd, and several run-of-the-mill motels, including the *Narrogin Motel* (☎ 9881 1660, 56 Williams Rd)*, which has singles/doubles for $50/60. A more interesting option is B&B at a local farmstay. *Chuckem Farm* (☎ 9885 9050) is on Chomley Rd, 27km south-west of town off Williams Rd, and *Stoke Farm* (☎ 9885 9018), on the Great Southern Hwy, 11km south of town. Both charge $55 per person for B&B and will provide dinner on request.

Wagin
pop 2300

Pronounced '**way**-jin' (and don't you forget it), this rural centre is 227km south-east of Perth. The Wagin tourist office (☎ 9861 1232) is in Kitchener St, at the charming **historical village**, which features buildings built in the late 19th century.

The town's 15m-high fibreglass **ram** is a tribute to the surrounding merino industry (and a sense of bad taste). **Mt Latham** ('Badjarning'), a granite rock 6km to the west of Wagin, offers good bushwalking.

The *Wagin Caravan Park* (☎ 9861 1177), on the corner of Arthur Rd and Scadden St, has tent/powered sites for $10/14. The *Wagin Motel* (☎ 9861 1888, 57 Tudhoe St) has singles/doubles for $58/68. The *Palace Hotel* (☎ 9861 1003), also on Tudhoe St, has simple rooms for $25/40.

Katanning

This town, south of Wagin and 277km south of Perth, has a large Muslim community from Christmas Island, who worship at their own **mosque** in Andrews Rd.

Other attractions include the **old flour mill** on Clive St, which houses the tourist office (☎ 9821 2634), open weekdays and Saturday mornings, and the ruins of an **old winery**. The **saleyards** here are the second-biggest inland saleyards in Australia.

The *Katanning Caravan Park* (☎ 9821 1066), on Aberdeen St, has tent/powered sites for $4/10. Single/double rooms at the *Katanning Motel* (☎ 9821 1657), on Albion St, start at $35/60. There's also a restaurant in the motel.

There are a handful of decent *cafes* that are good for coffees and lunches. *Hung Win's*, on Carew St, does Chinese food.

Kojonup
pop 1100

Some 39km south-west of Katanning, and on the southernmost extremity of the wheatbelt, Kojonup was established in 1837 as a military outpost to protect the mail run from Perth to Albany. The name is derived from the Aboriginal word *kodja*, meaning 'stone axe'. The tourist office (☎ 9831 1686) is in the old train station in Benn Parade. The **military barracks museum** still survives from the colonial era (circa 1845) and is worth a look.

Dumbleyung

Dumbleyung is on State Hwy 107 to the north-east of Lake Dumbleyung (where Donald Campbell broke the world speed record on water, setting 442.08km/h in *Bluebird* in 1964). Today the lake hosts a variety of birdlife. There is a good view of the lake from Pussy Cat Hill.

Surprise, there is the *Dumbleyung Caravan Park* (☎ 9863 4012), on Harvey St, and the *Dumbleyung Tavern Hotel* (☎ 9863 4028), on Bartram St.

Peppercorn Cottage (☎ 9864 1012), 20km east of Dumbleyung, off Lake Grace Rd, is good for a self-catering stay (minimum two nights); $65 for doubles.

THE MIDLANDS

Kukerin

Kukerin is 39km east of Dumbleyung. In wildflower season there is a worthwhile drive through the nearby **Tarin Rock Nature Reserve**.

Lake Grace

Lake Grace, 345km from Perth, takes its name from the shallow salt lake that is 9km west of town. The **Inland Mission Hospital**, built in 1925 by the famous 'Flynn of the Inland', founder of the Royal Flying Doctor Service, has recently been restored as a hospital museum.

Lake Grace Caravan Park (☎ *9865 1263)*, on Mathers St, has tent/powered sites for $8/12. Doubles at the *Lake Grace Hotel* (☎ *9865 1219)*, on Stubbs Terrace, cost $62.70, and at the *Lake Grace Motel* (☎ *9865 1180)*, on Griffith St, it is a little more expensive. You will have no trouble locating any of them – if you hit the desert, you have gone too far.

Lake King

Lake King, at the end of State Hwy 107, is where an old sand track heads off to the Frank Hann and Peak Charles National Parks. Lake King is a great place to see wildflowers in season.

On Varley Rd, there's the *Lake King Caravan Park* (☎ *9874 4060)* and the *Lake King Tavern/Motel* (☎ *9874 4048)*. The latter has singles/doubles starting at $60/70.

Hyden & Wave Rock

Wave Rock, 350km south-east of Perth and 4km east of the town of Hyden, is worth a visit – but only if you are nearby. The perfect surfer's wave is 15m high and 100m long and frozen in solid rock marked with different colour bands. The bands are caused by the run-off of waters containing carbonates and iron hydroxide. Unfortunately, a small concrete wall along its top detracts from its natural majesty.

Other interesting rock formations in the area bear names such as the **Breakers**, **Hippo's Yawn** and the **Humps**. Hippo's Yawn is a 20-minute walk from Wave Rock, and well worth the visit. The walls of

Mulka's Cave, 21km from Hyden, feature Aboriginal hand paintings. The tourist office (☎ 9880 5182), at the Wave Rock Wildflower Shop, provides information on how to get to these formations. Wave Rock is also renowned for its **lace collection**.

A Westrail bus travels to Hyden from Perth on Tuesdays ($30.60 one way).

Places to Stay & Eat At Wave Rock, the *Wave Rock Caravan Park* (☎ *9880 5022)* has tent/powered sites for $10/14 for two people, and cabins starting at $60. The very comfortable *Hyden Hotel Motel* (☎ *9880 5052, 2 Lynch St)* has singles/doubles starting at $55/85 and luxury rooms for quite a bit more. There's a pool for cooling summer dips. About 30 minutes' drive south-west of Wave Rock is *Joycraft Farmstays* (☎ *9880 5129)*, on the corner of Karlgarin Lake and Worland Rds, Karlgarin. It has B&B for $35 per person, and doubles as *Wave-a-Way Backpackers* with dorm beds for $17.

Meals are available at *Hyden Roadhouse* or at the hotel. There is a *coffee shop* at Wave Rock, but if you can, bring your own (BYO) picnic lunch.

Kondinin

Kondinin, in the heart of grain and sheepfarming country, boasts **Kondinin Cottage** (☎ 9889 1226), a restored mud-brick settler's home (built in 1923) that is classified by the National Trust and open daily except Wednesday. **Jilakin Rock**, about 25km south of Kondinin, is a spectacular grey-granite monolith overlooking Jilakin Lake, some 12 sq km in area. Near the edge of the lake is a stand of jarrah trees, rare in the wheatbelt and usually associated with forests 140km to the west.

Campers should head for *Kondinin Caravan & Camping* (☎ *9889 1006)*. *Kondinin Hotel/Motel* (☎ *9889 1009)*, on the corner of Rankin and Gordon Sts, has singles/doubles for $45/60, including breakfast.

Corrigin

An archetypal wheatbelt town 68km south of Bruce Rock and 230km south-east of Perth, Corrigin has a **folk museum** which has a collection of farm machinery; a **craft** cottage; and a **miniature railway**. The tourist office (☎ 9063 2203) is in Lynch St. About 5km west of town is a **dog cemetery**, one of the more bizarre sights in WA.

Powered sites at the *Corrigin Country Caravan Park (☎ 9063 2103)*, on Kirkwood St, cost $12. Dogs are allowed if they are kept on leashes. The *Corrigin Windmill Motel (☎ 9063 2390)*, on Brookton Hwy, has reasonably priced rooms. The tourist office can steer you towards farmstays.

Food is quite good in Corrigin – as long as you like yabbies! The Corrigin Windmill Hotel also has a licensed restaurant and the *Coffee Shop & Takeaway*, on Goyder St, is good for a snack.

Bruce Rock

Bruce Rock has a tourist office (☎ 9061 1002) in Johnson St and a **museum** comprising an original one-roomed school and a mud-brick settlers hut. The *Bruce Rock Shire Caravan Park (☎ 9061 1169)*, on Dunstal St, is good; tent sites cost $6.60, on-site vans cost $11 per person. The *Durham Roadhouse (☎ 9061 1174)*, on Johnson St, has single motel rooms with private bathroom for $35. The tourist office can help with farmstay accommodation.

If you wish to immerse yourself in agricultural delight, then the road between Quairading and Bruce Rock, 160km and 240km east of Perth respectively, is the place. Punctuating the sylvan scene of livestock and crops are a number of prominent rock formations, including **Kokerbin Rock**, a prominent granite outcrop reputed to be the third-biggest monolith in Australia. There are great views from its summit.

The road to Quairading passes through **Shackleton** (also known as Kwolyin), home of the smallest bank in Australia (no longer in use), just 4m by 3m.

Quairading

Quairading, 'home of the small bush kangaroo', has a tourist office (☎ 9645 1001) on Jennaberring Rd. The *Quairading Caravan Park (☎ 9645 1001)* and *Quairading Motel (☎ 9645 1054)* are in town.

Central Midlands

There are two road options inland of Dongara and Geraldton and both branch off from the Great Northern Hwy. The first option, State Hwy 116, is known locally as the Midlands Rd. It heads north from Bindoon and passes towns such as Moora, Coorow, Carnamah and Mingenew before emerging at the coastal town of Dongara.

The alternative route, roughly parallel with State Hwy 116 and east of it, branches off the Great Northern Hwy some 270km north-east of Perth at Wubin. It takes in the towns of Dalwallinu, Perenjori and Morawa before hitting Mullewa.

The big attraction for visitors to the central midlands region is the brilliant display of **wildflowers** here from July to November. Wilderness Wanderer (☎ 9397 0050) runs a four-day wildflower tour through this area in September, starting at $550, including meals and accommodation.

Safari Treks (☎ 9271 1271) and Gold 'n' Valley Tours (☎ 9401 1505) are two other companies operating trips focused on wildflowers.

Town tourist offices are usually only open for the wildflower season. Shire offices are a good alternative information source. The area is also a gateway to the Murchison goldfields. Several of its towns also contain evidence of a sojourn by prolific architect, Monsignor John Hawes (see the boxed text 'Monsignor John Hawes' in the Central West Coast chapter).

The other alternative for travelling north from Perth is the coastal route, the Brand Hwy, which heads slightly inland before it returns to the coast for some scenic oceanside driving to Dongara.

Locals in towns along the Brand Hwy cannot hide their glee at plans for a sealed road all the way up the coast from Lancelin (and by extension from Perth) to Cervantes. Developers are already laying claim to big blocks of land in towns such as Jurien and there's lots of talk about new resorts.

In the meantime, it takes four hours to travel the 4WD track linking Lancelin and Cervantes.

BRAND HIGHWAY
Cervantes & the Pinnacles Desert

The small seaport of Cervantes, 259km north of Perth, was named after a US whaling ship wrecked on nearby reefs. It is the entry point for the eerie and haunting Pinnacles Desert, in Nambung National Park. The Shell petrol station (☎ 9652 7041) acts as the tourist office, and the Pinnacles Beach Backpackers also has information. Peak times here are school holidays, long weekends, Easter and Christmas.

Some 19km from Cervantes, the sandy desert of the coastal Nambung National Park is punctured with peculiar, 30,000-year-old **limestone pillars**, some only a few centimetres high and others towering up to 5m. Some are coloured with lichen. To the south of the main group is an area known as the Tombstones, where dark spires protrude from the vegetated landscape. When Dutch sailors first saw the Pinnacles Desert from the sea they thought it was the ruins of an ancient city.

At peak times, early mornings are the best time to visit the Pinnacles Desert to avoid the crowds. Seeing the full moon over the Pinnacles Desert is an extraordinary, eerie experience, like stumbling onto the nocturnal meeting of some secret society

The Nambung National Park plays host to an impressive display of **wildflowers** from August to October.

Check in Cervantes before driving into the park – if conditions are bad, a 4WD may be necessary for the last 6km from the Hangover Bay turn-off. The trip takes about 25 minutes one way and entry to the park costs $8. The sand dunes along the coast north and south of Cervantes are spectacular.

Coastal Coachlines (☎ 9652 1036) runs a service from Perth to Cervantes ($20.50), Jurien ($21.50), Green Head and Leeman on Monday, Friday and public holidays.

Organised Tours Cervantes Pinnacles Adventure Tours (☎ 1800-623 212) operates from the corner of Aragon and Brown Sts. The Pinnacles tour includes a swim or snorkel at Hangover Bay, park entry fee and commentary ($20). The same company

offers a range of other tours including a crayfish (rock-lobster) factory tour ($5) and a five-hour outback farm visit ($5).

If the environmental impact of tearing around fragile sand dunes in a noisy, wheeled machine doesn't bother you, its coastal 4WD tour costs $20. Happyday Tours (☎ 9652 7244) will pick up passengers from the Greyhound Pioneer drop-off at the Cataby roadhouse on the Brand Hwy and take you on a two-hour Pinnacle tour for $30.

For a more personalised tour that is highly recommended, Turquoise Coast Enviro Tours (☎ 9652 7047) are run from 59 Seville St by a former park ranger with nearly 20 years' experience. A day tour ($85/50 adults/children) takes in the Pinnacles Desert, parts of Lesueur National Park, a walk through Stockyard Tunnel cave, and lunch and a swim at Lake Indoon.

Several tour operators visit the Pinnacles on their way up the coast to Perth, while others take day tours from Perth. Pinnacle Tours (☎ 9417 5555) has a day tour along the 4WD track linking Lancelin and Cervantes and on to the Pinnacles (and return) for $102.

Places to Stay & Eat *Pinnacles Caravan Park* (☎ *9652 7060)* is nowhere near its namesake, but on the beachfront in Cervantes. Its park cabins look a bit run down but they are cheap: $35/30 peak/off-peak. Tent/powered sites start at $12/15.50.

The friendly *Pinnacles Beach Backpackers* (☎ *9652 7377, 91 Seville St)* has the feel of a big, modern, family house. Dorm beds cost $15, and en suite doubles $50. Its other rooms can sleep up to five and start at $40 for two people.

A room in the brown-brick *Cervantes Pinnacles Motel* (☎ *9652 7145, 227 Aragon St)* costs $90, while self-contained units at *Cervantes Holiday Homes* (☎ *9652 7115)*, on the corner of Valencia Rd and Malaga Court, start at $65/$52 peak/off-peak.

If you want dinner, make sure you order it before 8.30 pm. The relaxed *Ronsard Bay Tavern*, on Cadiz St, serves counter meals and has live bands at the weekend. The local *pizza shop* has large supremes for

$16.90, and also serve burgers and chicken. The Cervantes Shell petrol station has a takeaway and a *restaurant* that opens from breakfast time. The Cervantes Pinnacles Motel has the licensed *Europa Anchor Restaurant*.

Jurien
pop 1100
This coastal town is 38km west of the Brand Hwy and 266km north of Perth. A new sealed road has cut the link to Cervantes from 53km to 21km.

Home to a large crayfishing fleet, Jurien is on a sheltered beach and offers good fishing and boating. The Jurien Bay Offshore Charter Co (☎ 9652 1563) takes an eight-hour deep-sea fishing trip including all equipment supplied for $100.

The **old jetty** was used in the late 1800s to load wool from inland stations onto boats bound for distant shores. Tourist information is available from the BP petrol station (☎ 9652 1444) on Bashford St.

Places to Stay & Eat The *Jurien Bay Caravan Park (☎ 9652 1595)* on Roberts St has tent/powered sites for $14/15, increasing by a dollar in the peak season. The *Jurien Bay Holiday Flats (☎ 9652 1172)*, on Grigson St, start at $60. The *Jurien Bay Hotel Motel (☎ 9652 1022)*, on Padbury St, has singles/doubles for $60/70 and serves meals. To find out about availability of holiday houses, contact Jennie Bryant Realty (☎ 9652 2077, 32a Bashford St), open seven days a week.

In Jurien, several new businesses with an eye on the planned new coast road to Perth are sprouting. One is the *Indian Ocean Cafe (36 Bashford St)*, which serves tasty home-made lunches, light meals and an all-day $7 breakfast.

Also on Bashford St, *Caffe Rusca* has Italian-style food.

Green Head
The most notable feature of Green Head, on the coast 27km north of Jurien, is the impressive **Dynamite Bay**, which is meant to be great for snorkelling and swimming – provided massive swells haven't filled it up with seaweed.

Green Head Caravan Park (☎ 9953 1131, 9 Green Head Rd) has tent/powered sites for $14/15 and on-site vans starting at $33. *Maccas Mooring (☎ 9953 1461, 1 Farley St)* is a B&B with bay views, cooked breakfasts, and a spa and sauna. Prices start at $50 per person.

Sea Lion Charters (☎ 9953 1012) takes tours from Green Head to view the sea lion colony at Fisherman Island.

National Parks
In addition to Nambung, there are several other interesting national parks not too far north of Perth. None of them have any tourist facilities though.

Stockyard Gully National Park, named after one of the stopping places once used by drovers on the North Rd stock route, is reached from the Coorow to Green Head road. Access to the park is by 4WD only, along the gravel Cockleshell Gully Rd.

Some 5.6km from the end of this road along a sandy track is the ancient underground river system of the 270m Stockyard Gully tunnel (torches/flashlights are needed). Turquoise Coast Enviro Tours (☎ 9652 7047) can take you there.

It's worth walking the 90-minute Badgingarra Trail in **Badgingarra National Park**. The park, on the west side of the Brand Hwy and opposite the town of Badgingarra, was established to protect the wildflowers that grow here.

Between the Brand Hwy and State Hwy 116, there are a number of national parks noted for their wildflowers. They include **Watheroo**, 443 sq km of sandy plain northeast of Badgingarra; **Alexander Morrison**, between Coorow and Green Head; and **Tathra**, east of Eneabba.

Lesueur National Park is one of the most diverse and rich wildflower areas in WA with over 900 species (perhaps 10% of the state's classified flora). It is also a breeding area for Carnaby's black cockatoo. Access is via a 4WD track off the gravel Cockleshell Gully Rd.

Bookings are required to visit or stay at the *Hi Vallee Farm* (☎ *9652 3035*), on Tootbardi Rd between Cervantes and Jurien and relatively close to Mt Lesueur National Park. The Williams family takes wildflower day tours for $110, including lunch. Dinner and B&B cost $55, camping $5 per person, and self-contained vans $11 per person.

MIDLANDS ROAD (STATE HIGHWAY 116)
Moora
pop 1800

Moora is a pleasant tree-lined town 172km north of Perth, on the banks of the Moore River. Tourist information is available at the shire office on Padbury St (☎ 9651 1401). Internet access is available at the Telecentre in the old railway station on Padbury St.

Some 19km east of town is the **Berkshire Valley Folk Museum**, which includes an old flour mill built in 1847. For opening times phone ☎ 9651 1644. About 20km north of Moora is **Coomberdale**, a flower farm with displays of dried flowers. Visitors are welcome from April to late October.

Places to Stay & Eat The grassy *Moora Caravan Park* (☎ *9651 1401*), on Dandaragan St, is next to the town pool and has tent/powered sites for $9/15. *The Moora Motel* (☎ *9651 1247*), on Roberts St, has decent singles/doubles for $65/75. *Rosewood B&B* (☎ *9651 1413, 180 Ferguson Rd*) has its entry on Clarke St and is a lovely rustic home with shady verandahs and peaceful gardens. Singles/doubles including breakfast with fresh juice, fruit and bread cost $65/85. Other B&Bs include *Rosemoore* (☎ *9651 1325*), closer to the town centre on Roberts St, where rooms cost $50/70 per night, and the modern-looking *Sangaree* (☎ *9651 1531, 229 Clarke St*), with rooms for $55/75. *Spencer Hill End Farmstay* (☎ *9651 7082*) is located near Watheroo National Park, about 47km north of Moora, and has B&B for $65 per double. Dinner costs $15 ($7.50 for children). Also in the vicinity is *Watheroo Station Tavern* (☎ *9651 7007*). Enter this pub on a quiet evening and be prepared for the whole bar

to stop talking and stare at you, nevertheless its relatively new motel rooms are not bad at $51/65.

Moora's *Pioneer Bakery (50 Padbury St)* has early breakfasts and its staff are competent on the espresso machine. It incorporates *Valtellina's Restaurant*, which offers main meals starting at $15.80. A Chinese restaurant is on Dandaragan St and the *Gourmet Cafe* on Gardiner St has meals and takeaways.

Mingenew

Mingenew's wildflowers bloom boldest in August and September. Its tourist office, open June to October, is next door to the post office on Midlands Rd. A good place to view wildflowers is the coal seam discovered by the Gregory brothers in 1846. It's some 32km north-east of town on the gorge of the Irwin River. The gravel road becomes inaccessible after heavy rain due to two river crossings.

Places to Stay & Eat On Lee Steere St, *Mingenew Caravan Park* (☎ *9928 1019*) is surrounded by handsome gum trees and has tent/caravan sites for $8/12. The *Schools Inn* (☎ *9928 1149*), on William St, has B&B for $70 a double. *Calomi Rose* (☎ *9929 1007*) offers farmstay and B&B, starting at $70 per double. The recently refurbished *Commercial Hotel* (☎ *9928 1002*), on Midlands Rd, has singles/doubles for $30/50 and it serves meals. Other sources of food are the *general store* and two *roadhouses* on Midlands Rd.

WONGAN HILLS TO MULLEWA
From the wheatbelt town of Wongan Hills you can head north on an inland route that runs roughly parallel to the Midlands Rd.

Perenjori
A couple of keen, young, local businesspeople give Perenjori, 350km north-east of Perth and 179km north of Wongan Hills, an energy that is lacking in many other comparable Midlands towns. Wildflowers are usually visible from July to October. The tourist office (☎ *9973 1105*) is in Fowler St.

Ask here for details of day drives as well as directions to the **garden of wildflowers**.

Monsignor John Hawes also touched this town with his design of the Catholic **Church of St Joseph** (see the boxed text 'Monsignor John Hawes' in the Central West Coast chapter).

There is a **museum** at the rear of the tourist office. There is a water hole, **Camel Soak**, 47km east of Perenjori.

Places to Stay & Eat The *Perenjori Caravan Park (☎ 9973 1193)*, on Crossing Rd, has an enthusiastic young owner who offers tent/powered sites for $3/12.50, on-site vans for $25 and self-contained park cabins for $85. In the town centre, the friendly *Perenjori Hotel (☎ 9973 1020)* has meals, including pizzas, and upstairs singles/doubles for $30/40 and motel units starting at $50. Tariffs include a light breakfast. *Perenjori News and Cafe* has takeaways and sandwiches and the *tourist office* does Devonshire teas in the tourist season.

Morawa

Wildflowers and the touch of Monsignor John Hawes are also the reasons for visiting this town. Hawes' **Church of the Holy Cross** features a tiny one-room stone hermitage where the monsignor lived for a time. The church, made of local stone and Cordoba tiles, is a fine example of Spanish-mission architecture.

The tourist office (☎ 9971 1204) is on Winfield St, but outside wildflower season it is only open by appointment. During the season a trip out to **Koolanooka Springs**, 24km east of town, is recommended.

Powered/unpowered sites at the small *Morawa Caravan Park (☎ 9971 1380)*, on White Ave, cost $12/8.50 for two people. On the corner of Solomon Terrace and Manning St, the old-fashioned *Morawa Motel Hotel (☎ 9971 1060)*, has single/double rooms for $20/35 and motel units for $45/60. Lunches and dinners are available here as well.

A *bakery and tearooms* are on the corner of White Ave and Winfield St.

Mullewa

Beautiful **wildflowers** are the main attraction here, especially the wreath flower, found in high concentrations. The Wildflower Show is held during the last week of August. Outside of wildflower season, Mullewa tries to attract visitors with murals depicting historical events painted on town buildings.

The tourist office (☎ 9961 1505), on the corner of Jose and Molster Sts, is open from July to October. At other times, *Foreman's Deli (☎ 9961 1110, 9 Jose St)* has information as well as hot food and coffee.

The Romanesque-style **Our Lady of Mt Carmel Church** in Doney St is the town's best feature. Prolific architect, Monsignor John Hawes designed and built it during his 20 years here as parish priest. Alongside, in Bowes St, he built the **Priest House** for himself and furnished the interior with jarrah pieces of his own design. It is more or less a museum honouring Hawes. The house is open from 10 am to noon Monday to Friday July to October.

The four-day, self-drive *Monsignor Hawes Heritage Trail* (pamphlet available from tourist offices for $3.50) takes in 15 of the buildings he designed in seven major towns of the Murchison region. The strength of his architectural vision and commitment – maintained in a land Hawes described as 'prosaic and mundane…full of hotels, beer, wool and sheep' – is truly remarkable. So are the complexity and style of his designs.

Places to Stay The *Mullewa Caravan Park (☎ 9961 1161, 1 Lovers Lane)* has tent/powered sites for $10/15. Singles/doubles at the *Railway Motel Hotel (☎ 9961 1050)*, on Gray St, cost $65/85 during peak times, $55/75 during off-peak.

Station stays north of Mullewa include *Tallering (☎ 9962 3045)*, which has B&B for $35 per person; it is situated some 26km north-east of Mullewa via a gravel road out of Pindar, off the Great Northern Hwy.

Also recommended is *Wooleen (☎ 9963 7973)*, 190km north of Mullewa off the Mullewa to Gascoyne Junction road, where homestead accommodation costs $100 per person including meals.

GREAT NORTHERN HIGHWAY

Although most people going to the Pilbara and the Kimberley travel up the coast, the Great Northern Hwy from Perth to Port Hedland is much more direct.

The road is sealed the total distance of 1636km – though parts are subject to flooding sometimes heavy enough to close it. The first section of this road, from Wubin to Meekatharra, skirts the Central Midlands on its eastern side.

The highway is one of Australia's least interesting, passing through country that is flat and featureless. Wildflower enthusiasts, however, will find something to whet their fancy from about July to November and the towns of Mt Magnet, Cue and Meekatharra help break the monotony.

The Great Northern Hwy (State Hwy 95) begins near Muchea, passes through Bindoon, New Norcia and Dalwallinu before heading north-east from Wubin. It is 272km from Perth to Wubin, 297km from Wubin to Mt Magnet, and 196km from Mt Magnet to Meekatharra.

Getting There & Away

SkyWest and Skippers Aviation share the Perth-Meekatharra route. Flights from Perth run on Mondays, Wednesdays and Fridays, returning on Fridays only. Maroomba Airlines services Mt Magnet from Perth every weekday except Thursday with same-day return flights. All these flights are booked through Ansett Australia (☎ 13 1300).

Greyhound Pioneer buses travel along the Great Northern Hwy from Perth to Port Hedland and Broome on Sunday and Friday, with a return service Sunday and Tuesday. Westrail runs bus services on Monday and Wednesday from Perth as far as

Out of Reverence for St Benedict

Intriguing New Norcia – named after the Italian town where St Benedict was born – began in 1846 as a mission settlement established by two Spanish monks. The community's first abbot, Dom Rosendo Salvado, was a charismatic and learned man who envisaged a self-sustaining village where Aborigines were encouraged to settle as land-holders as a way of becoming 'civilised'. While such attitudes seem patronising now, Salvado's approach was enlightened for the times. Sadly, according to some former residents, New Norcia's treatment of Aborigines in later years deteriorated. From the 1920s to 1973, hundreds of Aboriginal children were placed in orphanages here. Now grown men and women, some of them claim conditions were cruel and deprived.

Nevertheless, the monastery museum now gives an interesting insight into the monks' early relationship with local Aborigines, and it includes many photos and artefacts which relate both to monastic and community life. In 1849 Salvado took two Aboriginal boys to Rome, where they enthusiastically remained to study for the priesthood, becoming proficient in Italian. However, within a few years they became ill and died – one in Rome and one after returning home.

Under its second abbot, Dom Fulgentius Torres, New Norcia had boarding schools for non-indigenous children added to existing schools for Aboriginal boys and girls. The schools are prime examples of the town's remarkable European-style architecture. The National Trust has registered 27 of the 64 buildings here.

Vital elements in New Norcia's independence from the outside world were its sheep, its olive groves and orchards, and its flour mill and bakery. The monastery pressed its first olive oil in 1889. New Norcia oil went on to win a medal at the 1908 Franco-British Exhibition in London – as did the monastery-made macaroni. Ironically, since the closure of the schools late last century removed the community's main source of income, sales of its self-made products to the outside world today play a large part in keeping it afloat. Demand for New Norcia bread, baked both on site and in Perth, is huge and its nut cake and olive oil are delicious.

As for the man who started it all, Dom Salvado, he is still in New Norcia – buried beneath the Abbey Church.

Meekatharra, returning on the following days. A one-way fare to Mt Magnet is $56, to Cue $60.50 and to Meekatharra $67.30.

New Norcia

This village, 132km north of Perth, has a somewhat romantic feel very different from the matter-of-fact towns nearby. New Norcia is a curiously inspiring place – though its history does have controversial aspects (see the boxed text).

New Norcia's range of interesting and imposing Spanish-style buildings has gained the town a spot on the Register of the National Estate; 27 of the buildings are classified by the National Trust.

Established as a Spanish Benedictine mission in 1846, the whole town is still owned by that order. It's currently home to 18 monks, including four Spanish-born brothers ranging in age from 87 to 92. The monks own and operate everything in the town except the road.

The **museum** and **art gallery** include paintings by Spanish and Italian masters. Admission to both sites costs $4/1 for adults/children. They're in a building on the Great Northern Hwy which originally housed St Joseph's orphanage and school for Aboriginal girls.

The tourist office (☎ 9654 8056) in the same building opens from 9.30 am to 4.30 pm August to December and from 10 am the rest of the year. Though wares at the tourist office shop aren't cheap, any money spent here helps New Norcia keep going. Loaves of its fantastic bread are sold fresh daily. Also on sale are sweet baked goods, and oil made from the monastery olives.

Guided town **walking tours** ($10/5) leave the tourist office at 11 am and 1.30 pm and include the 150-year-old building where the bakery used to be, along with buildings otherwise inaccessible to the public. The monastery is not open to women, and is open to men only if they've been invited. The *New Norcia Heritage Trail* ($3 at the tourist office shop) includes a map for an additional 1.7km **river walk** that features a well sunk by town founder, Dom Salvado.

Places to Stay & Eat The grand *New Norcia Hotel* (☎ 9654 8034), set off the Great Northern Hwy behind the museum and art gallery, was designed in anticipation of a visit by Spanish Queen Isabella II that never eventuated. Instead it accommodated families visiting their children in the boarding schools, and now has singles/doubles with shared facilities for $45/65. The hotel bar offers sandwiches using the delicious local bread, and hot meals starting at $14.50. *New Norcia Roadhouse* (☎ 9654 8020), on the highway, also has meals.

As the Benedictine tradition emphasises hospitality, there is the small *Monastery Guesthouse* (☎ 9654 8002), accessed from the south-western corner of the monastery. Its twin rooms with en suites cost $40 per person, including a self-served breakfast and the same three-course lunch and light dinner as the monks. The monastery's serene atmosphere seeps through the guests' dining and sitting rooms and enclosed outdoor area. Male guests may ask to join the monks to eat, but should expect no dinner-party chitchat: Only one of the brothers is permitted to speak during meals and that's just to read the Bible out loud.

If there's no room at either inn, doubles at the farmstay *Napier Downs* (☎ 9655 9015) cost $120 with breakfast.

Getting There & Away Westrail buses pass through New Norcia three times a week ($13 one way from Perth). Greyhound buses cost $34 one way and go through twice a week.

Mt Magnet

Gold was found at Mt Magnet in the late 19th century and mining is still the town's main industry, thanks to the nearby Hill 50 Goldmine. If you're a woman travelling alone, especially outside wildflower season, prepare to be stared at by lots of tattooed men in dirty clothes. Mt Magnet was named after a prominent nearby hill which contained magnetic rocks. The town's wide main street with its once-grand old hotels is testament to an earlier, more prosperous era. The tourist office (☎ 9963 4172), on Hepburn St, opens during wildflower season.

THE MIDLANDS

A view of the town and the huge open-cut pits is available from **Warramboo** ('Camping Place') Hill. About 7km north of town are **The Granites**, a popular picnic spot where Aboriginal rock art can still be seen.

Places to Stay & Eat Recommended accommodation in Mt Magnet can be found at *Miners Rest (☎ 9963 4380)*, on Priestly St, a group of fibreglass shacks that once housed diamond miners and are now clean, self-contained single/double rooms costing $45/50. The *Swagman Roadhouse (☎ 9963 4844)*, at the northern end of town on the highway, has units for $40/50. It's open 24 hours and has hot food and coffee. The *Commercial Club Motel Hotel (☎ 9963 4021)*, on Hepburn St, has overpriced units for $70/90 and rooms for $45/60.

Avoid the run-down rooms at the *Mt Magnet Hotel (☎ 9963 4002)*, costing $45/50 – unless you think having lingerie-clad female bar staff downstairs compensates. The slightly bedraggled *Mt Magnet Caravan Park (☎ 9963 4198)*, on Hepburn St, has tent/powered sites for $8/15 and on-site vans for $25.

Some 40km south-west of Mt Magnet is *Wogarno Sheep Station (☎ 9963 5846)*, which charges $100 each person per night for full board. A bed in the shearers' quarters costs $15, or $20 with linen supplied.

Meals for around $15 are available from the town's *hotels*; the Commercial Club Motel Hotel is the most family-friendly. A cafe, *Diggers Diner*, two *supermarkets* and a *butcher* are on Hepburn St. The BP *petrol station* on Hepburn St at the southern end of town has takeaways.

Sandstone
pop 50
This town is not on the Great Northern Hwy but lies 160km east of Mt Magnet on a road impassable after heavy rain. Its name comes from the bronzed, rusty sandstone landscape surrounding it. The landscape, the wildflowers that appear from about late July to mid-September, and some fine goldfields-era architecture, are reasons to visit here. There were four principal mines in the area

during the peak mining period, 1908–1912. Around Sandstone are abandoned mining settlements. An updated *Sandstone Heritage Trail* pamphlet is in the pipeline.

South-east of town is the impressive basalt **London Bridge**, over 350 million years old. On the road to the bridge, among the cliffs, is the site of an **old brewery**.

Alice Atkinson Caravan Park (☎ 9963 5859), on Irvine St, has tent/powered sites for $6/12.50, and on-site vans for $20. *Sandstone Country Accommodation (☎ 9963 5869, 532 Thaduna Rd)* includes rooms from $40 to $50 with access to kitchen facilities. The *National Hotel (☎ 9963 5801)*, on Oroya St, has a restaurant.

Cue
pop 550
Cue is 80km north of Mt Magnet. **Austin St** has been classified by the National Trust due to its classic goldfields architecture, with many buildings of solid sandstone. Sadly, it's the street is now lined with empty shops, blank-windowed beneath their dented bull-nose verandahs. Away from the main street is a historic primary school and the dilapidated but impressive Masonic Lodge. The still-trading **Bell's Emporium** gives an idea of what shopping was like 100 years ago. A **lookout** on Cue Hill, about 1km out of town on an unsealed road branching off Sandstone Rd, gives great views of the area.

Near Cue are a number of **ghost towns**. The former sibling town of **Day Dawn** is 5km to the south. It once had a population of 3000 in the heyday of the Great Fingall Mine. About the only things left standing are the Great Fingall office and the gaunt chimneys of the Cue–Day Dawn Hospital.

Some 30km west is **Big Bell Mine**. The original town has a few remaining old buildings but access to the mine is restricted as mining has resumed.

Places to Stay & Eat The helpful *Cue Caravan Park (☎ 9963 1107)* has tent/powered sites for $10/14 for two people and the *Murchison Club Motel Hotel (☎ 9963 1020)*, in Austin St, has single/double motel units for $70/90.

Station stays near here include *Nallan Station* (☎ *9963 1054*), 11km north of Cue, which has camp sites/shearers' quarters/cottage hire for $5/15/35 per person, or a night in the homestead with dinner and breakfast for $80.

The Murchison Club Motel Hotel has a restaurant, and takeaway food is available from the *Ampol Roadhouse* (☎ *9963 1218*).

Wilgie-Mia & Walga Rock

The Murchison region has a number of significant Aboriginal sites. Two of the most celebrated are the Wilgie-Mia Red Ochre Mine and Walga Rock.

Unfortunately, due to safety concerns, tourists are discouraged from visiting Wilgie-Mia, some 100km from Cue on an unsealed road. Red ochre has been mined here by the Aborigines for possibly more than 30,000 years. They used stone hammers and wooden wedges to remove thousands of tonnes of rock to get to the ochre, believed to have been traded as far away as Queensland.

Walga Rock (also known as Walganna), about 50km south-west of Cue via Austin Downs Station, is a rock monolith that juts 50m out of the surrounding scrub. It is one of the most significant Aboriginal-art sites in WA. The 60m rock shelter at its base houses a gallery of desert-style paintings of lizards, birds and animals, and hand stencils in red, white and yellow ochre.

At the northern end of the gallery, a ship with twin masts, a funnel and four wavy lines beneath is depicted. Several theories have been advanced as to its origins, including one that it was painted by shipwrecked sailors and another that a shearer did it.

Meekatharra

pop 2000

Meekatharra, 764km north of Perth and 541km north-east of Geraldton, is a base for government services to the Murchison/east Gascoyne region. As a result, you feel just a little less conspicuous here as a traveller in off-peak times than you do in some of its neighbouring towns. Mining in this area employs 3000 people, with gold reserves expected to last several years more. The name means 'place of little water'.

Information is available at the town's shire office (☎ 9981 1002) on Main St. Next door is the Meekatharra Telecentre (☎ 9980 1811) for Internet access.

From 8 am to 10.30 am, visitors are welcome at the **School of the Air** (☎ 9981 1032), on High St, which has serviced remote students over a vast area since 1959. The **Royal Flying Doctor Service** (☎ 9981 1107) base, on Main St, is also open to visitors from 9 am to 2 pm weekdays.

From Meekatharra, you can travel south via Wiluna and Leonora (see The Southern Outback chapter for more information on these destinations) to the Kalgoorlie goldfields. It's more than 700km to Kalgoorlie-Boulder, partly on unsealed road. The unsealed road north-west from here to Mt Augustus is 337km.

Places to Stay & Eat All of Meekatharra's accommodation is located on Main St. The unremarkable *Meekatharra Caravan Park* (☎ *9981 1253*) has tent sites starting at $7, powered sites for $15 and cabins starting at $45. The *Commercial Hotel* (☎ *9981 1020*) has singles/doubles for $30/40. The *Royal Mail Hotel* (☎ *9981 1148*) has small motel rooms for $65/80. Rooms at *Auski Inland Motel Hotel* (☎ *9981 1433*) are big but could be cleaner at $95.

The *Balcony Coffee Shop*, on Main St, has a cappuccino machine, makes a good salad roll and holds regular 'Italian nights'. Also on Main St is *Ralph's Diner*, serving fish and chips. A *takeaway food van* operates on Friday nights. An $18.50 pasta at the Auski Inland Motel restaurant left a lot to be desired. All three of the town's hotels, on Main St, serve meals.

Central West Coast

This chapter covers a huge area of the Western Australia (WA) coast and interior. It extends from Dongara–Port Denison to the Gascoyne River and Carnarvon (about 500km as the crow flies) and out to the eastern apex of Mt Augustus, 350km from the Indian Ocean.

Batavia Coast

The strip of coast from Green Head north to Kalbarri is called the Batavia Coast, evoking the memory of the many shipwrecks here – especially the mutinous and bloody story of the *Batavia* (see the boxed text 'The Shipwreck Coast' later in this chapter).

The Batavia Coast combines rich history with many features of natural beauty. Take a look at the past in Greenough hamlet, the convict ruins near Port Gregory and the new museum at Geraldton. Wildflowers also feature heavily in this area, particularly beside the magnificent gorges of Kalbarri National Park. The beauty of the Houtman Abrolhos Islands is also striking from both the air and under the water.

The distance from Perth to Geraldton is 427km. From Perth, follow the Brand Hwy, also known as National Hwy 1, through the towns of Gingin and Badgingarra, and past turn-offs to the Pinnacles Desert and Jurien. The coastal towns of Leeman and Green Head are accessible from the turn-offs at Halfway Mill or Eneabba. The Brand Hwy joins the Midlands Rd (State Hwy 116) 8km east of Dongara–Port Denison and more or less hugs the coast from there to Geraldton. (See under Brand Highway in The Midlands chapter for more information on this route.)

DONGARA–PORT DENISON
pop 3000

The main road returns to the coast 358km north of Perth at Dongara, which is just north of Port Denison, over the Irwin River. These sibling towns have a pleasant seaside

HIGHLIGHTS

- Seeing the Murchison River thunder through Kalbarri National Park gorges
- Delving into the dramatic history of the Shipwreck Coast, brought to life at Geraldton Museum
- Touring Geraldton's crayfish processing plant
- Spotting dugongs and watching dolphins at play on a Shark Bay cruise
- Taking a sunset dip in the hot tubs of Francois Peron National Park
- Slurping on a fruit smoothie at Munro's Banana Plantation in Carnarvon
- Breathing in the spectacular isolation of the world's biggest rock, Mt Augustus

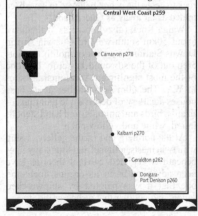

Central West Coast p259

Carnarvon p278

Kalbarri p270

Geraldton p262

Dongara–
Port Denison p260

feel with fine beaches, some high-quality accommodation and several restaurants with outdoor areas. Dongara was first settled in 1850, with a jetty built at nearby Port Irwin (later known as Denison) 10 years later. Dongara's main street is lined with Moreton Bay figs. The helpful Dongara–Port Denison tourist office (☎ 9927 1404) is housed in the historic original police station and court house at 5 Waldeck St. It opens from 9 am

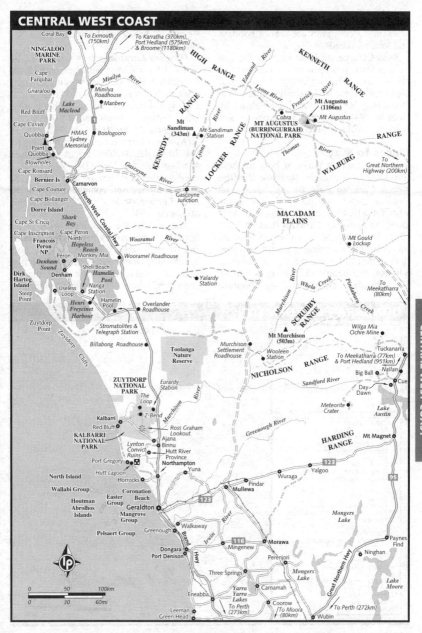

CENTRAL WEST COAST

Coral Bay

NINGALOO MARINE PARK

To Exmouth (150km)

To Karratha (370km), Port Hedland (575km) & Broome (1180km)

Cape Farquhar

Gnaraloo

Minilya River

Minilya Roadhouse

Manbery

HIGH RANGE

Edmund River

KENNETH RANGE

Lyons River

Frederick River

Mt Augustus (1106m)

Cobra

Mt Augustus

Red Bluff

Lake Macleod

Cape Cuvier

Quobba

Point Quobba

Blowholes

HMAS Sydney Memorial

Boologooro

Mt Sandiman (343m)

Mt Sandiman Station

KENNEDY RANGE

LOCKIER RANGE

MT AUGUSTUS (BURRINGURRAH) NATIONAL PARK

Thomas River

WALBURG RANGE

To Great Northern Highway (200km)

Cape Ronsard

Bernier Is

Carnarvon

Gascoyne River

Gascoyne Junction

Cape Couture

Cape Bollanger

Dorre Island

MACADAM PLAINS

Mt Gould Lookup

Cape St Cricq

Cape Inscription

Cape Peron North

Francois Peron NP

Hopeless Reach

Péron

Monkey Mia

Wooramel River

Wooramel Roadhouse

Shark Bay

Dirk Hartog Island

Denham Sound

Denham

Shell Beach

Hamelin Pool

Nanga Station

Yalardy Station

Murchison River

Whela Creek

Pindabarra Creek

To Meekatharra (80km)

Steep Point

Useless Loop

Henri Freycinet Harbour

Hamelin Pool

Overlander Roadhouse

Zuytdorp Point

Zuytdorp Cliffs

Stromatolites & Telegraph Station

Billabong Roadhouse

ZUYTDORP NATIONAL PARK

Toolanga Nature Reserve

Murchison Settlement Roadhouse

Wooleen Station

Mt Murchison (503m)

SCRUBBY RANGE

Wilga Mia Ochre Mine

Tuckanarra

To Meekatharra (77km) & Port Hedland (951km)

Nallan

NICHOLSON RANGE

Sandford River

Big Ball

Cue

Day Dawn

The Loop

Z-Bend

Eurardy Station

Murchison River

Greenough River

Meteorite Crater

Lake Austin

Kalbarri

Red Bluff

KALBARRI NATIONAL PARK

Ross Graham Lookout

Ajana

Binnu

Lynton Convict Ruins

Hutt River Province

Northampton

Port Gregory

Hutt Lagoon

Yuna

HARDING RANGE

Mt Magnet

North Island

Horrocks

Pindar

Mullewa

Wuraga

Yalgoo

123

95

Wallabi Group

Houtman Abrolhos Islands

Easter Group

Coronation Beach

Mangrove Group

Geraldton

Walkaway

Irwin River

Brand Hwy

116

Morawa

Mongers Lake

Paynes Find

Ninghan

Pelsaert Group

Greenough

Greenough

Dongara

Port Denison

Mingenew

Perenjori

Three Springs

Carnamah

Yarra Yarra Lakes

Coorow

Mongers Lake

Great Northern Hwy

Lake Moore

0   50   100km

0   30   60mi

Eneabba

Leeman

Green Head

To Perth (273km)

To Moora (80km)

To Perth (272km)

Wubin

to 5 pm weekdays and from 10 am to 2 pm weekends. Peak times are school holidays and long weekends.

Russ Cottage, on Point Leander Dr, was built in 1868; it is open from 10 am to noon on Sunday. The imposing brick **Royal Steamroller Flour Mill** is easily seen from the Brand Hwy but is accessed from Waldeck St. Built in 1894, its only purpose now is as a home for flocks of pigeons.

Places to Stay

The main caravan parks of both of these towns are all beachside. **Dongara Denison Beach Caravan Park** (☎ 9927 1131), on Denison Beach, has powered sites/on-site vans for $17/40 and park homes for $50. **Dongara Seaspray Caravan Park** (☎ 9927 1165, 81 Church St) is not as shady as the others but has a swimming pool. Camp sites here start at $14, vans at $25, and cabins at $40 for two people ($55 in peak times). Well-organised, clean and shady, **Dongara**

Denison Tourist Park (☎ 9927 1210), on George St, has on-site vans starting at $30 and tent/powered sites for $13/14.

Dongara Backpackers (☎ 9927 1581, 32 Waldeck St), affiliated with the Youth Hostel Association (YHA), is a charming, friendly place with rooms inside an old house and in a converted train carriage in the big garden. Dorm beds/twin rooms start at $14/32.

Dongara Motor Hotel (☎ 9927 1023), on Moreton Terrace, has pleasant rooms from $60/70 singles/doubles. Prices at **Dongara Marina Holiday Units** (☎ 9927 1486, 4 George St) in Port Denison start at $68 ($80 in peak times). Self-contained units at the **Lazy Lobster** (☎ 9927 2177, 45 Hampton St) start at $50.

The pick of the accommodation is the beautifully restored **Priory Lodge Historic Inn** (☎ 9927 1090, 6 St Dominics Rd), built in 1881. The Dominican Order bought it nine years later and for decades it was a nunnery and a girls' school. It now offers comfortable

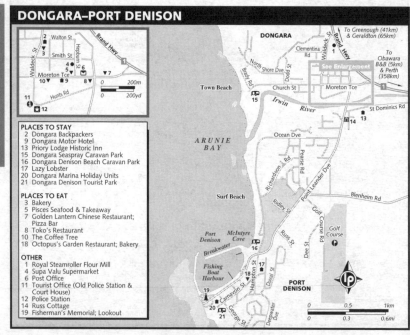

CENTRAL WEST COAST

DONGARA–PORT DENISON

PLACES TO STAY
2 Dongara Backpackers
9 Dongara Motor Hotel
13 Priory Lodge Historic Inn
15 Dongara Seaspray Caravan Park
16 Dongara Denison Beach Caravan Park
17 Lazy Lobster
20 Dongara Marina Holiday Units
21 Dongara Denison Tourist Park

PLACES TO EAT
3 Bakery
5 Pisces Seafood & Takeaway
7 Golden Lantern Chinese Restaurant; Pizza Bar
8 Toko's Restaurant
10 The Coffee Tree
18 Octopus's Garden Restaurant; Bakery

OTHER
1 Royal Steamroller Flour Mill
4 Supa Valu Supermarket
6 Post Office
11 Tourist Office (Old Police Station & Court House)
12 Police Station
14 Russ Cottage
19 Fisherman's Memorial; Lookout

accommodation with heaps of character, a pool and a separate bar and restaurant. Rooms here cost $40/55 singles/doubles.

B&Bs open and close constantly in this area – check at the tourist office. One option, **Obawara** *(☎ 9927 1043)*, 5km east of Dongara, is a sheep and cattle farm with doubles for $60 ($70 with breakfast).

Flower fans may like to spend time at **Western Flora Caravan Park** *(☎ 9955 2030)*, about 50km south of Dongara off the Brand Hwy. A daily guided wildflower walk is provided free if you stay here. It has camp sites, backpacker beds and chalets, and can organise B&B and meals.

Places to Eat

In Dongara, try **Toko's Restaurant** *(38 Moreton Terrace)*. Also on Moreton Terrace is the **Pisces Seafood & Takeaway**. Nearby is a **Supa Valu supermarket**. **The Coffee Tree** *(8 Moreton Terrace)* has tables under a massive fig tree and serves pots of loose-leaf tea. **Golden Lantern Chinese Restaurant** is next door to a *pizza bar* at the end of Moreton Terrace. A *bakery* on Waldeck St sells pies and fresh bread.

In Port Denison, the **Octopus's Garden Restaurant** *(60 Point Leander Dr)* has a pleasant verandah and plans for a bar and beer garden. Nearby is a good *bakery* for sandwiches and coffees.

GREENOUGH

About 40km north of Dongara and 20km south of Geraldton is Greenough. The Shire of Greenough encircles the city of Geraldton, so it is relatively large.

Just south of Greenough township is the fascinating **Greenough Historical Hamlet**. A day trip here from Geraldton or Dongara is well worth it. The hamlet contains a whole street of 19th-century buildings restored by the National Trust. Guided tours and a map are included in the admission ($4.50/ 2.50/10 adults/children/families).

West of the highway, along McCartney and Company Rds, other **historic buildings** include the old Wesley Church and the handsome Gray's Store. North of the hamlet is the popular Pioneer Museum, open 8 am to 4 pm

every day except Friday. The Geraldton-Greenough tourist office has the *Greenough-Walkaway Heritage Trail* pamphlet. Look for the **flood gums** – trees grown bent beneath salty ocean winds – in local paddocks.

Places to Stay & Eat

At the attractive **Greenough Rivermouth Caravan Park** *(☎ 9964 9845, 4 Hull St)*, 14km north of Greenough hamlet at Cape Burney, camp sites start at $15 for two, on-site vans start at $30 and cabins start at $50. Rooms at the over-decorated **Greenough River Resort** *(☎ 9921 5888)*, on Greenough River Rd, cost $110.

On Company Rd near Greenough hamlet is the restored **Hampton Arms** *(☎ 9926 1057)*, which has been accommodating travellers for almost 150 years. It has a restaurant and an out-of-print bookshop. Near the Pioneer Museum in a house with a fascinating history and an outdoor spa is **Rock of Ages** *(☎ 9926 1154)* B&B. Singles/doubles cost $55/65.

The historical hamlet has **tearooms** and Greenough River Resort has a *cafe* and *restaurant*.

GERALDTON
pop 21,000

Geraldton is unusual by WA standards in being a coastal town whose sole purpose is not just to pander to hordes of holiday-makers. Its textured history, thriving crayfish-export industry, and the delicate coral reefs of the Houtman Abrolhos Islands offshore make it a good place to spend a few days.

The area has a Mediterranean climate with an average maximum temperature of 28.8°C. It gets plenty of sun, although the constant wind – particularly from November to April – drives some people mad. But even that has its positive side: This town is one of world windsurfing's hotspots.

Orientation & Information

Geraldton stretches some distance along the Indian Ocean coast, but the main part of the city and its harbour is central. Most of its main businesses are on Marine Terrace. About 1.5km south-east of the town centre,

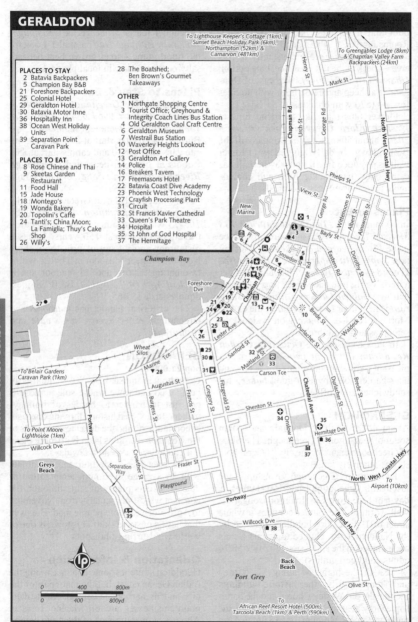

GERALDTON

PLACES TO STAY
2 Batavia Backpackers
5 Champion Bay B&B
21 Foreshore Backpackers
25 Colonial Hotel
29 Geraldton Hotel
30 Batavia Motor Inne
36 Hospitality Inn
38 Ocean West Holiday
   Units
39 Separation Point
   Caravan Park

PLACES TO EAT
8 Rose Chinese and Thai
9 Skeetas Garden
   Restaurant
11 Food Hall
15 Jade House
18 Montego's
19 Wonda Bakery
20 Topolini's Caffe
24 Tanti's; China Moon;
   La Famiglia; Thuy's Cake
   Shop
26 Willy's

28 The Boatshed;
   Ben Brown's Gourmet
   Takeaways

OTHER
1 Northgate Shopping Centre
3 Tourist Office; Greyhound &
   Integrity Coach Lines Bus Station
4 Old Geraldton Gaol Craft Centre
6 Geraldton Museum
7 Westrail Bus Station
10 Waverley Heights Lookout
12 Post Office
13 Geraldton Art Gallery
14 Police
16 Breakers Tavern
17 Freemasons Hotel
22 Batavia Coast Dive Academy
23 Phoenix West Technology
27 Crayfish Processing Plant
31 Circuit
32 St Francis Xavier Cathedral
33 Queen's Park Theatre
34 St John of God Hospital
35 The Hermitage
37 The Hermitage

To Lighthouse Keeper's Cottage (1km);
Sunset Beach Holiday Park (6km);
Northampton (52km) &
Carnarvon (481km)

To Greengables Lodge (8km)
& Chapman Valley Farm
Backpackers (24km)

Champion Bay

New Marina

Foreshore Dve

Wheat Silos

To Belair Gardens
Caravan Park (1km)

To Point Moore
Lighthouse (1km)

Greys Beach

Back Beach

Port Grey

To Airport (10km)

To
African Reef Resort Hotel (500m);
Tarcoola Beach (1km) & Perth (590km)

0   400   800m
0   400   800yd

CENTRAL WEST COAST

the Brand and North West Coastal Hwys meet at an appropriately important-looking roundabout.

The Geraldton-Greenough tourist office (☎ 9921 3999, fax 9964 2445) is in the Bill Sewell complex on Chapman Rd, diagonally opposite the old train station (which is now a bus station) and across the road from the Northgate shopping centre. It is open from 8.30 am to 5 pm weekdays, 9 am to 4.30 pm Saturday, and 9.30 am to 4.30 pm Sunday. Long weekends are peak tourist times.

The main post office is on Durlacher St and banks are scattered along Marine Terrace. Internet access is available at Phoenix West Technology at 220b Lester Ave.

If you are short of reading material, the House of Books, at 176 Marine Terrace, is packed with towers of paperbacks.

Geraldton Museum

This museum, in a specially designed building on the town's new marina, houses the enormous stone Batavia portico, meant as the gateway for a castle in Batavia (Jakarta) but lost from the ship of the same name when it sank near Geraldton in 1629 (see the boxed text 'The Shipwreck Coast' later in this chapter).

However, the new museum (due to open early in 2001) has been the focus of some controversy. Locals are desperate to have the remains of the old ship (the astonishingly intact stern and one piece of the side) returned to the area. Fremantle Maritime Museum, which currently houses the remains of the *Batavia*, has refused.

For the museum opening times and other inquiries call ☎ 9921 5080.

St Francis Xavier Cathedral

Geraldton's spectacular St Francis Xavier Cathedral is just one of a number of buildings in Geraldton and the state's midwest that were designed by the architect-cum-priest Monsignor John Hawes (see the boxed text).

Construction of the cathedral began in 1916, but building proceeded haltingly – at one stage it stopped for a whole decade – before it was completed in 1938.

Designing the Cathedral, Hawes aimed to catch 'a poem in stone'. He wanted to avoid slavishly imitating particular architectural styles, and to create beauty through simple, unornamented design. That also helped to keep costs down.

The cathedral's central dome has been compared with Brunelleschi's Duomo in Florence, Italy; and its central arched doorway is French Romanesque. But perhaps most striking is the joyous interior colour scheme of wide stripes of orange, dark grey and light grey. No description can do it justice – you have to go and see it for yourself. Guided visits are held at 10 am Monday and 2 pm Friday.

While he was working on the St John of God Hospital in Cathedral Ave, Hawes lived in **The Hermitage** across the road, in Onslow St. He designed this unusual dwelling, built for him in 1937 by a local contractor, as a possible place to retire. But he ended up leaving it for the Bahamas where he stayed until just before his death in 1956. It's open by appointment only.

Other Attractions

Geraldton Art Gallery, on the corner of Chapman Rd and Durlacher St, is open daily; entry is free. Built in 1870, the **Lighthouse Keeper's Cottage** on Chapman Rd, is now Geraldton Historical Society's headquarters, open from 10 am to 4 pm Thursday. You can look out over Geraldton from the **Waverley Heights Lookout**, on Brede St. **Point Moore Lighthouse**, on Willcock Dr, in operation since 1878, is worth a visit but you can't go inside. The **Old Geraldton Gaol Craft Centre**, on Chapman Rd in the Bill Sewell Complex, has locally made gifts and souvenirs for sale.

Organised Tours

The recommended Touch the Wild Safaris (☎ 9921 8435) takes a range of trips into the country around Geraldton with emphasis on local and natural history. The cost for adults/children is $95/65 for a full-day tour, $65/50 for a half-day.

The tours through the **crayfish processing plant**, at the end of Fisherman's Wharf Rd (about 4km from the tourist office), are

Monsignor John Hawes

The architect-cum-priest Monsignor John Hawes has left a magnificent legacy of buildings in the midwest. He was born in Richmond, England, in 1876. He trained as an architect in London, then, following his ordination as an Anglican priest in 1903, worked in the London slums as a missionary. He then went to the Bahamas where he helped rebuild a number of churches.

Two years later, he converted to Catholicism and went to study in Rome. He came to Australia in 1915 at the invitation of the Bishop of Geraldton and worked as a country pastor in the Murchison goldfields. For the next 24 years, he worked tirelessly as a parish priest at Mullewa and Greenough while designing 24 buildings – 16 of which were built.

His best works are the **Church of Our Lady of Mt Carmel** and the **Priest House** in Mullewa, the **Church of the Holy Cross** in Morawa, the **Church of St Joseph** in Perenjori and the beautiful, inspiring **St Francis Xavier Cathedral** in Geraldton.

Hawes left Australia in 1939 after witnessing the opening of his controversial Geraldton cathedral the previous year. His only regret at leaving Australia was that he couldn't take his fox terrier Dominie. He went to Cat Island in the Bahamas and lived as a hermit in a small stone building on a hilltop. He died in a Miami hospital in 1956 and his body was brought back to a tomb he had built for himself on Cat Island.

The *Monsignor Hawes Heritage Trail* pamphlet ($3.50) is available from the tourist office in Geraldton.

Geraldton's St Francis Xavier Cathedral has a striking interior colour scheme.

fascinating, cost nothing, and are held at 9.30 am and 2 pm on weekdays from November to June.

The processing plant has tanks that can hold 90 tonnes of live western rock lobster (crayfish) at a time. Staff have to keep close watch, though, because lobsters find other lobsters just as tasty as humans do.

Batavia Coast Dive Academy (☎ 9921 4229), at 153 Marine Terrace, offers dive charters, courses and night dives off the Geraldton coast.

Also available are boat and plane trips to the Houtman Abrolhos Islands and nearby reefs (see that section later in this chapter).

Special Events

The four-day Festival of Geraldton takes place in the October school holidays. There are dragon-boat races, parades and partying.

Places to Stay

Camping & Caravan Parks The neat *Belair Gardens Caravan Park* (☎ 9921 1997), on Willcock Dr at Point Moore, has powered sites/on-site vans for $15/27. The *Separation Point Caravan Park* (☎ 9921 2763), at the corner of Portway and Separation Way, shelters its sites with rows of athel pine trees; tent/powered sites cost $12/14, cabins start at $36. *Sunset Beach Holiday Park* (☎ 9938 1655), on Bosley St,

CENTRAL WEST COAST

is 7km north of town but is well maintained. Tent/powered sites cost $13/16, cabins $40 and chalets start at $55. Geraldton has other caravan parks – ask at the tourist office.

Hostels Budget travellers are spoilt for choice in Geraldton, where hostel accommodation is of high quality and caters to a range of tastes. The *Batavia Backpackers* (☎ 9964 3001) is in a century-old, National Trust–classified building on the corner of Chapman Rd and Bayly St next to the tourist office. It has breezy rooms big enough for you to sleep in with your windsurfer if you want. Dorm beds/doubles start at $13/30. The rambling, seaside *Foreshore Backpackers* (☎ 9921 3275, 172 Marine Terrace) is a real gem, described by one reader as like 'a beautiful country grandma house in Italy, France or England'. Dorm beds (no bunks!) start at $13 and doubles at $33. Both these backpacker places are YHA-affiliated.

If you want to get out of town, *Chapman Valley Farm Backpackers* (☎ 9920 5034), about 30km north-east of Geraldton, is in an historic house. Accommodation here costs $10 a night and staff will pick you up from town with 24 hours' notice if you stay at least two nights. However, you will have to take your own food.

B&Bs Among the best places we stayed is *Champion Bay Bed & Breakfast* (☎ 9921 7624, 31 Snowdon St). This sympathetically restored old house overlooking the bay is filled with beautiful objects and pictures. Host Frank is quite a character and may even treat you to a self-caught lobster cooked on the barbecue. Light-filled rooms start at $50/80 a single/double.

Locals swoon over *Greengables Lodge* (☎ 9938 2332, 7 Hackett Rd), a few kilometres out of town. Its master suite has its own spa and costs $105 a double with a cooked breakfast.

Hotels Although cheap beds are available in Geraldton's old hotels, the examples that we visited were pretty stomach-turning. Adults-only floor shows advertised in the bar downstairs were enough to turn us off

$30/40 singles/doubles at the *Geraldton Hotel* (☎ 9921 3700, 19 Gregory St), but the down-at-heel *Colonial Hotel* (☎ 9921 4444, 15 Fitzgerald St) at least had a homely feel.

When we visited, an upmarket hotel was under construction on Marine Terrace. Ask at the tourist office for details.

Motels Numerous motels, most belonging to well-known chains and similar looking, are found on and just off the Brand Hwy on the approach to the town centre. One is the *Hospitality Inn* (☎ 9921 1422, 169 Cathedral Ave), with singles/doubles for $95/105.

The *Batavia Motor Inne* (☎ 9921 3500, 54 Fitzgerald St) is more central and has singles/doubles for $75/85.

Also beachside is the *African Reef Resort Hotel* (☎ 9964 5566), on Broadhead Ave. It has a range of accommodation styles: A standard double costs $75, while an oceanview motel room is $105.

Other Accommodation *Ocean West Holiday Units* (☎ 9921 1047, 1 Hadda Way) are self-contained, close to the beach and will suit families. Prices start at $90.

Places to Eat

Open seven days, *Wonda Bakery* (98 Marine Terrace) makes good salad rolls. *Thuy's Cake Shop* (202 Marine Terrace) has cheap cakes, sandwiches and pastries. Residents recommend *Willy's* (239 Marine Terrace) for fish and chips. *Ben Brown's Gourmet Takeaways* (357 Marine Terrace) has woodfired pizzas and bread.

China Moon (198 Marine Terrace) has noodles and takeaways. *Rose Chinese and Thai* (9 Forrest St) and *Jade House* (57 Marine Terrace) are recommended. The Thai restaurant *Tanti's* (174 Marine Terrace) is popular. On the corner of Foreshore Dr and Fitzgerald St, *La Famiglia* does Italian food.

Another upmarket option is *Montego's* (103 Marine Terrace), which has an attractive balcony providing harbour views and good main meals starting at $17. Bookings are recommended at *Skeetas Garden Restaurant* (☎ 9964 1619, 9 George Rd), which is very popular with locals. Seafood restaurant. *The Boatshed (357 Marine Terrace)* is decorated like the set of a nautical musical. There's Italian food and pizza at *Topolini's Caffe (158 Marine Terrace)*.

Geraldton also offers plenty of options to satisfy junk-food cravings, with the famous franchises scattered through the town centre and a *food hall* on Durlacher St.

Entertainment

The *Freemasons Hotel* in the mall on Marine Terrace has a rollicking Irish bar, while the barn-sized *Breakers Tavern (41 Chapman Rd)* sometimes has live bands. The *Circuit* nightclub is on Fitzgerald St.

Getting There & Around

SkyWest Airlines has flights from Perth to Geraldton daily. It also flies direct from Geraldton to Carnarvon (Tuesday and Thursday) and Exmouth (Friday and Sunday).

Westrail has a daily bus service from Perth to Geraldton for $36, dropping off at the old train station. Its buses continue north-east to Meekatharra (twice weekly) or north to Kalbarri (thrice weekly). Greyhound's daily service from Perth to Geraldton costs $48 and stops outside the tourist office. It continues on Hwy 1 through Port Hedland and Broome to Darwin. Relatively new player Integrity Coach Lines runs buses from Perth to Geraldton four times a week for $38. Its buses also continue up Hwy 1 to Exmouth and Carnarvon, with plans to extend to Port Hedland. It also stops outside the tourist office.

A local bus service (☎ 9923 1100) costs $2 for an adult all-day ticket. Timetables and routes are available from the tourist office.

HOUTMAN ABROLHOS ISLANDS

There are 122 islands in this archipelago, located about 60km off the Geraldton coast.

The Shipwreck Coast

During the 17th century, ships of the Dutch East India Company, sailing from Europe to Batavia (now Jakarta), would head due east from the Cape of Good Hope then up the Western Australia coast to Indonesia. It only took a small miscalculation for a ship to run aground on the coast and a few did just that, usually with disastrous results.

Several wrecks of Dutch East India Company ships have been located, including the *Batavia* – the earliest and, in many ways, the most interesting.

In 1629 the *Batavia* went aground on the Houtman Abrolhos Islands, off the coast of Geraldton. The survivors set up camp, sent off a rescue party to Batavia in the ship's boat and waited. It took three months for a rescue party to arrive and in that time a mutiny had taken place and more than 120 of the survivors had been murdered. The ringleaders were hanged, and two mutineers were dumped on the coast just south of modern-day Kalbarri.

In 1656 the *Vergulde Draeck* struck a reef about 100km north of Perth and although a party of survivors made its way to Batavia, no trace other than a few scattered coins was found of the other survivors who had straggled ashore.

The *Zuytdorp* ran aground beneath the towering cliffs north of Kalbarri in 1712. Wine bottles, other relics and the remains of fires have been found on the cliff top. The discovery of the extremely rare Ellis van Creveld syndrome (rife in Holland at the time the ship ran aground) in children of Aboriginal descent poses the question: Did the *Zuytdorp* survivors pass the gene on to Aborigines they assimilated with 300 years ago?

In 1727 the *Zeewijk* followed the ill-fated *Batavia* to destruction on the Houtman Abrolhos Islands. Again a small party of survivors made its way to Batavia but many of the remaining sailors died before they could be rescued.

Many relics from these shipwrecks, particularly the *Batavia*, can be seen today in the museums in Fremantle and Geraldton. A good account is the *Islands of Angry Ghosts* by Hugh Edwards (1966), who led the expedition that discovered the wreck of the *Batavia*.

The island groups are Wallabi, Easter and Pelsaert; North Island stands alone at the top of the archipelago.

The beautiful but treacherous reefs surrounding the islands have claimed many ships over the years. The first to nearly run aground was Frederick de Houtman of the Dutch East India Company and it is believed that the name Abrolhos comes from the Portuguese expression *Abri vossos olhos* ('Keep your eyes open'). The most famous wreck was that of the *Batavia* on 5 June 1629 with 300 people aboard (see the boxed text).

The survivors' shelters – forts made of piled-up stones – still partially stand and were probably the first European structures on Australian soil.

The islands are now the centre of the area's crayfishing industry and about 200 boats are licensed to fish there.

Warm ocean currents make the Houtman Abrolhos Islands the most southerly coral islands of the Indian Ocean, and the Acropora family of corals – such as the well-known staghorn – are found in abundance. Sea anemones, plate corals, the hard Tubastrea corals and seaweeds such as sargassum are also here.

Getting There & Away

You are not allowed to spend the night on any of the Houtman Abrolhos Islands unless you're invited by one of the people working the cray boats there.

However, a fantastic way to experience them is by light plane. The excellent Shine Aviation Services (☎ 9923 3600) points out the spot where the *Batavia* was raised, the forts built by survivors of its wreck, and sea lions lazing on beaches. They then land for a snorkel across patches of coral teeming with life. A fixed-wing/seaplane flight costs $150/195 per person.

It takes 2½ hours to reach the Houtman Abrolhos islands by boat from Geraldton. The Abrolhos Islands Central Booking Agency (☎ 9964 7887) runs regular weekend ecotours for $240 per person per day, including food, on-board accommodation and fishing and snorkelling gear.

NORTHAMPTON
pop 1500

Northampton, 50km north of Geraldton, was settled soon after the establishment of the Swan River Colony. Copper was discovered nearby at Wanerenooka in 1842 and lead was discovered six years later. Convicts were brought into the region to relieve labour shortages and a convict-hiring facility was established at Lynton near Port Gregory from 1853 to 1856.

The helpful Northampton tourist office (☎ 9934 1488) is in the old police station on Hampton Rd. An agricultural centre, Northampton has a number of **historic buildings** and is also the closest town to the world-famous independent principality of Hutt River (see the boxed text 'Prince Leonard's Land' in this chapter).

St Mary's Convent, on Hampton Rd, is recognisable as the work of the ubiquitous Monsignor John Hawes and is built entirely of local stone. An early mine-manager's home, **Chiverton House**, is now a fine municipal museum (admission $2). The tourist office has $1 copies of the guide to the 2km *Hampton Road Heritage Walk*.

Places to Stay & Eat

The local *caravan park* (☎ 9934 1202), on the North West Coastal Hwy, has powered sites costing $12 for two people. There's well-maintained budget accommodation at the *Nagle Centre* (☎ 9934 1692), a former convent, on Hampton Rd. Two- and four-bed rooms cost $12 to $15 per person.

Northampton's three *hotels* have accommodation, but a more pleasant option is B&B at the *Old Miners' Cottages* (☎ 9934 1864, 14 Brook St), starting at $50. Its owners also run *Heidi's Restaurant* in town. The *Northampton Tourist Cafe* has tasty home made goodies and weak cappuccinos.

Some 95km north of Northampton on the North West Coastal Hwy north of the Kalbarri turn-off, *Eurardy Station* (☎ 9936 1038) offers accommodation on a working sheep farm along with wildflower tours and $15 meals (bookings required). B&B here starts at $25, camp sites cost $10 for two people.

CENTRAL WEST COAST

CENTRAL WEST COAST

Prince Leonard's Land

Down a dirt road in undulating farmland about 75km from Northampton lies an independent land. The Hutt River Province Principality was once part of Australia. That all changed when farmer Len Casley seceded from the State of Western Australia and the Commonwealth of Australia on 21 April 1970. His motivation was disgust at a government ruling that he could only sell a tiny portion of the massive crop of wheat he was about to harvest.

More than 30 years later, Mr Casley (or, as he is now known, Prince Leonard of Hutt) farms sheep instead of wheat on his 75-sq-km property-cum-country, which he shares with Princess Shirley, the royal couple's seven heirs, and about 20 other people. In the meantime, Hutt River – the residents of which pay no tax but receive no Australian government benefits – has become world-famous. In the winter, coach load after coach load of visitors drive the red-dirt road to pay their respects. The province has 13,000 citizens worldwide (a five-year passport costs $250), and its own army, navy and airforce (though only used for ceremonial purposes, Princess Shirley assures us).

Some look on the royal couple as a bit loopy, but in a world where average citizens are sick of feeling powerless against faceless bureaucrats making thoughtless decisions, Prince Leonard clearly inspires many others. Devotees from all over the world attended the province's 30th-anniversary celebrations. Placed around the property are also numerous monuments, sculptures and paintings created specifically for the royal couple by admirers.

While the notion of citizenship may not appeal once you've made the trek over the border into Hutt River, you can still buy stamps and postcards, exchange Australian for Hutt River money and admire the prince's crest ('death before dishonour').

There is a Web site at www.wps.com.au/hutriver/hut1.htm.

HORROCKS & PORT GREGORY

From Northampton you can head west through farming country to the coast at Horrocks and as far north as Port Gregory on sealed roads. By mid-2001 the next 58km to Kalbarri should be sealed.

Horrocks, 22km west of Northampton, is a holiday resort with a safe, sheltered bay. This area is described as an angler's paradise. The drive from Northampton to Port Gregory is 43km. The oldest port on the mid-west coast, Port Gregory supports a commercial fishing fleet and attracts lots of holiday-makers.

On the way to the coast you pass numerous ruins of the **Lynton Convict Settlement**. It was established as a convict-hiring facility (for men who had their ticket-of-leave) in 1853 and abandoned three years later.

Hutt Lagoon, just before Port Gregory, is a dry salt lake that sometimes looks like a small pink inland sea. The lagoon's pink colour is due to naturally occurring beta-carotene, a dye used in food colouring and pharmaceuticals.

The scenic coastal route from Port Gregory to Kalbarri takes you past all the wonderful sights of the southern part of Kalbarri National Park.

Places to Stay

Port Gregory Caravan Park (☎ 9935 1052), on Sandford St, has powered/unpowered sites for $14/12. Sites at the **Horrocks Beach Caravan Park** (☎ 9934 3039) cost $15/12 for two people. The charming **Olive Cottage** (☎ 9934 3093) is five minutes' drive from Horrocks and has B&B for $100 per couple – less if you stay longer than one night. The self-contained cottages at **Killara Holiday Village** (☎ 9934 3031) at Horrocks start at $40.

Lynton-on-Sea (☎ 9935 1040), a working farm next to the Lynton Convict Settlement, has B&B for a reasonable $30 and backpackers beds in a bunkhouse for $15 per person. The hill-top **Glenorie Lookout Lodge** (☎ 9935 1017), about half an hour from both Horrocks and Port Gregory, has doubles for $75.

KALBARRI
pop 1788

Kalbarri, popular with holiday-makers and backpackers, is nestled on the coast at the mouth of the Murchison River, 66km west of the main highway. On its way to the sea, the river has carved magnificent gorges through the sandstone-based landscape. These are protected within the 1860-sq-km Kalbarri National Park (see that entry later in this chapter).

In 1629 two *Batavia* mutineers (Wouter Loos and Jan Peleeromm) were marooned as punishment at Wittecarra Gully, an inlet just south of the town; it is marked today by an historical cairn.

The *Zuytdorp* was wrecked about 65km north of Kalbarri in 1712. Although diving on the *Zuytdorp* is treacherous due to a heavy swell and unpredictable currents, divers from the Geraldton Museum did manage to raise artefacts in 1986.

The ultra-efficient Kalbarri tourist office (☎ 9937 1104) on Grey St is open from 9 am to 5 pm daily. The post office is beside the Kalbarri Arcade in a service lane off Porter St at its Grey St end. Internet access is available at the library, in the same building as the tourist office, and at the Kalbarri Explorer shop next door to the post office. The national park office and ranger are on the Ajana–Kalbarri Rd, a little out of town.

Things to See & Do

The **Rainbow Jungle** has numerous, mostly Australian, breeds of parrot on display in cages. The park is 3.5km south of town towards Red Bluff and is worth a visit ($7/2 for adults/children). It's open 9 am (10 am Sunday) to 5 pm daily July to October, but closed Monday during other months. Displays at the **Black Rock Museum**, at 96 Grey St, include a mock gemstone mine ($4/3).

There are some excellent **surfing** breaks along the coast – Jakes Corner, 3.5km to the south of Kalbarri, is reputedly among the best in the state.

You can go **horse riding** through rugged bush at the Big River Ranch (☎ 9937 1214), 2km from town on the Ajana-Kalbarri Rd. A three-hour sunset beach ride costs $45.

Kalbarri **Camel Safaris** is based a few hundred metres south of Rainbow Jungle along Red Bluff Rd. It takes 45-minute rides through coastal bush ($16/12). The tourist office takes bookings.

The main focus for activity in Kalbarri is the river and the pristine country through which it runs. The *Kalbarri River Queen* does tours on the Murchison River up to twice daily ($20/15); book at the tourist office.

The more adventurous can hire their own vessel. Kalbarri Boat Hire (☎ 9937 1245), on the foreshore opposite Murchison Park Caravan Park, rents out power boats ($25 an hour), canoes ($10 an hour) and windsurfers ($15 an hour).

There's also daily (when the birds decide to show up) **pelican feeding** at 8.45 am on the riverbank opposite the Black Rock Museum.

Organised Tours

For tours over the spectacular Murchison River gorges, take a flight with Kalbarri Air Charter (☎ 9937 1130), starting at $35.

Kalbarri Coach Tours (☎ 9937 1161) does visits to The Loop and Z-Bend gorges and Nature's Window ($38). A full-day tour ($68) includes the above, plus the ocean gorges and Rainbow Jungle. Kalbarri Bush and Wildflower Safaris (☎ 9937 1742) has good-value tours that combine interesting natural history commentary with a look at the gorges. A half-day tour costs $35; a full-day tour including lunch costs $49.

Kalbarri Safari Tours (☎ 9937 1011) runs a full-day trek through the Z-Bend gorge for $50, or a day tour to Lucky Bay Lagoon, traversing some of the coast's dramatic sand dunes on the way, also for $50.

You can canoe between the Z-Bend and Loop gorges with Kalbarri Adventure Tours. The eight-hour tour includes 8km of bushwalking. Another way to experience the river gorges is to walk backwards down a cliff – you can do this by abseiling with Quentin. The tourist office has details.

As for ocean-based activities, several companies offer sunset cruises and deep-sea fishing all year round, and whale-watching trips August to December. Contact the tourist office to find out more.

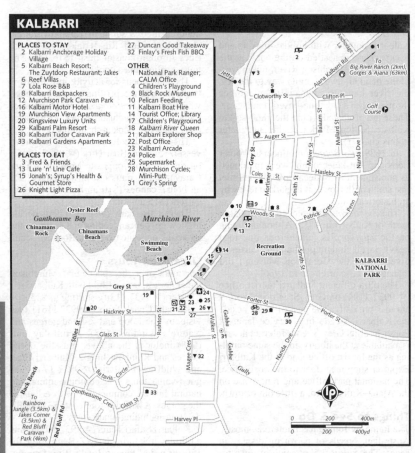

KALBARRI

PLACES TO STAY
2 Kalbarri Anchorage Holiday Village
5 Kalbarri Beach Resort; The Zuytdorp Restaurant; Jakes
6 Reef Villas
7 Lola Rose B&B
8 Kalbarri Backpackers
12 Murchison Park Caravan Park
16 Kalbarri Motor Hotel
19 Murchison View Apartments
20 Kingsview Luxury Units
29 Kalbarri Palm Resort
30 Kalbarri Tudor Caravan Park
33 Kalbarri Gardens Apartments

PLACES TO EAT
3 Fred & Friends
13 Lure 'n' Line Cafe
15 Jonah's; Syrup's Health & Gourmet Store
26 Knight Light Pizza

27 Duncan Good Takeaway
32 Finlay's Fresh Fish BBQ

OTHER
1 National Park Ranger; CALM Office
4 Children's Playground
9 Black Rock Museum
10 Pelican Feeding
11 Kalbarri Boat Hire
14 Tourist Office; Library
17 Children's Playground
18 Kalbarri River Queen
21 Kalbarri Explorer Shop
22 Post Office
23 Kalbarri Arcade
24 Police
25 Supermarket
28 Murchison Cycles; Mini-Putt
31 Grey's Spring

Places to Stay

Accommodation in Kalbarri tends to be bland and brown brick. Peak times are school holidays, when prices go up to match soaring demand, but at other times ask what special deals are available.

Camping & Caravan Parks The central *Murchison Park Caravan Park* (☎ 9937 1005), on Grey St, has powered sites for $15. On-site vans cost $35 off-peak, or $250 for a week at peak times. The riverside *Kalbarri Anchorage Holiday Village* (☎ 9937 1181), on Anchorage Lane, has tent/powered sites

for $12/15, and cabins starting at $48/32 peak/off-peak. The *Kalbarri Tudor Caravan Park* (☎ 9937 1077), on Porter St, has camp sites for $14 to $22, and cabins starting at $40/30 peak/off-peak.

Red Bluff Caravan Park (☎ 9937 1080), by the beach on Red Bluff Rd 4km south of town, has camp sites costing up to $12. Chalets start at $40/$35 peak/off-peak.

Hostels There are relatively few individual budget beds in Kalbarri – though splitting the bill for one of the dozens of holiday units with a group of companions would keep costs down. The lively *Kalbarri Backpackers* (☎ *9937 1430, 52 Mortimer St)*, has dorm beds starting at $14, as well as family and disabled units starting at $45. Guests can borrow snorkelling gear, boogie boards and golf clubs by leaving a deposit. It also has Internet access.

B&Bs The *Lola Rose B&B* (☎ 9937 2224, 21 Patrick Crescent) has singles/doubles starting at $45/75.

Motels Motel-style accommodation is harder to find. The *Kalbarri Motor Hotel* (☎ *9937 1000)*, on Grey St, has basic rooms with sea views for $55. The *Kalbarri Palm Resort (☎ 9937 2333, 8 Porter St)* has comfortable double rooms starting at $75/$55 peak/off-peak. It also has apartments, spa suites and family accommodation.

Other Accommodation Holiday units abound. *Kalbarri Beach Resort* (☎ *9937 1061)*, entered from Clotworthy St, has two-bedroom units starting at $120/95 peak/off-peak.

The clean *Murchison View Apartments* (☎ *9937 1096)*, on the corner of Grey and Rushton Sts, start at $120/$69. *Reef Villas* (☎ *9937 1165)*, on Coles St, has friendly management. Units start at $100/$70. Peaceful *Kalbarri Gardens Apartments (☎ 9937 2211, 33 Glass St)* could be better maintained for the cost – prices start at $90/$60.

A more upmarket option is the *Kingsview Luxury Units (☎ 9937 1274)*, on the corner of Stiles and Hackney Sts, costing $140.

Kalbarri's real estate agents (Roy Weston on Grey St and Ray White in the Kalbarri Arcade) also have *holiday homes* and *villas* for rent. For example, a three-bedroom house that sleeps seven costs $695/495 per week peak/off-peak.

Places to Eat
You won't go hungry in Kalbarri – though you might get sick of steak and seafood. You can eat good, big meals for $15 to $18 looking out over the river at the *Kalbarri Motor Hotel* on Grey St. *The Zuytdorp Restaurant*, on Clotworthy St, decorated

like the wreck it's named after, has an $18.50 smorgasbord. Behind it is *Jakes*, renowned for inexpensive, hearty meals. *Fred & Friends (☎ Shop 6, 108 Grey St)* is open from breakfast time and has main meals for $10 to $30.

Knight Light Pizza is on Walker St next door to *Duncan Good Takeaway*, which has cheap Mexican, Chinese and European dishes. For fish and chips try *Jonah's*, on Grey St. Several other *takeaway food* shops, a *bakery*, a *supermarket* and a *fruit and vegetable shop* are in the cluster of shops and the arcade in the service road off Porter St. A reader has recommended the *Lure 'n' Line Cafe* on Grey St for its good-value (Chinese) food and atmosphere.

The lunch favourite is *Syrup's Health and Gourmet Store*, on Grey St, for made-to-order salads, sandwiches, smoothies and that rare delicacy in these parts – a freshly squeezed juice. For dinner, we loved the outdoor *Finlay's Fresh Fish BBQ* on Magee Crescent for its enormous, tasty serves, low prices and especially its bizarre Wild-West-meets-beach-party ambience.

Getting There & Around
Western Airlines (☎ 1800-998 097) offers return flights from Perth to Kalbarri on Monday, Wednesday and Friday; one-way/return fares are $175/350. It costs $90 to fly from Kalbarri to Monkey Mia (or $522 Perth-Kalbarri-Monkey Mia-Perth).

Westrail buses from Perth travel to Kalbarri on Monday, Wednesday and Friday ($49/98 one way/return) returning Tuesday, Thursday and Saturday.

Greyhound Pioneer buses run from Perth to Kalbarri and return on Monday, Thursday and Saturday for $78.10/151.80 one way/return.

Bicycles can be rented from Murchison Cycles, on Porter St; if no-one is there, ask at the Mini-Putt complex next door.

KALBARRI NATIONAL PARK
This national park covers more than 1860 sq km of bushland, including several scenic gorges on the **Murchison River**. The Murchison River, which starts near Peak Hill, 80km

north of Meekatharra. It once flowed over a smooth red plain of Tumblagooda sandstone, but shifting of the earth's surface in the area about two million years ago caused the river to erode deep into the rock. This created the meandering 80km gorge.

From Kalbarri, it's about 40km to **The Loop** and **Z-Bend** gorge, two impressive gorges with steep banded cliffs. The road is unsealed but it is usually OK for 2WD; it's occasionally closed to all vehicles during extremely heavy rains.

Farther east along the Ajana Kalbarri Rd are two lookouts with excellent views: **Hawk's Head** and **Ross Graham** (he was a noted conservationist).

Short **walking trails** lead into the gorges from the road access points but there are also longer walks. The walk around The Loop, which begins and ends at Nature's Window, takes six hours.

Walkers tackling overnight or longer walks must check in with the ranger before they go. Five walkers is considered the minimum required for a safe trip. It takes about two days to walk between Z-Bend, a narrow ravine, and The Loop. The 38km walk from Ross Graham Lookout to The Loop requires a strenuous four days.

South of Kalbarri town there is a string of dramatic coastal cliff faces. These include **Red Bluff** (a red sandstone outcrop) and the banded **Rainbow Valley**. The sea has sculpted **Pot Alley**, **Eagle Gorge** and **Natural Bridge**.

All of these sights can be reached by car on a sealed road, with a few hundred metres' walk when you get there.

There is an 8km **coastal walking trail** from Eagle Gorge to Natural Bridge which takes three to five hours.

More than 1000 varieties of wildflowers bloom in Kalbarri National Park from July to November and the park is home to a range of other fascinating plant life, including the sand plain woody pear, from whose seed (the kalba) Kalbarri takes its name. Emus, euros, rock wallabies, and red and western grey kangaroos, as well as introduced animals such as wild pigs, are all found in the park.

Shark Bay

Shark Bay Marine Park, part of the Shark Bay World Heritage area, has spectacular beaches, important seagrass beds, and the ancient stromatolites at Hamelin Pool. The bay's peninsulas and nearby islands are sanctuaries for many endangered species. However, the main vehicles for Shark Bay's increasing popularity as an ecotourism destination are its most famous residents, the dolphins of Monkey Mia.

History

Prior to European colonisation, the Shark Bay region was inhabited by Aboriginal peoples, including the Malkana for whom there is evidence of habitation dating back some 22,000 years.

The first recorded landing on Australian soil by a European took place at Shark Bay in 1616 when Dutch explorer Dirk Hartog landed on the island that now bears his name. (See The Europeans under History in the Facts about Western Australia chapter.)

The area's many French place names are the legacy of the French explorers in the ships Le Géographe and Naturaliste (June 1801) but the name Bay of Sharks (now Shark Bay) was bestowed upon the area by William Dampier in August 1699. Mr Goodwin, Dampier's cook, is the first known European to have been buried on Australian soil.

Shark Bay is the name loosely applied to the two fingers of land that jut into the Indian Ocean and the lagoons that surround them. Denham, the main population centre of Shark Bay, is 129km off the main highway from the Overlander Roadhouse.

Monkey Mia, on the eastern finger, is 24km north-east of Denham on a sealed road. Shark Bay attained World Heritage listing in 1991.

KALBARRI TO DENHAM

The 177km stretch of rather dull highway between the turn-offs to Kalbarri and Shark Bay may well need breaking with a petrol, toilet or food stop – and there's two dusty roadhouses along the way depending on it.

The ***Billabong*** (☎ 9942 5980) is perched halfway between Geraldton and Carnarvon. The classic rock blasting out of the ***Overlander*** (☎ 9942 5916), near the turnoff to Shark Bay, will rouse you from any driving-induced stupor.

On the way into Denham, the first turnoff (27km from the highway) takes you 6km along a sealed road to **Hamelin Pool**, a marine reserve for the world's best known colony of **stromatolites** – evidence of the presence of some of the world's oldest living organisms (see the boxed text 'Stromatolites – A Special Sign' in this chapter). A boardwalk complete with kooky interpretive signs has been built to reduce damage to the delicate structures.

At Hamelin Pool, a tour of the old **Telegraph Station** (☎ 9942 5905) includes a video and other information on the stromatolites. The $5 tour takes half an hour and can be booked at the tea rooms nearby. A 1.5km return walk from the tearooms to the stromatolites boardwalk is signposted and takes you past an old shell quarry. You can also drive to the boardwalk.

Seagrasses

Shark Bay has the largest seagrass meadows and the most diverse collection of seagrass species of any single site in the world. Seagrass covers 4000 sq km (one-third) of the bay, including the 1030-sq-km Wooramel Bank meadow – the world's largest. The fields produce an estimated eight million tonnes of grass a year, helping keep the area's 10,000 dugongs nourished.

Seagrasses are not seaweeds. Seaweeds are algae without flowers or roots. In contrast, seagrasses grow in the sand of the sea bed, flowering and pollinating in a similar fashion to land plants. Their presence in Shark Bay has modified tidal movement and added to sediment build-up. This in turn has created the highly saline and protected environments required for the development of rare marine features such as the stromatolites (see the boxed text 'Stromatolites – A Special Sign' in this chapter).

About 50km north-west of Hamelin is the 2000-sq-km **Nanga Station**, with its old homestead constructed of cut shell blocks. Integrated into the station is the ***Nanga Bay Resort*** (☎ 9948 3992), which has a range of accommodation including comfortable motel rooms which start at $65, clean bunkhouse accommodation for $12 per person, and tent/powered sites for $12/16. It has a spa fed by an artesian bore, a safe swimming beach, a restaurant and a shop selling alcohol. This is a peaceful spot to spend a night or more, especially if you've just come from hectic Monkey Mia.

The 60km stretch of **Shell Beach** is solid shells nearly 10m deep. In some places in Shark Bay, the shells are so tightly packed that they can be cut into blocks and have been used for buildings.

Near Shell Beach, the 2m-high, electric **barrier fence** on the Taillefer Isthmus has been designed to keep out feral animals, contributors to the decline of native mammal populations.

DENHAM

The name Denham comes from Captain Henry Denham who charted the waters of Shark Bay in 1858 in HMS *Herald*. He was an early graffitist, inscribing his name into rock on the cliff face at Eagle Bluff. Once a pearling port, Denham is the most westerly town in Australia. The town has a church (1954) and a restaurant (1976) made of shell blocks – though such bricks can no longer be quarried in the area due to its World Heritage listing. That listing and a few dolphins who started letting fishermen feed them in the 1960s have turned Denham from a sleepy fishing village into a busy, cheerful seaside town.

The friendly and helpful Shark Bay tourist office (☎ 9948 1253), at 71 Knight Terrace, is open from 8 am to 6 pm daily. It has Internet access.

The Department of Conservation & Land Management (CALM) office (☎ 9948 1208), also on Knight Terrace, has information about the World Heritage area, including numerous publications, free and otherwise. Denham's peak tourist times are school holidays.

Stromatolites – A Special Sign

These part-submerged rock-like formations at Hamelin Pool are not dramatic to look at but were a major factor in Shark Bay getting World Heritage status. It takes a bit of imagination to understand why they're so remarkable: These are rarely seen evidence of the presence in high concentrations of some of the oldest life forms on earth.

These life forms are microbes: 3000 million of them can fit in 1 sq metre. Some of the microbes living at Hamelin Pool are thought to have descended from similar organisms that existed 1900 million years ago. Their family is therefore one of the oldest known continuous biological lineages. The evolution of such microbes was a vital development because it established the basic building block for future, more complex life forms.

The Hamelin Pool stromatolites – which are created when the microbes join together and trap sediment in the sticky surface of their cells – are no more than 3000 years old. But they are special because it's so rare to find the right conditions for their formation that growing examples only exist in two other places in the world – both in the Bahamas. The unusually still, salty water here means competitors and predators for the microbes that create the stromatolites can't survive.

Things to See & Do

There is an interesting **walk** along the shore from Denham to the Town Bluff – the two rows of curved rocks are believed to be an Aboriginal fish trap. A couple of kilometres down the road to Monkey Mia is the shallow and picturesque **Little Lagoon**.

Shark Bay Aquasports, on the foreshore opposite the Heritage Resort, rents out windsurfers for $50 a day, kayaks for $40, and snorkelling gear for $10. Bikes are for hire at the Shell petrol station on Knight Terrace for $25 a day. Ask at the tourist office about boat hire. About 4km from Denham on the Monkey Mia Rd is the turn-off to the spectacular **Francois Peron National Park** (see later in this section). An alternative wilderness destination, though harder to get to, is **Dirk Hartog Island**.

Organised Tours

You can book most tours for Denham, Monkey Mia and the Francois Peron National Park at Shark Bay's tourist office. Explorer Charters (☎ 9948 1246) offers a day-long wildlife cruise taking in the Zuytdorp Cliffs, Dirk Hartog Island and Steep Point three times a week ($85, including lunch). The same company offers deep-sea fishing trips ($120). Shark Bay Charter Service (☎ 9948 1113) will tailor fishing trips for one or more days to your requirements. Majestic Tours (☎ 9948 1640) runs 4WD trips around the World Heritage area. An all-day tour of the Francois Peron National Park costs $79. For more cruises and flights, see under Monkey Mia later in this chapter.

Places to Stay

The *Denham Seaside Caravan Park* (☎ 9948 1242), on Knight Terrace, is a friendly place on the foreshore with tent/powered sites for $12/16, basic cabins for $50 and new en suite cabins starting at $60. The *Blue Dolphin* (☎ 9948 1385), on Denham-Hamelin Rd tucked behind the Knight Terrace shops, has tent/powered sites for $10/16 and park cabins starting at $40. The *Shark Bay Caravan Park* (☎ 9948 1387, 4 Spaven Way) is a bit farther away from the beach but it has an 18m pool. Tent/powered sites cost $12/15.

Bay Lodge (☎ *9948 1278*), on Knight Terrace on the Denham foreshore, has backpackers beds for $14, and motel rooms and self-contained units starting at $75.

The friendly *Shark Bay Holiday Cottages* (☎ *9948 1206, 3–13 Knight Terrace*) has cottages starting at $55 for two people, increasing by about $5 in peak times. *Denham Villas* (☎ *9948 1264, 4 Durlacher St*) has spotless self-contained villas starting at $75. Neat units at *Tradewinds Holiday Village* (☎ *9948 1222*), on Knight Terrace, start at $70 per night for two people.

On Knight Terrace, singles/doubles at the excellent *Heritage Resort Hotel* (☎ *9948 1133*), are worth the $95/120 – especially if you score an upstairs front room with a balcony. *Shark Bay Hotel-Motel* (☎ *9948 1203, 43 Knight Terrace*), 'Australia's most western pub', has comfy doubles for $70 to $85.

To rent a privately owned cottage, call Ray White real estate (☎ 9948 1323).

Places to Eat
Denham's eat street is Knight Terrace. The *Loaves & Fishes Bakery* has pies and cakes and baked goods from the *supermarket* are also tasty. The *Bay Cafe* has an espresso machine. The lively *Shark Bay Hotel* has a bistro, while the *Heritage Resort Hotel* has a restaurant and bar meals, including a $15 buffet on Friday night and a $12 roast ($7 for children) on Sunday night. Pies at the shell-block *Old Pearler* restaurant are meant to be good for lunch, but a $19.50 prawn satay dinner was very ordinary.

Getting There & Away
Air Western Airlines (☎ 1800-998 097) has return flights from Perth on Monday, Wednesday and Friday; the one-way fare is $175 to Kalbarri and a further $90 from Kalbarri to Denham.

Bus North from Kalbarri, it's a fairly dull, boring and often very hot run to Carnarvon. The Overlander Roadhouse, 278km north of Geraldton, is at the turn-off to Shark Bay. Greyhound has a bus service from Denham and Monkey Mia to the Overlander that connects with interstate buses on Saturday, Monday and Thursday (both northbound and southbound). The fare from Perth to Denham is $135. It's $33/64 one way/return from Monkey Mia to the Overlander Roadhouse; $27/52 from Denham.

A daily local bus departs Denham (near the tourist office on Knight Terrace) at 8 am for Monkey Mia and returns at 4.30 pm. The fare is $16 return and bookings at the tourist office are essential.

FRANCOIS PERON NATIONAL PARK
This magnificent national park is named after the French naturalist who visited Shark Bay with Nicolas Baudin's *Le Géographe* expedition in 1801 and 1803. Baudin died of tuberculosis on the return voyage so it was left to François Péron to write up the narrative and scientific accounts of the expedition in his *A Voyage of Discovery to the Southern Hemisphere* (1809).

The 400-sq-km park is known for its arid scenery, tracts of wilderness and the landlocked salt lakes or *birridas*, which range from 100m to 1km wide. At the tip of the peninsula is Cape Peron with its dramatic colour contrasts.

An artesian bore in the grounds of the **Péron Homestead** provides 40°C water for a hot tub that you're welcome to soak in. The station is a reminder of the peninsula's former use as grazing land.

The park has camp sites with limited facilities at Big Lagoon, Gregories, Bottle Bay, South Gregories and Herald Bight. Always carry your own supplies of drinking water and carry out all rubbish. No fires are permitted but gas barbecues are provided at camp sites. Watch out for stonefish in shallow waters and keep well back from the unstable cliff edges at Cape Peron. Entry to the park is $8 per vehicle for a day visit.

The road to the homestead is sometimes suitable for 2WD vehicles but a 4WD with high clearance is necessary to go any farther into the park. Stick to the roads and *don't* try to cross any of the birridas – you will get bogged. Majestic Tours (☎ 9948 1640) has a tour option – see Organised Tours under Denham earlier in this chapter.

CENTRAL WEST COAST

DIRK HARTOG ISLAND

The site of one of the earliest known European landings in Australia (by Dutchman Dirk Hartog in 1616), this long, thin island now forms the western boundary of the Shark Bay World Heritage area. Its lack of road access ensures that you're likely to have the place almost entirely to yourself.

Dirk Hartog Island Homestead (☎ 9948 1211) offers full board to a maximum 16 guests for $150 per person per day. The homestead can charter a plane ($150 one way) or a boat ($300 one way) to get you there from Denham. Otherwise you can bring your 4WD over on a 20-minute barge trip from Steep Point ($625 return for a week) and camp.

Activities on Dirk Hartog Island include fishing, snorkelling, diving and swimming. Explorer Charters (☎ 9948 1246) offers a return island visitor's fare from Denham ($50). The *Sea Eagle* (☎ 9948 1113) also goes to the island.

MONKEY MIA

Everyone's got a different story about the origins of the name Monkey Mia for the sheltered beach on the other side of the peninsula from Denham. One theory is that it came from the schooner *Monkey*, which supposedly anchored in Shark Bay in 1834, with the Aboriginal word for house or home – *mia* – added, but this is disputed, as records indicate the *Monkey* was never near the eastern side of the Peron Peninsula. Then there was the pearling boat that had a monkey as a mascot, and then there was the fact that 'monkey' was slang at the time for Mongolian pearlers, and was also the colloquial expression for 'shepherd'. You may as well just make up your own theory.

Monkey Mia is 23km from Denham on a sealed road. Entry is $5 per person and $10 for a family. The visitor centre (☎ 9948 1366) is near the stretch of beach where the dolphins come in and has heaps of information and books. A redevelopment of this facility is planned. Electric self-drive glass-bottomed boats can be hired for $30 an hour and sea kayaks for $10 an hour from a tent on the beach.

No Monkey Business, Please

The Monkey Mia experience is carefully monitored. A ranger oversees proceedings in the dolphin-interaction area, where swimmers and boats are banned. Fish, supplied by the ranger, are fed to the dolphins in this area only and are sometimes offered to visitors so they can feed the dolphins.

To maximise the animals' survival chances, only adult females are fed and never more than one-third of their daily requirement.

Strict rules apply to interacting with the dolphins: Don't chase them; stroke them only along their sides with the back of your hand as they swim beside you; and don't touch their fins or their blowhole. The creatures sometimes come into other parts of the shore.

Monkey Mia – really no more than a camp ground and some holiday villas crammed together on a stretch of flattened dune – is worth avoiding in school holidays when it gets packed, hectic and expensive. Stay in Denham instead and take a day trip out there if you must.

Dolphins of Monkey Mia

If the only reason you've come all this way is to have a close and personal experience with Monkey Mia's 'world-famous' dolphins, be warned: that's also why throngs of other people are here. The dolphin experience usually consists of trying to catch a glimpse of one beyond the dozens of tourists standing with you in knee-deep water, rigorously overseen by a park ranger.

Three generations of bottlenose dolphins have been visiting Monkey Mia since the 1960s, probably initially attracted by fish thrown from boats. Today, as many as seven dolphins come into the beach on a regular basis, sometimes taking hand-held fish distributed to a couple of onlookers by the ranger. The record number of dolphins in one visit was 22.

There's no set time for their visit but you have a good chance of seeing some dolphins in the designated dolphin-viewing area from about 8 am.

The Gascoyne – Carnarvon 277

Organised Tours

While the beachfront dolphin experience is a dud compared with other meet-the-wildlife offerings in WA (such as swimming with whale sharks – see Ningaloo Marine Park in the Coral Coast & the Pilbara chapter), a cruise in the waters off Monkey Mia compensates. The *Shotover* (☎ 9948 1481) runs excellent 2½-hour dugong-spotting cruises for $40, throwing in a separate 1½-hour sunset cruise for free. As well as mysterious, ponderous dugongs, we saw dolphins and sea turtles. The *Aristocat* (☎ 9948 1446) runs similar cruises for similar prices. Family tickets on its wildlife cruises start at $70.

The glass-bottomed *Blue Lagoon Pearl* takes tours out to a pearl farm at Red Bluff ($18/7 adults/children). Monkey Mia Scenic Flights (☎ 9948 1445) takes a range of routes over the Shark Bay area starting at $35 per person for 15 minutes.

Places to Stay & Eat

The *Monkey Mia Dolphin Resort (☎ 9948 1320)* has all sorts of accommodation crammed up against the beach where the dolphins come in. Tent/powered sites start at $14/18 for two people; backpackers beds in fibreglass boxes smelling of mildew cost $14; canvas condos are $70 for four; on-site vans $35 for three; park homes $80 for four; and motel-style villas start at $140.

If self-catering, you're better off bringing supplies from Denham than buying them from the store here, as the range is limited and the prices fairly high. The *Peron Cafe* serves fresh sandwiches and light meals. The *Boughshed Restaurant* is efficient, friendly and has an interesting menu but, sadly, won our prize for coffee with the biggest price for least satisfaction in the north-west (a whopping $3.20 for a very ordinary brew).

The Gascoyne

The Gascoyne region takes its name from the 760km Gascoyne River, which together with its major tributary, the Lyons River, has a catchment area of nearly 70,000 sq km.

Seldom does the Gascoyne River flow above ground west of the Kennedy Range.

There are a number of attractions within this vast region but a good deal of driving is necessary to get to them. North of Carnarvon is an interesting stretch of coastline with blowholes and rocky capes. To the east is the impressive Kennedy Range, running north–south, and the massive bulk of Mt Augustus.

CARNARVON

pop 7000

Carnarvon is at the mouth of the Gascoyne River, which separates Babbage Island – where a heritage precinct is sited – from the main part of town. It's noted for its tropical fruit, particularly bananas, and fine climate. It can get very hot in the middle of summer and the area is periodically subject to floods and cyclones. Subsurface water, which flows even when the above-ground river is dry, is tapped to irrigate riverside plantations. Salt is produced at Lake Macleod near Carnarvon, and prawns and scallops are harvested in the area. The main street of Carnarvon is 40m wide, a reminder of the days when camel trains used to pass by.

In winter Carnarvon fills up with retirees from 'down south' escaping the cold. Apart from mild winters, the town's offerings to travellers are modest compared to other towns on the WA coast.

The Carnarvon tourist office (☎ 9941 1146), on Robinson St, is open from 8.30 am to 5 pm weekdays and from 9 am to noon weekends. Banks are among the shops on the Olivia Terrace end of Robinson St. The Wise Owl Book Exchange, on the corner of Robinson St and Babbage Island Rd, has books for sale or trade. Internet access is available at the library adjacent to the shire offices.

Things to See & Do

Carnarvon had a National Aeronautics and Space Administration **tracking station** (now the OTC, or Overseas Telecommunication, station) from 1966 to 1975. To get there, travel south on the North West Coastal Hwy from the Robinson St intersection and turn

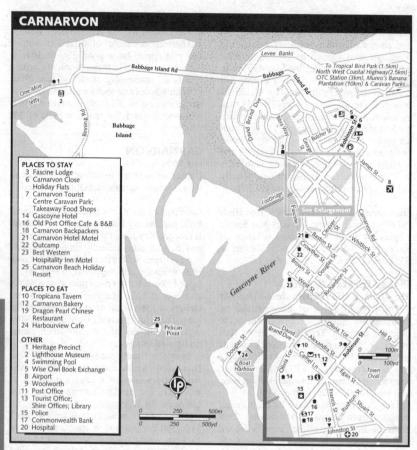

CARNARVON

PLACES TO STAY
3 Fascine Lodge
6 Carnarvon Close
Holiday Flats
7 Carnarvon Tourist
Centre Caravan Park;
Takeaway Food Shops
14 Gascoyne Hotel
16 Old Post Office Cafe & B&B
18 Carnarvon Backpackers
21 Carnarvon Hotel Motel
22 Outcamp
23 Best Western
Hospitality Inn Motel
25 Carnarvon Beach Holiday
Resort

PLACES TO EAT
10 Tropicana Tavern
12 Carnarvon Bakery
19 Dragon Pearl Chinese
Restaurant
24 Harbourview Cafe

OTHER
1 Heritage Precinct
2 Lighthouse Museum
4 Swimming Pool
5 Wise Owl Book Exchange
8 Airport
9 Woolworth
11 Post Office
13 Tourist Office;
Shire Offices; Library
15 Police
17 Commonwealth Bank
20 Hospital

left at Mahony Ave. The station is at the top
of the street. The site provides good views of
Carnarvon, and a museum in the pedestal of
the parabolic dish is set to open.

The **Fascine**, a riverside promenade lined
with palm trees, features some attractive old
houses and makes for a pleasant stroll.
Carnarvon is also developing its **heritage
precinct**, the old port 2.5km from the town
centre. You can catch a **tram**, 'The Coffee
Pot', along the historic **one mile jetty** ($4/2
for adults/children), or walk the jetty ($2).
It's a popular fishing spot. Nearby is the
Lighthouse Museum, in the old lighthouse

keeper's cottage. It's open 10 am to noon
and 2 to 4 pm daily ($3). From May until
the weather gets too hot, an old steam train
carries passengers from the jetty to the **footbridge** (open to pedestrians) for $4/2 for
adults/children.

Pelican Point, 5km to the south-west, is
a popular swimming and picnic spot. Other
good beaches, also south and off the Geraldton road, are **Bush Bay** (turn-off 20km)
and **New Beach** (37km).

Munro's Banana Plantation, about 10km
from town on South River Rd, has an informative plantation tour ($3) at 11 am daily

except Saturday. The cafe, set in tropical gardens, serves fantastic fruit smoothies ($3.80) and banana pancakes ($4.40).

The **Tropical Bird Park**, at 77 Angelo St, has 70 aviaries containing Australian birds. It opens 9.30 am to 4.30 pm daily ($4/2 for adults/children).

Carnarvon is a great place for fishing: grab a copy of *The Best Fishing Around Carnarvon*, free from the tourist office.

Organised Tours

Carnarvon Bus Charter departs from the tourist office and offers half-day tours around town for $25 and an all-day tour that includes Lake Macleod, Cape Cuvier, the *Korean Star* wreck and blowholes for $35.

Surfers can inquire after 'full-bore barrels with plenty of length' at the tourist office.

Whale-watching tours cost $75 and run from about June to November – inquire at the tourist office.

Paggi's (☎ 9941 1587) has scenic air tours down to Shark Bay and out over Mt Augustus; call and ask for prices. TropicAir Services (☎ 9941 2002) has a 70-minute blowholes coastal ride starting at $75 per person (depending on numbers) and flights over the Kennedy Range.

Places to Stay

Camping & Caravan Parks Carnarvon has a host of relatively unexciting caravan parks. Closest to the town centre is the *Carnarvon Tourist Centre Caravan Park* (☎ 9941 1438, 108 Robinson St). It has tent/powered sites for $12/15, and basic park homes without en suites starting at $45.

The *Marloo Caravan Park* (☎ 9941 1439), on Wise St, is targeted more towards 'mature' campers and not children. At busy times a vegetable stall is set up and there's an information room, message boxes for each site, and a pool. Camp sites start at $14 for two people.

The *Wintersun Caravan Park* (☎ 9941 8150), on Robinson St, has mini-golf and an eight-rink bowling green. Tent/powered sites here cost $15/16.75 for two people and new-looking en suite cabins for $65. Standard cabins start at $42.

Also on Robinson St, with prices similar to the other parks, are the shady *Carnarvon Caravan Park* (☎ 9941 8101) and *Plantation Caravan Park* (☎ 9941 8100).

Hostels *Carnarvon Backpackers* (☎ 9941 1095, 97 Olivia Terrace) is spacious and well-located in two houses overlooking the Fascine, but some of its kitchen facilities are a bit run-down. Dorm beds here cost $15 and doubles $30 to $40. Management can help you find local seasonal work.

B&Bs For the best breakfast in the north-west, as well as spotlessly clean, hospitable and personal accommodation, you can't go past the *Outcamp* (☎ 9941 2421, 139 Olivia Terrace) on the Fascine. The owners of this B&B, the Maslen family, have been in the Gascoyne region for generations and also own nearby Mardathuna station, so they're a veritable storehouse of local information and history.

Hotels & Motels There's OK rooms at the *Gateway Motel* (☎ 9941 1532, 379 Robinson St) for $90. Another motel option on a quieter road is the bland but clean and friendly *Fascine Lodge* (☎ 9941 2411, 1002 David Brand Dr), with singles/doubles for $90/95. The *Best Western Hospitality Inn Motel* (☎ 9941 1600), on West St, is in a quiet spot. Rooms cost $85/95.

The century-old *Gascoyne Hotel* (☎ 9941 1412, 88 Olivia Terrace) has double rooms upstairs for $40. New motel units at the rear cost $50/60. If you're desperate, motel-style units out the back of the blokey *Carnarvon Hotel Motel* (☎ 9941 1181), on Olivia Terrace, cost $40/60.

Other Accommodation The $70 self-contained *Carnarvon Close Holiday Flats* (☎ 9941 1317), on Robinson St, could do with a revamp. Better self-contained units in a beautiful spot on a private canal at *Carnarvon Beach Holiday Resort* (☎ 9941 2226), on Pelican Point, cost $75. The *Old Post Office Cafe & B&B* (☎ 9941 4231, 10 Robinson St) has singles/doubles for $45/60.

Places to Eat

The *Old Post Office Cafe & B&B* has meals including pizzas. A fine dinner of fish, chips, salad and a beer here costs $18.50. A trio of *takeaway shops* (burgers, chicken, pizzas) are on Robinson St beside the Carnarvon Tourist Centre Caravan Park. The best local fish and seafood meals and takeaways are said to be found at the *Harbourview Cafe*, overlooking the boat harbour.

Counter meals at the *Gascoyne Hotel* are reputedly good, as are those at *Tropicana Tavern* on Camel Lane. The Best Western Hospitality Inn also has a restaurant, *Sails*. The *Dragon Pearl (Francis St)* is a standard Chinese restaurant.

There is a *Woolworth supermarket* on Robinson St. The *Carnarvon Bakery*, also on Robinson St, has pies and sandwiches.

Getting There & Around

SkyWest Airlines (☎ 9334 2288) flies to Carnarvon return from Perth daily.

Greyhound Pioneer buses pass through Carnarvon daily on their way north and south. The one-way fare from Perth to Carnarvon is $126 ($240 return). Integrity Coach Lines runs four services a week to and from Perth ($100/185 one way/return), and two services north as far as Exmouth. Both of these stop outside the tourist office.

NORTH OF CARNARVON

Some 22km north of Carnarvon along a largely unsealed road is **Miaboolya Beach**, popular with anglers.

The spectacular **blowholes** 71km north of Carnarvon are worth the trip. They are reached along a sealed road via the North West Coastal Hwy. Water is forced through holes in the rock to a height of 20m.

The coastal road continuing north from the blowholes is unsealed. One kilometre south of the Quobba Station homestead is the **HMAS *Sydney* Memorial**, commemorating the ship sunk off the coast by the German raider *Kormoran* on 19 November 1941.

Cape Cuvier, where salt harvested from nearby Lake Mcleod is loaded on to ships bound for overseas, is 30km north of the blowholes. One kilometre farther north is

the *Korean Star*, which was grounded by Cyclone Herbie on 21 May 1988 (do not climb over the wreck as it is dangerous).

Places to Stay

There's a fine beach about a kilometre south of the blowholes with a primitive camp site (no fresh water available). You can camp at *Quobba Station (☎ 9941 2036)* for about $7 per person.

KENNEDY RANGE

This spectacular plateau is some 150km east of Carnarvon. It runs north from Gascoyne Junction for 195km and in places is 25km wide. The range is a huge mesa, pushed up from a sea bed millions of years ago. The southern and eastern sides have eroded to create dramatic 100m-high cliffs and canyons. The range is covered with red sand dunes and spinifex.

An expedition, led by Francis Gregory, explored the park in 1858. He named the range after the then governor of WA. The many artefacts attest to habitation by the Balardung and Warriyangga Aboriginal groups for some 20,000 years. The semi-precious coloured chert was used to make stone tools. The range has been explored for minerals and the mining potential has been deemed to be low.

Some 295 species of plant have been recorded in the park and 40% of these are annual wildflowers. Cliff-top eyries are perfect vantage points for the magnificent wedge-tailed eagle.

The eastern escarpment can be reached in a 2WD vehicle, depending on road conditions. Neither fuel nor water is available in the park so you have to come with adequate supplies.

Local tour operators include Stockman Safaris (☎ 9941 2421), which goes to the less-visited western side of the range ($95). Lindsay Orr's Outback Adventure Tours (☎ 9943 0550), based at Mt Sandiman Station, does 3½-day tours including the Kennedy Range and Mt Augustus for $485. Exmouth-based West Coast Safaris (☎ 9949 1625) takes four-day tours through the area for $550.

Places to Stay

Bush camping is permitted in the main visitor area at the base of the eastern escarpment of the Kennedy Range. The friendly *Mt Sandiman Station* (☎ *9943 0550*), 250km north-east of Carnarvon via Gascoyne Junction, offers dinner and B&B for $109 a double.

MT AUGUSTUS NATIONAL PARK

Mt Augustus (1106m), or Burringurrah as the local Wadjari people know it, is preserved in a national park 476km from Carnarvon. It's the biggest 'rock' in the world. Twice the size of Uluru (Ayers Rock) and three times as old, it looks less dramatic because of partial vegetation cover. The granite underneath the layered rocks of the mount is estimated to be 1700 million years old.

There are Aboriginal engravings at three main sites: **Ooramboo** has engravings of animal tracks on a rock face; at **Mundee** the engravings are in a series of overhangs; and **Beedoboondu**, the starting point for the climb to the summit, also has engravings of animal tracks and hunters.

From the car park near Beedoboondu, the strenuous excursion to the rock's top can take at least six hours and is 12km return. There is also a shorter walk of 6km (2½ hours return) from Ooramboo that also has elevated views.

Most visitors get to Mt Augustus via the remote **Gascoyne Junction** (175km east of Carnarvon on an unsealed road). There are unsealed roads into the area branching off the Great Northern Hwy from Meekatharra and off the North West Coastal Hwy, north of the turn-off to Giralia Station (see the Coral Coast & the Pilbara chapter).

In Gascoyne Junction, the *hotel* is also the general store, and is the only source of cold beer before you get to Mt Augustus or Meekatharra.

A copy of CALM's excellent *National Parks of the Gascoyne Hinterland*, covering the Kennedy Range and Mt Augustus ($2), is well worthwhile.

Places to Stay

Camping is not allowed in the area of Mt Augustus. The *Junction Hotel* (☎ *9943 0504*), where the Lyons River meets the Gascoyne River, has single/double rooms for $50/60. Some 37km north-west of Mt Augustus along an unsealed road is *Cobra Station Motel* (☎ *9943 0565*), with tent/powered sites for $13/15 for two people, guesthouse singles/doubles for $45/60, and motel rooms for $60/80.

Mt Augustus Outback Tourist Resort (☎ *9943 0527*), only 5km north-east of the rock, has tent/powered sites for $8/10 per person, and motel units for $60.

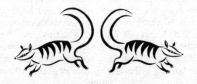

Coral Coast & the Pilbara

The Coral Coast, the area from Coral Bay to Onslow, is an incredibly rich ecotourism destination. The Pilbara, composed of the oldest rocks in the world, is an ancient, arid region with many natural wonders. It stretches from Onslow to north of Port Hedland and inland beyond Karijini National Park.

Coral Coast

The Coral Coast is replete with wildlife, and has a coral reef and a warm climate. Apart from the ecotourism possibilities, this is a good place to take it easy – lie on the beach and enjoy the magnificent fine weather, snorkel across the very accessible reef and have a meal of prawns or fresh fish.

CARNARVON TO NORTH WEST CAPE

From Carnarvon to Exmouth, via the North West Coastal Hwy, is about 370km. It is about 140km from Carnarvon to the first major roadhouse, at Minilya, then another 8km to the turn-off to the North West Cape via the Minilya-Exmouth Rd.

Turn off this road onto a 23km unsealed road to get to **Warroora Station** (☎ 9942 5920). Beach camping costs $5 per night. The homestead also has bunkhouse accommodation for $18 per person.

The turn-off to Coral Bay is 78km along the Minilya-Exmouth Rd from the highway. Some 52km farther north is a sealed road heading east to Giralia Station and on back to the North West Coastal Hwy.

Coral Bay

This tourist hamlet, around 150km south of Exmouth and 1132km north of Perth, is an important access point for Ningaloo Marine Park. Between April and November the temperature hovers around a pleasant 28°C. Peak times are April school holidays and June to mid-October. Basically a row of caravan parks with some holiday villas and

HIGHLIGHTS

- Swimming with magnificent whale sharks and manta rays near Exmouth
- Walking straight off the beach to snorkel over Ningaloo Reef at Coral Bay
- Cooling off in the oases of Millstream-Chichester National Park
- Taking in the view from Oxers Lookout, where four spectacular gorges meet in Karijini National Park
- Soaking up the atmosphere at historical Cossack
- Sinking a beer on the balcony at Trawlers Tavern, Point Samson
- Glimpsing the vast scale of the Pilbara's industry: Newman's Mt Whaleback mine tour and the sun sinking behind massive cranes and ships at Port Hedland

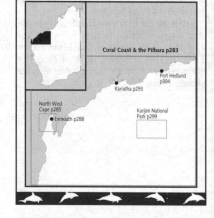

shops jammed in wherever there's a spare couple of square metres, Coral Bay can get packed and hectic, but the landscape and ocean surrounding it are exquisite.

The tiny township has been the scene of an age-old controversy: How much development can an ecotourism site take before the 'eco' part of the equation disappears?

CORAL COAST & THE PILBARA

Recently the Western Australia (WA) state government approved the building of a $180-million marina and a 2000-bed resort at Maud's Landing near Coral Bay. With the existing infrastructure (especially sewerage) already under strain, the locals are wondering how the land – not to mention the fragile and precious Ningaloo Reef – will cope. Construction on the new resort was expected to start in early 2001.

The helpful and friendly Coral Bay tourist office (☎ 9942 5877) is in the Coral Bay Shopping Village next to the People's Park. Internet access is available at Fin's Cafe and Ningaloo Reef Dive. Coral Bay's water comes from an artesian bore, which means that showers are salty and drinking water must be desalinated – so use it sparingly.

Underwater Activities Coral Bay is at the southern end of Ningaloo Marine Park and is a great place for snorkelling. You can walk straight in off the beach, put your head down into beautiful light-blue water and go for it. Keep in mind, though, that the usual dangers associated with tropical waters (stonefish, sea snakes, strong currents and sharks) also exist here.

Ningaloo Experience (☎ 9942 5877) does manta ray cruises, snorkelling tours and whale–watching tours; prices start at $85. It also arranges fishing charters, or you can go out on the *Mahi Mahi* (half-day $75; full-day from $110). Ningaloo Reef Dive (☎ 9954 5824) rents and refills diving tanks, and runs scuba tours and Professional Association of Diving Instructors (PADI) dive courses. An alternative for courses is Coral Dive (☎ 9942 5830). You can rent snorkelling equipment for $10 per day from the beach or go 'snuba' diving (using an air hose connected to a boat), starting at $45. Kim's Quad Treks uses four-wheel motorbikes to access secluded beaches and bush. A three-hour 'snorkel trek' (☎ 9942 5955) costs $55.

For those wanting to avoid submersion, trips on Glass Bottom Boats (☎ 9942 5932) or the Sub-Sea Explorer (☎ 9942 5955) start at $25 for two hours. Camels 'R' Us has its depot across from the Bayview Caravan Park. A one-hour sunset ride costs $30.

Places to Stay The following places are all located on Robinson St on the foreshore and are very easy to find. *Peoples Park Caravan Village* (☎ 9942 5933) has ablution blocks with poor drainage and unpowered/powered sites for $18/20 for two people. The *Bayview Holiday Village* (☎ 9942 5932) packs 'em in cheek-by-jowl in busy times and has tent/powered sites for $12/16.50 ($14.50/19.50 in peak). The *Coral Bay Lodge* (☎ 9942 5932) is connected to the Bayview Holiday Village and has units starting at $110. The pleasant *Ningaloo Reef Resort* (☎ 9942 5934) has rooms – many with good views – starting at $110 for two people ($10/5 for an extra adult/child).

As for backpackers, Coral Bay is the place to dust off that tent you've been lugging around all this time. A new coat of paint on the exterior of the *Bayview Backpackers* ($16) wasn't enough to conceal the run-down interiors of the kitchen and rooms. *Coral Bay Backpackers* (☎ 9942 5934), stuck up the back of the Ningaloo Reef Resort, isn't much better – although it is $1 cheaper.

Places to Eat For self-caterers, fresh food can be found at *Coral Bay Supermarket*. *Fin's Cafe* has good coffee and salad rolls and an interesting evening menu. A *bakery* and *supermarket* are in Coral Bay Arcade. The *general store* in the Coral Bay Shopping Village sells fresh local fish fillets. The Ningaloo Reef Resort has a *restaurant*, and the *Reef Licensed Restaurant*, next to the Bayview Holiday Village, has tasty steaks and pizzas.

NORTH WEST CAPE

The North West Cape, a finger of land jutting north into the Indian Ocean, is a fantastic ecotourism destination. Whale sharks, humpback whales and manta rays are found in and around the coral of Ningaloo Reef, while dramatic gorges and pristine landscapes can be visited out of the water. The cape's easily accessible activities, concentrated in a small (by WA standards) area, make it an excellent place to spend a few days or more.

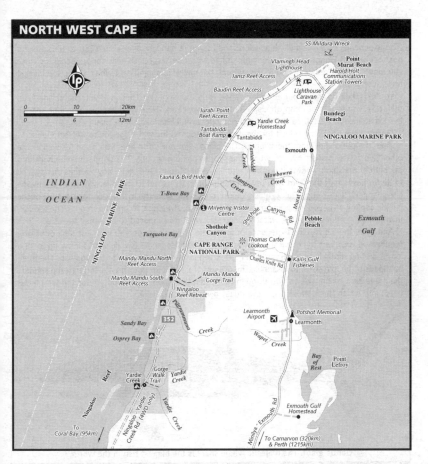

NORTH WEST CAPE

SS Mildura Wreck

Point Murat Beach
Vlamingh Head Lighthouse
Harold Holt Communications Station Towers
Jansz Reef Access
Baudin Reef Access
Lighthouse Caravan Park
Bundegi Beach
Jurabi Point Reef Access
Yardie Creek Homestead
NINGALOO MARINE PARK
Tantabiddi Boat Ramp
Tantabiddi
Tantabiddi Creek
Exmouth
INDIAN OCEAN
Fauna & Bird Hide
Mangrove Creek
Mowbowra Creek
Murat Rd
T-Bone Bay
Milyering Visitor Centre
Shothole Canyon
Pebble Beach
Exmouth Gulf
Turquoise Bay
Shothole Canyon
Thomas Carter Lookout
CAPE RANGE NATIONAL PARK
Charles Knife Rd
Kailis Gulf Fisheries
Mandu Mandu North Reef Access
Mandu Mandu Gorge Trail
Mandu Mandu South Reef Access
Ningaloo Reef Retreat
Yardinumuna
Learmonth Airport
Potshot Memorial
Learmonth
352
Sandy Bay
Creek
Wapet Creek
Osprey Bay
Bay of Rest
Point Lefroy
Reef
Gorge Walk Trail
Yardie Creek
Yardie Creek
Ningaloo Yardie Creek Rd (4WD only)
Yardie Creek
Exmouth Gulf Homestead
Ningaloo
Minilya - Exmouth Rd
To Coral Bay (95km)
To Carnarvon (320km) & Perth (1215km)

0   10   20km
0   6   12mi

The cape was once occupied by Aborigines, but about 150 years ago disease decimated the indigenous population. In this weathered country much of the evidence of their presence has faded rapidly.

During WWII the area near Wapet Creek on the eastern side of the cape was used as an advance and refuelling base for US submarines; codenamed 'Operation Potshot', the facility was destroyed by a cyclone in 1945.

Ningaloo Marine Park

Running alongside the North West Cape for 260km, from Bundegi Reef in the north-east to Amherst Point in the south-west, is the stunning Ningaloo ('point of land') Reef. In places, this miniature version of the Great Barrier Reef is less than 100m offshore.

There are eight sanctuary zones within the marine park – no fishing, only observing. Dugongs, greenback turtles (which lay their eggs along the cape beaches) and placid whale sharks can be seen in or just beyond the reef's waters.

More than 220 species of coral have been recorded in the waters of the park, ranging from the slow-growing bommies to delicate branching varieties. For eight or

The Biggest Fish in the World

'The experience of a lifetime', they call it, and as you're handing over your $250 to the grinning boat operator at Exmouth you're thinking: 'It had better be'. Especially considering there's a chance you may not even see what you're paying for – the majestic, magnificent whale shark, the biggest fish in the world.

You're picked up from your accommodation early the next day. They give you snorkelling gear, then take you to a boat ramp off Cape Range National Park. Here, you discover you'll be sharing this Experience of a Lifetime with not just one but several boatloads of people.

Once on the boat, you set off for the reef, staring across the water for you're-not-sure-what.

Then the call comes from the skipper: 'The plane's got one'. The boat you're on (as well as the other two boats) powers over to where the spotter plane is circling. The skipper manoeuvres into the path of the shark – not that you can actually see it. 'Group One, get ready', comes the cry. You jostle for position at the stern with seven other people, trying not to trip over your own or anyone else's flippers. 'Go! Jump! Quick, quick, quick!' comes the next cry. In you go, hoping none of the people coming after you are going to land on your head, struggling to breathe through the snorkel, madly kicking, your face in the water with no idea what it's supposed to be aimed towards.

And then, there it is – the Experience of a Lifetime, right alongside you with just a bit of kicking required on your part to keep it there. A vast, speckled filter-feeder (whale sharks grow up to 18m long), drifting serenely through the water, other fish in its slipstream – and now you too. The three boatloads of people seem to disappear, there's just the sound of your breath through the snorkel, the movement of the two of you through the water, the gloom all around you of the fathomless deep, into which the enormous fish eventually dives and disappears.

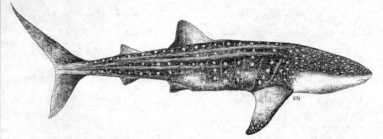

Gentle giant: The majestic whale shark is the biggest fish in the world.

nine nights after the full moon in March, there is a synchronised mass spawning of coral, with eggs and sperm released into the water simultaneously. Once fertilised, the larvae drifts until it settles and begins to build a skeleton, eventually forming into juvenile coral.

Every June and July humpback whales pass close by the coast on their way north to their calving grounds, probably near the Montebello Islands. They return to Antarctica in October and November.

In November turtles come up the beaches at night, when the tide is right, to lay their eggs. This usually happens from November to January near the top of North West Cape.

Contact the Department of Conservation & Land Management (CALM; ☎ 9949 1676) in Exmouth for more information. Its *Guide to Coral Coast Parks*, provided free with entrance to Cape Range National Park, is informative; CALM also publishes *The Marine Life of Ningaloo Marine Park and Coral Bay* ($14.95).

Interaction with Marine Life Whale sharks can be observed from late March to mid-June. The season begins at the time of coral spawning and there is a plankton bloom at the same time. The best way to see whale sharks is by licensed charter vessel (see the boxed text).

About eight boats are allowed to take trips out to the whale sharks. All provide transport, equipment and food – and similar experiences – for prices starting at $230. Some have extras such as videographers or a Japanese divemaster – ask at the tourist office for the excellent comprehensive list. Perhaps the only important distinguishing feature between operators is that some boats give you a second day out for free if no whale sharks are sighted first time round, and others don't.

Ningaloo Blue (☎ 9949 1119) does. For $250, it also has friendly staff, a tasty lunch, and snorkelling equipment supplied. We swam with manta rays as well as whale sharks and got to snorkel the reef.

The North West Cape area offers numerous opportunities to learn how to dive. Readers recommend the Exmouth Dive Centre (☎ 9949 1201). Its PADI open-water course takes up to five days, with a maximum group size of eight, and costs $270.

Coral Coast Dive (☎ 9949 1004) charges the same for a four-day course, with a maximum of six people.

Both companies take other courses, dive charters and trips to the Muiron Islands, 10km north-east of the cape.

These islands are a breeding sanctuary for three species of turtle: green, loggerhead and hawksbill. During dives it is possible to handfeed the 1.5m potato cod where they live in one of the lagoons (the 'cod house').

Dive charters are also provided by Western Australia Getaway Scuba and start at $65. Book through the tourist office.

Snorkel in Paradise (☎ 9949 1776) runs guided 6½-hour snorkelling tours for $40, including lunch, while tours with Adventure Snorkel and Marine Safari (☎ 9949 2255) are shorter and cheaper ($25 for backpackers).

Exmouth & Around
pop 2500

Exmouth was established in 1967 largely as a service centre for the huge US navy communications base. The Americans have moved out and now the town is a base for the many great eco-activities in the area. The well-staffed and helpful Exmouth tourist office (☎ 9949 1176), on Murat Rd, is open from 8.30 am to 5 pm daily. The CALM office (☎ 9949 1676) is on Nimitz St. Internet access is available at the Telecentre, 12 Learmonth St. Peak times in Exmouth are April to October.

Things to See & Do The **town beach** at the end of Warne St is a popular beachcombing spot. For swimming, the best beaches are on the west side of the cape in the Cape Range National Park, some half-hour's drive from Exmouth.

The wreck of the **SS *Mildura***, beached in 1907, and the **Vlamingh Head Lighthouse** are north of town and have sensational views.

Part of North West Cape is dominated by the 13 low-frequency transmitters of Harold Holt Communications Station. Twelve are higher than the Eiffel Tower and serve to support the 13th, which is 396m high.

Organised Tours Neil McLeod's Ningaloo Safari Tours (☎ 9949 1550) runs full-day tours exploring Ningaloo Reef, Cape Range National Park and the surrounding area, for $125; the cost includes boiled fruitcake made by Neil's mother. The tour also takes in a boat trip on Yardie Creek as well as an otherwise inaccessible drive over the top of the range.

Exmouth Cape Tourist Village (☎ 9949 1101) runs a scaled-down version of the Ningaloo Reef tour for $85.

The glass-bottom boat *Ningaloo Coral Explorer* (☎ 9949 2424) operates trips to view coral over Bundegi Reef on the east coast. Ningaloo Ecology Cruises (☎ 9949 2255) operates from Tantabiddi on the west coast. Sea Kayak Wilderness Adventures (☎ 9949 2952) runs a sea kayak full-day paddle along Ningaloo Reef for $95, including all equipment.

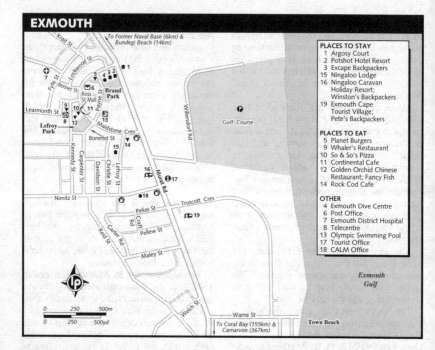

EXMOUTH

PLACES TO STAY
1 Argosy Court
2 Potshot Hotel Resort
3 Excape Backpackers
15 Ningaloo Lodge
16 Ningaloo Caravan
Holiday Resort;
Winston's Backpackers
19 Exmouth Cape
Tourist Village;
Pete's Backpackers

PLACES TO EAT
5 Planet Burgers
9 Whaler's Restaurant
10 So & So's Pizza
11 Continental Cafe
12 Golden Orchid Chinese
Restaurant; Fancy Fish
14 Rock Cod Cafe

OTHER
4 Exmouth Dive Centre
6 Post Office
7 Exmouth District Hospital
8 Telecentre
13 Olympic Swimming Pool
17 Tourist Office
18 CALM Office

Exmouth
Gulf

Town Beach

Exmouth Air Charter (☎ 9949 2182) does scenic flights over the reef ($49/69 for 30/60 minutes, minimum of two people).

Places to Stay Tidy *Exmouth Cape Tourist Village* (☎ *9949 1101*), on the corner of Truscott Crescent and Murat Rd, has powered sites for $20/19 peak/off-peak. Cabins and park homes start at $68/60 peak/off-peak.

Pete's Backpackers is incorporated into this park; beds start at $15. The *Ningaloo Caravan Holiday Resort* (☎ *9949 2377*), on Murat Rd, has been revamped in recent years. Tent/powered sites cost $18/24 ($14/16 off-peak). The new-looking, self-contained cabins start at $80/65 peak/off-peak. This park's *Winston's Backpackers* has pleasant doubles for $50 and dorm beds starting at $14.

Some 6km north of Exmouth, on the old US naval base, the *Exmouth Base Lodge* (☎ *9949 1474*) has $15 beds in neat twin rooms that once housed US sailors. You get the use of the base's 25m pool.

At Vlamingh Head, *Lighthouse Caravan Park* (☎ *9949 1478*) has powered sites for $19, cabins for $65/60 peak/off-peak and hilltop chalets ($120) with verandahs, from which you can sometimes watch whales frolicking. It also has a cafe and there is good surfing nearby.

The *Potshot Hotel Resort* (☎ *9949 1200*), on Murat Rd, has reasonable motel rooms starting at $85, as well as family-sized apartments starting at $125. The resort's *Excape Backpackers* (☎ *9949 1201*) has dorm beds starting at $14 ($13 if you stay for a week).

The clean and pleasant *Ningaloo Lodge* (☎ *9949 4949*), on Lefroy St, has en suite rooms for $60 to $80. Unpleasant, stale-smelling self-contained units at *Argosy Court* (☎ *9949 1177*), on Murat Rd, start at $60. Ray White Real Estate (☎ 9949 1144) rents out private houses.

The wheatbelt after harvest, near the town that means 'to rest a while' – Dalwallinu

A ghost-town feel, Cue

Mt Magnet mine

Cue's main street, from the central rotunda

Picturesque Little Lagoon in the Shark Bay World Heritage area, central west coast

Dolphin statue of compressed shells, Monkey Mia

The world's biggest 'rock', Mt Augustus

Hawk's Head lookout, Kalbarri NP

A carpet of wildflowers in the Murchison area

Places to Eat The beauty of Exmouth's natural surrounds is not replicated in the food its restaurants serve. The friendly *Potshot Hotel Resort* serves typical pub fare that you can eat by the pool. *Whaler's Restaurant*, on Kennedy St, had dismissive staff and a rather ordinary prawn salad for $11; mains start at $15. *So and So's Pizza*, on Maidstone Crescent in the main shopping precinct, is not bad. Nearby are *Golden Orchid Chinese Restaurant* and *Fancy Fish*, for fish and chips. The *Continental Cafe* facing on to the car park between Maidstone Crescent and the Ross St mall has fresh juices, sandwiches and an espresso machine.

A number of readers have recommended *Rock Cod Cafe* on Maidstone Crescent as good value. *Planet Burgers*, in a caravan across from Exmouth Dive Centre, attracts impressive queues. North of town at the naval base, the *Base Bar and Grill* has children's entertainment and serves steak, chicken and fish. About 26km south of town on Murat Rd, the *Kailis Gulf Fisheries* kiosk sells 1kg bags of cooked, cold prawns for $12.50.

Getting There & Away SkyWest Airlines flies between Learmonth airport (37km from Exmouth) and Geraldton once a week and has daily services to and from Perth. Book with Ansett (☎ 13 1300).

A Greyhound Pioneer bus service from Perth to Exmouth runs Sunday, Wednesday and Friday; from Exmouth to Perth, services are Saturday, Monday and Thursday ($185). Integrity Coach Lines bues are less frequent but $20 cheaper. Both companies stop outside the Exmouth tourist office.

Getting Around Exmouth township is not directly on the beach and is dozens of kilometres from the things you're here to see. Ningaloo Reef Bus (☎ 9949 1776) does a round trip six days a week (four days a week from October to March) from Exmouth to Ningaloo Reef Retreat – on the west coast of North West Cape in Cape Range National Park – with several stops along the way. A 34km return trip to the Vlamingh Head Lighthouse costs $6; to Turquoise Bay, also on the west side of North West Cape, return costs $20. Most of the guided tours include transport. In town, you can manage without a car, but if you're desperate to retain your independence, Marlin Car Hire has rates as low as $25 a day. Book through the tourist office. Allen's Car Hire (☎ 9949 2403) rents out Mazdas from $50 a day.

Station Stays

To get a glimpse of life on some of the largest and most isolated farms on earth, you could try a station stay during your visit to north-west Western Australia.

An example is the 2650-sq-km *Giralia Station* (☎ 9942 5937), 41km from the North West Coastal Hwy on the way to Exmouth. This working sheep station has worked hard to rebuild after the eye of Cyclone Vance passed over it in March 1999. It offers camp sites, clean compact 'quad' rooms with shared facilities ($55), or en suite homestead rooms with meals ($100). Guests are welcome to sample activities on the station, which runs 25,000 sheep.

Readers have recommended *Wooleen Station* (☎ 9963 7973), a cattle station 190km north of Mullewa. Rooms in the heritage-listed homestead cost $100, all meals included (minimum two-night stay). It's open from April to December. Also recommended – especially for its evening 'happy hour' – is *Indee Station* (☎ 9176 4968), some 49km south-west of Port Hedland.

Mt Florance Station (☎ 9189 8151) is halfway between the Millstream-Chichester and Karijini National Parks. In the Kennedy Range is *Mt Sandiman Station* (☎ 9943 0550) – see under Kennedy Range in the Central West Coast chapter for more information. *Erong Springs* (☎ 9981 2910) is 170km south of Mt Augustus and has camp sites and self-contained bungalows ($30/60).

Many stations also take 4WD tours to Aboriginal art sites, swimming spots, wildflower fields and other destinations. References to station stays are scattered throughout the text.

Cape Range National Park

The 510-sq-km park, which runs down the west coast of the cape, includes the modern Milyering visitor centre, a wide variety of rare flora and fauna, 50km of good swimming beaches, gorges (including scenic Yardie Creek) and rugged scenery. Entry to the main section of the park on the cape's west side costs $8 per car. When snorkelling and swimming here, beware of strong currents during outgoing tides.

Things to See & Do Unsealed roads off the Minilya-Exmouth Rd into the impressive Shothole and Charles Knife Canyons are, respectively, 16km and 23km south of Exmouth. The Charles Knife Rd actually follows the ridges of the canyon itself.

Weathering at the **Shothole Canyon** has, unusually for north-west WA, not occurred from permanent water but through periodic downpours and wind. The wind is a feature of the climate – it blows constantly, usually from west to east.

The view from the Thomas Carter lookout above **Charles Knife Canyon** is memorable. In front are the eroded limestone walls of the gorge and far beyond, the azure waters of Exmouth Gulf.

The Milyering visitor centre (☎ 9949 2808) is 52km from Exmouth on the west coast. A comprehensive display of the area's natural and cultural history can be seen here. It opens from 10 am to 4 pm year-round.

The gorge through which the saltwater **Yardie Creek** runs is 38km to the south of Milyering on a road that was expected to be sealed by the end of 2000. Here, the deepblue waters of the gorge are held back by a sand bar. You can easily see the black-footed wallaby on the multicoloured canyon walls. The 1.5km walk from the car park to the top of the gorge is recommended. CALM provides a *Visitor and Walk Trail Guide*.

Yardie Creek Tours (☎ 9949 2659) takes daily 75-minute boat trips into the gorge ($20/10 adults/children). South of Yardie Creek, 4WD vehicles can (with extreme caution) follow the coast south to Coral Bay. The road is signposted and there is a turn-off to the picturesque Point Cloates lighthouse.

Places to Stay Basic tent and some caravan sites are available in the park. Make sure you bring plenty of water; there are no supplies in the park. Just outside the park, around 34km from Exmouth, *Yardie Creek Homestead (☎ 9949 1389)* has a shop, a restaurant in peak season and camp sites for $16 per double. On-site vans start at $40/35 peak/off-peak and chalets at $75/70.

On the beach opposite the trail to Mandu Mandu Gorge is the serene *Ningaloo Reef Retreat (☎ 9949 1776)*. Aiming for minimum impact, accommodation is in swags under the stars. Food is served at pleasant shaded tables on decking beside a large tent. A package including meals, transport and guided snorkelling costs $90. Other packages are available. One reader says her stay here was the next best thing about her holiday 'right after meeting the man of my dreams'.

MINILYA TO KARRATHA

From Minilya it's about 110km north to the sealed road that heads west to Giralia Station – a good alternative route to the North West Cape. Watch for road signs about 50km north of Minilya where the Tropic of Capricorn crosses the highway. *Nanutarra Roadhouse (☎ 9943 0521)*, on the Ashburton River, is open 24 hours.

Just north of Nanutarra Roadhouse a road runs east to the mining towns of the Pilbara (Tom Price and Paraburdoo) and Karijini National Park. This road is sealed all the way to the Great Northern Hwy. About 40km north of the Karijini/Tom Price turn-off on the North West Coastal Hwy is the turn-off towards the coast to Onslow.

Continuing north along the highway, some 78km from the Onslow junction, is another easterly road to mining town Pannawonica (47km). About 43km beyond this is the *Fortescue River Roadhouse (☎ 9184 5126)*. It's around 100km farther on to Karratha (see under The Pilbara later in this chapter).

ONSLOW

pop 800

The original Onslow, near the mouth of the Ashburton River, came into being in 1883. It was the centre for pearling, mining and

Standing on Ground Zero

The Montebello Islands are a group of more than 100 flat limestone islands off the north-west coast of Western Australia (WA) between Onslow and Karratha. They range in size from Hermite, the largest at 1000 hectares, to small islets and rocks of less than one hectare. In 1992 they were gazetted as a conservation park administered by the Department of Conservation & Land Management (CALM).

In 1952 the British, in an operation codenamed Hurricane, detonated an atomic weapon mounted on HMS *Plym* anchored in Main Bay off Trimouille Island. In another display of ownership, the British named the islands: the bays, after wine varieties; the hills, after animals; and the points, after British prime ministers. They carried out two further atomic tests in 1956, on Alpha and Trimouille Islands.

Some 50 years later, we can step ashore on either of these islands and stand on 'ground zero' – the point of detonation of an atomic weapon. A few bits of old metal remain, as do the radiation warning signs. (CALM advises against touching the relics or digging in the ground.) You have to use your imagination to conceptualise the destruction caused by the blast, as nature has covered it over. The islands have thriving populations of both land and marine fauna and more than 100 plant species, including a stand of mangroves that is the most distant from the mainland in WA.

pastoral industries. Originally part of the Thalanyji people's lands, Old Onslow was abandoned in 1925 and relocated to Beadon Bay. The 'new' town, 81km from the North West Coastal Hwy, has the distinction of being the southernmost WA town to be bombed in WWII (in 1943). It was used by the British in the 1950s for nuclear testing in the Montebello Islands (see the boxed text).

Onslow is often hit by cyclones; one flattened the town in 1963. Today, it is the mainland base for offshore oil and gas exploration and production. The industrial-grade harvest of its newest industry, the Solar Salt project, goes overseas. Visit Onslow in winter for the superb fishing here then.

The helpful and friendly Onslow tourist office (☎ 9184 6644) is in the museum on Second Ave. The *Old Onslow Heritage Trail* ($1.50) is an informative guide.

Things to See & Do

The Onslow Goods Shed **museum**, on Second Ave, displays items of historical interest. There is good **swimming** and **fishing** in the area; anglers head for the Beadon Creek Groyne and Four Mile Creek or out to sea.

Old Onslow ruins, 48km west of town, include a gaol and a cemetery. Ashburton Air Services (☎ 9184 6037) takes **scenic flights**; prices start at $45 for 25 minutes, with a minimum of three people.

Places to Stay & Eat

Recommended as clean and comfortable, *Onslow Mackerel Motel* (☎ 9184 6444) is on the corner of Second Ave and Third St. Singles/doubles cost $85/100. *Onslow Sun Chalets* (☎ 9184 6058), on Second Ave, has rooms for $75/85.

The *Oceanview Caravan Park* (☎ 9184 6053), also on Second Ave, has tent/powered sites for $13/16 and park cabins starting at $50 for two people. The *Beadon Bay Village* (☎ 9184 6007), on Beadon Creek Rd, has tent/powered sites for $10/15.

Onslow has a *supermarket* incorporating a bakery and a liquor shop. Decent light meals are available at *Harry and Kay's Fish and Chips* and the *Main Street Cafe*. The *Beadon Bay Hotel*, on Second Ave, does counter meals. The town's only upmarket option is *Nikki's Restaurant*, on First Ave by the beach.

Getting There & Away

You really need your own transport to get in and out of Onslow. Greyhound Pioneer buses will drop you at the junction of Onslow Rd and the North West Coastal Hwy, but the daily northbound service passes at 3.25 am, so the driver won't leave you there unless you've organised a lift into town. Onslow Taxi (☎ 9184 6298) takes bookings. The one-way trip costs $28 per person.

DIRECTION & THEVENARD ISLANDS

Offshore, 11km and 22km respectively from Onslow, are Direction and Thevenard Islands, part of the Mackerel Islands group. There's accommodation available in *cabins* (☎ 9184 6444) on Thevenard Island, a 6km by 1.5km coral atoll. A group of two to three people gets all food, return transport to the island and a dinghy with an outboard motor for $825 per person for a week. You have to take your own linen.

Direction Island has only a single *cabin* (☎ 9388 2020) capable of sleeping eight people, which can be booked from March to November. Linen and food is not provided. This island has its own reef on one side and a beach on the other.

The Pilbara

Producing iron ore and natural gas, WA's Pilbara (meaning 'freshwater fish') region accounts for much of the state's prosperity. Gigantic machines tear the dusty red ranges apart and ridiculously long trains carry their yield hundreds of kilometres to coastal ports from where it's shipped overseas.

Neat company towns appear like mirages on the edge of enormous tracts of harsh, hot country. But this region has more to offer than the spectacles associated with its industry: the beautiful islands of the Dampier Archipelago, the gorges of Karijini National Park and historic towns such as Marble Bar and Cossack.

If travelling away from main highways in this area in your own vehicle, always carry a lot of extra water – 20L per person is a sensible amount – and check that you have enough fuel to get to the next petrol station. If travelling into remote areas, tell someone (the police, for ex-ample) your plans. Don't leave your vehicle if you are stranded.

KARRATHA
pop 10,800

Karratha ('good country'), the commercial centre for the coastal Pilbara, is on Nickol Bay and some 1535km from Perth. Hopes for renewed growth of the town are up with talk of new major projects starting in the area soon. The existing industry giants Hamersley Iron and Woodside LNG have been responsible for the town's prosperity until recent years.

Summer temperatures in Karratha reach beyond 40°C – winter is the best time to visit.

Information

The Karratha tourist office (☎ 9144 4600) is on Karratha Rd just before the T-junction of Dampier and Millstream Rds. When we last visited, management and staff here were not as friendly as in other north-west WA tourist offices, and were lacking the free tourist map available in other towns. The local CALM office (☎ 9143 1488) is more helpful and is out of town in the light-industrial area on Mardie Rd.

Karratha is something of a shopping-mall theme park, with three separate squat brick centres housing supermarkets and pretty much every other sort of shop, set amid seas of parking. Nearby are numerous takeaway food shops. Internet access is available at Adrienne's cafe in the Karratha City shopping centre. Banks line Port Hedland Place. A laundrette is in the Millars Well shopping centre. Karratha Cycle Hire is based at Karratha Backpackers (☎ 9144 4904), at 110 Wellard Way. Hiring a bike for a day costs $12.

Things to See & Do

There are good views from the lookout at **TV Hill**. The **Jaburrara Heritage Trail** near town is replete with evidence of Aboriginal occupation: carvings, grindstones, etchings and middens are all located on the 3.5km trail that starts near the tourist office. Jaburrara (pronounced 'yabura') is the name of the former Aboriginal inhabitants of the Karratha region. Tackle this walk in the early morning or in the evening. It will be more rewarding if you take *Jaburrara Heritage Trail* ($1.50 from the tourist office) with you.

Aboriginal carvings along the ridge were created with chert and dolerite tools and are estimated to be 5000 to 6000 years old. Flat rocks adjacent to one of the creeks on the trail were used for grinding

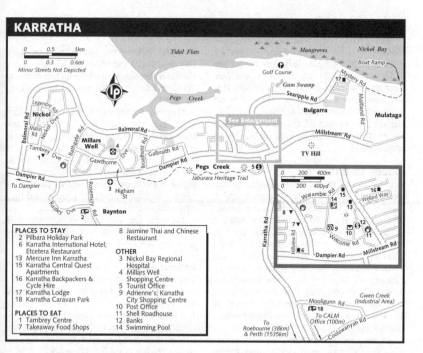

KARRATHA

PLACES TO STAY
2 Pilbara Holiday Park
6 Karratha International Hotel;
  Etcetera Restaurant
13 Mercure Inn Karratha
15 Karratha Central Quest
   Apartments
16 Karratha Backpackers &
   Cycle Hire
17 Karratha Lodge
18 Karratha Caravan Park

PLACES TO EAT
1 Tambrey Centre
7 Takeaway Food Shops

8 Jasmine Thai and Chinese
  Restaurant

OTHER
3 Nickol Bay Regional
  Hospital
4 Millars Well
  Shopping Centre
5 Tourist Office
9 Adrienne's; Karratha
  City Shopping Centre
10 Post Office
11 Shell Roadhouse
12 Banks
14 Swimming Pool

spinifex and other seeds. The *talu* sites, or spiritual repositories, are predominantly represented by physical features. The major talu here is the large dolerite outcrop Warramurrangka, the 'giant flying fox'.

Karratha is a good launching place for trips to the Millstream-Chichester and Karijini National Parks. Snappy Gum Safaris (☎ 9185 1278) has day trips to Millstream-Chichester National Park ($75/25 adults/children under 12). It can do Dampier and Roebourne pickups. It also takes two-/three-day Karijini tours for $235/320, which includes all food, sleeping swags, transport and park fees. The three-day trip is ideal for 'young people wanting a bit of excitement'; the two-day trip is more leisurely.

Places to Stay

Karratha's caravan parks – perched on the edge of town – aren't in the most scenic of locations but they seem to do the job. The owners say that the ***Pilbara Holiday Park*** (☎ 9185 1855), on Rosemary Rd, has been revamped in recent years. Tent/powered sites cost $14/18, on-site vans $39 and new-looking motel-style units $65.

Karratha Caravan Park (☎ 9185 1012), on Mooligunn Rd out of town in the light-industrial area, has powered sites for $18 and on-site vans for $40 for two people.

Karratha Backpackers (☎ 9144 4904, 110 Wellard Way) has been highly recommended by numerous travellers for its friendly, helpful host. Clean rooms and the use of the well-equipped facilities cost $15/30/40 for dorms/singles/doubles.

Shop around for cheap deals on Karratha hotels and motels – they often run special offers to attract residents of outlying company towns. The general standard of these places is high, although regular prices are expensive. The gleaming ***Karratha Central Quest Apartments*** (☎ 9143 9888), on the corner of Warambie and Searipple Rds, has

CORAL COAST & THE PILBARA

doubles starting at $120 (dropping to $79 on weekends). The **Karratha International Hotel** (☎ *9185 3111*), on the corner of Hillview and Dampier Rds, has rooms for $152 (weekends $125). The **Mercure Inn Karratha** (☎ *9185 1155*), on Searipple Rd, has comfortable rooms for $114 ($90 on weekends). A self-contained budget option, although a bit out of town, is **Karratha Lodge** (☎ *9144 4600*), on Walcott Way, with units for $55.

Places to Eat

The Karratha International Hotel has the nicely outfitted **Etcetera** restaurant and a poolside **cafe**. Its **Gecko's** saloon bar is one-time winner of a national award for best bar presentation and service. The **Mercure Inn Karratha** has a sparkling new bistro with good food (an enormous pasta dish costs $15). For family lunches, try the **Tambrey Centre**, off Tambrey Dr a few kilometres west of the town centre. Kids can play in the pool and get an icy pole and drink with their $6.50 meal; adults have access to a bar and counter meals.

Adrienne's, in the Karratha City shopping centre, has good coffee and fresh-squeezed juices. **Takeaway food shops** are scattered along Balmoral Rd. Also on this stretch is **Jasmine Thai and Chinese Restaurant**, where a horribly salty chicken curry cost us $13.80.

Getting There & Away

Qantas Airways/Airlink and Ansett Australia have direct daily jet services from Perth. Broome-based Northwest Regional Airlines (☎ 1300-136 629) flies a stopping-all-stations 'milk run' from Broome through Port Hedland, Karratha, Exmouth and back every day except Saturday.

Greyhound Pioneer (☎ 13 2030) has daily bus services ($146) from Perth; it uses the Shell roadhouse on Welcome Rd as its depot. Karratha Backpackers (☎ 9144 4904) has a free bus pickup and drop-off for booked guests.

Unless you just want to hang out in shopping malls, however, you're better off having a car in Karratha.

DAMPIER
pop 1600

Dampier, 20km from Karratha, is on King Bay and faces the other 42 islands of the Dampier Archipelago (named after explorer William Dampier, who passed by this area in 1699).

Dampier started out as a Hamersley Iron town and the port for Tom Price and Paraburdoo iron-ore operations. Gas from the extensive natural-gas fields of the North-West Shelf is piped ashore nearby on the Burrup Peninsula. From there, it gets piped to Perth or is liquefied as part of the huge Woodside Petroleum project and then exported to Japan and South Korea.

Dampier has mild, sunny winters with temperatures pushing 30°C, but in summer it is very hot.

Information

The office of the Dampier Community Association (☎ 9183 1243) is located just outside the shopping centre. Permits to drive along Hamersley Iron's service road to Millstream-Chichester National Park and Tom Price are available at the Hamersley Iron visitor centre, on Parker Point Rd, Dampier.

Things to See & Do

An inspection of the **port facilities** can be arranged (☎ 9144 4600); the cost is $5/3 adults/children. Admission to the **North-West Shelf Gas Project visitor centre** is free (☎ 9158 8292). It's open from 10 am to 4 pm weekdays from April to October.

The southern hemisphere's largest evaporative salt field can be viewed during a half-day tour of **Dampier Salt**. Tours depart the Karratha tourist office Tuesday and Thursday ($16/8).

In Dampier township, the **William Dampier Lookout** has a view over the harbour. Nearby **Hearson's Cove** is a popular beach and picnic area, as is **Dampier Beach**.

The **Burrup Peninsula** has some 10,000 Aboriginal rock engravings depicting creatures including fish, turtles, euros and wallabies. It is one of the most prolific sites for prehistoric rock art in the world. Karratha CALM (☎ 9143 1488) can tell you where the most easily accessible petroglyph sites can be found.

Dampier Archipelago This archipelago of 42 islands was formed some 6000 to 8000 years ago when rising sea levels flooded coastal valleys. The islands are within a 45km radius of Dampier; it is five minutes by boat to the nearest island and about two hours to the most distant.

The islands have seen the coming and going of pastoralism and whaling, along with development of pearling. For about three years in the late 1800s there was a whaling station on Malus Island, which processed humpback whales harpooned from longboats. The pots used to boil down the blubber are still on the island and are now heritage-listed.

The Dampier Archipelago is renowned as a game-fishing mecca and it hosts the Dampier Classic each year. Access to all of the islands in the archipelago is by boat from the ramps at Dampier, Point Samson, Wickham and Nickol Bay (Karratha).

There are numerous companies that offer a range of tours around the Dampier Archipelago. These include Deck'em Charters (☎ 9185 2691), which offers day-long snorkelling, fishing and other cruises for a cost of $120 per person.

The 12m catamaran the *Norcat* (☎ 9144 4250), takes day cruises for $88 and twilight cruises for $66.

Places to Stay & Eat
The *Dampier Transit Park* (☎ 9183 1109) has a three-night limit and camp sites costing from $9 to $16. The *Peninsula Palms Resort* (☎ 9183 1888), on The Esplanade, has motel units for $90 and self-contained family units for $132. The concrete-clad *Mercure Inn* (☎ 9183 1222), also on The Esplanade, has some rooms with water views. Motel units start at $100.

Barnacle Bob's, also on the Esplanade and with a balcony overlooking Hampton Harbour, is licensed and serves seafood. The shopping centre includes a *Chinese restaurant* and both of the town's motels have *restaurants*.

ROEBOURNE AREA
Roebourne, some 38km from Karratha, is the gateway to the historic buildings and picturesque beaches of the Point Samson Peninsula. Cape Lambert, on the peninsula's northern tip, is the port for the iron ore mined at Pannawonica.

Point Samson is a great fishing spot with some fine accommodation, and Cossack is a town steeped in history. This area holds the origins of European settlement of the north-west.

Aboriginal History
Aborigines have occupied the area around Roebourne for at least 20,000 years, according to radiocarbon dating of recovered artefacts. The Ngarluma people inhabited the flood country from the Maitland River to Peawah River, which covers about 6400 sq km. There were three divisions of this grouping: two of these were west and east of the Harding River and the other occupied the Burrup Peninsula and were known as the Jaburrara.

Numerous shell middens remain, including a number found just on the outskirts of Karratha. The Ngarluma people constructed spinifex fishing nets and etched symbolic motifs into thousands of rocks. The first settlers employed Aborigines as labourers and shepherds and paid them with goods. Introduced diseases, such as smallpox and measles, soon took their toll on the indigenous population.

There were a number of massacres and in one clash in 1868, known as the 'Flying Foam massacre', between 40 and 60 of the Aborigines were killed in retaliation for the spearing of four settlers. The Aborigines who remained were forced into working on pastoral leases, and others were forced to dive for pearl shells.

In the 1930s several neighbouring Aboriginal tribes, including the Yindjibarndi, Banjima and Martuthunira, were moved into reserves in Roebourne and Onslow. The main groups today in the Roebourne area are Yindjibarndi and Ngarluma. The Jaburrara are gone but their curious etchings survive.

CORAL COAST & THE PILBARA

Information

The friendly Roebourne District tourist office (☎ 9182 1060) is in the Old Gaol, on Queen St in Roebourne. If you're staying in the area for a night or more, Point Samson has the best range of accommodation, while Wickham has a good supermarket. This area gets very hot in summer. Its tourist season runs from late April to about October.

The *Emma Withnell Heritage Trail* brochure ($1.50) outlines a 52km walk/drive through Cossack, Roebourne, Wickham and Point Samson.

Roebourne

pop 1700

Once the capital of the state's north-west, Roebourne is the oldest existing town in the Pilbara. It has a history of grazing and gold and copper mining.

Fine historic buildings still stand. These include an **old gaol** (which now houses a free museum), the 1888 **Union Bank**, a **church** built in 1894 and the **Victoria Hotel**, the last of the five original pubs. The town was once connected to Cossack, 13km away on the coast, by a horse-drawn tram.

Roebourne's *Harding River Caravan Park* (☎ 9182 1063) has tent/powered sites costing $12/15 for two people. The BP roadhouse has takeaways and supplies.

Cossack

About 13km from Roebourne, Cossack is a fascinating historic hamlet with many intact early buildings. It was a bustling town and the main port for the district in the mid- to late 19th century. But its boom was short-lived and Point Samson soon supplanted it as the chief port for the area. The sturdy old buildings date from 1870 to 1898.

The town now includes an **art gallery** in the post office (1885), a **museum** in the 1895 stone-brick courthouse, and budget accommodation in the police barracks (1897). Other buildings include Galbraith's store (1891), a custom house/bond store (1896), and the schoolhouse (1897). Several sites where only stone floors now remain are believed to once have housed many of the many Chinese and Japanese people attracted to the area by gold,

pearls and the pastoral industry. Cossack's Chinatown, believed to have stretched from Mrs Pead's Boarding House (now just a wall, a stone floor and a stone path) along Perseverance St to the cemetery, once included two Chinese stores, a Japanese store, a Turkish bathhouse and several Japanese brothels.

Beyond town, the **pioneer cemetery** has a small Japanese section dating from the pearl-diving days. Cossack is in fact where pearling began in WA; it later moved to Broome in the 1890s. The brochure *Cossack Historic Walk* ($0.50) is helpful; all proceeds go towards restoration of the town.

The **Staircase to the Moon** (moonlight reflected on the tidal flats), viewed from Reader's Head Lookout, is legendary. It shines across an average of 50km of marsh and lasts for ages. You'll be fascinated to know that all seven of the species of mangrove found in the Pilbara grow near the Cossack boat ramp.

Places to Stay In the town's atmospheric old police barracks, *Cossack Backpackers* (☎ 9182 1190) recently got new mattresses. Dorm beds/family rooms cost $15/35. There's no shop and nowhere to eat in Cossack except a kiosk in the Customs House, so bring your own food. The Cossack's managers will pick you up from the bus depot in Roebourne.

Point Samson

pop 400

Point Samson, some 19km from Roebourne, took the place of Cossack when the old port silted up. In turn, it has since been replaced by the modern port facilities of Dampier and Cape Lambert, although it still has a big fishing fleet.

There are good beaches at Point Samson and at nearby **Honeymoon Cove**. You're best off timing your swim for high tide, though. At low tide, you can explore **Samson Reef** for coral and oysters. The area is also renowned for its excellent **fishing**, including at Sam's Creek and John's Creek. Point Samson Lodge (☎ 9187 1052) acts as an informal source of tourist information. It's also the base for a boat hire and charter company

(☎ 9187 1052) that organises extended **guided fishing trips** and rents out vessels (a 6.4m aluminium boat costs $210 a day).

Places to Stay & Eat The excellent *Point Samson Lodge Resort* (☎ *9187 1052, 56 Samson Rd*) could teach some of its big-name counterparts in other parts of WA a few things about considerate service and comfortable rooms. Spotless doubles start at $115 ($20/10 for extra adults/children). *Delilah's B&B* (☎ *9187 1471*), overlooking the harbour, has $85 doubles. The self-contained *Amani Cottage* (☎ *9187 0052, 1 McLeod St*) has singles/doubles for $70/80. Point Samson is flourishing as a holiday destination, so new B&Bs are sprouting up all the time – ask at the Roebourne tourist office.

The beachside *Solveig Caravan Park* (☎ *9187 1414*), on Samson Rd, has tent/powered caravan sites for $10/15 for two people, but is frequently booked out. At the time of writing, a new caravan park was touted for the town; again, check at the Roebourne tourist office.

Go the deep-fried option at the lively *Trawlers Tavern*, on Samson Rd – its $19 seafood salad was disappointing, but not so the $4.50 basket of chips. Its balcony is a great place for a beer. Downstairs, takeaway-oriented *Moby's Kitchen* offers well-priced fish and chips and children's meals.

COMPANY TOWNS

The Pilbara is the home of the 'company town'; most towns here only exist because big companies needed dormitories for their workers and administrative bases for their mining projects. They are designed much like nondescript new suburbs of cities in eastern states: vast shopping malls, wide main thoroughfares lined with takeaway food shops, and brick houses in curving dead-end streets.

Dampier, Karratha, Newman, Paraburdoo, Pannawonica and Tom Price all owe their existence to big mining companies. By the same token, the fortunes of some are waning as employees are laid off and 'fly-in, fly-out' (bringing workers by plane from

Perth for their shifts, rather than housing them in the town) increases.

Tom Price
pop 3400

This iron-ore town, south-west of Wittenoom, is the 'big daddy' of the Pilbara's company towns. Once owned by Hamersley Iron, it's now an 'open town' overseen by the Ashburton Shire. Built in 1962, it is named after mining expert Thomas Moore Price of the giant US Kaiser Steel Corporation. The iron ore mined here is taken to the coast at Dampier by rail. Tom Price is WA's highest town, with an elevation of 747m above sea level. Its tourist season runs from late April to early October.

The Tom Price tourist office (☎ 9188 1112) is on Central Rd. It takes bookings for daily (in peak season) tours to the huge open-cut mine works ($12/6 adults/children). It can advise on where to get a permit for Hamersley Iron's private road to Millstream-Chichester National Park.

Mt Nameless (1128m), 4km west of Tom Price, is one of the highest accessible mountains in the state. It offers good views of the area, especially at sunset.

Tom Price's main attraction is its proximity to Karijini National Park. Three companies offer outings from here to the park during tourist season. Lestok Tours (☎ 9189 2032) takes full-day trips for $85. Design A Tour (☎ 9188 1670) day trips cost $90. Both include lunch. Red Rock Abseiling Adventures (☎ 9189 2206) does half-/full-day abseiling and gorge walks for $95/150.

Places to Stay & Eat *Tom Price Tourist Park* (☎ *9189 1515*) has tent/powered sites for $14/18 for two people, and cabins starting at $75. *Karijini Lodge Motel* (☎ *9189 1110*), on Stadium Rd, has rooms starting at $119 and a *buffet restaurant*. The *Mercure Inn Tom Price* (☎ *9189 1101*) has rooms for $105, as well as a bistro.

For other sorts of food, head to the shopping mall, which has several *cafes* and *takeaways*. Self-caterers can buy ingredients from the *Coles supermarket* in Central Rd.

MILLSTREAM-CHICHESTER NATIONAL PARK

The impressive 2000-sq-km Millstream-Chichester National Park lies 150km south of Roebourne. It is reached by gravel road from the North West Coastal Hwy; the signposted turn-off is 27km past Roebourne. (Access is also possible along Hamersley Iron's private road, but you need a permit – see the Dampier section and the Tom Price entry under Company Towns earlier in this chapter for more information.) One of the features of this area is **Pyramid Hill**, a volcanic remnant comprised of reddish breccia and tuff, some 1800 million years old.

Millstream-Chichester National Park contains a number of freshwater pools formed by a spring from the underflow of the Fortescue River. **Python Pool**, different from the rest of Millstream, is a deep water hole at the base of a cliff. It was once an oasis for Afghani camel drivers and still makes a good place for a swim.

The road that heads over the Chichester Range is sealed for a good deal of the climb and descent. At the top of the range is **Mt Herbert** (366m), a good lookout and starting point for the **Chichester Range Camel Trail**, an 8km, two-hour walk through a rugged part of the range and via McKenzie Spring down to Python Pool. From the lookout you can see clay tablelands, basalt ranges and a cloak of pincushion spinifex.

The main part of the park is centred around Millstream Homestead and access is via a 30km loop road 11.5km off the Wittenoom-Roebourne Rd. The old homestead has been converted into an visitor centre with a wealth of detail on the Millstream ecosystems and lifestyle of the Yindjibarndi people.

The **Chinderwarriner Pool**, near the visitor centre, is another pleasant oasis with pools, palms (including the unique Millstream palm) and lilies; it is well worth a visit.

Places to Stay & Eat

There are basic *camp sites* (☎ *9184 5144)* at Snake Creek (near Python Pool), Crossing Pool and Deep Reach Pool; tent sites cost $10 for two people and $5.50 for each extra adult. Stock up on food in Karratha before tackling the Pilbara interior. Park entry fees ($9 per car) apply.

KARIJINI NATIONAL PARK

This national park, second-largest in the state after Rudall River, contains rugged scenery with few equals in Australia. It is about five hours from Roebourne and 3½ hours from Port Hedland.

The traditional owners of the region are the Banjima, Yinhawangka and Kurrama Aboriginal people. The name of the park recognises the significance of these people, who are known to have lived here for at least 20,000 years.

The park is rich with animals, birds and flowering plants. In the cooler months, look for yellow-flowering sennas (cassias) and acacias, mulla mulla and bluebells.

A visitor centre (☎ 9189 8121) is on Banjima Dr in the north-east corner of the park.

The Gorges

The gorges of Karijini National Park are spectacular both in their sheer, rocky faces and their varied colours.

A sealed road runs between the Great Northern Hwy and the visitor centre. This road leaves the highway about 35km south of the Auski Tourist Village and 155km north of Newman. In recent years, it was sealed all the way to Tom Price, linking the coastal and inland highways for 2WD vehicles (provided it's not too wet).

After 30km, turn north onto Banjima Dr and follow the sealed road to the visitor centre. You will come to a self-registration station where you pay entry fees ($9 per car, which includes a copy of *Karijini: Visitor Information/Walk Trail Guide*).

Dales Gorge is a good place to start your exploration of the many gorges. The 10km road into Dales Gorge starts just south of the visitor centre; there is a freshwater tank close to the turn-off for those needing to replenish supplies. At the end of this road you can get to **Circular Pool** and a lookout, and by a track to the bottom of **Fortescue Falls**. The walk from Circular Pool along Dales Gorge to the falls is recommended; you will be surprised how much permanent water is in the gorge.

KARIJINI NATIONAL PARK

To Port Hedland (230km)

CHICHESTER RANGE

Fortescue River

Great Northern Hwy

To Newman (145km)

Millstream Gorge

Auski Tourist Village

Mt George (832m)

34

18

Circular Pool

Dales Gorge

Fortescue Falls

30

Karijini Dve

Mt Windell (1107m)

Nanutarra-Munjina Rd

Yampire Gorge

Fig Tree Soak

Visitor Centre

10

To Great Northern Highway (36km)

24

(4WD only)

Kalamina Gorge

Banjima Dve

8

2

Juna Downs Rd

Local Traffic Only

24

Wittenoom

Kalamina Falls

6

19

Banjima Dve

Joffre Creek Gorge

Joffre

Wittenoom Roebourne Rd

Joffre Gorge

3

Red Gorge

Knox Gorge

10

Weano Gorge

Joffre Falls

3

Oxers Lookout

12

Bee Gorge

38

Mt Vigors (1161m)

Mt Oxer (1192m)

Karijini Dve

Mt Howieson (1113m)

Nanutarra-Munjina Rd

Hancock Gorge

Joffre Gorge

Range Gorge

Joffre Creek Gorge

26

Banjima Dve

To North West Coastal Highway (250km)

43

Mt King (1031m)

KARIJINI NATIONAL PARK

Mt Bruce (1235m)

Marandoo

Rio Tinto Gorge

Hamersley Gorge

Fortescue River South Branch

Hamersley Mount Bruce Rd

30

Marandoo Rd

22

To Tom Price (53km)

To Price (53km)

Tom Price

10km
5
0

6mi
3
0

★ 10 Distance in kilometres

Unsealed roads can vary
from excellent to impassable,
depending on many factors

Next, head west on Banjima Dr. Turn right 19km past the visitor centre for **Kalamina Gorge** (6km), with easy access to the bottom of the gorge. If you head left instead of right, 10km along Banjima Dr is the turn-off to the often dry but nonetheless spectacular **Joffre Falls**. If you drive 6km farther east, you'll come to **Knox Gorge**.

Three kilometres west of the Joffre Gorge turn-off on Banjima Dr is a T-junction. Head north at this junction for the remarkable **Oxers Lookout** (14km), at the point where **Red**, **Weano**, **Joffre** and **Hancock Gorges** all meet. This is repeatedly recommended as one of the Outback's greatest sights. If you wish to get down into the gorge proper, take the steps down to Handrail Pool (turn right at the bottom) in Weano Gorge.

Back at the T-junction of the Joffre Falls road and Banjima Dr you can head south to Tom Price. Follow Banjima Dr for 26km until it meets Karijini Dr. Turn right and continue for 2km and then head south for another 5km until you meet Marandoo Rd. Turn right on Marandoo Rd and after 35km it joins the Paraburdoo to Tom Price road; it is another 10km north-west to Tom Price. You'll pass **Mt Bruce** (1235m), the state's second-highest peak, on this route. (The state's highest mountain is **Mt Meharry** (1251m), near the south-east border of Karijini National Park.)

About 20km north-west of Tom Price you can take a side trip on the Nanutarra-Munjina road. Travel 61km north-east along this road to reach the turn-off to **Hamersley Gorge**, 5km from the main road. Evidence of the force of nature, reflected in the folded ribbons of rock, adds to the awe-inspiring landscape. Not far north is the **Rio Tinto Gorge**.

Although **Wittenoom**, north of the park, is now virtually a ghost town, a few of the inhabitants still cling tenaciously to their beleaguered homes. It's likely that there will be nothing there when you visit, as the WA state government is doing everything it can to close it down. Wittenoom has been removed from all official maps.

Wittenoom had an earlier history as a blue-asbestos mining town, but mining finally

Deadly Dust

Even though the asbestos mine closed in 1966, the Western Australia government warns there is a health risk in Wittenoom, and in Wittenoom and Yampire Gorges, from air-borne asbestos fibres. Avoid disturbing any asbestos tailings in the area and keep your car windows closed. If you are concerned, seek medical advice before going to these areas.

halted in 1966. A number of miners and baggers who once worked at the Wittenoom Gorge mine have subsequently 'died of the dust' (ie, died of mesothelioma, a debilitating lung condition).

The now infamous **Wittenoom Gorge** is immediately south of the former town. A road runs the 13km through this gorge, passing old asbestos mines and a number of smaller gorges and pretty pools.

Down the road around 24km east from Wittenoom there's a turn-off to the **Yampire Gorge**, where blue veins of asbestos can be seen in the rock. **Fig Tree Soak**, in the gorge, was used as a watering point by Afghani camel-drivers. The road (accessible by 4WD only) may be closed in future because of the asbestos risk.

Organised Tours
See the Karratha section and the Tom Price entry under Company Towns earlier in this chapter for park tours.

A great way to see the gorges of the Karijini National Park is by helicopter. One trip ($135, 30 minutes) departs from the Auski Tourist Village (☎ 9176 6979).

Places to Stay & Eat
There are several basic *camp sites* within the park, including at Dales Gorge, Weano Gorge and on Banjima Dr at the Joffre turn-off; contact the rangers (☎ 9189 8157) for information.

Almost 40 years after Wittenoom's infamous asbestos mine shut down, a hardy core of locals are still battling to keep the town open, arguing the air here contains no more asbestos dust than Perth air. The state government has bought and shut down the caravan park, but other accommodation is still available.

Wittenoom Holiday Homes (☎ 9189 7096), on Fifth Ave, has cottages for $72 per double. Dorm beds at the *Wittenoom Guesthouse (☎ 9189 7060)*, within an old convent, cost $10; single/twin rooms cost $20/35. The *Wittenoom Bungarra Bivouac Hostel (☎ 9189 7026, 71 Fifth Ave)* has cheap beds and is the base for Dave's Gorge Tours. However, Dave apparently only comes back to town to open these businesses during the busiest time of the year (in winter, and often as late as July).

Nomad Heights (☎ 9189 7068) is a small arid/tropical permaculture farm. You should book ahead and bring your own food. You can arrange to swap work on the farm for a bed, otherwise it's $8 a night.

Auski Tourist Village (☎ 9176 6988) is on the Great Northern Hwy some 42km east of Wittenoom, 260km south of Port Hedland and 200km north of Newman. Really no more than an oversized roadhouse, it has a range of accommodation and meals.

Mt Florance Station (☎ 9189 8151), halfway between Millstream-Chichester and Karijini National Parks, has beds in shearers quarters starting at $12, and camp sites for $5 per person.

NEWMAN
pop 2500
Newman is 414km north of Meekatharra and 450km south of Port Hedland on the Great Northern Hwy. It's like a little piece of Australian capital-city suburbia transplanted to the middle of the Outback. It was established in the 1970s to support Broken Hill Proprietary (BHP) Company's Mt Whaleback mine – the biggest iron-ore mine in the world. However, its fortunes are already in decline: In 1999, 275 workers accepted voluntary redundancies, emptying the town of hundreds more when they packed up their families and left.

Built of rammed earth, the helpful Newman tourist office (☎ 9175 2888) is at the corner of Fortescue Ave and Newman Dr. A **museum and art gallery** is housed here.

Guided tours (☎ 9175 2888) to watch massive machines digging at the walls of Mt Whaleback's 1.5km-by-5km hole are worth the $7 entry cost. The scales of the machines, the hole, and the trains used to get the ore to Port Hedland (426km away) are impressive.

The information-packed tours take about 1½ hours and leave the tourist office at 8.30 am daily except Sunday all year round, and at 1 pm from May to October.

The **scenic drive** north of Newman on the Great Northern Hwy is spectacular. The orange rocks lifted up against the subtle purples, yellows and greens of the Pilbara landscape are awe-inspiring. Wildflowers are seen along the road from August to October.

Places to Stay & Eat
Newman's caravan parks are as neat as the town itself. *Newman Caravan Park (☎ 9175 1428)*, on Kalgan Dr, has tent/powered sites for $12/16 for two people and backpacker cabins for $25 (with TV and access to cooking facilities). Cabins cost $65. The vast, friendly *Dearlove's Caravan Park (☎ 9175 2802)*, on Cowra Dr, has tent/powered sites for $14/17, motel-style cabins for $40/50 singles/doubles and single-room backpacker cabins with TV and air-con for $25. It also has a campers kitchen and barbecues.

The *Mercure Inn Newman (☎ 9175 1101)*, on Newman Dr, has double rooms starting at $110 – with a $6 discount if you've got a pension card. The *All Seasons Newman Hotel (☎ 9177 8666)*, on Newman Dr, has excellent doubles for $130 and good, clean, budget single/double rooms for $30/34.

Restaurants are concentrated in three blocks of shops in the signposted 'Town Centre'. The *Chinese Kitchen (☎ 9175 2274)*, in the Boulevard shopping centre, does tasty meals for $12 to $17. The *Newman Thai Restaurant (☎ 9177 8668)*, in the Hilditch Shopping Mall, has noodles and curries. Across the road at 1 Hilditch Ave is *TNT's Pizza (☎ 9177 8770)* and the more-upmarket *Palazzo Italiano*. Both the All Seasons Newman Hotel and the Mercure Inn Newman have *restaurants*.

Getting There & Away

Ansett Australia (☎ 13 1300) flies to and from Perth daily. Greyhound Pioneer (☎ 13 2030) has a bus service from Perth to Port Hedland (with connections to Broome) via Newman on Friday and Sunday, and in the other direction on Saturday and Monday.

MARBLE BAR

pop 350

Reputed to be the hottest place in Australia, Marble Bar had a period in the 1920s when temperatures topped 37°C for 160 consecutive days. On one occasion, in 1905, the mercury soared to 49.1°C. From October to March, daytime temperatures above 40°C are common – although it is dry heat and not too unbearable.

The town is 203km south-east of Port Hedland. There are plans to completely seal the road into Marble Bar from the Great Northern Hwy, but 40km remains unsealed at the time of writing and it can be rough for 2WDs and caravans. The town takes its name from a bar of red jasper across the Coongan River, 6km west of town. Tourist information is available from the service station (☎ 9176 1041) opposite the Ironclad Hotel. In late winter, as the spring wildflowers begin to bloom, Marble Bar is a pretty place and one of the most popular Pilbara towns to visit.

In town, the 1895 **government buildings** on the corner of General and McLeod Sts, made of local stone, are still in use. The **Comet Gold Mine**, 10km south of Marble Bar, is no longer in operation but has a souvenir shop and a mining museum; it's open 9 am to 4 pm daily. **Coppins Gap/Doolena Gorge**, about 70km north-east of Marble Bar, is a deep cutting which has impressive views, twisted bands of rock and an ideal swimming hole.

Places to Stay

The *Marble Bar Caravan Park* (☎ 9176 1067), on Contest St, has tent/powered sites for $14/18 and on-site vans for $50 (all prices for two people). Single/double rooms at the friendly *Ironclad Hotel* (☎ 9176 1066, 15 Francis St)* – a distinctive spot to drink – cost $70/80. Meals are available to house guests. The *Marble Bar Travellers Stop Motel* (☎ 9176 1166), on Halse Rd, has basic rooms with shared facilities for $35 and motel rooms for $77/88.

COLLIER RANGE & RUDALL RIVER NATIONAL PARKS

Two of the most isolated and interesting of the state's national parks are found in the Pilbara. Both parks are true wilderness areas, accessible only by 4WD. Travellers have to be self-sufficient with fuel, water, food and first-aid equipment; seek permission from property owners before using their roads.

The **Collier Range** is more readily accessible, as the Great Northern Hwy bisects it near the quaint Kumarina Roadhouse, 256km north of Meekatharra. Here, at the upper reaches of the Ashburton and Gascoyne Rivers, the ranges vary from low hills to high ridges bounded by cliffs.

Even more remote is the breathtakingly beautiful **Rudall River National Park**, a desert region of 15,000 sq km, which is accessible only to experienced drivers with 4WD vehicles. The best time to visit is in July and August when daytime temperatures are tolerable – although in the desert the nights can be exceptionally cold.

The park is reached via two routes. The first is from Marble Bar along the Telfer Mine Rd to the northern park boundary, about 420km. Permission to use this route must be obtained from Newcrest Mining's (☎ 9270 7070) Perth office. The second route is from Newman via Balfour Downs on the Talawana Track to the southern boundary, about 260km.

To give you an indication of the area you are entering, the Canning Stock Route, first travelled in 1906 and used to drive cattle from The Kimberley region south, skirts the park to the east. No 24 Well, one of 51 along the route, is to the south-east.

The Mardu people still live in this area and, as recently as the 1980s, established the Punmu and Parnngurr communities in the park.

Plateaus of sandstone and quartzite carved by glaciers 280 million years ago, sand plains covered with spinifex and desert oak, dunes and salt lakes are all features of the landscape. The rabbit-eared bandicoot (also dalgyte or bilby – see the boxed text 'The Bilby' in The Kimberley chapter) may still exist in the area.

At least two vehicles, both equipped with Royal Flying Doctor Service radios, are needed for this trip and travellers must be *totally* self-sufficient. There are absolutely no facilities in this park.

PORT HEDLAND
pop 15,000

This town handles the most export tonnage of any other port in Australia and is the place from which the Pilbara's iron ore is shipped overseas. The town is built on an island connected to the mainland by causeways. The main highway into Port Hedland enters along a 3km causeway – you can see the white mountain of Cargill Salt as you drive along it. The satellite community of South Hedland, some 20km away, was established to cope with the population overflow from Port Hedland.

The town was important even before the Marble Bar gold rush of the 1880s: It became a grazing centre in 1864, and during the 1870s a fleet of 150 pearling luggers was based there. By 1946, however, the population had dwindled to a mere 150. Iron-ore mining operations in the Pilbara ensured a rebirth of the port's importance. It's now the launching place for 57.5 million exported tonnes.

The port is on a mangrove-fringed inlet, so wildlife abounds, but the highlight of a visit to Port Hedland is watching the sun sink behind the massive, rust-coloured cranes and pylons of the port while enormous ships are guided in and out.

Information

The helpful tourist office (☎ 9173 1711), which has showers ($2), is at 13 Wedge St, across from the post office. It's open 8.30 am to 5 pm weekdays, 8.30 am to 4.30 pm Saturday, and from noon to 4 pm Sunday from May to October. Internet access is available at the tourist office and at the South Hedland Newsagent. Banks are on Wedge St.

Things to See & Do

Behind the tourist office a 26m **observation tower** provides views over the massive port machinery and stockpiles of ore. You must sign a waiver to climb the tower ($2/1 adults/children) and wear closed-in shoes. The iron-ore trains are up to 2.6km in length. At 9.30 am weekdays there's a 1½-hour BHP Iron Ore & Port Tour, which leaves from the tourist office ($10/2).

Pretty Pool, 7km east of the town centre on the waterfront, is a tidal pool safe for swimming – although wearing thick-soled shoes is advised due to stonefish. The **Royal Flying Doctor Service base**, at the airport, is open to visitors from 9 am to 2 pm weekdays.

Big Blue Dive (☎ 9173 3202) at 5 Wedge St runs both **fishing tours** and **sunset cruises** starting at $80 and $30 per person respectively.

Pilbara Astro Nights (☎ 9173 3454), held at Indee Station, 49km south-west of Port Hedland, are two-hour star-viewing sessions using an astronomical telescope. They cost $30/15 adults/children.

Turtle- & Whale-Watching The flatback turtle nests between October and March on some of the nearby beaches, including Cooke Point, Cemetery Beach and Pretty Pool. Turtles old enough to nest are believed to be aged at least 40. Inquire at the tourist office about their location during the nesting season.

Big Blue Dive (☎ 9173 3202) operates whale-watching trips from July to October. These take three hours and start at $60 per person. Departures are dependent on tides and numbers. Guest of honour is the humpback whale.

Places to Stay

Camping Opposite the airport, *Dixon's Caravan Park (☎ 9172 2525, Lot 945 North West Coastal Hwy)* is a fair way out of town, but handy if you're in transit. Tent/powered sites cost $2/18 for two people, cabins start at $45, and park homes at $65.

CORAL COAST & THE PILBARA

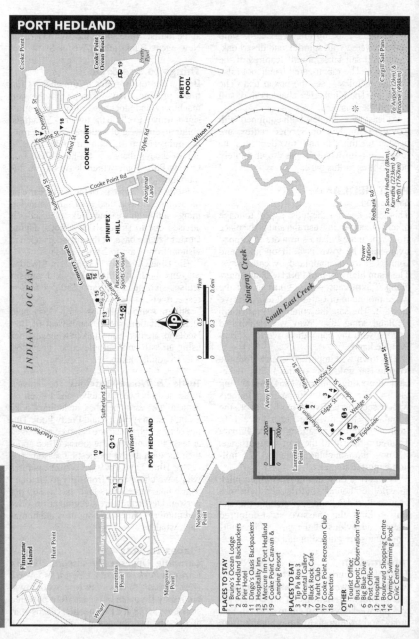

PORT HEDLAND

PLACES TO STAY
1 Bruno's Ocean Lodge
2 Port Hedland Backpackers
8 Pier Hotel
11 Dingo's Oasis Backpackers
13 Hospitality Inn
15 Mercure Inn Port Hedland
19 Cooke Point Caravan &
   Camping Resort

PLACES TO EAT
3 Tip Pa Ros 3
4 Oriental Gallery
7 Black Rock Cafe
10 Yacht Club
17 Cooke Point Recreation Club
18 Directors

OTHER
5 Tourist Office;
  Bus Depot; Observation Tower
6 Big Blue Dive
9 Post Office
12 Hospital
14 Boulevard Shopping Centre
16 Olympic Swimming Pool;
   Civic Centre

CORAL COAST & THE PILBARA

The village-like *Cooke Point Caravan and Camping Resort* (☎ 9173 1271), on the corner of Taylor and Athol Sts, is next to Pretty Pool. Powered sites cost $18 for two people, park cabins start at $55, and tent sites at $7.

The shady *South Hedland Caravan Park* (☎ 9172 1197), on Hamilton Rd, South Hedland, has tent/powered sites for $14/18 for two people and cabins starting at $50. Also in South Hedland, the brand-new *Blackrock Caravan Park* was due to open shortly at the time of writing.

The recommended *Indee Station* (☎ 9176 4968) offers camping for $10 a night per van (it has no powered sites). Some 49km south-west of Port Hedland, it's 9km off the Great Northern Hwy.

Hostels Basic but friendly, *Port Hedland Backpackers* (☎ 9173 3282, 20 Richardson St) has dorm beds/twin rooms for $15/34, as well as Internet access. The hostel runs three-day camping trips to Karijini National Park ($220), leaving once a week when road conditions allow.

The enthusiastic management of new-comer *Dingo's Oasis Backpackers* (☎ 9173 1000, 34 Morgans St) also has plans for tours and Internet access. The hostel has $15 dorm beds.

Hotels & Motels Good, reasonably priced accommodation in Port Hedland is scarce. On The Esplanade, The *Pier Hotel* (☎ 9173 1488) has scruffy single/double rooms for $60/70. Avoid the $60 motel rooms at *Bruno's Ocean Lodge* (☎ 9172 2635, 7 Richardson St), where you can tell the hair colour of the previous occupant just by having a shower.

The *Mercure Inn Port Hedland* (☎ 9173 1511), on Lukis St, is in a good spot for sunsets and has OK rooms for $130. The exorbitant price for a room at the *Hospitality Inn* (☎ 9173 1044), on Webster St, is $142. The *Mercure Inn Airport* (☎ 9172 1222), on the North West Coastal Hwy opposite the airport, is better value at $85.

In South Hedland, a budget option worth considering is the bizarre *Hedland Accommodation Centre* (☎ 9140 2925), on the corner of Hunt and Byass Sts, where vast warehouses are packed with rows of motel-style capsules. Singles/doubles cost $30/35.

Other motels in South Hedland include *The Lodge* (☎ 9172 2188), on Brand St, with doubles starting at $135, and the *South Hedland Motel* (☎ 9172 2222), in Court Place, with doubles starting at $110.

Places to Eat

Thai restaurant *Tip Pa Ros 3*, on Edgar St in an old Methodist church, has very good main courses for $14 to $17. Thai food and fish and chips are available from the *Yacht Club* on Sutherland St, opposite the hospital. Chinese food is found at the *Oriental Gallery*, corner of Edgar and Anderson Sts. Burgers in the bistro at the *Pier Hotel* are said to be tasty. Dinner at the *Mercure Inn Port Hedland* is good ($17.50 for fish and salad bar).

The *Black Rock Cafe*, on Wedge St, serves toasted sandwiches and weak coffees. The *Cooke Point Recreation Club*, on Keesing St, has a pizza bar and a bistro. On the same street is the reputedly upmarket alternative, *Directors*.

Getting There & Away

Ansett Australia (☎ 13 1300) flies two to three times daily between Perth and Port Hedland.

The Broome-based Northwest Regional Airline (☎ 1300-136 629) flies a stopping-all-stations 'milk run' from Broome, through Port Hedland, Karratha, Exmouth and back every day except Saturday.

By road it's 235km from Karratha to Port Hedland and 610km to Broome. Greyhound Pioneer (☎ 13 2030) runs a daily bus along the coast from Perth to Port Hedland, and inland via Newman (cutting four hours off the journey) on Friday and Sunday. Both services continue north to Broome, with connections to Darwin.

Greyhound Pioneer's depots are the tourist offices in South Hedland (Leake St) and Port Hedland (13 Wedge St). A one-way full fare from Perth costs $172.

Getting Around

The airport is 13km from town; the only way to get there is by taxi ($20). Hedland Bus Lines (☎ 9172 1394) runs a service between Port Hedland and South Hedland, which takes 40 minutes to an hour. Hire cars are available at the airport from the usual operators. Another option is Osborne Rentals (☎ 9140 2411) on Harwell Way in the Wedgefield light-industrial area.

The Kimberley

The rugged Kimberley, at the northern end of Western Australia (WA), is one of Australia's last frontiers. Despite enormous advances in recent years, this is still a little-travelled and remote area of great rivers and magnificent scenery.

It's generally agreed that the best time to visit is during the dry, between April and September, when daytime temperatures are warm but manageable and humidity and rainfall are low.

In the wet, torrential rains can turn creeks into raging rivers within 15 minutes. Watercourses can remain impassable for days – closing even Hwy 1, which runs through this part of WA as the Great Northern Hwy. It's not unknown for Kimberley towns to be cut off for three weeks. However, the wet is a spectacular time to visit, with dramatic thunderstorms, flowing waterfalls and a green, rejuvenated landscape.

The Kimberley's attractions include the dramatic gorges on the Fitzroy River, the remote Mitchell Plateau, Kalumburu and Gibb River Rds, the tidal waterfalls of Talbot Bay, Purnululu National Park, massive Lake Argyle and vibrant Broome.

The Kimberley – An Adventurer's Guide, by Ron and Viv Moon, has detailed information on various trails through the region. This publication is regularly updated.

Organised Tours

There are myriad organised tours available to give visitors on every budget a chance to explore different sections of the Kimberley, individually or combined. Tourist offices at each town have information on local operators. For Derby-based operators, see that section later in this chapter.

Over the Top Adventure Tours (☎ 9192 3977) in Broome operates budget two-day trips combining Windjana Gorge, Tunnel Creek and Geikie Gorge for $275, including meals, accommodation and transport.

East Kimberley Tours (☎ 9168 2213) provides a range of options, with departures

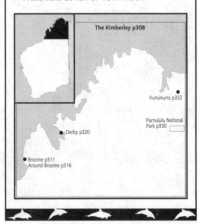

The Kimberley p308

Kununurra p332

Purnululu National Park p330

Derby p320

Broome p311
Around Broome p316

from Broome, Derby and Kununurra from May to October. A seven-day Mitchell Plateau and Gibb River Road (GRR) tour starts at $1700.

Australian Adventure Travel (☎ 9248 2355) has a 15-day trip from Broome to Kununurra return that includes the GRR, Purnululu National Park and the Mitchell Plateau. Prices start at $2250.

THE KIMBERLEY

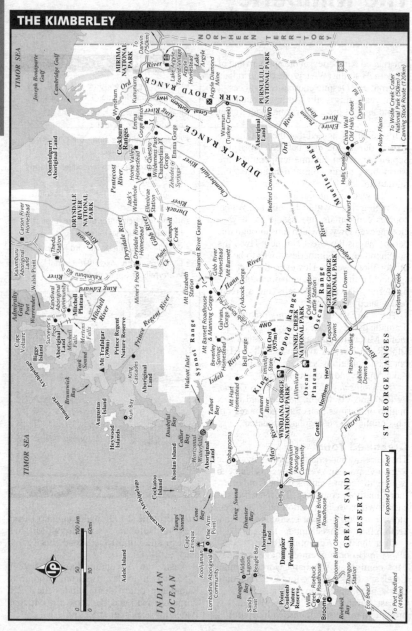

Kimberley Desert Inn 4WD Adventure (☎ 9169 1257) runs budget five-day camping trips along the GRR, including the Devonian Reef gorges, for $715. Kimberley Wilderness Adventures (☎ 9192 5741) has a seven-day GRR 4WD safari with mostly station accommodation, leaving from Kununurra and finishing in Broome; prices start at $1865. It runs other trips covering the major Kimberley destinations.

If you have limited time, flying is a good option. There are guided full-day trips to the Mitchell Plateau from Kununurra. Slingair (☎ 9169 1300) offers a range of trips over the Kimberley, from six hours (including a stop at Mitchell Falls) for $350 to three days (departing Kununurra, El Questro Wilderness Park or Broome) with various itineraries starting at $2375.

Broome Aviation (☎ 9192 1369) does flights from Broome to destinations along the Gibb River and Kalumburu Rds. Its Kimberley Explorer includes a Geikie Gorge boat cruise, lunch at Mt Hart Homestead, a look at the Buccaneer Archipelago, and a stop at Cape Leveque. Also Broome-based, King Leopold Air (☎ 9193 7155) has similar offerings.

If you've got $6000 or so to spare, a cruise with Broome-based North Star Charters

Horizontal Waterfalls

A remarkable feature of the rugged Kimberley coastline occurs when immense tidal currents rush in and out of its narrow gorges. With tides varying by up to 10m, the sea water gains rates of 30 knots as it moves in and out of some of the constricted sandstone gorges. Hence the name 'Horizontal Waterfalls'.

Included in many Kimberley flightseeing itineraries are the Horizontal Waterfalls of Talbot Bay. (The coast here is virtually inaccessible by land.) Two 30m-high gorges at the south end of the bay separate two smaller bays. At high tide, these fill with water – which is then squeezed back through the gorges as the tide goes out. The effect is impressive and is best seen around the full and the new moon.

(☎ 9192 1829) would be a great way to spend it. Its 34m cruise ship does several trips from April to August between Broome and Wyndham (and back). A one-way cruise takes 13 nights, and includes diving, walks and fishing. It's a luxurious way of seeing spectacular, isolated country, including the Prince Regent River and Mitchell Falls. The vessel even has its own helicopter. A double en suite berth on one of these trips costs $5950 per person.

Broome Region

The Pilbara and the Kimberley are separated by the westerly edge of the Great Sandy Desert, which extends all the way from the Northern Territory (NT) to the Indian Ocean. From the time you cross the De Grey River there is almost nothing until you reach Broome, an isolated town with a textured history that now fancies itself as a tropical paradise. Broome is nestled on the north side of Roebuck Bay and to the north is the Dampier Peninsula, home to a number of Aboriginal communities.

PORT HEDLAND TO BROOME

It is 610km from Port Hedland to Broome on what is probably Australia's most boring stretch of highway. Consequently, it proves to be a difficult day's drive. Get a copy of the handy leaflet *Port Hedland to Broome* from the tourist offices in Broome or Port Hedland. It describes attractive coastal camp sites, station stays and rest stops just off the highway. For that vital (and expensive) petrol stop, *Pardoo Roadhouse* (☎ *9176 4916*) and *Sandfire Roadhouse* (☎ *9176 5944*) are on the highway 460km and 318km south of Broome respectively.

Eco Beach (☎ *9193 5050*, ⓔ *ecobeach@ tpgi.com.au*), near Cape Villaret and the southern end of Roebuck Bay, is part of the traditional lands of the Yawuru people. It's off the highway 130km south of Broome and is usually accessible by 2WD. Accommodation is in open-walled, wooden huts on stilts with views to the ocean. The excellent menu here includes vegetarian options, but there's no air-con, no TV, and few telephones. Massages, horse riding and fishing charters are available. Wearing lots of insect repellent is advised.

Sadly, this thriving destination was badly damaged by Cyclone Rosita in April 2000, but the resort's determined Broome-based management is adamant it will rebuild. Pre-cyclone prices started at $110/90 peak/off-peak for two people, with meals costing $15 each. Call to find out whether the place is up and running again by the time you pass through.

BROOME
pop 13,700

Broome is booming – and you can see why. Its isolation makes it feel like a real escape, yet it still comes with all the comforts that city dwellers and other moneyed travellers hold dear, such as good coffee, outdoor bars with sunset views, and fresh food. Thus its population trebles with holiday-makers in June and July. But the tropical paradise theme – is it all an illusion? Just bear in mind: Those palm trees you see everywhere have been planted – they don't grow naturally here. This is the semiarid edge of the Great Sandy Desert.

'Old Broome' has certainly been sympathetically redeveloped, and architecture throughout the area has references to the town's Chinese and Japanese past (though there's a bit of overkill on the red and green lattice work). The town's textured history, good restaurants and beautiful beaches make a stay here a relaxing break.

History

The traditional owners of Broome are the Yawuru, Djugan and Goolarabooloo people. A council representing these three groups was established in 1994, and it contributes to the development of the Broome area. But relations between the indigenous and non-indigenous populations have not always been positive.

In the 1860s investigations into a convict's claim of a gold find in the area proved fruitless, so sheep were introduced instead. The Aboriginal inhabitants of Roebuck Bay resented the intrusion of the pastoralists, especially their fencing of traditional water holes. In November 1864 three members of the pastoralists' expedition were murdered by Aborigines, which resulted in open conflict. The pastoralists withdrew in 1867 only to be replaced by pearlers, working north from Cossack, in the 1870s.

The town was gazetted in 1883 and named after the then governor, Sir Frederick Napier Broome. Pearling in the sea off Broome started in earnest in the 1880s. Broome still remained very much a shantytown until the submarine telegraph cable was laid from Cable Bay, west of Broome, to Java (Indonesia) in 1889. This kept the pearling industry in close touch with price fluctuations and the industry began to expand rapidly. It peaked in the early 1900s when the town's 400 pearling luggers, worked by 3000 men, supplied 80% of the world's mother-of-pearl shell. However, it slowly declined in importance and it was not until the 1950s that it was revived, but on a much smaller scale. Today only a handful of boats operate.

Pearl diving was a dangerous occupation, as Broome's Japanese cemetery attests. The divers were from various Asian countries and the rivalries between different nationalities were intense, and sometimes took an ugly turn.

When Japan entered WWII in 1941, the 500 Japanese in Broome were interned for the duration of the war. On 3 March 1942, following the bombing of Darwin in February, the Japanese bombed Broome. A number of flying boats were destroyed and about 70 Dutch refugees were killed – the boat wrecks can today sometimes be seen at low tide from Town Beach.

Today, the main industry is beef and Broome's modern meat works can process 40,000 head during the season. Tourism is the other major industry and Broome's attractions and festivals bring hordes of visitors.

Orientation

The Great Northern Hwy becomes Hamersley St in town. Most of the action is in Chinatown, where the Paspaley shopping centre contains a Coles supermarket. The large

BROOME

PLACES TO STAY
1 Broome Caravan Park
18 Roebuck Bay Hotel Motel & Backpackers
28 Broome's Last Resort
29 Broome Motel
36 Ocean Lodge
37 Kimberley Klub
40 Mangrove Hotel
41 Moonlight Bay
43 Broome Apartments Park Court
45 The Temple Tree B&B
46 McAlpine House B&B
49 Broome Vacation Village
51 Tropicana Inn
54 Broometime Lodge
55 Palms Resort
58 Roebuck Bay Caravan Park
59 Mango Camping Ground

PLACES TO EAT
6 Shady Lane Cafe
7 Fong Sam's Bakehouse & Cafe

9 Bloom's
10 IceCreamery
14 Broome Pizza
15 Sheba Lane
27 noodlefish
31 Sanga's
57 Town Beach Cafe

OTHER
2 Post Office
3 Paspaley Shopping Centre
4 Woody's 4WD Hire
5 Nippon Inn
8 Sun Pictures
11 Dampier Creek Boat Tours
12 Pearl Luggers
13 Broome Telecentre
16 Kimberley Books
17 Fieldstar Consulting
19 Pearl Industry Statues
20 Tokyo Joe's
21 Shell Petrol Station

22 Tourist Office; Greyhound Bus Depot
23 Broome Bicycle Centre
24 Courthouse Markets
25 Courthouse
26 Broome Broome Car Hire
30 Avis
32 Hertz
33 Budget
34 Boulevard Shopping Centre
35 Aquatic Centre
38 Commonwealth Bank
39 Library; Civic Centre
42 Matso's Store
44 Hospital
47 Shell House
48 Goolarri Media Enterprises; GME GME Club
50 Topless Rentals
52 Broome Historical Society Museum
53 Magabala Books
56 Pioneer Cemetery
60 Flying Boat Wrecks

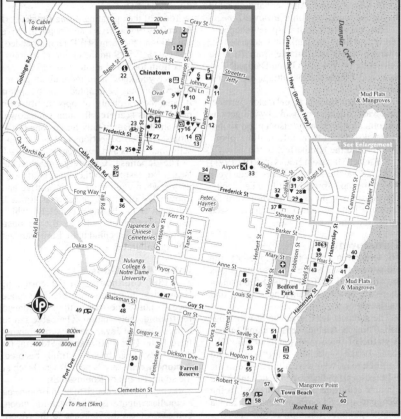

Boulevard shopping centre is out near the airport. Cable Beach is 6km north-west of Broome post office.

Information

The helpful though hectic Broome tourist office (☎ 9192 2222), on the corner of the Great Northern Hwy and Bagot St, is just across the sports field from Chinatown. It's open from 8 am to 5 pm weekdays and 9 am to 4 pm weekends from April to early October. During other months it's open from 9 am to 5 pm weekdays and 9 am to 1 pm weekends. It distributes a useful monthly guide to what's happening in and around Broome, a free copy of the annual *Kimberley Holiday Planner*. Another handy freebie during the tourist season is *Broome Time*.

The post office is in Paspaley shopping centre and there are banks in Carnarvon St. Internet access is available from Broome Telecentre (☎ 9193 7153), on Dampier Terrace, and Fieldstar Consulting, on Napier Terrace.

Kimberley Books, at 6 Napier Terrace, has a vast collection of books by indigenous and other authors and is also a good source of books and other information about Broome and the Kimberley.

Publisher Magabala Books (☎ 9192 1991) is at 2/28 Saville St. It produces exclusively Aboriginal and Torres Strait Islander books. The company name is the Yawuru word for the bush banana, which disperses its seed across the land.

Chinatown

The term 'Chinatown' is used to refer to the old part of town. Some Chinese merchants are still found on Carnarvon St, but most shops are now restaurants, pearl shops and tourist shops.

The signpost for Carnarvon St is in English, Chinese, Arabic, Japanese and Malay. A **statue** of three men stands nearby: Hiroshi Iwaki, Tokuichi Kuribayashi and Keith Dureau, who were all involved in the cultured-pearl industry. Alongside them is a life-size **sculpture** of a man dressed in the old pearl-diver's garb of hard-hat and a baggy, spaceman-like suit.

Pearling

Broome's pearling industry has provided the town with a fascinating multicultural past laced with stories of incredible tragedy, bravery and resourcefulness. **Broome Historical Society Museum** (☎ 9192 2075), on Saville St, has exhibits on Broome's history and on the industry and its dangers. It's in the old customs house and is open from 10 am to 4 pm weekdays and 10 am to 1 pm weekends from April to about October, and 10 am to 1 pm daily during the rest of the year.

To get a tangible sense of what life was like for hard-hat divers and their support crews, visit the excellent **Pearl Luggers**, at 44 Dampier Terrace. Tours taken by former divers cost $15.

Tours of the operating **Willie Creek Pearl Farm** (☎ 9193 6000) are also popular. Drive the 38km to the farm (4WD recommended) and pay $17.50/9 adults/children, or transport from town and a tour cost $45/23.

Once you know a bit more about the industry, you may be tempted to help support it, and there's plenty of opportunity with **pearl shops** scattered through Chinatown. The **Shell House**, in Guy St, has one of the largest seashell collections in Australia and sells shell crafts and jewellery.

The **Japanese Cemetery**, near Cable Beach Rd, testifies to the dangers of pearl diving when equipment was primitive and knowledge of diving techniques limited. Adjacent to the Japanese cemetery (which was renovated in 1983) is the **Chinese cemetery**, while behind it are European and Aboriginal graves.

Other Attractions

The 1888 **courthouse**, on the corner of Hamersley and Frederick Sts, was once used to house the transmitting equipment for the old cable station. The cable ran to Banyuwangi in Java, the ferry port across from Bali. The 1900 **Matso's Store**, at 60 Hamersley St, has been beautifully restored. A **pioneer cemetery** is near Town Beach at the southern end of Robinson St.

If you're lucky enough to be in Broome on a cloudless night when there is a full moon, you can witness the **Staircase to the Moon**.

The reflections of the moon from the rippling mud flats creates a wonderful golden stairway, best seen from the Roebuck Bay side of the peninsula. A lively **market** is held at Town Beach on these evenings. The effect is most dramatic about two days after the full moon. Check with the tourist office or the monthly holiday guide for exact dates and times.

The **Aquatic Centre** (☎ 9193 7677), on Cable Beach Rd, is open daily (call to check times as they change seasonally). Admission is $2.50/1.50 adults/children.

Organised Tours

A small hovercraft (☎ 9193 5025) makes one-hour trips ($60) daily around Roebuck Bay, stopping at points of interest. Lugger replica *The Willie* does sunset cruises from May to September ($50) – check with the tourist office for details. Dampier Creek Boat Tours (☎ 9192 1669) has a three-hour Roebuck Bay and creek fishing trip ($60/30 adults/children). You can also take a jet-boat (☎ 9193 6415) up the creek for $30/20.

WindRider Safaris (☎ 9192 2222) does full-day coastal sailing trips from Broome to Willie Creek. The price is $135, including individual minitrimarans and food.

Broome Sightseeing Tours' (☎ 9192 5041) self-guide kits include three cassettes, a booklet, a map and a discount pass ($20 for three days' hire; $35 with a Walkman). You can take yourself to up to 52 locations around town at your own pace.

To see Broome through Aboriginal eyes, try Mamabulanjin Tours (☎ 9192 2660). Baamba, AKA local actor and storyteller Stephen Albert (☎ 0417-988 328), takes a Chinatown tour at some times of the year. Once a year in winter, you can join the Goolarabooloo people (☎ 9192 2959) on their Lurujarri Dreaming Trail. It's a nine-day, 80km walk along the coast north of Broome, camping in the bush and learning about culture and country. The cost is $1200 ($600 for students or pensioners).

Fishing charters are available on the MV *Iceman* (☎ 0408-915 569) and with Broome Fishing Charters (☎ 9192 3829). Half-day 4WD tours to the northern beaches with

Walter (☎ 9192 3617) cost $90. George Swann of Kimberley Birdwatching (☎ 9192 1246) takes a range of natural-history trips. State-of-the-art watching equipment is provided, including tripod-mounted telescopes. With a minimum of four people, the cost of a three-hour shore-bird trip is $55; a five-hour trip around Broome's environs is $80.

Dougy's (beach) Buggies (☎ 0409-375 700) take two-hour town-and-beach tours for $60 per person. A half-day Kimberley Station Experience (☎ 9193 7267) runs Tuesday and Thursday (depending on numbers) and costs $70.

Special Events

As if this place needs any more reasons to attract even more visitors…

April

Easter Dragon Boat Regatta Local paddlers meet annually for this carnival, and for two days the town entertains the racers.

June

Broome Fringe Arts Festival Local artists highlight 'fringe arts' with markets, art installations, workshops and Aboriginal art exhibitions.

August

Opera Under the Stars World-class opera singers come to sing under the Kimberley's clear night skies.

Shinju Matsuri (Festival of the Pearl) This festival commemorates the early pearling years and the town's multicultural heritage. The town population swells and beds are scarce, so book ahead.

October

Stompen Ground This Aboriginal cultural festival features bands and food.

November

Mango Festival The town celebrates the mango harvest. Events include mango tasting, mardi gras and the Great Chefs of Broome Cook-off.

Places to Stay

The Broome tourist season starts in April, peaks in July and August and slows down by October. Outside the season some good deals can be had, but inside you're lucky to get a bed at all – let alone a cheap one.

Camping & Caravan Parks The *Roebuck Bay Caravan Park* (☎ 9192 1366), on Walcott St, has numerous sites overlooking the bay. Tent/powered sites cost $14/17.50 for two people, and on-site vans start at $45. *Broome Vacation Village* (☎ 9192 1057), on Port Dr, is set some distance out of town but has attractive park homes starting at $90 (less off-peak). Its tent/powered sites start at $17/20 for two people. From April to September, the Department of Conservation & Land Management (CALM) opens up its shady *Mango Camping Ground* (☎ 9192 1036), on Walcott St, for $7 per person. *Broome Caravan Park* (☎ 9192 1366) is on Wattle Dr, off the Great Northern Hwy.

Hostels The clean, spacious *Kimberley Klub* (☎ 9192 3233), on Frederick St, has impressive facilities, including bike hire, a tour-booking service, a bar, a swimming pool, and neat, airy rooms. Dorm beds start at $17/14 peak/off peak, and doubles cost $62/45. *Broome's Last Resort* (☎ 9193 5000), on Bagot St, has dorm beds starting at $16/14 and doubles for $50/40 in a rambling house. *Roebuck Bay Backpackers* (☎ 9192 1183), on Napier Terrace, is part of Broome's atmospheric and historic main pub. It's central and has OK dorm beds starting at $14. At the time of writing its $46 doubles were being refurbished.

B&Bs Luxurious *McAlpine House* (☎ 9192 3886, 84 Herbert St) – the former home of Lord Alistair McAlpine, founder of the original Cable Beach Resort – offers peaceful accommodation starting at $200/156 peak/off-peak, with breakfast and airport transfers included. Other options include *Harmony* (☎ 9193 7439), on the Great Northern Hwy about 5km from town, with singles/doubles for $50/80. *The Temple Tree* (☎ 9193 5728, 54 Anne St) has en suite singles/doubles for $75/95 peak and $60/80 off-peak.

Hotels & Motels Though some distance from both the beach and the town centre, the *Ocean Lodge* (☎ 9193 7700), on Cable Beach Rd, has a peaceful central courtyard.

Doubles cost $104/74 peak/off-peak. Comfortable rooms at the relatively new *Broome Motel* (9192 7775), on Frederick St, start at $95/68. The legendary *Roebuck Bay Hotel Motel* (☎ 9192 1221), in Chinatown, has lots of character, a pool, with double rooms for $110/83 (though wet-season specials can go as low as $60).

The brown-brick *Palms Resort* (☎ 9192 1898), on Hopton St, has unremarkable motel accommodation starting at $125/101. *Tropicana Inn* (☎ 9192 1204), on the corner of Saville and Robinson Sts, has OK rooms in a pleasant setting for $132/80.

The friendly, budget *Broometime Lodge* (☎ 9193 5067, 59 Forrest St) has doubles for $70/50. Units of comparable quality, though self-contained, are found at *Broome Apartments Park Court* (☎ 9193 5887, 2 Haas St). A one-bedroom unit starts at $88/64.

Some of the rooms at the *Mangrove Hotel* (☎ 9192 1303, 120 Carnarvon St) have great views across Roebuck Bay. Suites with balconies start at $165/130. More modest rooms cost $143/110. Nearby is the high-quality *Moonlight Bay* (☎ 9193 7888), also bayside and with an enormous pool. Apartments here start at $186/150.

Habitat Beach Resort (☎ 9158 3520) is beside the golf course. A pleasant one-bedroom self-contained unit costs $140/110.

The exclusive *Cockatoo Island Resort* (☎ 8946 4455) is a one-hour flight from Broome ($320 return). It offers fishing, bushwalking, cruises and whale-watching during the season. The cost of $470 per double includes all meals.

Places to Eat

Broome has a good range of cafes and restaurants, which, combined with the offerings of Cable Beach just down the road, will make it difficult for self-caterers to stick to their spartan rice-and-pasta regimen.

Bloom's, on Carnarvon St, has good breakfasts and some of the best coffee in the north-west. Also serving good coffee, tea in pots, and tasty food is *Town Beach Cafe*, in a beautiful spot overlooking Roebuck Bay. *Sanga's*, on Coghlan St behind the Frederick St BP, has high-quality takeaway Thai food – a delicious phad Thai packed with seafood costs just $12.50. *Shady Lane Cafe*, on Johnny Chi Lane, has home-made sausage rolls for $2.50. *Broome Pizza*, on Napier Terrace, does a roaring trade (tasty small/large pizzas cost $9/14).

Fong Sam's Bakehouse and Cafe, on the corner of Carnarvon and Short Sts, has some baked goods but also does fast, hot meals. The Paspaley shopping centre has a *Coles supermarket*. The *IceCreamery*, on Carnarvon St, is usually busy and does smoothies. Outside the wet, the Saturday *Courthouse Markets* sell fresh organic produce, freshly squeezed juices and takeaway Asian-style food.

The bistro at the *Roebuck Bay Hotel Motel* is reputedly quite good. Locals also recommend *noodlefish*, on Frederick St, for casual, Asian-inspired meals – though it closes during the wet. *Sheba Lane*, on Napier Terrace, is an upmarket Asian-style restaurant with an excellent reputation. *Tropicana Inn* has a restaurant and bar and grill. The Mangrove Hotel has the indoor *Charters* restaurant and the outdoor *Tides* – where the food is good but the serenity of a Roebuck Bay sunset may be shattered by blaring classic rock.

Entertainment

The atmospheric *Roebuck Bay Hotel Motel* ('Roey') is popular with locals and travellers alike. It regularly has bands.

A Place in the Sun

Opened in 1916, Sun Pictures in Broome is believed to be the world's oldest operating picture garden. The silent movies shown here were accompanied by music played by 'Fairy', the pianist, until the projector was adapted for sound in 1933. The first 'talkie' screened was the musical comedy *Monte Carlo*, starring Nelson Eddy and Jeanette MacDonald.

There is nothing quite like watching a movie while lying back in a deck chair under the stars. The snack bar still serves that old favourite, the 'chocolate bomb' – vanilla ice cream in a cone, dipped in chocolate and frozen.

Goolarri Media Enterprises (☎ *9192 1325, 16 Blackman St)* holds events such as film launches, and band and karaoke nights at its *GME GME Club* (the acronym is pronounced 'gimmee'). Call first to find out what's on.

Dating from 1916, *Sun Pictures (27 Carnarvon St)*, in Chinatown, is believed to be the world's oldest operating open-air cinema (see the boxed text). It shows recent releases seven nights a week. For extra comfort, take your own pillow or blanket.

Nightclubs in town include the *Nippon Inn*, on Dampier Terrace, and *Tokyo Joe's*, on Napier Terrace.

Getting There & Away

Ansett Australia (☎ 13 1300) offers daily direct flights into and out of Broome from Perth, Darwin and Alice Springs, with connections to other Australian cities. Qantas Airways (☎ 13 1313) offers similar routes about twice a week.

Northwest Regional Airlines (☎ 1300-136 629) does a 'milk run' daily except Saturday from Broome to Exmouth via Port Hedland and Karratha; and every day except Sunday from Broome to Halls Creek via Fitzroy Crossing.

Greyhound Pioneer Australia (☎ 13 2030) buses run through Broome on the daily Perth to Darwin run. The Greyhound Pioneer depot is in the same building as the tourist office.

Getting Around

To/From the Airport There are plenty of taxis (☎ 1800-880 330) at the airport. A taxi to Chinatown costs $5 and to Cable Beach about $11.

Bus The Town Bus Service (☎ 9193 6000) plies hourly between the town (including stops near most places to stay) and Cable Beach. Fares cost $2.50/1 adults/children; a day pass is $8/4. The first service of the day (7.30 am from Chinatown) runs one way to Gantheaume Point for those feeling like an early morning walk to Cable Beach. Be warned: It's a 5km hike along the beach, so take water and a hat.

THE KIMBERLEY

Car Numerous rental companies make car hire in Broome very competitive. Prices fluctuate depending on the season, the weather and how busy the town is, so it's worth shopping around.

Several operators are based at the airport. Hertz (☎ 9192 1428), Budget (☎ 9193 5355) and Avis (☎ 9193 5980) all have a presence in Broome. Other companies include Topless Rentals (☎ 9193 5017) and Broome Broome (☎ 9192 2210).

Woody's 4WD Hire (☎ 9192 1791), on Dampier Terrace, is renowned for having the cheapest petrol in town.

Bicycle Broome is flat and interesting to ride around, and the stretch between Cable Beach and town (6km) is manageable. Backpacker hostels such as the Kimberley Klub have the best-value bike hire ($10 per day). The Broome Cycle Centre, on the corner of Hamersley and Frederick Sts, sells and repairs bikes as well as hires them out ($15 per day).

AROUND BROOME
Cable Beach

Some 6km from the Broome post office, the little town of Cable Beach has almost enough facilities to make it a holiday destination in its own right – although it's lacking its neighbour's interesting history. A classic beach with white sand, turquoise water, and a backdrop of red pindan cliffs, it takes its name from the cable that once linked Broome and Indonesia.

The possible presence of poisonous box jellyfish makes it dangerous to swim here from about November to March (if in doubt, check at the Broome tourist office).

Surfboards and other equipment are available for hire on the beach. Parasailing is also sometimes available; call (☎ 0407-446 106).

Situated on the northern side of an outcrop of rocks just north of the car park, it's not exactly a nudist beach but clothes are optional. You can also take vehicles (other than motorcycles) onto this part of the beach, although at high tide access is limited because of the rocks, so take care not to get stranded.

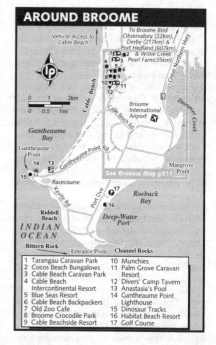

AROUND BROOME

1 Tarangau Caravan Park	10 Munchies
2 Cocos Beach Bungalows	11 Palm Grove Caravan
3 Cable Beach Caravan Park	Resort
4 Cable Beach	12 Divers' Camp Tavern
Intercontinental Resort	13 Anastasia's Pool
5 Blue Seas Resort	14 Gantheaume Point
6 Cable Beach Backpackers	Lighthouse
7 Old Zoo Cafe	15 Dinosaur Tracks
8 Broome Crocodile Park	16 Habitat Beach Resort
9 Cable Beachside Resort	17 Golf Course

A number of companies run **camel rides** along the beach. The best time to ride is at sunset. Prices are about $30 per hour, with discounts available for children. For more information and bookings, contact the Broome tourist office.

Also on Cable Beach Rd is the **Broome Crocodile Park** (☎ 9192 1489), established in 1983. It's open from 10 am to 5 pm weekdays, 2 to 5 pm weekends, in the dry season. Feeding tours are held at 3 pm Wednesday to Sunday. In the wet it's open from 3.30 to 5 pm daily, with a feeding tour at 3.45 pm. Admission is $14/7/35 adults/children/families.

Places to Stay On Millington Rd, *Cable Beach Caravan Park* (☎ 9192 2066) has a leafy, grassy old section and a new section with very little shade, the latter of which is less likely to be booked out. Tent/powered sites cost $16/20 for two people. *Tarangau Caravan Park* (☎ 9193 5084), farther north on Millington Rd, has tent/powered sites for $13/18.50 and on-site vans for $31.50. *Palm Grove Caravan Resort* (☎ 9192 3336), on Cable Beach Rd, has tent/van sites for $16/21. Its camping area is a bit like a car park, but its clean, modern park homes and cottages are great value, starting at $95/75 peak/off-peak for a one-bedroom.

Some facilities at *Cable Beach Backpackers* (☎ 9193 5511), on Lullfitz Dr, looked a bit grimy, but there is a big kitchen, a bar, a pool and a free shuttle bus to town. It's a short walk to Cable Beach and it has surfboard and moped hire ($10 and $25 per day). A bed in a quad dorm starts at $16; doubles start at $48.

New, more-upmarket places to stay are emerging all the time around Cable Beach. Most existing accommodation is also relatively new, so standards are usually high.

The clean, spacious, self-contained apartments at *Cable Beachside Resort* (☎ 9193 5545), on the corner of Cable Beach and Murray Rds, are in a peaceful setting. A one-bedroom unit costs $170/125 peak/off-peak.

Cocos Beach Bungalows (☎ 9192 3873, 11 Lullfitz Dr) is ideal for families or large groups. In a spacious, peaceful setting, the bungalows have big verandahs and three bedrooms. They cost $170/125. Rooms at the *Blue Seas Resort* (☎ 9192 0999, 27–31 Lullfitz Dr) all face onto a main courtyard and swimming pool; they cost $110/174.

The main reason for staying at the *Cable Beach Intercontinental Resort* (☎ 1800-199 099) is because this is where Broome's renaissance as a tourist mecca began, thanks to British millionaire Lord Alistair McAlpine. But, if you're not into bragging to your friends about having stayed here, there are other options at Cable Beach that are much better value. While rooms at the Intercontinental are beautifully furnished, with prices starting at $261/203 for two people the bathroom we saw was not nearly big enough or luxurious enough.

Places to Eat The Intercontinental resort has the upmarket *Pandanus* restaurant and the more economical pasta and salad bar at *Lord Mac's*. A beer at an outdoor table at

the resort's *Sunset Bar* is a great way to end the day. The *Old Zoo Cafe*, on Challenor Dr, serves tasty breakfasts, lunches and dinners. Try the amazing apricot lassi ($3.50), laced with rosewater.

Munchies, near the Palm Grove Caravan Resort, has cafeteria-style hot meals for $10 and less. Counter meals at the *Divers' Camp Tavern* are reputedly good – mains start at $16.50.

At the time of writing a new *restaurant* and *kiosk* were under construction, directly overlooking Cable Beach at its main access point from the car park.

Gantheaume Point

The long sweep of Cable Beach eventually ends at Gantheaume Point, 7km south of Broome along a sandy road. The red, craggy cliffs have been eroded into curious shapes. At extremely low tides, **dinosaur tracks**, made 120 million years ago by a carnivorous species, are exposed. At other times you can inspect cement casts of the footprints on the clifftop. **Anastasia's Pool**, an artificial rock pool believed to have been built by a former lighthouse keeper for his crippled wife, is on the north side of the point; it fills at high tide.

Broome Bird Observatory

The Birds Australia Broome Bird Observatory (☎ 9193 5600), 25km south-east of Broome on Roebuck Bay, is rated as one of the top four nonbreeding grounds for migrant Arctic waders. Each year, the bay is visited by 150,000 migratory birds from the northern hemisphere.

The observatory is a good base for seeking out birds in a variety of habitats. Please ring beforehand to find out the best viewing times. It organises two-hour tours ($25/45 from the observatory/Broome) to see birds of the bush, shore and mangroves (binoculars are provided).

Access to the observatory is via an unsealed road off the Great Northern Hwy, 9km north of town. *Camp sites* near the observatory cost $16 for two people; bunk rooms cost $32 for two people; and a six-bed, self-contained chalet is $80 a double ($10 for each extra person).

DAMPIER PENINSULA

It's about 220km from the turn-off 10km out of Broome to the Cape Leveque lighthouse at the tip of the Dampier Peninsula. To get there, you need a 4WD as the sandy road becomes impassable in the rain. (It's also unsuitable for caravans.) Check road conditions with the Broome tourist office before setting out.

The drive is long and pretty boring, but the spectacular red pindan cliffs and beautiful beaches at the end make it worthwhile. Several of the Aboriginal communities along here allow visitors and some offer accommodation, mud-crabbing and bush-tucker walks.

Originally, the peninsula was inhabited by the Bardi people, and during the early pearling days a number of Aborigines dived for pearl shell.

The **Beagle Bay Aboriginal Community** (☎ 9192 4913), 118km from Broome, has a fascinating church, in the middle of a green, built by monks and completed in 1918. A few nuns and monks still live here, including one who grows organic vegetables and produces honey. Inside the church is an altar decorated with pearl shell. A fee of $5 is charged for entry into the community and you must contact the office on arrival; petrol and diesel are available from 8 am every day except Sunday. Camping is not permitted.

You can *camp* at **Middle Lagoon** (☎ 9192 4002), on the coast north of Beagle Bay (33km off the Cape Leveque Rd). This picturesque spot offers snorkelling, fishing and swimming. Unpowered sites cost $10; beach shelters with a pine floor cost $30 for two people; and cabins with fridges (you must bring linen and towels) cost $80 for four. An entry fee of $5 per vehicle applies.

About 20km from the cape on the Cape Leveque Rd is the **Lombadina Aboriginal Community** (☎ 9192 4936), which has a church clad in corrugated iron, lined with paperbark and supported by bush timber. One-day and overnight mud-crabbing and traditional fishing tours are available; contact the Broome tourist office for details. Fuel (unleaded and diesel) is available on weekdays. Four-bed, backpacker-style units

The Bilby

Conservation authorities are seeking help to locate the rare remaining populations of the bilby. Once widespread across Australia, this type of bandicoot with rabbit-like ears is now restricted to arid north-western regions. The Department of Conservation & Land Management (CALM) says that the reasons for its decline are not really known (though introduced predators, such as foxes and cats, are likely to be a factor). To increase knowledge about the conditions required for the species' survival, CALM asks that you report any sightings.

The bilby is a little bigger than a rabbit and has long ears, silky grey fur, a black-and-white tail and strong claws. Spotting the creature is rare – it spends its days in a burrow up to 2m deep, and emerges at night to feed on witchetty grubs, seeds, fruit, termites and ants.

More often, the presence of bilby colonies (of two to five animals sharing several hectares) is identified through clues. For example, the burrow entrances are usually circular, about 15cm wide and tucked between clumps of plants. Tracks are like those of a kangaroo (two parallel lines for hind feet, alternating with two dots in a line for front feet). Its droppings ('scats') are also distinctive – 2.5cm long and 1.2cm wide, cylindrical and smooth.

Keep your eyes peeled and you'll perhaps contribute to the survival of this unique Australian animal.

KN

cost $38.50 per person. Fully self-contained units, which sleep four, cost $132 (linen and towels provided). Camping is not permitted.

Cape Leveque has a lighthouse and some exquisite beaches. About 5km from the lighthouse is **One Arm Point**, another Aboriginal community (☎ 9192 4930).

Kooljaman (☎ *9192 4970*), just by the beach on Cape Leveque, has tent/powered sites for $12/15, beach shelters for $36 for two people, family units for $80, cabins starting at $100 and safari tents for $160. Bookings are essential.

Bush-tucker, mud-crabbing tours and fishing charters are available. Unleaded and diesel fuel can be purchased here. The *restaurant* is open April to October, and the *store* year-round for limited hours daily.

Take note that while you can look around or purchase goods, Aboriginal communities won't want you to stay on their land. Permission to visit other areas must be obtained in advance.

On the western coast of Dampier Peninsula, along the unsealed Cape Bertholet Rd, is **Point Coulomb Nature Reserve**. This conservation area was set up to protect the unique pindan vegetation of the peninsula and may still harbour the endangered rabbit-eared bandicoot or bilby (see the boxed text). Bilbies may be seen in the nocturnal house at the CALM offices in Herbert St, Broome.

Organised Tours

Although a 'Dampierland' trip with Over the Top Adventure Tours (☎ 9193 3977) was slightly disorganised, it included some interesting stops at Beagle Bay and Lombadina Aboriginal Communities. The cost of $175 included 4WD transport, lunch, an afternoon on the Cape Leveque beach and a sunset barbecue with bad wine. Flak Track (☎ 9192 1487) also runs a day tour to the peninsula ($170).

Cape Leveque is included on some flight-seeing itineraries. For example, King Leopold Air (☎ 9193 7155) does a 2½-hour flight over the Horizontal Waterfalls and Cockatoo Island with a landing at Cape Leveque for $259.

Gibb River Road

The GRR is impassable in the wet; do not attempt it from December to April. The best time is from May to November; ring the Department of Main Roads (☎ 1800-013 314) for up-to-date information on road conditions. There are a number of rules to observe; see the boxed texts 'Safe Driving' and 'Responsible Camping' in this chapter.

Fuel is available at Iminitji Store (diesel only), Mt Barnett Roadhouse at Manning Gorge, and El Questro Wilderness Park. The Kimberley gorges are the major reason for taking this route. You could also make a side trip to the Windjana Gorge and Tunnel Creek (see Devonian Reef National Parks later in this chapter). Get a copy of the excellent *Gibb River and Kalumburu Roads Travellers Guide* – $2 at tourist offices.

There's no public transport along the GRR – in fact there's very little traffic of any sort, so don't bother trying to hitch! Take note that in many cases prior bookings are essential for homestead accommodation.

DERBY
pop 5000
The West Kimberley is a vast area that includes Broome to Fitzroy Crossing, the Devonian Reef national parks, the Gibb River and Kalumburu Rds and the remote and rugged north-west coast. The main town of the region is Derby, only 220km from Broome and a major administrative centre. It is a good point from which to travel to the spectacular gorges in the region.

Derby is on King Sound, north of the mouth of the Fitzroy, the mighty river that drains the West Kimberley. The area has been occupied by Aborigines for many thousands of years.

Derby was officially proclaimed a town site in 1883 and the first wooden jetty was built there two years later. The Australian Aerial Medical Service, later to become the Royal Flying Doctor Service (RFDS), started operation at Derby airport in 1934, largely funded by donations from the state of Victoria.

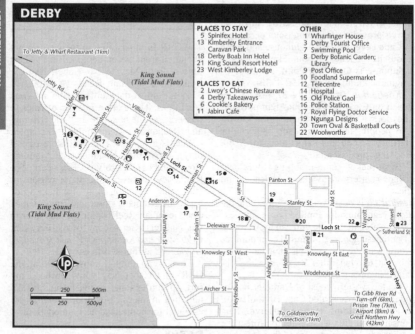

DERBY

PLACES TO STAY
5 Spinifex Hotel
13 Kimberley Entrance Caravan Park
18 Derby Boab Inn Hotel
21 King Sound Resort Hotel
23 West Kimberley Lodge

PLACES TO EAT
2 Lwoy's Chinese Restaurant
4 Derby Takeaways
6 Cookie's Bakery
11 Jabiru Cafe

OTHER
1 Wharfinger House
3 Derby Tourist Office
7 Swimming Pool
8 Derby Botanic Garden; Library
9 Post Office
10 Foodland Supermarket
12 Telecentre
14 Hospital
15 Old Police Gaol
16 Police Station
17 Royal Flying Doctor Service
19 Ngunga Designs
20 Town Oval & Basketball Courts
22 Woolworths

To Jetty & Wharf Restaurant (1km)

King Sound (Tidal Mud Flats)

King Sound (Tidal Mud Flats)

Jetty Rd
Elder St
Johnston St
Villiers St
Hardman St
Nevill St
Clarendon St
Rowan St
Loch St
Hensman St
Anderson St
Marmion St
Fairbairn St
Delewarr St
Swan St
Panton St
Stanley St
Juld St
Knowsley St West
Heytesbury St
Archer St
Holman St
Ashley St
Brand St
Loch St
Knowsley St East
Wodehouse St
Camarvon St
Stanwell
Waycott St
Sutherland St
Derby Hwy

0   250   500m
0   250   500yd

To Goldsworthy Connection (1km)

To Gibb River Rd Turn-off (6km), Prison Tree (7km), Airport (8km) & Great Northern Hwy (42km)

Derby is part of the largest shire in Australia – 102,706 sq km – with more than 45% of the shire population comprising Aborigines. Mowanjum ('settled at last'), on the outskirts of Derby, was one of the first independent Aboriginal communities established in the Kimberley.

It has the highest tidal range in Australia; the highest astronomical tide is 11.8m and the lowest astronomical tide is 1.3m.

Information

The friendly Derby tourist office (☎ 9191 1426), at 1 Clarendon St, is open from 8.30 am to 4.30 pm weekdays, 9 am to 1 pm weekends, April to October. It's open the same hours weekdays and 9 am to noon Saturday from November to March. The Telecentre on Clarendon St has Internet access. The Woolworths supermarket in Loch St is open daily. The BP Colac Roadhouse petrol station (☎ 9191 1256) is open 5.30 am to 7.30 pm Monday to Saturday, 6 am to 6 pm Sunday. There's a Foodland supermarket on Clarendon St and a Shell petrol station on the corner of Hardman and Clarendon Sts.

Things to See & Do

Derby's **botanic garden**, on Loch St, has a collection of palms and features a sandstone rockery.

A small museum is housed in **Wharfinger House**, once the residence of the harbour master, at the end of Loch St. Ask at the tourist office for the key.

The original **old Derby police gaol**, which was constructed in the late 1880s, is next to the present Derby police station and is worth driving past for a look. The **RFDS** building, in Clarendon St, welcomes visitors at 9 and 11 am and 2 pm weekdays.

Ngunga Designs, on Stanley St, has a range of attractive clothing and materials screen printed with Aboriginal designs. It also sells carved boab nuts and paintings.

Summer temperatures in the Pilbara town of Karratha reach above 40°C

The honeymoon suite, outback style, Karijini NP

Swimming at Fortescue Falls, Karijini NP

The Great Northern Hwy, Karijini NP

The high cliffs of Knox Gorge, Karijini NP

JOHN HAY

Cockburn Range, the Kimberley

JOHN HAY

Corrugated-iron architecture, Broome

ILSA COLSON

Eco Beach, southern end of Roebuck Bay, near Broome

JOHN HAY

El Questro Homestead, the Kimberley

RICHARD I'ANSON

Mitchell Falls at the Mitchell Plateau, the Kimberley

RICHARD I'ANSON

Bungle Bungle Range, Purnululu NP

PETER PTSCHELINZEW

Spinifex grass, Great Sandy Desert

RICHARD I'ANSON

Rocky Gantheaume Point, Roebuck Bay

Derby's lofty **jetty** has in recent years got a new lease on life thanks to a new facility opening for lead and zinc exports. The jetty was built in 1894, to handle wool and pearl-shell exports. This impressive D-shaped structure stands on legs long enough to support it above occasional 11m king tides.

Derby is surrounded by huge expanses of mud flats, baked hard in the dry and sometimes home to crocodiles.

The **Prison Tree**, near the airport, 7km south of town, is a huge boab tree with a hollow trunk 14m around. It is said to have been used as a temporary lock-up years ago. One interpretation is that police enjoyed the shelter and shade of the tree's interior after chaining their prisoners around its exterior. Nearby is **Myall's Bore**, a 120m-long cattle trough filled from a 322m-deep artesian bore.

Organised Tours

Scenic flights to the nearby islands of the Buccaneer Archipelago are available. Aerial Enterprises (☎ 9191 1132) and Derby Air Services (☎ 9193 1375) provide 1½-hour flights for about $120 to the archipelago.

Outside busy times there's a minimum of four passengers.

Four Derby-based boat-charter outfits take cruises into the Buccaneer Archipelago. They say their biggest advantage is that it takes them an hour to cruise to the islands, compared with the 10 hours required from Broome. Kimberley Thousand Island Charters (☎ 9191 1851) and Unreel Adventure Safaris (☎ 9193 1999) offer fishing trips. One Tide Charters (☎ 9193 1358) has four- to eight-day cruises. Buccaneer Sea Safaris (☎ 9191 1991) takes three- to 21-day trips into the archipelago, sometimes combined with 4WDs. Buccaneer's Prince Regent River Explorer trip includes the Horizontal Falls of Talbot Bay (see the boxed text 'Horizontal Waterfalls' earlier in this chapter).

Bush Track Safaris (☎ 9191 1547) operates four- to 10-day tours into the remote Walcott Inlet area starting at $195 per day. West Kimberley Tours (☎ 9193 1442) operates tours to the Devonian Reef gorges ($80 per person) and GRR gorges ($300 for two days). A six-day Hotland Safaris (☎ 9193 1312) tour of the West Kimberley region costs $1080.

Upside-Down Trees

Boab trees are a common sight in the Kimberley; the biggest specimens are many thousands of years old. It's probable that seeds from African baobabs floated to Australia and the boab or *Adansonia gregorii* evolved from there.

The boab is a curious-looking tree with branches rising like witches' fingers from a wide trunk that is sometimes elegantly bottle-shaped, and other times squat and powerful looking. Boabs

shed all their leaves during dry periods, making their spindly branches look like roots.

One local story is that the boab was once a magnificently proportioned tree that formed too high an opinion of itself and grew too close to heaven. This displeased the gods so much they ended up pulling it out of the ground – and then thrusting it back in upside-down.

The curious-looking boab is a common sight in the Kimberley.

Places to Stay

Tent/powered sites at **Kimberley Entrance Caravan Park** (☎ 9193 1055), on Rowan St, cost $15/18 for two people. It won't take bookings for stays of less than 30 days, but can usually find everyone a spot somewhere in the 3.2 hectares of grounds.

West Kimberley Lodge (☎ 9191 1031) is in a peaceful spot on the corner of Sutherland and Stanwell Sts. It has neat singles/doubles starting at $45/55 and a shared kitchen. In a bush setting a short drive out of town is the **Goldsworthy Connection** (☎ 9193 1246, Lot 4 Guildford St). It has clean self-contained homes that sleep seven for $150. It also has plans for establishing backpacker accommodation.

Accommodation at the **Spinifex Hotel** (☎ 9191 1233), on Clarendon St, is pretty basic no matter how much you're paying, but the place has character. It has budget rooms for $40/50, motel units for $50/65, and backpacker beds for $15.

Derby Boab Inn Hotel (☎ 9191 1044), on Loch St, has motel rooms not much better than at the Spinifex Hotel but costing $95. Its budget rooms cost $65/75. Double rooms in need of a good airing at **King Sound Resort Hotel** (☎ 9193 1044), on Loch St, cost $105; singles cost $95.

Places to Eat

Wharf Restaurant (☎ 9191 1195), at the end of Jetty Rd, has some of the best food in the north-west and this alone is reason enough to visit Derby. An enormous serve of Thai-flavoured barramundi 'wings' costs $22.50, and can be eaten at comfortable outside tables surrounded by tropical plants and overlooking the jetty. **Lwoy's Chinese Restaurant**, on Loch St, reputedly serves reasonable food. All three **hotels** also serve meals. Fast food is available from **Derby Takeaways** (☎ 9191 1131), next to the tourist office. Options for lunch include **Cookie's Bakery** and **Jabiru Cafe**, on Clarendon St.

Getting There & Away

Skippers Aviation flies to and from Broome six days a week. Book through Ansett Australia (☎ 13 1300). Greyhound Pioneer's daily Perth-Darwin bus service stops in Derby at the tourist office.

DERBY TO MT BARNETT

From Derby, travel 119km along the GRR for the turn-off to Windjana Gorge (a farther 21km) and Tunnel Creek (51km). For more information see Devonian Reef National Parks later in this chapter. From either, you can continue to the Great Northern Hwy near Fitzroy Crossing.

At 120km along the GRR you cross the Lennard River bridge and at 145km you pass through the Yamarra Gap in the King Leopold Ranges. At 181km is the Inglis Gap, where the road descends into the **Broome Valley**.

At 184km you can turn off to the beautiful **Mt Hart Homestead** (☎ 9191 4645), which is another 50km along a rough dirt road. Bookings are essential; B&B with dinner costs $130/65 adults/children.

Back on the GRR some 30km beyond the Mt Hart Homestead turn-off is the turn-off to the **Bell Gorge**, 29km off the road along a 4WD-only track. This gorge is 5km long and has a waterfall just north of its entrance; the nearby pool is great for a refreshing dip.

You can **camp** here along Bell Creek or along Silent Grove for $7/1 adults/children. There is no access from mid-December to mid-April. A ranger is here from May to September.

Some 221km on the GRR from Derby is the **Iminitji Store** (☎ 9191 7471) and com-

---

Safe Driving

- When driving off the main roads, carry spare parts and repair kits, and enough water and food to last four days longer than planned.
- If your vehicle breaks down, stay with it and conserve water.
- Be prepared to stop for stray cattle or wildlife, such as emus and kangaroos, especially at night.
- If approaching or overtaking a road train, remember it needs to stay on the road.
- Not all roads are for public access – seek permission to drive on private land.

munity; you can buy diesel and there's a mobile mechanic based here.

At 246km you can turn off to the **Old Mornington Cattle Station** (☎ *9191 7035*), 100km off the GRR on the Fitzroy River. You can camp for $8 per person or enjoy comfortable tent accommodation (with hot showers) for $85/42.50, fully inclusive.

At 251km is the road into *Beverley Springs Homestead* (☎ *9191 4646*), a working cattle station, 43km off the GRR. You can camp here, and B&B homestays and chalets with dinner cost $115. Bookings are requested. You can also gain access to Walcott Inlet by arrangement.

The turn-off to **Adcock Gorge** is at 267km. This gorge is 5km off the road and is good for swimming. If the waterfall is not flowing too fiercely, climb above it for a good view of the surrounding country.

Horseshoe-shaped **Galvans Gorge** is less than 1km off the road at the 286km mark. Camping is not permitted. The rock paintings here include one of a Wandjina head – said by many local Aborigines to be the shadow of an ancestor imprinted on the rock.

MT BARNETT & MANNING GORGE

The *Mt Barnett Roadhouse* (☎ *9191 7007*), 306km from Derby, is owned and run by the Aboriginal Kupungarri community. A small *general store* has groceries and is open 7 am to 5 pm from May to September. It's also the access point for **Manning Gorge**, which lies 7km off the road along a dirt track. There's an entry fee of $4 per person and *camping* costs another $7 per adult.

The camp site is by the waterhole, but the best part of the gorge is about a 1¼-hour walk along the far bank – walk around the right of the waterhole to pick up the marked track. It's a strenuous walk and, because the track runs inland from the gorge, you should carry drinking water. At the end you're rewarded with a beautiful gorge and a waterfall.

BEYOND MT BARNETT

Turn-off to the **Barnett River Gorge** 328km from Derby. This is another good swimming spot, 3km down a side road.

The *Mt Elizabeth Station* (☎ *9191 4644*) lies 30km off the road at the 338km mark. B&B homestead accommodation is available but this must be arranged in advance ($105/60 per adult/child with dinner). The cost for camping is $10 per person. Scenic flights over the Horizontal Waterfalls and Bell Gorge, among other sights, depart from here May to September.

The GRR passes through magnificent scenery for the 100km past the Kalumburu Rd. There is no camping at Campbell Creek (451km from Derby) and the Durack River (496km). At 476km there is a turn-off to *Ellenbrae Station* (☎ *9161 4325*), a farther 6km down a side road; camping starts at $7 and B&B with dinner costs $105 (bookings are essential). *Jack's Waterhole* on the **Durack River Station** (☎ *9161 4324*) is 500m down a side road at the 524km mark. Bookings are required for homestead B&B with dinner ($60). Camping, including hot showers, costs $6/2 adults/children.

At 579km you get some excellent views of the Cockburn Range to the north, and to the Cambridge Gulf and the twin rivers (the Pentecost and the Durack). A kilometre farther on is the turn-off to *Home Valley Homestead* (☎ *9161 4322*), 1km off the GRR, with camping for $6/2 adults/children. Dinner plus B&B in the homestead costs $50 per person. There's also a swimming pool and emergency repairs can be done. Backpackers are welcome here.

The large **Pentecost River** is forded at 590km. Exercise extreme caution at this crossing if there's water in the river, and watch out for saltwater crocodiles if you're fishing. There's no camping.

El Questro Wilderness Park (☎ *9169 1777)*, 16km off the GRR at the 614km mark, offers a range of accommodation, facilities and activities. Luxurious accommodation at *The Homestead*, with everything included, starts at $675 a night per double (no children under 16 years) with a minimum stay of two nights.

The property also has the attractive *El Questro Bungalows*, starting at $115/150 singles/doubles, with the *Steakhouse* restaurant and *Swinging Arm Bar* nearby.

Camping options in the park include *El Questro Riverside Camping* for $10 to $15.

Activities available from El Questro Wilderness Park include 4WD and boat trips to the **Chamberlain Gorge** (starting at $37), which include a look at some Wandjina paintings. Horse rides ($30 an hour) and helicopter trips are also available. Other gorges are accessible from the park – ask one of the rangers.

The GRR's final attraction before the Great Northern Hwy is **Emma Gorge**; turn off at 623km.

Some 2km off the GRR, the *Emma Gorge Resort* (☎ *9169 1777)* is run by El Questro and has singles/doubles in tented cabins starting at $70/103. It also has a restaurant, bar, shop, swimming pool and laundry. Bookings are essential. From the resort, it's about a 40-minute walk to the spectacular gorge.

At 630km you cross King River (no camping) and at 647km you finally hit the bitumen road; Wyndham lies 48km to the north, while it's 52km east to Kununurra.

Northern Kimberley

KALUMBURU ROAD

This is a natural earth road that traverses rocky, isolated terrain. To travel it, you must be self-sufficient and well prepared. All distances given are from where the Kalum-

buru Rd leaves the GRR. This junction is 406km from Derby and 241km from the Great Northern Hwy between Wyndham and Kununurra.

It is recommended that you obtain a permit before entering the Kalumburu Aboriginal lands. Call ☎ 9161 4300 (fax 9161 4331) from 7 am to noon weekdays.

Gibb River Road to Mitchell Plateau

The Gibb River is crossed at 3km and Plain Creek at 16km. You can *camp* at both places. The first fuel is at the *Drysdale River Homestead* (☎ *9161 4326)*, 1km off the Kalumburu Rd at the 59km mark. The homestead has a licensed dining room and bar, and accommodation for $80 per double. Camping costs from $3.50 to $10 per adult. Scenic flights and 4WD tours – including trips to see examples of the ancient Bradshaw rock art (see boxed text 'Kimberley Art' later in this chapter for more information) – are also based here.

Back on the Kalumburu Rd you can turn off to *Miner's Pool* camping ground at 62km. It is 3.5km to the river and camping costs $3.50/2.50 adults/children. Just after Miner's Pool turn-off is the Drysdale River Crossing; you cannot camp here.

At 162km turn off for the Mitchell Plateau. From this junction it is 70km along the Mitchell Plateau road to the turn-off to the spectacular multitiered **Mitchell Falls**. (Most years you can't get to the falls until late May or when the wet ends.) It's a steep 16km farther (including a 3km walk) down to the falls, so allow a full day for the excursion. The walk alone can take up to six hours return and, first passes by Merten's Falls.

From May through September, Heliwork (☎ 9169 1300) bases a helicopter at the Mitchell Falls car park, meaning that you can replace that six-hour walk with a six-minute, $40 helicopter ride.

The Mitchell Plateau is also known for its ancient, tall, fan palms, its remnant rainforests, Wandjina paintings, the King Edward River and the Surveyor's Pool.

You can *camp* at King Edward River (don't use soap in the watercourse), at Camp

Creek (away from the Kandiwal Aboriginal Community) and at Mitchell Falls car park.

Kimberley Coastal Camp (☎ 9161 4410, April to October) is in a remote spot on the eastern side of Port Warrender, with access by boat from Walsh Point, 7km away. With a maximum of eight guests at any one time, the cost is $350 per person for 24 hours, which includes luxury camp-style accommodation, meals and guides.

Mitchell Plateau to Kalumburu

At 198km, *Theda Station (☎ 9161 4329)* is 1km off the road. A working cattle station, it has a store, mechanical repairs, and camping with hot showers for $9/3. Rooms with shared facilities cost $30. It offers tours of **Bradshaw art sites** and scenic flights. Access along a private road to Drysdale River National Park is also possible with the approval of the station owners.

From the Mitchell Plateau turn-off, the Kalumburu Rd heads north-east towards Kalumburu, crossing the Carson River at 247km. About 1km farther on, a road runs east to **Carson River Homestead** on the fringe of the Drysdale River National Park.

Without prior approval from the Kalumburu Aboriginal Community, there is no access to the park via this homestead. (Accommodation is not available at the homestead.)

The **Kalumburu Aboriginal Community** (☎ 9161 4300) is 267km from the GRR and about 5km from the mouth of the King Edward River and King Edward Gorge. The picturesque mission is set among giant mango trees and coconut palms, and it has accommodation. Entry is $25 per vehicle and an additional fee is levied to camp at McGowan's Island and Honeymoon Beach. The *store* is open from 8.30 to 10.50 am and 1.30 to 3.50 pm weekdays, 8.30 to 10.50 am Saturday. Fuel is available from the mission from 7 to 11 am and 1.30 to 4 pm weekdays, from 7 to 11 am Saturday.

Fishing, trekking, and scenic flights can be arranged here.

DRYSDALE RIVER NATIONAL PARK

Very few people get into Drysdale River, WA's most northern national park, 150km west of Wyndham. Apart from being one of the most remote parks in Australia – it has no

---

Kimberley Art

The Kimberley is one of the greatest ancient art galleries in the world. Many different styles of rock art are scattered through this area, but two of the better known are the Wandjina and the Bradshaw.

In 1838 the explorer George Grey, travelling in the Glenelg River region, was probably the first European to see the Wandjina paintings. These large mouthless figures in headdress are among the most famous of Aboriginal images.

Wandjina paintings are believed to be the shadows of ancestors, imprinted on the rock as they pass by. Each Wandjina traditionally had its own custodian family and, to ensure good relations between Wandjina and people, the images should be retouched annually. The sites still hold a great deal of significance for Aboriginal people, so if you stumble across one treat it with respect and don't touch the paintings.

The Bradshaw figures (some 10,000 to 30,000 years old) are much older than the Wandjina, but both their source and their significance have been forgotten and most local people now don't consider the Bradshaws part of their story.

The paintings take their name from Joseph Bradshaw, who explored the area in 1891. He said of them: 'The most remarkable fact in connection with these drawings is that wherever a profile face is shown, the features are of a most pronounced aquiline type, quite different from those of any native we encountered.'

The best way to see examples of Kimberley art is with a guide from one of the stations. Drysdale River Station (☎ 9161 4326), Theda (☎ 9161 4329), and Mt Elizabeth Station (☎ 9191 4644) run tours.

public road access – it is the largest park in the Kimberley with an area of 4482 sq km.

This park is home to a number of unique plants, diverse animals, open woodlands, rugged gorges, and the meandering Drysdale River. Rainforest – its existence not recognised until 1965 – is found in pockets along the Carson escarpment and in some gorges.

The King George River drains from the northern part of the park. At the mouth of this river are the spectacular, split **King George Falls**, best seen from the air.

Permission to access this park is required from either the Kalumburu Aboriginal Community (if travelling via Carson River Homestead) or Theda Station (to use its private route). CALM also asks that you register with its Kununurra office before making the trip in.

PRINCE REGENT NATURE RESERVE

This 6350-sq-km wilderness is one of Australia's most isolated reserves, and there are no roads into it; it is best seen from the air or its edges explored by boat. Notable features include the mesa-like **Mt Trafalgar** and **Mt Waterloo**, the cliffs of the straight **Prince Regent River** and the photogenic **King Cascade**.

Buccaneer Sea Safaris (☎ 9191 1991), based in Derby, runs cruises out of Cockatoo Island to destinations including the Prince Regent River. Prices start at $230 per person per day. Derby Air Services (☎ 9193 1375) offers a half-day West Coast Discovery flight ($330 per person) that includes the Prince Regent Reserve area – although this company shuts down in the wet season. Ask at the Derby tourist bureau for other tour options.

Great Northern Highway

DEVONIAN REEF NATIONAL PARKS

The West Kimberley boasts three national parks, based on gorges which were once part of a western 'great barrier reef' in the Devonian era, 375 to 350 million years ago

(see Geology in the Facts about Western Australia chapter). The geological mysteries of this region are unravelled in the CALM pamphlet *Geology of Windjana Gorge, Geikie Gorge and Tunnel Creek National Parks* (1985), by Phillip Playford.

Geikie Gorge National Park

The magnificent Geikie Gorge, named after the British geologist Sir Archibald Geikie, is 18km north of Fitzroy Crossing on a sealed road. Part of the gorge, on the Fitzroy River, is in a small national park only 8km by 3km. During the wet, the river rises nearly 12m and in the dry it stops flowing, leaving a series of water holes.

The vegetation here is dense and there is much wildlife, including freshwater crocodiles. Sawfish and stingrays, usually only found in or close to the sea, have adapted to the fresh water and can be seen in the river. Visitors are only permitted to walk along the prescribed part of the west bank, where there is an excellent 1.5km **walking track**.

During the April to November dry season there are one-hour boat trips ($20/2.50 adults/children) up the river, at 9.30 and 11 am and 3 pm. Times can vary – check at the Fitzroy Crossing tourist office. The trips cover 16km of the gorge; tickets are sold at the CALM information centre at the gorge.

You can also visit the gorge from April to October with Danggu Aboriginal guides (☎ 9191 5355), who show you a lot more than rocks and the water. These Bunuba people reveal interesting secrets of bush tucker, stories of the region and Aboriginal culture. The trip includes a river excursion and lunch beside the Fitzroy River for $95. It leaves from the boat ramp at the gorge at 8 am, returning at 1.30 pm.

Windjana Gorge & Tunnel Creek National Parks

You can visit the spectacular ancient rock formations of Windjana Gorge and Tunnel Creek from the Leopold Downs Rd, off the Great Northern Hwy between Fitzroy Crossing and Derby.

The near-vertical walls at the 3.5km-long Windjana Gorge soar 90m above the Lennard

River, which rushes through in the wet but becomes just a series of pools in the dry. Fossil bones of the extinct giant marsupial *Diprotodon* have been found here. Nightly *camping* fees, which include firewood, are $9/2 adults/children.

Three kilometres from the river are the ruins of **Lillimilura**, an early homestead converted to a police station in 1893.

Tunnel Creek is a 750m-long tunnel cut by the creek through a spur of the Napier Range. The tunnel is 3m to 15m wide, and you can walk all the way along it. You'll need light but sturdy shoes; be prepared to wade through very cold, chest-deep water in places.

Near the north entrance to the tunnel are **cave paintings**. At the other entrance is the black dolerite and basalt that was fashioned by the Aborigines into stone axes. A cave near the tunnel was used as a hide-out by Aboriginal tracker Jundumarra, also known as Pigeon, between 1894 and 1897 (see the boxed text).

FITZROY CROSSING
Fitzroy Crossing is on the Great Northern Hwy 256km beyond the Derby turn-off and 288km from Halls Creek.

Aboriginal people have lived in this area for many thousands of years and more than 34 Aboriginal communities still exist in the Fitzroy valley. One of these, the **Buyulu community**, about 12km south of Fitzroy Crossing, welcomes visitors.

The **old Fitzroy Crossing** site is on Russ Rd, about 4km north-east of the present town on the north bank of Brooking Creek. The **Crossing Inn**, on the south side of Brooking Creek, established as a shanty inn by Joseph Blythe in the 1890s, is the oldest pub in the Kimberley and still has lively nights. On Skuthorp Rd is a **cemetery** containing the graves of many early European pioneers.

The Fitzroy River flows for 750km through the hills and plains of the King Leopold Ranges. When in flood it takes on Amazonian proportions, extending as wide as 30km.

The helpful Fitzroy Crossing tourist office (☎ 9191 5355) is on Flynn Dr.

Places to Stay & Eat
On the Great Northern Hwy, *Fitzroy River Lodge & Caravan Park* (☎ *9191 5141*) is in a great spot, stretching across a vast lawn and tree-covered area alongside the river. It has tent/powered sites for $17/19 for two people, and safari tents (in the dry) starting at $110 for doubles. Unfortunately, it shamelessly exploits its captive market for half-decent motel rooms. A $145 room was acceptable for its great view over the flood plain – until we found the still-dirty ashtray and then had our water cut off without warning as we were having our morning showers.

Darlngunaya Backpackers (☎ *9191 5140)*, on Russ Rd, is in the old post office, about 4km from town. It has beds starting at $15 and self-contained houses for $110 for two people. It also has bikes and canoes for hire. Pick-up from the Greyhound bus (which stops outside the tourist office about 1.25 am) costs $5. Swollen waterways can make Darlngunaya inaccessible by car, so it closes in the wet.

Fitzroy Crossing has a *supermarket*. Both *roadhouses* on the Great Northern Hwy serve meals – with the Ngiyali BP said to be superior. Several items on the menu at the *Fitzroy River Lodge & Caravan Park* restaurant were unavailable, but the $23.50 steak was enormous and tasty.

On the Run

Windjana Gorge, Tunnel Creek and Lillimilura hosted the adventures of an Aboriginal tracker called Jundumarra or 'Pigeon'. In October 1894 Pigeon shot a policeman (PC William Richardson) and then went on the run with a band of dissident Aborigines.

Hiding out in the seemingly inaccessible gullies of the Napier Range, the group skilfully evaded search parties for more than two years. The deaths of several more settlers were attributed to Pigeon before he was finally trapped and killed in Tunnel Creek in early 1897. For more information get hold of a copy of the *Pigeon Heritage Trail* from the Derby tourist office ($2.50).

HALLS CREEK

pop 1200

The area around the new town of Halls Creek, in the centre of the Kimberley and on the edge of the Great Sandy Desert, was traditionally the land of the Jaru and Kija people. Graziers took over in the 1870s and virtually used these people as slave labour on stations. Now, Aboriginal communities in the Kimberley are buying more and more of these stations as they come on the market. The Shire of Halls Creek population is 65% Aboriginal.

The region was the site of WA's first gold rush in 1885. The gold soon petered out and today the town services the surrounding cattle country. The new town on the Great Northern Hwy is 15km from its much more picturesque original site where some crumbling remains can still be seen.

Halls Creek is doing its best to overcome an earlier negative reputation with regards to what it offers visitors. The town has established a shady park on its main street and has plans for a new tourist complex. In the existing tourist office, copies of the Shire of Halls Creek's 'Strategic Plan' are available. It states its vision as 'promoting participation and a sense of unity to all people'.

The Halls Creek tourist office (☎ 9168 6262), on the Great Northern Hwy, is open from 8 am to 4 pm weekdays from April to October; it is closed for the remainder of the year. It provides an excellent free map.

Things to See & Do

Artefacts and paintings produced in outlying communities are sold at an **Aboriginal art shop** on Duncan Rd.

Six kilometres east of Halls Creek and about 1.5km walk off Duncan Rd (be sure to shut the gate behind you!), there's a 6m-high natural quartz wall, called the **China Wall**, due to its supposed resemblance to the Great Wall of China.

The Halls Creek **old town** is 16km along the unsealed Duncan Rd and is definitely worth a visit. Situated in attractive hilly country, the old town town once boasted 3000 inhabitants. The only obvious remains are the walls of the old post office, made

from ant mounds and spinifex; the town's cemetery; and a huge broken bottle pile where a pub once stood. Gold can still be found in these hills.

You can swim in **Caroline Pool, Sawpit Gorge** and **Palm Springs**. A popular picnic and camping spot, Palm Springs is a natural spring located where the Black Elvire River crosses Duncan Rd. It once supported a market garden, which supplied vegetables to the area. Caroline Pool is a natural waterhole off Duncan Rd near old Halls Creek and Sawpit Gorge is a popular fishing and swimming spot on the Black Elvire River.

Oasis Air (☎ 9168 6462) operates **scenic flights** out of Halls Creek, including to the Wolfe Creek Crater ($100, 70 minutes), Purnululu National Park ($120, 80 minutes), and the Prince Regent River with a stop at Mt Hart Homestead ($360, 4½ hours). There are also plans for 4WD tours out of Halls Creek. Contact the tourist office for details.

Places to Stay

Halls Creek Caravan Park (☎ 9168 6169), on Roberta Ave towards the airport, has tent/powered sites for $14/16 for two, on-site vans for $40 per double, cabins for $50 and individual backpacker cabins for $18 per person.

A much prettier option (though check that the road is passable) is *Halls Creek Lodge* (☎ 9168 8999), in the old town on Duncan Rd. Peaceful and well-elevated with views of the surrounding hills, it has tent/powered sites for $10/12 for two, air-con rooms for $25/40 singles/doubles and dorm beds for $15. Its restaurant opens for dinner – $12.50 includes cake and coffee.

Kimberley Hotel Motel (☎ 9168 6101), on Roberta Ave, has a pleasant setting but is another place that holds travellers to ransom because of a virtual absence of competition. Its standard rooms are overpriced at $80 and its 'deluxe' rooms are comfortable but cost $140. *Halls Creek Motel* (☎ 9168 6001), on the Great Northern Hwy, has small, old-fashioned single/double rooms for $65/$80.

Places to Eat

Halls Creek Bakery, on the Great Northern Hwy, has delicious $2.20 sausage rolls, as well as other pastries and salad sandwiches. Pizza night there is Friday. The *Kimberley Hotel* has a large restaurant as well as a couple of bars. Try the $14 entree of crocodile and camembert.

Getting There & Away

From Halls Creek, Kununurra is 359km north-east and Derby 544km west. Greyhound Pioneer buses pass through Halls Creek early in the morning (northbound) and late at night (southbound).

WOLFE CREEK CRATER NATIONAL PARK

The 835m-wide and 50m-deep Wolfe Creek Crater is the second-largest known meteorite crater in the world. It is estimated to be about 300,000 years old. To the Aborigines, the crater is 'Gandimalal', a place where, according Aboriginal mythology, one of the snakes emerged from the ground.

The turn-off to the crater (the Tanami Desert Rd) is 18km out of Halls Creek towards Fitzroy Crossing and from there it's 112km by unsealed road to the south. It's easily accessible without 4WD in the dry season (April to November). Check road conditions with the Halls Creek shire office.

You can walk for about 200m along a track up to the steep crater lip. Loose rocks make it unsafe, so take care. The trees in the centre have been growing only since the 1980s when the reserve was fenced to keep out cattle.

Oasis Air takes scenic flights over the crater – see the Halls Creek section earlier.

HALLS CREEK TO KUNUNURRA

The drive from Halls Creek to Kununurra takes 3½ to four hours. The only petrol stop on the highway is at **Warmun** (Turkey Creek), 163km north-east of Halls Creek. The *Turkey Creek Roadhouse* (☎ 9168 7882) is not a bad place to take a break. It has takeaway food including 'game burgers' and fresh fruit salad. Tent/powered sites here cost $15/20, motel units $70 and dorm beds $20.

Warmun is known mainly for its close proximity to the Purnululu National Park. Heliwork (☎ 9168 7337) has an office at the roadhouse and runs chopper rides over the area, giving an excellent overview of the park's fern-fringed gorges and amazingly striped sandstone domes. A 45-minute flight with a well-informed, friendly pilot is well worth the $170 per person (minimum two passengers).

East Kimberley Tours (☎ 9168 2213) also runs Purnululu tours out of Warmun. A 13-hour 'express' 4WD trip leaves at 5.30 am and makes stops including Echidna Chasm and Cathedral Gorge and costs $136.

Opposite the roadhouse is the **Daiwul Gidja Culture Centre** (☎ 9168 7580), open on weekdays from November to March and daily from April to October. It has interpretive displays, videos and staff on hand to give an insight into the culture and knowledge of the Gidja people, inhabitants of the Warmun area for thousands of years. The centre also offers half-day and full-day cultural and bush-tucker tours for $48/98.

PURNULULU NATIONAL PARK

The 350-million-year-old **Bungle Bungle Range** at the Purnululu National Park is an amazing spectacle: impressive rounded sandstone towers, with an exterior crust striped in bands of orange (iron oxide) and blackish-green (cyanobacteria). The range is a plateau that is more than 200m above the surrounding plain and at its edges are the curious beehive domes.

Traditionally the land of the Kija and Jaru people, who still live in settlements in the East Kimberley, the park contains Aboriginal art and a number of burial sites, though these are not accessible to the public. Tourists did not start visiting the 'Bungles' until after the area was filmed by a TV crew in 1982. By the end of the 1990s, visitor numbers were approaching 15,000 annually.

The national park and adjoining conservation reserve (totalling 3100 sq km) are 165km (four hours) from Halls Creek and 305km (five hours) from Kununurra. The range is hard to get to and access is limited to 4WDs with good clearance; no caravans

THE KIMBERLEY

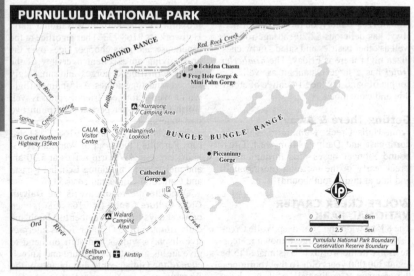

PURNULULU NATIONAL PARK

OSMOND RANGE

Red Rock Creek

Frank River

Bellburn Creek

Spring Creek

Spring

Spring

Echidna Chasm

Frog Hole Gorge &
Mini Palm Gorge

Kurrajong
Camping Area

CALM
Visitor
Centre

Walanginidji
Lookout

BUNGLE BUNGLE RANGE

To Great Northern
Highway (35km)

Piccaninny
Gorge

Cathedral
Gorge

Piccaninny Creek

Walardi
Camping
Area

Ord River

Bellburn
Camp

Airstrip

0   4   8km
0   2.5   5mi

Purnululu National Park Boundary
Conservation Reserve Boundary

or trailers are permitted. Visitors are asked to stay on authorised tracks as new tracks quickly erode in the wet. The park is closed from 1 January to 31 March; this is extended if the weather is bad. Visitors to the park are charged an entry fee of $9 per vehicle. *Camping* costs $9/2 adults/children.

From the main highway it's 53km along the Spring Creek Track to Three Ways, where the ranger's headquarters and CALM visitor centre are located.

There is much to see once you have made the long trip to the park, but it will all be a little bewildering unless you have some means of interpreting what you are looking at. The CALM visitor centre is open 7 am to noon and 1 to 4 pm daily from May to September. Information and souvenirs are available. You can also buy the *Bungle Bungle Range* guide book by the Australian Geological Survey Organisation here.

Things to See & Do
Walking is the only means of access into the gorges so this is the main activity in the park. **Echidna Chasm** in the north and **Cathedral Gorge** in the south are each about a two-hour return walk from the nearest car

parks. The soaring **Piccaninny Gorge** is a 30km round trip that comfortably takes two days to walk. **Frog Hole** walking trail takes about two hours return and leads to a small pool at the base of the Bungle Bungle Range, while **Mini Palms Gorge** is a 5km return walk that has some difficult parts and takes about three hours return. It leads to a natural amphitheatre where many young palms grow.

Walanginjdji Lookout, just a couple of kilometres from the visitor centre, is an easy 500m return walk and gives views of the western side of the range.

The narrow gorges in the northern part of the park can only be seen from the air. They too are a spectacular sight, choked in fan palms. The Kimberley's southernmost patches of rainforest are found around Osmond Creek. The rock formations of the Bungle Bungle Range are fragile – you're not allowed to climb them.

Organised Tours
As the range is so vast, and many parts are inaccessible from the ground, flights and helicopter rides prove to be money well spent. For flights and tours operating out of

Warmun and Halls Creek, see the Halls Creek and Halls Creek to Kununurra sections earlier in this chapter.

Alligator Airways (☎ 9168 1333) does 135-minute scenic flights from Kununurra over the Bungle Bungle Range for $170/90 adults/children. Combined with a 4WD ground trip and walk through Cathedral Gorge, the cost is $375. Slingair (☎ 9169 1300) also does flights from Kununurra, starting at $170/130 adults/children.

Kimberley Desert Inn 4WD Adventure (☎ 9169 1257) takes three-day tours into the Bungle Bungle Range for $430.

Broome-based Kimberley Wilderness Adventures (☎ 9192 5741) has a two-day drive-in, fly-out option for $575/475. East Kimberley Tours (☎ 9168 2213) has trips from Kununurra starting at $318 (plus $30 park fee). You can also drive yourself in by 4WD and pay to stay at its Bellburn Camp for $80 per person, including dinner and breakfast; bookings are required.

Places to Stay

It's 20 minutes north from CALM's visitor centre to *Kurrajong Camping Area* and 30 minutes south to *Walardi Camping Area*. Both areas are for casual visitors – they have long-drop toilets, untreated water and fireplaces firewood supplied. (Bellburn Creek Camp is reserved for fly/drive visitors and licensed tour operators.) Camping fees apply.

There is no rubbish disposal so take all your rubbish out of the park.

Getting There & Away

The turn-off to the single-access track to the park, known as Spring Creek Track, is 110km north of Halls Creek and 50km south of Warnum. This 4WD-only track traverses rugged country with numerous creek crossings and, although it's only 53km between the highway and Three Ways, it takes 2½ hours to drive. From Three Ways it is 12km to the Walardi Camping Area (30 minutes); 20km to the Echidna Chasm car park (45 minutes); 7km to Kurrajong Camping Area (20 minutes); and 27km to the Piccaninny Creek car park (one hour).

KUNUNURRA
pop 4800

In the Miriwoong language the region is known as 'Gananoorrang' ('meeting of the waters') – Kununurra is the European translation of this. As in most parts of the rugged Kimberley, Aborigines have occupied the area for thousands of years. Nearby, Hidden Valley is of great significance to the Aboriginal people and has ancient rock art and axe grooves.

Founded in the 1960s, Kununurra, in the centre of the Ord River Irrigation Scheme, is a striking green, attractive, bustling little place. Much of its history features in Mary Durack's *Kings in Grass Castles* and *Sons in the Saddle*. In the past it was just a stopover on the main highway and there was little incentive to linger. Now there's enough to keep you here for several days plus. The main part of town branches off the Victoria Hwy, which skirts Lily Creek Lagoon. This lagoon is part of Lake Kununurra – created by the Kununurra Diversion Dam, built across the Ord River in 1963. Upstream some 72km by road from Kununurra is the much bigger Ord Dam, built in 1971. By almost completely plugging the Ord River's massive wet season rush of water, the dam created the largest body of fresh water in Australia: Lake Argyle.

The town is a popular place to look for work. The main fruit-picking season starts in May and ends about September. Contact Kimberley Group Training (☎ 9168 3808) in the Commonwealth Building on Konkerberry Dr for further information.

Information

Kununurra tourist office (☎ 9168 1177), on Coolibah Dr, is open from 8 am to 5 pm weekdays, 8 am to 4 pm weekends, from April to September. The rest of the year it is open from 9 am to 4 pm weekdays, 9 am to noon Saturday. It was working towards having Internet terminals set up for public use by mid-2000.

Internet access is also available at the Telecentre (☎ 9169 1868), on Coolibah Dr. The CALM office (☎ 9168 0200) is on Konkerberry Dr and a laundrette is in Banksia St.

THE KIMBERLEY

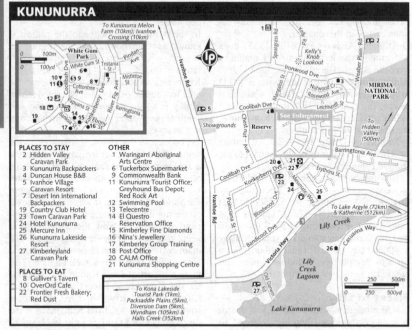

KUNUNURRA

To Kununurra Melon Farm (10km); Ivanhoe Crossing (10km)

White Gum Park

To Kununurra Melon Farm (10km); Ivanhoe Crossing (10km)

Kelly's Knob Lookout

MIRIMA NATIONAL PARK

See Enlargement

Showgrounds

Reserve

To Hidden Valley (500m)

To Lake Argyle (72km) & Katherine (512km)

Lily Creek

Lily Creek Lagoon

Lake Kununurra

To Kona Lakeside Tourist Park (1km); Packsaddle Plains (5km); Diversion Dam (5km); Wyndham (105km) & Halls Creek (352km)

PLACES TO STAY
2 Hidden Valley Caravan Park
3 Kununurra Backpackers
4 Duncan House B&B
5 Ivanhoe Village Caravan Resort
7 Desert Inn International Backpackers
19 Country Club Hotel
23 Town Caravan Park
24 Hotel Kununurra
25 Mercure Inn
26 Kununurra Lakeside Resort
27 Kimberleyland Caravan Park

PLACES TO EAT
8 Gulliver's Tavern
10 OverOrd Cafe
22 Frontier Fresh Bakery; Red Dust

OTHER
1 Waringarri Aboriginal Arts Centre
6 Tuckerbox Supermarket
9 Commonwealth Bank
11 Kununurra Tourist Office; Greyhound Bus Depot; Red Rock Art
12 Swimming Pool
13 Telecentre
14 El Questro Reservation Office
15 Kimberley Fine Diamonds
16 Nina's Jewellery
17 Kimberley Group Training
18 Post Office
20 CALM Office
21 Kununurra Shopping Centre

Kununurra's time is 1½ hours behind that of Katherine in the NT. Kununurra is free of the Mediterranean fruit fly, so strict quarantine regulations apply when entering WA from the NT.

Peak season in Kununurra is during the dry; in the wet, roads into the town are sometimes completely impassable, cutting it off for weeks.

Mirima National Park

This national park, with a steep gorge, some great views and a few short walking tracks, covers an area of 18 sq km. This is a rugged area of 300-million-year-old sandstone hills and valleys, and is often described as a 'mini Purnululu'.

Mirima is the name given to the park by the Miriwoong people. Shelter and permanent water made it a meeting place and a *corroboree* ground.

Within the park you will see small boab trees growing out of the valley walls. It is believed that rock-wallabies carried the seeds in their droppings.

Three short walking trails within the park are the **Lily Pool** (100m return), where there are stone-axe grooves; **Wuttuwutubin** ('short and narrow', 500m return), which enters a steep-sided gorge; and **Didbagirring** (1km return), which affords great views over Kununurra and the banded-rock formations of the park.

Other Attractions

The **Waringarri Aboriginal Arts Centre** is on Speargrass Rd. You get a certificate of authenticity with any painting purchased, and biographies of artists are available. It also sells carved boab nuts. **Red Rock Art** is another gallery, located in the same building as the tourist office.

To see some of the gleaming products of the Argyle Diamond Mine, go to Nina's Jewellery or Kimberley Fine Diamonds, both on Konkerberry Dr.

There are good views of the irrigated fields from **Kelly's Knob Lookout**, a short drive from the town centre. During the wet, distant thunderstorms can be spectacular when viewed from here, although caution is needed as the Knob is frequently struck by lightning.

Lake Kununurra has plentiful birdlife and thousands of freshwater crocodiles (See the boxed text 'Freshies & Salties' later in this chapter). There's good fishing downstream of Diversion Dam (watch for dangerous saltwater crocodiles) and also on the Ord River at **Ivanhoe Crossing** – also a salty hang-out, so don't swim there.

Packsaddle Plains, 6km out of town, has a zebra rock gallery and a small wildlife park. On Research Station Rd 11km from town, the **Kununurra Melon Farm** (☎ 9168 1400) has tours and tastings.

The **swimming pool** (☎ 9168 2120) on Coolibah Dr is open daily ($2.50/1.50 adults/children).

Organised Tours & Flights

Canoe trips on the Ord River between Lake Argyle and the Diversion Dam are popular. The recommended Kimberley Canoeing Experience (☎ 1800-805 010) has one- to three-day tours for $95 to $160, with gear supplied, including transport to the dam.

Barramundi is the major fishing attraction, but other fish are also caught. Arnie Birch (☎ 9169 1820) is an indigenous guide who claims to have caught his first barramundi when he was just four years old. His day-long Fishing Adventures include gear, lunch and billy tea for $210. The price is the same for a day at Macka's Barra Camp (☎ 9169 1759), on the lower Ord River. Ultimate Adventures (☎ 9168 2310) can organise float-plane transfers for catered remote-location fishing trips – call for prices.

The excellent Triple J Tours (☎ 9168 2682) operates daily 110km-return cruises from Kununurra along the Ord River to the Ord Dam wall. The scenery is spectacular and the commentary, from a well-informed skipper, adds a whole new dimension.

During our tour, we saw wild donkeys, freshwater crocodiles, an amazing array of birdlife, cliff-living wallabies, and bats (the best bit). The cost of $75/40 adults/children includes an afternoon tea of pumpkin scones. An alternative is Duncan's Ord River Tours (☎ 9168 1823).

Kununurra is the base for numerous companies taking tours and scenic flights to other parts of the Kimberley. For example, East Kimberley Tours (☎ 9168 2213) runs a wide range of fly/drive trips to destinations including the GRR, Mitchell Plateau and the Devonian Reef Gorges for $850 to 2250. Slingair (☎ 9169 1300) does full-day scenic flights over Purnululu National Park, Lake Argyle and the Argyle Diamond Mine from April to November for $525, including 4WD ground tours of the Bungle Bungle Range. Alligator Airways (☎ 9168 1333) does Purnululu National Park fly-overs, taking in Lake Argyle and Argyle Diamond Mine for $170/90 adults/children.

Kimberley Desert Inn 4WD Adventure (☎ 9169 1257) does budget trips out of Kununurra along the GRR (five days) for $715, and through the Purnululu National Park (three days) for $430. Lake Argyle Cruises (☎ 9168 7361) provides a coach transfer from Kununurra to its tours of massive Lake Argyle, some 70km south-east of Kununurra – a two-hour cruise with transfer costs $46/25 adults/children.

Day tours are available to El Questro Wilderness Park, including Emma Gorge, Zebedee Springs and the Chamberlain River, for $125. Bookings can be made at the El Questro Reservation Office (☎ 9169 1777), in Banksia St.

Places to Stay

Camping & Caravan Parks Kununurra has beautiful caravan parks. The central *Town Caravan Park (☎ 9168 1763)*, on Bloodwood Dr, has tent/powered sites starting at $8/18, on-site vans starting at $60/50 peak/off-peak, and en suite villas starting at $90/70. *Hidden Valley Caravan Park (☎ 9168 1790)*, on Weaber Plain Rd at the base of the national park, has unpowered/powered sites for $14/16 for two people. The fastidiously maintained *Ivanhoe Village Caravan Resort (☎ 9169 1995)*, on Coolibah Dr, has a range of accommodation from unpowered/powered sites for $16/18 to good-value cabins for $89/75 peak/off-peak.

Kona Lakeside Tourist Park (☎ 9168 1031) is in a picturesque, leafy spot about 2km from town on Lake Kununurra. Tent /powered sites start at $8.50/19.50, on-site vans start at $45, and park cabins and bungalows cost from $55 to $105. Sites at *Kimberleyland Caravan Park* (☎ 9168 1280), on the lake's edge on the Victoria Hwy, cost $16/18.50 for two people.

Hostels One pair of travellers at *Desert Inn International Backpackers* (☎ 9168 2702), on Tristania St, told us: 'When you meet the owner of this place, you will fall in love with her'. While we wouldn't quite go that far, this hostel is certainly friendly, comfortable and well organised. Dorm beds start at $15 and doubles at $40. Prices are similar at *Kununurra Backpackers* (☎ 9169 1998, 22 Nutwood Crescent), in a couple of adjacent houses with a shady garden. Both hostels have pools.

B&Bs The best place we saw in Kununurra was *Duncan House B&B* (☎ 9168 2436, 167 Coolibah Dr). Quality en suite rooms start at $90/110 singles/doubles.

Hotels & Motels At either end of the peak season it's worth shopping around because special deals are sometimes available. Tariffs are otherwise pretty high in the dry.

The central *Country Club Hotel* (☎ 9168 1024, 47 Coolibah Dr) has relatively new, light motel rooms starting at $120/105 per double peak/off-peak. The tiredness of the friendly *Hotel Kununurra* (☎ 9168 1344), on Messmate Way, is reflected in its room prices: doubles cost $55 to $90 peak; $50 to $70 off-peak. Kununurra also has a *Mercure Inn* (☎ 9168 1455), on the corner of Victoria Hwy and Messmate Way, with rooms for $140/105 peak/off-peak. *Kununurra Lakeside Resort* (☎ 9169 1092), on Casuarina Way, is in a great spot overlooking Lily Creek Lagoon, but the service was a bit hit-and-miss when we visited early in the season. Tariffs are $130 in peak season, but special off-peak deals can go as low as $78.

Places to Eat
The *OverOrd Cafe*, next to the tourist office, has reasonable coffee and does Thai takeaway as well as sandwiches and breakfasts. *Frontier Fresh Bakery*, on River Fig Ave, makes tasty salad rolls. Part of the bakery is *Red Dust*, which has gourmet pizzas starting at $14.95. You can sometimes buy home-baked rye bread from the *Tuckerbox supermarket*. The Country Club Hotel has good Chinese food in its *Chopsticks* restaurant; its *Kelly's Bar & Grill* opens in the peak season and serves pizzas and Italian food by the pool. *Gulliver's Tavern* (196 Cottontree Ave) has a bar and also The George Room restaurant. The *Hotel Kununurra* also has meals. The restaurant at the *Mercure Inn* was under renovation when we visited.

Getting There & Away
Ansett Australia (☎ 13 1300) has flights to and from Perth, Darwin and Broome daily. Greyhound (☎ 13 2030) buses pass through Kununurra daily on the Darwin to Perth route; they pick up and drop off outside the tourist office. The northbound bus arrives 9 am; the southbound at 5.45 pm.

LAKE ARGYLE
Created when the mighty Ord River was dammed in 1971, Lake Argyle is the largest body of fresh water in Australia, holding up to 30 times as much water as Sydney Harbour and containing about 90 islands. Prior to its construction, there was too much water in the wet season and not enough in the dry to sustain profitable agriculture. A regular water supply has encouraged farming – especially of tropical fruit, including bananas and melons – on a massive scale.

The lake is 72km from Kununurra by sealed road. Near the lake is the reconstructed **Argyle Homestead**, once home to prominent pioneer family the Duracks and was moved here when its original site was flooded. It now houses a **pioneer museum**, open from 8.30 am to 4.30 pm daily from April to October (admission is $2).

Lake Argyle Tourist Village, located east of the Ord Dam, is the base for trips out onto this enormous inland sea. Lake Argyle

Cruises (☎ 9168 7361) runs a six-hour, 120km cruise daily from June to August and on demand from September to May. You can see a vast range of wildlife, have a fossick on one of the islands and enjoy a sunset beer or wine ($95/60 adults/children). The same company runs fishing tours ($70/50), sunset cruises ($35/17.50) and diving trips to the submerged **Argyle Downs homestead**. Alligator Airways (☎ 9168 1333) offers a float-plane flight over the Bungle Bungle Range to Lake Argyle, meeting up with other tours. Prices start at $210/140.

Places to Stay & Eat
Near the Ord Dam, *Lake Argyle Tourist Village (☎ 9168 7360)* has unpowered/powered sites for $12/15.50 for two people, and rooms starting at $65. It's nothing flash but its bar reputedly has good food, including locally caught silver cobbler or barramundi. It screens a video showing the construction of the huge neighbouring dam on request.

ARGYLE DIAMOND MINE
About 250km south of Kununurra is Argyle Diamond Mine – the world's largest – which produces around one-third of the world's diamonds, although most of these are of industrial quality.

Belray Diamond Tours (☎ 9168 1014) join with Slingair to offer several different trips. A seven-hour combined Purnululu National Park fly-over and mine visit costs $295 per person, lunch included. Its road-tour option to the mine costs $155. Once at the mine, visitors see most of its major features including the open-cut pit, the processing plant and security room.

WYNDHAM
pop 1500
Well worth the 105km side trip from Kununurra, Wyndham has an untouched feel and one of the most amazing look-outs in the north-west. Its port, a short drive north of the newer part of town, has an atmospheric main street featuring several buildings from the gold rush era.

Towering over the port, Mt Bastion (330m) provides the breathtaking **Five Rivers Lookout**, accessible via a steep sealed 4km of road. From here you see the King, Pentecost, Durack, Forrest and Ord Rivers enter the Cambridge Gulf.

In 1819 Lieutenant Phillip Parker King, in the *Mermaid*, sailed into the inlet where Wyndham now stands; he named the gulf after the Duke of Cambridge.

There are **paintings** of great antiquity in the Wyndham region, evidence of the Aboriginal culture that thrived here for thousands of years.

Wyndham was the starting point for two record-breaking flights to England in 1931 and the finish of an England to Australia flight in 1933.

The enthusiastic owners of the Mobil petrol station (☎ 9161 1281) have heaps of tourist information and advice.

Things to See & Do
A number of **historic buildings** survive in the port – the old post office, Durack's store (now a hardware shop), and the old Court House (now a museum, $2).

From the wharf and floating pontoon next to the boat ramp you can sometimes see large, saltwater (estuarine) **crocodiles**, originally attracted to the area by the blood drain from the now-defunct abattoir. Keep well back from the water's edge – they are extremely quick, crafty and powerful, and don't mind a bit of human flesh for dinner. For a closer, safer look at these awesome reptiles, visit the **Wyndham Zoological Gardens and Crocodile Park** (☎ 9161 1124), on Barytes Rd. It is open daily from March to November ($11); guided tours and crocodile feeding (of whole chickens, in one gulp) are held at 11 am.

The park also runs a breeding program for the rare Komodo dragon, the world's largest lizard, and has six of these endangered Indonesian natives in an enclosure with a viewing platform.

Not far from Wyndham is a protected bird sanctuary – **Marlgu Billabong** in Parry Lagoons Nature Reserve – featuring a bird hide and boardwalk. The Parry

Freshies & Salties

The Kimberley is home to two types of crocodiles: one that rarely eats anything bigger than a bat, and one that, come dinner time, views humans as a satisfactory substitute for cow or dingo. The former is the freshwater crocodile (*Crocodylus johnstoni*), or 'freshy'. The latter is the saltwater or estuarine crocodile (*C. porosus*) – the massive, prehistoric-looking 'salty'.

Northern Australia's salties are the world's largest remaining crocodile species. Male salties grow to an average 5m, though one has been measured at 7.3m. They can weigh up to three-quarters of a tonne. Just by looking at a large male you can see that, once he has reached maturity, he's pretty much invincible in the wild. Salties can live to more than 70 years. Reproductive age for males is 16; for the smaller female, it's 14. Breeding season is the wet.

Salties – which can inhabit fresh as well as salt water – have been known to lie in wait for prey (for example, a cow) for days, getting to know its routines. In attack, it propels itself out of the water with its tail and clamps its vast jaw around the cow's head. Then it goes into a death roll – spinning its body to topple the cow over before pulling it into the water and drowning it. Very occasionally it will do the same to people – but to keep things in perspective, in the last 20 years there has been less than one fatal crocodile attack per year.

In contrast, the freshy is, if anything, scared of people and would only cause you injury by snapping at you if you happened to step on it. It eats insects, birds, small fish and bats, and very occasionally may attack a dingo at the water's edge. Males grow to a maximum 3.3m; females to 1.85m. They live no longer than 50 years.

Lily Creek Lagoon in Kununurra is a good spot to see freshies. Take a high-powered torch down at dusk and see hundreds of pairs of eyes glinting on the water's surface. As for salties, if you're close enough to get a good look at one in the wild, you're probably also close enough to get eaten. Crocodile farms in Broome and Wyndham are a better option.

Creek flood plain has been listed as a 'wetland of international importance' under the Ramsar Convention, established to protect migratory birds that in some cases fly from as far as Siberia each year.

The Kununurra office of CALM (☎ 9168 0200) conducts bird-watching tours during the dry.

Kimberley Pursuits (☎ 9161 1029) offers horse treks of two to seven days duration starting at $260. Joining a 10-day annual June cattle muster costs $800.

Places to Stay & Eat

Featuring an enormous boab tree, *Wyndham Caravan Park* (☎ 9161 1064), on Baker St, has tent/powered sites for $14/17 for two people. Standard/budget rooms in the atmospheric *Wyndham Town Hotel* (☎ 9161 1202), on O'Donnell St, cost $80/50.

Across the road, the town's only budget option for self-caterers is the *Gulf Breeze Guest House* (☎ 9161 1401), in the old postmaster's house. It has a pool, breezy verandahs and a homely feel, and singles/doubles cost $30/45. On the Great Northern Hwy south of town, motel rooms at the *Wyndham Community Club* (☎ 9161 1130) were being refurbished when we visited and cost $49.50/$60.50.

Parry's Creek Farm (☎ 9161 1139) is 7km off the Great Northern Hwy on a road that's impassable when wet. Situated in an internationally protected bird reserve (see Things to See & Do earlier), it has camping for $7 per person, and a double and a twin room for $45. Meals are available in peak season.

Burgers and fish and chips at *Captain Robb's Port Takeaway*, across the road from Wyndham Town Hotel and partly overlooking the harbour, are recommended. Both the hotel and Wyndham Community Club have meals. On the Great Northern Hwy, the *bakery* has pastries, and a kiosk in the *Tuckerbox supermarket* makes up sandwiches.

Glossary

back of beyond – very remote area
billabong – water hole in dried-up riverbed
birridas – salt lakes
boomerang – Aboriginal curved, flat wooden hunting instrument
booze bus – police van used for random breath-testing for alcohol
bottle shop – liquor shop
boys and girls in blue – police officers
bull bar – outsize front bumper on vehicle, used as a barrier against animals
bull dust – fine, powdery and sometimes deep dust on Outback roads
bush – treed-covered area; the country
bushranger – Australia's equivalent of the outlaws of the American Wild West
bush tucker – food available naturally in the wild
BYO – Bring Your Own (alcohol)

Centre, the – the remote interior of Australia
chopper – helicopter
corroboree – a sacred or festive Aboriginal gathering
counter meal – pub meal

didgeridoo – cylindrical, wooden Aboriginal musical instrument
dormitory suburb – a suburb from which most residents commute to work in a nearby large town
dry, the – the dry season

Eftpos – Electronic Funds Transfer at Point of Sale

flightseeing – aerial sightseeing
fossick – hunt for semiprecious stones
freshy – freshwater crocodile

green, the – alternative term for *the wet*

homestead – the residence of a *station* owner or manager

kampong – Malay village
Koori – Aborigine

mallee – low, shrubby, multistemmed eucalypt; also 'the mallee' – the *bush*
marron – freshwater crayfish
midden – refuse; remains
milk bar – small shop selling milk and other provisions
Modern Australian – cuisine borrowing from foreign influences

Nyungar – Aboriginal people of the south-western region

off the beaten track – unfamiliar territory
Outback, the – remote part of the *bush*

paddock – a fenced area of land, usually intended for livestock; field
Perth Hills – local name for the Darling Range
pindan – semiarid country of south-western Kimberley region

rammed earth – compacted earth used as building material
(park) ranger – person employed to patrol public parks
roadhouse – a restaurant or cafe, usually with a petrol station, on the side of a road
road train – very long articulated truck
roo bar – *bull bar*

salty – saltwater crocodile
scrub – stunted trees and bushes in a dry area; a remote, uninhabited area
sealed road – tarred road
sea wasp – box jellyfish; also known as a 'stinger'
splurge – spend extravagantly
station – large sheep or cattle farm

thongs – flip-flops; casual summer footwear
twitcher – bird-watcher
two-up – traditional heads/tails game

WACA – Western Australian Cricket Association (pronounced 'WAKKA')
wet, the – rainy season

yabbie – small freshwater crayfish

Acknowledgments

Thanks

Thanks to Tim Winton for permission to use the extract from his *Land's Edge* (published in 1993 by Pan Macmillan Australia), which appears on page 11 of this book.

Many thanks to the travellers who used the last edition and wrote to us with helpful hints, useful advice and interesting anecdotes. Your names follow:

Barbara & Chris Addy, Karinda Agnew, Shan & John Allert, H E Arnold, Nicola Bates, Michael Bau, Maria Berger, Peter Beyerle, Wendy Bignami, Georgina Bingham, Ina Birkenbeul, Eugen Birnbaumer, Jesper Boegeskov, Mandy Borsberry, Simon Bowker, David Braidwood, Enid S Brett, David M Brice, Jill & Paul Bromhead, Angela Brooks, Sarah Broughton, Joan Brown, David Burkart, Sandra Butler, Jane Caldwell, Barry Carter, Connie Chai, Kay Courtney, Julia Cox, Belinda Creswell, Duncan Davidson, Elizabeth Docking, Dawn Dybing, Anne Evans, Rob Fariel, Tony Ferrell, Pat Frost, G Gardnerina, Paddy Garthwaite, Pistor Gerhart, Peter Gillen, Russell Glass, Justine Griffith, Godfrey Guinan, Rita Gupta, Lyn Halliday,

M G Hampton, Simon Harris, Ian Harrison, Digby Hart, Abby Harwood, Fiona Heggie, Axel Hein, Kim Hind, Carl R Holm, Orlando Huber, Brendan Jones, Gregory Jones, M & H Jones, Lorenza Kasner, Robert & Caro Kay, S Kay, Daniel Kelly, Ky Khan, Holger Koetzle, Rex Hu Ton Kwong, D Langley, Amanda Larkin, Stephen Le Breton, Aileen Lee, Kathryn Levi, Deborah Ling, Derek Lister, Stephen Litvin, Mary Lou Tucker, Jill Maguire, Lisa Marion, Marg Mason, Chris McLaughlin, John McLeod, A P Cullen MengBeng, Rosanne & Tim Moore, Daniel Morrissy, Michael Moylan, Daniel Mrier, John Musca, Caroline Norton, S O'Brien, Nick O'Neil, Ann & Eddie Parcell, Susan Park, Kaaren Payne, Chris Peach, Sylvia van der Peet, J & R Pilcher, Norman Poulter, Liz Power, Philippe Quix, Eleanor Rairi, Andrea Ream, Eamonn Richardson, Sean & Carol Richardson, Jeff Riley, Mallory Rome, Jeff Ross, Rick Roylance, Ross Rutherford, Trish Ryding, Mike Scott, Meg Slooman, A Sompopsakul, Mary Steen, Dave Stewart, Gunnar Stoelsvik, Tom Suffling, Nicole Sunier, Christina Tassell, Elisa Tembras, Anne Thomson, Aisha Timol, Dr Klaus Truoel, Cathy Viero, Jane Wall, Anne Wallis, Tim Lohmann Holger & Katrin Wiesel, Laura Wilson, Miriam Wilson

LONELY PLANET

You already know that Lonely Planet produces more than this one guidebook, but you might not be aware of the other products we have on this region. Here is a selection of titles that you may want to check out as well:

Australia
ISBN 1 86450 068 9

Outback Australia
ISBN 0 86442 504 X

Australian phrasebook
ISBN 0 86442 576 7

Aboriginal Australia
ISBN 1 86450 114 6

Cycling Australia
ISBN 1 86450 166 90

Walking in Australia
ISBN 0 86442 669 0

Watching Wildlife Australia
ISBN 1 86450 032 8

New South Wales
ISBN 0 86442 706 9

Victoria
ISBN 0 86442 734 4

Australia Road Atlas
ISBN 0 86450 065 4

South Australia
ISBN 0 86442 716 6

Healthy Travel Australia, NZ & the Pacific
ISBN 1 86450 052 2

Northern Territory
ISBN 0 86442 791 3

Queensland
ISBN 0 86442 590 2

Tasmania
ISBN 0 86442 727 1

Available wherever books are sold

LONELY PLANET

Guides by Region

Lonely Planet is known worldwide for publishing practical, reliable and no-nonsense travel information in our guides and on our Web site. The Lonely Planet list covers just about every accessible part of the world. Currently there are 16 series: Travel guides, Shoestring guides, Condensed guides, Phrasebooks, Read This First, Healthy Travel, Walking guides, Cycling guides, Watching Wildlife guides, Pisces Diving & Snorkeling guides, City Maps, Road Atlases, Out to Eat, World Food, Journeys travel literature and Pictorials.

AFRICA Africa on a shoestring • Cairo • Cairo City Map • Cape Town • Cape Town City Map • East Africa • Egypt • Egyptian Arabic phrasebook • Ethiopia, Eritrea & Djibouti • Ethiopian (Amharic) phrasebook • The Gambia & Senegal • Healthy Travel Africa • Kenya • Malawi • Morocco • Moroccan Arabic phrasebook • Mozambique • Read This First: Africa • South Africa, Lesotho & Swaziland • Southern Africa • Southern Africa Road Atlas • Swahili phrasebook • Tanzania, Zanzibar & Pemba • Trekking in East Africa • Tunisia • Watching Wildlife East Africa •   Watching Wildlife Southern Africa • West Africa • World Food Morocco • Zimbabwe, Botswana & Namibia
Travel Literature: Mali Blues: Traveling to an African Beat • The Rainbird: A Central African Journey • Songs to an African Sunset: A Zimbabwean Story

AUSTRALIA & THE PACIFIC Auckland • Australia • Australian phrasebook • Australia Road Atlas • Bushwalking in Australia •Cycling New Zealand • Fiji • Fijian phrasebook • Healthy Travel Australia, NZ and the Pacific • Islands of Australia's Great Barrier Reef • Melbourne • Melbourne City Map • Micronesia • New Caledonia • New South Wales & the ACT • New Zealand • Northern Territory • Outback Australia • Out to Eat – Melbourne • Out to Eat – Sydney • Papua New Guinea • Pidgin phrasebook • Queensland • Rarotonga & the Cook Islands • Samoa • Solomon Islands • South Australia • South Pacific • South Pacific phrasebook • Sydney • Sydney City Map • Sydney Condensed • Tahiti & French Polynesia • Tasmania • Tonga • Tramping in New Zealand • Vanuatu • Victoria • Walking in Australia • Watching Wildlife Australia • Western Australia
Travel Literature: Islands in the Clouds: Travels in the Highlands of New Guinea • Kiwi Tracks: A New Zealand Journey • Sean & David's Long Drive

CENTRAL AMERICA & THE CARIBBEAN Bahamas, Turks & Caicos • Baja California • Bermuda • Central America on a shoestring • Costa Rica • Costa Rica Spanish phrasebook • Cuba • Dominican Republic & Haiti • Eastern Caribbean • Guatemala • Guatemala, Belize & Yucatán: La Ruta Maya • Healthy Travel Central & South America • Jamaica • Mexico • Mexico City • Panama • Puerto Rico • Read This First: Central & South America • World Food Mexico • Yucatán
Travel Literature: Green Dreams: Travels in Central America

EUROPE Amsterdam • Amsterdam City Map • Amsterdam Condensed • Andalucía • Austria • Baltic States phrasebook • Barcelona • Barcelona City Map • Berlin • Berlin City Map • Britain • British phrasebook • Brussels, Bruges & Antwerp • Brussels City Map • Budapest • Budapest City Map • Canary Islands • Central Europe • Central Europe phrasebook • Corfu & the Ionians • Corsica • Crete • Crete Condensed • Croatia • Cycling Britain • Cycling France • Cyprus • Czech & Slovak Republics • Denmark • Dublin • Dublin City Map • Eastern Europe • Eastern Europe phrasebook • Edinburgh • Estonia, Latvia & Lithuania • Europe on a shoestring • Finland • Florence • France • Frankfurt Condensed • French phrasebook • Georgia, Armenia & Azerbaijan • Germany • German phrasebook • Greece • Greek Islands • Greek phrasebook • Hungary • Iceland, Greenland & the Faroe Islands • Ireland • Istanbul • Italian phrasebook • Italy • Krakow • Lisbon • The Loire • London • London City Map • London Condensed • Madrid • Malta • Mediterranean Europe • Mediterranean Europe phrasebook • Moscow • Mozambique • Munich • the Netherlands • Norway • Out to Eat – London • Paris • Paris City Map • Paris Condensed • Poland • Portugal • Portuguese phrasebook • Prague • Prague City Map • Provence & the Côte d'Azur • Read This First: Europe • Romania & Moldova • Rome • Rome City Map • Russia, Ukraine & Belarus • Russian phrasebook • Scandinavian & Baltic Europe • Scandinavian Europe phrasebook • Scotland • Sicily • Slovenia • South-West France • Spain • Spanish phrasebook • St Petersburg • St Petersburg City Map • Sweden • Switzerland • Trekking in Spain • Tuscany • Ukrainian phrasebook • Venice • Vienna • Walking in Britain • Walking in France • Walking in Ireland • Walking in Italy • Walking in Spain • Walking in Switzerland • Western Europe • Western Europe phrasebook • World Food France • World Food Ireland • World Food Italy • World Food Spain
Travel Literature: Love and War in the Apennines • The Olive Grove: Travels in Greece • On the Shores of the Mediterranean • Round Ireland in Low Gear • A Small Place in Italy • After Yugoslavia

INDIAN SUBCONTINENT Bangladesh • Bengali phrasebook • Bhutan • Delhi • Goa • Healthy Travel Asia & India • Hindi & Urdu phrasebook • India • Indian Himalaya • Karakoram Highway • Kerala • Mumbai (Bombay) • Nepal • Nepali phrasebook • Pakistan • Rajasthan • Read This First: Asia & India • South India • Sri Lanka • Sri Lanka phrasebook • Tibet • Tibetan phrasebook • Trekking in the Indian Himalaya • Trekking in the Karakoram & Hindukush • Trekking in the Nepal Himalaya
Travel Literature: The Age of Kali: Indian Travels and Encounters • Hello Goodnight: A Life of Goa • In Rajasthan • A Season in Heaven: True Tales from the Road to Kathmandu • Shopping for Buddhas • A Short Walk in the Hindu Kush • Slowly Down the Ganges

ISLANDS OF THE INDIAN OCEAN Madagascar & Comoros • Maldives • Mauritius, Réunion & Seychelles

MIDDLE EAST & CENTRAL ASIA Bahrain, Kuwait & Qatar • Central Asia • Central Asia phrasebook • Dubai • Hebrew phrasebook • Iran • Israel & the Palestinian Territories • Istanbul • Istanbul City Map • Istanbul to Cairo on a shoestring • Jerusalem • Jerusalem City Map • Jordan • Lebanon • Middle East • Oman & the United Arab Emirates • Syria • Turkey • Turkish phrasebook • World Food Turkey • Yemen
Travel Literature: Black on Black: Iran Revisited • The Gates of Damascus • Kingdom of the Film Stars: Journey into Jordan

NORTH AMERICA Alaska • Boston • Boston City Map • California & Nevada • California Condensed • Canada • Chicago • Chicago City Map • Deep South • Florida • Great Lakes • Hawaii • Hiking in Alaska • Hiking in the USA • Honolulu • Las Vegas • Los Angeles • Los Angeles City Map • Louisiana & The Deep South • Miami • Miami City Map • New England • New Orleans • New York City • New York City City Map • New York City Condensed • New York, New Jersey & Pennsylvania • Oahu • Out to Eat – San Francisco • Pacific Northwest • Puerto Rico • Rocky Mountains • San Francisco • San Francisco City Map • Seattle • Southwest • Texas • USA • USA phrasebook • Vancouver • Virginia & the Capital Region • Washington DC • Washington, DC City Map • World Food Deep South, USA • World Food New Orleans
Travel Literature: Caught Inside: A Surfer's Year on the California Coast • Drive Thru America

NORTH-EAST ASIA Beijing • Beijing City Map • Cantonese phrasebook • China • Hiking in Japan • Hong Kong • Hong Kong City Map • Hong Kong Condensed • Hong Kong, Macau & Guangzhou • Japan • Japanese phrasebook • Korea • Korean phrasebook • Kyoto • Mandarin phrasebook • Mongolia • Mongolian phrasebook • Seoul • Shanghai • South-West China • Taiwan • Tokyo
Travel Literature: In Xanadu: A Quest • Lost Japan

SOUTH AMERICA Argentina, Uruguay & Paraguay • Bolivia • Brazil • Brazilian phrasebook • Buenos Aires • Chile & Easter Island • Colombia • Ecuador & the Galapagos Islands • Healthy Travel Central & South America • Latin American Spanish phrasebook • Peru • Quechua phrasebook • Read This First: Central & South America • Rio de Janeiro • Rio de Janeiro City Map • Santiago • South America on a shoestring • Santiago • Trekking in the Patagonian Andes • Venezuela
Travel Literature: Full Circle: A South American Journey

SOUTH-EAST ASIA Bali & Lombok • Bangkok • Bangkok City Map • Burmese phrasebook • Cambodia • Hanoi • Healthy Travel Asia & India • Hill Tribes phrasebook • Ho Chi Minh City • Indonesia • Indonesian phrasebook • Indonesia's Eastern Islands • Jakarta • Java • Lao phrasebook • Laos • Malay phrasebook • Malaysia, Singapore & Brunei • Myanmar (Burma) • Philippines • Pilipino (Tagalog) phrasebook • Read This First: Asia & India • Singapore • Singapore City Map • South-East Asia on a shoestring • South-East Asia phrasebook • Thailand • Thailand's Islands & Beaches • Thailand, Vietnam, Laos & Cambodia Road Atlas • Thai phrasebook • Vietnam • Vietnamese phrasebook • World Food Thailand • World Food Vietnam

ALSO AVAILABLE: Antarctica • The Arctic • The Blue Man: Tales of Travel, Love and Coffee • Brief Encounters: Stories of Love, Sex & Travel • Chasing Rickshaws • The Last Grain Race • Lonely Planet Unpacked • Not the Only Planet: Science Fiction Travel Stories • Lonely Planet On the Edge • Sacred India • Travel with Children • Travel Photography: A Guide to Taking Better Pictures

Index

Text

Bold indicates maps.

Boxed Text

Bold indicates maps.

MAP LEGEND

CITY ROUTES

Freeway	Freeway
Highway	Primary Road
Road	Secondary Road
Street	Street
Lane	Lane
	On/Off Ramp

	Unsealed Road
	One-Way Street
	Pedestrian Street
	Stepped Street
	Tunnel
	Footbridge

HYDROGRAPHY

	River; Creek
	Lake
	Dry Lake; Salt Lake
	Spring; Rapids
	Waterfalls

AREA FEATURES

	Building
	Park; Garden
	Market
	Sports Ground
	Beach
	Cemetery

TRANSPORT ROUTES & STATIONS

	Train
	Underground Train
	Cable Car; Chairlift
	Ferry

	Walking Trail
	Walking Tour
	Path
	Pier; Jetty

BOUNDARIES

	International
	State

REGIONAL ROUTES

	Tollway; Freeway
	Primary Road
	Secondary Road
	Minor Road

POPULATION SYMBOLS

✪ CAPITAL	National Capital	⊙ CITY	City
◉ CAPITAL	State Capital	○ Town	Town
		● Village	Village
			Urban Area

MAP SYMBOLS

▪	Place to Stay
▼	Place to Eat
●	Point of Interest

Airfield	Cinema	▲ Mountain	Swimming Pool
Airport	Cycle Shop/Path	Museum; Gallery	Swimming Beach
Bank	Embassy	National Park	Surf Beach
Bus Station	Golf Course	Parking	Taxi
Bus Stop	Hospital	Picnic	Telephone
Camping Ground	Internet Cafe	Police Station	Theatre
Caravan Park	Lighthouse	Post Office	Toilet
Cathedral; Church	Lookout	Pub; Bar; Nightclub	Tourist Information
Cave	Monument	Shopping Centre	Winery
		Ski Field	Zoo

Note: Not all symbols displayed above appear in this book

LONELY PLANET OFFICES

Australia
Locked Bag 1, Footscray, Victoria 3011
☎ 03 9689 4666 fax 03 9689 6833
email: talk2us@lonelyplanet.com.au

USA
150 Linden St, Oakland, CA 94607
☎ 510 893 8555 TOLL FREE: 800 275 8555
fax 510 893 8572
email: info@lonelyplanet.com

UK
10a Spring Place, London NW5 3BH
☎ 020 7428 4800 fax 020 7428 4828
email: go@lonelyplanet.co.uk

France
1 rue du Dahomey, 75011 Paris
☎ 01 55 25 33 00 fax 01 55 25 33 01
email: bip@lonelyplanet.fr
www.lonelyplanet.fr

**World Wide Web: www.lonelyplanet.com *or* AOL keyword: lp
Lonely Planet Images: lpi@lonelyplanet.com.au**